HOW TO GET A

JOB

IN

Europe

Robert Sanborn and Cheryl Matherly

The Insider's
Guide Series

SURREY BOOKS
CHICAGO

HOW TO GET A JOB IN EUROPE

Published by Surrey Books, Inc., 230 E. Ohio St., Suite 120, Chicago, IL 60611.

Copyright © 1999 by Surrey Books, Inc. All rights reserved, including the right to reproduce this book or portions thereof in any form, including any information storage and retrieval system, except for the inclusion of brief quotations in a review.

This book is manufactured in the United States of America.

4th Edition. 1st printing, May, 1999 1 2 3 4 5

Library of Congress Cataloging-in-Publication data:
Sanborn, Robert, 1959-
    How to get a job in Europe/Robert Sanborn and Cheryl Matherly.—4th ed.
      p. cm.
    Includes bibliographical references and index.
    ISBN 1-57284-027-7 (pbk.)
      1. Americans—Employment—Europe. 2. Job hunting—Europe.
I. Matherly, Cheryl. II. Title.
HF5549.5.E45S26 1999
650.14'094—dc21
                                    99-17261
                                      CIP

AVAILABLE TITLES IN THIS SERIES—$18.95

How To Get a Job in Atlanta
How To Get a Job in Chicago
How To Get a Job in Dallas/Fort Worth
How To Get a Job in Denver and Central Colorado
How To Get a Job in Europe ($21.95)
How To Get a Job in New York City and the Metropolitan Area
How To Get a Job in the San Francisco Bay Area
How To Get a Job in Seattle and Western Washington
How To Get a Job in Southern California

Single copies may be ordered directly from the publisher. Send check or money order for book price plus $4.00 for first book and $1.50 for each additional book to cover insurance, shipping, and handling to Surrey Books at the above address. For quantity discounts, please contact the publisher.

Editorial production by Bookcrafters, Inc., Chicago.
Cover and book design by Joan Sommers Design, Chicago.
Typesetting by On Track Graphics, Inc., Chicago.
"How To Get a Job" series is distributed to the trade by Publishers Group West.

Acknowledgments

This edition of the book would never have been possible, and the book is certainly better for, the hard work, creativeness, and perseverance of Ann Peterson. Her insights were invaluable. We also want to thank Armanda Lewis for her work as research assistant, diligently rooting out information via the Internet, the library, and the telephone. We acknowledge Anderson Brandao for all his help and diligence in helping us put the original edition of the book together. Also providing hard work through the years were J.R. Smiljanic, Don Kindred, Linda Breed, Alan Ying, Victoria Mejia, and Tam Truong. We would also like to thank Rebecca Durrer, Claire Saxton, Kristin Baker, Ariel Strichartz, Biff Clay, Andi Galt, and Sandra De Los Santos. All contributed valuable and hard work to the completion of this volume. We both thank the staff of the Rice University Career Services Center for their assistance. Bob thanks his strongest support system, his wife Ellen and his lovely daughter Virginia Elisabet. Cheryl adds her special thank you to Steven Wilson.

NOTE TO OUR READERS

The author and editors have made every effort to supply you with the most useful, up-to-date information available to help you find the job you want. Each name, address, and phone number has been verified by our staff of fact checkers. But offices move and people change jobs, so we urge you to call or write before you visit. And if you think we should include information on companies, organizations, or people that we've missed, please let us know.

The publisher, authors, and editors make no guarantee that the employers listed in this book have jobs available.

DROP US A LINE

Among the features in this edition are "Dear Bob and Cheryl" letters—short notes from working travelers like yourself, recounting their experiences in Europe. For this feature to be a success in future editions, we need your input. So if you've crushed wine with your bare feet in Italy, au paired in Austria, penned copy on Fleet Street, or have any other such experiences you think fellow readers might be interested in, do write to us in care of Surrey Books. Not only could your experiences be published but you will have helped your fellow humans with their respective search for jobs in faraway lands. Send your stories to:

Dear Bob and Cheryl
Europe Stories
c/o Surrey Books
230 E. Ohio St., Suite 120
Chicago, IL 60611

JOB HUNTING?

These books, covering 8 major markets, plus Europe, can help you achieve a successful career

HOW... to get the job you want: Each book gives you more than 1,300 major employers, numbers to call, and people to contact.

WHERE... to get the job you want: How to research the local job market and meet the people who hire.

PLUS... how to use the World Wide Web, local networks, and professional organizations; how to choose a career; advice on employment services; how to sell yourself in the interview; how to write power resumes and cover letters; and hundreds of names and numbers, many available nowhere else!

ORDER FORM

Please send the following at $18.95 each

___ **HOW TO GET A JOB IN ATLANTA**
___ **HOW TO GET A JOB IN CHICAGO**
___ **HOW TO GET A JOB IN DALLAS/FORT WORTH**
___ **HOW TO GET A JOB IN DENVER**
___ **HOW TO GET A JOB IN EUROPE ($21.95)**
___ **HOW TO GET A JOB IN NEW YORK**
___ **HOW TO GET A JOB IN SAN FRANCISCO**
___ **HOW TO GET A JOB IN SEATTLE**
___ **HOW TO GET A JOB IN SOUTHERN CALIFORNIA**

Enclosed is my check/money order for $_____

☐ Visa ☐ MasterCard ☐ AmEx ☐ Discover

_____
CARD NUMBER

_____
EXP. DATE

_____
SIGNATURE

_____
NAME

_____
ADDRESS

_____
CITY   STATE   ZIP

_____
PHONE

For Easier Ordering Call 1-800-326-4430

Send check or money order, and include $4.00 for first book and $1.50 for each additional book to cover insurance, shipping, and handling to: Surrey Books, 230 E. Ohio St., Suite 120, Chicago, IL 60611. Or call toll-free: 1-800-326-4430. Allow 2-4 weeks for delivery. Satisfaction Guaranteed or your money back.

Contents

Part I

Getting a Job in Europe

So You Want To Get a Job in Europe

Rome, Paris, London...yes, Americans are fascinated with Europe. Many Americans have lived and worked in Europe before moving on to greater things. Thomas Jefferson and Benjamin Franklin both worked in Europe during their careers. Ernest Hemingway spent part of his career in Spain. Jim Morrison spent some time in Paris. Bill Clinton studied in England. International work has always been a ticket to glamour, adventure, and career advancement.

You can work in Europe in jobs ranging from investment banking in Frankfurt to teaching English in Prague to bartending in a London pub. These jobs and many more are available—or can be created—to satisfy your desire for a European work experience. This book offers a variety of options and resources for Americans seeking work in Europe.

How much do you know about international work? A European job may not entail constant travel (if any), and you will often be expected to work for less money than in the United States. You may have to speak a foreign language, and your two years of high school French may do little more than allow you to converse with kindergartners. Your living conditions will probably be more cramped than you are used to (unless you are moving from Manhattan, of course).

Chances are, however, that if you are reading this book, you're ready for all that. It's the adventure—both good and bad—that is motivating you to find international work.

Myths about International Work

1. Foreign languages get you a job.
Many Americans think that knowing a foreign language means they are qualified for an international job. We have met countless students and graduates who want to work abroad and think it shouldn't be a problem to locate international work because they have majored in a foreign language. This is the equivalent of saying, "If you speak English, you can get any job in the United States." Foreign languages can and certainly do help. Fluency (or at least a willingness to become fluent) in the language of the country in which you wish to work is a must, but it is not the sole factor in your eligibility for a position. Employers look for skills and experience. Knowledge of a foreign language is taken for granted.

2. Classes on Europe and similar topics help you get a job.
Most college students have the opportunity to take courses on European history, current events, and other international relations courses. Again, many people assume that having taken several international affairs classes has prepared them for working abroad. An understanding of current and historical events in your country of interest is needed, but as with foreign language experience, it will be taken for granted. You should take these courses and have this knowledge, but don't expect to sell employability based on the knowledge acquired through your international relations course work.

3. My American MBA degree will not be useful in Europe.
Many Americans are under the impression that technical graduate degrees such as an MBA don't count for much in Europe. The reality is that the American MBA is highly thought of in Europe. Many European schools (see Chapter 2) now offer MBA degrees, often designed on the American model. The American MBA can be especially useful when accompanied by fluency in a European language and knowledge of the job market. Also, with the increasing presence of American business in Europe, your chances for employment improve if you have an MBA.

4. American subsidiaries hire lots of Americans.
Most American firms in Europe are run and staffed by Europeans. Americans are hired by American firms in Europe, but these are most likely to be people who have skills that are needed in Europe and who have worked with a particular company for some time, proving their abilities. Employment opportunities do exist with these companies, but you must prove you have the skill to be needed in Europe, know the right people in the company, simply be in the right place at the right time—or all of the above.

5. If you go to Europe you are bound to find something.

Americans, especially American college students, often go to Europe with the idea that once they arrive, some type of job opportunity will simply materialize. This is a risky assumption. Without planning, you are likely to end up unemployed with few prospects for changing the situation. Looking for work once you are in Europe can be done, but it's not as easy as just hopping the next plane and reading the help-wanted ads in the newspaper. Figure out all the angles first, and know what's in store for you. Chapter 4 outlines the steps needed for preparation.

An American in Europe

Michael Yeaman is an American with the good fortune of working professionally in London. How did he do it? The hard way, some might say. After receiving his undergraduate and master's degrees in geophysics from Stanford University, he worked in the United States for a number of years in the international division of his company, Amoco Oil. After about eight years, he joined the U.S. office of an Australian oil firm. He was hired because of the skills and knowledge he developed at Amoco. After less than a year, he was transferred to London. Moving expenses paid, a professional position, good salary—this is what many people dream of in contemplating a successful transfer to Europe. It took Michael nine years to get there, of course, but he did so on his own terms.

Using This Book

The book will be most useful when read in its entirety, but it is organized so that you can skip among the chapters to find the areas most relevant to your particular search. We cover the best ways to get to Europe, how to prepare for your job search, and tips for uncovering potential employers.

You may notice that the book does not cover some European countries, specifically the Balkans and the Russian states. After much deliberation, we decided that at the time the book went to press, economic and political conditions were so volatile in these regions that it was impossible to provide relevant and current advice for job seekers. Hopefully by the time we prepare the 5th edition of *How to Get a Job in Europe* this situation will be different and we can again include a complete picture of the European job market.

Before You Go

Don't let the romance of the perfect European job cloud your judgment about your chances for finding international work. Chapter 2 focuses on the qualifications needed for work in Europe and provides insight into educational opportunities in Europe and in the United States that best prepare you for an international career.

Chapter 3 focuses on the European economy and the political and economic upheavals that affect the job seeker. These changes in Europe suggest benefits and limitations for Americans looking for work abroad

Chapter 4 can help you decide what kind of job you are looking for. You have a number of options, from professional positions in banking, non-profit organizations, and education to temporary positions in agriculture, child care, and resort work.

If you're interested in a professional career in Europe, Chapter 8 will give you career ideas. The chapter covers everything from international banking to positions with the United States federal government to working as a correspondent with a major newspaper.

PERIODICALS FOR THE INTERNATIONAL JOB SEEKER

Preparation is the key to an international job search, and your research can make the difference between success and failure. There are several books and magazines that provide useful background information for helping direct your efforts.

The Economist is a weekly magazine that examines business and current events in Europe. It is probably the one best source of information on current political and economic happenings and as such is a must for the prospective job seeker interested in learning more about the current scene in Europe. It is widely available at bookstores or, for those who prefer, by subscription:

The Economist
Subscription Department
P.O. Box 58524
Boulder, CO 80322-8524
Tel.: (800) 456-6086
Fax: (303) 443-5080
www.economist.com

For service outside North America, contact:

The Economist
Subscription Office
P.O. Box 14, Harold Hill
Romford, Essex RM3 8EQ, England
Tel.: (212) 541-5730
Fax: (212) 541-9378

Here are a few daily business newspapers that can also give insight into current business conditions in Europe and ongoing employment trends:

The Financial Times of London
Business Information Limited
Towerhouse, South Hampton Street
London WC2E 7HA, England

Available in the United States at:

The Financial Times of London
14 East 60th Street
New York, NY 10022
Tel.: (212) 752-4500

The Wall Street Journal
Dow Jones
420 Lexington Avenue
New York, NY 10170
www.wsj.com
(Also publishes a European edition)

A number of business weeklies are published in both the United States and Europe and provide coverage of European business and economic activity:

Bloomberg
499 Park Ave.
New York, NY 10022
Tel.: (212) 318-2000
Fax: (212) 980-4585
www.bloomberg.com

Business Week
McGraw-Hill Building
1221 Avenue of the Americas
New York, NY 10020
Tel.: (212) 512-2000
www.wsj.com

Forbes
Subscriber Services
P.O. Box 10048
Des Moines, IA 50340-0048
Tel.: (800) 888-9896
www.forbes.com

Fortune
Time, Inc.
Time & Life Building
Rockefeller Center

New York, NY 10020-1393
Tel.: (800) 621-8000
www.pathfinder.com/fortune/

Red Herring
1550 Bryant Street, Suite 450
San Francisco, CA 94103
Tel.: (415) 865-2277
Fax: (415) 865-2280
www.redherring.com

The *International Herald Tribune*, published by the *Washington Post* and the *New York Times*, is the only pan-European English daily offering broad coverage of daily business and political events in Europe:

International Herald Tribune
850 3rd Avenue
New York, NY 10022
Tel.: (212) 752-3890
Fax.: (212) 755-8785
www.iht.com

In Europe:

International Herald Tribune
181 Avenue Charles-de-Gaulle
F-92521 Neuilly-sur-Seine, France
Tel.: [33] 1 46.37.93.00
Fax: [33] 1 41.43.93.38

EUROPE magazine focuses on European affairs and the relationship between the European Union and the U.S. Published ten times a year, the magazine is available from P.O. Box 2115, Knoxville, IA 50197-2115.

You'll also want to read European newspapers, often available at large bookstores or newsstands, that are primarily devoted to events within their own country. If you intend to job search and live in one particular country or region of Europe, these newspapers may be your best job-search resource. Chapters 11 through 21 include lists of these papers and periodicals under specific country headings.

Another outstanding resource for the European job search is *Transitions Abroad*. This bi-monthly magazine is packed with information on work, study, and travel abroad. The magazine is especially targeted to students, although there are articles that will be of interest to anyone considering living abroad.

Transitions Abroad
Transitions Abroad Publishing, Inc.
18 Hulst Road
P.O. Box 1300
Amherst, MA 01004

BOOKS ON WORKING ABROAD

Check any bookstore and you'll likely find the shelves sagging with books on how to get an international job—some truly helpful, some only so-so. The following titles are particularly informative.

Adventure Careers. Alex Hiam and Susan Angle. Career Press, 180 Fifth Avenue, P.O. Box 34, Hawthorne, NJ 07507. Not specifically on working abroad, but a thoughtful guide to those pondering international or other non-traditional career paths.

Alternative Travel Directory. Clay Hubbs. Transitions Abroad Publishing, Inc., P.O. Box 1300, Amherst, MA 01004-1300.

The Back Door Guide to Short Term Job Adventures. Michael Landes. Ten Speed Press, P.O. Box 7123, Berkeley, CA 94710, www.backdoorjobs.com. A guide to internships, extraordinary experiences, seasonal jobs, and volunteering for everyone from college students to senior citizens. One section lists 200 programs overseas.

The Canadian Guide to Working and Living Overseas. Jean-Marc Hachey. Intercultural Systems, P.O. Box 588, Station B, Ottawa, Ontario, Canada K1P 5P7. A highly regarded source covering practically every aspect of working and living abroad.

The Complete Guide to International Jobs & Careers. Krannich & Krannich. Impact Publications, 9104-N Manassas Drive, Manassas Park, VA 22111. An overview of career strategies and opportunities in the international arena, emphasizing professional positions. Readers may also find useful *The Almanac of International Jobs and Careers,* a companion volume to the *Complete Guide,* which lists contact information on organizations providing overseas opportunities.

The Directory of Jobs and Careers Abroad. Andre de Vries. Peterson's Guides Inc., 202 Carnegie Center, Princeton, NJ 08543-2123. A guide to career options the world over, with especially good notes on descriptions, outlook, and resources involving particular careers.

Employment Abroad: Facts and Fallacies. Rachel Theus, ed. International Division, Chamber of Commerce of the United States, 1615 H Street NW, Washington, DC 20062. A practical look at the realities of working overseas.

Great Jobs Abroad. Arthur H. Bell. McGraw Hill, 11 West 19th St., New York, NY 10011. Useful lists of resources for the international job searcher.

How to Find an Overseas Job with the U.S. Government. Cantrell and Modderno. Worldwise Books, P.O. Box 3030, Oakton, VA 22124. Details the types of jobs available—and how to get them—with the organization that employs the greatest number of Americans working internationally.

The International Consultant. H. Peter Guttman. Worldwise Books, P.O. Box 3030, Oakton, VA 22124-9030. Provides advice and an overview of feasible options.

International Jobs. Eric Kocher. Addison-Wesley Publishing Company, 202 Carnegie Center, Reading, MA 01867. A handbook of career opportunities around the world.

Overseas Summer Jobs. David Woodworth, ed. Distributed in the U.S. by Peterson's, 202 Carnegie Center, Princeton, NJ 08543-2123. A country-by-country listing of summer and temporary international jobs.

Passport to Overseas Employment. Dale Chambers. Simon & Schuster, 1230 Avenue of the Americas, New York, NY 10020. Covers the general spectrum of working-abroad information—career options, employment regulations, and so on, plus an informative chapter on student discount information.

Taking Off. Lauren Tarshis. Simon & Schuster, 1230 Avenue of the Americas, New York, NY 10020. A "how-to" guide on alternative ways to spend one's first year out of college; also relevant to job changers and those interested in taking a year's sabbatical. Includes U.S. and international opportunities.

Work Abroad: The Complete Guide to Finding a Job Overseas. Clay Hubbs and Jason Whitmarsh, eds. Transitions Abroad Publishing, P.O. Box 1300, Amherst, MA 01004-1300. Useful collection of essays on all options for working abroad.

Work Your Way Around the World. Susan Griffith. Distributed in the U.S. by Peterson's, 202 Carnegie Center, Princeton, NJ 08543-2123. Extremely thorough guide to how to work in almost any country in the world.

The European Job Search

Many prospective job seekers romanticize about finding work in Europe. Anyone who thinks that a European job search will be easy will be disappointed. Europe is a tough place to find employment, some countries more than others. Getting a good job—especially a permanent one—involves a great deal of work. For those who work hard, network, and have a lot of gumption, though, the rewards of international work can be well worth the effort.

Chapter 4 outlines the steps for finding a job in Europe. Chapter 6 offers tips on effective interviewing. Chapter 5 gives details and samples of resumes and cover letters for the international job search. Chapter 7 details how placement organizations can and can't help you in your search. The summer or temporary job search is discussed in Chapter 9. Chapter 10 looks at particular options for teaching English abroad. Part II of the book, Chapters 11 through 20, focuses on the European countries themselves and what they have to offer in terms of employment.

BOOKS ON LIVING ABROAD

The Adventure of Working Abroad. Joyce Sautters Osland. Jossey-Bass Publishers, 350 Sansome Street, San Francisco, CA 94104. Looks at experiences of expatriates.

An American's Guide to Living Abroad. Louise Guido, ed. Living Abroad
  Publishing, Inc., 199 Nassau Street, Princeton, NJ 08540. Includes editions on
  western and eastern Europe.

The Art of Crossing Cultures. Craig Sorti. Intercultural Press, P.O. Box 700,
  Yarmouth, ME 04096. Focuses on the personal challenges in living abroad.

European Customs and Manners. Nancy Braganti and Elizabeth Devine. Simon
  & Schuster, 1230 Avenue of the Americas, New York, NY 10020. A compendi-
  um of tips on such things as greetings, dress, legalities and safety, key phrases,
  and business etiquette in 24 European countries.

Evaluating an Overseas Job Opportunity. John Williams. Pilot Books, 103 Cooper
  Street, Babylon, NY 11702. Step-by-step guide to understanding a company's
  offer for an international job.

Gestures: The Do's and Taboos of Body Language Around the World. Robert
  Axtell. John Wiley & Sons, New York. An entertaining primer on intercultural
  communications.

A Handbook for Citizens Living Abroad. Doubleday, 1990. A guide to some of the
  practicalities of life overseas, including information on moving, taxes, consular services, voting, and the like.

International Travel Health Guide. Travel Medicine, Inc., 351 Pleasant Street,
  Suite 312, Northampton, MA 01060. Provides current information on health
  concerns for those traveling or living abroad.

Moving Abroad: A Guide to International Living. Virginia McKay. VLM
  Enterprises, P.O. Box 7236, Wilmington, DE 19803. Covers many of the practicalities of living overseas.

Survival Kit for Overseas Living. Robert Kohls. Intercultural Press, P.O. Box 700,
  Yarmouth, ME 04096. Focuses on the adaptations one has to make in adjusting
  to life in a foreign land.

When Cultures Collide. Richard D. Lewis. Nicholas Brealey Publishing, 17470
  Sonoma Highway, Sonoma, CA 95476. A cross-cultural guide that is a must-
  read for professionals living and working overseas; explores the cultural roots
  of national behavior.

Women's Guide to Overseas Living. Nancy Piet-Pelon and Barbara Hornby.
  Intercultural Press, P.O. Box 700, Yarmouth, ME 04096. Examines international
  career motives and options; moving, culture shock, health concerns, etc.

Another potentially good source for information on living in Europe is the
Network for Living Abroad, basically a matching service. Members pay an annual fee (six months, if they prefer), fill out a questionnaire, and are given names of
others who are interested in studying, working, or retiring in the same geograph-
ical area. For more information, write to: Network for Living Abroad, 13351-D
Riverside Drive, Suite 101, Sherman Oaks, CA 91423.

For a quick overview of whatever country or countries you might be interested in, "Culturegrams" are another option. These are four-page summaries of essential information—customs, manners, and the like—on dozens of cultures worldwide, and are updated annually. Single copies are available, or you may purchase the entire set. Send inquiries to Publication Services, David M. Kennedy Center of International Studies, Brigham Young University, 280 HRCB, Provo, UT 84602.

Similar to "Culturegrams" is the U.S. government's "Background Notes" series. Each pamphlet gives an overview of the history, geography, cultures, and foreign relations of a particular country. "Background Notes" are available individually, as an annual subscription, or as a set from the Superintendent of Documents, U.S. Government Printing Office, Washington, DC 20402.

Know before you go

For up-to-date information on any country in the world, including political, economic, and cultural data, contact the U.S. Department of State's Citizens Emergency Center at (202) 647-5225. The Citizens Emergency Center not only deals with emergencies involving Americans abroad; they also provide Consular Information Sheets and Travel Warnings. These include information on crime and security, health concerns, immigration, currency, unrest and instability, and embassy and consulate locations abroad. Each call to the Center's automated switchboard allows you to listen to recordings on as many as three countries of your choice and to order printed information about those countries if you would like. For those who prefer, this information is also available from the Overseas Advisory Council at http://ds.state.gov/osacmenu.cfm.

ADDRESSES OF CHAMBERS OF COMMERCE

Chambers of commerce, whether located in the United States or in Europe, can offer information on businesses and organizations in the country of your choice. Information on economic trends and living conditions is also often available. The following list provides the addresses for the major chambers of commerce for each country included in this book. Where possible, a U.S. location is specified. For more complete listings of chambers of commerce, please refer to the individual country chapters in Part II of this book.

AUSTRIA
United States-Austrian Chamber of
Commerce
165 West 46th Street, #1112
New York, NY 10036
Tel.: (212) 819-0117
Fax: (212) 819-0117

BELGIUM
Belgian-American Chamber of
Commerce in the United States
Empire State Building
1330 Avenue of the Americas, 26th
Floor
New York, NY 10019
Tel.: (212) 969-9940
Fax: (212) 969-9942
www.belcham.org

BULGARIA
Bulgarian Chamber of Commerce and
Industry
42 Parchevich Str.
BG-1000 Sofia, Bulgaria
Tel.: [359] (2) 987-2631
Fax: [359] (2) 987-3209

CYPRUS
Cyprus Trade Center
13 East 40th Street
New York, NY 10017
Tel.: (212) 213-9100
Fax: (212) 213-2918
www.cyprus-tradeny.org

CZECH REPUBLIC
Czechoslovak Chamber of Commerce
and Industry
Argentinska 38
CS-170 05 Prague 7, Czech Republic
Tel.: [42] (2) 872 41 11
Fax: [42] (2) 879 134

DENMARK
Danish-American Chamber
of Commerce
885 2nd Avenue, 18th Floor

New York, NY 10017
Tel.: (212) 980-6240
Fax: (212) 754-1904

FINLAND
Finnish-American Chamber of
Commerce
866 UN Plaza #249
New York, NY 10017
Tel.: (212) 821-0225
Fax: (212) 750-4417
www.finlandtrade.com

FRANCE
French-American Chamber of
Commerce in the United States
1350 Avenue of the Americas,
6th Floor
New York, NY 10019
Tel.: (212) 765-4460
Fax: (212) 765-4650

GERMANY
German-American Chamber of
Commerce
40 West 57th Street
New York, NY 10019
Tel.: (212) 974-8830
Fax: (212) 974-8867
www.gac-com.org

GREECE
Hellenic-American Chamber of
Commerce
Atlantic Bank Building, Suite 1204
960 Avenue of the Americas
New York, NY 10001
Tel.: (212) 629-6380

HUNGARY
Hungarian-American Chamber of
Commerce
10 Twin Dolphin Drive, #B-500
Redwood City, CA 94065
Tel.: (650) 595-1448
Fax: (650) 591-1448

IRELAND
Ireland Chamber of Commerce in the U.S.
1305 Post Road, #205
Fairfield, CT 06430
Tel.: (203) 255-1630
www.iccusa.org

ITALY
Italy-America Chamber of Commerce
730 5th Avenue, #600
New York, NY 10019
Tel.: (212) 459-0044
Fax: (212) 459-0090
www.italchambers.net/newyork

LIECHTENSTEIN
Liechtenstein Chamber of Commerce and Industry
Postfach 232
L-9490 Vaduz, Liechtenstein
Tel.: [41] (75) 232 2744
Fax: [41] (75) 238 1503

LUXEMBOURG
Luxembourg Chamber of Commerce
825 3rd Avenue, 36th Floor
New York, NY 10022
Tel.: (212) 888-6701

MALTA
Malta Chamber of Commerce
Exchange Buildings
Republic Street
VLT05 Valletta, Malta
Tel.: [356] 24 72 33
Fax: [356] 24 52 23
www.chamber-commerce.org.mt

NETHERLANDS
The Netherlands Chamber of Commerce in the U.S.
One Rockefeller Plaza, #1420
New York, NY 10020
Tel.: (212) 265-6460
Fax: (212) 265-6402

NORWAY
Norwegian-American Chamber of Commerce
800 3rd Avenue
New York, NY 10022

Tel.: (212) 421-9210
Fax: (212) 838-0374

POLAND
Polish-U.S. Economic Council
1615 H Street NW
Washington, DC 20062-2000
Tel.: (212) 463-5482
Fax: (202) 463-3114

PORTUGAL
Portugal-U.S. Chamber of Commerce
590 5th Avenue
New York, NY 10036
Tel.: (212) 354-4627
Fax: (212) 575-4737
Email: anao-sori@ix.netcom.com

ROMANIA
Romanian Chamber of Commerce and Industry
22 Boulevard Nicolae Balcescu
R-79302 Bucharest, Romania
Tel.: [40] (1) 312 1312
Fax: [40] (1) 312 3830

SLOVAK REPUBLIC
Slovak Chamber of Commerce and Industry
Gorkeho 9
816 03 Bratislava, Slovakia
Tel.: [421] (7) 533 3272
Fax: [421] (7) 533 0754
www.scci.sk

SPAIN
Spain-U.S. Chamber of Commerce
350 5th Avenue, Suite 2029
New York, NY 10118
Tel.: (212) 967-2170
Fax: (212) 564-1415
Email: spuscha@aol.com

SWEDEN
The Swedish-American Chamber of Commerce
599 Lexington Avenue, 13th Floor
New York, NY 10022
Tel.: (212) 838-5530
Fax: (212) 755-7953

SWITZERLAND
Swiss American Chamber of
Commerce
608 5th Avenue, Suite 309
New York, NY 10020
Tel.: (212) 246-7789
Fax: (212) 246-1366

TURKEY
Union of Chambers of Commerce,
Industry, Maritime Commerce, and
Commodity Exchanges
Atatürk Bulvari 149

06582 Bakanliklar, Ankara, Turkey
Tel.: [90] (312) 125 5614
Fax: [90] (312) 118 1002

UNITED KINGDOM
British-American Chamber of
Commerce
52 Vanderbilt Avenue, 20th Floor
New York, NY 10017
Tel.: (212) 661-4060
Fax: (212) 661-4074
www.ba-cc.org

Getting to Europe from the U.S.: The Best Way to Go

You have many options for getting to Europe. Any travel agent can help. You can just pick up the phone and make all of your travel plans yourself. You may choose to surf the Web and look for your best deals. If you're interested in economy, though, you'll want to look around.

One inexpensive—and perhaps unconventional—way to go is to travel as an air courier. This involves escorting time-sensitive business documents or other materials for international freight companies. Typically, you are met both at your airport of departure and arrival by an agent of the company. You are responsible for the port-to-port transport of the documents you've been hired to carry. Serving as an air courier can mean traveling at true bargain rates, but it isn't for everyone. Some people may not feel comfortable with the idea of escorting goods that don't belong to them. Frequently, you can only travel with carry-on luggage because you must commit your luggage space for the documents you are carrying. You must leave and return according to the schedule of the company that hires you to transport documents. *Transitions Abroad* magazine occasionally carries ads for air courier services and courier information sources. Those interested might also wish to consult *The Insiders Guide to Air Courier Bargains: How to Travel Worldwide for Next to Nothing* by Kelly Monaghan. (Available from The Intrepid Traveler, Box 438, New York, NY 10034-0438; (800) 356-9315.)

For readers interested in more conventional travel arrangements, so-called "bucket shops" or consolidators are your best bet for locating non-advertised, bottom-barrel rates. These ticket handlers, often found in large cities such as New York, get tremendous discounts on bulk ticket buying. Savings are passed on to the customer, but the tickets usually have very strict travel restrictions and are always non-refundable. Students—and sometimes teachers—can also get discounts through agents who specialize in student discount travel.

Cards with clout

The International Student Identity Card, International Teacher Identity Card, and GO 25 Card are available to students, teachers, and anyone aged 12 through 25, respectively. These cards entitle their owner to sometimes substantial discounts—up to 50%—on commercial airfares and other travel-related expenses like ground transportation, accommodations, and ticket prices for museums, theaters, and so on. With medical and accident insurance, a toll-free traveler's assistance service, and informational travel handbooks thrown in as well, the cards are well worth investigating for those who qualify. The cards are sponsored by the Council on International Educational Exchange and are available at a very reasonable cost through any Council Travel office (see below).

SELECTED TRAVEL AGENCIES

Finding a travel agency that suits your particular needs is, of course, up to you. The following list is given not to endorse the agencies listed but to provide the reader with a starting point for investigating his or her own travel options. *Bon voyage!*

Anderson Travel
863 Main Street
Hackensack, NJ 07601
Tel.: (800) 733-9430
General discounter and full-service agency. Contact: Sylvia Roy.

Council Travel
205 East 42nd Street
New York, NY 10017
Tel.: (888) COUNCIL
www.ciee.org
Emphasizes student discounts, with over 30 offices in major cities throughout the United States, plus nine offices in France, Germany, and the U.K.

International Student Exchange Flights
5010 East Shea Blvd., Suite A-104
Scottsdale, AZ 85254
Tel.: (602) 951-1700
Tel.: (800) 255-8000
Student discounter.

STA Travel
5900 Wilshire Blvd., Suite 2110
Los Angeles, CA 90036
Tel.: (213) 937-1150
Tel.: (800) 777-0112
www.sta-travel.com/
Emphasizes student discounts. Offices in Berkeley, Boston, Cambridge, Los Angeles, New York, Philadelphia, San Francisco, Santa Monica, Westwood, and throughout Europe.

Travac
989 6th Avenue, 16th Floor
New York, NY 10018
Tel.: (212) 563-3303
Tel.: (800) 872-8800
www.travac.com
General discounter, with offices also in Los Angeles, Orlando, San Francisco, Geneva, London, Vienna, and Zurich.

two

Do You Qualify for an International Job?

Many factors affect whether you can get a job in Europe. You must have enough interest. (Since you're reading this book, we'll take that as a given.) You must have the determination to work hard to find a job. You need to be flexible enough to adapt to the challenges of living in another culture. It helps if you speak another language and if your education or previous work experience has prepared you with a marketable set of skills. Take a close look at what you have to offer an employer to evaluate your qualifications for working abroad.

Adapting to International Living

People who have lived and worked overseas always have stories about the interesting, amusing, and outrageous incidents they have experienced. They like to gossip about the seemingly inexplicable behavior of people from the different country, perhaps to make sense of it or to simply entertain others. These stories often reveal how people who have lived and worked abroad inevitably question their basic assumptions about themselves, their culture, their interpersonal relationships, and their management style.

International living provides many stressors, both positive (such as adventure or novelty) and negative (feelings of inadequacy or language barriers). The cross-cultural setting can be so stressful that it demands that ordinary people respond in extraordinary ways and thereby discover strengths that they would have never developed in their own culture. Many people living abroad challenge themselves, first to survive the differences and changes, then to be effective, and finally to develop explanations for the ambiguity of their new experiences.

Obviously, you do not have to leave the U.S. to undergo this type of personal growth, but there is no question that the international experience can be fertile ground for personal development. Still, not all people take advantage of this opportunity when they leave the country. Some people go abroad for a variety of reasons that have nothing to do with personal growth. They can be motivated by hardship, pay, and a reputedly glamorous lifestyle; others are polishing their resume for future job hopping; others grab international assignments as a way to escape personal, family, or even legal problems. Research suggests, however, that the people who are most successful living abroad are those who have a positive attitude about work and possess a strong sense of self. People with a grounded, stable personality have the wherewithal to handle the normal pressures of an international assignment without "going native" or turning to other coping mechanisms such as drugs or alcohol. Additionally, people who are flexible, adaptable, and open-minded are best prepared for a cross-cultural experience.

European Employment Regulations

Each country in Europe has different laws regarding foreign workers. One unfortunate fact is true of all countries: it is difficult to get permission to work. Many countries mandate that you must secure employment before you can apply for a work visa, while employers require a work visa before they'll hire you. Chapters 11 through 20 outline specific work visa regulations for each country. If you want to work for a large multinational corporation, the company itself can often obtain the documentation necessary for international employment. This process, however, is very time-consuming, labor intensive, and expensive. Most companies won't do this unless you offer a very specific skill they cannot find in their European location. This is part of the reason that we stress the importance of identifying your most marketable skills.

Students often have an easier time of circumventing employment regulations. Several work exchange programs provide the necessary documents for American students seeking jobs and internships (Chapters 7, 9). The Council on International Educational Exchange and BUNAC sponsor Americans to work abroad in casual jobs that can be ideal for students who want to work abroad for the summer.

Many Americans seeking work in Europe don't bother with regulations and search for employment that ranges from grape-picking to working in a pub. While some people are successful at finding work without legal permission, this is risky. Many employers will not consider hiring you because they can be fined for violating their country's employment laws. Also, you have no recourse if you have trouble with your employer, such as a dispute over wages. Finally, if you are discovered to be working illegally in the country, you can be deported.

Foreign Language Requirements

Clearly, foreign language skills improve your employment opportunities in Europe. Although you may have studied a foreign language in high school or college, it may not be sufficient for the workplace. An employer may be impressed by your ability to translate medieval Spanish literature, but they're still looking for employees who can read technical manuals and communicate with clients.

A good gauge of your language skills is your ability to use a foreign language to engage in small talk and basic conversations about the industry. If a potential employer contacts you by telephone in a foreign language, you should be able to respond and converse until you can gracefully shift into English. Only send a cover letter in a foreign language if you speak as fluently as your letter would indicate.

Fluency, although tremendously helpful, is not necessary when applying for an international job. You must, however, demonstrate a willingness to improve your language skills, perhaps by enrolling in foreign language classes while you are job searching. The best courses usually emphasize practical skills, such as business terminology, rather than a tourist-oriented vocabulary. Intensive conversational foreign language courses with qualified instructors are available at most community colleges and continuing education programs at universities. Commercial courses are more expensive, but often emphasize business language skills.

Some countries are more particular about your ability to speak the native language than others. For instance, few companies in Denmark expect foreigners to learn Danish. In France, however, poor language skills are fatal to your job search. Chapters 11 through 20 examine this issue country by country.

Easiest Jobs To Find

Some international jobs are easier for Americans to find than others. Teaching English is always a good way to work in Europe. Work permits are easier to come by for English teachers, and the demand is great. Working in resort areas or in any hospitality-oriented business is another area where work is relatively easy to find. This is especially true in countries such as Greece, where English speakers are needed to cater to tourists from the British Isles and Scandinavia. Agriculture or other similarly low-skilled, manual labor jobs are available at the right time of year. For opportunities in these jobs to be available to outsiders, however, you should look in countries where unemployment is relatively low. Au pair work (child care and housework) is also readily available for Americans. Chapter 9 discusses ways to find summer and temporary work. Non-profit organizations can sometimes provide low-paid work if you arrange things before arriving in Europe. (Opportunities in non-profits are discussed in the country chapters and in Chapter 8.)

Areas Where Jobs for Americans Are Scarce

Americans will find some areas offer few opportunities. Small European companies engaged in non-tourism or trade-related business, for instance, have little use for American workers. This type of company will only hire you if you provide some skill not readily available from local workers, such as computer programming.

The competition for the few positions with the United Nations or international government organizations is especially keen. These organizations have highly bureaucratic hiring processes and a surplus of applicants. You can enhance your odds of securing this kind of work by earning a graduate degree and allowing ample time, sometimes as much as two years, for your application to filter through the process.

As we mentioned earlier, there are few opportunities for Americans with U.S. firms operating abroad. These companies prefer to hire local workers because the company does not have to confront the legal issues associated with hiring foreign workers. You should approach American firms operating abroad strategically. Consider how to build a *career* rather than just landing a *job*.

Higher Education and the International Career

The best way to work abroad is to get the right education—education that will provide you skills that will put you in high demand. Computer programming, accounting, and business are a few areas in which a graduate degree can significantly increase your odds of finding work. Although your political science and history classes won't get you a job, a graduate degree from a top school of international affairs can open many doors.

TOP GRADUATE AND PROFESSIONAL SCHOOLS OF INTERNATIONAL AFFAIRS

Columbia University
School of International and Public Affairs (SIPA)
420 West 118th Street, Room 1427
New York, NY 10027
Tel.: (212) 854-8690
www.columbia.edu/cu/business

Georgetown University
Edmund A. Walsh School of Foreign Service
301 ICC
Washington, DC 20057
Tel.: (202) 687-5696
www.georgetown.edu

Harvard University
John F. Kennedy School of
Government
Cambridge, MA 02138
Tel.: (617) 495-1154
www.harvard.edu

Johns Hopkins University
School of Advanced International
Studies (SAIS)
1740 Massachusetts Avenue NW
Washington, DC 20036
Tel.: (202) 663-5700
www.johnshopkins.edu

Princeton University
Woodrow Wilson School of Public
and International Affairs
Princeton, NJ 08544
Tel.: (609) 258-4831
www.princeton.edu

Tufts University
Fletcher School of Law and
Diplomacy
Medford, MA 02155
Tel.: (617) 381-3040
www.tufts.edu

A Master of Business Administration (MBA) degree from a school that offers a specialization in international business can make you marketable to an international employer. Many MBA programs offer this type of degree, with various emphases and specializations. Look at a variety of MBA programs to find one that best meets your objectives. (Be sure to inquire about the schools' international placement success rates from their career centers.)

TOP INTERNATIONAL MBA PROGRAMS (U.S.)

Columbia University
Graduate School of Business
3022 Broadway
105 Uris Hall
New York, NY 10027
Tel.: (212) 854-1961
Email: gohermes@claven.gsb.colum-
bia.edu
www.columbia.edu/cu/business

Harvard University
Graduate School of Business
Administration
Master's Program
595 Commonwealth Avenue
Boston, MA 02215-1704
Tel.: (617) 495-6127
Email: admissions@hbs.edu
www.hbs.edu/mba/admissions

Monterey Institute of International
Studies
425 Van Buren Street
Monterey, CA 93940
Tel.: (408) 647-4123

New York University
Stern School of Business
Administration
Department of International Business
44 West 4th Street, Suite 11-58
New York, NY 10012-1126
Tel.: (212) 998-0600
Email: sternmba@stern.nyu.edu
www.stern.nye.edu

Thunderbird: The American
Graduate School of International
Management
15249 North 59th Avenue
Glendale, AZ 85306-6000
Tel.: (602) 978-7100
Email: tbird@t-bird.edu
www.t-bird.edu

University of Chicago
Graduate School of Business
1101 East 58th Street
Chicago, IL 60637
Tel.: (312) 702-7369
http://gsbwww.uchicago.edu

University of Pennsylvania
Wharton School, Joseph H. Lauder
Institute
Steinberg-Deitrich Hall, Suite 1030
Philadelphia, PA 19104-6368
Tel.: (215) 898-3430
Email:
mba.admissions@wharton.upenn.edu
www.wharton.upenn.edu

University of South Carolina
Graduate School, College of Business
Administration
Program in International Business
Studies
Columbia, SC 29208
Tel.: (803) 777-3176

EUROPEAN MBA PROGRAMS

Europe offers a number of business programs that grant the MBA degree. These programs are widely accepted in Europe and offer a quality education. All classes are taught in English. At INSEAD, the most prestigious of the European schools, roughly 10 percent of the students are American. These schools can provide an ideal starting point for those interested in European business. The following schools are considered the best by European employers; the first two, INSEAD and IMD, are arguably among the top ten MBA schools in the world. Cambridge and Oxford universities have recently initiated MBA programs and should also provide interesting opportunities.

INSEAD—The European Institute of
Business Administration
Admission Office
Boulevard de Constance
F-77305 Fontainebleau Cedex, France
Tel.: [33] 1 60.72.42.15
Email: admissions@insead.fr
www.insead.fr

IMD—International Institute for
Management Development
MBA Information Service
Chemin de Bellerive 23
CH-1007 Lausanne, Switzerland
Tel.: [41] (21) 618 10 11
Fax: [41] (21) 617 71 54

The London Business School
Sussex Place
Regent's Park
London NWI 4SA, England
Tel: [44] (171) 262 5050
Email: mba-info@lbs.lon.ac.uk
www.lbs.lon.ac.uk

IESE—European Graduate School of
Business and Management
Avenida Pearson 21
E-08034 Barcelona, Spain
Tel.: [34] (3) 204 40 00
Fax: [34] (3) 280 11 70

Manchester Business School
Booth Street West
Manchester M15 6PB, England

Rotterdam School of Management
Burgmeester Oudlaan 50
P.O. Box 1738
NL-3000 DR Rotterdam, Netherlands

Scuola di Direzione Aziendale
Via Bocconi 8
I-20136 Milan, Italy

Instituto de Estudios Superiores de la
Empresa
Avenida Pearson 21
E-08034 Barcelona, Spain

Internships

There are many programs for college students seeking international internships. These internships are often available for academic credit and can be unpaid. You do, however, receive valuable work experience that can be the ticket to launching your international career.

The best place to find out about internship programs is through the career center or the international programs office at your university. Program details—types of programs offered, number of placements available, application requirements—vary from year to year, so become familiar with your campus resources for international exchanges. The following books can also be helpful for identifying internships.

Directory of International Internships. Career Development and Placement Service Office of Michigan State University, 113 Student Services Building, East Lansing, MI 48824. Lists internships across a wide spectrum of interests.

International Directory of Youth Internships. Apex Press, Publications Office, P.O. Box 337, Croton-on-Hudson, NY 10520. Lists United Nations agencies and affiliated organizations that offer internship and volunteer opportunities.

International Internships and Volunteer Programs. Cantrell and Modderno. Worldwise Books, P.O. Box 3030, Oakton, VA 22124.

Internships. Peterson's Guides. P.O. Box 2123, Princeton, NJ 08543-2123. Concentrates mostly on opportunities in the United States, but also includes a chapter on the international arena.

Internships: Travel and Hospitality Industries. Gale Research, 27500 Drake Road, Farmington Hills, MI 48331.

Internships in Foreign and Defense Policy: A Complete Guide for Women (and Men). Seven Locks Press, P.O. Box 27, Cabin John, MD 20818.

The specific country-by-country reports in Part II include information on organizations that arrange regional internships. Three internship programs, however, are worth mentioning here. **The American-Scandinavian Foundation** (725 Park Avenue, New York, NY 10021; (212) 879-9779) offers paid internships in Finland, Norway, Denmark, and Sweden in engineering, horticultural, forestry, and agricultural fields. **IASTE,** the **International Association for the Exchange of Students for Technical Experience** (10400 Little Patuxent Parkway, Suite 250, Columbia, MD 21044-3510; (410) 997-3068) places students studying science, engineering, math, agriculture, or architecture into internships in 65 different countries. **CDS International, Inc.** (330 7th Avenue, New York, NY 10001; (212) 760-1400) offers internships in Germany in fields ranging from engineering to business.

Interning with Uncle Sam

Don't overlook the U.S. government for possible overseas opportunities. The Department of State, for example, offers spring, summer, and fall internships to upper-level undergraduates and graduate students. While most of these positions are at the Department's Washington, D.C., headquarters, opportunities are available to serve as Junior Foreign Service Officers—performing professional-level work in research, writing, computer science, international law—at U.S. embassies and consulates abroad. For more information, write to the Intern Coordinator, Recruitment Division, Department of State, P.O. Box 9317, Arlington, VA 22219. As with any bureaucracy, processing of applications takes time. Be advised that application deadlines are generally six to eight months before one's time of potential employment.

Temporary Jobs

Jobs such as au pair work, workcamps, agriculture work, and menial labor that don't require a formal education are relatively easy to obtain. Au pairs are in constant demand, and there are many agencies that place Americans in European homes. This work is time-consuming and often doesn't leave much free time for travel. Work camps and agricultural work are plentiful during specific seasons. During fruit picking season, for example, laborers are in high demand. Working in resorts, as in agriculture, is also seasonal. Chapter 9 presents a rundown of possibilities for these and other temporary positions. Resources for temporary work are included in the country-by-country reports in Part II of this book.

three

Key Employment Sectors in the New Europe

n 1992 the 12 member countries of the European Union (E.U.) formed a single market, a market which some have referred to as a "United States of Europe." Previously known as the "European Community" or "Common Market," the European Union features common financial regulations, trade and labor standards, and free access to members' products and jobs. This merger created a unified economic system, increasing European economic power and mobility. Member nations remain independent, but trade, manufacturing, finance, and transportation have largely become pan-European efforts. With over 330 million prosperous consumers, the European Union has become the world's largest market and a large employment market as well. This market and the Union should continue to expand. The E.U. has grown from its original 12 to 15 members.

The Single Market

The E.U.'s objective is to create an internal market without restrictions on movement of goods, services, labor, and capital. Trade and movement in such a market are as open as among the states of the U.S. Foreign companies, too, are allowed to compete in previously protected areas.

Although the single market benefits economic growth and standards of living in the E.U. as a whole, it will take time to develop. Initial competition among companies for market position in the European Union creates lower prices and unemployment. But as the companies grow, expand, and profit, the single market is expected to create at least 2 million new jobs in the next decade.

The southern European economies, especially Greece, Spain, Portugal, and parts of Italy, will receive structural development funds from Brussels, the capital of the European Union, to provide them greater parity with the richer northern members, and they should prosper from increased European investment.

Opening trading lines and dismantling restrictions among the European countries create opportunities for expansion in the European marketplace. Italian companies that only sold merchandise in France, for example, can now produce the same items and market them across Europe without prohibitive restrictions, taxes, or national alterations to the product. Since these companies are opening themselves up to a more competitive market, mergers between companies and expansions among the larger ones is now the rule of business, as national firms attempt to acquire international expertise and enter new markets.

Decisions by European companies to merge with both European and American companies have helped to cut costs, increase productivity, and form strategic alliances. U.S. multinational companies that have been enjoying a large market now must face new competition from these larger and more powerful European companies. With the new changes in the European market, American companies must consider their competitors' improved positions and reformulate their European business strategies.

Who's who in the European Union

Current members: Austria, Belgium, Britain, Denmark, Finland, France, Germany, Greece, Ireland, Italy, Luxembourg, the Netherlands, Portugal, Spain, and Sweden.

Good future bets for the E.U.: Switzerland, Slovenia, the Czech Republic, Hungary, Poland, Iceland.

Long shots: Turkey, Malta, Cyprus, Bulgaria, Romania, Albania, Slovakia, Croatia, Bosnia, Macedonia, Serbia-Montenegro, Moldova.

Real long shots: Russia, Morocco, Tunisia, Ukraine, Belarus.

A Common Currency

Beginning January 1, 1999, members of the E.U. adopted a single European currency, newly named the Euro. The economic case for a single currency in Europe rests on three main claims: 1) that it will lower transaction costs for traders and travelers; 2) that it is necessary to complete the Single Market, and 3) that participants will benefit from a strong, inflation-free currency with a reputation inherited from the deutsche mark. Prior to the introduction of the Euro, a tourist who successively changed $100 into the currency of Member States would end up with roughly $50 after paying commission charges and adjusting for different exchange rates. Arguments for the single European currency rest on the hope that it will usher in permanent low inflation. With low inflation, markets will work more efficiently, the quality of savings and investment decisions will improve, tax distortions can be removed, and incomes can be more evenly distributed.

There may also be problems with the Euro. In a single currency area, local wages and price levels take the strain of the readjustment. It could also result in large migrations of workers seeking employment in prosperous areas.

There is great uncertainty about the end economic result of a single European currency, and European businesses will be under great pressure to prepare new price lists and invoices in that currency.

Who's who in the EMU:
European Monetary Union members: Austria, Belgium, Finland, France, Germany, Ireland, Italy, Luxembourg, the Netherlands, Portugal, and Spain.

Central Europe

Almost ten years have passed since the communist governments of East Germany, Poland, Czechoslovakia, and Hungary collapsed and were replaced by democratically elected leaders. In Romania, instability continues despite the Communist Party's fall from power. Bulgaria's leaders have also pursued slower changes. The former state of Yugoslavia finds itself embroiled in ethnic tensions and civil war, although the former republics of Croatia and Slovenia have elected democratic governments and favor economic liberalization.

Foreign investment provides the developing Central European economies with funds, expertise, and technology for continued fast-paced growth. The developing countries in return supply the foreign investors with inexpensive development and labor costs. Poland, Hungary, and the Czech Republic have attracted the bulk of foreign investment in Central Europe. In addition to being the closest to Western style democracy, these countries have liberalized their economies. Poland, the Czech Republic, and Hungary's privatization efforts provide opportunities for foreign investors, although some have been more successful than others.

Privatization, foreign investment, unemployment, and convertible currencies will severely challenge these economies. The initial transformations into market economics will dislodge traditional relationships and radically alter national development. Central Europe will face economic and possibly political instability and uncertainty in the near future. Foreign investment in such an environment may be limited by such concerns. Despite the obstacles, these economies boast educated, well-trained work forces, an existing industrial infrastructure, and proximity to the E.U. marketplace. These advantages should help Central Europe compete for investment with East Asia and Latin America.

Democratization also attracts development aid from the Western powers. American companies entering the Central European marketplace will face competition from E.U. firms, especially German companies. German banks have already assumed the lead in lending to Central Europe.

The region's future relationship to the E.U. remains unresolved. While aid from the E.U. to Central Europe has been forthcoming, the poorer southern members of the E.U. fear that foreign investments, which would have been made in their own low-cost economies, will shift to Central Europe. Japan's Suzuki Motor Co., for example, decided to build its new European plant in Hungary instead of Spain as previously announced. The outlook is good for Central Europe; the outcome, however, is still undecided.

What European Business Expansion Means to Americans Seeking Jobs

With the expansion of American firms into the European market, you might assume that jobs for Americans would be abundant, but that is not necessarily the case. Basic regulations within each country ensure that a certain percentage of jobs are held by citizens of that country. Most of the jobs open to Americans in these countries are short-term in nature, for those with specific skills, or for top-level executives.

Another competitive disadvantage for Americans is the fact that workers from E.U. countries do not have to obtain work permits. They are allowed to travel and obtain employment in other E.U. countries without any restrictions. A worker from Italy can travel to Greece, for example, to locate employment without worrying about a visa or work permit. European workers can easily gain employment in any E.U. member country, providing employers with a large pool of European applicants to choose from before they have to consider foreigners.

There are still, of course, many openings that Americans can fill after mastering the paperwork. Many American accountants, consultants, investment lawyers, and mergers and acquisitions specialists have settled in Europe's financial capitals to take advantage of the upcoming general business expansion.

Americans can overcome employment roadblocks by emphasizing their unique skills and intelligently marketing themselves to potential employers. Writing an effective international resume and highlighting the education, training, and experience desired by European employers are certainly keys. The most practical route to employment in Europe is to find a position in the U.S. and transfer abroad later. U.S.-based multinational manufacturers and exporters, internationally oriented consulting and law firms, and communication companies present opportunities for employment in Europe. Summer work and internships in Europe also serve to introduce a potential employer to an applicant's talents.

Language skills certainly help promote an American's employment opportunities in Europe. Within the E.U. bureaucracy, French and English dominate, although German is spreading. English predominates at the lower levels, with French still important in the higher branches. In business, French and German are widespread although a host country's language may range from Flemish to Portuguese to Magyar.

Employment Sectors in the E.U.

Various fields have been affected in different ways by the establishment of the European Union. American business and employment opportunities will reflect these changes in each country. However, a few sectors hold special promise and potential for American job seekers.

Manufacturing and trading. Joint ventures and mergers between American and European manufacturing and trading firms are becoming increasingly important and necessary. The Daimler-Benz and Chrysler merger illustrates how companies are looking to become more competitive by taking advantage of economies of scale. Within five years, Daimler-Benz anticipates that it expects to save an additional $3 billion annually by sharing engineering and manufacturing know-how. The two companies will share each other's factories, infrastructure, and intellectual capacities.

Americans attempting to find jobs with U.S. companies should demonstrate an ability to satisfy local needs such as providing local connections to suppliers, bureaucracies, and distribution networks needed to succeed in new markets. This type of expertise usually comes through previous work or internship experience in the country, and at a minimum, superior language ability. Specific technical or business skills are also highly sought after and should be a focal point for any American applicant. Otherwise, an applicant's skills, experience, and/or research in the industry should be emphasized.

Retail. The retail industry in Europe grew significantly in the 1980s as European consumers became richer and correspondingly spent more money. Currently, however, retailers face slower growth because as consumers get richer, they spend a lower portion of their incomes on basic necessities such as food and clothing. European supermarket chains have already formed joint-purchasing agreements to reduce costs. Retailers expect that expansion across Europe will take time and extensive consumer preference research. National and regional variations in consumer tastes will probably frustrate the quest for the common "Euroconsumer." Eventually, retailing should benefit from the elimination of trade barriers, which reduces prices of goods. American retailers have yet to exploit fully the European market; but European retailers are very active in the U.S. This should be seen as a real employment opportunity for Americans with big-picture experience in retailing.

Eastern European retailing is erupting out of state-controlled inefficiency and shortages, as new business opportunities in the industry emerge. East European shops are overstaffed and undersupplied, and distribution systems are largely inept. The region's retail industry is likely to expand anyway because of huge consumer savings awaiting spending. Again, Americans who are in a position to offer senior experience and management know-how have a number of employment options. The pay, however, may not be up to Western standards.

Agriculture. The E.U. contains over 10 million politically astute and highly efficient farmers. Many farmers have found that increasing efficiency by eliminating excess labor increases their E.U. subsidies. Employment in agribusiness probably won't skyrocket anytime soon, although low-skill seasonal employment in agriculture, especially in wine-producing areas, is generally abundant for Americans.

Management consulting and finance. Consulting is growing by 20 percent annually in the U.S. and even faster overseas. With the tremendous surge of business activity in Europe, accompanied by increased global competition and uncertainty, management consulting will be in even greater demand. Many consulting firms are already operating overseas, but with European integration, these firms and others will be expanding at record rates.

The $8 billion merger between Deutsche Bank and Banker's Trust illustrates the extent to which being competitive in financial markets depends on being a global player. The purchase gives Germany's biggest bank control of the eighth-largest U.S. bank, but one suffering from heavy losses in emerging markets and heated competition in investment banking. Deutsche Bank would gain a major U.S. foothold after failing to build a U.S. investment-banking business that can compete with Wall Street firms like Merrill Lynch & Co. and Goldman, Sachs & Co.

Hotels and tourism. This industry should prosper throughout Europe. Eastern Europe's tourist trade is only now beginning to draw American attention but has lured West Europeans, especially Germans, for years. Short-term work is often available for Americans. Higher-level management positions demand high-level experience.

Non-profit organizations in Europe may be found in Brussels and Strasbourg, the sites of the E.U. administration and the European Parliament, and various United Nations agencies reside in Geneva and Paris. Many global relief and development organizations are based in London and Rome. Environmental groups exist throughout the E.U. but especially in Germany and northern Europe, where air pollution has been most severe. Specialized knowledge and experience along with familiarity with languages and culture are the key to non-profit jobs. Any time a job seeker can offer a type of experience not easily found locally the chances for getting a job increase substantially.

Education employment in Europe assumes several forms: English language teaching is fairly common; secondary and university education positions are usually unionized and difficult to acquire; American primary and secondary schools in Europe are quite common and offer numerous opportunities. English language teaching, while easy to find, won't make you rich. It will, however, provide you with a little spending money. If you speak English and have a college degree, you are usually qualified. Teaching in an American school is not as easy. You must be certified to teach and usually have at least a few years of experience.

four

The 9-Step Job Search

The good news is that anyone with gumption and gusto can successfully find work abroad. The bad news is that no one is waiting in line to hand you your dream international job. Successful job searching, especially for one in Europe, is hard work. It hinges on your ability to effectively develop a strategy to reach the right employers. This chapter is devoted to helping you find the right resources to get the best results from the time you invest in your job search.

9 Steps to Getting a Job in Europe

STEP 1. Know why you want to work in Europe.
What do you want to get out of an international job? The answer to this question is key for focusing your job search. You need to know if you are looking for an international career or an international job. An international job is work that you do with the primary objective of supporting yourself while you live abroad. Your job may or may not be related to your long-term career plans. For example, you might work as an au pair for a year in Spain in order to improve your Spanish. An international career, by contrast, may take several years (and a graduate degree) to achieve. Most Americans working for multinationals in Europe have international careers. Your

goal—short- or long-term—for international work will direct the techniques you use to find a job. Here are a few other practical matters to consider:

Where do you want to do this job? Do you want to do this job in a German- or English-speaking country? Do you want to be in Western Europe, Central Europe, or the Balkans? Do you want to be on the beach, in the mountains, or in the city?

What special skills do you possess that might interest an employer? As we've already discussed, employers will hire you for a particular skill they need. Think first about your academic preparation. An accounting or finance degree can make you very marketable. Consider also those hidden skills that you may not have used much in your jobs in the U.S. For example, if you are good with children, you might find an employer willing to hire you as a child-care worker. If you have strong grammar and are a clear speaker, you might try teaching English.

How strong are your language skills? If you speak another language or languages fluently, you may be qualified for certain jobs. For example, most jobs in the hospitality industry, regardless of the position, require that you speak fluently at least one other European language.

What kind of experience do you want from this job? Is your primary motivation to go to Europe or are you trying to build an international career?

How important is money? Be honest! Some of the most interesting and rewarding opportunities are with volunteer organizations.

STEP 2. Identify jobs that match your background.

Think about your abilities, skills, areas of special knowledge, and your interests, particularly those you've developed through your education or previous jobs. Employers will expect that you bring a particular set of skills, and often your accounting, finance, or computer science degree may prepare you with what you need. You may also find that you possess special abilities that can also place you in demand. For example, if you like working outside, agricultural work might be a good fit. If you are an excellent cook, you might apply as a chef in a guesthouse or ski resort.

STEP 3. Research your country.

Your next step is to become completely familiar with the country in which you would like to work. The best place to begin is by reading local newspapers. Chapters 11-20 include lists of major newspapers in each country in Europe, often available at larger newsstands or university libraries. Additionally, many newspapers also maintain sites on the World Wide Web. Also contact the appropriate chambers of commerce and world trade centers. Your goal is to become knowledgeable about key industrial sectors, economic trends, and relevant employment laws. You should be familiar with any cross-culture issues that will affect your job search.

The following list of directories can help with your research. A more complete list is included in the International Business section of Chapter 8. Professional organizations—which you should seek out on your own, according to your particular career interests—are also a resource for your research.

DIRECTORIES

Directory of American Firms Operating in Foreign Countries. (UniWorld Business Publications, 50 East 42nd Street, Suite 509, New York, NY 10017) Covers around 3,000 American firms with branches in Europe.

Europe's 15,000 Largest Companies. (ELC Publishing, 109 Uxbridge Road, Ealing, London W5 5TL, England) Includes rankings of Europe's 500 most profitable and 125 least profitable firms.

Human Rights Directory: Western Europe. (c/o Human Rights Centre, University of Ottawa, 57 Louis Pasteur, Ottawa, ON KIN 605) Covers around 850 human rights organizations in Western Europe.

International Directory of Importers. (Interdata, 1480 Grove Street, Healdsburg, CA 95448) The edition on Europe contains information on most major importers.

Major Companies of Europe. (Distributed in the U.S. by Kluwer, Inc., 101 Philip Drive, Assinippi Park, Norwell, MA 02061) Lists approximately 6,500 top firms.

Medium Companies of Europe. (Available from Kluwer, Inc.) Approximately 8,000 listings.

Pan-European Associations: A Directory of Multi-National Organizations in Europe. (CBD Research, 15 Wickham Road, Beckenham, Kent BR3 2JS, England) Over 17,000 multinational organizations listed and described.

Ward's Business Directory. (Gale Research, Book Tower, Detroit, MI 48226) Covers 15,000 of the larger international corporations.

WORLD TRADE CENTERS

World Trade Centers can provide information on international businesses, regional job markets, and influential people in the international business world. Here is a list of World Trade Centers in major U.S. cities:

Atlanta
World Trade Center Atlanta
One SunTrust Plaza
Lower Lobby, Suite 100
303 Peachtree Street NE
Atlanta, GA 30308-3235
Tel.: (404) 880-1550, (404) 880-1551
Fax: (404) 880-1555
Email: wtcatl@mindspring.com
www.wtcatlanta.com

Boston
World Trade Center, Boston
164 Northern Avenue
Executive Offices, Suite 50
Boston, MA 02210-2004
Tel.: (617) 385-5000,
Fax: (617) 385-5033
Email: wti@wtcb.com
www.wtcb.com/

Chicago
200 World Trade Center Chicago,
Suite 2400
Chicago, IL 60654
Tel.: (312) 467-0550
Fax: (312) 467-0615
Email: info@wtcc.org
www.wtcc.org

Denver
World Trade Center, Denver
1625 Broadway, Suite 680
Denver, CO 80202
Tel.: (303) 592-5760
Fax: (303) 592-5228
Email: wtcdenver@worldnet.att.net
www.wtcdn.com

Detroit
1251 Fort Street
Trenton, MI 48183
Tel.: (313) 479-2345
Fax: (313) 479-5733
Email: wtcdw@sprintmail.com

Houston
Houston World Trade Association
1200 Smith, Suite 700
Houston, TX 77002
Tel.: (713) 844-3637
Fax: (713) 844-0200
Email: pfoley@houston.org
www.houston.org

Indianapolis
54 Monument Circle, Suite 250
Indianapolis, IN 46204
Tel.: (317) 756-8102
Fax: (317) 756-8122
www.wtcin.com

Los Angeles
Los Angeles World Trade Center
Greater Los Angeles World Trade
Center Association
350 S. Figueroa Street, Suite 172
Los Angeles, CA 90071
Tel.: (310) 680-1888
Fax: (310) 680-1878
Email: enter@glawtca.latrade.org

Miami
World Trade Center, Miami
5600 N.W. 36th Street, Suite 601
Post Office Box 590508
Miami, FL 33159-0508
Tel.: (305) 871-7910
Fax: (305) 871-7904
Email: info@worldtrade.org
www.worldtrade.org

New York
World Trade Center, New York
The Port Authority of New York and
New Jersey
Suite 88 West
New York, NY 10048
Tel.: (212) 435-7168
Fax: (212) 435-2810
Email: dmay@panynj.gov

Philadelphia
Greater Philadelphia World Trade and
Financial Center
Carl Marks & Co.
135 East 57th Street
New York, NY 10022
Tel.: (212) 909-8400
Fax: (212) 980-2631

San Francisco
World Trade Center of San Francisco
250 Montgomery Street, 14th Floor
San Francisco, CA 94104
Tel.: (415) 392-2705
Fax: (415) 392-1710
Email: leina@bawtc.baytrade.org

Seattle
Seattle World Trade Center
CRG Hospitality
2200 Alaskan Way, Suite 410
Seattle, WA 98121
Tel.: (206) 441-5144
Fax: (206) 441-6369
Email: wtcseattle@crgnet.com

St. Louis
World Trade Center, St. Louis
St. Louis County Economic Council
121 South Meramec, Suite 1111
St. Louis, MO 63105

Tel.: (314) 854-6141
Fax: (314) 862-0102
Email: wtcst@co.st-louis.mo.us
www.st-louis.mo.us/st-
louis/county/wtc

Washington, D.C.
World Trade Center, Washington, DC
245 Davis Avenue SW
Leesburg, VA 20175
Tel.: (703) 779-2014
Fax: (703) 779-8611
Email: runde@usa.net

World Trade Centers are also located in the following U.S. cities (check local listings for contact information): Baltimore, Bridgeport, Charleston, Columbus, Fort Lauderdale, Honolulu, Irvine, Jacksonville, Kansas City, Las Vegas, Long Beach, McAllen, Milwaukee, New Orleans, Norfolk, Orlando, Oxnard, Phoenix, Pittsburgh, Portland, Raleigh-Durham, San Antonio, St. Paul, Tacoma, Tampa, Wichita, Wilmington.

STEP 4. Write a resume and cover letter.

Your international resume and cover letter resemble those you prepare for an American job search, but there are important differences. First, you should describe your education in a way that someone not familiar with the American educational system will understand. For example, instead of listing a GPA, use "Grade Point Average" or a class ranking, such as "top 25% of class." Do not use acronyms or abbreviations that would be unfamiliar to a European employer. Emphasize the specific, practical skills you offer an employer, such as programming or business skills. Include any previous international experience to assure the employer that you are familiar with working or living in a cross-cultural setting. If you are applying through a program such as BUNAC, which arranges your work permit, be sure to include that information. Finally, most European employers expect you to include personal information, such as your age, marital status, and health. There are examples of good resumes and cover letters included in Chapter 5.

STEP 5. Use a variety of job-search strategies.

Generally, the more techniques you use to find job leads the faster you'll find work. Job search strategies fall into three categories: identifying specific openings, targeted mailings, and networking. Depending on your interests, some of these approaches may be more effective than others. For example, non-profit organizations frequently do not advertise job openings, and networking is the best way to uncover these leads. On the other hand, the federal government is required to advertise every vacancy.

Job openings are advertised in a variety of locations, and you should take advantage of all of them. They include local newspapers, employment agencies, professional organization newsletters, and job bulletins. International positions are frequently advertised in *The Economist* and the *International Herald Tribune* (see Chapter 1). European employers, especially in the U.K. and Ireland, are increasingly listing jobs on the World Wide Web. Each chapter in Part II lists useful websites for job seekers in that country.

SOURCES LISTING INTERNATIONAL OPENINGS

ACCESS: Networking in the Public Interest
50 Beacon Street
Boston, MA 02108
Tel.: (617) 720-JOBS
Listings are primarily for community work within the U.S. but occasionally include international positions with non-profit organizations.

International Career Employment Opportunities
Route 2, Box 305
Stanardsville, VA 22973
Tel.: (804) 985-6444
Fax: (804) 985-6828
Email: intlcareers@internemci.com
Includes listings in agriculture, business, computers, construction, education, social services, and more. Published every other week.

International Employment Gazette
2200 North Main Street, Suite 100
Greenville, SC 29601
Tel.: (800) 822-9188
Fax: (803) 235-3369
Lists private-sector business and technical jobs and teaching and volunteer experiences.

International Employment Hotline
Will Cantrell, Editor
P.O. Box 3030
Oakton, VA 22124
Tel.: (703) 620-1972
Fax: (703) 620-1973

Overseas Employment Newsletter
1255 Laird Blvd., Suite 208
Town of Mount Royal
Quebec, Canada H3P 2T1
Tel.: (514) 739-1108
Fax: (514) 739-0795

USEFUL WEBSITES FOR EUROPEAN JOB LISTINGS

www.businesseurope.com
Gives economic forecasts for European countries.

www.topjobs.co.uk
A detailed and efficiently laid out website of worldwide job offerings.

www.escapeartist.com/jobs/overseas1.htm
Wonderful, comprehensive website that has job offerings for Europe.

www.europages.com
Search engine with a multi-country capacity with multi-language queries.

www.job-office.com
Uncomplicated database featuring European job offerings.

accom.finder.co.uk:80
Impressive website that finds accommodations.

www-europe.hp.com/JobPosting
Hewlett Packard has job postings for European countries.

www.tesol.net/tesljob.html
Information about teaching jobs in Europe.

Targeted mailings can be effective if done properly. A targeted mailing is not synonymous with a mass mailing. With a mass mailing, you might send a letter and resume to 50 or more employers. You will probably receive little response for the money you spend on postage. With a targeted mailing, however, you identify a select number of employers to whom you want to apply. Your criteria for setting up a targeted mailing might include: 1) Type of employer; 2) Geographic location; 3) Size of employer; 4) Hiring history (for example, have they hired Americans with your background?). Your advantage with a targeted mailing is that you work with a select number of companies to which you can write carefully drafted letters explaining your qualifications. You also can better manage effective follow-up.

Your initial list should include no more than 20 carefully selected employers. Try to get your package to a specific person who manages a department in which you would like to work. (You could also send the same package to the personnel department, although since their job is to process employment information, not make hiring decisions, they are less likely to be able to provide the kind of attention you need.) In each package, send an individualized cover letter (see the section on cover letters in Chapter 5) and a resume. Be prepared to follow-up by telephone, letter, or email on every package you mail. To get an idea of which organizations and people to target, talk to your contacts, use library resources, directories, and chambers of commerce.

The electronic international job search
The explosion of the Internet makes the international job search easier and much less costly. An increasing number of European employers are listing positions on Internet job-posting sites, such as the **Monsterboard** (www.monster.co.uk/). Most large companies maintain a Web page, including a site with employment information. Lists of useful websites for the job searcher are included in each country report in Part II. Get an Email address if you don't

already have one; Yahoo! offers free Email accounts. This will make following up with employers much easier.

Consider developing an electronic version of your resume that you can submit to an employer by email. An electronic resume resembles your regular resume except that all of the text embellishment, such as boldface, italics, or underlining, has been removed. Finally, consider creating a personal Web page on which you can post your resume. Your goal is to be as accessible as possible to a potential European employer!

Check out Joyce Lain Kennedy's *Hook Up, Get Hired* (John Wiley & Sons) for complete information on conducting an electronic job search. Margaret Dikel (the former Margaret Riley) maintains the **Riley Guide** (www.dbm.com/jobguide/), a complete site for job searching on the Web.

Finding your job online

Dear Bob and Cheryl:

I decided I wanted something other than the usual summer-abroad work experience—something other than waitstaffing, bartending, or temping. I really wanted a job in a high-tech industry because my major in college is computer science, so I started looking for high-tech jobs in London. I didn't have too much luck with my international summer job search while only pursuing the usual job search routes, such as contacting alumni and computer companies listed in work abroad books. As an alternative to these approaches, I decided to post my resume on about ten of the major online job banks, and I used the job banks to apply online to specific high-tech jobs posted on the Internet.

In a few weeks, I received a solicitation to interview with a London-based network administrator. That administrator became my boss in a few weeks. My job as a computer support analyst is still the best summer job I've ever had. My boss and I still keep in touch, and it's great to know that not only do I have an international friend, but I also have an international industry contact.

Jyoti Gupta
Houston, Texas

STEP 6. Network.

Networking, or talking with people you know who can help you in your job search, will generally yield your best results. Employers, especially those who have not previously hired Americans, are more likely to consider you if you have been referred by someone they trust. Potential contacts include friends, people you meet through professional organizations, relatives, alumni, speakers at on-campus events, professors, former employers, and many others. Find creative ways to expand the number of your contacts. Most networking happens informally. You meet someone at a party who knows someone working for a company in Paris in which you are interested. You can create occasions for "spontaneous" networking by telling many people about your job search.

Networking for a job on a different continent can be difficult, but it's not impossible. You will probably be surprised at how many people you already know who are able to provide you with leads—at least for other contacts. World Trade Centers also provide a good starting point, and international alumni from schools you attended can also be helpful. Use professional associations and international chambers of commerce as resources to make helpful contacts.

One assertive technique for making contacts in a particular field is the information interview. These are not the same as job interviews. You are not asking your contact for a job, rather for information about their company or industry. The purpose of the information interview is to teach you more about a particular career field and help you build a useful network. As you begin your international job search, conducting information interviews with local people can help you learn more about particular companies and find connections to helpful people living and working in Europe.

The following is a list of questions you may want to ask in an information interview. It is your responsibility to understand the nature of your visit (i.e., to get information, not a job), to know the basics about the organization ahead of time (so as not to waste time), and to take responsibility for the progress of the interview.

JOB DESCRIPTION

- What are your major duties and responsibilities?
- How does your position fit into the structure of the organization?
- With what people in the organization (superiors, subordinates, peers) do you have the most contact?
- Describe a typical day.
- What aspects of your job do you find most interesting?
- What aspects do you enjoy least?
- What changes do you see occurring in this field? Will the type and number of jobs change significantly over the next 10 years? What, if any, will be the effect of changing technology on the field?

CAREER PATH

- What are the typical entry-level jobs in this field?
- What is the best way to find this job in Europe?
- What were the positions you had that led to this one?
- How long does it usually take to move from one step to the next in this field?
- Are there any specifically defined prerequisites for advancement—for example, years in service, examinations, advanced degrees, board interviews, and so on?
- What are the best jobs in this field for career advancement?
- Are there other areas of this field to which people in it may be transferred? What are they?

PREPARATION

- What are the academic and experience prerequisites for entry-level jobs in this field?
- Is the degree I'm working on/I have suitable?
- Are there any specific courses I might take that would be particularly useful?
- Are there any extracurricular or other experiences (work, volunteering, internships, etc.) that would enhance my chances of employment?
- What types of training do companies give persons entering the field?
- What advice would you give to someone planning to enter this field?

GENERAL

- What is the current demand for employees at entry level in this field? And higher?
- What are the salary ranges at various levels in the field?
- How many hours a week does someone typically work in this field?
- Where might I find job descriptions and other specifications for some of the positions in this field?
- Are the content and format of my resume appropriate for someone seeking a job in this field?
- Is there anyone else in the field with whom you would suggest I talk?

Don't let the information interview end without asking this last question. This is how you expand your network. Remember, your job search depends on who you know, and networking is the way you meet them.

Alumni networking

One networking option you may want to try is your university alumni association. Many alumni associations have a contact service that can put you in touch with alumni overseas who are willing to help graduates of their *alma mater.* While this by no means assures you of a job, since the alumni abroad may have nothing to do with hiring, it can provide you with contacts in various overseas companies. The individual alumnus may be able to provide information on the local job market, help you get an interview, help you find accommodations in an area you would visit for an interview, or perhaps even provide a place for you to stay during your visit.

STEP 7. Organize your job search.

Approach your job search deliberately. Keeping records, a daily planner, and scheduling each day's activities will improve your job search's efficiency. A few other tips:

Decide how to spend your time each day. An international job search can be very, very slow, and the long periods you will spend waiting for an employer to respond to your letters may zap your motivation. The successful job seekers, however, are persistent. Structure your job search tasks and plan to spend regular time each week working to accomplish them.

Keep a personal calendar for your appointments.

Keep all of your contact information (see below for specifics) organized in a notebook or index-card file so you'll have complete records ready for follow-up.

Don't expect quick success. A job search in the U.S. takes at least 6 months, and an international job search can take much longer.

Develop a support system. Job searching can be frustrating, especially if you are receiving little response to your hard work. Know which of your friends and family can provide emotional support. Better yet, form a job-search group of friends who also want to work abroad.

Allow free time to do fun things, and give yourself breaks. Remember why you decided to work in Europe in the first place!

For *each* employer you contact, keep the following information:
- Name, address, phone number, fax, and email of the employer.
- Brief description of the employer.
- Name and title of contact person(s) within the firm.
- Where you found out about the job (publication, professor, friend, etc.).
- Specific or possible openings.
- Date you sent initial resume.
- Follow-up by you or employer. (If the employer doesn't contact you within two weeks of your mailing, you should call them).
- Date of interview and other interview information (place, interviewer, any information gleaned from the interview, and so on).

- Date you sent thank-you letter.
- Resolution: what happened with this employer, and (to the best of your knowledge) why.

STEP 8. Follow-up on all calls and letters; keep talking to people.

Employers, especially international employers, are more likely to treat you seriously if you promise to follow-up on your initial calls or letters. They are less likely to shove your resume under a stack of personnel files if you make it clear that you will be calling back soon. Follow-up phone calls to Europe from the United States are a possibility and can indicate a true interest on your part in getting a particular job. Email can be an equally effective and less costly alternative for contacting employers.

Improving response and follow-up

Nothing is more frustrating than sending off letters and getting little or no response. Three tips can help. First, many European companies make extensive use of faxing as a part of their day-to-day activities. While faxing unsolicited resumes or letters of inquiry isn't a good plan, you might better your chances for a prompt response if you include a fax number with your initial correspondence. A fax number also indicates to potential employers that you could speedily provide whatever additional information they might need.

Second, you might improve your chances not only of a prompt follow-up but of actual employment if you can tell employers you already have a work permit. CIEE, BUNAC, and IASTE are three organizations that can provide students with temporary work permits for certain European countries (see Chapter 9). Many employers would be glad not to have to secure an employment permit for you.

Finally, be aware that smaller organizations—especially non-profits—simply don't have the funds to respond to every inquiry they receive (including both unsolicited resumes and requests for information). By enclosing International Reply Coupons (IRCs) available from your local post office, you incur the cost of the return mailing, not them.

STEP 9. Go to Europe and make personal contact.

There is no substitute for face-to-face interviews. No matter how professional your resume is, it can only help your chances of securing a job if you establish contact in person. By visiting the companies yourself, you will impress them with the seriousness of your interest in working with them. Also, if you have the opportunity to visit the organizations you are interested in, you'll have a better idea of where you would or wouldn't feel comfortable working. Only plan to travel to Europe once you have established some solid job leads or firm appointments for informational interviews.

There are no magic spells to make an international job search move quickly. The requirements for success are rather mundane—persistence, organization, and aggressiveness. There are many resources to help you with your job search, but ultimately, success is up to you. And you will feel tremendous satisfaction knowing that you made it happen. *Bonne chance!*

five

The International Resume

Your resume is a tool to get you a job or an interview. Although most of the components of an international resume are similar to those you would use for a U.S. job search, there are important differences. European employers expect to see personal information, including marital status, age, and health information on the resume. You will want to make sure you have clearly explained all your experiences, especially your education, in terms that are meaningful to employers not familiar with the U.S. Most important, you must stress those points that make you unique in the international job market. Many Europeans are accustomed to resumes that are long and tell a life story. However, the short one-page version, with select highlighted information areas, is becoming increasingly popular. This type of resume should focus only on the information that will be most important to a prospective employer.

The purpose of a resume is to concisely tell an employer:

- Who you are.
- What you have done.
- What you do now.
- What you can do.

Resume Format

There is no one "right" style or format—at home or abroad. You can choose any format that works well for you and that you find appealing. Here are the most common formats:

Chronological: The chronological resume is the traditional style most often used in the workplace and job search. In this format, you would list your experience in chronological order, beginning with your most recent experience and working backward. The advantage of this format is that it is familiar and easy for employers to read.

Functional: The functional resume is most common among career changers, people reentering the job market after a lengthy absence, and those wishing to highlight aspects of their experience not related directly to employment. This resume places the emphasis on the skills you possess rather than the places you obtained them. A functional skills resume is the most difficult to write, but can be very effective at demonstrating to an employer what you know how to do.

Combination: The combination resume combines the best features of a functional resume and a chronological resume. You can highlight skills and accomplishments while maintaining the somewhat traditional format of a reverse chronological resume.

LAYOUT AND APPEARANCE

Employers won't read your resume; they will skim it. Make sure information is clear and concise.

Some general format tips for all resumes:
- Use one-inch margins on all sides.
- Place material in order of importance.
- Use a reverse chronological sequence.
- Highlight important points by underlining or using boldface print.
- Fit the resume on one page unless you have a long work history.

Here are some additional hints:
- Use the jargon of your profession.
- Stress your assets; downplay your liabilities.
- Do not exaggerate, and be prepared to provide hard proof of your credentials (i.e., copies of certificates, diplomas, pay stubs from previous employment).
- Use the present tense for current experiences and the past tense for previous experiences.
- Write in telegraphic style, which avoids using personal pronouns.
- Avoid abbreviations; write everything out in full.

- Have clear copies made on good-quality bond paper, preferably on European-sized A-5 (21x29.7cm.) white paper.
- Use same-sized paper for both your resume and your cover letter.
- Proofread carefully for grammatical, spelling, or typographical errors.
- Have the draft of your resume reviewed by a friend or someone in the field before making a final copy.

THE ELECTRONIC RESUME

If you are applying for many jobs overseas, it may be easier and cheaper to send an electronic resume than a paper copy. An electronic resume is similar to a conventional resume, but it is designed to be read by a computer. You will use this version when you post a resume to a website or submit your resume to an employer via email. The format you choose for your conventional resume will work here, but you will want to take advantage of a few peculiarities of the electronic version:

- Develop a list of key words from company literature, job descriptions, or trade magazines. Add a "keywords" list at the top of your resume. These are words that a computer scan will search for. List computer skills and other required job skills you possess.
- Use a font size between 10 and 14 points.
- Avoid graphics, bolding, underlining, or other text embellishment.
- Leave a large margin all the way around the resume.

Check out *Resumes in Cyberspace* by Pat Criscito (Barron's Educational Series, 250 Wireless Blvd., Hauppauge, NY 11788) for more tips and examples.

Contents of an International Resume

All international resumes should contain the following information:

Name, Address, Phone: This information should appear at the top of the page. If you list two addresses or phone numbers, label them appropriately. Include the area codes with your phone number and fax number. Make sure that you include a phone number where employers can reach you or leave a message for you during their work day. Also list your email address and personal Web page.

Professional Objective: This is optional, especially if you are including a cover letter in which you specifically tailor your career objective to the job for which you are applying. You may want to use a few different resumes, highlighting different objectives and perhaps tailoring each resume to a particular employer. If you do choose to include an objective, write one that is concise, specific, and which makes sense in terms of the particular job you are applying for.

Education: Make sure you have presented your education in a format easily understood by an employer not familiar with the American system of education. List your expected or earned degrees in reverse chronological order with the dates, names, and locations of the institutions and concentrations or major fields of studies. Include your grade point averages if they enhance your presentation. If you do include grade point averages, be sure to indicate the range of the scale since these vary both domestically and internationally. (For example, write "3.5/4.0," not just "3.5.") If you include academic honors or special achievements, add a couple of words to explain it to an international employer.

Experience: This is probably the most important section of your resume. Use action words and avoid phrases like "my duties included" or "my responsibilities were." In addition to describing duties, mention special skills or accomplishments. Your work experience should be listed in reverse chronological order and should include job titles, dates of employment, names and locations of employers. Include volunteer work here only if it is career-related. Make sure that an employer reading your experience section can clearly identify your marketable skills.

International Experience: This section should include anything that will demonstrate your ability to work effectively in a foreign country. Employers are looking for your ability to adapt to different cultures and work environments.

Languages: Mention your language skills, whether you are fluent, have a working knowledge, or simply have studied a foreign language. Any exposure at all is a plus. Specify your level of knowledge, being careful not to exaggerate. You will be sorely embarrassed the first time your prospective employer calls on the phone and attempts to converse in the language. Most international employers, unless the job specifically requires complete fluency in another tongue, will be concerned mainly that you have had some experience in a language and/or are trying to acquire conversational skills (e.g., taking courses at a language school).

Additional Information: This can include hobbies, volunteer work, memberships, awards, travel, and so on. Remember that your resume is only one page, so only include information that will enhance your presentation. For example, include foreign travel since you are applying for international jobs.

References: Do not list references by name, but you can include a statement that "references will be furnished upon request." Prepare a separate sheet that lists your references, including phone numbers and email addresses. Most European employers take past employer references very seriously. Because you are not European, the employer is less familiar with your background and may consider you a risky hire. Make sure you receive permission before using anyone as a reference.

ACTIVE VERBS

Here is a partial list of active verbs useful in resume writing:

Administer: a department of people; programs; a specific activity, such as a test.

Analyze: quantitative data, statistical data, human/social situations.

Appraise: evaluate programs or services, judge the value of property, evaluate performance of individuals.

Budget: outline costs of a project; assure that money will not be spent in excess of funds; use money efficiently and economically.

Compile: gather numerical, statistical data; accumulate facts in a given topic area.

Control: exercise financial control, environmental control; control a crowd, or children.

Coordinate: numerous events involving groups of people, quantities of information, activities in several locations, events in a time sequence.

Create: artistically (visual arts, etc.); new ideas for an organization; new ways to solve mechanical problems; invent new apparatus, equipment.

Deal with pressure: risks toward self, physical and otherwise; risks toward others; time pressure, deadlines for getting work done.

Delegate: distribute tasks to others, give responsibility to others on a work team.

Distribute: products to people personally; market products, make them available to customers.

Edit: newspaper, magazine pieces, book manuscripts, etc.

Estimate: judge likely costs of an operation, project possibilities of future income, judge physical space accurately.

Evaluate: assess a program to determine its success, judge the performance of an individual.

Imagine: new ways of dealing with old problems, theoretical relationships, artistic ideas or perspectives.

Initiate: personal contacts with strangers; new ideas, ways of doing things; new approaches.

Interpret: other languages, obscure phrases or passages in English, meaning of statistical data, relative import of situations.

Interview: evaluate applicants for organizations, obtain information from others.

Investigate: seek information that may be hard to obtain, seek the underlying causes of a problem.

Listen: to conversations between others, to extended conversation from one person in order to help, to recording devices or other listening situations.

Manage: be responsible for the work of others, have responsibility for the processing of information, guide activities of a team, have responsibility for meeting objectives of an organization or department.

Monitor: follow progress of another person, observe progress of equipment or apparatus.

Negotiate: financial contracts, between individuals or groups.

Plan: anticipate future needs of a company or organization, schedule a sequence of events, arrange an itinerary for a trip.

Process: the orderly flow of data and/or information, introduce an individual to the routines and procedures of an organization, identify human interactions taking place in a group, channel information through a system.

Program: for computers; develop and arrange a sequence of events.

Promote: through written media; on a personal level, one-to-one; arrange financial backing.

Recruit: attempt to acquire the services of people for an organization.

Research: extract information from library, archives, etc.; obtain information from other people (surveys); obtain information from physical data.

Review: observe, inspect, summarize a collection of documents, information, etc.; assess effects of a program; assess performance of an individual.

Sell: convince an individual or organization to purchase or accept a product, service, idea, policy.

Speak: address an audience, individual, or group, in person or through electronic media.

Supervise: hold direct responsibility over the work of others, final responsibility; oversee the maintenance of a physical plant, building, etc.

Teach: instruct students in an academic setting; train individuals to perform certain tasks; familiarize or orient people in the context of a given system.

Translate: express words of one language in another language; reduce sophisticated language to simpler terms.

Troubleshoot: find sources of difficulty in human relations, systems, or physical apparatus.

Write: copywrite for sales; creative writing; reports or memos.

Sample Resume #1—Chronological

James K. Kindred
5411 Baton Rouge Street
Washington, DC 20052
Tel. (202) 555-0909
Fax (202) 555-0910

EDUCATION:	**Georgetown University,** Washington, DC M.B.A., May 1999, Concentration in Marketing Extensive course work in International Business Chair of International Society **Northern Illinois University,** DeKalb, Illinois B.A. Economics, May 1995 Presidential Scholar, cum laude Course work in International Relations and Spanish
EXPERIENCE:	MANAGEMENT CONSULTANT, **Ernst & Young,** Houston, Texas. Provided consulting services to the energy industry. Involved in developing an international client base. June 1995-1997; Summer 1998 MARKETING ASSISTANT, **Health and Fitness Magazine,** Chicago, Illinois. Initiated a new marketing strategy to increase circulation of the magazine in the Chicago restaurant community. August 1994-April 1995. COMPUTER CONSULTANT, **Northern Illinois University,** DeKalb, Illinois. Advised students in using Microsoft Word and other software programs for the Macintosh SE. January 1993-July 1994
INTERNATIONAL ACTIVITIES:	Fluent in French and Spanish; elementary Swedish. Have traveled throughout Western Europe.
LEADERSHIP ACTIVITIES:	Youth City Representative, P. W. Williams Campaign for Governor President, Student Government Tutor, Student Volunteer Program
PERSONAL:	Date of Birth: 23/09/73 Marital Status: Single Health: Excellent
REFERENCES:	Available upon request

Sample Resume #2—Functional

Deborah B. Williams
111 Kent Street
Yakima, Washington 00030
(823) 555-1313

CAREER OBJECTIVE   Position as an English teacher.

AREAS OF EXPERTISE

Interpersonal/Communication Skills
- Conducted 20-30 parent-teacher conferences per month.
- Counseled individual students as needed.
- Supervised and advised one student teacher per semester for three years.
- Interviewed applicants for employment; provided supervision and training.
- Successfully sold and marketed merchandise to customers.
- Served in leadership capacity with educational association.

International
- Fluent in French and German.
- Volunteered for 2 months in Senegal.
- Lived in Paris for one year during High School.

Planning
- Initiated and executed seminars and meetings.
- Developed lesson plans for all subjects taught.
- Assisted with leadership goals of the school and district.
- Planned and developed educational programs for in-service teacher groups.

EXPERIENCE   *Teacher,* fourth grade, Yakima School District, Yakima, Washington. 1995-present.
Assistant Manager, The Limited, Seattle, Washington. 1993-1995 (summers).
Administrative Aide, Shearson Brothers, Portland, Oregon, 1991-1992 (summers).

EDUCATION   University of Washington, Seattle, Washington
B.S., Elementary Education, 1995
G.P.A.: 3.7/4.0

HONORS/ ACTIVITIES   Dean's List, 6 semesters
Vice-President, Drab Residential Hall

Sample Resume #3—Combination

Cheryl Jordan
100 Charles Street
Houston, Texas 77306
(713) 555-1000

OBJECTIVE:
A computer programming related position, preferably involving software engineering skills.

EDUCATION:
Louisiana State University, Baton Rouge, Louisiana
B.S., Computer Science, May 1997

QUALIFICATIONS:
Career-related projects:
- Designed and implemented multi-tasking operating system for the IBM PC.
- Designed electronic mail system using PSL/PSA specification language.

Computer languages and operating systems:
- Proficient in Ada, Modula-2, Pascal, COBOL.
- Familiar with C++, Fortran, Lisp, Prolog, dBaseIII, SQL, QBE.
- Experienced in UNIX, MS-DOS, XENIX, CP/M operating systems.

Hardware:
- IBM PC (MS-DOS, Xenix), Pyramid 90x (UNIX), Cyber 990 (NOS).
- Data General MV/10000 (UNIX, AOS/VS).

International:
- Speak Spanish and Portuguese.
- Have traveled throughout Europe and South America.
- Lived in Madrid, Spain, for one year.

WORK EXPERIENCE:
Gonzalez Programming Services, Houston, Texas 10/94-Present
- UNIX Programmer—Responsible for porting MS-DOS database applications to IBM-PC/AT; running Xenix System V; system administration.

Wortham Arts Center, Houston, Texas 9/93-9/94
- Computer Programmer—Performed daily disk backup on Burroughs B-1955 machine. Executed database update programs and checks. Assisted customers with user problems.

REFERENCES: Furnished upon request.

Sample Resume #4—Chronological

Michael M. Montrose
8423 Hearth
White Plains, New York 00090
(714) 555-5309

CAREER OBJECTIVE: Position in economic analysis and management with a multinational firm.

EDUCATION: **Columbia University,** School of International and Public Affairs.
Master's degree in International Econometrics, May 1999.
Specialization: Western Europe.

Emory University, Atlanta, Georgia.
Bachelor's degree in Econometrics, May 1997.

University of Tübingen, Tübingen, Germany.
Studies in International and German Affairs, 1995-96.

RELEVANT COURSE WORK: Finanacial Management and Statistical Analysis.
International Trade Analysis.

EXPERIENCE: **Dresdner Bank,** Frankfurt, Germany, Summer 1998.
Assisted in Central Office, International Division, North America.
Responsible for learning German and U.S. banking rules, Euromarket instruments and activities, and aiding team members on correspondence and investment banking projects dealing with U.S. banks and corporations.

Emory University, Atlanta, Georgia, 1996-97.
Teaching Assistant. Taught first semester micro- and macro-economics courses.

ADDITIONAL INFORMATION: Knowledge of Lotus 1-2-3, SPSSP, C++, and word processing packages.

LANGUAGES: Fluent in German, fair knowledge of Italian.

REFERENCES: Available upon request

Sample Resume #5—Chronological

Ellen B. Souvlaki
12929 Houston Street
Washburn, Maine 00056
Tel./Fax (207) 555-3748

OBJECTIVE: Position in International Banking

EXPERIENCE: CITICORP, Asia Pacific Group, New York
Banking Associate: 1991-present
  • Developed marketing strategy for Japanese institutional and corporate clients.
  • Formatted department's cost structure and budget expenses on Lotus 1-2-3.
  • Researched bank's competitive position vis-à-vis Japanese banks in U.S. markets.

BUDGET HOTELS, Ltd., Brighton, U.K.
Consultant: March 1987-July 1991
  • Analyzed cost and pricing structure of unprofitable hotel.
  • Designed and executed audio/visual sales presentations.

DENMART, A/S, Otterup, Denmark
Marketing Intern: July 1986-February 1987
  • Designed two-year strategy for welding machine sales to U.S. market.
  • Promoted products at trade shows in U.S. and Europe.

AIESEC-OHIO, International Exchange Program
President: 1985
Director of Corporate Fundraising: 1984
  • Launched sales campaign resulting in 15 internships for foreign and American students.
  • Raised $5,000 in corporate contributions.

EDUCATION: Harvard University, Graduate School of Business Administration, Cambridge, Massachusetts, 1986
MBA in International Finance and Banking.

Florida State University, Tallahassee, Florida
Bachelor of Science: May 1984
  • National Merit Scholar
  • Semester abroad: University of East Anglia, England

LANGUAGES: Danish, Norwegian, beginning Japanese.

The Cover Letter

Your cover letter, along with your resume, serves to introduce you to a potential employer and to develop sufficient interest in you to warrant a personal interview. It should be addressed to a particular person. It should be short (one page at most), concise, and designed to be read by someone with limited time. Cover letters should always be (or at least look) individually prepared. Cover letters should be specifically tailored to the organization.

You should always organize your cover letter around the requirements of the job to which you are applying. This way you can demonstrate exactly how your previous background, experience, or skills can be of value to the employer. Of course, some "requirements" are universal: intelligence, assertiveness, imagination, good interpersonal skills. These can be demonstrated either experientially (work) or inferentially (academic or extracurricular achievements, interests, hobbies).

Contact the American affiliate of a particular company, if possible, by telephone to find out exactly where resumes should be sent. Also, if you don't want your resume put immediately in the inactive file, you should include in your cover letter words to the effect: "I will be contacting you within three weeks regarding...." In this way, you prompt a timely response; and if they do not respond, they should expect your follow-up.

Another method that often prompts a quick response is to send a copy of your letter and resume to the Department Head or Manager within the division you are interested in. This puts more responsibility on the recipient of your letter, letting them know that they will not be the only person in that organization to read it. In this way, your resume has a better chance of ending up in the right hands.

Basics of the Cover Letter

First Paragraph: This is a quick introduction: who you are; why you are writing; how you heard of the opening; what position you seek; who suggested you write; or what it is about the organization that is motivating you to write.

Second Paragraph: Referring to your work and/or academic background, demonstrate why you are both interested and qualified for the position, the organization, or the field. Try not simply to repeat the resume but to amplify your background—briefly! It is better to highlight how well you did something than just what you did.

Third Paragraph: In the concluding paragraph, you ask for an interview. You have several options on how to manage this. You can await a written or phoned reply, or you can follow up with a phone call or email yourself. You are more likely to get an interview if you follow up on your correspondence. The phone call is particularly appropriate to local organizations, where travel will not be a problem. If you are writing a distant company and are planning to be in the area, let them know this. However, organizations usually will not pick up your expenses merely on the basis of a letter and a resume.

Sample Cover Letter #1

8425 Shadybrook Lane
Houston, Texas 77554

April 9, 1999

M Jacques C. Guroid
Manager, International Division
Snodgrass and Humperdinkle
7 Rue d'Argent
F-75631 Paris, France

Dear M Guroid:

As a second-year graduate student at Rice University's Jones School of Business Administration, I was intrigued to learn about the expansion of your international division. (*Wall Street Journal*, March 16, 1999.) I am writing to express an interest in joining your marketing department.

My MBA requirements have included intensive course work in international marketing, accounting, and finance. These have provided me with a firm foundation from which to begin an international business career. In addition, I have held intern positions at Citicorp and AT&T, both of which strengthened my understanding of international markets and marketing practices. I am fluent in French and Spanish.

The enclosed resume provides a more detailed description of my qualifications. I hope you will agree that my academic and work experiences make me well-suited to contribute to Snodgrass and Humperdinkle's future international expansion. I will call you in a few weeks to discuss my application further. In the interim, feel free to call me at (713) 555-5454.

Thank you for your consideration.

Sincerely,

J. Evelyn Stone

Sample Cover Letter #2

November 9, 1998

912 East 37th Street
Chicago, Illinois 60664
(312) 555-5454

Mr. J. R. Ixer
Recruiting Coordinator
International Banc d'Argent (IBA)
123 Wall Street
New York, NY 10001

Dear Mr. Ixer:

I am writing to inquire about opportunities with the foreign trading group at International Banc d'Argent. I received your name from Ms. Julia de la Torre, finance manager with IBA. I believe my substantial work experience in foreign trade will make me a valuable addition to your group.

I am currently a foreign trade analyst at First National Bank in Chicago. At First National I have focused on international finance. My work brings me into daily contact with the international aspects of trade, economics, and foreign policy analysis.

As my resume indicates, I also have strong experience in working in a research environment and have successfully managed numerous projects involving the supervision of personnel.

Again, I would like to express my interest in a position with IBA and assure you of my proven ability to perform well. I look forward to hearing from you soon and giving you a chance to assess for yourself my qualifications. I will be calling you within the next two weeks regarding the position. Thank you for your consideration.

Sincerely,

Thomas Anderson

cc: Ms. Julia de la Torre, Finance Manager, IBA

six

The International Interview

Getting a job in Europe sometimes may not necessitate interviewing at all. Since you live across the ocean, the employer might trust that your written credentials represent you well. If you are looking for work with a corporation with offices in the United States, a representative from their American office may interview you. Finally, for those lucky few seeking a professional position in Europe, you may be flown in for an interview, though this does not happen often. No matter how you are interviewed, you must be prepared to represent yourself in the best way possible.

The purpose of an interview is to give you and an employer the opportunity to evaluate each other. The interview should be an active two-way exchange of information. The interviewer wants to evaluate your personality in terms of the position and the organization. You can use the interview to find out if the position interests you, to "sell" yourself by highlighting your positive points, and to gain a job offer. Remember that the employer wants to hire you if you can convince him or her that you are right for the job.

Because of travel constraints in the international job search, an employer may choose to interview you by telephone. It is to your advantage to practice well ahead of time what you intend to say so that you will sound smooth and articulate over the phone, because the prospective employer's impression of you is heavily dependent on verbal communication skills. You should have a quiet place to call from, with no noises, distractions, or potential interruptions to break the flow of your interview. It's a good idea to write down points you want to bring up in response to potential interview questions so you don't forget anything. Questions asked during the phone interview will probably be the same as during a regular interview. You should also come up with a list of questions about the job or the company in case you're given the opportunity to ask questions.

Qualities on Which You Are Evaluated

These are some qualities on which a typical interviewer might evaluate you:

Personal appearance: You should look neat and professional. In Europe, however, what constitutes "professionalism" varies slightly from what you're accustomed to in the U.S. Depending on where you are, the standards may be more or less formal than in the States. If you're familiar with the standards of professional dress in the country in which you'll be interviewing, wear clothes that are appropriate. If you aren't familiar or aren't comfortable with professional dress habits abroad, don't let it bother you. Your potential employer should realize that standards of professional dress vary across cultures, and you will seldom go wrong if you present yourself well by American standards.

Work experience: Articulate your pertinent work experience, its value, and how it might relate to the job you are applying for. Even if the work experience is unrelated to your field, employers look upon any previous work experience as an asset.

Education: The importance of degrees and grades varies from job to job and from organization to organization. You should always be prepared, however, to answer questions about your academic background, special interests or achievements, or any possible deficiencies.

Verbal communication skills: Effective communication includes effective listening as well as the articulate, confident, and poised expression of ideas. Because verbal communication skills are so important, you should be careful to accurately portray your foreign language abilities on your resume. Unless the employer has indicated that foreign language skills are required for the job, you will likely be interviewed in both English and the second language. Make sure you have basic business terminology at your fingertips so that you can discuss your interest in the position.

General personality qualities: Poise, sincerity, enthusiasm, self-confidence, maturity, and motivation are valued by most employers. Of course, depending on the personality of the organization and the available position, some of these qualities may be stressed more than others.

Skills: The interviewer will evaluate your skills for the job, such as organization, analysis, and research. It is important to emphasize the skills that you feel the employer is seeking and to give specific examples of how you developed them.

Goals/Motivation: Employers will assess your ability to articulate your short- and long-term goals. You should be ambitious, yet realistic about the training and qualifications needed to advance. You should demonstrate interest in the functional area or industry to which you are applying for work and a desire to succeed and work hard. Be prepared to thoroughly discuss your interest in working in Europe, in particular how this experience will relate to your long-term goals.

Before the Interview

- **Identify your strengths, skills, goals, and personal qualities.** This self-assessment is crucial to knowing what you have to offer an employer and to conveying it effectively.
- **Research the organization by reading annual reports and other literature.** This will demonstrate that you are sincerely interested in the position and prepare you to ask intelligent questions. An interview is supposed to be a dialogue; you want to learn about them just as they want to learn about you.
- **Rehearse what you plan to say during the interview.** Practice answers to commonly asked questions and determine how you will emphasize your strengths and skills. This is especially important if you will be interviewing in a foreign language.
- **Dress professionally and conservatively.** If you make a negative first impression you may not be fairly considered for the job. Women should wear a tailored suit or dress. Limit jewelry and cosmetics and keep hair neat. Men should wear a suit and tie, with hair and beard/mustache trimmed.
- **Be prepared for questions about the country in which you are working.** It's a good idea to do some research about the region, its customs, people, political situations, and so on. You might want to pick up an English copy of a recent newspaper from the area so you will have a bit of small talk to draw from. Anything that will make you sound informed about the area will make you appear as a serious job candidate and give you an advantage.

During the Interview

- **Make sure that you arrive for your interview on time or a few minutes early.**
- **Greet the interviewer by his or her last name, offer a firm handshake and a warm smile.**
- **Be aware of your non-verbal behavior.** Wait to sit until you are offered a chair. Sit straight, look alert, speak in a clear, strong voice, and stay relaxed. Make good eye contact, avoid nervous mannerisms, and listen carefully to the questions the employer asks. Smile.

- **Follow the interviewer's lead,** but try to get the interviewer to describe the position and duties to you fairly early in the interview so that you can later relate your background and skills in context.
- **Be specific, concrete, and detailed in your answers.** The more information you volunteer, the better the employer can evaluate your qualifications for the position.
- **Don't mention salary in a first interview unless the employer does.** If asked, give a realistic range and add that the opportunity is the most important factor for you. Make sure you have correct information about salaries in Europe; they can be much lower than for comparable positions in the U.S.
- **Offer examples of your work and references that will document your best qualities.**
- **Answer questions as truthfully and as frankly as you can.** Never appear to be "glossing over" anything, yet don't over-answer questions. The interviewer may steer the interview into ticklish political or social questions. If this occurs, answer honestly, trying not to say more than is necessary.
- **Never make derogatory remarks about present or former employers or companies.**

Questions You May Be Asked During an Interview

Although it may appear differently, the employer has a reason for each question he or she asks. Try to put yourself in the interviewer's shoes and ask why you were asked a particular question. This can help you focus your answer with the most relevant information. Direct your responses toward the particular position for which you are applying. What follows are some questions that employers often ask during interviews. Rehearse answers to these questions prior to your interview so you can appear relaxed and confident.

Ice breakers

These are designed to put you at ease and engage you in informal conversation. Be yourself, act natural, and be friendly. For example:
  a. Did you have any trouble finding your way here?
  b. How was your plane flight?
  c. Can you believe this weather?
  d. I see you're from Omaha. Is this your first trip to Europe?

Work history and education

These are to assess whether your background and skills are appropriate for the position. Be prepared to talk about your skills and relate them to the job to be filled. Give specific examples of how you used skills in the past. Also, remember that questions you are asked concerning your past will help the employer determine how you might react and make decisions in the future.

a. Tell me about yourself.

b. Tell me about the most satisfying job/internship you ever held.

c. Tell me about the best boss you ever had. The worst.

d. What have you learned from some of the jobs you've held?

e. For what achievements were you recognized by your superiors at your last position?

f. What are you looking for in an employer?

g. What are you seeking in a position?

h. Why did you choose to get a degree in the area that you did?

i. In what activities have you participated outside of class?

j. How did you finance your education?

Ambitions and plans

These are questions to evaluate your ambition, how clearly you have thought about your future goals, their feasibility, and how actively you seek to meet them.

a. Are you a joiner or a loner? A leader or a follower? A committee member or chairperson? Keep in mind that a ship full of captains will founder as badly as a ship with none at all.

b. What job in our company would you choose if you were free to do so?

c. What does success mean to you? How do you judge it?

d. Assuming you are hired for this job, what do you see as your future?

e. What personal characteristics do you think are necessary for success in this field?

f. Will you fight to get ahead in your career?

g. Are you willing to prove yourself as a staff member of our firm? How do you envision your role?

h. Are you willing to work overtime?

i. Where do you see yourself five years from now? Ten years?

j. How much money do you hope to earn in five years? Ten years?

Company or organization

These questions are to determine if you have conscientiously researched the company and if you would be a "match" for them. They also indicate your interest in the company.

a. Do you prefer working for a small or large organization?

b. Do you prefer a private or non-private organization? Why?

c. What do you know about our organization?

d. Why did you choose to interview with us?

e. What kind of work are you interested in doing for us?

f. What do you feel our organization has to offer you? What do you feel you have to offer us?

Values and self-assessment

These help the interviewer get to know you better and to determine how well you understand yourself. They also help to inform the interviewer of what motivates you.

a. What kinds of personal satisfactions do you hope to gain through work?
b. If you had unlimited funds, what would you do? Where would you live?
c. What motivates you?
d. What are your strengths and weaknesses?
e. How would you describe yourself?
f. What do you do with your free time?
g. What kind of people do you like to work with?
h. How do you adapt to other cultures?

They want to know *what?*

Don't be surprised if in a European job interview you are asked questions that strike you as strictly personal and not at all relevant to your potential employment. Questions and practices that are considered discriminatory—and illegal—in the United States are perfectly acceptable—and common—in Europe. To begin with, you may be asked to submit a photograph with your resume or other application materials. In many European countries, this is standard. Both men and women are likely to be asked about their marital status, but for women seeking a potentially long-term position within a company, inquiries about their married life—for example, how long they've been married—may be a subtle way of finding out whether they intend to have children in the near future. (In some European countries, companies are obligated to pay a woman's salary while she is on an extended maternity leave; hence the potential employer's concern.) Some interviewees don't have any qualms about lines of questioning that are personal. If you think you'd likely take offense, though, be prepared. Knowing to expect personal questions and deciding ahead of time the best way to deal with them will serve you in good stead.

Closing and Post-Interview

- **Don't be discouraged.** Often, no definite offer is made or specific salary discussed.
- **If you get the impression that the interview isn't going well and that you've already been rejected, don't let your discouragement show.**

Once in a while, an interviewer who is genuinely interested in you may seem to discourage you to test your reaction.

- **Be prepared with questions to ask the employer at the end of the interview.** If those questions have been answered in the course of the interview, refer to them, saying that they have now been answered to your satisfaction.
- **At the conclusion of the interview, ask when a hiring decision will be made.** This is important not only because it reconfirms your interest in the position but also so you'll know when, realistically, to expect a response. Don't forget, of course, to thank your interviewer for his or her time and to make clear your interest in the position if you feel there may be any doubt about this point.
- **Take notes on what you feel you could improve upon for your next interview and on what you feel went particularly well.** After all, experience is only valuable to the extent that you're willing to learn from it.
- **If you are interested in the position, type a brief thank-you letter to the interviewer,** indicating your interest and appreciation.
- **Accept or reject all job offers in writing.**

Soft-sell thank-you letters

Most job applicants in the United States view the thank-you letter not so much as an expression of simple thanks but as one more step in the self-marketing process. Letters are brief, snappy, and assertively confident. Candidates typically make mention of key points that were discussed during the interview, try to state one or two additional reasons why they would be an asset if hired, reiterate their continued interest in the possibility of employment, and, as if it isn't already obvious, close by indicating their desire for favorable consideration. This type of "hard sell" may not be so effective in Europe, where (a) a more subtle approach is often the norm, and (b) in some countries the post-interview thank-you note isn't usually part of the employment process. In writing a thank-you letter for a European job interview, your best approach may be to compose something more along the lines of a genuine and simple expression of thanks rather than a Madison-Avenue blitz. If you mention your qualifications, say something truly substantive—for example, something relevant that didn't come up during the interview. Anything else may be viewed as an uncouth and unwelcome attempt to curry favor.

After the Interview

The interview is over, and now the waiting begins. There may be many reasons why a company is slow to reply to you after the interview. It could be that the interview process hasn't concluded or that other commitments have kept the company from making a decision. However, if much time has passed and you haven't heard anything from a company in which you are particularly interested, a telephone call or an email message asking about the status of your application is appropriate. This inquiry should be stated in a manner that is not pushy but shows your continued interest in the company. Remember that waiting is an integral part of the job hunt, but a demonstration of your continued interest is appropriate.

The Rejection

When you receive a rejection letter or phone call, as everyone does at one time or another in the job-hunting process, evaluate the reasons why you may have received it. Did you not receive an offer because you were really not suited for the position? Perhaps your job search should be more specifically designed and targeted. Were you rejected because your personal and professional goals were different from those of the company? Make sure, as you prepare for each interview, that you have realistic expectations regarding initial positions and career paths. Could it be that you simply did not interview well? Perhaps you were not well enough prepared or you were a bit preoccupied that day. In that case, you could benefit from feedback regarding your interviewing skills. Try a mock interview with a career counselor. Don't let a rejection get you down; if you learn from one job interview, the next may be more successful.

The Offer

When your hard work finally pays off, make sure to get your offer in writing. Your employer should include your starting date, salary, responsibilities, location, and the date by which you must respond. Maintain a healthy skepticism even when celebrating the successful outcome of your hard work. Perhaps more than even with an American job offer, closely evaluate your offer to make sure it is as great as it seems at first. The employer has made you an offer that is in the company's best interest; make sure it is fair to you as well.

Evaluating job offers. Take a close look at the salary and make sure it is reasonable for the city in which you will be living. Evaluate your base salary, housing allowances, and relocation benefits. Also calculate the bite taxes and national health insurance will take from your paycheck. Ask questions about medical coverage and, depending on the length of time you'll be living abroad, contributions to pension plans.

Response date. Make sure the response date gives you time to complete negotiations with other employers if possible. Up to two weeks is generally considered a reasonable response time. Be very skeptical if an organization tries to rush your decision—they may have a reason why they don't want you to carefully evaluate your decision! You may have to make a decision before you have complete information on all possible job offers. However, you should only accept an offer if you really intend to stick with it. Remember, if the company to which you are applying is based in Europe, it will take longer for your acceptance letter to reach the organization within the acceptable time, so you may have to send it in a bit earlier or fax it.

Starting date. Companies with formal training programs have specific starting dates. However, with many other employers you can negotiate a start date that is acceptable to both of you. If you want to take a vacation before starting, try to arrange it before accepting the offer.

Evaluate your offer!

So your hard work has paid off and now you have a job offer in hand. It sounds like a good deal, but how do you know? John Williams has written a useful little booklet, *Evaluating an Overseas Job Offer* (Pilot Books, 103 Cooper Street, Babylon, New York, 11702) that walks you through the process. His three big tips? First, don't believe everything you are told. The company has made you an offer that is in *their* best interests, and it is up to you to decide how good it is for you. Second, investigate the offer and company thoroughly before making any commitment. Third, make sure you and the employer sign a written agreement.

seven

International Placement Organizations

Placement organizations run the gamut from executive search firms, which specialize in helping high-level businesspeople with experience and special skills, to non-profit organizations, which specialize in placing students in summer jobs abroad. Reputable organizations can be very helpful in putting you in touch with employers who are actually hiring. There are many shady organizations, however, that place ads offering "jobs on luxury cruise lines" in order to dupe enthusiastic job searchers out of their money. Thoroughly investigate a placement agency before you sign any contracts for services.

Many U.S. agencies will charge a fee to cover the cost of locating employment or providing help in obtaining working papers and related materials. Some of this help is well worth the minor cost. Paying $200 to receive working papers, for example, could be money well spent. Some agencies, however, simply aren't trustworthy. Always find out exactly what you're getting in return for your money and always ask for a list of where they have placed clients in the past. Employment agencies located in the U.K. (with the exception of those placing au pairs or models) are not permitted to charge an up-front fee.

The ideal placement agency would not charge any fee for their services and would identify a number of European job leads for you. Such an agency does not exist. What real-world placement agencies can do is complete some of the leg work for you, but this carries a price tag. There are a number of different types of placement organizations: executive search firms, non-profit and student-oriented firms, and temporary placement agencies.

Executive Search Firms

The executive search firm is one that caters to the businessperson, engineer, or other professional with specific skills and with a good deal of experience. Their fees are paid by the company who has the vacant position. Executive search firms can give you an idea of your value in Europe and whether a placement is possible. Because they are paid by the hiring organization, they usually won't waste their time with someone they can't place. Be very leery of executive search firms that charge a fee; the most reputable organizations do not charge the job searcher. The following publications list executive recruiters in Europe.

The Executive Grapevine: The International Directory of Executive Recruitment Consultants. Published annually by Executive Grapevine International, 79 Manor Way, London SE3 9XG, England. Provides information on 1,000 executive search firms in major cities outside the U.K.

Executive Moves. Published by Blackheath Court Press, 79 Manor Way, London SE3 9XG, England. Lists executive recruiting firms in the U.K.

Key European Executive Search Firms and Their U.S. Links. Published by Kennedy Publications, Templeton Road, Fitzwilliam, NH 03447. Lists about 500 search firms in the U.S. and 23 European nations.

EXECUTIVE SEARCH FIRMS IN THE UNITED STATES

You may want to check with some of the following American placement agencies that handle international employment to determine their usefulness for you. We do not imply any recommendation of these firms through our listing of them.

Dunhill Employment Agency
59 Elm Street
New Haven, CT 06510
Tel.: (203) 562-0511
Places workers in upper-level management positions throughout Europe.

General Industrial Technologies
900 Ellison Avenue
Westbury, NY 11590
Tel.: (516) 222-0000
Provides placements for industrial, architectural, and engineering positions.

Group Fischer
160 Newport Center Drive, Suite 200
Newport Beach, CA 92660
Tel.: (714) 759-3374
Operates a database of employment opportunities and publishes a newsletter, "The Fischer Report."

Robert Half International
1901 Avenue of the Stars
Los Angeles, CA 90067
Tel.: (310) 286-6800
An accounting and finance placement firm that operates internationally.

International Staffing Consultants
500 Newport Center Drive, Suite 300
Newport Beach, CA 92660-7003
Tel.: (714) 721-7990
Provides placements in oil and gas, refinery and chemical, mining, power, and related energy businesses throughout Europe and around the world. Publishes a weekly "International Jobs Report" which includes a variety of positions, including non-technical.

Korn/Ferry International
1800 Century Park East, Suite 900
Los Angeles, CA 90067
Tel.: (213) 552-1834
Operates branches throughout Europe.

Snelling and Snelling
12801 North Central Expressway, Suite 700
Dallas, TX 75243
Tel.: (214) 239-7575
Operates a branch in Romania. An additional office will be opening soon in Bulgaria.

TRS-Total Recruiting Service
3333 Michelson Drive, A1-30
Irvine, CA 92730
Tel.: (714) 975-3630
Arranges placement for all types of jobs all over the world.

World Vision International
121 East Huntington Drive
Monrovia, CA 91016
Tel.: (818) 303-8811
An interdenominational Christian humanitarian agency that lists employment opportunities throughout the world.

PLACEMENT AGENCIES IN EUROPE

A number of agencies can also be found in Europe. You should also check the individual country chapters to see what other resources are available. Again, listings are meant to inform readers, not to endorse the agencies included.

Anders Glaser Wills
4 Maddison Court
Maddison Street
Southampton, SO1 0BU England
Tel.: [44] 703 223511
Fax: [44] 703 227911
Five offices in the U.K., plus contacts on the European mainland and in the Middle East. In partnership with International Staffing Consultants (see above).

Angel Recruitment
Angel House, 50 Fleet Street
London EC4Y 1BE, England
Placement emphasis is primarily upon the Middle East, but operates in Europe as well.

Forgeot, Weeks
Personal Career Consultants
3 rue du Faubourg Saint Honoré
Paris, France 75008
Tel.: [33] (1) 46.54.20.0
Fax: [33] (1) 40.07.00.67

also
9 route des Jeunes
Geneva, Switzerland 1227
Tel.: [41] (22) 425249

Parc Limited
St. John's Court, Swords Road
Santry, Dublin 9
Ireland
Tel.: [353] (1) 8429933
Fax: [353] (1) 8429259
Focuses on placement in Ireland and the U.K.

PLACEMENT AGENCIES ON THE INTERNET

www.bceurope.com/
Bertram Consulting, an executive search in the IT industry and the management of start-ups in European high-tech enterprises.

www.internet-solutions.com/itjobs.htm
Links to websites for IT recruitment agencies based in the U.K. and an increasing number of links to agencies based in the U.S. and Europe.

www.jobserve.com
Specializes in IT positions in Europe.

www.netline.com
Includes the largest site of recruiters, employment agencies, and search firms.

www.nationjob.com/rob half
The international job site for Robert Half International.

Summer, Student, and Temporary Placement Agencies

Chapter 9 lists agencies that place people in summer and temporary positions. These positions include au pair work, agricultural work, secretarial positions, positions teaching English, and work in vacation areas. Workcamps located throughout Europe provide volunteer opportunities in activities ranging from construction to ecological work to children's camps.

The Council for International Educational Exchange (Council) is one of the oldest and best known non-profit organizations. It sponsors the International Student Identity Card (ISIC) and organizes charter flights, work programs and tours in Europe, and various language and exchange programs. For a reasonable cost, Council will acquire three- to six-month work permits for you for temporary and summer jobs in Ireland, France, and Germany. For more information, contact Council directly at 205 East 42nd Street, New York, NY 10017; (888) COUNCIL.

Temporary placement agencies can be a very good place to look for short-term clerical or retail assignments. Usually temporary agencies have a large number of positions to fill, and if you are not too picky or have excellent clerical skills, they can find you work quite quickly.

eight

The International Professional Career

As United States companies invest in Europe, career opportunities for Americans in business and other professional areas will increase. Opportunities are increasing for the job seeker interested in building a professional international career.

This chapter contains information, resources, and employer listings for international business, international law, international media and communications, international non-profit opportunities, the federal government, and teaching in Europe. Building an international career is a long-term proposition. It usually requires a combination of the right education and appropriate work experience with a multinational corporation that has an international career track. The following sections will give you a clear picture of an international career and the options that are available in Europe. The sections are as follows:

- International Business, with sub-sections on:
  - International Trade
  - International Banking and Finance
  - International Economics
  - International Consulting
- International Law
- International Media and Communications

- International Non-Profits
- The U.S. Federal Government
- International Teaching

International Business

Employment in Europe in business fields will very likely increase in the new European marketplace. American firms are expanding into the European Union while European companies are actively engaged in mergers and acquisitions as a part of their own expansion plans. Foreign companies are usually required to hire European nationals unless the company can show that a foreigner has some special skill not readily available locally. Remember, your best strategy is to first work for the company in the U.S., prove your abilities, and request a transfer to Europe later.

International business is a broad category of jobs and careers, so this section is sub-divided into four sections: International Trade, International Banking and Finance, International Economics, and International Consulting. Each will have its own list of resources, but the following list is a useful summary of general international business resources.

INTERNATIONAL BUSINESS RESOURCES

America's Corporate Families and International Affiliates. Published by Dun & Bradstreet Information Services, Dun & Bradstreet Co., 3 Sylvan Way, Parsippany, NJ 07054-3896. Lists 1,700 U.S. parent companies and their over 13,000 foreign subsidiaries, and 2,500 parent companies abroad and their over 6,000 U.S. subsidiaries.

Directory of American Firms Operating in Foreign Countries. New York: Uniworld Business Directories. An annual 3-volume compilation of information on 2,600 U.S. corporations that operate abroad, cataloged by firm name and geographic location.

Directory of European Businesses. Published by K.G. Saur, Reed Reference Publishing, 121 Chanlon Road, New Providence, NJ 07974. Includes information on accounting, law, and market research firms, management consultants, banks, manufacturers, government agencies, regulatory bodies, newspapers, and business periodicals in 35 eastern and western European countries.

Directory of U.S. Companies Doing Business in Central Eastern Europe and the Commonwealth of Independent States. Published quarterly by Wetherling International, P.O. Box 5393, Arlington, VA 22205. Covers over 450 U.S. firms with interests in the CIS and central eastern Europe.

Dun's Europa. Published annually by Dun & Bradstreet Information Services, Dun & Bradstreet Co., 3 Sylvan Way, Parsippany, NJ 07054-3896. Covers 50,000 leading manufacturers, distributors, financial and service companies throughout Europe.

Eastern European Business Directory. Published by Gale Research, 27500 Drake Road, Farmington Hills, MI 48331. Includes information on over 7,000 firms and organizations in Bulgaria, Czech Republic, Hungary, Poland, Romania, the former East Germany, and the western part of the former Soviet Union.

Eastern European Top 200 (on disk). Published by European Business Press Group, Research Park Zellik, De Haak, B-1731 Zellik, Belgium. Covers companies in 11 central and eastern European countries, including names and titles of key personnel, plus interviews with company executives.

Europages: The European Business Directory. Available annually from EUREDIT S.A., 7 Coldbath Square, London EC1R 4LQ, England. Covers 150,000 companies in 18 countries.

European Business Rankings. Published by Gale Research, 27500 Drake Road, Farmington Hills, MI 48331. Includes over 2,250 citations of European company rankings, including the top 10 entries from each list cited.

Europe's 15,000 Largest Companies. Published annually by ELC Publishing, 109 Uxbridge Road, Ealing, London W5 5TL, England. Lists over 10,000 leading industrial, trading, insurance, and transportation companies, plus banks, hotels and restaurants, ad agencies, and other enterprises. Includes a ranking of Europe's 500 most profitable and 125 least profitable firms.

Faulkner & Gray's European Business Directory. Published annually by Faulkner & Gray, 11 Penn Plaza, New York, NY 10001. Lists over 2,000 accountants, attorneys, consultants, commercial and investment banks, search firms, translators, and other concerns in Europe and the United States engaged or interested in European business.

Major Business Organizations of Eastern Europe and the Commonwealth of Independent States. Published annually by Graham & Trotman Ltd., Sterling House, 66 Wilton Road, London SW1V 1DE, England. Available in the U.S. from Kluwer Inc., 101 Philip Drive, Assinippi Park, Norwell, MA 02061. Lists over 2,500 ministries, chambers of commerce, banks, manufacturers, and trading organizations in Albania, Bulgaria, Czech Republic, Hungary, Poland, Romania, the former Yugoslavia, the Baltic Republics, and the CIS.

Major Companies of Europe. Published annually in three volumes by Graham & Trotman Ltd., Sterling House, 66 Wilton Road, London SW1V 1DE, England. Available in the U.S. from Kluwer Inc., 101 Philip Drive, Assinippi Park, Norwell, MA 02061. Lists approximately 6,500 top firms, including company name, address, and phone, names and titles of key personnel, number of employees, and so on.

Medium Companies of Europe. Published annually in three volumes by Graham & Trotman Ltd.; available in the U.S. from Kluwer Inc. (see entry above). Approximately 8,000 listings.

Principal International Business. New York: World Marketing Directory. Published annually. Presents up-to-date information on about 50,000 leading enterprises in 143 countries throughout the world.

The Times 1000, The Indispensable Annual Review of the World's Leading Industrial and Financial Companies. Published annually by Times Books Ltd., 77/85 Fulhan Palace Road, Hammersmith, London W1R 4BN, England. A directory containing company names, main activities, chairmen, and managing directors. Contains 500 leading European companies.

Western European Top 500. Published by European Business Press Group, Research Park Zellik, De Haak, B-1731 Zellik, Belgium. Describes and ranks (by sales) 2,500 leading businesses in 19 countries.

Who Owns Whom: Continental Europe. Published by Dun & Bradstreet Ltd., Holmers Farm Way, High Wycombe, Buckinghamshire HP12 4UL, England. Available in the U.S. from Dun & Bradstreet Information Services, Dun & Bradstreet Co., 3 Sylvan Way, Parsippany, NJ 07054. Provides information on 7,900 parent companies and their domestic and foreign subsidiaries and affiliates for 15 Western European nations.

Who's Who in European Business and Industry. Published by Triumph Books, 1436 West Randolph Street, Chicago, IL 60607. In two volumes, lists 9,500 European executives and the 1,400 companies that employ them.

World's Largest Market: A Business Guide to Europe. Available from AMACOM, 135 West 50th Street, New York, NY 10020. Focuses on U.S. government resources and cooperative research and development programs. Also gives European country profiles and relocation information.

Worldwide Branch Locations of Multinational Companies. Published by Gale Research Inc., 27500 Drake Road, Farmington Hills, MI 48331. Lists 20,000 subsidiaries, sales branches, and other affiliates of over 500 multinational corporations worldwide.

GENERAL BUSINESS PUBLICATIONS

Hoover's Handbook of American Business. Published by Reference Press Inc., 6448 Highway 290 East, Suite E-104, Austin, TX 78723. Profiles over 500 major companies worldwide; also includes lists on various themes—for example, 20 largest airline companies in the world, 20 largest ad agencies in the U.S., and so on.

How to Find Information About Companies. Washington, DC: Washington Researchers Publishing. An excellent guide to sources; deals with federal government agencies and commissions that provide information, citing organizations in both the legislative and executive branches, as well as non-governmental sources. Among the government organizations cited are: the International Development Corporation Administration, the International Trade Commission, and the Department of Commerce. Non-government sources include trade and professional associations and unions, business databases, job-search services, and investigative services.

Moody's Manuals and *Standard & Poor's Register of Corporations* are also important resources if you're investigating a public corporation. They are available at any public library. Knowledge of a company's products, assets, sales volume, and recent acquisitions can be quite helpful in an interview.

U.S. Employment Opportunities. U.S. government publication. Contains general information regarding industry classifications, required qualifications, and future trends in business. Highlights the best opportunities, tells whom to contact, and lists resource books, associations, and journals.

TOP 20 INTERNATIONAL COMPANIES
(1997, by market value)

1. Royal Dutch/Shell (The Netherlands)
2. Roche Holding (Switzerland)
3. British Petroleum (UK)
4. Glaxo Wellcome (UK)
5. HSBC Holdings (UK)
6. Sandoz (Switzerland)
7. Nestle (Switzerland)
8. Unilever plc/NV (The Netherlands)
9. ENJ (Italy)
10. Allianz Holding (Germany)
11. Ciba (Switzerland)
12. BT (UK)
13. Smithkline Beecham (UK)
14. Lloydes TSB Group (UK)
15. Siemens (Germany)
16. Daimler-Benz (Germany)
17. Bayer (Germany)
18. Veba (Germany)
19. Astra (Sweden)
20. Union Bank of Switzerland (Switzerland)

International Trade

Jobs in international trade are actually advertised in newspaper classifieds. The Thursday employment section of the *Wall Street Journal* is a good place to look, along with the *International Herald Tribune,* the Sunday *New York Times,* and *International Opportunities Newsletter.* There are also two trade publications, the *Export Bulletin* and the *Import Bulletin,* that have classified job ads. *The Economist* may have a few international trade position listings, but it also provides excellent coverage and analysis of international trade. For leads on international trade openings, it is also worthwhile to write to these business chambers of commerce:

International Chamber of Commerce
38 Cours Albert 1
F-75008 Paris, France
Tel.: [33] 49.53.28.28
Fax: [33] 49.53.29.42
www.iccwbo.org/

U.S. Chamber of Commerce
1615 H Street NW
Washington, DC 20062
Tel.: (202) 659-6000

Prospective employers are looking for fluency in a relevant foreign language, foreign experience, and a strong economics background. You should emphasize course work or experience in international economics, international business, or even development economics. Familiarity with a specific business product, a particular area of the world, or knowledge of the trade process (traffic, documentation, etc.) is helpful.

You will need excellent oral communication skills, demonstrated sales experience, and excellent written skills. You also must demonstrate that you can work well under pressure. Willingness to travel is a definite plus, as is some relevant work experience. Good places to get experience in this field are with commodity trading companies, Capitol Hill offices, trade associations, consulting firms, and government agencies that deal with trade (e.g., Dept. of Commerce). Complete as many internships as possible.

International trade is very sensitive to protectionist measures and fluctuations of interest rates. You might follow these indicators to identify trends in the market that would work to your advantage or disadvantage.

Several international organizations (U.N., I.M.F., World Bank) employ international economists interested in trade, but the number of available places is limited because turnover is low and the organizations must maintain a proportionate geographic balance. Most of the people employed in these positions have completed a Ph.D. in economics. Another place to look for jobs in the field of international trade is with the large banks listed under the "International Banking and Finance" section of this chapter.

One job-search resource in international trade that some job seekers overlook is the U.S. Department of Commerce. Although it is a government agency, it is an important center for information about international trade in general and U.S. trade in particular. U.S. import and export statistics are available from:

U.S. Department of Commerce
Foreign Trade Reference Room, Room 2233
14th Street & Constitution Avenue NW
Washington, DC 20230
Tel.: (202) 482-2000
Fax: (202) 482-2741
www.doc.gov/

World import and export statistics ("World Trade Statistics") can be obtained from the same address, Room 2022. There is also a Dept. of Commerce Library in New York City at 26 Federal Plaza. The Foreign Traders Index, which is supplied by U.S. Foreign Commerce attachés, gives information on 140,000 foreign-based import companies in 130 countries (use address listed above).

Other U.S. Department of Commerce Services

- World Traders' Data Reports: describes company financial references, activities, reputation, area of operation, date established, number of employees, and general profiles. Written by U.S. Commercial Service attachés abroad.
- Country Desk Offices: specific country files on U.S. and foreign businesses.
- Foreign Commercial Service: assists U.S. corporations through export promotions, market research, counseling, and liaison with foreign businesses and government officials.
- Trade Operations Program: specifies products, countries of interest, and opportunities through Foreign Service telex updates.
- Export Counseling Service: coordinates information and consults with new export businesses through nationwide district offices, helping direct representation and sales to foreign government tenders.

BUSINESS AND CAREER RESOURCES IN INTERNATIONAL TRADE

ABC Europe Production Europe xR (European Exporters). Published in English, German, French, and Spanish by ABC der Deutschen Wirtschaft Verlagsgesellschaft, Europ Export Edition GmbH, Berliner Allee 8, Postfach 4034, D-6100 Darmstadt 1, Germany. Distributed in the U.S. by Western Hemisphere Publishing, P.O. Box 847, Hillsboro, OR 97123-0847. Lists 100,000 export manufacturers in 32 countries.

American Register of Exporters and Importers. New York: American Register of Exporters and Importers Corp. Updated each May. Covers 42,000 U.S. manufacturers and distributors in the import/export trade and service firms assisting foreign private and public customers. Lists company name, address, and product.

Continental Europe Market Guide. A semiannual publication of Dun & Bradstreet Information Services, Dun & Bradstreet Co., 3 Sylvan Way, Parsippany, NJ 07054-3896. Covers over 200,000 firms in 21 western European nations.

Directory of Foreign Trade Organizations in Eastern Europe. Published every other year by International Trade Press, 1650 Borel Place, Suite 130, San Mateo, CA 94402-3403. Lists over 3,500 organizations involved in foreign trade in Eastern Europe.

Dun & Bradstreet Exporter's Encyclopedia, World Marketing Guide. New York: Dun & Bradstreet International. Guide to exporting, organized by country. Updated annually.

Kompass (database). Updated quarterly by AFFARSDATA, Hollandargatan 13, P.O. Box 3188, S-10363 Stockholm, Sweden. Includes data on 400,000 manufacturers and distributors of 70,000 products and services in Belgium, Denmark, Finland, France, Germany, Italy, Luxembourg, Netherlands, Norway, Spain, Sweden, Switzerland, and the U.K.

National Trade and Professional Associations of the United States and Canada and Labor Unions. C. Colgate, ed. Washington, DC: Columbia Books. Updated annually. Listing of 5,800 organizations alphabetically, geographically, by names of executives, amount of budget, and type of product or field.

Standard & Poor's Register of Corporations, Directors and Executives. New York: Standard & Poor's Corp. Updated annually. Eleven volumes include listings of manufacturers by special product and leading trade and brand names, as well as an alphabetical listing with addresses, branch offices, subsidiaries, products, and estimated capitalization.

World Trade Centers Association World Business Directory. Published by Gale Research, 27500 Drake Road, Farmington Hills, MI 48331. Covers over 100,000 companies in 190 countries engaged in international trade.

The World Trade System. Available from Longman Group U.K., Westgate House, 6th Floor, The High, Harlow, Essex CM20 1YR, England. Lists national and international trade groups.

SELECTED AMERICAN EMPLOYERS ENGAGED IN INTERNATIONAL TRADE

3M
3M Center
St. Paul, MN 55144
Tel.: (612) 733-1110
(Adhesive, abrasive, imaging, and paper products; 45% foreign sales)

American Cyanamid Company
One Cyanamid Plaza
Wayne, NJ 07470
Tel.: (201) 831-2000
(Pharmaceutical manufacturer; 37% foreign sales)

Boeing Company
7755 E. Marginal Way South
Seattle, WA 98108
Tel.: (206) 655-2121
(Aeronautical products; 50% foreign sales)
www.boeing.com

Chase Manhattan Corp.
1 Chase Manhattan Plaza
New York, NY 10081
Tel.: (212) 552-2222
(Individual and wholesale banking; 43% foreign sales)
www.chase.com

Citicorp
399 Park Avenue
New York, NY 10043-0001
Tel.: (212) 559-1000
(Banking and financial services; 36% foreign sales)
www.citicorp.com

Compaq Computer Corp.
20555 State Hwy. 249
Houston, TX 77070
Tel.: (713) 370-0670
(Personal computers; 45% foreign sales)
www.compaq.com

CPC International
International Plaza, Box 8000
Englewood Cliffs, NJ 07632-9976
Tel.: (201) 894-4000
(Food processing; 60% foreign sales)

Digital Equipment Corp.
146 Main Street
Maynard, MA 01754
Tel.: (508) 493-5428
(Computer hardware and software;
60% foreign sales)

Dow Chemical Company
2030 Dow Center
Midland, MI 48674
Tel.: (517) 636-1000
(Chemicals and plastics; 50% foreign
sales)
www.dow.com

Eastman Kodak
343 State Street
Rochester, NY 14650
Tel.: (716) 724-4000
(Imaging equipment; 41% foreign
sales)
www.kodak.com

Ford Motor Company
The American Road
Dearborn, MI 48121
Tel.: (313) 322-3000
(Automobiles, agricultural equipment,
financial services; 33% foreign sales)
www.ford.com

General Motors
3044 W. Grand Blvd.
Detroit, MI 48202
Tel.: (313) 556-5000
(Motor vehicles; 20% foreign sales)
www.gm.com

Hewlett-Packard
3200 Hillview Avenue
Palo Alto, CA 94304-1208
Tel.: (415) 857-5016
(Computers; 21% foreign sales)
www.hp.com

Intel Corp.
3065 Bowers Avenue
Santa Clara, CA 95052
Tel.: (408) 765-8080
(Computer systems and components;
43% foreign sales)
www.intel.com

McDonnell Douglas
P.O. Box 516
St. Louis, MO 63166
Tel.: (314) 232-0232
(Aeronautical products; 23% foreign
sales)

Mobil Corp.
3225 Gallows Road
Fairfax, VA 22037
Tel.: (703) 849-3000
(Petroleum exploration and processing; 65% foreign sales)
www.mobil.com

Motorola, Inc.
1303 East Algonquin Road
Schaumburg, IL 60196
Tel.: (708) 576-5000
(Electronic products, systems, and
components; 38% foreign sales)
www.motorola.com

PepsiCo, Inc.
700 Anderson Hill Road
Purchase, NY 10577
Tel.: (914) 253-2000
(Beverages, foods, and restaurants;
20% foreign sales)

Texaco, Inc.
2000 Westchester Avenue
White Plains, NY 10650
Tel.: (914) 253-4000
(Petroleum exploration and processing; 40% foreign sales)
www.texaco.com

Union Carbide
39 Old Ridgebury Road
Danbury, CT 06817
Tel.: (203) 794-2000
(Manufactures chemicals and plastics;
17% foreign sales)

Unisys Corp.
P.O. Box 500
Blue Bell, PA 19424
Tel.: (215) 986-1101
(Manufactures computers; 20% for-
eign sales)
www.unisys.com

International Banking and Finance

As a result of the internationalization of the world's financial markets and the deregulation of several important capital markets in the 1980s, notably London and Frankfurt, an increasing number of financial institutions are devoting more attention to their international operations. Thus, there will be a need for personnel with wide-ranging backgrounds in economics, politics, business, foreign languages, and international experience.

In government and semi-public financial institutions, there is also a need for talented people who understand the complex global financial markets and who can analyze private-sector investment activities. International banking and finance offers an expansion of career opportunities for people who want to be in global markets, serving as a bridge between capital-raising entities and capital-providing investors.

Many banking jobs depend on the kinds of financial services the bank extends to the community, such as retail banking, commercial banking, trust banking, and investment banking.

An MBA is not necessary to be considered seriously by international businesses, but basic business knowledge is essential. Accounting is the most important prerequisite; it is necessary for insight into overall company policy and prospects. An understanding of economics can be very valuable, especially on the corporate ladder. Finance experience or course work is also crucial. Larger banks are more likely to have less stringent requirements for previous experience because they are able to provide in-house training to new hires.

The prognosis for a career in international finance will be determined by:

1. *Continuing internationalization of financial markets,* as banks and their customers stake out new positions in international markets.

2. *Technological change,* since the impetus for much growth and diversification in services comes from the development of new technology.

3. *Deregulation and regulation:* whatever the government stance, banks will need to have a counter-stance.

4. *Changes in political stability and economic progress* in foreign countries affect long-term sources of growth since stability by definition requires time; given the competitive nature of the marketplace, flexibility is required so that changes don't take the bank by surprise.

All banks are expanding the range of services they offer. Since many of these new services involve international money markets, this expansion bodes well for those with a background in accounting and finance. It is important to remember, however, that not all banks are experiencing international growth. Many have pulled back from overseas markets, especially in response to soft Asian, Latin American, and Russian markets. Some are concentrating on specific regions; California banks, for instance, are focusing on Asia and the Pacific Rim. Others want to specialize in specific industries, such as energy, or in foreign governments and banks. Some banks are moving aggressively and indiscriminately into any new market. These differences in outlook are reflected in banks' respective annual reports, especially over several years; that is one reason why annual reports are such important resources in the job search.

If your ultimate goal is to land a job in a European capital, you should realize that many banks hire foreign nationals for their foreign subsidiaries, making it easier to find a job in the U.S. than abroad. Training and several domestic assignments will facilitate transferring abroad. Fluency in a language is a definite asset in the job search but does not guarantee that you will find a job outside the U.S.

Regardless of the specific area you want to work in, it is important to look at the needs of individual banks. Your prospects are considerably enhanced if you can see the connection between the combination of language, international affairs, and business experience that you can present to a bank in response to their specific growth objectives.

RESOURCES IN INTERNATIONAL BUSINESS AND FINANCE

Publications:

Business Week
The Economist
The Financial Times
The New York Times
The Wall Street Journal

Books & Articles:

The Economies of Money, Banking, and Financial Markets. Mishkin, Frederic. Columbia University: Little, Brown and Co., 1986. Basic textbook on money and financial markets.

Financial Markets and the World Economy. Van Horne, James. Englewood Cliffs, NJ: Prentice-Hall, 1984. Chapters 3 and 4 discuss how interest rates are determined.

Guide to Careers in World Affairs. New York: Foreign Policy Association, Inc. Pages 53-64 provide an excellent point of departure for finance and many other occupational areas. Contains addresses and suggestions for specific institutions, although given the rapid pace of change in the industry, this book should not be used by itself.

International Jobs. Kocher, Eric. Reading, MA: Addison-Wesley Publishing Co. Provides a similar and somewhat more timely approach than the Foreign Policy Association's book above.

Occupational Outlook Handbook and Quarterly. Washington, DC: U.S. Department of Labor Statistics. A directory of 100 state employment agencie that provide career information on over 250 occupations.

SELECTED EUROPEAN AND AMERICAN BANK EMPLOYERS:

Allied Irish Bank
405 Park Avenue
New York, NY 10022-4405
Tel.: (212) 339-8000

American Express Bank
American Express Tower, 24th Floor
New York, NY 10285
Tel.: (212) 298-3962

American Scandinavian Banking
Corp.
437 Madison Avenue
New York, NY 10022-7001
Tel.: (212) 371-1090

Bank of Boston
100 Federal Street
Boston, MA 02110
Tel.: (212) 434-2200

Bank of New York
48 Wall Street
New York, NY 10286
Tel.: (212) 495-1784

Bankers Trust
280 Park Avenue
New York, NY 10017
Tel.: (212) 250-2500

Brown Brothers Harriman
59 Wall Street
New York, NY 10005-2818
Tel.: (212) 483-1818

Chemical Bank
270 Park Avenue, 2nd Floor
New York, NY 10017
Tel.: (212) 270-6000

Continental Bank International
231 South LaSalle Street
Chicago, IL 60697-0002
Tel.: (312) 828-2345

Creditanstalt-Bankverein
245 Park Avenue, 27th Floor
New York, NY 10167
Tel.: (212) 856-1000

Dillon, Read and Co.
535 Madison Avenue
New York, NY 10022
Tel.: (212) 906-2000

European American Bank
811 Vermont Avenue NW
Washington, DC 20571
Tel.: (202) 566-8990

Federal Reserve Bank of New York
33 Liberty Street
New York, NY 10045
Tel.: (212) 720-5000

First Boston Corp.
55 East 52nd Street
New York, NY 10055
Tel.: (212) 909-2000

First Fidelity Bank
123 South Broad Street
Philadelphia, PA 19109-1199
Tel.: (215) 985-6000

First Interstate Bancorp
633 West 57th Street
Los Angeles, California 90071
Tel.: (213) 614-3001

First National Bank of Boston
100 Federal Street
Boston, MA 02110-1802
Tel.: (617) 434-2200

French American Banking Corp.
200 Liberty Street, 20th Floor
New York, NY 10281
Tel.: (212) 978-5700

Goldman Sachs
85 Broad Street
New York, NY 10004-2456
Tel.: (212) 902-1000

Keefe, Bruyette, and Woods
Two World Trade Center, 85th Floor
New York, NY 10048
Tel.: (212) 323-8300

Kidder Peabody and Co.
10 Hanover Square
New York, NY 10005
Tel.: (212) 510-3000

Kleinwort, Benson, Lonsdale
200 Park Avenue, 25th Floor
New York, NY 10166
Tel.: (212) 983-4000

Marine Midland Bank
One Marine Midland Center
Buffalo, NY 14202-2842
Tel.: (716) 841-2424

Mellon Bank Corp.
Mellon Bank Center
Pittsburgh, PA 15258
Tel.: (412) 234-5000

Merrill Lynch & Co. International Bank
World Financial Center—North
Tower, 16th Floor
New York, NY 10281-1361
Tel.: (212) 449-3022

Morgan Stanley Group
1251 Avenue of the Americas
New York, NY 10020
Tel.: (212) 703-4000

Northern Trust Co.
50 South LaSalle Street
Chicago, IL 60675-0002
Tel.: (312) 630-6000

Paine-Webber
1285 Avenue of the Americas

New York, NY 10019-6093
Tel.: (212) 713-2000

Republic New York Corp.
452 5th Avenue, P.O. Box 423
New York, NY 10018-2706
Tel.: (212) 525-5000

Salomon Brothers
7 World Trade Center
New York, NY 10048
Tel.: (212) 783-7000

Shawmut National Corp.
One Federal Street
Boston, MA 02211
Tel.: (617) 292-2000

Smith Barney Shearson
1345 Avenue of the Americas
New York, NY 10105
Tel.: (212) 399-6000

United States Trust Company of New York
114 West 47th Street
New York, NY 10036
Tel.: (212) 852-1000

Wells Fargo Bank International
420 Montgomery Street
San Francisco, CA 94104-1205
Tel.: (415) 477-1000

Western Bancorporation
1251 Westwood Boulevard
Los Angeles, CA 90024-4811
Tel.: (310) 477-2401

International Economics

Skills and experience associated with international economics can be applied to virtually any international career. International economists work in many fields: banking, finance, business, consulting, development, government, and trade. They also work in the related fields of security policy, human rights, and media.

Most economists in this specialization find positions in either private-sector finance or business. In the private sector, fields for international economists include economic analysis, corporate profitability, securities, sales and trading, professional banking, community banking, and auditing.

RESOURCE ORGANIZATIONS IN INTERNATIONAL ECONOMICS

The American Economic Association. 2014 Broadway, Suite 305, Nashville, TN 37203-2418. (Publishes *Job Openings for Economists* bi-monthly.)

The National Association of Business Economists. 28790 Chagrin Boulevard, Suite 300, Cleveland, OH 44122. (Publishes job listings periodically, also *Business Economic Careers.*)

National Economic Association. c/o Alfred L. Edwards, University of Michigan, School of Business, Ann Arbor, MI 48109-1234. (Publishes job listings.)

SELECTED EMPLOYERS OF ECONOMISTS

Developing expertise that would be of interest to any of these organizations requires smart thinking about skills complementary to economics—accounting, finance, trade, development, and policy analysis, for example, depending on your interests.

Agency for International Development (A.I.D.)
International Development Intern Recruitment
Office of Personnel and Management
320 21st Street NW
Washington, DC 20523

Central Intelligence Agency
Office of Personnel
P.O. Box 12727, Dept. A
Washington, DC 20505

Foreign Commercial Service
Department of Commerce
14th and Constitution Avenue NW
Washington, DC 20230

International Development Cooperation Agency (I.D.C.A.)
320 21st Street NW
Washington, DC 20523

International Monetary Fund (I.M.F)
700 19th Street NW
Washington, DC 20431

Office of International Cooperation and Development (O.I.C.D.)
U.S. Department of Agriculture
Personnel Office, Room 430
Washington, DC 20250
Tel.: (202) 653-9241

Overseas Private Investment Corporation (O.P.I.C.)
1129 20th Street NW
Washington, DC 20527

United Nations
Recruitment Programs Sections
Office of Personnel Services
First Avenue & 46th Street
New York, NY 10017

(or through the U.S. Dept. of State)
United Nations Recruitment Staff
Bureau of International Organization Affairs
Department of State
Washington, DC 20520

U.S. Department of Commerce/Bureau of Economic Analysis
1401 K Street NW
Washington, DC 20230

U.S. Department of Energy
Office of the Assistant Secretary for International Affairs and Energy Emergencies
Forrestal Building
1000 Independence Avenue SW
Washington, DC 20585

U.S. Department of Labor
Bureau of International Labor Affairs
OASAM
200 Constitution Avenue, Room S-2235
Washington, DC 20210

U.S. Department of State
Bureau of Economic and Business
Affairs
2201 C Street NW, Room 6828
Washington, DC 20520

U.S. Department of the Treasury
Office of the Assistant Secretary for

International Affairs
15th & Pennsylvania Avenue NW,
Room 3432
Washington, DC 20220

U.S. International Trade Commission
500 E Street SW
Washington, DC 20436

World Bank
Career Information Center
1818 H Street NW
Washington, DC 20455

International Consulting

What is consulting? It is helping companies or organizations improve their performance through strategic planning. There are three main types of consulting:

General management consulting, which includes the analysis of market trends, feasibility studies, and impact studies of broader market economic issues.

Government consulting relates to government functions such as defense/military, foreign aid, international trade, and economic issues.

Specialized consulting focuses on specific areas, for example, benefits, technology, agriculture, trade, and the like.

Consulting firms as a group are rather diverse. Some firms began in accounting and expanded into management consulting as an additional service. Others were founded specifically for management or more technical consulting. While a few firms boast several hundred employees worldwide and recruit intensively, many are small operations, emphasizing the experience and high-level skills of their staffs.

Management consulting firms are probably the best known. Although some management consulting firms trace their origins back to the nineteenth century, consulting as a profession has only recently become a major player in business and government. Several of the larger firms began to merge or buy out smaller firms in the 1980s, producing a relative consolidation and stabilization in the industry.

When hiring new employees, consulting firms look for analytical skills, the ability to quickly and systematically break down problems and analyze them, client-relations skills, common sense, confidence, communication skills, initiative and creativity, independent thinking, and the technical expertise that is reflected in a master's degree.

Management consulting, the sector we will focus on here, may be further broken down into five sub-categories:

Pure Strategy–provides overall corporate direction; hired directly by CEOs. Usually small, prestigious firms that hire MBAs.

Traditional–strategic but area-specific consulting, such as finance. More diversified than pure strategy consulting firms.

Accountancy–strong in information-technology work; the fastest-growing type of management consulting firm.

Human Resources–people management, including pay structures and pension plans; most political branch.

Specialists–area experts, such as information technology or data processing. Usually small firms.

RESOURCES IN CONSULTING

Organizations:

American Association of Political Consultants. 5335 Wisconsin Avenue NW, Suite 700, Washington, DC 20015. Membership roster available.

Council of Consulting Organizations (management consulting organizations). 521 Fifth Street, 35th Floor, New York, NY 10175. Incorporating the Association of Management Consultants, the Association of Management Consulting Firms (formerly the Association of Consulting Management Engineers—ACME), the Institute of Management Consultants, and the Society of Professional Management Consultants. Membership directory available.

Publications:

Consultants and Consulting Organizations: Directory and Supplements. Gale Research, 27500 Drake Road, Farmington Hills, MI 48331. Updated annually.

Directory of Management Consultants. Kennedy Publications, Templeton Road, Fitzwilliam, NH 03447.

Directory of Management Consultants in the U.K. Alan Armstrong & Associates Ltd., 72-76 Park Road, London NW1 4SH, England.

Dun's Consultants Directory. Extremely extensive; divided alphabetically, geographically, and by specialty.

International Consultants: A Worldwide Professional Directory. Seminar Services S.A., 1 Passage Perdonnet, CH-1005 Lausanne, Switzerland.

Management Consulting. Boston, MA: Harvard Business School Press, Harvard University.

Management Consulting: A Guide to the Professions. M. Kubr, ed. International Labor Organization, CH-1211 Geneva, Switzerland.

Who's Who in Consulting: A Reference Guide to Professional Personnel Engaged in Consulting of Business, Industry, and Government. Gale Research, 27500 Drake Road, Farmington Hills, MI 48331.

SELECTED INTERNATIONAL CONSULTING EMPLOYERS

1. MANAGEMENT CONSULTING FIRMS

American Management Systems
1777 North Kent Street
Arlington, VA 22209
Tel.: (703) 841-6000

Andersen Consulting
69 Washington Street
Chicago, IL 60602-3094
Tel.: (312) 580-0069
Systems and consulting services, involving planning, design, and installation of information systems for management planning and control. Also performs analytical studies to support management decision making.

Bain and Co.
2 Copley Place
Boston, MA 02117-0897
Tel.: (617) 572-2000
Specialists in strategy consulting in such areas as developing and establishing corporate strategy, developing market programs, handling acquisitions and divestitures. Over 800 employees worldwide.

Theodore Barry and Associates
1520 Wilshire Blvd.
Los Angeles, CA 90017
Tel.: (213) 413-6080

Roland Berger and Partner GMBH
8000 Munchen 81
Munich, Germany

Booz, Allen, and Hamilton
101 Park Avenue
New York, NY 10178
Tel.: (212) 697-1900
International management and technology consulting firm; federal government specialists; oriented to senior executives. Assignments are diverse, ranging from strategic planning and acquisitions to global marketing, energy policy designing, and technology advancement. Second-highest firm in revenue.

Boston Consulting Group
Exchange Place
Boston, MA 02109
Tel.: (617) 973-1200
International firm best known for long-range strategic business planning. Over 350 employees worldwide.

Cresap, McCormack and Paget
245 Park Avenue, 18th Floor
New York, NY 10167
Tel.: (212) 935-7000

Data Resources
11 Broadway, 6th Floor
New York, NY 10004
Tel.: (212) 208-1200

Deloitte and Touche
10 Westport Road
Wilton, CT 06897
Tel.: (203) 761-3000

Economic and Management Consultants
25 St. James Street
London SW1, England

Ernst and Young
787 7th Avenue, 14th Floor
New York, NY 10019
Tel.: (212) 407-1500

A.T. Kearney
222 West Adams
Chicago, IL 60606
Tel.: (312) 648-0111

KPMG Peat-Marwick
767 5th Avenue
New York, NY 10153
Tel.: (212) 909-5000
Strategic planning, financial management, human resources, management information systems, operations management, and executive search.

Arthur D. Little
25 Acorn Park
Cambridge, MA 02140
Tel.: (617) 498-5000

McKinsey and Co.
55 East 52nd Street
New York, NY 10022
Tel.: (212) 446-7000
General management consulting, with emphasis on strategy, organization, and operations. Specialties are staff management and research. 38 offices worldwide. Top firm in revenues and prestige. "Up or out" reputation.

Mercer Consulting Group
1166 Avenue of the Americas
New York, NY 10036
Tel.: (212) 345-5000
Employee benefits consulting service specializes in design, implementation, communication, and marketing of employee benefit plans. Sells to commercial concerns worldwide.

PriceWaterhouse Coopers
1251 Avenue of the Americas
New York, NY 10020
Tel.: (212) 819-5000
Assists management in designing and implementing improved information structures and systems. Specialists in over 35 industries and government.

Kurt Salmon Associates
1355 Peachtree Street NE
Atlanta, GA 30309
Tel.: (404) 892-0321

2. BUSINESS & FINANCE CONSULTING FIRMS

Checchi and Co.
1730 Rhode Island Avenue NW, Suite 910
Washington, DC 20036
Tel.: (202) 452-9700

Hay, Huggins Co.
229 South 18th Street
Philadelphia, PA 19103
Tel.: (215) 875-2300

J.D. Henson & Associates
12265 South Dixie Hwy., Suite 907
Miami, FL 33156
Tel.: (305) 595-7934

Hewitt Associates
100 Half Day Road
Lincolnshire, IL 60069
Tel.: (708) 295-5000

ICME Business Consultants
Restelbergstrasse 49
8044 Zurich, Switzerland

International Business-Government Counselors
818 Connecticut Avenue NW, 12th Floor
Washington, DC 20006
Tel.: (202) 872-8181

Robert R. Nathan Associates
2101 Wilson Blvd., Suite 1200
Arlington, VA 22201
Tel.: (703) 516-7700

3. MARKETING & SALES CONSULTING FIRMS

Demby and Associates
141 East 44th Street, Suite 310
New York, NY 10017
Tel.: (212) 692-9220

Frost and Sullivan
106 Fulton Street
New York, NY 10038
Tel.: (212) 233-1080

4. OTHER

Chemonics International Consulting
2000 M Street NW, Suite 200
Washington, DC 20036
Tel.: (202) 466-5340
International development consulting firm.

Data Resources
24 Hartwell Avenue
Lexington, MA 02173
Information services and communications consulting firm.

Experience, Inc.
123 North 3rd Street, Suite 304
Minneapolis, MN 55401
Tel.: (612) 338-7844
Agricultural consulting firm.

A.L. Nellum Associates
1900 L Street NW, Suite 405
Washington, DC 20036
Tel.: (202) 466-4920
Human resources and development consulting.

Towers Perrin
245 Park Avenue
New York, NY 10167
Tel.: (212) 309-3400
International firm, specializing in total compensation, pay and benefits, actuarial and communications consulting. Through its Cresap, McCormick, and Paget division, T.P.F.&C. offers general management and management services in the areas of strategy, human resource management, and management processes.

International Law

International law practice describes a scope of work rather than a specific kind of work. International lawyers are generally first-class domestic lawyers who have established themselves within their firms and have earned the right to claim the "plum" international cases. Lawyers who practice "internationally" are expected to be familiar with most business, trade, and corporate law, as well as the civil law system and how it may conflict with the common law system.

Practicing law in Europe is generally very difficult. In fact, you will not be able to practice legally in Europe unless you have attended a European law school. Lawyers employed by American companies, however, can practice in Europe for their employer.

Employers invariably cite excellent undergraduate and law school academic records as the primary hiring criteria. Fluency in foreign languages (especially Spanish, French, and Japanese), knowledge of international economics, and international work or study experience are also important factors. An understanding and appreciation of other cultures and their attitudes is, of course, a basic prerequisite to successfully practicing international law.

Employment experience or academic backgrounds in international affairs may not provide a job-hunting advantage over other lawyers. Few firms, if any, specifically hire international lawyers out of law school. A few years of successful domestic practice are normally required before a lawyer gets an international case. Individuals with international academic or employment backgrounds do, however, possess an edge, providing an employer with a record of grades to examine or the certainty that the prospective lawyer has international business skills and a knowledge of world affairs that would be an asset to the firm. Specialization in a particular area (such as Great Britain, the E.U., or German law) might be helpful.

Several law schools offer strong international law programs, consisting mainly of international course electives and activities such as international law societies, international law journals, and an international law moot court team. It would be impossible to participate in all of these activities and "get the grades" at competitive law schools. Firms repeatedly emphasize the importance of high academic performance. It is also more important to consider the law school's overall reputation and quality of faculty; employers will usually consider an applicant's place in his or her law school class, not his or her place among graduates who may pursue international law.

Large firms tend to dominate international law practice in the U.S. Geographic location often influences a firm's area of international practice: New York City for international business, Washington, DC, for international public affairs, San Francisco for the Pacific Rim, Houston for Latin America, and Miami for international financing. Some firms also maintain offices abroad, but that does not always mean that most attorneys in those firms practice internationally.

In recent years, medium-sized firms have also begun to enter the international law market. International law can also be practiced in the federal government (the State Department., I.N.S., etc.), private corporations (as in-house counsel), non-profit organizations (World Bank, Inter-American Bank), and academia (law school teaching), although the hefty pay is generally still in the large law firms.

Potential law school applicants should realize that international law is not actually a field of law, such as tax or environmental law, but merely a term that describes the practice of various types of law across national boundaries, not always involving travel. Most international cases are assumed by senior partners, often on the insistence of the international client. International lawyers have generally "paid their dues" and proven themselves as excellent domestic lawyers before being assigned an international case. Having reached that point, however, lawyers often cite international law as the most exciting and interesting area of practice.

RESOURCES IN INTERNATIONAL LAW

Organizations:

American Bar Association, Section of International Law and Practice. 1800 M Street NW, Suite 450-S, Washington, DC 20036, (202) 331-2239.

Association of Student International Law Societies. A branch of the ILSA in Washington (see last entry).

International Law Institute. 1615 New Hampshire Avenue NW, Washington, DC 20009, (202) 483-3036.

International Law Society of America (American Society of International Law). 2223 Massachusetts Avenue NW, Washington, DC 20008, (202) 265-4313.

Publications:

The American Journal of Comparative Law.

The American Journal of International Law.

Career Preparation and Opportunities in International Law. Williams, John, ed. Chicago: American Bar Association, 1984.

Directory of Opportunities in International Law. Brinkman, Paul, ed. John Bassett Moore Society of International Law, University of Virginia School of Law, Charlottesville, VA 22901.

The ILSA Guide to Education and Career Development in International Law. Available from the ILSA in Washington (see above). Tel.: (202) 265-0386.

The International Lawyer. Journal of the A.B.A. Section of International Law and Practice.

International Lawyers Newsletter.

Martindale Hubbell Law Directory. Published annually by Martindale Hubbell, Inc., 121 Chanlon Road, New Providence, NJ 07974.

TOP 10 LAW SCHOOLS PUBLISHING INTERNATIONAL LAW JOURNALS

1. **Harvard University Law School**
   Harvard International Law Journal
   Cambridge, MA 02138

2. **Yale University Law School**
   Yale Journal of World Public Order
   New Haven, CT 06520

3. **University of Michigan Law School**
   Michigan Yearbook of International Legal Studies
   Ann Arbor, MI 48104

4. **Columbia University School of Law**
   Columbia Journal of International Law
   New York, NY 10027

5. **Stanford University Law School**
   Stanford Journal of International Studies
   Stanford, CA 94305

6. **University of Virginia School of Law**
   Virginia Journal of International Law
   Charlottesville, VA 22901

7. **New York University School of Law**
   Journal of International Law and Politics
   New York, NY 10012

8. **University of Texas School of Law**
   Texas International Law Journal
   Austin, TX 78705

9. **Georgetown University Law Center**
   Law and Policy in International Business
   Washington, DC 20001

10. **Cornell University Law School**
    Cornell International Law Journal
    Ithaca, NY 15853

Not a lawyer? Try paralegal work.

Many people with an interest in international law often find positions as legal assistants or paralegals within law firms that have large international practices. Working as a paralegal offers a number of benefits to those interested in law. It gives you the chance to view the law environment from the inside. You also learn a valuable skill that can be highly sought after and well paid. While not as glamorous as being a lawyer, paralegals work in the same locale, do similar work, and can derive immense pleasure from their jobs. This can also be excellent work if you are considering attending law school at some point in the future.

SELECTED INTERNATIONAL LAW FIRMS

Cleary, Gottlieb, Steen, and Hamilton
One Liberty Plaza
New York, NY 10006
Tel.: (212) 225-2000

Covington and Burling
1201 Pennsylvania Avenue NW
Washington, DC 20004
Tel.: (202) 662-6000

Gibson, Dunn, and Crutcher
333 South Grand Avenue
Los Angeles, CA 90071
Tel.: (213) 229-7000

Mudge, Rose, Guthrie, Alexander, and Ferdon
180 Maiden Lane
New York, NY 10038
Tel.: (212) 510-7000

Patton, Boggs, and Blow
2550 M Street NW, 8th Floor
Washington, DC 20037
Tel.: (202) 457-6000

Pennie and Edmonds
1155 Avenue of the Americas, 22nd Floor
New York, NY 10036
Tel.: (212) 790-9090

White and Case
1155 Avenue of the Americas
New York, NY 10036
Tel.: (212) 819-8200

International Media and Communications

The international communications field includes newspaper journalism and broadcasting as well as magazine and book publishing. These jobs are in great demand, so finding them requires a considerable amount of patience and determination. Even those who follow everything suggested here will need much talent and luck to land a good job. Our recommendations are focused more on journalism than publishing, since most people interested in international media and communications are aiming for jobs as foreign correspondents.

Many editors consider a journalism degree too narrow. They claim to prefer candidates who have a broad liberal arts background and a knowledge of politics, history, and international affairs. Fluency in more than one language is helpful in the communications field as well. Reporters are sent mainly to western European capitals, financial centers such as London, Frankfurt, Paris, and Rome, and "hot spots" like Eastern Europe and Northern Ireland.

News organizations want, first and foremost, good writing, editing, and reporting skills. These can best be developed through work experience and internships, although taking courses at a journalism school, especially a "writing and report" course, is also helpful.

It is essential to have a file of "clips," published articles with your byline. A good work experience or internship will allow you to accumulate them. Generally, successful applicants for reporting jobs already have several internships under their belts. Internships can also lead directly to jobs through an improved network of contacts or simply by being hired by the organization where you interned.

The largest employers of foreign correspondents are the wire services. The Associated Press, for example, has 200 reporters stationed around the world. *The New York Times* has the largest overseas staff of any newspaper by far, with more than 100 correspondents. *The Los Angeles Times, The Wall Street Journal, The Washington Post, Time* magazine, and *Newsweek* also have large overseas staffs. Other large metropolitan papers keep overseas staffs of anywhere from 10-50. Other internationally oriented publications, such as *The International Herald Tribune,* owned by the *Washington Post* and *The New York Times,* and *The Christian Science Monitor,* employ many Americans abroad.

Getting on a staff is best accomplished through contacts, luck, or simple, physical courage. Willingness to jump into the thick of the fighting in the site of latest international conflict has often been the ticket to employment as a foreign correspondent, as has being next to the editor's desk when something big happens on an empty beat.

But if you are hired by a wire service, they'll probably assign you first to a smaller office in the U.S. If you are good and make your interest in foreign reporting known, you may eventually be transferred to the foreign desk in New York, from whence you can be sent overseas. Experienced, senior personnel are likely to occupy the desirable European capital bureaus. Another approach would be to work for an English-language paper overseas. They often need native English speakers as writers and editors.

Newspapers and magazines are less systematic than the large wire services, but you still must work up to the foreign jobs from within the organization. Getting a job on a newspaper, large or small, is no mean feat. Blanket the market with resumes and clips, addressed to the managing editor in most cases. Newspapers are not as efficiently managed as other corporations, so you will probably have to follow up more assiduously than usual to arrange an interview.

Once you get a job, don't let your contacts in other news organizations dwindle. Journalism is a nomadic profession, and most people change positions every 2-3 years, at least in the beginning. And keep in mind that "news organization" may be a broader term than what first comes to mind. Every international foundation, corporation, or organization, for example, has a public relations staff. For instance, one of the best magazines in the Middle East is published by Aramco, the Arab-American oil company. You should also keep up your "special" skills after you have been hired, even if you don't use them in your current position. If a paper needs to fill its Athens bureau, your knowledge of Greek might make all the difference.

Publishing companies also maintain subsidiaries overseas, either for distribution of books published in the U.S. or for production abroad. As in journalism, excellent writing skills are key. Publishing involves marketing and other clearly typical business endeavors. The industry is not particularly profitable and companies are not always very efficient. Achieving a position in Europe would involve language fluency (although Britain is the overseas focus of most publishing houses) and proven experience in the industry.

RESOURCES IN INTERNATIONAL COMMUNICATIONS AND MEDIA

Broadcasting/Cablecasting Yearbook. R.R. Bowker Co., 121 Chanlon Road, New Providence, NJ 07954.

Careers in International Affairs. Sheehan, Gerard. Washington: Georgetown University School of International Affairs.

Editor and Publisher International Yearbook. Editor and Publisher Company, 11 W. 19th Street, New York, NY 10011, (212) 675-4380.

Guide to Careers in World Affairs. New York: Foreign Policy Association, 1987.

International Jobs: Where They Are, How to Get Them. Kocher, Eric. Reading, MA: Addison-Wesley, 1989. Author is a former dean of Career Education at Columbia.

International Literary Marketplace. Found, Peter, ed. R.R. Bowker Company, 121 Chanlon Road, New Providence, NJ 07954.

Literary Marketplace. New Jersey: R.R. Bowker Co. (see above). Directory of American book publishing, updated annually.

O'Dwyer's Directory of Corporate Communications. J.R. O'Dwyer Company, 271 Madison Avenue, 6th Floor, New York, NY 10016, (212) 679-2471. Lists public relations and communications departments of America's largest companies and trade associations.

Publisher's International Directory. New Jersey: R.R. Bowker Co. (see above). Contains names and addresses of 20,000 publishers in 144 countries.

Student Guide to Mass Media Internships. Intern Research Group, Journalism Department, Buzzard Building, Eastern Illinois University, Charelston, IL 61920. Information on internships with newspapers, magazines, public relations firms, publishers, TV and radio stations. Listings by subject and location.

Ulrich's International Periodicals Directory. New Jersey: Reed Reference Publishing, 121 Chanlon Road, New Providence, NJ 07974, (908) 464-6800. Lists 66,000 periodicals from all over the world in 557 subject areas.

SELECTED INTERNATIONAL COMMUNICATIONS EMPLOYERS

BROADCASTING

ABC/Capital Cities
77 West 66th Street
New York, NY 10023
Tel.: (212) 456-7777

American Women in Radio and Television
1101 Connecticut Avenue NW, Suite 700
Washington, DC 20036
Tel.: (202) 429-5102

AP Broadcast Services
1825 K Street NW, Suite 710
Washington, DC 20006
Tel.: (202) 736-1100

Board for International Broadcasting
1201 Connecticut Avenue NW, Suite 400
Washington, DC 20036

Cable News Network (CNN)
100 International Blvd.
One CNN Center
Atlanta, GA 30303
Tel.: (404) 827-1500

CBS Inc.
51 West 52nd Street
New York, NY 10019
Tel.: (212) 975-4321

The Discovery Channel
7700 Wisconsin Avenue
Bethesda, MD 20814
Tel.: (301) 986-1999

International Radio and Television Society
420 Lexington Avenue
New York, NY 10170
Tel.: (212) 867-6650

Lehrer News Hour
3620 27th Street S.
Arlington, VA 22206

Museum of Broadcasting
One East 53rd Street
New York, NY 10022

National Broadcasting Company (NBC)
30 Rockefeller Plaza
New York, NY 10112
Tel.: (212) 664-4444

Radio Free Europe/Radio Liberty
1201 Connecticut Avenue NW
Washington, DC 20036-2605
Tel.: (202) 457-6900

Turner Broadcasting System
100 International Blvd.
One CNN Center
Atlanta, GA 30303
Tel.: (404) 827-1700

MAGAZINES

Business Week
1221 Avenue of the Americas,
39th Floor
New York, NY 10020
Tel.: (212) 512-2511
www.businessweek.com

The Economist
The Economist Building
111 West 57th Street
New York, NY 10019
Tel.: (212) 541-5730
www.economist.com

Editor and Publisher
11 West 19th Street
New York, NY 10011
Tel.: (212) 675-4380

Euromoney Publications
Nestor House, Plyhouse Yard
London EC4VM 5EX, England

Forbes, Inc.
60 5th Avenue
New York, NY 10011
Tel.: (212) 620-2200
www.forbes.com

Foreign Affairs Journal
58 East 68th Street
New York, NY 10021
Tel.: (212) 734-0400

Fortune Magazine
Time and Life Building
Rockefeller Center
New York, NY 10020
Tel.: (212) 522-1212
www.fortune.com

Investment Dealers' Digest
2 World Trade Center, 18th Floor
New York, NY 10048

The Nation
72 5th Avenue
New York, NY 10011
Tel.: (212) 242-8400
www.nation.com

National Geographic Society
1145 17th Street NW
Washington, DC 20036
Tel.: (202) 857-7000

Newsweek, Inc.
444 Madison Avenue
New York, NY 10022
Tel.: (212) 350-4000
www.newsweek.com

New Yorker Magazine
25 West 43rd Street, 17th Floor
New York, NY 10036
Tel.: (212) 840-3800

Time, Inc.
Time and Life Building
Rockefeller Center
New York, NY 10020
Tel.: (212) 522-1212
www.time.com

MOTION PICTURES/TV
PRODUCTION

Columbia Pictures Entertainment
10202 West Washington Blvd.
Culver City, CA 90232
Tel.: (310) 280-8000

Tri-Star Pictures
711 5th Avenue
New York, NY 10022
Tel.: (212) 751-4400

Viacom International
1515 Broadway
New York, NY 10036-5794
Tel.: (212) 258-6000

Warner Communications
239 Lorraine Avenue
Upper Montclair, NJ 07043-1495
Tel.: (201) 746-7900

NEWSPAPERS

Christian Science Monitor
1 Norway Street
Boston, MA 02115
Tel.: (617) 450-2000

Financial Times
14 East 60th Street
New York, NY 10022
Tel.: (212) 752-4500

Gannett Company
535 Madison Avenue
New York, NY 10022
Tel.: (212) 715-5300

Hearst Corp.
959 8th Avenue
New York, NY 10019-3795
Tel.: (212) 649-2000

International Herald Tribune
850 3rd Avenue, 8th Floor
New York, NY 10022
Tel.: (212) 752-3890
www.iht.com

Knight-Ridder, Inc.
One Herald Plaza, 6th Floor
Miami, FL 33132
Tel.: (305) 376-3800

Los Angeles Times
Times Mirror Square
Los Angeles, CA 90053
Tel.: (213) 237-5000
www.latimes.com

New York Times
229 West 43rd Street
New York, NY 10036
Tel.: (212) 556-1234
www.nytimes.com

Wall Street Journal
Dow Jones and Co.
200 Liberty Street
New York, NY 10281
Tel.: (212) 416-2000
www.wsj.com

Washington Post
1150 15th Street NW
Washington, DC 20071
Tel.: (202) 334-6000

NEWS SERVICES

Associated Press
50 Rockefeller Plaza
New York, NY 10020-1666
Tel.: (212) 621-1500

Foreign Press Association
110 E. 59th Street, 2nd Floor
New York, NY 10022-1304

Gannett News Service
1000 Wilson Blvd.
Arlington, VA 22229
Tel.: (703) 276-5800

Hearst News Service
1701 Pennsylvania Avenue, Suite 610
Washington, DC 20006
Tel.: (202) 298-6920

Interlink Press Service
777 UN Plaza
New York, NY 10017

Reuters America
1333 H Street NW, Suite 410
Washington, DC 20005-2289
Tel.: (202) 898-8300

Reuters Information Services
85 Fleet Street
London EC4P 4AJ, England

United Press International
1400 I Street NW, Suite 800
Washington, DC 20005-2289
Tel.: (202) 898-8000

PUBLISHING

Association of American Publishers
220 East 23rd Street
New York, NY 10010
Tel.: (212) 689-8920

Bantam Doubleday Dell Publishing Group
66 5th Avenue
New York, NY 10103
Tel.: (212) 765-6500

Burson-Marsteller, Inc.
230 Park Avenue S.
New York, NY 10003
Tel.: (212) 614-4000

Conde Nast Publications
6300 Wilshire Blvd., 12th Floor
Los Angeles, CA 90048
Tel.: (213) 965-3400

Doubleday and Co.
245 Park Avenue
New York, NY 10167
Tel.: (212) 984-7561

Harwood Academic Publishers
P.O. Box 786, Cooper Station
New York, NY 10276

Macmillan Publishing Co.
866 3rd Avenue
New York, NY 10022
Tel.: (212) 202-2000

Prentice-Hall Simon & Schuster
Route 9W
Prentice-Hall Building
Engelwood Cliffs, NJ 07632
Tel.: (201) 592-2000

OTHER

CN Communications International
1441 Irving Street
Rahway, NJ 07065

Facts on File
460 Park Avenue S.
New York, NY 10016-7382
Tel.: (212) 683-2244

Grey Advertising
777 3rd Avenue
New York, NY 10017
Tel.: (212) 546-2000

Hughes Communications
1990 East Grand Avenue
El Segundo, CA 90245-5030
Tel.: (310) 607-4000

International Non-Profits

Non-profit organizations offer a wide array of opportunities for the international affairs professional. These range from analyst positions in think tanks to managerial positions in issue-specific non-profits. Non-profits are among the largest industries in the U.S., employing an estimated one-eighth of all professionals. Many people are attracted to a chance to work in socially relevant work.

Non-profit organizations have fostered great social change, from civil rights to elderly care. This sector's wages, however, are lower than the for-profit sector, and since a large amount of their funding depends on grant money, fund-raising becomes a very important task.

If you decide that you want to work in the non-profit field, your first task will be to clarify your interests. Which issues do you wish to deal with: European integration, the environment, human rights, development, international security, etc.? What kind of work do you wish to do: fund-raising, research, program planning, etc.?

Your second challenge will be to ferret out job openings. This is not easy in the non-profit sector because most organizations are small, have little turnover, and can't afford to spend resources on extensive recruitment. Therefore, it takes persistence on your part to make contacts and learn about openings. In the long run, it will pay off in the amount of satisfaction you will feel, knowing that you are making a valuable contribution to society.

For those interested in opportunities in European governmental affairs, *The European Community,* published by MacMillan Publishers (4 Little Essex Street, London WC2R 3LF, England) might be of interest. Updated biennially, it provides location and other information on European Union institutions and departments, such as the European Parliament, the Court of Justice, Council of Ministers, and so on.

SELECTED INTERNATIONAL NON-PROFIT EMPLOYERS

American Association for the
International Commission of Jurists
777 UN Plaza, Suite 9E
New York, NY 10017
Tel.: (212) 972-0883

American Council on Germany
14 East 60th Street, Suite 606
New York, NY 10022
Tel.: (212) 826-3636

American Enterprise Institute for
Public Policy Research
International Programs
1150 17th Street NW
Washington, DC 20036
Tel.: (202) 862-5800

American-European Community
Association
13 Short Gardens
London WC2H 9AT, England

American Red Cross
430 17th Street NW
Washington, DC 20006-0000
Tel.: (202) 737-8300

American-Scandinavian Foundation
725 Park Avenue
New York, NY 10021
Tel.: (212) 879-9779

American Society of International Law
2223 Massachusetts Avenue NW
Washington, DC 20008-2864
Tel.: (202) 265-4313

Amnesty International of the U.S.A.
322 8th Avenue
New York, NY 10001
Tel.: (212) 807-8400

Arms Control Association
11 DuPont Circle NW, Suite 250
Washington, DC 20036
Tel.: (202) 797-4626

Atlantic Council of the U.S.
1616 H Street NW
Washington, DC 20006
Tel.: (202) 347-9353

Business Council for International
Understanding
420 Lexington Avenue
New York, NY 10170
Tel.: (212) 490-0460

CARE
151 Ellis Street
Atlanta, GA 30303
Tel.: (800) 521-CARE

Center for Defense Information
1500 Massachusetts Avenue NW
Washington, DC 20005
Tel.: (202) 862-0700

Center for International
Development and Environment
1709 New York Avenue, 7th Floor
Washington, DC 20006

Center for Strategic and International
Studies
1800 K Street NW, Suite 400
Washington, DC 20006

Centre for Social Development and
Humanitarian Affairs
UN Vienna International Centre
Postfach 500
A-1400 Vienna, Austria

Citizen Exchange Council
12 West 31st Street, 4th Floor
New York, NY 10001
Tel.: (212) 643-1985

Committee for Economic Development
2000 L Street NW, Suite 700
Washington, DC 20036
Tel.: (202) 296-5860

Committee to Protect Journalists
16 East 42nd Street, 3rd Floor
New York, NY 10017
Tel.: (212) 983-5355

Council for a Livable World
20 Park Plaza, No. 602
Boston, MA 02116
Tel.: (617) 542-2282

Doctors Without Borders U.S.A.
30 Rockefeller Plaza, Suite 5425
New York, NY 10112
Tel.: (212) 649-5961

Economic and Social Research Institute
11490 Commerce Park Drive
Reston, VA 22091

Foreign Policy Association
729 7th Avenue, 8th Floor
New York, NY 10019-6860
Tel.: (212) 764-4050

Hudson Institute
Herman Kahn Center
5395 Emerson Way, P.O. Box 26-919
Indianapolis, IN 46226
Tel.: (317) 545-1000

Institute for Policy Studies
1601 Connecticut Avenue NW, 5th Floor
Washington, DC 20009
Tel.: (202) 234-9382

International Labor Organization
4 Route des Morillons

CH-1211 Geneva 22, Switzerland
Tel.: (41 22) 799 6111

International Republican Institute
1212 New York Avenue, Suite 900
Washington, DC 20005
Tel.: (202) 408-9450

National Democratic Institute for International Affairs
1717 Massachusetts Avenue NW, Suite 503
Washington, DC 20036
Tel.: (202) 328-3136

Nature Conservancy International
1815 Lynn Street
Arlington, VA 22209
Tel.: (703) 841-5300

Save the Children Federation
54 Wilton Road
Westport, CT 06880-3108
Tel.: (203) 226-7271

Tolstoy Foundation
200 Park Avenue S., Room 1612
New York, NY 10103
Tel.: (212) 677-7770

Union of Concerned Scientists
26 Church Street
Cambridge, MA 02238
Tel.: (617) 547-5552

U.S. Committee for UNICEF
333 East 38th Street, 6th Floor
New York, NY 10016
Tel.: (800) FOR KIDS

Women's Action for New Directions (nuclear disarmament group)
P.O. Box B
Arlington, MA 02174
Tel.: (617) 643-6740

Women Strike for Peace
105 2nd Street NE
Washington, DC 20002
Tel.: (202) 543-2660

Women's International League for Peace and Freedom
1213 Race Street
Philadelphia, PA 19107-1691
Tel.: (215) 563-7110

The U.S. Federal Government

This section focuses on international affairs positions in the federal government, one of the greatest potential employers for individuals interested in working in Europe. Many U.S. government agencies will become involved with business and trade issues, as well as political concerns, in the post-common currency Europe.

The U.S. government presence in Europe includes the Foreign Service, Commerce Department, trade missions, and security and defense personnel. Finding a position in Washington can be a very good route to eventually transferring abroad. You should realize that most federal employers with international affairs offices aren't necessarily focused exclusively upon Europe, and you may not receive a European assignment.

Foreign-oriented agencies, such as the Central Intelligence Agency or the Department of State, generally conduct their own recruiting processes. Domestic-oriented agencies that are involved with international activities, such as the Department of the Treasury or the Department of Commerce, recruit through the Office of Personnel Management, which is the human resource office of the federal government. To learn more about applying for federal jobs, write:

Office of Personnel Management
1900 E Street NW
Washington, DC 20415
Tel.: (202) 606-1800
www.opm.gov/

EXECUTIVE BRANCH EMPLOYERS

Office of Management and Budget
725 17th Street
Washington, DC 20503
Tel.: (202) 395-3000
Staff of 600. International Affairs Division includes Trade, Monetary, Investment Policy, Summer Internships.

Office of U.S. Trade Representative
600 17th Street NW
Winder Building
Washington, DC 20506
Tel.: (202) 395-3204
Staff of 140. One-year unsalaried Internship Program; 18% acceptance rate.

Department of Agriculture
14th Street and Independence Avenue SW
Washington, DC 20250
Tel.: (202) 720-2791
The department has a management development program; most foreign service assignments are made through the ranks on a merit basis. Employs Global/Regional Trade Analysts, Managers, Agricultural Policy Analysts, Statisticians. The following divisions are concerned with international issues:
 • World Agricultural Outlook Board
 • International Economics Division
 • Foreign Agricultural Service
 • Office of International Cooperation and Development
 • PL 480 Surplus Commodity and Export Credit Programs

Department of Commerce
14th Street and Constitution Avenue NW
Washington, DC 20230
Tel.: (202) 482-2000
The International Trade Administration uses the Cooperative Education Program extensively to recruit and train mid-level management. Employs: Systems Analysts, Statisticians, Economists, Trade Analysts, Writer/Editors, Consulate Posts, Regional/Program Managers, Policy Analysts. The following divisions are concerned with international issues:
 • International Trade Administration
 • Bureau of Economic Analysis
 • Bureau of Export Administration
 • U.S. Travel and Tourism Administration
 • Center for International Research
 • Foreign Trade Program

Department of Defense
Office of the Assistant Secretary for Security Affairs
The Pentagon
Washington, DC 20301-1155

Department of Education
Office of Inter-Government and Inter-Agency Affairs
400 Maryland Avenue SW
Washington, DC 20202
Tel.: (202) 401-1576

Department of Energy
Office of the Assistant Secretary for International Affairs and Energy Emergencies
1000 Independence Avenue SW
Washington, DC 20585
Tel.: (202) 586-5000

Department of Health and Human Services
Office of International Health
200 Independence Avenue SW
Washington, DC 20201
Tel.: (202) 690-7000

Department of Housing and Urban Development
Office of International Affairs
H.U.D. Building, 451 7th Street SW
Washington, DC 20410
Tel.: (202) 708-0980

Department of the Interior
Office of Territorial and International Affairs
18th and C Streets NW, Room 4310
Washington, DC 20240
Tel.: (202) 208-4822

Department of Labor
Bureau of International Labor Affairs
200 Constitution Avenue NW, Room S-2235
Washington, DC 20210
Tel.: (202) 219-6043

Department of State
2201 C Street NW
Washington, DC 20520
Tel.: (202) 647-6575

Department of Transportation
Office of Policy and International Affairs
400 7th Street SW
Washington, DC 20590
Tel.: (202) 366-4000

Department of the Treasury
Office of the Assistant Secretary for International Affairs
15th Street and Pennsylvania Avenue NW, Room 3432
Washington, DC 20220
Tel.: (202) 622-1080

The Foreign Service

The Department of State's Foreign Service has its own separate entrance procedure, consisting of a number of steps. (Certain specialist positions—for example, security officers, couriers, secretaries, doctors, nurses—summer employment, and internships do not require this procedure.) The written exam, usually offered in November, lasts about four hours and includes a test of job-related knowledge, one of English expression, and a biographic information questionnaire. The knowledge test is fairly wide-ranging and generally includes questions on world geography, the historical antecedents of international affairs, basic economic principles, U.S. history, contemporary cultural trends, and the like. The English expression test assesses one's knowledge of English grammar, punctuation, and spelling. The biographic information questionnaire is designed to compare personal characteristics of applicants with those of successful federal government professionals and administrators. There is no fee for taking the Foreign Service Exam. Registration for the written portion closes in early October. In recent years, the exam has been offered in alternate years.

Roughly 14,000 applicants worldwide take the written exam. Of those 14,000, about 3,000 are invited to participate in the next step in the process, the oral assessment. Normally conducted within nine months of the written exam, the oral assessment lasts a full day and consists of the following exercises: (a) a démarche (a role-playing exercise in which the candidate plays the part of a foreign service officer abroad and presents a position statement to two representatives of a foreign government, played by examination assessors), (b) a written report and analysis of the démarche, (c) an essay, (d) an oral exam consisting of three hypothetical questions, one each from three of the Foreign Service's six functional fields (administrative, consular, economic, political, information/cultural, and commercial), and (e) a group exercise, structured as a budget meeting, designed to measure oral presentation, negotiating, and teamwork skills.

At the end of the day, participants in the oral assessment are given either a personal interview (if they pass) or an exit interview (otherwise). The exit interview is a short, "thanks and regrets." The personal interview is more like a traditional job interview, wherein the assessors review your personal information (application forms and so on) and ask you questions based on that. The number of applicants invited to continue on in the process varies yearly, depending on the Foreign Service's current hiring needs.

For those who successfully complete the personal interview, there are security and medical clearances to attain (which can take months), and then one's name is placed on a register. Then as positions become available, applicants who make it to the register may be given an offer. Candidates' names remain on the register for 18 months. The State Department expects to hire 240 people for 1999.

Appointees are trained and oriented in Washington for a period of 2-12 months, which is usually followed by a 4-year probationary period. Initial assignments are entirely at the discretion of the respective divisions. You may not get an assignment in Europe. Advancement is highly competitive, dependent upon periodic review and evaluation. For an application and information packet, contact:

The Department of State
Recruitment Division
P.O. Box 9317
Arlington, VA 22219
Tel.: (703) 875-7490
www.state.gov/www/careers/index.html

SELECTED U.S. GOVERNMENT AGENCIES WITH INTERNATIONAL AFFAIRS DIVISIONS

Most of these agencies, like the Environmental Protection Agency, conduct their own recruitment. Employment information is generally available on the agencies' websites, or you can contact them directly for information on how to apply for jobs.

Agency for International Development
Main State Building, 2201 C Street NW
Washington, DC 20523
Tel.: (202) 663-1291

Central Intelligence Agency
P.O. Box 1925
Department S, Room 4N20
Washington, DC 20013
www.odci.gov/cia/

Congressional Budget Office
2nd & D Streets SW
Washington, DC 20515
Tel.: (202) 226-2628
www.cbo.gov/

Customs Service
1301 Constitution Avenue NW,
Room 3422
Washington, DC 20229
Tel.: (800) 944-7725
www.customs.ustreas.gov/

Defense Intelligence Agency
Civilian Staffing Operations Division
200 MacDill Boulevard
Civilian Personnel Division(DAH-2)
Washington, DC 20340-5100
Tel: (800) 526-4629
http://140.47.5.4/

Drug Enforcement Administration
Information Services Section (CPI)
700 Army-Navy Drive
Arlington, VA 22202
www.usdoj.gov/dea/

Environmental Protection Agency
401 M Street SW
Washington, DC 20460
Tel.: (202) 260-2090
www.epa.gov/

Federal Communications Commission
1919 M Street NW
Washington, DC 20554
Tel.: (202) 418-0200
www.fcc.gov/

Federal Maritime Commission
1100 L Street NW, Room 10103
Washington, DC 20573-0001
Tel.: (202) 523-5773

Federal Reserve System
20th Street & Constitution Avenue NW
Washington, DC 20551
Tel.: (202) 452-3000
www.bog.frb.fed.us/

Federal Trade Commission
6th Street & Pennsylvania Avenue NW
Washington, DC 20580
Tel.: (202) 382-4357
www.ftc.gov/

General Accounting Office
441 G Street NW
Washington, DC 20548
Tel.: (800) WORK-GAO
www.gao.gov/

House Foreign Affairs Committee
2170 Rayburn House Office Building
Washington, DC 20515-0001
Tel.: (202) 225-5021

Immigration and Naturalization Service
1425 I Street NW
Washington, DC 20536
Tel.: (202) 514-4301
www.ins.usdoj.gov/

International Trade Commission
500 E Street SW, Room 314
Washington, DC 20436

Tel.: (202) 205-2000
www.usitc.gov/

National Aeronautics and Space Administration
Washington, DC 20546
Tel.: (202) 358-0000
www.nasa.gov/

National Security Council
Office of Civilian Personnel
Recruitment Branch
Fort Meade, MD 20755-6000
Tel.: (301) 859-6444
www.whitehouse.gov/WH/EOP/NSC/html/nschome.html

Securities and Exchange Commission
450 5th Street NW

Washington, DC 20549
Tel.: (202) 942-7040
www.sec.gov/

Senate Foreign Relations Committee
423 Dirksen Building
Washington, DC 20510-0001
Tel.: (202) 224-4651
www.senate.gov/committee/foreign.html

Smithsonian Institution
Office of Personnel Administration
900 Jefferson Drive SW
Washington, DC 20560
Tel.: (202) 287-3100
(202) 287-3102 (vacancies)
www.si.edu/organiza/start.htm

RESOURCES ON FEDERAL EMPLOYMENT

The Book of U.S. Government Jobs. Damp, Dennis. D-Amp Publications, Moonship Township, PA.

Congressional Quarterly. Washington, DC: Congressional Quarterly, Inc. Annual list of registered lobbyists.

Congressional Yellow Book. Monitor Publishing Co., New York, NY. Annual.

Federal Agencies. Government publication. Published annually.

Federal Career Opportunities and *Federal Jobs Newsletter.* P.O. Box 1059, Vienna, VA 22075.

Federal Jobs for College Graduates. Goldenkoff & Morgan, eds. New York: Arco/Prentice Hall. Provides profiles and contact information for over 60 federal agencies.

Federal Yellow Book. Monitor Publishing Co., New York, NY. Annual.

How to Find an Overseas Job with the U.S. Government. Cantrell, Will, & Francine Modderno. Worldwise Books, P.O. Box 3030, Oakton, VA 22124.

U.S. Government Manual. Published annually by the Office of the Federal Register, Washington, DC.

Washington Information Directory. Washington, DC: Congressional Quarterly, Inc. Published annually.

International Teaching

Positions for American teachers can be found throughout Europe, and the demand remains constant. The small class sizes, historical settings, and diverse student populations—often multinational and multilingual—all provide for an intimate, stimulating, and rewarding teaching experience.

Elementary and Secondary School Teaching

To teach at the elementary and secondary school levels, most overseas schools require a bachelor's degree and teacher certification in addition to at least two years' teaching experience. Appointments for positions at most schools are made months before the school year begins, so you should apply well ahead of time.

The biggest employers of teachers at the pre-university level in Europe are (1) American-sponsored schools; (2) international schools; and (3) Department of Defense Dependent Schools. American-sponsored schools are private schools that accept American and multinational students and are founded by American citizens but not controlled by the U.S. government. International schools are independent but usually feature an American or British curriculum. Department of Defense Dependent Schools are for the dependents of military and civilian employees working on overseas bases.

The Department of State maintains information on American-sponsored schools. The information can be obtained by writing:

Office of Overseas Schools
U.S. Department of State
Room 245, SA-29
Washington, DC 20522-2902
(703) 875-7800
www.state.gov/www/about_state/schools/oteaching.html

For information on international schools, one good bet is to consult *The ISS Directory of Overseas Schools,* compiled by International Schools Services, Inc. This is a directory of international schools all over the world and throughout Europe. While the directory is aimed primarily at the prospective student, an address is included for each school, so you can write individual schools for more information. ISS also assists teachers in placement overseas, including annual recruitment fairs and monthly newsletters. Their New Perspectives program places applicants who are certified but lack experience. If you use ISS facilities, you must pay an initial fee as well as a secondary fee if you are placed in a job. For information, contact:

International Schools Services
Educational Staffing
P.O. Box 5910
Princeton, NJ 08543
Tel.: (609) 452-0990
Fax: (609) 452-2690

Teaching without certification

While you generally need certification (and experience) to teach at the elementary or secondary level in Europe, those without official credentials needn't abandon hope.

Overseas Academic Opportunities (72 Franklin Ave., Ocean Grove, NJ 07756; (908) 774-1040), for example, lists K-12 positions open to those without certification or experience. Working as a tutor or language instructor in English as a second language may be another option. Check out Chapter 10 to explore teaching English abroad.

For more information about independent international schools, here are some more directories:

International Schools Directory. Published by the European Council of International Schools (ECIS), 21B Lavant Street, Petersfield, Hampshire GU32 3EL, England. The ECIS also holds annual recruitment fairs in London.
The ISS Directory of Overseas Schools. Published by Peterson's Guides, Inc., P.O. Box 5910, Princeton, NJ 08543.
Schools Abroad of Interest to Americans. Published by Porter Sargent Publications, 11 Beacon Street, Boston, MA 02108.

For specific job leads, the following publications can be helpful:

The International Educator
International Educator's Institute
P.O. Box 513
Cummaquid, MA 02637
Tel.: (508) 362-1414

The Times Educational Supplement
Times Newspapers Ltd.
Priory House
St. John's Lane
London EC1M 4BX, England

The International Employment Hotline (P.O. Box 3030, Oakton, VA 22124), although not geared exclusively toward educators, lists teaching and other education-related positions abroad and also provides information on upcoming recruitment fairs. *Transitions Abroad* magazine (18 Hulst Road, P.O. Box 1300, Amherst, MA 01004) is another good resource on international teaching, providing both general information and listings of program opportunities in specific countries when available.

In addition to those sponsored by ISS, international recruitment fairs are sponsored by the following organizations:

Ohio State University
Office of Career Services
150 Arps Hall
1945 North High St.
Columbus, OH 43210-1172
Tel: (614) 292-2741

Queen's University
Placement Office
Faculty of Education
Kingston, Ontario K7L 3N6, Canada
Tel.: (613) 545-6222
Fax: (613) 545-6584

Search Associates
P.O. Box 636
Dallas, PA 18612
Tel.: (717) 696-5400
Fax: (717) 696-9500

University of Northern Iowa
Overseas Placement Service for
Educators
Cedar Falls, IA 50614-0390
Tel.: (319) 273-2083
Fax: (319) 273-6998

If you would like to work for the Department of Defense, you should be aware of a few things. While your preferences are taken into account, you must prepare to be assigned anywhere worldwide. Also, in addition to teaching certification and work experience, you must pass physical examinations. For more information, write:

Department of Defense Dependents' Schools
Teacher Recruitment Section
4040 North Fairfax Drive
Arlington, VA 22203-1634
(703) 696-3269

Another option for those interested in elementary or secondary teaching is to look into programs sponsored by the U.S. Department of Education. They offer programs such as teacher exchanges, in which you would exchange positions with a teacher abroad. Summer seminars are another alternative to consider. For information on both of these programs, write:

Teacher Education Branch
Division of International Services and Improvement
International Education Programs
U.S. Department of Education
Washington, DC 20202

College-Level Teaching

If you are interested in a teaching position in a college or university, there are several options you should investigate. You do not have to search for specific programs in order to teach in a university abroad. Foreign universities routinely recruit in the United States for teaching positions. Placement offices and various publications will prove helpful in finding these jobs. Several helpful publications are the *Chronicle of Higher Education,* the *New York Times,* and the *London Times Higher Education Supplement.*

You should also consider teaching in international organizations such as the United Nations, the Peace Corps, or the YMCA Overseas Service Corps. The United Nations agency in charge of education, UNESCO (United Nations Educational, Scientific, and Cultural Organization), recruits teachers with doctoral degrees and at least five years' experience. For information, write:

UNESCO Recruitment
Division of International Education
U.S. Department of Education
Washington, DC 20202

For information about educational assignments abroad with the Peace Corps, write:

Peace Corps
1990 K Street NW, Room 9320
Washington, DC 20526
Tel: (800) 424-8589
www.peacecorps.gov/

The Fulbright Commission sponsors the most prestigious exchanges for college teachers. Write:

Fulbright Scholar Awards Abroad: Grants for Faculty and Professionals
Council for International Exchange of Scholars
3007 Tilden Street NW, Suite 5M
Washington, DC 20008-3009
Tel: (202) 686-4000
Email: info@ciesnet.cies.org

OTHER SOURCES OF INFORMATION

Experiment in International Living
School for International Training
P.O. Box 676
Kipling Road
Brattleboro, VT 05301
Tel.: (800) 257-7751, ext. 258
Provides information on teaching positions around the world.

Friends of World Teaching
P.O. Box 1049
San Diego, CA 92112
Tel.: (619) 275-4066
Provides information on positions at all levels of teaching in over 100 countries worldwide.

Fulbright Teacher Exchange Program
E/ASX, USIA
600 Maryland Avenue SW, Room 235
Washington, DC 20024-2520
Tel.: (800) 726-0479
Fax: (202) 401-1433
Email: advise@usia.gob
Opportunities Abroad for Educators provides program descriptions and application materials for opportunities at all levels of education.

nine

Summer and Temporary Jobs in Europe

There are many good summer jobs in Europe, but finding them takes effort and forethought. In almost every country you must have secured employment before a work permit will be issued, yet a work permit is required before you'll be allowed into the country for employment. This may make working overseas legally sound like mission impossible, but it is really not. As you read this book, thousands of Americans are at work in various jobs in Europe, which means that every one of them has successfully mapped their way through (or around) the regulatory labyrinth. And if they can do it, so can you. Specific employment regulations for Americans are found in the individual country chapters in Part II of this book.

In addition to the legal hurdles you will jump as you hunt for short-term employment, there also may be specific job requirements that stand in your way. Most employers, for example, specify age, experience, language, and availability preferences. Many jobs require basic conversational skills. Seasonal work, such as tourism and agriculture, generally demands that an employee commit for the entire period advertised.

You will often be able to find unofficial summer work. Such jobs will enable you to bypass the cumbersome and restrictive bureaucratic procedures for gaining employment in Europe, and some workers avoid local taxes and deductions as well. Unfortunately, the informal nature of these jobs means you also forfeit government labor regulations that protect you against exploitative practices. You run the risk of working long hours at wages below the legal minimum, and if your employer fails to pay you, your options are very limited.

One route to short-term employment is to go through one of several non-profit organizations (listed below) that work on an exchange basis with European countries. The services of these organizations aren't free, but they will arrange all of your paperwork and working permits. Some can go a step beyond this and actually find employment for you within a number of European countries.

This chapter lists sources for general summer and other temporary employment information, types of short-term jobs available in Europe, and short-term job opportunities available in Europe. Volunteer opportunities and short-term employers are listed in the individual country chapters of the book (Chapters 11 through 21), so if you're interested in that type of work, be sure to look in Part II.

WORK EXCHANGE ORGANIZATIONS

AIESEC-U.S.
135 West 50th Street, 20th Floor
New York, NY 10020
Tel.: (212) 757-3774
AIESEC, a French acronym for the International Association of Students in Economics and Business Management, is a work-exchange program that focuses on undergraduate students interested in business-related careers. AIESEC is composed of about 100 student-run chapters at American universities. Local chapter members develop exchange positions for international students. In turn, the American students become eligible for international positions in other participating countries. The only real requirement for securing overseas employment through this program is that the student work with his or her local chapter to develop positions for in-bound students.

The American-Scandinavian Foundation
725 Park Avenue
New York, NY 10021
Tel.: (212) 879-9779
Email: contrib@amscan.org
www.amscan.org/training.htm
This foundation organizes trainee programs for college juniors majoring in a technical area. (Participants must be full-time students.) Overseas assignments are for a maximum of 18 months. Emphasis is on engineering opportunities, and most of the positions are in Denmark and Finland.

BUNAC
16 Bowling Green Lane,
London EC1R 0QH
Tel.: [44] (171) 251-3472
www.bunac.org.uk

OR
P.O. Box 430
Southbury, CT 06488
Tel.: (800) GO-BUNAC or (203) 264-0901
Fax: (203) 264-0251
www.bunac.org
Each year thousands of American students obtain special blue card work permits that allow them to work at both paid and unpaid jobs through Britain. BUNAC is also a resource and support center for American students participating in their programs. You are responsible for finding your own job using the resources available through the program or your own personal contacts. Participants rarely have problems earning enough to cover living and travel expenses.

Council on International Educational Exchange (CIEE)
205 East 42nd Street
New York, NY 10017-5706
(888) COUNCIL; (212) 882-2600
www.ciee.org
The CIEE's Work Abroad Program is a good bet for obtaining work permits before locating a position. For a fee, the organization will acquire three- to six-month work permits for you for temporary and summer jobs in Ireland, France, and Germany, plus provide you with a program handbook detailing general information on the country you have chosen to visit, employment tips and contacts, hints on travel and housing, and so on. The CIEE's International Voluntary Service Department also recruits hundreds of volunteers per year for positions in workcamps in several European nations, plus other countries throughout the world. These camps bring together volunteers from around the world for tasks that range from environmental conservation to castle restoration.

IAESTE Trainee Program
c/o Association for International Practical Training
10 Corporate Center, Suite 250
10400 Little Patuxent Parkway
Columbia, MD 21044
Tel.: (410) 997-2200
www.aipt.org/iaste.html
This program is set up as a one-to-one exchange program and offers exchanges among 63 countries and the United States for students in architecture, computer sciences, engineering, the natural and physical sciences, and mathematics. Juniors, seniors, and graduate students are eligible for summer placements and for long-term placements of from 3 to 12 months.

InterExchange
161 6th Avenue
New York, NY 10013
Tel.: (212) 924-0446
Fax: (212) 924-0575
www.interexchange.org
Coordinates work-exchange positions in the Czech Republic, Finland, France, Germany, Hungary, Norway, and Switzerland and au pair jobs in Austria,

Finland, France, Germany, Italy, Norway, and Spain. Work-exchange positions include jobs in agriculture, environmental protection, resorts and camps, teaching English, and marketing and foreign trade. Most positions require some knowledge of languages.

YMCA of the USA
International Office for Europe
2200 Prospect Avenue
Cleveland, OH 44115
Tel.: (216) 344-0095
The YMCA's Europe office coordinates programs ranging from teaching English or sports to working in summer camps to assisting with development projects. A strong YMCA background is a must.

Types of Summer and Temporary Jobs in Europe

Agricultural Work

Agricultural work is often physically demanding, but for those with the strength and endurance there is almost always work to be found in Europe throughout the summer and into fall. Tasks include planting, shearing, picking, and every sort of heavy lifting. Finding work in agriculture primarily means being in the right place at the right time. A farmer may advertise in a local pub, hostel, or market, but in general, jobs aren't advertised. The quickest route to employment may be to approach a farmer in the field directly. As a result, agricultural work is best sought from within the country.

Competition for agricultural work is fairly keen because the work requires little complex skill and attracts many workers from less-developed countries. The following organizations are involved in pan-European international agricultural placement. More specific agricultural employment information for some countries is given in the individual country chapters in Part II.

Future Farmers of America
National FFA Center
Student Services—International
P.O. Box 15160
Alexandria, VA 22309-0160
Coordinates the Work Experience Abroad Program. Stays range from one month to a year, and participating countries include Austria, Belgium, Bulgaria, the Czech Republic, Denmark, Finland, France, Germany, Greece, Hungary, Ireland, Italy, Luxembourg, the Netherlands, Norway, Poland, Slovakia, Sweden, and the U.K.

Global Outreach
P.O. Box 15160
Alexandria, VA 22116-3291
Sends students to Germany, Hungary, Romania, the U.K., and Russia.

International Agricultural Exchange Association
IAEA Servicing Office
1000 1st Avenue S.
Great Falls, MT 59401
Arranges work exchange programs in Europe, Australia, New Zealand, and
Japan. Participants must have at least one year's experience in farming and be
between 19 and 30 years of age.

Au Pair Work

There are many positions available in most European countries for au pair work.
Au pairs, traditionally young women, usually live with families and help them
with housework, child care, and other domestic tasks. For this they are given
room and board and perhaps a small salary. The primary goal of the au pair's stay
is educational: the opportunity to become familiar with the customs and language of another country in an intimate setting is the au pair's true reward. Other
benefits include the chance to build up a network of friends and future employment contacts, plus (with a bit of luck) the opportunity to travel with one's host
family. One helpful resource for those considering au pair work is *The Au Pair
and Nanny's Guide to Working Abroad* by Susan Griffith and Sharon Legg. The
book details what life as an au pair is like and provides employment information.
For ordering information, contact Vacation Work Publishing, 9 Park End Street,
Oxford OX1 1HJ, England.

Some degree of competency in the language of the country you hope to live
in is generally required for au pair work; you do need to be able to communicate
with your host family. And many hiring agencies (and family employers) require
a minimum commitment of two to three months and sometimes as much as a
year. Program fees vary, so explore your options. The following organizations
place au pairs throughout Europe. More specific employment information for
some countries is given in the country-by-country section of this chapter.

Au Pair Homestay
World Learning Inc.
1015 15th Street NW, Suite 750
Washington, DC 20005
Tel.: (202) 408-5380
Fax: (202) 408-5397
Email: 7084391@MCXIMail.com
Sends au pairs of both sexes to Britain, France, Germany, Iceland, Finland,
Netherlands, Norway, Switzerland, and Argentina.

WISE (Worldwide Internships & Service Education)
303 South Craig Street, Suite 202
Pittsburgh, PA 15213
Tel.: (412) 681-8120
Fax: (412) 681-8187
Sends au pairs to Finland, France, Netherlands, Switzerland, and Germany.

Au Pair in Europe
P.O. Box 68056
Blakely Postal Outlet
Hamilton, Ontario L8M 3M7, Canada
Tel.: (800) 665-6305; (905) 545-6305
Fax: (905) 544-4121
Email: aupair@princeent.com
Places au pairs in 18 countries.

American Institute for Foreign Study
102 Greenwich Avenue
Greenwich, CT 06830
Tel.: (800) 727-AIFS
Email: info@aifs.org
www.aifs.org
Sends au pairs to France, Spain, and Germany.

Office and Clerical Work

Secretaries and typists with good office and language skills are needed for high-level appointments in many European countries. If you don't mind the insecurity of working as a temporary office worker, you can interview before you leave with an American temporary agency that has offices in the European city where you are interested in working. (Manpower, for example, is the world's largest temporary agency and has offices throughout Europe and the United States. Check your local business or *Yellow Pages* for locations near you.)

Some large temporary agencies will allow you to take their aptitude tests in the U.S. and forward the results to their overseas branch. You must be fluent in the language of the employer's country. Some short-term contracts are available, but most are on a longer-term basis. You must have office experience and be committed to the job. A number of full-time job placement agencies may also prove helpful. These are listed in Chapter 7. Check out the websites listed in the individual country chapters in Part II for the best listings of clerical positions.

Recreational Resort Work

There is a growing demand for sports instructors and teachers due to the increase in "Club Med"-type vacation centers and resorts. Tourist resort work also includes jobs as drivers, security personnel, food servers, and various other forms of low-skilled labor. Employers generally require language proficiency and relevant work experience. These jobs also require a written application, and the employers often request letters of reference. Specific resort and hotel employment information, as well as a listing of major hotels and hotel chains for some countries is found in the individual country chapters in Part II of this book. The following organizations are involved in international resort placement:

Club Méditerranée (Club Med)
106-110 Brompton Road
London SW3 1JJ, England

If you speak fluent French, are single, are able to work from May to October, and are over 21, this could be for you. Club Med staffs workers in France, Greece, Israel, Italy, Morocco, Romania, Spain, Switzerland, Tunisia, Turkey, and elsewhere. Applications must be received by January 31. (Club Med recruits in the U.S. primarily for North American positions—especially at entry level. For those willing to earn their way to European employment by first proving themselves closer to home, Club Med's U.S. recruitment hotline is: (407) 337-6660.)

Eurocamp Summer Jobs
P.O. Box 170
Liverpool L70 1ES, England.
Tel.: [44] 1565 625522
Provides work on European campsites as couriers, drivers, youth leaders, etc. Must speak at least one European language. Campsites located in Austria, Belgium, France, Germany, Italy, Spain, Switzerland, Netherlands, and Denmark.

Eurosites
Wavell House, Holcombe Road
Helmshore
Lancashire BB4 8EP, England
Hires campsite representatives for Austria, Germany, Spain, France, and Italy. Must be able to work between March 1 and October 31. Accommodations available in tents.

Inghams/Bladon Lines Travel Ltd.
56-58 Putney High Street
London SW15 1SF, England
Tel.: [44] 181 785 2200
Hires staff for winter ski resorts in France, Italy, Austria, and Switzerland.

Openwide International Ltd.
103A Oxford Street
London W1R 1TL, England
Tel.: [44] (171) 494-2321
Fax: [44] (171) 439-2037
Hires entertainers for hotels in Spain, Cyprus, Greece, and Turkey. Must be able to work a minimum of 4 months. Knowledge of German, Spanish, or French is helpful but not required.

Thomson Holidays
Overseas Personnel Department
Greater London House
Hampstead Road
London NW1 7SD, England
Hires entertainers, children's activities leaders, and general staff for resorts throughout Europe. Opportunities are mostly for summer work (April to October), but limited winter resort opportunities may be available as well. Fluency in at least one European language required.

Youth hostels also are a good source to look into. Many hostels will provide room and board in exchange for manual labor and other help.

American Youth Hostel Association
P.O. Box 36713
Washington, DC 20013-7613
Provides a list of hostels around the world.

For those interested in summer camp work, the following volunteer opportunity may be of interest:

YMCA International Camp Counselor Program
YMCA International Program Services
356 West 34th Street
New York, NY 10001
Tel.: (212) 727-8800
Places a small number of volunteers aged 21 to 29 years of age as summer camp counselors overseas. Positions are strictly volunteer; participants are responsible for all travel and living expenses. Previous YMCA work experience is required.

Shipping out for fun and profit

Dear Bob and Cheryl:

I just finished six months of working on a cruise ship and thought I might share a few things. The ship I was on started off in the Mediterranean, then headed off to Southeast Asia and Australia. As you might imagine, cruise work is a great way to see the world! This can depend on your position on board, though. I worked in the ship's boutique. This made for eleven-hour days at sea but meant that my time was my own in port (the boutique was closed then). Other workers weren't so lucky (kitchen help, for example), and always seemed to have something requiring their attention, whether we were at sea or not. The privileges you have on board may also vary by position. On my ship, staff members—ship officers, entertainment and fitness staff, and those of us in retail—could use the passenger pool and gym in our off hours. Crew members—stewards, waiters, and sailors—weren't allowed to be seen in public recreation areas after hours and could only use the crew facilities.

What did I like best about the job? Port time! What did I like the least? To be honest, being one of only 30 women on a ship with 270 men wasn't an experience I'd recommend to just anyone. I have a strong personality, but being so constantly the focus of so much attention got to be a bit much. For those willing to deal with both the up- and the downside of cruise work, though, a word of advice in parting: both during the hiring process and on the job, be prepared and be patient. Oh—and going to Europe while you're waiting for an offer can work in your favor. Otherwise, those who are more immediately available might be hired before you.—Kate Riley

For information on opportunities at sea, readers might want to consult the *Guide to Cruise Ship Jobs* (Pilot Books, 103 Cooper Street, Babylon, NY 11702) or *How to Get a Job with a Cruise Line* (Ticket to Adventure, Inc., P.O. Box 41005, St. Petersburg, FL 33743).

Tourism, Hotels, and Restaurants

There are many hotels and restaurants throughout Europe that hire Americans for work. The pay is not the best, and if business becomes exceedingly hectic, they might expect you to work overtime and perform other duties without compensation of money or time off. Hotel work is, however, one of the most abundant opportunities for employment in Europe. If you are interested in hotel work, you can find hotel guides in libraries, or, better yet, information on hotels can be found through national tourist offices, which have lists of the largest, centrally located hotels throughout Europe.

Shortcut to tourism jobs

Many summer or temporary jobs can be found in areas dominated by the tourist and hospitality industries. Finding a job can often be as simple as locating a hotel or resort in a popular area that needs some extra help during high season—summer for beach areas, winter for ski resorts. Thus, the question for the job seeker becomes, "What are the hot vacation spots in the country where I want to work?" For the answer, turn to the country's national tourism office. It can often provide information on hotels, resorts, restaurants, and other "tourist traps"—i.e., potential job markets.

Simply write or call the office of the country or countries you're interested in, requesting information on that country (or region of the country) and the vacation areas within it. Then as that information arrives, write to the establishments of interest and hope for the best. Tourist offices for each country (in-country and in the United States, where applicable) are listed in the individual country chapters in Part II.

Volunteer Opportunities

While it is sometimes difficult to obtain a work permit and find a job in Europe if you aren't an E.U. national, positions in workcamps are usually available and are relatively easy to obtain. Most camps offer work in fields such as agriculture, building construction and renovation, ecological and environmental work, forest clearing, and children's camps. Some workcamps offer small wages in addition to free room and board, as well as evening activities like sports or language classes.

Specific information about workcamp organizations can be found under "Volunteer Opportunities" in the individual country chapters in Part II. Workcamps aren't the only option when it comes to volunteering in Europe, of course. Volunteer positions run the gamut from archaeology to teaching (and not just English) to—well, let your imagination wander. It's amazing how opportunities open up when you're willing to work for free.

VOLUNTEER OPPORTUNITIES RESOURCES

The International Directory of Voluntary Work by David Woodworth. Available from Peterson's Guides, 202 Carnegie Center, Princeton, NJ 08543-2123.

International Internships and Volunteer Programs by Cantrell and Modderno. Published by Worldwise Books, P.O. Box 3030, Oakton, VA 22124.

International Workcamp Directory. Available from Volunteers for Peace, International Workcamps, 43 Tiffany Road, Belmont, VT 05730; (802) 259-2759.

Volunteer! The Comprehensive Guide to Voluntary Service in the U.S. and Abroad. Published by the CIEE (see "Work Exchange Organizations," earlier this chapter, for contact information). The CIEE also publishes *International Workcamps,* which is updated annually and available free upon request.

Selected organizations that recruit Americans for volunteer positions in Europe are:

Council on International Educational Exchange
205 East 42nd Street
New York, NY 10017-5706
Tel.: (800) COUNCIL; (212) 882-2600
Email: ivpbrochure@ciee.org
www.ciee.org

Service Civil International
5474 Walnut Level Road
Crozet, VA 22932
Tel.: (804) 823-1826

Volunteers for Peace
43 Tiffany Road
Belmont, VT 05730
Tel.: (802) 259-2759
Fax: (802) 259-2922
Email: vfp@vermontel.com
www.vermontel.com/~vfp/home.htm

"WWOOF" your way across Europe

Need a break from big-city hassles and concrete jungles? WWOOFing might be just the ticket. Working Weekends on Organic Farms (WWOOF) was founded in Britain in 1971 with the intention of giving city-dwellers brief exposure to organic farming principles. WWOOF provides a variety of tasks, since organic farming is more labor-intensive than conventional modern agriculture. Heavy machinery is rarely used, nor are chemical pesticides. The latter means that volunteers may be asked to perform tasks never dreamed of in the nine-to-five workaday world, such as gathering ladybugs, praying mantises, or other garden predators for use as natural pesticides. The WWOOF network extends across Europe and throughout the world. For more information contact WWOOF International, 19 Bradford Road, Lewes, Sussex BN7 1RB, England.

ten

Teaching English Abroad

I f you're a native speaker of English and have at least a bachelor's degree, you may already be qualified for a job in Europe teaching English. Factors ranging from the formation of the European Union to the fall of communism in Eastern Europe have made English language skills a hot commodity. The greatest opportunities are in countries that don't require their students to learn English in school, such as Spain, Italy, Germany, Greece, and most of the Eastern European countries. This chapter focuses on teaching English abroad, a good option for people who are not certified teachers. Chapter 8 covers international careers for professional teachers.

Some schools will consider you qualified to teach if you are simply a native speaker of English. More credible organizations, however, will expect you to have a bachelor's degree, some prior teaching experience, and be willing to sign a 9-month contract. Although it is possible to find work without a Teaching English as a Foreign Language (TEFL) certificate, this accreditation can make you more competitive in the job market. The pros and cons of TEFL certification are discussed later in this chapter.

Although you are expected to have a firm grasp of English grammar, native speakers are almost always hired to lead conversations rather than diagram sentences. You are likely to be placed in a "total immersion" classroom, one in which English is the only language used for instruction, and therefore your job search will not be handicapped by weak foreign language skills. English teaching, especially if you are new to it, can be an exciting way to experience another culture. It can also be grueling work. Remember that most English language classes sponsored by private companies are taught in the evenings and on weekends!

English teaching assignments vary widely, from school to school, from country to country. That is why it is very important to thoroughly investigate the organization that is hiring you to teach English. Many fly-by-night operations each year hire teachers to work in very unsatisfactory work conditions! Especially if you are unfamiliar with an organization or you are being asked to pay up-front for placement, be sure to ask for references from other people for whom they have successfully found work.

USEFUL BOOKS

There are many useful books on the market for people interested in teaching English abroad. Some are "how-to" manuals for job searchers; others are useful bags of tricks that you can reference when looking for classroom teaching techniques.

More Than a Native Speaker: An Introduction for Volunteers Teaching Abroad. Don Snow. (TESOL, 1600 Cameron St., Sutie 300, Alexandria, VA 22314) Ideas for English teaching techniques

Opportunities in Teaching English to Speakers of Other Languages. Blyth Camenson. (VGM Career Horizons, 4255 West Touhy Avenue, Lincolnwood, IL 60646-1975). Overview of careers in teaching English as a foreign language.

The Practice of English Language Teaching. Jeremy Harmer. (Longman Publishing Group, 10 Bank St., White Plains, NY 10602-1951) A thorough reference book for techniques for teaching ESL.

Teaching English Abroad. Susan Griffith. (Peterson's Guides, 202 Carnegie Center, Princeton, NJ 08543-2123) Probably the most comprehensive guide to teaching English abroad.

Teaching English Guides. (In Print Publishing Ltd., Coleridge House, 45 Coleridge Gardens, London NW6 3QH, England) Titles available include "Teaching English in Italy" and "Teaching English in Eastern and Central Europe."

Work Abroad: The Complete Guide to Finding a Job Overseas. Clay Hubbs and Jason Whitmarsh. (Transitions Abroad Publishing, P.O. Box 1300, Amherst, MA 01004-1300) Contains an extremely thorough section on finding work as an English teacher, even if you do not have TEFL certification.

Freelance teaching?

An alternative to teaching in a language school is to hang out your own proverbial shingle and market yourself as a freelance English teacher. You can often undercut the price of an established language school and pocket the change. Freelancing also gives you the flexibility to set your own hours and teaching load. Of course, your salary is dependent on your success in attracting and retaining students. Your clients will cancel and postpone lessons with an irritating frequency. Usually, freelancing is not a good option if you plan to stay in a country for less than six months—it takes at least that long to network your way into a stable base of students!

TEFL Certification

TEFL certification can significantly enhance your prospects for finding work, especially for inexperienced teachers. Most TEFL programs are month-long training institutes that include practice teaching sessions, observation, and job-placement assistance. Especially in western Europe, a TEFL certificate is a useful way to pry open the door to a language school. TEFL certified teachers also usually command higher salaries. TEFL certification is not required to find a job teaching English, and especially if you are only planning to work for less than a year, the cost of the certificate may make it prohibitive.

CERTIFICATION PROGRAMS

American English Programs
17 South Street
Northampton, MA 01060
Tel./Fax: (413) 582-1812
Email: eflworld@crocker.com

EFL Teacher Training
Lado Enterprises, Inc.
2233 Wisconsin Avenue NW
Washington, DC 20007
Tel.: (202) 223-0023
Fax: (202) 337-1118

Hamline TEFL Certificate Course
Hamline University
1536 Hewitt Avenue
St. Paul, MN 55104
Tel.: (800) 888-2182
Fax: (612) 641-2489

New World Teachers
605 Market Street, Suite 800
San Francisco, CA 94105
Tel.: (800) 644-5424
Email: teacherssf@aol.com
www.goteach.com

RSA/Cambridge CELTA
English International
655 Sutter Street, Suite 200
San Francisco, CA 94102
Tel.: (415) 749-5633
Email: 103326.1743@compuserve.com

University of Cambridge CELTA
St. Giles Language Teaching Center
1 Hallidie Plaza, 3rd Floor
San Francisco, CA 94102
Tel./Fax: (415) 788-3552

MAJOR LANGUAGE SCHOOL CHAINS

Berlitz International
Research Park, 239 Wall Street
Princeton, NJ 08540
Most TEFL placements are in Spain, Italy, Germany, and France.

Inlingua Teacher Service
Essex House
27 Temple Street
Birmingham B2 5DB, England
Most vacancies are in Germany, Italy, and Spain.

International House
106 Picadilly
London W1V 9FL, England
Operates nearly 100 schools around the world.

Placement Services

Working with a placement service can make finding a teaching job much easier. Many teaching services are non-profit organizations that see their purpose as promoting cultural exchanges. Others are for-profit organizations that have been hired by schools for help in finding teachers. Placement services, including cultural exchange programs, often charge fees that range from a few hundred dollars to several thousand. Be sure to compare costs before deciding to work with a particular service.

TEACHER PLACEMENT SERVICES

ASSIST (American Slavic Student Internship Service Training Corporation)
1535 SW Upper Hall
Portland, OR 97201
Tel.: (503) 220-2535
Email: assistusa@aol.com
Places teachers in schools and businesses in Moscow or St. Petersburg for any length of time, any time of year.

Brethren Volunteer Services
1451 Dundee Avenue
Elgin, IL 60120
Tel.: (847) 742-5100/(800) 323-8039
Fax: (847) 742-6103
Most teaching positions are in Poland and require a 2-year commitment.

Central European Teaching Program
Beloit College
P.O. Box 242
700 College Street
Beloit, WI 53511
Tel.: (608) 363-2619
Fax: (608) 363-2689
Email: mullenm@beloit.edu
www.beloit.edu/~cetp
Placements for a school year in elementary and high schools throughout Hungary, Romania, and Albania.

English for Everybody
655 Powell Street, Suite 505
San Francisco, CA 94108
Tel.: (415) 789-7641
Fax: (415) 433-4733
Offers placement assistance for teaching jobs in eastern Europe, Russia, and Austria.

Fandango
1613 Escalero Road
Santa Rosa, CA 95409
Tel./Fax: (707) 539-2722
A recruitment agency specializing in the Czech Republic, Russia, Poland, the Baltic States, and Hungary.

Foundation for a Civil Society
Masaryk Fellowship Program
1270 Avenue of the Americas, Suite 609
New York, NY 10020
Tel.: (212) 332-2890
Fax: (212) 332-2898
Email: 73303.3024@compuserve.com
Coordinates 1-month placements in
the Czech Republic and Slovakia
during the summer.

**Fulbright English Teaching
Assistantship**
U.S. Student Programs Division
Institute of International Education
809 United Nations Plaza
New York, NY 10017-3580
Tel.: (212) 984-5330
www.iie.org
One-year positions available for
Belgium, Luxembourg, Austria,
France, and Germany.

InterExchange
161 6th Avenue
New York, NY 10013

Tel.: (212) 924-0446
Fax: (212) 924-0575
www.interexchange.org
Year-long placements to teach English
in the Czech Republic (mostly Prague)
and Hungary (mostly Budapest).
Semester or year-long placements are
also available in Finland.

Peace Corps
PRU Box 941
Washington, DC 20526
Tel.: (800) 424-8580, ext. 2293
www.peacecorps.gov
Two-year positions teaching English,
math, and science are available in
eastern Europe.

WorldTeach
Harvard Institute for International
Development
1 Eliot Street
Cambridge, MA 02138-5705
Tel.: (617) 495-5527
Places volunteers in positions in several
countries, including Poland and Russia.

Part II

Where the Jobs Are:
A Country-by-Country Look

eleven

The United Kingdom: England, Northern Ireland, Scotland, and Wales

MAJOR EMPLOYMENT CENTERS: London, Birmingham, Glasgow

MAJOR BUSINESS LANGUAGE: English

LANGUAGE SKILL INDEX: Pretty much the only language around

CURRENCY: British pound

TELEPHONE COUNTRY CODE: 44

TIME ZONE: EST+5

PUNCTUALITY INDEX: Protocol and formality in England are generally more important than in the U.S., although the Welsh and Scots may be more informal. Prior appointments and punctuality are generally expected

AVERAGE DAILY TEMPERATURE, HIGH/LOW: January, 44/35°F; July, 73/55°F (London)

AVERAGE NUMBER OF DAYS WITH RAIN: January, 17; July, 12

BEST BET FOR EMPLOYMENT:

FOR STUDENTS: Apply to BUNAC and work in London

PERMANENT JOBS: Banking and finance in London

CHANCE OF FINDING A JOB: Pretty good if you aren't picky

TRIVIA: For the most part, the British are very keen on rules: wait in line or queue up, and try not to use too many shortcuts in the job search

Britain is in northwestern Europe, surrounded by the English Channel, North Sea, and the north Atlantic Ocean. Ireland and France are its nearest neighbors. Britain is about the size of Oregon. The northern part of England and much of Wales and Scotland consist of highlands while the rest of the country is characterized by a low, rolling landscape. "Britain," or "Great Britain," refers to England, Wales, and Scotland; the "United Kingdom" also includes Northern Ireland.

English is spoken throughout the United Kingdom, but Welsh is spoken in western Wales by about 20% of the population, and Gaelic is spoken in some parts of Northern Ireland. The Church of England is Britain's established church, with a following among 20% of the population. Also significant are the Church of Wales, the Church of Scotland, the Church of Ireland, the Roman Catholic Church, and Methodist, Baptist, and Jewish institutions. Northern Ireland is two-thirds Protestant and one-third Catholic and suffers from sectarian unrest.

Britain served as one of the Roman Empire's farthest outposts until being overrun by various Norse and Germanic tribes. The Normans crossed the Channel and conquered England in 1066. The English defeated the ruling house of Wales in 1283. England and Scotland were eventually peacefully united in 1603 when James VI of Scotland became England's James I. A long struggle between Parliament and the monarchy resulted in civil war, the declaration of a republic, a restoration, and a Bill of Rights. Parliamentary sovereignty was established by the early nineteenth century.

Meanwhile, Britain had established an extensive empire in the Americas, Africa, and Asia. Despite the loss of most of its North American possessions, the British Empire stretched across the world during the Victorian period in the late nineteenth century. Britain provided a significant portion of the Allied efforts in both world wars. The British war effort extended beyond Europe into Africa, the Middle East, the Far East, and India. The empire began dissolving, generally peacefully, after World War II. The Commonwealth of Nations is an association of former British colonies.

Under Clement Atlee, Britain established an extensive social welfare system in the late 1940s. By the 1970s the country's visible economic stagnation led to popular disillusionment with the social welfare consensus and the election of a Conservative parliamentary majority in 1979. Prime Minister Margaret Thatcher and her successor, John Majors, emphasized private-sector economic growth and low taxation.

In 1997, the Labour Party shed its socialist mantle and swept national elections and ousted the conservative government. Prime Minister Tony Blair has, among other policies, backed referenda that have established that Scotland and

Wales should be given greater degrees of self-government and London should acquire a New-York style mayor.

The on-again-off-again peace process with Northern Ireland has gained momentum since the 1997 elections. In June 1997, Dr. Mo Mowlam, Britain's new Northern Ireland Secretary, promised to admit Sinn Féin to all-party talks following a new cease-fire. This cleared the way for talks chaired by former U.S. Senator George Mitchell, which produced the Good Friday agreement on April 10, 1998. This agreement allowed the people of Northern Ireland to decide their political future by majority vote. The agreement also established a new Northern Irish parliament and high-level political links between the Republic and Northern Ireland. The agreement was approved by 71% of the voters in referendums held on both sides of the Irish border. The Irish and British remain hopeful that peace will finally come to Northern Ireland.

It is important to understand that the inhabitants of Scotland are "Scots," but the adjective for virtually everything else is "Scottish." Also remember that although they are often combined for statistical purposes, the English and the Welsh are two separate cultures, and you must avoid confusing them.

Business hours are generally from 9 a.m. to 5 p.m., Monday-Friday. Most shops are open on Saturdays from 9 a.m. to 5 p.m. and, except in rural areas, on Sundays from 10 a.m. to 4 p.m. In country towns, some shops may observe an early closing day, usually Tuesday or Wednesday afternoon.

Current Economic Climate

Economic growth in the U.K. has quickened over the last few years. The unemployment rate is around 3% in Britain, with slightly higher rates in Northern Ireland and areas like Liverpool. The economic situation in Great Britain is improving, and the technology boom is adding to the creation of many jobs in the country. Even though Britain will not initially participate in the European single currency, economists do not foresee any grave changes in its economy.

The United Kingdom's combined work force is 60% services, 25% manufacturing, and 5% agricultural. Major industries in England and Wales include: steel, automobiles, shipbuilding, textiles, chemicals, financial and banking services, and machinery. Scotland's primary industries are: machinery, automobiles, electronic products, and petroleum products. Northern Ireland's major industries are shipbuilding and textiles. Historically, manufacturing dominates the north of England as well as Scotland, while service industries have prospered in the wealthier southern part of the country, especially London. The U.S. and E.U. provide the vast majority of Britain's trade.

U.K.'S 10 LARGEST COMPANIES

(1997, composite ranking)
1. Unilever
2. British Post Office
3. B.A.T. Industries
4. British Telecommunications
5. J. Sainsbury
6. BTR
7. HSBC Holdings
8. BET
9. Lonrho
10. National Westminster Bank

Using the phone, fax, and Internet

Public phones are all owned by British Telecom and operate either with coins or with a phonecard, which can be bought at post offices. Some old phones require payment upon answering. London has two area codes: 171 for the inner London area and 181 for outer London. You need to use these prefixes if dialing between the two zones. The operator can be reached by dialing 100; information is 192 for the U.K. and international directory assistance, 153. The national emergency number is 999. International calls can be made from booths designated "intercontinental" or from British Telecom offices. British newspapers frequently advertise companies that offer low-cost alternatives for placing international calls.

To use your own mobile phone in Britain you will need to contact the company you purchased your phone from and they will be able to advise you on what you have to do. If you prefer to rent a mobile phone for the duration of your visit, there are a few companies that offer this service. Also, due to the introduction of a Global System for Mobile Communication (GSM), it is now possible to rent a portable phone for use in more than one country.

Many private shops offer fax services. Cybercafes have exploded throughout Britain and make it convenient to access Email.

Getting Around in Great Britain

British Rail operates a very extensive, but also rather expensive, rail network. InterRail passes are accepted, but not Eurail. Various special passes are available, depending upon distance and time of usage. The bus system is quite convenient and cheap, especially within cities.

Employment Regulations and Outlook for Americans

U.S. citizens do not need a visa to enter Britain or to stay for fewer than six months. Those intending to work, however, must present a work permit from an employer in Britain when arriving in the country. British employers usually request work permits for foreign employees from the Department of Employment. The Immigration Office provides residence authorization. The Department of Employment will not issue work permits for unskilled and semiskilled workers. Nonetheless, unofficial jobs for non-E.U. nationals are still available.

Job Centres are located throughout the country and contain bulletin boards on which jobs, especially agricultural work, are posted. Tourist work is readily found in London, Wales, Scotland, the Lake District in northwestern England, and along the southern coast of England. Hotels and restaurants, including fast-food chains, offer work at low wages. Jobs can also be found bartending in pubs if an employer is unconcerned about the lack of a work permit.

If you are a student, you can bypass the usual employment restrictions by contacting BUNAC (British Universities North America Club), which can provide a permit allowing an American student to work in Britain for up to six months. BUNAC has resources to help the student job searcher who arrives in London without a job or a place to stay. Most students working through BUNAC work in "casual" jobs, such as waiting tables, clerical assignments, or retail jobs. Students, however, can make enough money to cover their living and travel expenses for their stay, making the program quite a good deal for those who qualify. For more information, contact the BUNAC at:

BUNAC
16 Bowling Green Lane
London ECIR 0QH, England
Tel.: [44] (171) 251-3472
Fax: [44] (171) 251-0215
Email: wib@bunac.org.uk
www.bunac.org

-or-

P.O. Box 49
South Britain, CT 06487
Tel.: (203) 264-0901
Fax: (203) 264-0251

One BUNAC participant's experiences in London

I arrived in London with no money (well, practically none), no job, no friends, no flat—nothing. Having nowhere to go, I did exactly what the BUNAC tells you not to: I arrived at their door, luggage in hand. Serves me right for bucking their advice, too. They were closed. Although I had to wait a day to get started, the notices board at BUNAC found me everything I needed. Apartment. Job. And through those, friends and money.

My first, tide-me-over type job was a week at the perfume counter at Harrod's. That job had its advantages, the main one being that Harrod's is like a big, really chic campus, with lots of socializing after hours. Plus, working there gave me time to interview elsewhere on my day off. The people I interviewed with were all wonderful—very receptive.

I ended up, through a little luck and a little planning, taking a job as a law clerk with one of the largest law firms in the world. "Luck," I say, because you never know what kind of jobs you might find posted at BUNAC. Pub work. Sheepherding in Scotland. You just never know. Planning was involved too, because just as with any job search, experience counts. My academic background—economics and, especially, Spanish—helped a lot.

Another important part of planning is to take decent clothes! It may sound obvious, but I was surprised at the number of people who apparently hadn't thought of this. No matter what kind of work you hope to find, you'll at least need one nice outfit for interviewing. Beyond that, take clothes that are specifically appropriate for the kind of job you want. This won't guarantee that you'll find exactly the job you had in mind, but if it does come along you'll be ready.—Karen Crook

Short-term and Temporary Work

Many British agencies can help with placement as an au pair. There are also many summer camps throughout the U.K. that regularly need temporary help. BUNAC (see pg. 131) offers the best help if you are looking for casual work, such as waiting tables.

Anglia Au Pair & Nanny Agency
70 Southsea Avenue
Leigh-on-Sea
Essex SS0 2BJ, England
Tel.: [44] (1702) 471 648
Places au pairs throughout the U.K.

Cura Domi-Care at Home
8 North Street
Guildford
Surrey GUI 4AF, England
Tel.: [44] (1483) 302 275
Fax: [44] (1483) 304 302

Recruits help for elderly and disabled people in their own homes. Some positions are residential.

Euroyouth Ltd.
301 Westborough Road
Westcliff
Southend-on-Sea
Essex SS0 9PT, England
Tel.: [44] (1702) 341 434
Fax: [44] (1702) 330 104
Places au pairs throughout Britain.

Nord-Anglia International Limited
10 Eden Pl.
Cheadle, Stockport
Cheshire SK8 1AT, England
Tel.: [44] (1285) 644 727
Places over 500 people into English-language summer schools in Britain and Ireland as language and sports instructors.

PGL Adventure
Alton Coruth
Penyard Lane
Ross-on-Wye
Herefordshire HR9 5 NR, England
Tel.: [44] (1989) 767 833
Hires over 500 people as sports instructors, counselors, and general staff for summer camps in Britain.

Internship Programs

Several internship programs offer students opportunities to obtain professional experience. Some programs, such as those run by Boston University and Northern Illinois University, also offer an opportunity to earn academic credit.

Academic Internships
Northern Illinois University
Williston Hall, 4th Floor
DeKalb, IL 60115
Tel.: (815) 752-0700
Fax: (815) 753-1488
Email: ca0ams1@wpo.cso.niu.edu

Boston University International Programs
232 Bay State Road, 5th Floor
Boston, MA 02215
Tel.: (617) 353-9888
Fax: (617) 353-5402
Email: abroad@bu.edu
www. bu.edu/abroad
Offers internships in advertising, marketing, broadcasting, business, journalism, and politics.

Brethren Colleges Abroad
605 College Avenue
N. Manchester, IN 46963
Tel.: (219) 982-5244
Fax: (219) 982-7755
Email: bca@manchester.edu
www.bcanet.org/
Business, teaching, political science, and social work internships.

Fashion Design and Merchandising
London College of Fashion
20 John Princes Street
London W1M 0BJ, England
Tel: [44] (171) 514 7411
Fax: [44] (171) 514-7490
Email: lcfdali@londonfashion.ac.uk

Professionally oriented internships in public relations, design, marketing, retailing, trend forecasting, and design companies.

Hansard Scholar Programme
The Hansard Society
St. Philips, Building North
Sheffield Street
London WC2A 2EX, England
Tel.: [44] (171) 955 7478
Fax: [44] (171) 955 7492
Internship program for students who want to become involved in British government and Parliament.

IASTE-US
10400 Little Patuxent Parkway, Suite 250 L
Columbia, MD 21044-3510
Tel.: (410) 997-3068
Fax: (410) 997-5186
Email: iaeste@aipt.org
www.aipt.org/iaste.html
Arranges reciprocal internships in 63 different countries. Specifically for students in technical fields.

University of North London
Office of International Programs
228 Miller Bldg., Box 2000
SUNY Cortland
Cortland, NY 13045
Tel.: (607) 753-2209
Fax: (607) 753-5989
www.cortland.edu/html/ipgms.html
Internship opportunities in Parliament, hospitals, promotion agencies, radio/TV.

Volunteer Opportunities

The BTCV (British Trust for Conservation Volunteers) is Britain's largest volunteer organization, sponsoring over 60,000 individuals in hundreds of rural and urban conservation and environmental projects. BTCV's counterpart organization in Scotland is the Scottish Conservation Trust. The National Trust also maintains hundreds of workcamps throughout the United Kingdom in various environmental, construction, and preservation projects. Christian Movement for Peace operates additional workcamps for volunteers in children's camps, farm work, clearing work, and international political solidarity. The United Nations Association provides workcamps utilizing volunteers in Wales. These workcamps focus upon children's camps, ecological work, clearing work, archaeological excavation, and gardening. Volunteers for Peace is a major international workcamp organization based in the U.S.

International Voluntary Service (IVS) offers workcamps throughout the United Kingdom. In England, IVS recruits volunteers for children's camps, the mentally disabled, the handicapped, ecological work, agriculture, and building construction and renovation. IVS's 17 workcamps in Scotland field 168 volunteers in the same range of activities. In Northern Ireland, IVS sponsors workcamps for volunteers in children's camps, clearing work, and construction.

British Trust for Conservation Volunteers
36 St. Mary's Street, Wallingford
Oxfordshire OX10 0EU, England
Tel.: [44] (1491) 3976 6824602

Council on International Educational Exchange
205 East 42nd Street
New York, NY 10017
Tel.: (888) COUNCIL
Email: ivpdirectory@ciee.org
www.ciee.org

International Voluntary Service—Britain
Old Hall, East Bergholt
Colchester CO7 6TQ, England

International Voluntary Service—United States
SCI-USA
Route 2, Box 506
Crozet, VA 22932
Tel.: (804) 823-1826

The National Trust Working Holidays
P.O. Box 84
Cirencester, Glouscester GL7 1RQ,

England
Tel.: [44] (1285) 644 727

Scottish Conservation Projects Trust
Balallan House, 24 Allen Park
Stirling FK8 2QG, Scotland
Tel.: [44] (1786) 79697

United Nations Association (Wales)
International Youth Service (UNAIYS)
Welsh Center for International Affairs
Temple of Peace, Cathays Park
Cardiff CF1 3AP, Wales
Tel.: [44] (222) 223 088

Volunteers for Peace
International Workcamps
43 Tiffany Road
Belmont, VT 05730
Tel.: (802) 259-2759
Fax: (802) 259-2922
Email: VFP@VFP.prg
www.vfp.org

Several other organizations also offer volunteer services involving either very specific types of work or work at specific sites in Britain:

Cathedral Camps
16 Glebe Avenue
Flitwick, Bedfordshire MK45 1HS,
England
Tel.: [44] (1525) 716 237
Volunteers work in maintenance, conservation, and restoration of cathedrals.

Community Service Volunteers
237 Pentonville Road
London N1 9NJ, England
Tel.: [44] (171) 278 6601
www.csv.org.uk/home.htm
Involves nearly 2,000 individuals annually in projects assisting the mentally and physically handicapped.

Leonard Cheshire Foundation
Leonard Cheshire House
26/29 Maunsel Street
London SW1P 2QN, England
Tel.: [44] (171) 828 1822
Volunteers help in home for disabled adults, most with physical disabilities.

The Monkey Sanctuary
Looe
Cornwall PL13 1NZ, England
Tel.: [44] (1503) 262 532
Volunteers work in a sanctuary that houses colony of South American wooly monkeys.

The Wildlife Trust West Wales
7 Market Street
Haverfordwest
Dyfed, Wales SA61 1NF, U.K.
Tel.: [44] (1437) 765 462
Volunteers serve as assistant wardens on Skomer Island, a National Nature Reserve off the Welsh coast.

Winged Fellowship Trust
Angel House
20-32 Pentonville Road
London N1 9XD, England
Tel.: [44] (171) 833 2594
Recruits volunteers for help in summer camps for people with disabilities.

NEWSPAPERS IN THE UNITED KINGDOM

Aberdeen Press and Journal
P.O. Box 43
Lang Stracht, Mastrick
Aberdeen AB9 8AF, Scotland
Tel.: [44] (224) 690222
Fax: [44] (224) 663575
www.pressandjournal.co.uk

Belfast Telegraph
124-144 Royal Avenue
Belfast BT1 1EB, Northern Ireland
Tel.: [44] (1232) 264 000
Fax: [44] (1232) 554 506
www.belfasttelegraph.co.uk

Daily Record
1 Canada Square
Canary Wharf
London E14 5AP, England
Tel.: [44] (171) 293 3000
Fax: [44] (171) 293 3280
www.record-mail.co.uk

Daily Telegraph
1 Canada Square
Canary Wharf
London E14 5DT, England
Tel.: [44] (171) 538 5000
Fax: [44] (171) 538 6242
www.telegraph.co.uk

Financial Times
1 Southwark Bridge
London SE1 9HL, England
Tel.: [44] (171) 873 3000
Fax: [44] (171) 873 5700
www.FT.com

The Guardian
119 Farringdon Road
London EC1R 3ER, England
Tel.: [44] (171) 278 2332
Fax: [44] (171) 837 2114
www.guardian.co.uk

The Independent
1 Canada Square
Canary Wharf
London E14 5AP, England
Tel.: [44] (171) 293 2000
Fax.: [44] (171) 293 2435
www.independent.co.uk

The Times
P.O. Box 495
1 Virginia Street
London E1 9XY, England
Tel.: [44] (171) 782 5000
Fax.: [44] (171) 782 5438
www.the-times.co.uk

Resources for Further Information

USEFUL WEBSITES FOR JOB SEARCHERS

The Internet is a good place to begin your job search. Many British employers list job vacancies, especially those in technical fields, on the World Wide Web. There are also many websites that provide useful information for job searchers researching the British job market. (Britain is second only to the U.S. in its number of websites.)

The Appointments Online (TAPS)
http://taps.com
A very large database of British job resources, including job postings.

BCL International
www.bcl.com
A source of technical job listings.

Britain in the USA
http://britain-info.org/index.htm
Information for travelers and workers; economic information; work regulations; many links to other helpful organizations.

British Airways
www.british-air.com/inside/employme/
employme.shtml
Maintains a large section for Employment Opportunities.

Career Advisory Services
www.prospects.csu.man.ac.uk
Graduate employers and vacancies.

Chadwick Nott (Legal Recruitment)
www.chadwick-nott.co.uk
Recruitment database for legal professionals.

Dot Jobs
www.dotjobs.co.uk
Listings of electronics and engineering jobs.

International IT Recruitment Exchange
www.dmcl.com/it
Has a very large directory of agencies in the U.K. that find, offer, or recruit for IT (technical) jobs.

Job.Net
www.vnu.co.uk/cc (check under "Job World" link)
Jobs in information technology and finance.

Unixis IT Connections
www.it-connect.com
Technical job list.

EMBASSIES AND CONSULAR OFFICES

American embassies and consulates have commercial and/or economic sections that can provide you with business information and explain aspects of the local economy. Inquiries about business opportunities should be addressed either to "Commercial Officer" or "Commercial Section," followed by the appropriate street address.

Representation of the United Kingdom in the United States

Embassy of Great Britain
3100 Massachusetts Avenue NW
Washington, DC 20008
Tel.: (202) 462-1340
Fax: (202) 588-7870

British Consulates General: Atlanta, (404) 524-5856; Boston, (617) 248-9555; Chicago, (312) 346-1810; Houston, (713) 659-6270; Los Angeles, (310) 477-3322; New York, (212) 745-0200; San Francisco, (415) 981-3030

Representation of the United States in the United Kingdom

American Embassy
24/31 Grosvenor Square
London W1A 1AE, England
Tel.: [44] (171) 499 9000
Fax : [44] (171) 409 1637
www.usembassy.org.uk/

American Consulate General—
Northern Ireland
Queen's House, 14 Queen Street
Belfast BT1 6EQ, Northern Ireland

Tel.: [44] (1232) 241279
Fax: [44] (1232) 248482

American Consulate General—Scotland
3 Regent Terrace EH7 5BW
Edinburgh, Scotland
Tel.: [44] (131) 556 8315
Fax: [44] (131) 557 6023

CHAMBERS OF COMMERCE

Chambers of commerce consist of firms in both countries interested in international trade. These are appropriate companies to initially target in the job search.

American Chamber of Commerce (U.K.)
75 Brook Street
London W1Y 2EB, England
Tel.: [44] (171) 493-0381
Fax: [44] (171) 493-2394
Email: acc@amcham.demon.co.uk
www.amcham.org.uk/

British-American Chamber of Commerce
52 Vanderbilt Avenue, 20th Floor
New York, NY 10017
Tel.: (212) 889-0680
Fax: (212) 661-4074
Email: RFursland@bacc.org
www.ba-cc.org

WORLD TRADE CENTERS IN THE UNITED KINGDOM

World Trade Centers usually include many foreign companies operating in the country.

World Trade Center Bristol
c/o WTC Ltd.
University Gate
Park Row, Bristol BS1 5UB, England
Tel.: [44] (117) 900 8220
Fax : [44] (117) 900 8166
Email: mapf94@dial.pipex.com
www.wtcuk.co.uk/

Cardiff World Trade Center
Cardiff International Arena
Mary Ann Street
Cardiff CF1 2EQ Wales, England

Tel.: [44] (1222) 234 900
Fax : [44] (1222) 234 901
Email: debbie@worldtradecenter.btinternet.com
http://homer.cwtc.co.uk/cwtc/

London World Trade Center Association
2 Harbour Exchange Square
Exchange Tower, Suite 703
London E14 9GB, England
Tel.: [44] (171) 987 3456
Fax : [44] (171) 537 0880
Email : nicola.pettitt@capitalandprovident.com

OTHER INFORMATIONAL ORGANIZATIONS

Foreign government missions in the U.S. such as national tourist offices can furnish visas and information on work permits and other important regulations. They may also offer economic and business information about the country.

British Information Services
845 Third Avenue
New York, NY 10022-6691
Tel.: (212) 752-5747
Fax: (212) 758-5395

British Tourist Authority
551 Fifth Avenue, 7th Floor
New York, NY 10176-0799
Tel.: (212) 986 2200
Toll free: (800) GO 2 BRITAIN

Email: travelinfo@bta.org.uk
www. visitbritain.com

British Tourist Authority, UK
Thames Tower
Black's Road
London W6 9EL, England
Tel.: [44] (181) 846 9000
Fax: [44] (181) 563 0302

BUSINESS DIRECTORIES

Although not always easy to find, business directories can prove invaluable in the international job search. Most directories list company names, addresses, products, and phone numbers. Some directories include executive names and titles and financial information about the company. These sources provide you with the names of the people to contact for employment information as well as financial data, which can tell you how strong a company's position in a country may be.

A-Z of Careers and Jobs. Published by Kogan Ltd., 120 Petonville Road, London N1 9JN, England. Lists British sources for information on careers.

Britain's Privately Owned Companies. The Top 10,000. Published annually by Jordan Ltd., 21 St. Thomas Street, Bristol, Avon BS1 6JS, England. Describes and ranks 10,000 British companies according to various criteria.

Britain's Top 3,000 Foreign-Owned Companies. Available annually from Jordan Ltd., 21 St. Thomas Street, Bristol, Avon BS1 6JS, England. Covers major foreign-owned firms.

British-American Chamber of Commerce. Published annually by the British-American Chamber of Commerce, 52 Vanderbilt Avenue, 20th Floor, New York, NY 10017; www.ba-cc.org. Lists 600 British and American firms engaged in bilateral trade.

British Consultants Bureau—Directory. Published in odd years by the British Consultants Bureau, 1 Westminster Palace Gardens, 1-7 Artillery Row, London SW1P 1RJ, England. Covers about 220 consulting firms in Great Britain engaged in worldwide practice in such specialties as engineering, architecture, management, and so on.

British Exports. Published annually by Kompass, Reed Information Services, East Grinstead House, Windsor Court, East Grinstead, West Sussex RH19 1XD, England. Lists 14,000 British exporters.

Directory of British Importers. Published biennially by Trade Research Publications, 2 Wycliffe Grove, Werrington, Petersborough PE 4 5DE, England. Lists British importers and foreign suppliers.

Directory of Directors. Published annually by Professional Publications, Reed Information Services, East Grinstead House, Windsor Court, East Grinstead, West Sussex RH19 1XE, England; email: ntillin@reedinfo.co.uk. Lists executives of British firms.

Directory of Foreign Firms Operating Abroad: United Kingdom. World Trade Academy Press, 257 Central Park West, Suite 10A, New York, NY 10024-4110; email: uniworldbp@aol.com; www.uniworldbp.com. Lists names and addresses of parent companies in the U.S. and their subsidiaries and affiliates in the U.K.

Kelly's Business Directory. Published annually by Reed Information Services, East Grinstead House, Windsor Court, East Grinstead, West Sussex RH19 1XE, England; email: ntillin@reedinfo.co.uk. Lists 84,000 British and foreign firms.

Key British Enterprises. Available annually from Dun & Bradstreet Ltd., Holmers Farm Way, High Wycombe, Buckinghamshire, HP1 24U, England. Describes 50,000 leading British firms.

Kompass United Kingdom. Published annually by Kompass, Reed Information Services, Windsor Court, East Grinstead House, East Grinstead, West Sussex RH19 1XD, England. Lists over 46,000 British manufacturing and service firms.

London Directory for Trade and Industry. Published annually by Guardian Communications, McMillan group, Charles Roe House, Chestergate, Macclesfield, Cheshire SK11 602, England. Lists 7,000 firms in the London area.

Oliver's Guide to the City of London. Published in even years by A. P. Information Services, Roman House, 296 Golders Green Road, London NW11 9PZ, England. Describes over 8,000 firms in London's financial district.

Scotland's Top 2,000 Companies. Published annually by Jordan Information Services, 21 St. Thomas Street, Bristol, Avon BS1 6JS, England. Describes Scotland's leading firms.

U.K.'s 10,000 Largest Companies. Published annually by ELC Publishing, 30 Eastbourne Terrace, W2 6LG London, England. The U.K.'s leading businesses, ranked by sales.

Who Owns Whom: United Kingdom and Republic of Ireland. Available annually from Dun & Bradstreet Ltd., Holmers Farm Way, High Wycombe, Buckinghamshire HP12 4UL, England. Lists 15,000 British and Irish parent companies and their 155,000 domestic and foreign subsidiaries.

Leading Employers in the United Kingdom

The following companies are classified by business area: Banking and Finance; Industrial Manufacturing; Retailing and Wholesaling; and Service Industries. Company information includes firm name, address, phone and fax numbers, specific business, and American parent company, where applicable. In the case of American parent firms, your chances of achieving employment abroad are substantially better if you contact the subsidiary company in Europe rather than the parent company in the U.S. The following list is subdivided into England, Northern Ireland, Scotland, and Wales. Each section lists American companies, followed by major European—mostly British—companies in each region.

AMERICAN COMPANIES IN ENGLAND

BANKING AND FINANCE

Alexander Howden Group Ltd
8 Devonshire Square
London EC2M 4PL, England
Tel.: [44] (171) 623 5500
Fax: [44] (171) 621 1511
(Insurance)
Howden Holdings Ltd.

Allen-Bradley International Ltd.
Pitfield,
Milton Keynes
Buckinghamshire MK 11 3RD, England
Tel.: [44] (190) 883 8800
Fax: [44] (190) 836 8618
www. rockwell.com
(Holding co.)
Rockwell International Corp.

American Standard (U.K.) Ltd.
90 Newbold Road
Rugby, Warwickshire CV21 2NL, England
Tel.: [44] (1 718) 853 2532
Fax: [44] (1 788) 570 366
www.americanstandard.com
(Holding co.)
Ideal-Standard Ltd.

Bank of America National Trust and Savings Association
1 Alie Street
London E1 8DE, England
Tel.: [44] (171) 634 4000
Fax: [44] (171) 248 1244
www.bankamerica.com
(Bank)
BankAmerica Corp.

Chase Manhattan Bank, Ltd.
125 London Wall
London EC2Y 5AJ, England
Tel.: [44] (171) 777 2000
Fax: [44] (171) 777 4727
www.chase.com
(Bank)
Chase Bank

Chemco Equipment Finance Ltd.
Chemical Bank House, 180 Strand
London WC2R 1ET, England
Tel.: [44] (171) 379 7474
(Financial services)
Chemical Banking Corp.

Chemical Bank
The Adelphi
1-11 John Adam Street
London AC2N 6HT, England
Tel.: [44] (171) 932 3000
Fax: [44] (171) 839 8380
www. chemicalbank.com
(Bank)
Chemical Banking Corp.

Cigna Services UK Ltd.
Cigna House, London,
London EC3M 7NA, England
Tel.: [44] (171) 560 8000
Fax: [44] (171) 560 8339
(Insurance)
Cigna U.K. Corp.

Citibank International PLC
336 The Strand
London WC2R 1HD, England
Tel: [44] (171) 500 5000
Fax: [44] (171) 438 1695
(Bank)
Citibank

First National Bank of Boston (Guernsey) Ltd.
Bank of Boston House
London SW1H 0ED, England
Tel.: [44] (171) 799 3333
Fax: [44] (171) 222 5649
(Bank)
Bank of Boston Corp.

First National Bank of Chicago Ltd.
First Chicago House
London WC2E 9RB, England
Tel.: [44] (171) 240 7240
Fax: [44] (171) 836 7167
(Bank)
First Chicago Corp.

Kidder Peabody Securities Ltd.
107 Cheapside
London EC2V 6DD, England
Tel.: [44] (171) 480 8200
(Securities)
General Electric Co.

Merrill Lynch Europe PLC
Ropemaker Place 25, Ropemaker Street
London EC2Y 9LY, England
Tel.: [44] (171) 628 1000

Fax: [44] (171) 867 4818
www.merrilllynch.com
(Securities)
Merrill Lynch and Co. Inc.

Moody's Investors Services Ltd.
51 Eastcheap, 6th Floor Front
London EC3M 1LB, England
Tel.: [44] (171) 621 9068
(Commercial ratings service)
The Dun and Bradstreet Corp.

Morgan, J.P., Sterling Securities
60 Victoria Embankment
London EC44 0JP, England
Tel.: [44] (171) 723 0111
(Securities)
Morgan, J.P., & Co. Inc.

Morgan Stanley Intl.
25 Cabot Square, Canary Wharf
London E14 4QA, England
Tel.: [44] (171) 513 8000
Fax: [44] (171) 425 8990
(Securities)
Morgan-Stanley Group Inc.

Prudential Financial Services LTD
142 Holborn Bars
London EC1N 2NH, England
Tel.: [44] (171) 405 9222
Fax: [44] (171) 548 3802
www.prudential.com
(Holding co.)
Prudential Securities Group

INDUSTRIAL MANUFACTURING

Abbott Laboratories Ltd.
Abbott House
Maidenhead
Berkshire SL6 4XE, England
Tel.: [44] (162) 877 3355
Fax: [44] (162) 964 4305
(Pharmaceuticals)
Abbott Laboratories

Albright & Wilson PLC
Hagley Road West
Warley
West Midlands B68 ONN, England
Tel.: [44] (121) 429 4942
Fax: [44] (121) 420 515
(Chemicals)

Amerada Hess Ltd.
Greater London House
160 Hampstead Road
London NW1 7QN, England
Tel.: [44] (171) 388 5151
(Petroleum products)
Amerada Hess Corp.

Amoco (U.K.) Ltd.
Amoco House, West Gate
London W5 1XL, England
Tel.: [44] (181) 991 5639
Fax: [44] (181) 849 7329
(Petrochemicals)
Amoco Corp.

Analog Devices Ltd.
Walton House, Station Avenue
Walton-on-Thames, Surrey KT12 1PF,
England

Tel.: [44] (193) 223 2222
(Semiconductors)
Analog Devices Inc.

Armstrong World Industries Ltd.
Fleck Way
Stockton-on-Tees
Cleveland TX17 9JT, England
Tel.: [44] (189) 525 1122
Fax: [44] (189) 523 1517
(Floor and ceiling coverings)
Armstrong World Industries Inc.

AT&T Istel
P.O. Box 5
Redditch, Worcestershire B97 4DQ,
England
Tel.: (152) 751 8181
Fax: (152) 740 2408
(Industrial machinery)

Avon Cosmetics Ltd.
Nunn Mills Road
Northampton, Northamptonshire
NN1 5PA, England
Tel.: [44] (160) 423 2425
Fax: [44] (160) 423 2444
(Cosmetics and toiletries)
Avon Products Inc.
avon.com

Base Ten Systems Ltd.
12 Eelmoor Road
Farnsborough
Hampshire GU14 7QN, England
Tel.: [44] (125) 251 7665
(Measuring and controlling devices)
Base Ten Systems Inc.

Bechtel Ltd.
Bechtel House
London W6 8DP, England
Tel.: [44] (181) 846 5111
Fax: [44] (181) 846 6940
(Engineering)
Bechtel Corp.

Borden (U.K.) Ltd.
Rownhams Road
North Baddesley
Southampton S052 9ZB, England
Tel.: [44] (1703) 732 131
(Resins and plastics)
Borden Inc.

Bristol-Myers Squibb Pharmaceuticals Ltd.
Squibb House, Hounslow
Middlesex TW3 3JA, England
Tel.: [44] (181) 572 7422
Fax: [44] (181) 577 1756
(Pharmaceuticals)
Bristol-Myers Squibb Co.

J.I. Case Europe Ltd.
Wheatley Hall Road
Doncaster, South Yorkshire
DN2 4PG, England
Tel.: [44] (130) 273 3401
Fax: [44] (130) 273 3419
(Heavy equipment)
CASECORP

Caterpillar Ltd.
Peckleton Lane, Leicester
Leicestershire LE9 9JT, England
Tel.: [44] (145) 582 6826
Fax: [44] (145) 582 6900
www.caterpillar.com
(Earthmoving equipment)
Caterpillar Inc.

Colgate-Palmolive Ltd.
Guildford Business Park
Guildford
Surrey GU2 5LZ, England
Tel.: [44] (1 483) 302 222
Fax: [44] (1 483) 303 003
(Toiletries, cleaning products)
Colgate-Palmolive Co.

Compaq Computer Ltd.
Hotham House, Richmond
Surrey TW9 1EJ, England
Tel.: [44] (181) 332 3000
Fax: [44] (181) 332 1960

www.compaq.com
(Computers and software)
Compaq Computer Corp.

Conoco Ltd.
Park House, 116 Park Street
London W1Y 4NN, England
Tel.: [44] (171) 408 6000
Fax: [44] (171) 408 6660
www. conoco.com
(Petroleum)
Du Pont E.I. de Nemours and Co.

CPC (United Kingdom) Ltd.
Claygate House, Esher
Surrey KT10 9PN, England
Tel.: [44] (1 372) 462 181
Fax: [44] (1 372) 468 775
(Food products)
CPC International Inc.

Cyanamid of Great Britain Ltd.
Cyanamid House, 154 Fareham Road
Gosport, Hampshire PO13 OAS, England
Tel.: [44] (1329) 224 000
Fax: [44] (1329) 202 13
(Medical instruments)
American Cyanamid Co.

Digital Equipment Co. Ltd.
Digital Park, Worton Grange
Imperial Way
Reading, Berkshire RG2 OTE, England
Tel.: [44] (734) 868 711
Fax: [44] (734) 867 969
(Computers)
Digital Equipment Corp.

Dow Chemical Co. Ltd.
Lakeside House, Stockley Park
Uxbridge, Middlesex UB11 1BE, England
Tel.: [44] (181) 848 8688
www.dow.com
(Chemicals)
Dow Chemical Co.

DuPont and Fujifilm Electronic Imaging Ltd.
Wedgwood Way, Stevenage
Hertfordshire SG1 4QN, England
Tel.: [44] (1 438) 734 000
Fax: [44] (1 438) 734 154
(Chemicals)
E.i. DuPont de Nemours & Co.

Emerson Electric (U.K.) Ltd.
39 Portman Square
London W1H 9FH, England
Tel.: [44] (171) 486 2755
Fax: [44] (171) 487 2747
(Portable electric tools)
Emerson Electric Co.

Esso Petroleum Co. Ltd.
Esso House, Victoria Street
London SW1E 5JW, England
Tel.: [44] (171) 834 6677
Fax: [44] (171) 245 2556
(Petroleum products)
Exxon Corp.

Exxon Chemical Ltd.
P.O. Box 12, Fareham
Hampshire PO15 7AP, England
Tel.: [44] (148) 988 4597
Fax: [44] (148) 988 4477
www.exxon.com
Exxon Corp.

Ford Motor Co. Ltd.
Eagle Way, Brentwood
Essex CM13 3BW, England
Tel.: [44] (127) 725 3000
Fax: [44] (127) 723 2374
www.ford.com
(Automobiles)
Ford Motor Co.

General Electric International
3 Shortlands
London W6 8BX, England
Tel.: [44] (181) 741 9900
Fax: [44] (181) 741 9460
(Electronic equipment)
General Electric Co.

General Foods Ltd.
St. George's House, Bayshill Road
Cheltenham, Gloucestershire GL50 3AE,
England
Tel.: [44] (242) 236 101
(Food processing)
Philip Morris Companies Inc.

General Motors Holdings
Griffin House, Luton
Bedforshire LU1 3YT, England
Tel.: [44] (242) 236 101
(automobiles)

Gillette Industries Ltd.
Gillette Corner, Great West Road
Isleworth, Middlesex TW7 5NP, England
Tel.: [44] (181) 847 7800
Fax: [44] (181) 568 1712
(Shaving equipment)
The Gillette Co.

Goodyear Great Britain Ltd.
Stafford Road, Wolverhampton
West Midlands WV10 6DH, England
Tel.: [44] (1 902) 22090
Fax: [44] (1 902) 22090
(Tires)
Goodyear Tire & Rubber Co.

W.R. Grace Ltd.
Northdale House, North Circular Road
London NW10 7UH, England
Tel.: [44] (181) 965 0611
Fax: [44] (181) 961 8620
(Chemical products)
W.R. Grace & Co.

Harcourt Brace Jovanovich Ltd.
24/28 Oval Road
London NW 17DX, England
Tel.: [44] (171) 267 4466
(Publishing)
Harcourt Brace Jovanovich Inc.

H.J. Heinz Co. Ltd.
Hayes Park, Hayes
Middlesex UB4 8AL, England
Tel.: [44] (181) 573 7757
Fax: [44] (181) 848 2325
(Processed foods)
H.J. Heinz Co.

Honeywell Ltd.
Honeywell House, Charles Square
Bracknell, Berkshire RG12 1EB, England
Tel.: [44] (1344) 826 000
Fax: [44] (1344) 416 240
(Process control systems)
Honeywell Inc.

IBM United Kingdom Holdings Ltd.
P.O. Box 41, Portsmouth
Hampshire PO6 3AU, England
Tel.: [44] (1705) 561 000
Fax: [44] (1705) 388 914
(Data processing equipment)
IBM Inc.

Ingersoll-Rand Co. Ltd.
P.O. Box 2
Bolton BL6 6JN, England
Tel.: [44] (1204) 69 06 90
Fax: [44] (1204) 69 03 88
Ingersoll-Rand Co.

Kellogg Co. of Great Britain Ltd.
Kellogg Building, Talbot Road
Manchester M16 0PU, England
Tel.: [44] (161) 869 2000
Fax: [44] (161) 869 2100
(Food processing)
Kellogg Co.

Kimberly-Clark Ltd.
Larkfield, Aylesford
Kent ME20 7PS, England
Tel.: [44] (1622) 616 000
Fax: [44] (1622) 616 001
(Paper products)
Kimberly-Clark Corp.

Kodak Ltd.
Kodak House
P.O. Box 66
Station Road, Hemel
Hempstead, Hertfordshire HP1 1JU,
England
Tel.: [44] (1442) 611 22
Fax: [44] (1442) 240 609
(Photographic supplies)
Eastman Kodak Co.

Levi-Strauss (U.K.) Ltd.
Levi's House, Moulton Park
Northampton NN3 1QG, England
Tel.: [44] (1604) 790 436
Fax: [44] (1604) 790 400
(Clothing)
Levi-Strauss Inc.

Eli Lilly Group Ltd.
Kingsclere Road, Basingstoke
Hampshire RG21 6XA, England
Tel.: [44] (1256) 315 000
Fax: [44] (1256) 485 710
(Pharmaceuticals)
Eli Lilly & Co.

Mars UK Ltd.
3D Dundee Road, Slough
Berkshire SL1 4JX, England
Tel.: [44] (1753) 550 055
Fax: [44] (1753) 533 172
(Confectionery)
Mars Inc.

**McDonnell Douglas Information
Systems Ltd.**
Maylands Park South, Boundary Way
Hemel Hempstead, Hertfordshire
HP2 7HU, England
Tel.: [44] (1442) 232 424
Fax: [44] (1442) 244 896
(Computers and software)
McDonnell Douglas Corp.

McGraw-Hill Book Co. (U.K.) Ltd.
McGraw-Hill House
Shoppenhangers Road
Maidenhead, Berkshire SL6 2QL, England
Tel.: [44] (1628) 623 432
(Publishing)
McGraw-Hill Inc.

Merck Sharp & Dohme (Holdings) Ltd.
West Hill, Hertford Road
Hoddesdon, Hertfordshire EN11 9BU,
England
Tel.: [44] (1992) 467 272
Fax: [44] (1992) 467 270
(Chemicals and pharmaceuticals)
Merck and Co. Inc.

Mobil Oil Co. Ltd.
Mobil House, Milton Keynes
Buckinghamshire MK9 1ES, England
Tel.: [44] (190) 885 300
Fax: [44] (190) 885 3999
(Petroleum products)
Mobile Oil Corp.

Monsanto PLC
P.O. Box 54
High Wycombe, Buckinghamshire HP12
4HL, England
Tel.: [44] (149) 447 4918
(Chemicals and plastics)
Monsanto Corp.

Motorola Ltd.
Church Road, Crawley
West Sussex RH11 0PQ, England
Tel.: [44] (129) 340 4343
Fax: [44] (175) 353 7390
(Electronic equipment)
Motorola Inc.

National Semiconductor (U.K.) Ltd.
Larkfield Industrial Estate, Greenock
Renfrewshire PA16 0EQ, England
Tel.: [44] (181) 568 8855
(Electronic components)
National Semiconductor Corp.

NCR Ltd.
206 Marylebone Road
London NW1 6LY, England
Tel.: [44] (171) 723 7070
Fax: [44] (171) 725 8224
(Data processing equipment)
NCR Corp.

Occidental Petroleum (Caledonia) Ltd.
123 Buckingham Palace Road
London SW1 9SW, England
Tel.: [44] (171) 828 5600
(Petroleum products)
Occidental Petroleum Corp.

Otis Elevator PLC
Otis Building
London SW9 0JZ, England
Tel.: [44] (171) 735 9131
Fax: [44] (171) 735 4639
(Elevators and escalators)
United Technologies Corp.

Pfizer Group Ltd.
P.O. Box 24, Ramsgate Road
Sandwich, Kent CT13 9NJ, England
Tel.: [44] (1304) 616 161
Fax: [44] (1304) 616 221
(Pharmaceuticals)
Pfizer Inc.

Phillips Electronics UK Ltd.
Phillips Center 420-30
London Road, Croydon
Surrey CR9 3QR, England
Tel.: [44] (181) 689 2166
Fax: [44] (181) 689 9179
(Electronics)
Phillips Petroleum Co.

Pitney Bowes PLC
The Pinnacles, Harlow
Essex CM19 5BD, England
Tel.: [44] (1279) 426 731
Fax: [44] (1279) 449 275
(Business equipment)
Pitney Bowes Inc.

Polaroid (U.K.) Ltd.
Ashley Road
St. Albans, Herts AL1 5PR, England
Tel.: [44] (727) 59 191
(Photographic equipment)
Polaroid Corp.

Procter & Gamble Ltd.
Hedley House, St. Nicholas Avenue
Newcastle-upon-Tyne
Tyne&Wear NE99 1EE, England
Tel.: [44] (191) 279 2000
Fax: [44] (191) 279 2282
(Toiletries and soaps)
Procter & Gamble Co.

Quaker Oats Ltd.
P.O. Box 24, Bridge Road
Southall, Middlesex UB2 4AG, England
Tel.: [44] (181) 574 2388
(Processed foods)
The Quaker Oats Co.

Rank Xerox Ltd.
Parkway, Marlow
Buckinghamshire SL7 1YL, England
Tel.: [44] (1628) 890 0000
Fax: [44] (1628) 889 2001
(Office equipment)
Xerox Corp.

Raychem Ltd.
Faraday Road
Swindon, Wiltshire SN3 5HH, England
Tel.: [44] (1793) 528 171
Fax: [44] (1793) 572 516
(Material science components)
Raychem Corp.

Raytheon United Kingdom Ltd.
King's House, Harrow
Middlesex I1A1 1YD, England
Tel.: [44] (181) 861 2525
Fax: [44] (181) 863 0599
(Electronic equipment)
Raytheon Co.

Readers Digest Association Ltd.
Berkeley Square House
London W1X 6AB, England
Tel.: [44] (171) 629 8144
Fax: [44] (171) 499 9751
(Publishing)
Readers Digest Association

Rockwell International Ltd.
Greenbank Street
Preston PR1 7LA, England
Tel.: [44] (177) 225 7571
Fax: [44] (177) 288 0464
(Industrial equipment and components)
Rockwell International Corp.

Rohm & Haas (U.K.) Ltd.
Lennig House, 2 Masons Avenue
Croydon, Surrey CR9 3NB, England
Tel.: [44] (181) 686 8844
(Chemicals)
Rohm & Haas Co.

Scott Ltd.
Thames House
Crete Hall Road
Gravesend
Northfleet DA11 9AD, England
Tel : [44] (1474) 33 60 00
(Paper products)
Kimberly-Clark Holding Ltd.

Texaco Ltd.
1 Westferry Circus
London EI4 4HA, England
Tel.: [44] (171) 930 00
Fax: [44] (171) 719 5109
(Petroleum products)
Texaco Inc.

Texas Instruments Ltd.
Manton Lane
Bedford MK41 7PA, England
Tel.: [44] (234) 270 111
(Electronic components)
Texas Instruments Inc.

3M U.K. Holdings PLC
3M House
P.O. Box 1
Bracknell, Berkshire RG12 1JU, England
Tel.: [44] (344) 858 000
(Diversified products)
Minnesota Mining and Manufacturing
Corp.

Union Texas Petroleum Ltd.
5th Floor, Bowater House
68-114 Knightsbridge
London SW1X 7LR, England
Tel.: [44] (171) 581 5533
(Petroleum products)
Union Texas Petroleum Holdings Inc.

Unisys Ltd.
Bakers Court, Uxbridge
Middlesex UB8 1RG, England
Tel.: [44] (1895) 237 137
Fax: [44] (1895) 862 093
(Data processing equipment)
Unisys Corp.

RETAILING AND WHOLESALING

Amdahl (U.K.) Ltd.
Viking House, 29-31 Lampton Road
Hounslow TW3 1JD, England
Tel.: [44] (181) 572 7383
(Computer equipment)
Amdahl Corp.

AT&T Holdings Ltd.
Highfield House Redditch
Worcestershire B97 5ED, England
Tel.: [44] (1527) 55 0330
Fax: [44] (1527) 40 4350
(Computer systems)
AT&T Corp, USA

Baxter Healthcare Ltd.
Caxton Way
Thetford, Norfolk IP24 3SE, England
Tel.: [44] (1842) 75 4581
Fax: [44] (1842) 76 7083
(Medical supplies)
Baxter International Inc.

Black & Decker International
Westpoint, The Grove
Slough, Berkshire SL1 1QQ, England
Tel.: [44] (175) 351 1234
Fax: [44] (175) 355 1155
(Handheld power tools)
Black & Decker Manufacturing Co.

Charles River (U.K.) Ltd.
74 Oldfield Road
Hampton, Middlesex TW12 2HR,
England
Tel.: [44] (95) 478 2020
(Laboratory animal breeding)
Bausch and Lomb

Hewlett-Packard Ltd.
Cain Road, Bracknell
Berkshire RG12 1HN, England
Tel.: [44] (1344) 360 000
Fax: [44] (1344) 363 344
(Computers and calculators)
Hewlett-Packard Co.

Ilford Group Ltd.
Town Lane, Knutsford
Cheshire WA16 7 JL, England
Tel.: [44] (156) 565 000
Fax: [44] (156) 587 2734

Jaguar PLC (Jaguar Cars Ltd.)
Browns Lane, Allesley, Coventry
West Midlands CV5 9DR, England
Tel.: [44] (1203) 402 121
Fax: [44] (1203) 405 451
(Automobiles)
Ford Motor Co., USA

Tandem Computers Ltd.
Tandem House, 7 Roundwood Avenue
Stockley Park, Uxbridge UB11 9AU,
England
Tel.: [44] (181) 569 1290
(Computer sales and marketing)
Tandem Computers

Time Warner Entertainment Ltd.
Interpark House, London
London W1Y 7DS, England

SERVICE INDUSTRIES

Booz Allen & Hamilton International (U.K.) Ltd.
30 Charles II Street
London SW1 Y4AE, England
Tel.: [44] (171) 930 8144
(Consulting)
Booz Allen and Hamilton Inc.

Brown & Root (U.K.) Ltd.
150 The Broadway, London
London SW19 1RX, England
Tel.: [44] (181) 544 5000
Fax: [44] (181) 544 6951
(Engineering and construction)
Halliburton Co.

Leo Burnett Ltd.
48 St. Martins Lane
London WC2N 4EJ, England
Tel.: [44] (171) 836 2424
(Advertising)
Leo Burnett International

D'Arcy & Masius Benton & Bowles
1-2 St. James's Square
London SW1Y 4JN, England
Tel.: [44] (171) 839 3422
(Advertising)
D'Arcy & Masius Benton & Bowles

Dun & Bradstreet (U.K.) Ltd.
Holmers Farmway, High Wycombe
Buckinghamshire HP12 4UL, England
Tel.: [44] (149) 442 2000
Fax: [44] (149) 442 2260
(Information services)
The Dun and Bradstreet Corp.

England ADP Ltd.
ADP House, 2 Pine Trees,
Chertsey Lane
Staines TW18 3DS, England
Tel.: [44] (784) 451 355

Tel.: [44] (171) 290 6000
Fax: [44] (171) 290 6050
(Periodicals)
Time Warner Co. LP

Wang (U.K.) Ltd.
Wang House, 1000 Great West Road
Brentford, Middlesex TW8 9HL, England
Tel.: [44] (181) 568 9200
(Data processing equipment)
Wang Laboratories Inc.

(Software and office supplies)
Automatic Data Processing Inc.

Grey Communications Group Ltd.
215-227 Great Portland Street
London W1N 5HD, England
Tel.: [44] (171) 636 3399
(Advertising)
Grey Advertising Inc.

Interpublic Ltd.
4 Golden Square London
London W1R 3AE, England
Tel.: [44] (171) 734 7116
Fax: [44] (171) 439 0289
(Advertising)
Interpublic Group of Companies Inc.

McCann-Erickson Advertising Ltd.
McCann-Erickson House
36 Howland Street
London W1A 1AT, England
Tel.: [44] (171) 580 6690
(Advertising)
Interpublic Group of Companies Inc.

McDonald's Ltd.
11-59 High Road, East Finchley
London N2 8AW, England
Tel.: [44] (181) 700 7000
Fax: [44] (181) 700 7050
(Restaurant operations)
McDonald's Corp.

A.C. Nielsen Co. Ltd.
Nielsen House, London Road
Oxford, Oxfordshire OX3 9RX, England
Tel.: [44] (186) 574 2742
Fax: [44] (186) 574 2222
(Market research)
The Dun and Bradstreet Corp.

The Ogilvy Group (Holdings) Ltd.
Brettenham House, Lancaster Place
London WC2E 7EZ, England
Tel.: [44] (171) 836 2466
(Advertising)
The Ogilvy Group Inc.

Sothebys International Inc.
34-35 New Bond Street
London W1A 2AA, England
Tel.: [44] (171) 493 8080
Fax: [44] (171) 409 3100
(Art auctioning)
Sothebys Holdings Inc.

J. Walter Thompson UK Holdings Ltd.
40 Berkeley Square
London W1X 6AD, England

Tel.: [44] (171) 629 9496
(Market research and advertising)
J. Walter Thompson Co.

Time Warner Ltd.
Unit 1, London
London W8 4LD, England
Tel.: [44] (171) 376525
Fax: [44] (171) 938 3986
(Motion picture theaters)
Warner Communications Inc.

Young & Rubicam Group Ltd.
Greater London House, Hampstead Road
London NW1 7QP, England
Tel.: [44] (171) 387 9366
Fax: [44] (171) 611 6570
(Advertising)
Young & Rubicam Inc.

EUROPEAN COMPANIES IN ENGLAND

The following are major non-American firms operating in the country. These selected companies can be either domestic or foreign, but are usually British. Such companies will generally hire their own nationals first but may employ Americans.

BANKING AND FINANCE

AAH Holdings PLC
76 South Park
Lincoln LN5 8ES, England
Tel.: [44] (192) 857 9393
Fax: [44] (192) 857 9757
(Holding co.)

Barclays Bank PLC
54 Lombard St.
London EC3P 3AH, England
Tel.: [44] (171) 626 1567
Fax: [44] (171) 488 0020
(Commercial bank)

B.A.T. Industries PLC
P.O. Box 345, Windsor House
50 Victoria Street
London SW1H ONL, England
Tel.: [44] (171) 222 7979
Fax: [44] (171) 222 0122
(Financial services)

Commercial Union Assurance Co. PLC
St. Helen's, 1 Undershaft
London EC3P 3DQ, England
Tel.: [44] (171) 283 7500
Fax: [44] (171) 662 8070
(Insurance)

Guardian Royal Exchange PLC
Royal Exchange
London EC3V 3LS, England
Tel.: [44] (171) 283 7101
Fax: [44] (171) 621 2599
(Insurance)

Lloyds Bank PLC
71 Lombard Street
London EC3P 3BS, England
Tel.: [44] (171) 626 1500
Fax: [44] (171) 929 2901
(Bank)

Midland Bank
PLC27/32 Poultry
London EC2P 2BX, England
Tel.: [44] (171) 260 8536
Fax: [44] (171) 260 8249
(Banking and financial services)

National Westminster Bank PLC
41 Lothbury
London EC2P 2BP, England
Tel.: [44] (171) 726 1000
Fax: [44] (171) 726 1035
(Banking and financial services)

Prudential Assurance Co. Ltd.
1 Stephen Street
London W1P 2AP, England
Tel.: [44] (171) 405 9222
Fax: [44] (171) 548 3850
(Insurance)

Royal Insurance Holdings PLC
1 Cornhill
London EC3V 3QR, England
Tel.: [44] (171) 283 4300
Fax: [44] (171) 283 4841
(Insurance)

INDUSTRIAL MANUFACTURING

Laura Ashley Holdings PLC
Laura Ashley House, 3rd Floor
London SW1X 7LQ, England
Tel.: [44] (171) 880 5100
Fax: [44] (171) 880 5300
(Clothing)

Associated British Foods PLC
Weston Centre, Bowater House
68 Knightsbridge
London SW1X 7LQ, England
Tel.: [44] (171) 589 6363
Fax: [44] (171) 584 8560
(Processed foods)

Bayer PLC
Bayer House
Newbury, Berkshire RG14 1JA, England
Tel.: [44] (163) 556 3000
Fax: [44] (163) 556 3393
(Chemicals)
Bayer Co., Germany

BBA Group PLC
P.O. Box 18, Cleckheaton
West Yorkshire BD19 6HP, England
Tel.: [44] (1274) 853 000
Fax: [44] (1274) 871 633
(Automotive and aviation products)

BICC PLC
Devonshire House, Mayfair Place
London W1X 5FH, England
Tel.: [44] (171) 629 6622
Fax: [44] (171) 409 0070
(Transmission equipment)

Blue Circle Industries
PLC84 Eccleston Square

Standard Chartered Bank1
Aldermanbury Square
London EC2V 7SB, England
Tel.: [44] (171) 280 7500
Fax: [44] (171) 280 7112
(Banking and financial services)

Sun Alliance & London Insurance
1 Bartholomew Lane
London EC2N 2AB, England
Tel.: [44] (171) 588 2345
Fax: [44] (171) 826 1159
(Insurance)

London SW1V 1PX, England
Tel.: [44] (171) 828 3456
Fax: [44] (171) 245 8272
(Building materials)

The Body Shop International PLC
Hawthorn Road, Littlehampton
West Sussex BN17 6LS, England
Tel.: [44] (1903) 731 500
Fax: [44] (1903) 726 250
(Personal care products)

Bowater Industries PLC
Bowater House, Knightsbridge
London SW1X 7NN, England
Tel.: [44] (171) 584 7070
(Building materials)

British Aerospace PLC
Warwick House, Farnborough
Hampshire GU14 6YU, England
Tel.: [44] (125) 237 3232
Fax: [44] (125) 238 3000
(Aircraft, defense equipment and space
systems)

The British Petroleum Company PLC
Britannic House, Moore Lane,
London EC2M 7BA, England
Tel.: [44] (171) 496 4000
Fax: [44] (171) 496 4630
(Petroleum products)

British Steel PLC
9 Albert Embankment
London SE1 7SN, England
Tel.: [44] (171) 735 7654
Fax: [44] (171) 587 1142
(Iron and steel)

B.S.G. International PLC
Seton House, Warwick
Warwickshire CV34 6DE, England
Tel.: [44] (192) 640 0040
Fax: [44] (192) 640 6300
(Automotive products)

BTR PLC
Silvertown House
Vincent Square
London SW1P 2PL, England
Tel.: [44] (171) 834 3848
Fax: [44] (171) 834 3879
(Construction, agricultural, and aircraft
equipment)

Bunzl PLC
110 Park Street
London W1Y 3RB, England
Tel.: [44] (171) 495 4950
Fax: [44] (171) 495 4953
(Paper and plastic products)

The Burmah Castrol PLC
Burmah Castrol House
Pipers Way Swindon
Wiltshire SN3 1RE, England
Tel.: [44] (1793) 511 521
Fax: [44] (1793) 513 506
(Chemical products and gas)

Cadbury Schweppes PLC
25 Berkeley
London W1X 6HT, England
Tel.: [44] (171) 409 1313
Fax: [44] (171) 830 5157
(Confectionery and beverages)

Ciba-Geigy PLC
Hulley Road, Macclesfield
Cheshire SK10 2NX, England
Tel.: [44] (1625) 421 933
Fax: [44] (1625) 619 637
(Chemicals)

Coats Viyella PLC
28 Saville Row
London W1X 2DD, England
Tel.: [44] (171) 734 4030
Fax: [44] (171) 437 2016
(Textiles, clothing, thread)

Courtlands PLC
50 George St.
London W1A 2BB, England
Tel.: [44] (171) 612 1000
Fax: [44] (171) 612 1520
(Coatings, sealants, packaging)

Daily Mail & General Trust PLC
Northcliffe House, 2 Derry Street
Kensington, London W8 5TT, England
Tel.: [44] (171) 938 6000
Fax: [44] (171) 938 4626
(Publishing)

Dalgety PLC
100 George Street
London W1H 5RH, England
Tel.: [44] (171) 486 0200
Fax: [44] (171) 935 3120
(Agribusiness, processed foods)

Delta PLC
1 Kingsway
London WC2B 6XF, England
Tel.: [44] (171) 836 3535
Fax: [44] (171) 836 4511
(Electrical equipment)

Electrolux Ltd.
Electrolux Works, 101 Oakley Road
Luton, Bedfordshire LU4 9QQ, England
Tel.: [44] (1582) 491 234
Fax: [44] (1582) 490 214
(Electrical appliances)

Elf Aquitaine UK PLC
30 Buckingham Gate
London SW1E 6NN, England
Tel.: [44] (171) 963 5000
Fax: [44] (171) 963 5197
(Petroleum products)
Elf Aquitaine, France

Fisons PLC
RPR House, Eastborne
East Sussex BN21 3YG, England
Tel.: [44] (132) 353 4000
Fax: [44] (132) 353 4080
(Medical and veterinary products)

The General Electric Co. PLC (GEC)
1 Stanhope Gate
London W1A 1EH, England
Tel.: [44] (171) 493 8484
Fax: [44] (171) 493 1974
(Electrical and electronic equipment)

GKN PLC
P.O. Box 55
Redditch
Worcestershire B98 0TL, England
Tel.: [44] (1 527) 517 715
Fax: [44] (1 527) 517 700
(Motor components)

Glaxo Holdings PLC
Stockley Park West, Uxbridge
Middlesex UB11 1BU, England
Tel.: [44] (181) 990 9100
Fax: [44] (181) 990 4343
(Pharmaceuticals)

Glynwed International PLC
Headland House, 54 New Coventry Road
Sheldon, Birmingham B26 3AZ, England
Tel.: [44] (121) 742 2366
Fax: [44] (121) 742 0403
(Steel and engineering)

Guinness PLC
39 Portman Square
London W1H OEE, England
Tel.: [44] (171) 164 100
Fax: [44] (171) 935 5500
(Brewing and distilling)

Hanson PLC
1 Grosvenor Place
London SW1X 7JH, England
Tel.: [44] (171) 245 1245
Fax: [44] (171) 235 3455
(Mining, chemicals)

Harrisons & Crosfield PLC
One Great Tower Street
London EC3R 5AH, England
Tel.: [44] (171) 711 1400
Fax: [44] (171) 711 1401
(Chemicals)

Hoechst UK Ltd.
Hoechst House
Middlesex TW4 6 JH, England
Tel.: [44] (181) 570 7712
Fax: [44] (181) 577 1854
(Chemicals and synthetic fibers)

Imperial Chemical Industries PLC
Imperial Chemical House
9 Millbank
London SW1P 3JF, England
Tel.: [44] (171) 834 4444
Fax: [44] (171) 83442042
(Chemicals, pharmaceuticals, plastics)

Lonrho PLC
4 Grosvenor Place
London SW1X 7AL, England
Tel.: [44] (171) 201 6000
Fax: [44] (171) 201 6100
(Holding company with interests in
mining, agribusiness, hotels, and other
land-related concerns)

Lucas LTD
Brueton House, New Road
West Midlands B91 3TX, England
Tel.: [44] (1216) 276 000
Fax: [44] (1216) 276 171
(Aerospace and automotive components)

MacMillan Publishers Ltd.
25 Eccleston Place
London SW1W 9NF, England
Tel.: [44] (171) 881 8000
Fax: [44] (171) 881 8001
(Publishing)

Meyer International PLC
Aldwych House
London WC2B 4HQ, England
Tel.: [44] (171) 400 8888
Fax: [44] (171) 400 8700
(Building and timber products)

Parker Pen Ltd.
Parker House, 652 Railway Road
Newhaven, East Sussex BN9 0AU, England
Tel.: [44] (1273) 513 233
Fax: [44] (1273) 514 773
(Writing instruments)
Parker Pen Holdings

Peugeot Talbot Motor Co. Ltd.
Aldermoor House, P.O. Box 227
West Midlands CV3 1LT, England
Tel.: [44] (1618) 868 1111
Fax: [44] (1618) 765 705
(Automobile manufacturing)
Peugeot, France

Pilkington Distribution Services Ltd.
Prescot Road, St. Helens
Merseyside WA10 3TT, England
Tel.: [44] (1744) 695 695
Fax: [44] (1744) 692 047
(Glass products)

Polygram UK Ltd.
P.O. Box 1420, 1 Sussex Place
London W6 9XS, England
Tel.: [44] (181) 910 5000
Fax: [44] (181) 741 4901
(Records, cassettes, CDs)

Ranks Hovis Ltd.
The Lord Rank Center, High Wycombe
Buckinghamshire HP12 3QS, England
Tel.: [44] (1494) 428 000
Fax: [44] (1494) 428 428
(Processed foods)
Rank Hovis McDougall Ltd.

Reckitt & Colman PLC
One Burlington Lane
London W4 2RW, England
Tel.: [44] (181) 994 6464
Fax: [44] (181) 994 8920
(Household goods and pharmaceuticals)

Reed International PLC
Michelin House, London
London SW3 6RB, England
Tel.: [44] (171) 581 9393
Fax: [44] (171) 589 8419
(Business publishing and information)

RMC Group PLC
RMC House, Coldharbour Lane
Thorpe, Egham, Surrey TW20 8TD,
England
Tel.: [44] (1932) 568 833
Fax: [44] (1932) 568 933
(Construction materials)

Rolls-Royce PLC
65 Buckingham Gate
London SW1E 6AT, England
Tel.: [44] (171) 222 9020
Fax: [44] (171) 227 9179
(Engines and aircraft equipment)

Rothmans UK Holdings LTD
15 Hill Street
London W1X 7FB, England
Tel.: [44] (171) 491 4366
Fax: [44] (171) 493 8404
(Tobacco products, luxury consumer
goods)
Rothmans International LTD

Rover Group Holdings PLC
International House, Bickenhill Lane
West Midlands B37 7HQ, England
Tel.: [44] (1214) 825 845
Fax: [44] (1214) 817 000
(Automobiles)

Rowntree MacKintosh Ltd.
P.O. Box 202
York Y01 1XY, England
Tel.: [44] (904) 653071
(Confectionery)

The RTZ Corporation PLC
P.O. Box 133
6 St. James's Square
London SW1Y 4LD, England
Tel.: [44] (171) 930 2399
Fax: [44] (171) 930 3249
(Mining)

Sandoz Products Ltd.
Calverley Lane, Horsforth
Leeds LS18 4RP, England
Tel.: [44] (532) 584646
(Chemicals and pharmaceuticals)

Simon Engineering PLC
Simon House, London
London SW1W 9BJ, England
Tel.: [44] (171) 730 0777
(Heavy equipment)

Smith Industries PLC
765 Finchley Road, Childs Hill
London NW11 8DS, England
Tel.: [44] (181) 458 3232
Fax: [44] (181) 458 4380
(Aviation, marine, and medical
equipment)

SmithKline Beecham PLC
SmithKline Beecham House
Middlesex TW8 9BD, England
Tel.: [44] (181) 975 2000
Fax: [44] (181) 975 2773
(Pharmaceuticals)

Smith & Nephew PLC
2 Temple Place, Victoria Embankment
London WC2R 3BP, England
Tel.: [44] (171) 836 7922
Fax: [44] (171) 240 7088
(Medical and health care products)

Steetley PLC
P.O. Box 53, Brownsover Road
Rugby, Warwickshire CV21 1UT, England
Tel.: [44] (788) 535 621
(Quarrying and conversion)

Tate & Lyle PLC
Sugar Quay, Lower Thames Street
London EC3R 6DQ, England
Tel.: [44] (171) 626 6525
Fax: [44] (171) 895 5514
(Food processing)

TI Group PLC
50 Curzon Street
London W1Y 7PN, England
Tel.: [44] (171) 499 9131
Fax: [44] (171) 493 6533
(Specialized engineering products)

Total Oil Great Britain Ltd.
33 Cavendish Square, London
London W1 3TX, England
Tel.: [44] (171) 629 1111

(Petroleum products)
Total Oil Holdings Ltd.

The Union International PLC
14 West Smithfield
London EC1A 9JL, England
Tel.: [44] (171) 248 1212
(Food processing)

United Biscuits Holdings PLC
Church Road, West Drayton
Middlesex UB7 7PR, England
Tel.: [44] (895) 432 100
Fax: [44] (1895) 448 848
(Food processing)

United News & Media PLC
Ludgate House
245 Blackfriars Road
London SE1 9UY, England
Tel.: [44] (171) 921 5000
Fax: [44] (171) 928 2728
(Publishing)

Vauxhall Motors Ltd.
Osbourne Road, Luton
Bedfordshire LU1 3YT, England
Tel.: [44] (1582) 21 122
Fax: [44] (1582) 42 7400
(Motor vehicles)
VHC Sub-Holdings Ltd.

RETAIL AND WHOLESALING

Allied-Lyons PLC
Allied House, 24 Portland Place
London W1N 4BB, England
Tel.: [44] (171) 323 9000
(Food products)

Argyll Group PLC
6 Millington Road
Hayes, Middlesex UB3 4AY, England
Tel.: [44] (181) 848 8744
(Food products)

Asda Group PLC
Asda House, Southbank, Great Wilson
Street
Leeds LS11 5AD, England
Tel.: [44] (1132) 435 435
Fax: [44] (1132) 418 666
(Food, furnishings)

Vickers PLC
Vickers House, Millbank
London SW1P 4RA, England
Tel.: [44] (171) 828 7777
Fax: [44] (171) 828 6585
(Automobiles, military vehicles, medical
equipment)

Waterford Wedgwood UK PLC
Barlaston, Stoke-on-Trent
Staffordshire ST12 9ES, England
Tel.: [44] (1782) 204141
Fax: [44] (1782) 204402
(Table and gift ware)

Wellcome Foundation Ltd.
Landsdowne House, London
London W1X 6BQ, England
Tel.: [44] (171) 387 4477
Fax: [44] (171) 408 0228
(Pharmaceuticals)
Wellcome PLC

Whitbread & Co. PLC
Brewery, Chiswell Street
London EC1Y 4SD, England
Tel.: [44] (171) 326 6611
Fax: [44] (171) 615 1000
(Eating places)

Boots Company PLC
1 Thane Road West
Nottingham NG2 3AA, England
Tel.: [44] (1159) 506 111
Fax: [44] (1159) 592 727
(Pharmaceuticals)

British Gas PLC
Rivermill House, 152 Grosvenor Road
London SW1V 3JL, England
Tel.: [44] (171) 821 1444
(Gas)

The Burton Group PLC
214 Oxford Street
London W1N 9DF, England
Tel.: [44] (171) 636 8040
Fax: [44] (171) 580 8634
(Clothing, furniture)

Dixons Group PLC
200 The Campus, Hemel Hempstead
Hertfordshire HP2 7TG, England
Tel.: [44] (1442) 353 000
Fax: [44] (1442) 233 218
(Consumer electronics)

Gallaher Ltd.
Members Hill, Brooklands Road
Weybridge, Surrey KT13 0QU, England
Tel.: [44] (1932) 859 777
Fax: [44] (1932) 832 508
(Tobacco products and housewares)

Grand Metropolitan PLC
8 Henrietta Place, London
London W1M 9AG, England
Tel.: [44] (171) 518 5200
Fax: [44] (171) 518 4600
(Food and beverages)

Kingfisher PLC
North West House, 119 Marylebone Road
London NW1 5PX, England
Tel.: [44] (171) 724 7749
Fax: [44] (171) 724 1160
(Specialty stores)

The Littlewoods Organisation PLC
JM Centre
100-110 Old Hall Street
Liverpool, Meyerside L70 1AB, England
Tel.: [44] (1512) 352 222
Fax: [44] (1512) 354 900
(Mail order and chain stores)

Marks and Spencer PLC
Michael House, 37-67 Baker Street
London W1A 1DN, England
Tel.: [44] (171) 935 4422
Fax: [44] (171) 268 2608
(Clothing, food, household goods)

Mocatta & Goldsmith Ltd.
Mocatta House, 4 Crosby Square
London EC3A 6AQ, England
Tel.: [44] (171) 638 3636
(Gold and silver bullion)

William Morrison Supermarkets PLC
Hilmore House, Thornton Road

Bradford, West Yorkshire BD8 9AX,
England
Tel.: [44] (1274) 494 166
Fax : [44] (1274) 49 48 31
(Supermarkets)

J. Sainsbury PLC
Stamford House, Stamford Street
London SE1 9LL, England
Tel.: [44] (171) 921 6000
Fax: [44] (171) 921 6132
(Food products)

Selfridges Ltd.
400 Oxford Street
London W1A 1AB, England
Tel.: [44] (171) 629 1234
Fax: [44] (171) 495 8321
(Department stores)
Sears Investment Trust Ltd.

W.H. Smith Ltd.
Audrey House
London EC1N 6SN, England
Tel.: [44] (171) 730 1200
Fax: [44] (171) 730 1200
(Printed materials)
W.H. Smith Group PLC

Storehouse PLC
Marylebone House, London
London NW1 5QD, England
Tel.: [44] (171) 262 3456
Fax: [44] (171) 262 4740
(Furniture, household goods)

Tesco PLC
Tesco House, Delamare Road, Cheshunt
Waltham Cross, Hertfordshire EN8 9SL,
England
Tel.: [44] (1992) 632 222
Fax: [44] (1992) 630 794
(Food products)

Thorn PLC
37 Windsor Street, Chertsey
Surrey KT16 8AT, England
Tel.: [44] (1932) 570 033
Fax: [44] (1932) 571 740
(Household appliances)

SERVICE INDUSTRIES

Abbott Mead Vickers PLC
191 Old Marylebone Road
London NW1 5DW, England
Tel.: [44] (171) 402 4100
Fax: [44] (171) 723 3432
(Advertising)

Amec PLC
Sandiway House, Hartford
Northwich, Cheshire CW8 2YA, England
Tel.: [44] (1606) 883885
Fax: [44] (1606) 688 3996
(Engineering and construction)

BAA PLC
130 Wilton Road
London SW1V 1LQ, England
Tel.: [44] (171) 834 9449
Fax: [44] (171) 932 6699
(Airport operations)

Bass PLC
20 North Audley Street, London
London W1Y 1WE, England
Tel.: [44] (171) 409 1919
Fax: [44] (171) 409 8503
(Pub, hotel, and restaurant operation)

BET PLC
Stratton House, Piccadilly
London W1X 6AS, England
Tel.: [44] (171) 629 8886
Fax: [44] (171) 499 5118
(Distribution services)

British Airways PLC
Speedbird House, Hounslow
Middlesex TW6 2JA, England
Tel.: [44] (181) 759 5511
Fax: [44] (181) 897 2157
(Airline)

British Railways Board
Euston House
P.O. Box 100
London NW1 1DZ, England
Tel.: [44] (171) 928 5151
Fax: [44] (171) 922 6545
(Railway services)

British Telecommunications PLC
BT Centre, 81 Newgate Street
London EC1A 7AJ, England
Tel.: [44] (171) 356 5000
Fax: [44] (171) 3565520
(Telecommunication services)

Costain Group PLC
111 Westminster Bridge Road
London SE1 7UE, England
Tel.: [44] (171) 705 8444
Fax: [44] (171) 705 8599
(Engineering and construction)

Delta PLC
1 Kingsway
London WC2B 6XF, England
Tel.: [44] (171) 836 3535

Dowty Group PLC
Arle Court, Cheltenham
Gloucestershire GL51 0TP, England
Tel.: [44] (242) 221 133
(High-technology engineering)

Hawker Siddeley Industries Ltd.
Silvertown House
London SW1P 2PL, England
Tel.: [44] (171) 834 3848
Fax: [44] (171) 834 3879
(Machine tools)
Hawker Siddeley Management Ltd.

Inchcape PLC
33 Cavendish Square, London
London W1M 9HF, England
Tel.: [44] (171) 546 0022
Fax: [44] (171) 321 0604
(International marketing and distribution)

Johnson Matthey PLC
2-4 Cockspur Street, Trafalgar Square
London SW1Y 5BQ, England
Tel.: [44] (171) 269 8400
Fax: [44] (171) 269 8433
(Materials technology)

Ladbroke Group PLC
Maple Court, Watford
Hertfordshire WD1 1HZ, England
Tel.: [44] (1923) 434 000
Fax: [44] (1923) 434 001
(Casinos, hotels)

John Laing PLC
133-39 Page Street, Mill Hill
London NW7 2ER, England
Tel.: [44] (181) 959 3636
Fax: [44] (181) 906 5297
(Engineering and construction)

LEP Group PLC
LEP House, 87 East Street
Epsom, Surrey KT17 1DT, England
Tel.: [44] (372) 729 595
(Freight forwarding)

London Regional Transport
Albany House, 55 Broadway
London SW1H 0BD, England
Tel.: [44] (171) 222 1234
Fax: [44] (171) 222 5719
(Public transportation)

Manpower Holdings PLC
International House, London
London W1M 1PR, England
Tel.: [44] (171) 224 6688
Fax: [44] (171) 224 5267
(Staff recruitment services)

John Mowlem & Co. PLC
White Lion Court, Swan Street
Isleworth, Middlesex TW7 6RN, England

Tel.: [44] (181) 568 9111
Fax: [44] (181) 847 4802
(Engineering and construction)

NFC PLC
The Merton Centre, 45 St. Peters Street
Bedford MK40 2UB, England
Tel.: [44] (1234) 272 222
Fax: [44] (1234) 270 900
(Transport, home services, distribution
and travel)
NFC Holdings Ltd.

Nokia UK Ltd.
Lancaster House
Huntingden, Cambridgeshire PE18 6XU
Tel.: (1480) 434 444
Fax: (1480) 432 300
(Electrical appliances)

Ocean Group PLC
Ocean House, Bracknell
Berkshire RG12 1N, England
Tel.: [44] (1344) 302 000
Fax: [44] (1344) 710 031
(Freight management)

**The Peninsular & Oriental Steam
Navigation Co.**
79 Pall Mall
London SW1Y 5EJ, England
Tel.: [44] (171) 930 4343
Fax: [44] (171) 908572
(Shipping, construction)

The Post Office
Royal Mail House
London EC1V 9HQ, England
Tel.: [44] (171) 490 2888
Fax: [44] (171) 250 2632
(Postal services)

Reuters Holdings PLC
85 Fleet Street
London EC4P 4AJ, England
Tel.: [44] (171) 250 1122

Fax: [44] (171) 542 5896
(News and business information services)

Severn Trent PLC
2297 Coventry Road
West Midlands B26 3JZ, England
Tel.: [44] (1217) 224 000
Fax: [44] (1217) 224 800
(Water and waste treatment)

Tarmac PLC
Hilton Hall, Essington
Wolverhampton, Westmidlands WV11
2BQ, England
Tel.: [44] (1902) 307 407
Fax: [44] (1902) 307 408
(Engineering and construction)

**Trafalgar House Balfour Beatty Joint
Venture**
M1-A1 Link Road, Leeds
West Yorkshire LS15 9JJ, England
Tel.: [44] (113) 204 4000
Fax: [44] (113) 204 4001
(Engineering and construction; hotel
operations)

Transport Development Group PLC
Windsor House, 50 Victoria Street
London SW1H 0NR, England
Tel.: [44] (171) 222 7411
Fax: [44] (171) 222 2806
(Storage, packing, and distribution)

Trusthouse Fort PLC
166 High Holborn
London WC1V 6TT, England
Tel.: [44] (171) 836 7744
(Hotels and catering)

George Wimpey PLC
26-28 Hammersmith Grove
London W6 7EN, England
Tel.: [44] (181) 748 2000
Fax: [44] (181) 748 0076
(Engineering and construction services)

AMERICAN COMPANIES IN NORTHERN IRELAND

Hewlett-Packard Ireland Ltd.
Temple House, Temple Road
Blackrock, Northern Ireland
Tel.: [44] (1) 88 3399
Fax: [44] (1) 88 3742
(Computer systems and software)
Hewlett-Packard Co.

Invercon Papermills Ltd.
P.O. Box 4, Larne
Antrim BT40 1HT, Northern Ireland
Tel.: [44] (574) 260323
Fax: [44] (574) 260324
James River Corp.

Lee Apparel Ltd.
16 Comber Road Newtownards
County Down BT23 4HY, Northern
Ireland
Tel.: [44] (247) 819000
Fax: [44] (247) 819845
(Clothing)
V.F. Corp.

United Technologies Corp. Ltd.
Londonderry, Northern Ireland
Tel.: [44] (504) 251 581

(Electrical systems and motors)
United Technologies Corp.

VF Corp Ltd.
16 Comber Road, Newtownards
Down County BT23 4HY, Northern
Ireland
Tel.: [44] (1247) 800 200
Fax: [44] (1247) 819 845
Lee Bell Inc.

EUROPEAN COMPANIES IN NORTHERN IRELAND

European Components Co. Ltd.
770 Upper Newtownrds Road
Belfast BT16 OUL, Northern Ireland
Tel.: [44] (1232) 480 595
Fax: [44] (1232) 480 786
(Textiles)

**Harland & Wolff Shipbuilding & Heavy
Ind. Ltd.**
Queen's Island, Belfast BT3 9DU
Northern Ireland
Tel.: [44] (1232) 458 456
Fax: [44] (1232) 458 515

Hoechst Fibre Industries U.K. Ltd.
P.O. Box LTS/1, Limavady
Londonderry BT49 0JT, Northern Ireland
Tel.: [44] (5047) 629 11
Fax: [44] (5047) 661 11
(Pharmaceuticals)
Hoechst AG, Germany

James Maxton & Co.
Queen's Road
Belfast BT3 9DT, Northern Ireland
Tel.: [44] (1232) 458 238

Fax: [44] (1232) 456 428
(Shipping and offshore platform services)
Det Norske Veritas, Germany

Northern Telecom
Doagh Road
Newtownabbey, Antrim County BT36
6XA, Northern Ireland
Tel.: [44] (1232) 365 111
Fax: [44] (1232) 635 285
(Telephones)
Nortel Ltd.

**Thomson Corporation—Belfast
Telegraph Newspapers Ltd.**
124 Royal Avenue
Belfast BT1 1EB, Northern Ireland
Tel.: [44] (1232) 321242
(Publishing)

Ulster Bank Ltd.
P.O. Box 232, 47 Donegall Place
Belfast BT1 5AU, Northern Ireland
Tel.: [44] (232) 244744
Fax: [44] (1232) 898587
(Commercial bank)

AMERICAN COMPANIES IN SCOTLAND

BANKING AND FINANCE

Cigna Insurance Co. of Europe, SA/NV
Crusader House, Cartsdyke Avenue
Cartsburn East
Greenock, Strathclyde PA15 1DT,
Scotland

Tel.: [44] (131) 892 224
Fax: [44] (131) 248 94
(Insurance)
Cigna Worldwide Inc.

INDUSTRIAL MANUFACTURING

ARCO British Ltd.
Greenbank Road, East
Tullos Industrial Estate
Aberdeen AB1 4BP, Scotland
Tel.: [44] (224) 873143
Fax: [44] (224) 878 8653
(Petroleum production)
Atlantic Richfield Co.

Compaq Computer Manufacturing Ltd.
Erskine Ferry Road, Bishopton
Renfrewshire PA7 5PP, Scotland
Tel.: [44] (141) 814 800
Fax: [44] (141) 812 7745
(Business and personal computers)
Compaq Computer Corp.

Digital Equipment Scotland Ltd.
Masshill Industrial Estate
Ayr, Ayrshire PA6 6BE, Scotland
Tel.: [44] (1292) 266 955
Fax: [44] (1292) 883 198
(Computers and software)
Digital Equipment Corp.

Ethicon Ltd.
P.O. Box 408, Bankhead Avenue
Edinburgh, Midlothian EH11 4HE,
Scotland
Tel.: [44] (131) 453 5555
Fax: [44] (131) 453 6011
(Medical supplies)
Johnson & Johnson

Kodak Ltd.
24 Hanover Street
Edinburgh EH2 2EN, Scotland
Tel.: [44] (131) 225 4525
(Photographic equipment)
Eastman Kodak Co.

Motorola Ltd.
Colvilles Road
Glasgow G75 0TG, Scotland
Tel.: [44] (41) 391 01
Fax: [44] (41) 345 82
(Semiconductors)
Motorola Inc.

NCR (Mfg.) Ltd.
Kingsway West
Dundee, Angus DD2 3XX, Scotland
Tel.: [44] (1382) 611 511
Fax: [44] (1382) 622 722
(Office equipment)
NCR Corp.

Polaroid (U.K.) Ltd.
Vale of Leven Industrial Estates
Dumbarton G82 3PW, Scotland
Tel.: [44] (1382) 54141
Fax: [44] (1382) 55101
(Photographic equipment)
Polaroid Corp.

Rockwell Assemblies Ltd.
Kelvin Industrial Estate, Singer Road
Glasgow, Strathclyde G75 0YE, Scotland
Tel.: [44] (41) 3552 49100
Fax: [44] (41) 3553 63557
(Industrial equipment and machinery)
Rockwell International Corp.

Scotts Porage Oats, A&R Scott
Uthrogle Mill, Cupar
Fife KY15 4PA, Scotland
Tel.: [44] 334 52961
Fax: [44] 334 56307
(Cereal products)
Quaker Oats Co.

RETAILING AND WHOLESALING

General Dynamics International Corp.
Scotland Field Support Office
Holly Loch, Scotland

(Aircraft and other military equipment)
General Dynamics Corp.

SERVICE INDUSTRIES

Datastream International
Miller House, 18/20 George Street
Edinburgh EH2 2PF, Scotland
Tel.: [44] (131) 220 2301
Fax: [44] (131) 220 2727
(Business information services)
The Dun & Bradstreet Corp.

Kelly Temporary Services Ltd.
Pacific House, 4 Cadogen Street
Glasgow, Lanarkshir G2 6VA, Scotland
Tel.: [44] (141) 204 1551
(Temporary labor)
Kelly Services Inc.

Ogilvy & Mather (Scotland) Ltd.
Sutherland House, 108-114 Dundas Street
Edinburgh, Midlothian EH3 5DQ,
Scotland

Tel.: [44] (131) 557 0987
(Advertising)
Ogilvy Group Inc.

EUROPEAN COMPANIES IN SCOTLAND

BANKING AND FINANCE

Bank of Scotland
The Mound, Edinburgh
Midlothian EH1 1YZ, Scotland
Tel.: [44] (131) 442-7777
Fax: [44] (131) 243-5437
(Bank)

Grampian Holdings
Stag House, Castlebank Street
Glasgow, Lanarkshire G11 6DY, Scotland
Tel.: [44] (141) 357 2000

Fax: [44] (141) 334 8709
(Industrial holding co.)

Royal Bank of Scotland PLC
42 St. Andrew Square
Edinburgh, Midlothian EH2 2YE,
Scotland
Tel.: [44] (131) 556 8555
Fax: [44] (131) 557 6140
(Bank)

INDUSTRIAL MANUFACTURING

ABB Vetco Gray UK LTD
Broadfold Road, Aberdeen
Aberdeenshire AB23 8EY, Scotland
Tel.: [44] (122) 485 2000
Fax: [44] (122) 485 2427
(Oil & gas machinery)
ABB Holdings Co.

Alcan Metal Centres (Northern) Ltd.
24 Baronald Street
Rutherglen, Glasgow G73 1PH, Scotland
Tel.: [44] (41) 647 9317
Fax: [44] (41) 647 4765
(Aluminum products)
Alcan Aluminium Ltd.

Brown & Root Highlands Fabricators LTD
P.O. Box 4, Tain
Rossshire IV19 1QY, Scotland
Tel.: [44] (186) 285422
Fax: [44] (186) 285422
(Gas & oil machinery)

Ciba-Geigy Pigments
Hawkhead Road
Paisley PA2 7BG, Scotland
Tel.: [44] 887 1144
Fax: [44] 887 1663
(Chemicals and dyes)
Ciba Geigy Ltd.

Elf Enterprise Caledonia LTD
1 Claymore Drive, Aberdeen
Aberdeenshire AB23 8GB, Scotland

Tel.: [44] (122) 425 5500
Fax: [44] (122) 423 3838
(Petroleum)

Harper Collins Publishers Ltd.
Westerhill Road, Bishopbriggs
Glasgow G64 2QT, Scotland
Tel.: [44] (141) 772 3200
Fax: [44] (141) 306 3119
(Publishing)

Highland Distilleries Co. PLC
106 West Nile Street
Glasgow G1 2QY, Scotland
Tel.: [44] (141) 332 7511
(Whisky distilling)

Modern Structural Plastics Ltd.
1.9 Telford Road
Cumbernauld, Strathclyde G67 2AX,
Scotland
Tel.: [44] (23) 67 29595
(Industrial plastics)
Electrolux AB

Scottish & Newcastle Breweries PLC
Abbey Brewery, Holyrood Road
Edinburgh, Midlothian EH8 8YS,
Scotland
Tel.: [44] (131) 556 2591
Fax: [44] (131) 556 4665
(Alcoholic beverages)

RETAILING AND WHOLESALING

William Grant & Sons Distillers Ltd.
Strathclyde Business Park, Motherwell
Lanarkshire ML4 3AN, Scotland
Tel.: [44] (169) 884 3843
Fax: [44] (169) 884 4788
(Liquors)

John Menzies PLC
Hannover Buildings, Edinburgh
Midlothian EH2 2YQ, Scotland
Tel.: [44] (131) 225 8555
Fax: [44] (131) 226 3752
(Publishing, confectionery, toys, and
learning centers)
Russel Corp. UK Ltd.

Russel Corp. UK Limited
1 Dunlap Square, Livingston
West Lothian EH54 85B, Scotland

Tel.: [44] (150) 641 9444
Fax: [44] (150) 641 9494
(Furnishings)

Scotsman Publications Ltd.
P.O. Box 56
Midlothian EH1 1YT, Scotland
Tel.: [44] (131) 225 2468
Fax: [44] (131) 225 5473
(Newspapers)
Boston Holdings Ltd.

Uniroyal Englebert Tyres Ltd.
Newbridge, Midlothian EH28 8LG
Scotland
Tel.: [44] (131) 333 2700
Fax: [44] (131) 333 4668
(Tires)
Continental Tyre Group Ltd.

SERVICE INDUSTRIES

ABB Wylex Production and Development Ltd.
57/58 Nasmyth Road
South Field Industrial Estate
Glenrothes, Scotland
Tel.: [44] (592) 774 002
Fax: [44] (592) 630 627
(Engineering and construction)
ABB Asea Brown Boveri (Holdings) Ltd.

Det Norske Veritas
Magnet House, 59 Waterloo Street
Glasgow G2 7BP, Scotland
Tel.: [44] (41) 221 4802
Fax: [44] (41) 221 3365
(Shipping and offshore platform services)
Det Norske Veritas

Kvaerner Energy Ltd.
Glasgow Road, Clydebank
Dunbartonshire G81 1YA, Scotland

Tel.: [44] (141) 952 2030
Fax: [44] (141) 307 8896
(Engineering)
Kvaerner John Brown Holdings PLC

National Australia Group Services Ltd.
350 Vincent Place, Glasgow
Lanarkshire G1 2HL, Scotland
Tel.: [44] (141) 223 2041
Fax: [44] (141) 223 2123
(Business services)

Todd & Duncan Ltd.
Lochleven Mills, Kinross
Kinrossshire KY13 7DH, Scotland
Tel.: [44] (157) 786 3521
Fax: [44] (157) 786 4533
(Fabric mills)

AMERICAN COMPANIES IN WALES

INDUSTRIAL MANUFACTURING

Alcoa Manufacturing (GB) Ltd.
P.O. Box 68, Waunarlwydd Works
Swansea, West Glamorgan SA1 1XH,
Wales
Tel.: [44] (792) 873301
(Aluminum products)
Aluminum Company of America

Cyanamid Aerospace Products Ltd.
Abenbury Way, Wrexham Industrial Estate
Wrexham, Clwyd LL13 9UF, Wales
Tel.: [44] (978) 61971
(Aerospace products)
American Cyanamid Co.

Dow Corning Ltd.
5 Barry Plant, Barry
South Glamorgan CF63 2YL, Wales
Tel.: [44] (144) 673 2350
Fax: [44] (144) 674 7944
(Chemicals)
Dow Corning Corp.

Fram Europe Ltd.
Llantrisang, Pontyclun
Mid Glamorgan CF7 8YU, Wales
Tel.: [44] (443) 22 3000
Fax: [44] (443) 22 5459
(Automotive filters)
Allied-Signal Inc.

Hoover Ltd.
Dragonparc, Merthyr Tydfil
Mid. Glamorgan CF48 1PQ, Wales
Tel.: [44] (1685) 721 222

Fax: [44] (1685) 382 946
(Home appliances)
Hoover Corp.

James River Corp.—Wrexham Plant
Wrexham Industrial Estate, Bridge Road
Wrexham, Clwyd LL20 8AE, Wales
Tel.: [44] (978) 661 541
Fax: [44] (978) 661 541 33
(Paper products)
James River Corp.

Owen-Corning Fiberglass G.B. Ltd.
Bryn Lane, Wrexham Clwyd LL13 9JU
Wales
Tel.: [44] (1978) 661 51
Fax: [44] (1978) 660 382
(Fiberglass products)
IPM Inc.

EUROPEAN COMPANIES IN WALES

Allied Steel & Wire Ltd.
P.O. Box 83, Cardiff
South Glamorgan CF1 5XQ, Wales
Tel.: [44] (122) 247 1333
Fax: [44] (122) 258 2001
(Steel manufacturing)
ASW Holdings

Det Norske Veritas
Cremona House, 2 Lon Ucha
Cardiff, South Glamorgan CF4 6HL,
Wales
Tel.: [44] (836) 74 1936
(Shipping and offshore platform services)
Det Norske Veritas

Kwik Save Group PLC
Warren Drive, Prestatyn
Clwyd LL19 7HU, Wales
Tel.: [44] (174) 588 7111
Fax: [44] (174) 588 2302
(Food retailing)
Kwik Save Group PLC

Matsushita Electric Ltd.
Wyncliffe Road, Cardiff
S. Glamorgan CF2 7XB, Wales
Tel.: [44] (122) 254 0011
Fax: [44] (122) 254 0041
(Video equipment)
Matsushita Electric Industrial Co., Ltd.

Pirelli General PLC
Harriet Street,
P.O. Box 1
Mid Glamorgan CF44 7EN, Wales
Tel.: [44] (685) 87 0170
Fax: [44] (685) 87 7071
(Tires)
Pirelli SpA

Rowan Foods Ltd.
Ash Road South
Wrexham, Clwyd LL13 9UG, Wales
Tel.: [44] (197) 866 1966
Fax: [44] (197) 866 1856
(Frozen specialties)
Hazelwood Frozen Products Ltd.

South Wales Electricity PLC
Newport Road, Cardiff
S. Glamorgan CF3 9XW, Wales
Tel.: [44] (122) 279 2111
Fax: [44] (122) 277 7759
(Electric services)
Hyder PLC

Wallace Evans Ltd.
Plymouth House, Penarth
S. Glamorgan CF64 3YF, Wales
Tel.: [44] (122) 270 4321
Fax: [44] (122) 270 9793
(Engineering services)

INTERNATIONAL NON-PROFIT EMPLOYERS IN THE UNITED KINGDOM

Amnesty International
1 Easton Street
London WC1X 8DJ, England
Tel.: [44] (171) 413 5500

Friends of the Earth
26-28 Underwood Street
London N1 7JQ, England
Tel.: [44] (171) 490 1555

**International Headquarters of the
Salvation Army**
c/o Gen. Eva Burrows
101 Queen Victoria Street
P.O. Box 249
London EC4 4EP, England
Tel.: [44] (171) 236 5222

International Youth Hostel Federation
9 Guessens Road
Welwyn Garden City
Herstford AL8 6QW, England
Tel.: [44] (707) 324 170

Oxfam
274 Banbury Road
Oxford OX2 7DZ, England
Tel.: [44] (865) 311 311

Royal Society for the Arts
8 John Adam Street
London WC2N 6EZ, England
Tel.: [44] (171) 930 5115

INTERNATIONAL SCHOOLS IN THE UNITED KINGDOM

**American Community School
"Heywood"**
Portsmouth Road
Cobham, Surrey KT11 1BL, England
Tel.: [44] (1932) 869 744
Fax: [44] (1932) 869 789
Email: trouillard@acs-england.co.uk
www.acs-england.co.uk
(U.S./International Baccalaureate
curriculum, pre-K-13)

The American School in London
2-8 Loudoun Road
London NW8 0NP, England
Tel.: [44] (171) 449 1200
Fax: [44] (171) 449 1350
Email: admission@asl.org

TASIS England American School
Coldharbour Lane
Thorpe, Surrey TW20 8TE, England
Tel.: [44] (1932) 565 252
Fax: [44] (1932) 564 644
Email: ukadmissions@tasis.com
(U.S. school, pre-K-12)

United World College of the Atlantic
St. Donat's Castle
Llantwit Major
South Glamorgan, Wales
Tel.: [44] (446) 792 530
Fax: [44] (446) 794 163
Email: atlantic@rmplc.co.uk
(I.B. curriculum)

Republic of Ireland

twelve

MAJOR EMPLOYMENT CENTER: Dublin

MAJOR BUSINESS LANGUAGE: English

LANGUAGE SKILL INDEX: Plan to speak English; Gaelic is not used in the business place

CURRENCY: Euro; the Irish pound (punt) will remain the currency in circulation until 2002

TELEPHONE COUNTRY CODE: 353

TIME ZONE: EST+5

PUNCTUALITY INDEX: Attitudes toward punctuality are flexible, so you should schedule business meetings accordingly

AVERAGE DAILY TEMPERATURE, HIGH/LOW: January, 47/35°F; July, 67/51°F (Dublin)

AVERAGE NUMBER OF DAYS WITH RAIN: January, 18; July, 14

BEST BET FOR EMPLOYMENT:

  FOR STUDENTS: CIEE in Dublin

  PERMANENT JOBS: High-tech industry

CHANCE OF FINDING A JOB: Poor country, great scenery, few jobs

TRIVIA: Ireland may be the best country in the world for hitchhiking

reland, or Eire, approximately the size of West Virginia, is across the Irish Sea from Britain in northwestern Europe. The country covers about 83% of the island that bears its name and encompasses several low mountain ridges near the coasts, surrounding a low-lying interior. In the fourth century B.C. the Celts arrived and assimilated the local peoples, the Picts and the Erainn, to establish a Gaelic civilization. By the fifth century A.D., Gaelic culture had spread to Scotland and elsewhere and St. Patrick had largely converted the country to Christianity. Norse invaders were defeated in 1014. Over 95% of the population is Catholic and about 5% Protestant. Gaelic is spoken in the northwestern parts of the country, although virtually everyone speaks English as well.

In the twelfth century, England received Ireland as a papal fief as Henry II began the English invasions. In 1801 Britain and Ireland became the United Kingdom of Great Britain and Ireland. A devastating famine and economic decline in the late nineteenth century eventually led to independence efforts. An unsuccessful rebellion in 1916 led to civil war until 1921, when the major part of Ireland received dominion status. Britain maintained Ulster as Northern Ireland. In 1949 the Irish Free State declared itself the Republic of Ireland and withdrew from the British Commonwealth. Ireland is a member of the European Union and the United Nations.

Ireland has a parliamentary system of government. The prime minister, currently Bertie Ahern, is officially known in Gaelic as *Taoiseach* (pronounced "tea shock"). The president of Ireland is elected for seven years. The current president is Mary McAleese, replacing Mary Robinson, president from 1991-1997, who is now the U.N. High Commissioner on Human Rights. The main political parties are Fianna Fáil and Fine Gael. The Labour Party has gained some popular support because of voters' disenchantment with the major parties. The Liberal Progressive Democrats and the socialist Democratic Left are also important political players.

Offices are usually open Monday-Friday from 9 a.m. to 5 p.m. On Thursday or Friday, many shops will stay open late.

Current Economic Climate

Ireland, with a population of only 3.66 million, has a small but highly open economy. It has had the most rapidly expanding economy in the industrialized world. Ireland's growth and per capita income now surpass that of Britain. The healthy state of the economy means that Ireland is now well prepared to take part as a founding member of the European single currency. It has a low inflation rate (about 2.2%) and the unemployment rate, now at 9%, is expected to decrease over the next few years. Ireland is second only to the U.S. in the export of computer software, and information technology is now contributing more to economic growth than agriculture.

Ireland's literary perq

The Irish are very proud of their literary tradition. Ireland has produced many important writers including Oscar Wilde, W. B. Yeates, George Bernard Shaw, Sean O'Casey, James Joyce, Samuel Beckett, and more recently, Roddy Doyle. Ireland is so serious about its literary history that it currently does not tax writers.

IRELAND'S 10 LARGEST COMPANIES
(1997, composite ranking)
1. Jefferson Smurfil Group
2. Allied Irish Banks
3. CRH
4. Aer Lingus
5. Bank of Ireland
6. Waterford Wedgwood
7. Avonmore Foods
8. Kerry Group
9. Fitzwilton
10. Lyons Irish Holdings

Using the phone, fax, and Internet

Public phones in Ireland almost exclusively use phone-cards, available from Telecom Éireann. In September 1998, seven-digit phone numbers were introduced throughout Ireland. A new prefix was placed between the area code and an existing five-digit or six-digit number. Directory assistance for help with these new numbers is "1190."

Faxes can be sent from post offices or other specialist offices. Email cafes are springing up in major cities like Dublin, Dork, and Galway.

Getting Around in Ireland

Since the rail network focuses primarily upon Dublin, buses serve as a convenient alternative in areas not covered by trains. Bus fares may be more expensive. Ferries provide passage across the English Channel and along the English and Irish coastline. Eurail and InterRail passes are accepted throughout Ireland, and pass holders are given various discounts on trains, ferries, and airplanes. Ireland's major airline, Aer Lingus, connects Dublin with London but is more expensive than several available ferry services. Ryan Air also connects Ireland and Britain.

Employment Regulations and Outlook for Americans

Ireland's high unemployment rate increases the difficulty of finding work. Unlike E.U. or U.K. residents, U.S. citizens who wish to work must have a work permit from a prospective employer upon arriving in Ireland. A visa is not required for stays of less than 90 days.

Agricultural work is almost impossible to find because of the high rural unemployment rate. Tourist work in hotels, bars, and restaurants may occasionally be found in Cork and Dublin.

If you are a student, you can bypass the usual employment restrictions by contacting the Council for International Educational Exchange (CIEE) about their Work in Ireland Program, which grants permits allowing American students to work in Ireland for up to four months. The Union of Students in Ireland Travel Service (USIT), which cooperates with the CIEE in administering the program, can be very helpful in finding a job.

CIEE	**USIT**
205 East 42nd Street	19 Aston Quay
New York, NY 10017	O'Connell Bridge
Tel.: (888) COUNCIL	Dublin 2, Ireland
Email: wabrochure@ciee.org	Tel.: [353] (1) 677 8117
www.ciee.org	Fax: [353] (1) 677 8098

Short-term and Temporary Work

A good bet for casual work in Ireland is to work as an au pair. There are also ample opportunities to work in pubs or hotels, especially in tourist centers such as Dublin, but these employers require you to apply in person. USIT (see above) can be most helpful with this work.

Job Options Bureau (Irish representative of the International Au Pair Association)	**Langtrain International**
Tourist House	Torquay Road
40-41 Grand Parade	Foxrock
Cork, Ireland	Dublin 18, Ireland
Tel.: [353] (21) 27 39 06	Tel.: [353] (1) 289 3876
	English teaching center and an au pair placement agency.

Internship Programs

Several professional internship programs offer students opportunities to obtain professional experience. Some programs, such as Dublin Internships, also offer an opportunity to earn academic credit.

Dublin Internships
8 Orlagh Lawn
Scholarstown Road
Dublin 16, Ireland
Tel./Fax: [353] (1) 494 5277
Places students in internships from all majors. Positions are generally full-time and non-salaried; students get credit through their home institutions.

IASTE-US
10400 Little Patuxent Parkway, Suite 250 L
Columbia, MD 21044-3510
Tel.: (410) 997-3068
Fax: (410) 997-5186

Email: iaeste@aipt.org
www.aipt.org/iaste.html
Arranges reciprocal internships in 63 different countries. Specifically for students in technical fields.

Internships in Dublin
Office of International Programs
Box 2000
SUNY Cortland
Cortland, NY 13045
Tel.: (607) 753-2209
Fax: (607) 753-5989
www.cortland.edu/html/ipgms.html
Internships in public administration, government, or political science.

Volunteer Opportunities

International Voluntary Service (IVS) maintains 19 workcamps for 148 volunteers to work with the physically and mentally handicapped, in community centers and children's camps, and doing gardening and clearing. Comhchairdeas is a workcamp network centered in Ireland's poorer districts that involves volunteers in construction and conservation programs designed to further community development. Volunteers for Peace offers three workcamps concentrating upon international understanding and peace issues and includes 20 Americans each time.

Comhchairdeas
c/o Council on International Educational Exchange
205 East 42nd Street
New York, NY 10017
Tel.: (888) COUNCIL
Email: ivpdirectory@ciee.org
www.ciee.org

Conservation Volunteers Ireland
P.O. Box 3836
Ballsbridge
Dublin 4, Ireland
Tel.: [353] (1) 668 1844
Unpaid environmental working holidays.

International Voluntary Service
SCI-USA
Route 2, Box 506

Crozet, VA 22932
Tel.: (804) 823-1826

Irish Youth Hostel Association
61 Mountjoy Street
Dublin 1, Ireland
Tel.: [353] (1) 830 4555
Places people into voluntary work with hostels.

Volunteers for Peace
International Workcamps
43 Tiffany Road
Belmont, VT 05730
Tel.: (802) 259-2759
Fax: (802) 259-2922
Email: VFP@VFP.prg
www.vfp.org

NEWSPAPERS IN IRELAND

Irish Independent
Independent House
90 Middle Abbey Street
Dublin 1, Ireland
Tel.: [353] (1) 873 13 33
Fax: [353] (1) 873 17 87

The Irish Press
Parnell House, Parnell Square

Dublin 1, Ireland
Tel.: [353] (1) 871 33 33
Fax: [353] (1) 874 68 68

The Irish Times
10-16 D'Olier Street
Dublin 2, Ireland
Tel.: [353] (1) 679 20 22
Fax: [353] (1) 679 39 10

Resources for Further Information

USEFUL WEBSITES FOR JOB SEARCHERS

The Internet is a good place to begin your job search. Many Irish employers list job vacancies, especially those in technical fields, on the World Wide Web. There are also many websites that provide useful information for job searchers researching the Irish job market.

Corporate Skills Ltd.
www.corporateskills.com
Ireland's biggest computer jobs agency; good resource for technical job seekers.

Infolive
www.infolive.ie/
Excellent resource; gives tourist work permit information; offers links to job search pages; probably a good starting place for the job search.

Irish Jobs
www.exp.ie/
Page for recruiters and job seekers to contact each other; excellent resource for all types of job seekers.

The Skills Group Recruiting Consultancy
www.skillsgroup.ie/
Finds jobs for those with training in engineering, business, etc.

EMBASSIES AND CONSULAR OFFICES

American embassies and consulates have commercial and/or economic sections that can provide you with business information and explain aspects of the local economy. Inquiries about business opportunities should be addressed either to "Commercial Officer" or "Commercial Section," followed by the appropriate street address.

Representation of Ireland in the United States

Embassy of Ireland
2234 Massachusetts Avenue NW
Washington, DC 20008
Tel.: (202) 462-3939
Fax: (202) 232-5993

Irish Consulates General: Boston, (617) 267-9330; Chicago, (312) 337-1868; New York, (212) 319-2555; San Francisco, (415) 392-4214

Representation of the United States in Ireland

American Embassy
42 Elgin Road, Ballsbridge
Dublin, Ireland

Tel.: [353] (1) 668 8777
Fax: [353] (1) 668 9946
www.indigo.ie/usembassy-usis/

CHAMBERS OF COMMERCE

Chambers of commerce consist of firms in both countries interested in international trade. These are appropriate companies to initially target in the job search.

Chamber of Commerce of Ireland
22 Merrion Square
Dublin 2, Ireland
Tel.: [353] (1) 661 2888
Fax: [353] (1) 661 2811
Email: chambers@iol.ie

U.S. Chamber of Commerce in Ireland
20 College Green

Dublin 2, Ireland
Tel.: [353] (1) 793 733

Ireland Chamber of Commerce in the US
1305 Post Road, Suite 205
Fairfield, CT 06430
Tel.: (203) 255-1630
www.iccusa.org

OTHER INFORMATIONAL ORGANIZATIONS

Foreign government missions in the U.S. such as the Irish Tourist Board can furnish visas and information on work permits and other important regulations. They may also offer economic and business information about the country.

Ireland-U.S. Council
460 Park Avenue, 22nd Floor
New York, NY 10022-1906
Tel.: (212) 751-2660
Fax: (212) 751-8951

Irish Tourist Board
345 Park Ave.
New York, NY 10154

Tel.: (212) 418-0800
Fax: (212) 371-9059

Irish Tourist Board
Baggot St. Bridge
Dublin 2, Ireland
Tel.: [353] (1) 765 871
www.visit.ie/dublin

BUSINESS DIRECTORIES

Although not always easy to find, business directories can prove invaluable in the international job search. Most directories list company names, addresses, products, and phone numbers. Some directories include executive names and titles and financial information about the company. These sources provide you with the names of the people to contact for employment information as well as financial data, which can tell you how strong a company's position in a country may be.

American Business Directory. Published annually by the U.S. Chamber of Commerce in Ireland, 20 College Green, Dublin 2, Ireland; email: amcham@iol.ie. Lists the 350 members of the U.S. Chamber of Commerce in Ireland as well as U.S.-related businesses in Ireland.

Directory of Foreign Firms Operating Abroad: Ireland. World Trade Academy Press, 257 Central Park West, Suite 10A, New York, NY 10024-4110; email: uniworldbp@aol.com; www.uniworldbp.com. Lists names and addresses of parent companies in the U.S. and their subsidiaries and affiliates in Ireland.

Ireland: A Directory. Published annually by the Institute of Public Administration, 57-61 Lansdowne Road, Dublin 4, Ireland. Includes 2,000 major firms, government agencies, various associations, and media organizations.

Ireland's Top Companies. Belenos Publications Ltd., 50 Fitzwilliam Square, Dublin 2, Ireland; email: belenos@tinet.ie. Lists top 1,000 business and finance firms.

Irish Financial Services Directory. Kompass Register of Irish Industry and Commerce, Parnell Court, Granby Row, Dublin 1, Ireland; email: info@kompass.ie; www.kompass.ie. Lists top financial services firms.

Kompass Ireland. Published annually by Kompass Register of Irish Industry and Commerce, Parnell Court, Granby Row, Dublin 1, Ireland; email: info@kompass.ie; www.kompass.ie. Lists 20,000 manufacturing and industrial companies in Ireland.

Overseas Companies in Ireland. A continuously updated computer printout published by the Industrial Development Authority of Ireland, Wilton Park House, Wilton Place, Dublin 2, Ireland. Covers 1,000 international firms with operations in Ireland.

Thom's Commercial Directory. Published annually by Thom's Directories, 38 Merrion Square, Dublin 2, Ireland. Lists 93,000 manufacturers, service companies, government agencies, banks, trade unions, and company executives.

Who Owns Whom: United Kingdom and Republic of Ireland. Available annually from Dun & Bradstreet Ltd., Holmers Farm Way, High Wycombe, Buckinghamshire HP12 4UL, England. Lists 15,000 British and Irish parent companies and 155,000 domestic and foreign subsidiaries. Available in the U.S. from Dun & Bradstreet Information Services, 3 Sylvan Way, Parsippany, NJ, 07054.

AMERICAN COMPANIES IN IRELAND

Many American firms operate in Ireland. The following companies are classified by business area: Banking and Finance; Industrial Manufacturing; Retailing and Wholesaling; and Service Industries. Company information includes firm name, address, phone and fax numbers, specific business, and American parent company. Your chances of achieving employment abroad are substantially better if you contact the subsidiary company in Europe rather than the parent company in the U.S. Most major enterprises in Ireland are foreign rather than domestic—hence the limited number of Irish companies listed below.

BANKING AND FINANCE

Chase Manhattan Bank (Ireland) PLC
La Touche House EFSC
Custom House Docks (1)
Dublin, Ireland

Tel.: [353] (1) 790 31 11
Fax: [353] (1) 790 31 23
(Commercial and investment bank)

INDUSTRIAL MANUFACTURING

Abbott Ireland Ltd.
Ballytivnan, Sligo, Ireland
Tel.: [353] (71) 45271
Fax.: [353] (71) 556 01
(Pharmaceuticals and nutritional formulas)
Abbott Laboratories

Analog Devices BV
Raheen Industrial
Raheen, Limerick, Ireland
Tel.: [353] (61) 22 90 11
Fax: [353] (61) 30 84 48
(Semiconductors)
Analog Devices Inc.

Amdahl Ireland Ltd.
Balheary, Swords
Dublin, Ireland
Tel.: [353] (1) 840 3001
Fax: [353] (1) 840 3776
(Computers)
Amdahl International Corp.

Apple Computer Ltd.
Hollyhill Industrial Estate
Hollyhill, Cork, Ireland
Tel.: [353] (21) 28 40 00
Fax: [353] (21) 39 22 20
(Personal computers)
Apple Computer Inc.

Bausch & Lomb Ireland
Waterford Industrial Estates
Waterford, Ireland
Tel.: [353] (51) 55 001
Fax: [353] (51) 35 56 39
(Contact lenses)
Bausch & Lomb Inc.

Borden Co. Ltd.
West End Mallow, Ireland
Tel.: [353] (22) 21327
Fax: [353] (22) 215 31
(Food processing)
Borden Inc.

Braun Ireland Ltd.
Industrial Estate, Dublin Road
Carlow, Ireland
Tel.: [353] (503) 423 01
Fax: [353] (503) 764 05
(Consumer appliances)
Gillette Co.

Coca-Cola Bottlers Ireland
Western Industrial Estate
Nass Road
Dublin 12, Ireland
Tel.: [353] (1) 456 53 77
Fax: [353] (1) 460 21 69
(Soft drinks)
The Coca-Cola Co.

Colgate-Palmolive
Unit C Airport Industrial Estate
Dublin 9, Ireland
Tel.: [353] (1) 842 4711
(Toiletries)
Colgate-Palmolive Corp.

Dataproducts (Dublin)
Clonshaugh Industrial Estate
Coolock, Dublin 17, Ireland
Tel.: [353] (1) 474855
(Printers)
Dataproducts Corp.

Digital Equipment Corp.
Balybrit Industrial Estate
Galway, Ireland
Tel.: [353] (91) 57651
(Data processing equipment)
Digital Equipment Corp.

RETAILING AND WHOLESALING

Becton Dickinson & Co. Ltd.
Pottery Road
Dun Laoghaire, Ireland
Tel.: [353] (1) 285 48 00
Fax: [353] (1) 285 43 32

Fruit of the Loom International Ltd.
Ballymacarry Buncrana, Ireland
Tel.: [353] (77) 62 222
Fax: [353] (77) 623 33
(Clothing)
Fruit of the Loom Inc.

Goblin Ireland Ltd.
Clash Industrial Estate
Tralee, Ireland
Tel.: [353] (66) 21 444
Fax: [353] (66) 214 60
(Industrial vacuum cleaners)
Shop-Vac Corp.

Intel Ireland Ltd.
Collinstown Industrial Park
Leixlup County, Kildare Island, Ireland
Tel.: [353] (1) 606 70 00
Fax: [353] (1) 606 70 70
(Computer software)
Intel Corp.

The Kellog Co. of Ireland, Ltd.
Unit 4, Airways Industrial Estate
Clonshaugh, Dublin 17, Ireland
Tel.: [353] (1) 842 91 00
Fax: [353] (1) 842 99 74
(Breakfast cereals)
Kellog Co.

Microsoft Manufacturing BV
Blackthorn Road
Dublin 18, Ireland
Tel.: [353] (1) 295 38 26
Fax: [353] (1) 295 35 81
(Computer software)
Microsoft Corp.

Pepsi-Cola Manufacturing
Little Island Industrial Estate
Cork, Ireland
Tel.: [353] (21) 353 921
(Soft drinks)
PepsiCo Inc.

Pfizer Pharmaceuticals Production Corp.
Ringaskiddy, Ireland
Tel.: [353] (21) 37 87 01
Fax: [353] (21) 37 83 53
(Pharmaceuticals)
Pfizer Inc.

(Surgical equipment)
Becton Dickinson & Co.

Conoco Ireland Ltd.
Conoco House, Deansgrange

Blackrock,
Dublin, Ireland
Tel.: [353] (1) 289 66 44
Fax: [353] (1) 289 74 38
(Petroleum)
Conoco Inc.

CPC Foods Ireland Ltd.
Goldenbridge, Inchicore
Dublin 12, Ireland
Tel.: [353] (1) 455 76 38
 (Cereals and soups)
CPC International

Esso Ireland Ltd.
Esso House, Stillorgan
Blackrock
Dublin, Ireland
Tel.: [353] (1) 2881 16 61
Fax: [353] (1) 288 73 03
(Petroleum products)
Exxon Corp.

Henry Ford & Son Ltd.
Elm Court, Boreenmanna Road
Cork, Ireland
Tel.: [353] (21) 32 92 77
Fax: [353] (21) 96 26 34
(Motor vehicles)
Ford Motor Co.

General Motors Distribution Ireland Ltd.
Belgard Road, Tallaght
Dublin 24, Ireland
Tel.: [353] (1) 514033

(Motor vehicles)
General Motors Corp.

IBM Ireland Ltd.
2 Burlington Road
Dublin 4, Ireland
Tel.: [353] (1) 660 37 44
Fax: [353] (1) 660 06 38
(Data processing equipment)
IBM World Trade Corp.

Master Foods Ltd.
7/8 Harcourt Street
Dublin 2, Ireland
Tel.: [353] (1) 478 49 55
Fax: [353] (1) 478 36 87
(Confectionery)
Mars Inc.

Rank Xerox (Ireland) Ltd.
Unit 75 Lagan Road
Dublin Industrial Estate
Dublin 11, Ireland
Tel.: [353] (1) 830 18 33
Fax: [353] (1) 830 78 84
(Copier equipment)
Xerox Corp.

Texaco (Ireland) Ltd.
Texaco House, 83 Pembroke Road,
Ballsbridge
Dublin 4, Ireland
Tel.: [353] (1) 558 68 22
Fax: [353] (1) 668 48 90
(Petroleum products)
Texaco Inc.

SERVICE INDUSTRIES

American Express Ireland Ltd.
Temple House, Temple Road
Blackrock, Dublin, Ireland
Tel.: [353] (1) 205 51 11
Fax: [353] (1) 288 34 29
(Travel and financial services)
American Express Co.

Arthur Andersen & Co.
Andersen House
IFS Centre Dublin 1, Ireland
Tel.: [353] (1) 670 10 00
Fax: [353] (1) 670 10 10
(Accounting and management consulting)
Arthur Andersen

Dun & Bradstreet Ltd.
455a Holbrook House, Holles Street
Dublin 2, Ireland
Tel.: [353] (1) 676 42 39
Fax: [353] (1) 678 93 01
(Business information)
The Dun & Bradstreet Corp.

Kelly Temporary Services Ltd.
21/22 Grafton Street
Dublin 2, Ireland
Tel.: [353] (1) 667 931 11
(Temporary labor)
Kelly Services Inc.

EUROPEAN COMPANIES IN IRELAND

BANKING AND FINANCE

Allied Irish Banks PLC
Bankcentre
Dublin 4, Ireland
Tel.: [353] (1) 677 76 23
Fax: [353] (1) 702 52 30
(Bank)

Bank of Ireland
Lower Baggot Street
Dublin 2, Ireland
Tel.: [353] (1) 615 933

Fax: [353] (1) 661 5101
(Bank)

Ulster Bank Ltd.
33 College Green
Dublin 2, Ireland
Tel.: [353] (1) 677 76 23
Fax: [353] (1) 679 79 41
(Bank)

INDUSTRIAL MANUFACTURING

BP Oil Ltd.
BP House
Setanta Place
Dublin 2, Ireland
Tel.: [353] (1) 775 131
(Petroleum products)

Cadbury Ireland PLC
Malahide Road, Coolock
Dublin 5, Ireland
Tel.: [353] (1) 848 00 00
Fax: [353] (1) 847 29 05
(Confectionery)
Cadbury Schweppes PLC

Guinness Ireland Group
St. James Gate
Dublin 8, Ireland
Tel.: [353] (1) 453 67 00
Fax: [353] (1) 453 69 38
(Beverages)

Irish National Petroleum Ltd.
Warrington House, Mount Street Crescent
Dublin 2, Ireland
Tel.: [353] (1) 660 79 66
Fax: [353] (1) 660 79 52
(Petroleum products)

Kerry Group PLC
Princes Street, Tralee
County Kerry, Ireland
Tel.: [353] (66) 224 33
Fax: [353] (66) 223 53
(Food products)

Unilever PLC
Whitehall Road Rathfarnham
Dublin 14, Ireland
Tel.: [353] (1) 298 43 44
Fax: [353] (1) 296 15 98
(Consumer products)
Unilever NV/PLC, Netherlands

RETAILING AND WHOLESALING

Birds Eye Foods Ltd
Whitehall Road
Dublin 14, Ireland
Tel.: [353] (1) 298 41 11
Fax: [353] (1) 298 43 97
(Frozen goods)
Van den Bergh Foods

Irish Shell Ltd.
Shell House
Beech Hill Clonskeagh
Dublin 4, Ireland

Tel.: [353] (1) 202 88 88
Fax: [353] (1) 283 83 18
(Petroleum products)

Nestlé (Ireland) Ltd.
Blessington Road, Tallaght
Dublin 24, Ireland
Tel.: [353] (1) 451 22 44
Fax: [353] (1) 451 28 23
(Food products)

SERVICE INDUSTRIES

Aer Lingus PLC and Aerlinte Eireann PLC
Dublin Airport, Co.
Dublin, Ireland
Tel.: [353] (1) 705 22 22
Fax: [353] (1) 705 38 32
(Air services)

Bell Freight Transport Group Ltd
Bell House
Dublin 2, Ireland
Tel.: [353] (1) 40 26 00

Fax: [353] (1) 405 26 96
(Transportation service)

McInerney Properties PLC
McInerney House
27-28 Herbert Place
Dublin 2, Ireland
Tel.: [353] (1) 661 87 44
Fax: [353] (1) 661 87 54
(Civil engineering and construction)

INTERNATIONAL SCHOOLS IN IRELAND

St. Andrew's College
Booterstown Avenue
Blackrock, Dublin
Ireland
Tel.: [353] (1) 228 27 85

Fax: [353] (1) 283 16 27
(U.S./International Baccalaureate
curriculum, 1-12)

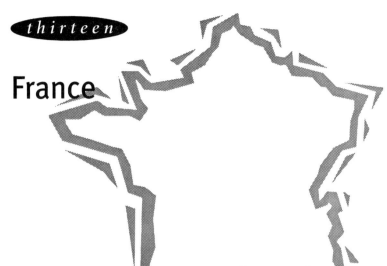

thirteen

France

MAJOR EMPLOYMENT CENTERS: Paris, Marseilles, Lyon, Toulouse

MAJOR BUSINESS LANGUAGE: French

LANGUAGE SKILL INDEX: Absolutely necessary. The French are particularly proud of their language and will generally not respond to inquiries initiated in English. If your French is weak, begin in French and attempt to shift into English later

CURRENCY: Euro; the French franc will remain the currency in circulation until 2002

TELEPHONE COUNTRY CODE: 33

TIME ZONE: EST+6

PUNCTUALITY INDEX: Somewhat lax. Paris is stricter

AVERAGE DAILY TEMPERATURE, HIGH/LOW: January, 42/32°F; July, 76/55°F (Paris)

AVERAGE NUMBER OF DAYS WITH PRECIPITATION: January, 15; July, 12

BEST BET FOR EMPLOYMENT:

FOR STUDENTS: Use CIEE or find agricultural work

PERMANENT JOBS: Computer science + French could = Job

CHANCE OF FINDING A JOB: Good for those with technical expertise and language skills

TRIVIA: Don't look for a job in August; the whole country is on vacation

Threst of the French Republic, larger than California but smaller than Texas, is in western Europe. Shaped like a pentagon, France borders the Bay of Biscay to the west, Spain, Andorra, and the Mediterranean to the south, Italy, Switzerland, and Germany to the east, and the English Channel (La Manche), Belgium, and Luxembourg to the north. The Alps, the Vosges, and the Pyrenees mountains form France's eastern and southern borders. The rest of the country consists of river basins and a large central plateau.

In addition to French, minorities speak German, Flemish, Italian, Breton, Basque, and Catalan. About 80% of the population is Roman Catholic, with significant Protestant and Jewish groups. France maintains an overseas province, French Guyana, in South America and several dependencies in the Caribbean and the Pacific, such as French Caledonia.

The Romans, under Julius Caesar, conquered Gaul in the first century B.C. and ruled the region until the Frankish invasions in the fifth century A.D. and Charlemagne's subsequent empire. The Carolingian, Valois, and Bourbon dynasties ruled France until the Revolution in 1789. France had established itself as a preeminent power, especially under ambitious rulers such as Louis XIV, the "Sun King." Napoleon Bonaparte eventually consolidated his power, replacing the republican government and creating the French Empire, which spread over the Continent. By 1815, France had been militarily defeated but remained one of Europe's major powers.

Two monarchies and two republics took turns ruling France until World War I, when the country suffered severe losses. The Third Republic finally collapsed in World War II in the face of German military power. The Nazi-installed Vichy regime survived until 1946, when a provisional government was installed. The Fourth Republic collapsed in 1958 in the midst of escalating tensions in French Algeria. Charles de Gaulle wrote a new constitution, creating a powerful president, and was elected to that office to inaugurate the Fifth Republic. France is a member of the European Union and the North Atlantic Treaty Organization, although French troops do not belong to N.A.T.O.'s central command structure.

In 1981 François Mitterrand won election as the first Socialist president of France. In 1986, parliamentary elections gave the right-wing opposition, led by Jacques Chirac, a majority in the National Assembly. Mitterand was forced to work with the opposition, an unprecedented arrangement in French government that became known as "cohabitation." In 1995, Chirac was elected president of France with 52% of the vote. He was re-elected as president in 1997, but his party lost support to a coalition of Socialists, Communists, and Greens that was led by Lionel Jospin who became prime minister. Once again, France entered into a period of cohabitation. This time, however, Chirac is on the other side.

Business hours in France vary by region and industry but almost always include a midday break from noon to 2:00 p.m. In the south, midday closures may continue until 3:30 or 4:00 p.m. Traditionally, stores close on Monday but are now usually open in the larger cities. Some stores open on Sunday morning as well.

Current Economic Climate

France was hit especially hard by the recession in the early 1990s and is still recovering. The sluggish rise in the gross domestic product will keep France's relatively high unemployment near 12%, a figure that has not budged for several years. The country's high-tech industrial base and well-educated work force result in a per capita income of over $9,000. Large numbers of immigrants from North Africa perform much of the unskilled labor in France. The E.U. and the U.S. are France's major trading partners, but the former African, Caribbean, and Pacific colonies are also important.

Perhaps one of the most defining features of the French economy is union activity, strongest in the public sector where strikes are often a daily occurrence. The power of French unions to disrupt business distorts their size. Only about 15% of the French work force is unionized—among the lowest rates in the E.U.—although France is one of the most industrialized nations in the world.

The country's major industries include steel, automobiles, chemicals, textiles, foodstuffs, and electronics. Approximately 46% of the work force is engaged in service industries, 45% in manufacturing, and 9% in agriculture. The relatively large number of workers employed in agriculture is a reason for the French farmers' periodic protests against cheaper imports.

FRANCE'S 10 LARGEST COMPANIES
(1997, composite ranking)
 1. SCNF
 2. Compagnie Générale des Eaux
 3. Alcatel Alsthom Compagnie Générale
 4. France Télécom Group
 5. Lyonnaise des Eaux Dumez
 6. Accor
 7. Peugeot Citroën
 8. Régie Nationale de Usines Renault
 9. Compagnie Générale des Etablissements
10. Electricité de France

Using the phone, fax, and Internet
You can dial direct from any phone in France to almost anywhere in the world. Most public phones require phonecards (*télécartes*), which are sold at post offices, tobacconists shops, supermarkets, and Paris metro ticket

counters. All public telephones can take incoming calls, making it easy for people to return your calls. France is divided into five telephone zones and all telephone numbers dialed from within France are 10-digit (add a "0" before the zone). Information is "12," and you should dial "17" in case of emergency. Virtually all post offices can send and receive faxes. Cybercafes are becoming increasingly common, especially in big cities, making it easy to access your Email.

Getting Around in France

France enjoys one of the world's most extensive and efficient rail networks, the SNCF. It offers numerous discount specials for the frequent traveler, and Eurail passes are accepted. Seat reservations should be made in advance. Flying is expensive but fares are cheaper with discount packages that combine train travel with flights. Traveling by bus is cheap but slow.

Employment Regulations and Outlook for Americans

U.S. citizens normally do not need visas for stays of less than 30 days. If you intend to work, a work permit, obtained by your prospective employer at the Office des Migrations, must be presented upon arrival. A residence permit must also be arranged with the local Prefecture de Police or with the French Consulate. At present, the government's concern about unemployment levels in France discourages further immigration, while stringent new rules regarding employment make it nearly impossible for foreigners to find a job.

The national employment agency, Agence National pour l'Emploi (ANPE), maintains regional offices throughout France but isn't considered to be very efficient. These offices normally contain job postings that provide you with employers to contact directly. One professional employment agency, l'Association pour l'Emploi des Cadres (APEC), publishes a weekly job bulletin, the *Courrier-Cadres.* APEC attempts to place management personnel and may be helpful for some Americans with management experience.

Unskilled work is fairly plentiful in France. Employers are very likely to hire foreign workers, especially in the tourist industry. Manual labor in hotels and restaurants in the south of France is readily found, but employers are often unscrupulous about paying the minimum wage to non-E.U. nationals. Tourist jobs are available in the Alps during the winter and on the Cote d'Azur in the summer. Americans may be able to find opportunities teaching English either at foreign language schools or to private individuals. Most universities also employ English speakers to work in their language labs. Agricultural work throughout the country can usually be found in the summer, picking various kinds of fruits. Grape picking is usually plentiful, but the work is particularly unpleasant. Competition for all types of farm work is intense owing to the huge foreign labor pool.

If you are a student, French Cultural Services in New York will send you a free booklet, *Employment in France for Students.* (Contact information is listed below under "Other Informational Organizations.") One of the 32 regional Centres d'Information et de Documentation Jeunesse (CIDJ) is a useful point for student workers looking for information on seasonal agricultural work and on regulations affecting foreign students. Students can bypass the usual employment restrictions by contacting the Council for International Educational Exchange (CIEE), which can provide a permit allowing American students to work in France for up to three months. The American Church (65 quai d'Orsay, Paris 7, France) maintains a notice board with job listings.

ANPE (main office)
Le Galilée
4 rue Galilée
F-93198 Noisy-le-Grande, France
Tel.: [33] (1) 49 31 74 00

APEC
51 boulevard Brune
F-75689 Paris 14, France

Centres d'Information et de Documentation Jeunesse (CIDJ)
101 Quai Branly
F-75740 Paris Cedex 15, France
Tel.: [33] (1) 44 49 12 00
Fax: [33] (1) 40 65 02 61

CIEE
205 East 42nd Street
New York, NY 10017
Tel.: (888) COUNCIL
Email: wabrochure@ciee.org
www.ciee.org

Short-term and Temporary Work

The best bet for casual work is as an au pair. It is also possible to find casual work in the hospitality industry, but that requires very strong French language skills. It is best to use CIEE for help with finding these sorts of casual jobs (see above).

Alliances Abroad
2830 Alameda
San Francisco, CA 94103
Fax: (415) 621-1609
Email: AlliancesA@aol.com
Places au pairs; applicants must have studied French for at least 3 years.

American Institute for Foreign Study (AIFS)
102 Greenwich Ave.
Greenwich, CT 06830-5577
Tel.: (800) 727-2437
Email: info@aifs.org
www.aifs.org
Places students with French language skills as au pairs.

Butterfly et Papillon
avenue de Geneve 5
F-74000 Annecy, France
Tel.: [33] (4) 50 67 03 51
Email: aupair.France@wanadoo.fr
Places au pairs for 3-18 month
assignments.

Federation Unie des Auberges de Jeunesse
27 rue Pajol
F-75018 Paris, France
Tel.: [33] (1) 44 89 87 27
Short-term work at youth hostels
throughout France.

Inter-sejors
179 rue de Courcelles
F-75017 Paris, France
Tel.: [33] (1) 47 63 06 81
Places au pairs throughout France.

Nature et Progrès
3 place Pasteur
F-84000 Avignon, France
Sells lists of organic farmers who need
temporary assistance. Request "Les Bonnes
Addresses de la Bio."

Internship Programs

Several professional internship programs offer students opportunities to obtain professional experience. Some programs, such as that run by Boston University, also offer an opportunity to earn academic credit.

Boston University International Programs
232 Bay State Road, 5th Floor
Boston, MA 02215
Tel.: (617) 353-9888
Fax: (617) 353-5402
Email: abroad@bu.edu
www.bu.edu/abroad
Offers internships in advertising,
marketing, broadcasting, business,
journalism, and politics.

Brethren Colleges Abroad
605 College Avenue
N. Manchester, IN 46963
Tel.: (219) 982-5244
Fax: (219) 982-7755
Email: bca@manchester.edu
www.bcanet.org/
Business, teaching, political science, and
social work internships.

IASTE-US
10400 Little Patuxent Parkway, Suite 250 L
Columbia, MD 21044-3510
Tel.: (410) 997-3068
Fax: (410) 997-5186

Email: iaeste@aipt.org
www.aipt.org/iaste.html
Arranges reciprocal internships in 63
different countries. Specifically for
students in technical fields.

Penn-in-Compiegne
Penn Summer Abroad
University of Pennsylvania
3440 Market Street, Suite 100
Philadelphia, PA 19104-3335
Tel.: (215) 898-5738
Fax: (215) 573-2053
Arranges short-term internships with
banks, government offices, advertising
agencies, hospitals, etc.

Skidmore College in Paris
Department of Foreign Language and
Literature
Skidmore College
Saratoga Springs, NY 12866-1632
Tel.: (518) 581-7400 ext. 2383
Coordinates credit-bearing internships for
students majoring in business, music,
journalism, or government.

Life as a State Department intern

I served for nine months as a State Department intern at the American embassy in Paris. For those considering an internship with State, here are a few tips to help you through the application process.

Most internships last a semester, although they may last longer depending on your availability and the needs of the office you're assigned to. You should apply early; application materials are due in March, for example, for candidates hoping to start in September. Candidates interested in European postings should apply through the Department's Bureau of European and Canadian Affairs.

State Department internships are unpaid. Some posts provide housing, if available (Paris, London, and Bonn, to name a few); others don't. Since internships are unpaid and the costs of getting to Europe and supporting yourself there aren't cheap, internships tend to attract something of a "country club" set: those who can support themselves with their own resources. For those without pockets deep enough for such a venture, hope is available in the way of private fellowships. I was able to obtain one through my university, for example.

Interns work in one of four functional areas: administrative, consular, economics, or political science. For the last two, fluency in the language of the country you hope to work in can play a big part in your acceptance. I worked in the political section, which was incredibly exciting. There's the glamour of it, for one thing: being privy to top-secret cables, and feeling like you're really at the center of world affairs. As for the work itself, my job was part writing and analysis (reports and cables to and from Washington, briefings for the ambassador, and the like), and part busy work (clerical tasks, answering phones, running errands).

I would certainly recommend a State Department internship to anyone considering a career in the Foreign Service. The application and screening process for professional State Department careers is long and rigorous. What better way to find out whether, for you, the result would be worth the effort than to sample State Department life as an intern?
—Elizabeth Bailey

Volunteer Opportunities

Volunteers in France must present a work visa upon arrival. Service Civil International (SCI) operates workcamps for volunteers in fields such as children's camps, environmental and ecological work, peace issues, Esperanto, building renovation, and agriculture. Jeunesse et Reconstruction (JR) runs workcamps, using over 1,100 volunteers. JR's workcamps include environmental, ecological, and forest work; building renovation and construction; and archaeological excavations. Another organization, Concordia, offers workcamps, placing over volunteers throughout France. These camps involve environmental work, building restoration and construction, and path clearing.

Concordia
27 rue de Metz
F-75018 Paris, France
Tel.: [33] (1) 45 23 00 23
Projects involve construction, restoration work, conservation, and social work.

Council on International Educational Exchange
205 East 42nd Street
New York, NY 10017
Tel.: (888) COUNCIL
Email: ivpdirectory@ciee.org
www.ciee.org

Jeunesse et Réconstruction
10 rue de Trévise
F-75009 Paris, France
Tel.: [33] (1) 47 70 15 88

Arranges workcamps throughout France and recruits grape-pickers.

Service Civil International—U.S.A.
Route 2, Box 506
Crozet, VA 22932
Tel.: (804) 823-1826

Volunteers for Peace
International Workcamps
43 Tiffany Road
Belmont, VT 05730
Tel.: (802) 259-2759
Fax: (802) 259-2922
Email: VFP@VFP.prg
www.vfp.org
Major U.S.-based international workcamp coordinator.

Several smaller organizations also offer volunteer service at specific sites in France:

ATD Quart Monde
107 avenue du General Leclerc
F-95480 Pierrelayle, France
Tel.: [33] (3) 30 37 11 11
Maintains workcamps involving construction and gardening to benefit the poor.

Chantiers d'Etudes Medievales
4 rue du Tonnelet Rouge
F-67000 Strasbourg, France
Tel.: [33] (3) 88 37 17 20
Organizes restoration of several medieval sites.

Direction des Affaires Culturelles
Service Regional de l'Archéologie
6 fure de la Manufacture

F-45000 Orleans, France
Tel.: [33] (1) 38 78 85 41
Maintains lists of excavations in need of volunteers (division of the Ministry of Culture).

Club de Vieux Manoir
10 rue de la Cossonnerie
F-75001 Paris, France
Tel.: [33] (1) 45 08 80 40
Restores historical sites throughout France.

REMPART
1 rue des Guillemites
F-75004 Paris, France
Tel.: [33] (1) 42 71 96 55
Fax: [33] (1) 41 71 73 00

Organizes restoration workcamps at buildings and sites with historical or cultural value.

La Sabranenque
Centre International
rue de la Tour del'Oume
F-30290 Saint Victor la Coste, France
Tel.: [33] (4) 66 50 05 05

-or-

217 High Park Blvd.
Buffalo, NY 14226

Tel.: (716) 836-8698
Recruits volunteers to help preserve and restore monuments.

Service Archeologique d'Arras
80 rue Meaulens Prolongée
F-62000 Arras, France
Tel.: [33] (3) 21 50 86 32
Conducts archaeological projects in Douai. Knowledge of French is recommended.

NEWSPAPERS IN FRANCE

Le Figaro
37 rue du Louvre
F-75002 Paris, France
Tel.: [33] (1) 42 21 62 00
Fax: [33] (1) 42 21 28 82

France Soir
37 rue du Louvre
F-75070 Paris Cédex 02, France
Tel.: [33] (1) 44 82 87 00
Fax: [33] (1) 44 82 88 45

International Herald Tribune (English)
181 avenue Charles de Gaulle
F-92521 Neuilly-sur-Seine, France
Tel.: [33] (1) 46 37 93 00
Fax: [33] (1) 46 37 93 70

Le Monde
21 bis rue Claude-Bernard
F-75242 Paris Cédex 05, France
Tel.: [33] (1) 42 17 20 00
Fax: [33] (1) 42 17 21 21

Le Parisien
25 avenue Michelet
F-93408 Saint-Ouen Cédex, France
Tel.: [33] (1) 40 10 30 30
Fax: [33] (1) 40 10 51 51

Le Provençal
4 rue Cougit
F-13105 Marseilles Cédex 3, France
Tel.: [33] (4) 91 84 45 45
Fax: [33] (4) 91 84 49 95

Resources for Further Information

USEFUL WEBSITES FOR JOB SEARCHERS

The Internet is a good place to begin your job search. Many French employers list job vacancies, especially those in technical fields, on the World Wide Web. There are also many websites that provide useful information for job searchers researching the French job market.

An Anglophone's Resource on Paris, Paris-Anglophone
http://paris-anglo.com
Here is the place to start: housing, living, studying, working, etc.

Archive of French Job Offers
www.loria.fr/news/fr.emplois.offres.html
French job offers.

French Classifieds
http://locaflat.com/franceclassified.html
Housing & jobs.

Government Information on Working in France
www.france.diplomatie.fr/
Information from government about working in France.

Kelly Services
www.kellyservices.fr
Temporary work.

Le Monde Informatique
www.lmi.fr/
Job offers from Le Monde.

Nomade: Emploi Guide
www.nomade.fr/enseignement_emploi/
Huge database of job opportunities.

Steria Enterprise (IT)
www.steria.fr
A French software engineering and services specialist includes job offers on their website.

See job lists on the phone

Be sure to check out the French Telecom subscriber services Minitel, a computerized information system which operates via a screen that plugs into an ordinary telephone. With the screen, you can access a variety of databases listing job vacancies (as well as other information). The databases are available at all information centers and post offices. Try 3615 TOPJOBS for general job listings or 3614 ALPES for winter resort vacancies. A list of Minitel services for the job searcher is available at www.argia.fr/.

EMBASSIES AND CONSULAR OFFICES

American embassies and consulates have commercial and/or economic sections that can provide you with business information and explain aspects of the local economy. Inquiries about business opportunities should be addressed either to "Commercial Officer" or "Commercial Section," followed by the appropriate street address.

Representation of France in the United States

Embassy of France
4101 Reservoir Road NW
Washington, DC 20007
Tel.: (202) 944-6000
Fax: (202) 944-6166

French Consulates General: Chicago, (312) 787-5359; Los Angeles (Westwood), (310) 235-3200; New York, (212) 606-3600; San Francisco (415) 397-4330

Representation of the United States in France

American Embassy
2 avenue Gabriel
F-75382 Paris Cédex 08, France
Tel.: [33] (1) 42 96 12 02
Fax: [33] (1) 42 66 97 83

American Consulate
2 rue St. Florentin
F-75382 Paris, Cédex 08
Tel.: [33] (1) 43 12 48 40
Fax: [33] (1) 42 61 61 40

American Consulate General—Marseilles
12 boulevard Paul Peytral
F-13286 Marseilles Cédex 06, France
Tel.: [33] (4) 91 54 92 00
Fax: [33] (4) 91 55 09 47

American Consulate General—Strasbourg
15 avenue D'Alsace
F-67082 Strasbourg Cédex, France
Tel.: [33] (3) 88 35 31 04
Fax: [33] (3) 88 24 06 95

CHAMBERS OF COMMERCE

Chambers of commerce consist of firms in both countries interested in international trade. These are appropriate companies to initially target in the job search.

American Chamber of Commerce in France
21 avenue George V
F-75008 Paris, France
Tel.: [33] (1) 40 73 89 90
Fax: [33] (1) 47 20 18 62
www.amchamfr.com

Bordeaux Chamber of Commerce
9 Place de la Bourse
F-33076 Paris, France
Tel.: [33] (1) 56 90 91 28

Chamber of Commerce and Industry
27 avenue de Friedland, Cédex 08
F-75383 Paris, France
Tel.: [33] (1) 42 89 70 26
Fax: [33] (1) 42 89 70 70
Email: jdmarzolf@ccip.fr
www.ccip.fr

French-American Chamber of Commerce in the U.S.
1350 Avenue of the Americas, 6th Floor
New York, NY 10019
Tel.: (212) 765-4460
Fax: (212) 765-4650

French Chamber of Commerce
9 boulevard Malesherbes
F-75998 Paris, France
Tel.: [33] (1) 42 65 12 66

Marseilles Chamber of Commerce and Industry
Palais de la Bourse
F-13001 Marseilles, France
Tel.: [33] (4) 91 91 42 25

WORLD TRADE CENTERS IN FRANCE

World Trade Centers usually include many foreign companies operating in the country.

World Trade Center Bordeaux
2, Place de la Bourse
F-33076 Bordeaux, France
Tel.: [33] (5) 56 79 50 22
Fax : [33] (5) 56 79 52 65
Email: wtc.bx.so@gci-sa.fr

World Trade Center Grenoble
P.O. Box 1509
F-38025 Grenoble, Cédex 1, France
Tel.: [33] (4) 76 28 28 43
Fax: [33] (4) 76 28 28 35
Email: grex@esc-grenoble.fr

World Trade Center Lille
58 Rue de L'Hopital
Militaire
BP 209
F-59029 Lille Cédex, France
Tel.: [33] (3) 20 57 05 07, [33] (3) 20 63 08 51
Fax: [33] (3) 20 40 04 55
Email: wtcll@etnet.fr
www.lille.cci.fr

World Trade Center Lyon
16 Rue de la Republique
F069002 Lyon, France
Tel.: [33] (4) 72 40 57 52
Fax: [33] (4) 72 40 57 61
Email: wtc@wtc-lyon.org
www.wtc-lyon.org

World Trade Center Marseilles
Centre Mediterraneen de Commerce Int'l.
2 Rue Henri Barbusse
F-13241 Marseilles Cédex 01, France
Tel.: [33] (4) 91 39 33 58
Fax: [33] (4) 91 39 34 53
Email: cii-crdi@lac.gulliver.fr

World Trade Center Metz-Saarbrücken
Club WTC
Tour B, 2 Rue Augustin Fresnel Case 88248
F-57082 Metz Cédex 3, France
Tel.: [33] (3) 87 75 85 00
Fax: [33] (3) 87 75 85 29
Email: wtc-metz@moselle.cci.fr
www.moselle.cci.fr/wtc

World Trade Center Montpellier
Immeuble La Coupole
275 Rue Leon Blum, BP 9531
F-34045 Montpellier, Cédex 01 France
Tel.: [33] (4) 67 13 60 60
Fax : [33] (4) 67 13 60 64
Email: wtc@mlrt.fr
www.tech-montpellier.com

World Trade Center Nantes
Centre Atlantique de Commerce International
16 Quai Ernest Renaud, BP 90517
F-44105 Nantes Cédex 4, France
Tel.: [33] (2) 40 44 60 55
Fax: [33] (2) 40 44 63 80
Email: wtc@nantes.cci.fr
www.nantes.cci.fr

World Trade Center Paris
Palais Des Congres 2, place de la Porte Maillot
B.P. 18
F-75853 Paris Cédex 17, France
Tel.: [33] (1) 40 68 14 25
Fax: [33] (1) 40 68 14 21
Email: wtcparis@ccip.fr
www.ccip.fr

World Trade Center Strasbourg
Maison du Commerce International de Strasbourg (MCIS)
4 Quai Kleber
F-67080 Strasbourg Cédex, France
Tel.: [33] (3) 88 76 42 24
Fax: [33] (3) 88 76 42 00
Email: wtc.eic@strasbourg.cci.fr

OTHER INFORMATIONAL ORGANIZATIONS

Foreign government missions in the U.S. such as National Tourist Offices and embassies and consulates can furnish visas and information on work permits and other important regulations. They may also offer economic and business information about the country.

French Cultural Services
972 Fifth Avenue
New York, NY 10021
Tel.: (212) 439-1400

French Government Tourist Office
444 Madison Avenue
New York, NY 10022
Tel.: (212) 838-7800
Fax: (212) 838-7855

French Institute/Alliance Française
22 East 60th Street
New York, NY 10022
Tel.: (212) 355-6100
Fax: (212) 935-4119
www.fiaf.org/

Paris Tourism Office
127 Avenue de Champs-Élysées
F-75008 Paris, France
Tel.: [33] (1) 47 23 61 72

Fruit-picking dates in France

Brittany: apples (mid-Sept—late Oct.), cherries (mid-May—early July)

Languedoc: apples (mid-Sept.—late Oct.), strawberries (mid-May—late July), peaches (mid-June—mid-Sept.)

Normandy: apples (mid-Sept—late Oct.), cherries (mid-May—early July)

Paris region: peaches (mid-June—mid-Sept.), pears (mid-July—mid-Nov.), tomatoes (late Aug.—early Sept.)

BUSINESS DIRECTORIES

Although not always easy to find, business directories can prove invaluable in the international job search. Most directories list company names, addresses, products, and phone numbers. Some directories include executive names and titles and financial information about the company. These sources provide you with the names of the people to contact for employment information as well as financial data, which can tell you how strong a company's position in a country may be.

American Chamber of Commerce in France Membership Directory. Published annually by the American Chamber of Commerce in France, 21 avenue George-V, F-75008 Paris, France; email: amchamfr@club-internet.fr; www.amchamfr.com. Lists American and French companies engaged in bilateral trade.

American Subsidiaries and Affiliates of French Firms. Published by French Embassy Trade Office, 810 7th Avenue, 38th Floor, New York, NY 10019-5818. Lists of American subsidiaries in France.

Annuaire Telexport—French Exporters and Importers. Published annually in French, English, German, and Spanish by the Paris Chamber of Commerce and Industry, c/o Association Telexport, 92 bis, rue Cardinet, F-75017 Paris, France. Covers 38,000 French companies involved in international trade.

Bottin Professions. Published annually in French by Bottin SA, 4 rue Andre Boulle, F-94961 Gretul Cédex 9, France. Describes over 100,000 French businesses, including financial data.

Directory of Corporations and Corporate Officers. Published annually by DAFSA, 25 rue Leblanc, F-75010 Paris, France. Lists 13,000 corporation board members and 1,200 companies listed on the French stock exchange.

Directory of Foreign Firms Operating Abroad: France. World Trade Academy Press, 257 Central Park West, Suite 10A, New York, NY 10024-4110; email: uniworldbp@aol.com; www.uniworldbp.com. Lists names and addresses of parent companies in the U.S. and their subsidiaries and affiliates in France.

ESSOR. Published annually in French, English, German, and Spanish by Union Française d'Annuaires Professionnels, 130 avenue de Bouleaux, F-78192 Trappes Cédex, France; email: info@enorcontacts.tm.fr. Describes 170,000 trade-related firms and agencies.

L'Expansion—Le Classement Annuel des 1000 Premieres Enterprises Françaises. Published annually in French by Groupe Expansion, 14 boulevard Poissonnierc, F-75008 Paris Cédex 9, France. Lists the annual changes in financial status of France's 1,000 leading firms.

France 30,000. Published annually in French by Dun & Bradstreet France, avenue de Choisy, F-75643 Paris Cédex 13, France. Describes 30,000 largest French firms.

French Company Handbook. Published annually by International Business Development, International Herald Tribune, 181 avenue Charles de Gaulle, F-92200 Neuilly, France. Describes 120 major French companies.

Kompass France. Published annually in French by Kompass France, 55 quai du Marechal Joffre, F-92415 Courbevoie Cédex, France; email: kompass@pratique.fr; www.kompass.com. Lists 115,000 French manufacturing and service companies.

Membership Directory of the French-American Chamber of Commerce in the U.S. Published annually by the French-American Chamber of Commerce in the U.S., 1350 Avenue of the Americas, 6th Floor, New York, NY 10019. Lists French and American companies engaged in bilateral trade.

Qui Represente Qui en France. Published annually in French by Kompass France, 66 quai de Marechal Joffre, F-92145 Courbevoie Cédex, France; email: kompass@pratique.fr; www.kompass.com. Lists French importers and distributors representing foreign firms in France.

Working in Corsica

Corsica is a full province, or department, of France but has a distinctly Mediterranean character. Corsicans are much closer to Sardinians than they are to other French people. The island is mostly poor and underdeveloped, but it does provide opportunities in the tourist industry and in agriculture. Competition for most manual work comes from a very large number of Arab workers. Female workers often find the attention received from the single migrant Arab workers highly annoying.

The tourist industry centers around Ajaccio, Bastia, Bonifacio, and Propriano. Resorts are located throughout the coastal areas. Hotels, bars, and restaurants often advertise for jobs in some of the mainland newspapers, especially in Nice and Marseilles. German speakers are especially sought due to the high levels of German tourists in Corsica.

Fruit-picking is available on the eastern coast from mid-November through December. The tropical fruits that grow on the island require hard work to pick. In addition, the midday heat mandates that work starts around dawn. The grape harvest occurs on the northern coast from September to early October. North African workers dominate the agricultural labor market in much of Corsica.

AMERICAN COMPANIES IN FRANCE

Many American firms operate in France. The following companies are classified by business area: Banking and Finance; Industrial Manufacturing; Retailing and Wholesaling; and Service Industries. Company information includes firm name, address, phone and fax numbers, specific business, and American parent company. Your chances of achieving employment abroad are substantially better if you contact the subsidiary company in Europe rather than the parent company in the U.S.

BANKING AND FINANCE

American Express Bank SA
12 rd pt Champs Elysées
F-75008 Paris, France
Tel.: [33] (1) 47 14 50 00
Fax.: [33] (1) 42 68 17 17
(Bank)
American Express

Chase Manhattan Bank.
42 rue Washington
F-75008 Paris, France
Tel.: [33] (1) 53 77 10 00
Fax: [33] (1) 53 77 10 50
(Bank)
Chase Manhattan Corporation

Natwest
23 rue Balzac
F-75001 Paris, France
Tel.: [33] (1) 53 93 13 00
Fax: [33] (1) 40 15 07 37
(Bank)
Natwest

INDUSTRIAL MANUFACTURING

Aussedat Rey SA
1 rue du Petit-Clamart
F-78141 Vélizy-Villacoublay Cédex,
France
Tel.: [33] (1) 40 83 44 53
Fax: [33] (1) 46 31 18 96
(Paper products)
International Paper Corp.

Bridgestone Firestone France
avenue G. Washington
F-62400 Béthune, France
Tel.: [33] (3) 21 64 77 00
Fax: [33] (3) 21 64 77 77
(Tires and tubes)
Firestone Tire & Rubber Co.

Case Poclain
avenue Georges Bataille
F-60330 Le Plessis-Belleville, France
Tel.: [33] (3) 44 63 27 12
Fax: [33] (3) 44 60 55 33
(Construction equipment)
Tenneco Inc.

Caterpillar France SA
40 avenue Léon Blom
38100 Grenoble, France
Tel.: [33] (4) 76 23 70 00
Fax: [33] (4) 76 40 14 31
(Earth-moving machinery)
Caterpillar Inc.

Colgate Palmolive
55 boulevard de la Mission-Marchand
F-9240 Courbevoie Cédex, France
Tel.: [33] (1) 47 68 60 00
Fax: [33] (1) 47 68 64 82
(Household, personal care products)
Colgate Palmolive Corp.

Corning France
44 avenue de Valvins
F-77210 Avon Cédex, France
Tel.: [33] (1) 64 69 75 00
Fax: [33] (1) 60 72 21 75
(Telephone cables)
Corning

Republic National Bank New York
20 Place Vendôme
F-75001 Paris, France
Tel.: [33] (1) 44 86 18 61
Fax: [33] (1) 40 20 94 85
(Bank)
Bank of New York

John Deere France
10 rue du Paradis
F-45140 Ormes, France
Tel.: [33] (2) 38 72 30 00
Fax: [33] (2) 38 74 86 65
(Farm machinery)
Deere & Company

Dow France
300 route des Crêtes, BP 203
F-06904 Sophia Antipolis, France
Tel.: [33] (4) 92 94 40 00
Fax: [33] (4) 92 94 40 90
(Chemicals and pharmaceuticals)
Dow Chemical Co.

Du Pont de Nemours France SA
137 rue de l'Université
F-75007 Paris, France
Tel.: [33] (1) 45 50 65 50
Fax: [33] (1) 47 53 09 65
(Chemical and electronic products)
E.I. Du Pont de Nemours & Co.

Esso SAF
2, rue des Martinets, Rueil Malmaison
F-925569 Rueil Malmaison Cédex, France
Tel.: [33] (1) 47 10 60 00
Fax: [33] (1) 47 10 66 00
(Petroleum products)
Exxon Corp.

Exxon Chemical Polymeres SNC
rue President Kennedy
F-76330 Notre Dame De Gravenchon,
France
Tel.: [33] (2) 35 39 51 51
Fax: [33] (2) 35 39 51 97
(Chemicals)
Exxon Corp.

Goodyear France SA
101 avenue la Châtaigneraie
F-92506 Rueil Malmaison Cédex, France
Tel.: [33] (1) 47 16 23 08
Fax: [33] (1) 47 16 23 13
(Rubber products)
Goodyear Tire and Rubber Co.

Johnson Francaise SA
10 rue St. Hilaire
Boite Postale 606
F-95310 St. Ouen l'Aumône, France
Tel.: [33] (1) 34 21 21 21
Fax: [33] (1) 30 37 42 36
(Household products)
S.C. Johnson & Son Inc.

Kodak-Pathe
26 rue Villiot
F-75012 Paris, France
Tel.: [33] (1) 40 01 30 00
Fax: [33] (1) 40 01 46 50
(Photographic equipment and optical lenses)
Eastman Kodak Co.

Lilly France SA
203 Bureaux de la Colline
F-92210 St. Cloud Cédex, France
Tel.: [33] (1) 49 11 34 34
Fax: [33] (1) 46 02 27 67
(Pharmaceuticals)
Eli Lilly & Co.

Mars Alimentaire SA
3 chemin de Sandlach
Boite Postale 36
F-67500 Haguenau, France
Tel. [33] (3) 88 05 10 01
Fax: [33] (3) 88 05 10 02
(Confectionery)
Mars Company

Merck Sharp & Dohme-Chibret, Laboratories
3 avenue Hoche
F-75008 Paris, France
Tel.: [33] (1) 47 54 87 00
Fax: [33] (1) 47 66 99 91
(Pharmaceuticals)
Merck & Co. Inc.

Mobil Oil Francaise
20 avenue André Prothin
F-92976 Paris la Defense Cédex, France
Tel.: [33] (1) 41 45 42 41
Fax: [33] (1) 41 45 42 93
(Petroleum products)
Mobil Oil Corp.

Motorola Semiconducteurs SA
avenue de General Eisenhower
F-31000 Toulouse, France

Tel.: [33] (5) 61 19 90 00
Fax: [33] (5) 61 40 44 99
(Semiconductors)
Motorola Corp.

Parke-Davis
11 avenue Dubonnet
F-92400 Courbevoie Cédex, France
Tel.: [33] (1) 49 04 07 01
Fax: [33] (1) 49 04 07 44
(Gourmet foods)
Warner-Lambert Corp.

Procter & Gamble France
96 avenue Charles de Gaulle
F-92201 Neuilly-sur-Seine, France
Tel.: [33] (1) 40 88 55 11
Fax: [33] (1) 40 81 58 58
(Household products)
Procter & Gamble Co.

Rohm & Haas France SA
185 rue de Bercy
F-75012 Paris 12 E, France
Tel.: [33] (1) 40 02 50 00
Fax: [33] (1) 43 45 28 19
(Chemicals)
Rohm & Haas Co.

SmithKline Beecham Laboratories
6 Esplanade Charles de Gaulle
F-92000 Paris, France
Tel.: [33] (1) 46 98 48 48
Fax: [33] (1) 46 98 49 00
(Pharmaceuticals)
SmithKline Beecham Corp.

Texas Instruments France
821 avenue Jack Kilby, BP 5
F-06271 Villeneuve Loubet Cédex, France
Tel.: [33] (4) 93 22 27 05
Fax: [33] (4) 93 22 27 66
(Electronic equipment)
Texas Instruments Inc.

3M France SA
boulevard de l'Oise
F-95006 Cergy, France
Tel.: [33] (1) 30 31 61 61
Fax: [33] (1) 30 31 74 26
(Adhesives, coatings, sealants, etc.)
Minnesota Mining and Manufacturing Corp.

RETAILING AND WHOLESALING

Control Data France SA
55 avenue des Champs Pierreux
Le Capitole
F-92012 Nanterre Cédex, France
Tel.: [33] (1) 41 37 80 63
Fax: [33] (1) 41 37 80 01
(Software)
Control Data Corp.

Digital Equipment France
Parc du Bois Briard
9-13 avenue du Lac
F-91007 Evry Cédex, France
Tel.: [33] (1) 69 87 51 11
Fax: [33] (1) 69 87 13 60
(Data processing equipment)
Digital Equipment Corp.

Ford France SA
344 avenue Napoléon-Bonaparte
F-92500 Rueil Malmaison Cédex, France
Tel.: [33] (1) 47 31 60 00

Fax: [33] (1) 47 32 63 47
(Automobiles and automobile parts)
Ford Motor Co.

Intel Corporation SARL
103 3 quai de Grenelle
F-75015 Paris, France
Tel.: [33] (1) 45 71 71 71
Fax: [33] (1) 45 71 70 00
(Electronic components)
Intel Corporation

Rank Xerox
7 rue Touzet Gaillard
F-93586 Saint-Ouen Cédex, France
Tel.: [33] (1) 49 48 27 00
Fax: [33] (1) 49 48 43 21
(Office equipment)
Xerox Corp.

SERVICE INDUSTRIES

Andersen Consulting
Tour Gan la Défense 2
16 place de 1 Iris
F-92400 Courbevoie, France
Tel.: [33] (1) 41 99 24 24
Fax: [33] (1) 53 23 53 23
(Consulting)
Andersen Consulting

Diebold France SA
146 boulevard Haussmann
F-75008 Paris, France
Tel.: [33] (1) 40 76 00 30
(Consulting and public relations)
Diebold, John, Inc.

Dun & Bradstreet France SA
35 avenue G Clemenceau
F-75013 Paris, France
Tel.: [33] (1) 41 35 17 00
Fax: [33] (1) 41 35 17 77
(Information services)
Dun & Bradstreet Information Services
Europe

Euro Disney SCA
Service du Recruitement-Casting
Disneyland Paris
BP 110

77777 Marne-la-Valléd Cédex, France
F-93160 Noisy-le-Grand, France
Tel.: [33] (1) 31 19 99
(Theme parks, recreational services)
Walt Disney Co.

I.B.M. France
2 avenue Gambetts
Tour Descartes La Defense
F-92400 Courbevoire, France
Tel.: [33] (1) 49 05 70 00
Fax: [33] (1) 49 05 69 23
(Information systems)

McKinsey & Co. Inc. France
79 avenue de Champs Élysées
F-75008 Paris, France
Tel.: [33] (1) 40 69 14 00
Fax: [33] (1) 40 69 93 93
(Consulting)
McKinsey & Co.

Ogilvy & Mather International
40 avenue George V
F-75008 Paris, France
Tel.: [33] (1) 53 23 30 00
Fax: [33] (1) 53 23 30 30
(Advertising and public relations)
Ogilvy & Mather International Inc.

Saatchi & Saatchi Advertising
30 boulevard Vital-Bouhot
F-92521 Neuilly Cédex, France
Tel.: [33] (1) 40 88 40 00
(Advertising)
Saatchi & Saatchi Co.

Young et Rubicam France SA
23 rue Maillasson
F-92100 Boulogne Billancourt, France
Tel.: [33] (1) 46 84 33 33
(Advertising)
Young & Rubicam

EUROPEAN COMPANIES IN FRANCE

The following are major non-American firms operating in the country. These selected companies can be either French or other European. Such companies will generally hire their own nationals first but may employ Americans.

BANKING AND FINANCE

Assurances Générales de France (AGF)
87 rue de Richelieu
F-75002 Paris, France
Tel.: [33] (1) 44 86 20 00
(Insurance)

AXA Banque
5-7, rue de Milan
F-75009 Paris, France
Tel.: [33] (1) 44 63 30 00
Fax: [33] (1) 44 63 30 34
(Bank)

AXA SA
100-101 Terrasse Boieldieu
F-92042 Paris la Défense Cédex, France
Tel.: [33] (1) 47 76 82 00
Fax: [33] (1) 47 76 83 75
(Insurance)

Banque Indosuez
44 rue de Courcelles
F-75008 Paris, France
Tel.: [33] (1) 44 20 20 20
Fax: [33] (1) 44 20 29 56
(Bank)

Banque Nationale de Paris (BNP)
16 boulevard des Italiens
F-75009 Paris, France
Tel.: [33] (1) 40 14 45 46
Fax: [33] (1) 40 14 79 97
(Bank)

Barclay's Bank PLC
21 rue Laffitte
F-75009 Paris, France
Tel.: [33] (1) 44 79 79 79
Fax: [33] (1) 44 79 72 52
(Bank)

Compagnie Financiére de Paribas
5 rue d'Antin
F-75002 Paris, France

Tel.: [33] (1) 42 98 12 34
Fax: [33] (1) 42 98 11 42
(Bank)

Compagnie Financiére Edmond de Rothschild
47 rue du Saint-honoré
F-75008 Paris, France
Tel.: [33] (1) 40 17 25 25
Fax: [33] (1) 40 17 24 02
(Bank)

Crédit Commercial de France
103 avenue des Champs-Elysées
F-75008 Paris, France
Tel.: [33] (1) 40 70 70 40
Fax: [33] (1) 40 70 70 09
(Bank)

Credit Lyonnais
19 blvd des Italiens
F-75002 Paris, France
Tel.: [33] (1) 42 95 70 00
Fax: [33] (1) 42 95 50 49
(Bank)

Deutsche Bank
3 avenue de Friedland
F-75008 Paris, France
Tel.: [33] (1) 44 95 64 00
Fax: [33] (1) 75 07 01
(Bank)

GTM-Entrepose
61 avenue Jules-Quentin, BP 306
F-92000 Nanterre, France
Tel.: [33] (1) 46 95 70 00
(Real estate development)

Union des Assurances de Paris
3 boulevard Diderot
F-75012 Paris, France
Tel.: [33] (1) 45 26 40 38
(Insurance)

INDUSTRIAL MANUFACTURING

Aerospatiale
37 boulevard de Montmorency
F-75781 Paris Cédex 16, France
Tel.: [33] (1) 42 24 24 24
Fax: [33] (1) 45 25 54 14
(Aerospace equipment)

Alcatel Alsthom
54 rue La Boetie
F-75008 Paris, France
Tel.: [33] (1) 40 76 10 10
Fax: [33] (1) 40 76 14 00
www.Alcatel.com
(Communications, energy, engineering)

Arianespace
boulevard de l'Europe
F-9100 Evry, France
Tel.: [33] (1) 60 87 60 00
Fax: [33] (1) 60 87 62 47
(Aerospace)

Arjomari Diffusion SNC
66 rue du Dessous de Bergés
F-75013 Paris, France
Tel.: [33] (1) 44 06 28 00
Fax: [33] (1) 45 84 61 59
(Paper products)

BP France
8 rue des Gémeaux
F-95800 Cergy, France
Tel.: [33] (1) 34 22 40 00
Fax: [33] (1) 34 22 44 17
(Petroleum products)

BIC SA
11 rue Petit
F-92110 Clichy, France
Tel.: [33] (1) 45 19 52 00
 (Writing instruments)

BSN Emballage
64 bd 11 Novembre 1918
F-69100 Villeurbanne, France
Tel.: [33] (4) 72 82 51 71
Fax: [33] (4) 72 82 52 38
(Glass and hollow-ware)

Compagnie de Saint-Gobain
Les Miroirs
18 rue D'alsace
F-92400 Courbevoie, France
Tel.: [33] (1) 47 62 34 00
(Glass products)

Dumez Ile de France
2 rue Jacques Brel
F-92240 Malakoff, France

Tel.: [33] (1) 41 08 27 00
Fax: [33] (1) 41 08 28 20
(Engineering and construction)

Electricité de France
23 rue Vienne
F-75383 Paris Cédex 08, France
Tel.: [33] (1) 42 93 59 65
(Electricity production)

Elf Aquitaine SA
2 place de la Coupole
F-92078 Paris la Defense, France
Tel.: [33] (1) 47 44 45 46
Fax: [33] (1) 47 44 45 46
(Oil)

Fromageries Bel
4 rue d'Anjou
F-75008 Paris, France
Tel.: [33] (1) 40 07 72 50
Fax: [33] (1) 42 66 99 61
(Dairy business)

IMETAL
3 avenue du Maine
F-75755 Paris, France
Tel.: [33] (1) 45 38 48 48
Fax: [33] (1) 45 38 74 78
(Metals and building materials)

L'Air Liquide
57 avenue Carnot
F-94500 Champigny Sur Marne, France
Tel.: [33] (1) 49 83 55 55
(Gases and medical equipment)

Legrand SA
128 avenue du Mal de Lattre de Tassignay
F-87000 Limoges, France
Tel.: [33] (5) 55 06 74 74
 (Electrical equipment)

L'Oreal
1 avenue Eugéne Schueller
F-93600 Aulnay Sous Bois, France
Tel.: [33] (1) 48 68 96 00
Fax: [33] (1) 48 68 95 13
(Cosmetics and toiletries)

Michelin
ZI N 11 rue Gutenberg
F-37300 Joue Les Tours, France
Tel.: [33] (2) 47 48 60 00
 (Tires and rubber products)

Leroy-Somer Electric Motors SA
boulevard Marcellin Leroy
F-16015 Angouléme, France

Tel.: [33] (5) 45 64 45 64
Fax: [33] (5) 45 64 45 04
(Machinery)

Pechiney SA
6 Place de Vosges
Immeuble Balzac
F-92400 Courbevoie, France
Tel.: [33] (1) 46 91 46 91
Fax: [33] (1) 46 91 51 13
(Aluminum and packaging products)

Pernod Ricard
142 boulevard Haussmann
F-75008 Paris, France
Tel.: [33] (1) 40 76 77 78
 (Alcoholic beverages)

Perrier Vittel
F-30130 Vergaze, France
Tel.: [33] (1) 40 75 38 00
Fax: [33] (1) 45 63 22 99
(Beverages and confections)

Peugeot SA
75 avenue de la Grande Armée
F-75116 Paris, France
Tel.: [33] (1) 44 74 84 39
Fax: [33] (1) 43 44 39 45
(Automobiles and parts)

**Regie Nationale des Usines Renault
(RENAULT)**
34 quai du Pont du Jour
F-92109 Boulogne Billancourt, France
Tel.: [33] (1) 41 04 50 50
Fax: [33] (1) 53 24 41 20
(Automobiles)

Roussel Uclaf SA
102 111 route De Noisy
F-93235 Romainville, France
Tel.: [33] (1) 49 91 49 91
Fax: [33] (1) 40 62 49 49
(Chemicals and pharmaceuticals)

**SAGEM (Societe D'Applications
Generales D'Electricite et de Mecanique)**
6 avenue d'Iéna
F-75783 Paris, France
Tel.: [33] (1) 40 70 63 63
Fax: [33] (1) 47 20 39 46
(Communications and other electronic
equipment)

Skis Rossignol SA
Le Menon rue Butterlin
F-38500 Voiron, France
Tel.: [33] (4) 76 66 65 65
Fax: [33] (4) 76 65 67 51
(Sporting goods)

TOTAL
Tour Total
24 cours Michelet
F-92800 Puteaux, France
Tel.: [33] (1) 47 67 42 00
Fax: [33] (1) 49 06 02 10
www.total.com
(Oil and gas exploration)

Usinor Sacilor
11/13 Cours Valmy
F-92800 Paris, France
Tel.: [33] (1) 41 25 60 10
Fax: [33] (1) 41 25 56 75
(Steel)

RETAILING AND WHOLESALING

Auchan SAMU SA
40 avenue de Flandres
F-59264 Croix, France
Tel.: [33] (3) 20 81 68 00
Fax: [33] (3) 20 89 69 09
www.auchan.fr
(Hypermarkets, restaurants)

Compagnie Générale des Eaux SA
52 rue d'Anjou
F-75008 Paris, France
Tel.: [33] (1) 49 24 49 24
Fax: [33] (1) 49 24 69 99
(Water & energy; real estate & construction)

E. Remy-Martin et Compagnie
20 rue de la Societe Vinicole
F-1610 Cognac, France
Tel.: [33] (5) 45 35 76 00
Fax: [33] (5) 45 35 02 85
(Alcoholic beverages)

France Télécom Group
2 rue de la Herse
F-28400 Nogent Le Routrou, France
Tel.: [33] 800 14 20 14
(Communications)

Galeries Lafayette SA
40 boulevard Haussmann
F-75009 Paris, France

Tel.: [33] (1) 42 82 34 56
Fax: [33] (1) 42 82 30 51
(Department stores)

Lyonnaise des Eaux SA
72 avenue de la Liberte
92000 Nanterre, France

SERVICE INDUSTRIES

Accor SA
62 avenue de Saxe
F-75738 Paris Cédex 15, France
Tel.: [33] (1) 53 78 53 78
Fax: [33] (1) 45 57 04 22
(Hotels and restaurants)

Air France
45 rue de Paris
F-95747 Roissy Charles de Gaulle Cédex,
France
Tel.: [33] (8) 02 80 28 02
Fax: [33] (1) 49 69 53 80
www. airfrance.com
(Airline)

Club Méditerranée SA
Chemin du Glacier
F-74400 Chamonix Mont Blanc, France
Tel.: [33] (4) 50 53 08 29
Fax: [33] (4) 50 53 57 84
(Tourism)

CE Hachette Livre Industrie et Services
1 Gutenberg
F-78310 Maurepas, France
Tel.: [33] (1) 30 66 20 66
Fax: [33] (1) 30 66 24 29
www.Hachette.es/elle
(Publishing)

Havas
3-5 rue Danton
F-92200 Levallois Perret, France
Tel.: [33] (1) 40 89 65 65
Fax: [33] (1) 47 57 46 82
(Communications and travel)

Tel.: [33] (1) 46 95 50 00
Fax: [33] (1) 45 95 51 80
(Water & electricity)

Jeumont-Schneider Transformateurs
84 avenue Paul Santy, Lyon
F-69008 Lyon, France
Tel.: [33] (4) 78 01 88 00
Fax: [33] (4) 78 00 31 14
(Electrical engineering design)

Michelin
46 avenue de Bréteuil
F-75234 Paris, France
Tel.: [33] (1) 45 66 12 34
Fax: [33] (1) 45 66 11 63
(Publishing)

Publicis SA
133 avenue des Champs-Elysées
F-75008 Paris, France
Tel.: [33] (1) 44 43 78 00
Fax: [33] (1) 44 43 78 77
(Advertising)

SNCF (Société Nationale des Chemins de Fer Français)
42 rue Riquet
F-75018 Paris, France
Tel.: [33] (1) 46 07 04 95
Fax: [33] (1) 46 07 04 96
(Railway transport)

Union Miniere France
40 rue Jean Jaurès
F-93170 Bagnolet, France
Tel.: [33] (1) 49 72 42 42
Fax: [33] (1) 49 60 52 58
(Engineering in mining and industrial waste)

INTERNATIONAL NON-PROFIT EMPLOYER IN FRANCE

U.N.E.S.C.O.
7 place de Fontenoy Trésor
F-75007 Paris, France
Tel.: [33] (1) 45 68 10 00

INTERNATIONAL SCHOOLS IN FRANCE

American School of Paris
41 rue Pasteur
F-92210 Saint-Cloud, France
Tel.: [33] (01) 46 02 54 43
Fax: [33] (01) 46 02 23 90
(U.S./I.B., pre-K-12)

The International School of Monaco
12 Quai Antoine 1er
98000 Monte Carlo, Monaco
Tel.: [33] (93) 25 68 20
Fax: [33] (93) 25 68 30
Email: intlschl@monaco.mc
(Curriculum in English and French)

International School of Paris
6 rue Beethoven
F-75016 Paris, France
Tel.: [33] (01) 42 24 09 54
Fax: [33] (01) 45 27 15 93

Email: isp@compuserve.com
www.isparis.com
(U.S./U.K./I.B. curriculum, pre-K-12)

Marymount School
72 boulevard de la Saussaye
F-92200 Neuilly-sur-Seine, France
Tel.: [33] (01) 46 24 10 51
Fax: [33] (01) 46 37 07 50
 (U.S. curriculum, pre-K-8)

Mougins School
615 avenue de Maurice Donat
F-06250 Mougins, France
Tel.: [33] (93) 90 15 47
Fax: [33] (93) 75 31 40
Email: mouginsschool@riviera.fr
www.riviera.fr/
(U.K., pre-K-12)

fourteen

Italy

MAJOR EMPLOYMENT CENTERS: Rome, Milan, Naples, Turin

MAJOR BUSINESS LANGUAGE: Italian

LANGUAGE SKILL INDEX: Really should know it

CURRENCY: Euro; the lira will remain the currency in circulation until 2002

TELEPHONE COUNTRY CODE: 39

TIME ZONE: EST+6

PUNCTUALITY INDEX: Punctuality means being twenty minutes late

AVERAGE DAILY TEMPERATURE, HIGH/LOW: January, 54/39°F; July, 88/64°F (Rome)

AVERAGE NUMBER OF DAYS WITH PRECIPITATION: January, 11; July, 1

BEST BET FOR EMPLOYMENT:

FOR STUDENTS: Unofficial resort work

PERMANENT JOBS: Specialized skills and assignment from an American company

CHANCE OF FINDING A JOB: Not so good, thanks to relatively high unemployment rates

TRIVIA: Faxes are widely used in Italy for business purposes. Make initial business contacts by fax, if possible, and confirm arrangements by fax rather than phone

taly stretches into the Mediterranean Sea from south-central Europe. The country is about the size of Arizona, and it borders France, Switzerland, Austria, and the former Yugoslavia to the north. The Adriatic Sea separates Italy from the Balkan peninsula to the east. North Africa is across the Mediterranean to the south. Sardinia and Sicily form the western edge of the Tyrrhenian Sea. The Apennine Mountains traverse the length of the peninsula, and the Alps form the northern borders.

The western Roman Empire lasted until the fifth century A.D. The northern Italian city-states developed into flourishing cultural and commercial centers in the late Middle Ages and during the Renaissance. France, Austria, and Spain continuously fought over territory and influence in Italy, thereby contributing to the country's political fragmentation. By the mid-nineteenth century, the House of Savoy had become a significant European power, and in 1861 Victor Emmanuel II of Sardinia was proclaimed King of Italy. The country fought with the Allies in World War I, but Benito Mussolini's Fascists assumed power in 1922, allying with the Nazis in Germany. Following its military defeat and liberation, Italy changed sides to the Allies in World War II and became a republic in 1946. Italy was a founding member of both the European Union and the North Atlantic Treaty Organization.

Italy, with nearly fifty governments in the post-World War II era, has a reputation for having a political revolving door. The governments have consisted, for the most part, of various reincarnations of the same five political parties: the Christian Democrats, Socialists, Republicans, Social Democrats, and the Liberals. In 1996, the Olive Tree coalition, a center-left coalition, was elected to office. Despite this tradition, Romano Prodi, the head of the coalition, has remained in power for more than two years with no serious signs of instability. He might be able to realize one of his political promises: to fulfill a five-year term, a first in Italian post-war politics.

Many businesses close daily from 1:00 to 3:00 p.m. for siesta. Banking hours from Monday to Friday are from 9:00 a.m. to 1:00 p.m., and then again from 2:30 to 4:00 p.m. The postal system is notoriously inefficient; urgent or overnight mail should be sent through private carriers.

Using the language

Finding work in Italy generally requires a knowledge of Italian since, after Americans, Italians are considered the least likely people to learn a foreign language. Don't expect people to respond to inquiries in English.

Current Economic Climate

Although Italy has the fifth largest economy in the world, it is currently experiencing moderate economic trouble. Italy's current unemployment rate is 11.8%. The country experienced a severe economic crisis in 1992-93 that resulted in a succession of governments attempting extreme measures such as the privatization of the country's large public sector. Additionally, the Olive Tree coalition has had to work hard to meet the Maastricht criteria for entry in the European Monetary Union by cutting the budget deficit and lowering inflation in order to be included with the first group of countries in 1999.

Italy's labor force is 58% government and services, 32% industrial, and 10% agricultural. Major industrial products include machinery, automobiles, and textiles. The E.U. and the U.S. constitute the majority of Italy's trading partners. American firms, already big investors in Italy, have begun improving their position in the country.

Despite privatization efforts, many of Italy's large conglomerates are still owned by the state and are considered fairly well run. These giant corporations usually own interests in numerous industries throughout the country. The state-controlled economy does occasionally become involved in political patronage. The large state-owned banks, for example, are each allotted to the Christian Democrats and Socialists, matching bank assets with party strength in parliament. The private sector is also very centralized in the form of huge holding companies. These private conglomerates are generally dominated by one family and represent most of the capitalization of Italy's stock markets.

ITALY'S 10 LARGEST COMPANIES
(1997, composite ranking)
 1. Istituto per la Ricostruzione Industriale
 2. Fiat
 3. Società Finanziaria Telefonica
 4. Enel
 5. Telecom Italia
 6. Ente Nazionale Idrocarburi
 7. Finmeccanica
 8. Pirelli
 9. Assicurazioni Generali
10. Olivetti

Using the phone
Public phones in Italy accept either tokens or cards. Token-operated phones usually require depositing several coins when initiating a call, but they will return the unused portion. Cards can be bought from vending machines. Long-distance telephone rates offered by Italian carriers are

among the highest in Europe, and if possible, you will find it more affordable to use U.S. long-distance services such as AT&T when making international calls.

In 1998, all telephone numbers in Italy were changed in order to bring the country in line with E.U. regulations. All prefixes, including the zero, were incorporated into the actual phone numbers. In December 2000, all phone numbers will change again. The zero will be replaced with a 4 for all phone numbers for fixed telephones and a 3 for mobile telephones.

Getting Around in Italy

Italy's modern railway system still offers relatively inexpensive fares. Eurail and InterRail passes are accepted on all railways. In some mountainous regions, buses are sometimes faster than trains. Buses also serve as a better alternative transportation within cities. Since the Italian highway system, the *autostrade,* is well-kept and expressways available, renting a car can be a good option. Tolls, however, can be expensive. Alitalia is Europe's fifth largest airline. Traveling becomes congested in August, a vacation period in most parts of the country.

Employment Regulations and Outlook for Americans

Italy's high unemployment rate continues to limit job opportunities for foreigners. U.S. citizens do not need visas for stays fewer than 90 days but must obtain one if staying past the 90-day limit. The Ministry of Home Affairs must grant a prospective employee a residence permit for employment. A work permit from an employer must be obtained prior to arrival. Employers must also provide a statement explaining that no Italians in the area can perform the job. Visitors should register with the local police headquarters, the Questura, within three days of arrival. The police headquarters also provides residence permits.

Job opportunities are available to those with specialized skills (working for American companies) and to those willing to work in lower-skill occupations. Most au pair agencies in Europe deal primarily with Italy, where the program is well established. English speakers can also find jobs teaching English for private agencies, individuals, or as readers at universities.

Agricultural work in Italy is done by North Africans, decreasing your chances for jobs on farms. Tourist work in hotels and restaurants is generally difficult to find because of the plentiful supply of local labor. Employers also find the bureaucratic hassle of filling out the paperwork for foreigners discouraging. Individual contacts are very important in Italy. Employers are more likely to consider a foreigner if they have been recommended by someone.

Short-term and Temporary Work

The best bet for temporary and casual work in Italy is to work as an au pair.

Au Pair International
via S. Stefano 32
I-40125 Bologna, Italy
Tel.: [39] 05 126 75 75
Fax: [39] 05 123 65 94

ARCE
via XX Settembre 2/44
I-16121 Genoa, Italy
Tel.: [39] 01 05 83 020

Fax: [39] 01 05 83 092
Long-established au pair agency.

Summer Camps
via Roma 54
I-1803 San Remo, Ligueria, Italy
Tel./Fax: [39] 01 84 50 60 70
Recruits for help in summer camps
throughout Italy.

Internship Programs

Several internship programs offer students opportunities to obtain professional experience. Some programs, such as that run by the American University in Rome, also offer an opportunity to earn academic credit.

American University in Rome
via Pietro Roselli 4
I-00153 Rome, Italy
Tel.: [39] 06 583 30 919
Fax: [39] 06 583 30 992
Internships for students interested in
international business.

IASTE-US
10400 Little Patuxent Parkway, Suite 250 L
Columbia, MD 21044-3510
Tel.: (410) 997-3068
Fax: (410) 997-5186
Email: iaeste@aipt.org
www.aipt/iaste.html

Volunteer Opportunities

Christian Movement for Peace
c/o Volunteers for Peace
International Workcamps
43 Tiffany Road
Belmont, VT 05730
Tel.: (802) 259-2759
Fax: (802) 259-2922
Email: VFP@VFP.prg
www.vfp.org

Emmaus Italia
via la Luna No.1
I-52020 Pergine Valdarno Arezzo, Italy
Organizes 20 workcamps, primarily in
Rome and Milan, around such issues as

fire prevention, site preservation, and
housing renovation, plus opportunities
working with disabled persons and in
theater and film.

Movimento Cristano per la Pace
via Rattazzi 24
Rome, Italy

Service Civil International—Italy
via del Laterani 28
Rome, Italy

Service Civil International—U.S.A.
Route 2, Box 506
Crozet, VA 22932
Tel.: (804) 823-1826

Several smaller organizations also offer volunteer service at specific sites in Italy:

Gruppi Archeologici d'Italia
via Tacito 41
I-00193 Rome, Italy
Tel.: [39] 06 687 4028
Organizes archaeological digs throughout Italy.

Italia Nostra
via Cappelletta 3
Verona, Italy
Organizes archaeological digs.

Kronos
via G.B. Vico 20
I-00196 Rome, Italy
Operates fire-fighting camps in Calabria.

Mani Tese
via Cavenaghi 4
I-20149 Milan, Italy
Tel.: [39] 02 46 97 188
Conducts fund-raising for the Third World.

Servizio Volontariato Gionvanile
Piazza Vanvitelli 8-10
I-81100 Caserta, Italy
Tel.: [39] 08 23 32 25 18
Places volunteers in archaeological camps around Naples.

NEWSPAPERS IN ITALY

Corriere della Sera
via Angelo Rizzoli 2
I-20132 Milan, Italy
Tel.: [39] 02 63 39
Fax: [39] 02 29 00

Il Giornale d'Italia
via Parigi 11
I-00185 Rome, Italy
Tel.: [39] 06 47 49 01
Fax: [39] 06 46 34 35

Il Giornale di Napoli
via Diocleziano 109
I-80125 Naples, Italy

Tel.: [39] 08 17 62 43 00
Fax: [39] 08 17 62 45 44

La Republica
Piazza Indipendenza 11/b
I-00185 Rome, Italy
Tel.: [39] 06 498 21
Fax: [39] 06 498 229 23

La Stampa
via Marenco 32
I-10126 Turin, Italy
Tel.: [39] 01 16 56 81
Fax: [39] 01 16 55 306

Resources for Further Information

USEFUL WEBSITES FOR JOB SEARCHERS

The Internet is a good place to begin your job search. Many websites provide useful information for job searchers researching the Italian job market; there are also several that list job vacancies, especially in technical industries.

La Bacheca
http://www.bacheca.com
Job listings for Italy.

Firenze Online
http://www.fionline.it/lavoro
Posts a wide range of job listings, in Italian.

Irsea Jobs
http://www.starfarm.it/irsea/job.htm
Job search site, in Italian.

Joy Soluzioni Multimedia
http://www.joy.it/occasione/offertel.htm
Posts technical job listings, in Italian.

Lavoro Online
http://www.ba.dada.it/lavoro.html
Database that includes links to Italian companies; posts job listings, in Italian.

EMBASSIES AND CONSULAR OFFICES

American embassies and consulates have commercial and/or economic sections that can provide you with business information and explain aspects of the local economy. Inquiries about business opportunities should be addressed either to "Commercial Officer" or "Commercial Section," followed by the appropriate street address.

Representation of Italy in the United States

Embassy of Italy
1601 Fuller Street NW
Washington, DC 20009
Tel.: (202) 328-5500
Fax: (202) 483-2187
www.italyemb.nw.dc.us:80/Italy/

Italian Consulates General: Chicago, (312) 467-1550; Los Angeles, (310) 820-0098; New York, (212) 737-9100

Representation of the United States in Italy

American Embassy
via Veneto 119/A
I-00187 Rome, Italy
Tel.: [39] 06 46 741
Fax: [39] 06 46 742 217
www.usis.it/

American Consulate General—Florence
Lungarno Amerigo Vespucci 38
I-50123 Florence, Italy
Tel.: [39] 05 52 39 82 76
Fax: [39] 05 52 84 08 8

American Consulate General—Milan
Via Principe Amedeo 2/10
I-20121 Milan, Italy

Tel.: [39] 02 29 03 51
Fax: [39] 02 29 00 11 65

American Consulate General—Naples
Piazza della Republica 2
I-80122 Naples, Italy
Tel.: [39] 08 15 83 81 11
Fax: [39] 08 17 61 18 69

U.S. Information Service
Via Bigli 11
I-20121 Milan, Italy
Tel.: [39] 02 77 19 03 1
Fax: [39] 02 77 19 03 25

CHAMBERS OF COMMERCE

Chambers of commerce consist of firms in both countries interested in international trade. These are appropriate companies to initially target in the job search.

American Chamber of Commerce in Italy
via Cantù, 1
I-20123 Milan, Italy
Tel.: [39] 02 869 0661
Fax: [39] 02 805 7737
www.amcham.it

Italy-America Chamber of Commerce
730 Fifth Avenue, Suite 600
New York, NY 10019

Tel.: (212) 459-0044
Fax: (212) 459-0090
www.italchambers.net/newyork

Chamber of Commerce of Bologna
Piazza Affari
Piazza Costituzione 8
I-40129 Bologna, Italy
Tel.: [39] 05 16 09 31 11
Fax: [39] 05 16 09 34 51

Milan Chamber of Commerce
via Meravigli 9/B-11
I-20123 Milan, Italy
Tel.: [39] 02 85 15 1
Fax: [39] 02 85 15 42 32

Rome Chamber of Commerce
via de Burro 147
I-00186 Rome, Italy
Tel.: [39] 06 52 08 21
Fax: [39] 06 58 23 38

WORLD TRADE CENTERS IN ITALY

World Trade Centers usually include many foreign companies operating in the country.

World Trade Center Genoa
Via De Marini 1
I-16149 Genoa, Italy
Tel.: [39] 01 02 42 30 01
Fax: [39] 01 02 64 56 802
Email: wtc_ge@tn.villate.it

World Trade Center Milan
World Trade Center Milano
Via Tamburini 13
I-20123 Milan, Italy
Tel.: [39] 02 46 32 60
Fax: [39] 02 48 56 161

OTHER INFORMATIONAL ORGANIZATIONS

Foreign government missions in the U.S. such as national tourist offices can furnish visas and information on work permits and other important regulations. They may also offer economic and business information about the country.

Italian Cultural Institute
686 Park Avenue
New York, NY 10021

Italian Government Travel Office
630 Fifth Avenue, 15th Floor
Rockefeller Center
New York, NY 10111

Tel.: (212) 245-4822
Fax: (212) 586-9249

United Nations Information Center
Palazzetto Venezia
Piazza San Marco 50
Rome, Italy

BUSINESS DIRECTORIES

Although not always easy to find, business directories can prove invaluable in the international job search. Most directories list company names, addresses, products, and phone numbers. Some directories include executive names and titles and financial information about the company. These sources provide you with the names of the people to contact for employment information as well as financial data, which can tell you how strong a company's position in a country may be.

Annuario delle Banche e Finanziarie (Banking and Finance). Published by Bancaria Editrice, Piazza del Gesu 49, I-00186 Rome, Italy. Directory of banks, credit and financial institutions.

Directory of Foreign Firms Operating Abroad: Italy. World Trade Academy Press, 257 Central Park West, Suite 10A, New York, NY 10024-4110; email: uniworldbp@aol.com; www.uniworldbp.com. Lists names and addresses of parent companies in the U.S. and their subsidiaries and affiliates in Italy.

Guide to the Italian Clothing Industry. GESTO, via Mercatoe 28, I-20121 Milan, Italy; email: gesto@sente.it. Over 5,000 apparel manufacturers.

ITALI. Published in Italian by SEAT, SS 148 Pontina, KM 29, 100, I-00040 Rome, Italy. Lists 260,000 Italian companies in all businesses.

Italian American Business Directory. Published annually by the American Chamber of Commerce in Italy, via Cesare Cantu 1, I-20123 Milan, Italy; email: amcham@amcham.it; www.amcham.it. Describes 40,000 Italian and American firms engaged in bilateral trade.

Italian General Directory. Published annually by Guida Monaci, via Vitorchiano 107/109, I-00189 Rome, Italy; email: guidamonaci@italybygm.it; www.italygygm.it. Lists 100,000 industrial and commercial firms.

Kompass Italia. Published annually in Italian by Kompass Italia, fia Servais 125, I-10146 Turin, Italy. Includes 40,000 manufacturing and service companies.

United States–Italy Trade Directory. Published annually by the Italy-America Chamber of Commerce, 730 Fifth Avenue, Suite 600, New York, NY 10119. Lists 4,000 American firms with Italian business interests.

AMERICAN COMPANIES IN ITALY

Many American firms operate in Italy. The following companies are classified by business area: Banking and Finance; Industrial Manufacturing; Retailing and Wholesaling; and Service Industries. Company information includes firm name, address, telephone and fax number where possible, specific business, and American parent company. Your chances of achieving employment abroad are substantially better if you contact the subsidiary company in Europe rather than the parent company in the U.S.

BANKING AND FINANCE

Chase Manhattan Bank Association
piazza Meda 1
Casella Postale 10932
I-20121 Milan, Italy
Tel.: [39] 02 8542 1
(Bank)
Citicorp

INDUSTRIAL MANUFACTURING

Abbott SPA
Strada Statale 148 Km. 52
I-04010 Aprilia, Italy
Tel.: [39] 06 92 89 21
Fax: [39] 06 92 53 193
(Pharmaceuticals)
Abbott Laboratories

Avon cosmetics SPA
via XXV Aprile 15
I-22077 Olgiate Comasco (CO), Italy
Tel.: [39] 03 19 98 11 1
Fax: [39] 03 19 98 31 2
(Cosmetics and perfumes)
Avon Products Inc.

Beloit Italia SPA
via Martiri del XXII 1921, 76
I-10064 Pinerolo, Italy
Tel.: [39] 01 21 23 11
Fax: [39] 01 21 39 76 37
(Machinery)
Beloit Corp.

Black & Decker Italia SPA
via del Crotto 1
I-23862 Civate Lc, Italy
Tel.: [39] 03 41 58 91 11
Fax: [39] 03 41 55 10 51
(Handheld power tools)
Black & Decker Co.

Bridgestone Firestone Italia SPA
Contrada Gambetta 9
I-70026 Modugno, Italy
Tel.: [39] 08 05 06 31 11
Fax: [39] 08 05 06 33 33
(Tires)
Firestone Tire & Rubber Co.

Bristol-Myers Squibb SPA
via Paolo di Dono 73
I-00143 Rome, Italy
Tel.: [39] 06 250 396
Fax: [39] 06 250 396 530
(Pharmaceuticals and chemicals)
E.R. Squibb & Sons Inc.

Chiquita Italia SPA
via Tempio del Cielo 3
I-00144 Rome, Italy
Tel.: [39] 06 52 08 31
Fax: [39] 06 52 95 49 9
(Fruit and fruit products)
Chiquita Brands International Inc.

Colgate Palmolive SPA
via Palmolive 18,
I-00042 Anzio, Rome, Italy
Tel.: [39] 06 983 91
Fax: [39] 06 98 98 84 33
(Soap, toiletries, cosmetics)
Colgate Palmolive Corp.

Cyanamid Italia SPA
via Franco Gorgone 6
I-95121 Catania, Italy
Tel.: [39] 09 55 98 11 1
Fax: [39] 09 57 18 01 34
(Chemicals)
American Cyanamid Co.

Digital Equipment SPA
viale Fulvio Testi 280/6
I-20126 Milan, Italy
Tel.: [39] 02 26 61 81
Fax: [39] 02 66 10 25 95
(Electronic equipment)
Digital Equipment Corp.

Dow Italia SPA
via Patroculo 21
I-20151 Milan, Italy
Tel.: [39] 02 48 221
Fax: [39] 02 48 22 43 66
(Chemicals and plastics)
Dow Chemical Co.

DuPont de Nemours Italiana SPA
via Volta 16
I-20093 Cologno Monzese, Italy
Tel.: [39] 02 25 30 21
Fax: [39] 02 25 47 76 5
(Chemicals)
E.I DuPont de Nemours & Co.

Exxon Chemical Mediterranea SPA
via Paleocapa 7
I-20121 Milan, Italy
Tel.: [39] 02 88 031
Fax: [39] 02 88 03 231
(Chemicals)
Exxon Corp.

Ford Italiana SPA
viale Pasteur 8/10
I-00144 Rome (RM), Italy
Tel.: [39] 06 54 47 1
(Automobiles)
Ford Motor Co.

Gillette Group Italy SPA
via Pirelli 18
I-20124 Milan, Italy
Tel.: [39] 02 66 78 1
Fax: [39] 02 66 78 101
(Toiletries)
Gillette Co.

Goodyear Italiana SPA
piazza G Marconi 25
I-00144, Rome, Italy
Tel.: [39] 06 54 39 01
Fax: [39] 06 54 39 02 31
(Tires)
Goodyear Tire & Rubber Co.

Grace Italiana SPA
via Trento 7
I-20017 Rho, Italy
Tel.: [39] 02 93 32 1
Fax: [39] 02 93 32 555
(Chemicals and pharmaceuticals)
W.R. Grace & Co.

Honeywell Information Systems SPA
via Pirelli 32
I-20124 Milan, Italy
Tel.: [39] 02 67 79 1
Fax: [39] 02 67 79 23 60
(Computers and software)
Honeywell Information Systems Inc.

Ingersoll-Rand Italiana SPA
Strada Provinciale Sassanese
I-20060 Vignate, Italy
Tel.: [39] 02 95 05 61
Fax: [39] 02 95 60 315
(Industrial equipment and machinery)
Ingersoll-Rand Co.

International Paper Italia SPA
via Ornago 55
I-20040 Bellusco, Italy
Tel.: [39] 06 27 45 1
Fax: [39] 06 96 22 366
(Paper products)
International Paper Co.

Johnson Wax SPA
piazza M. Burke 3
I-20020 Arese, Italy
Tel.: [39] 02 93 37 1
Fax: [39] 02 93 37 407
(Household cleaning products)
S.C. Johnson & Son, Inc.

Kraft General Foods SPA
via Montecuccoli 21
I-20147 Milan, Italy
Tel.: [39] 02 41 35 1
Fax: [39] 02 41 35 45 00
(Food processing)
Kraft General Foods, Inc.

Levi Strauss Italia SPA
Cso Como 15
I-20154 Milan, Italy
Tel.: [39] 02 29 02 31
Fax: [39] 02 29 00 36 81
(Clothing)
Levi Strauss & Co.

Litton Italia SPA
via Pontina Km 27.800
I-00040 Pomezia, Italy
Tel.: [39] 06 91 19 21
Fax: [39] 06 91 22 51 7
(Computers)
Litton International SA

Mattel Toys SPA
via Vittorio Veneto 119
I-28040 Oleggio Castello (NO), Italy
Tel.: [39] 03 22 23 13 11
Fax: [39] 03 22 23 14 94
(Toys and games)
Mattel Inc.

RETAILING AND WHOLESALING

Apple Computer SPA
via Milano
I-20093 Cologno Monzese, Italy
Tel.: [39] 02 73 26 1
Fax: [39] 02 27 32 65 55
(Computers and software)
Apple Computer Corp.

Merck Sharp & Dohme (Italia) SPA
via Fabbroni 6
I-00191 Rome, Italy
Tel.: [39] 06 36 19 11
Fax: [39] 06 36 30 86 19
(Pharmaceuticals)
Merck Sharp & Dohme (International)
Ltd.

Mobil Oil Italiana SPA
via vittorio Brancati 60
I-00144 Rome, Italy
Tel.: [39] 06 50 51 32 12
(Petroleum products)
Mobil Corp.

Motorola SPA
Centro Milanofiori Str. 2
I-20090 Assago, Italy
Tel.: [39] 02 82 201
(Electronic equipment)
Motorola Co.

Pfizer Italiana SPA
via Valbondone 113
I-00188 Rome, Italy
Tel.: [39] 06 33 18 2
Fax: [39] 06 33 62 60 19
(Chemicals and pharmaceuticals)
Pfizer Inc.

Pharmacia and Upjohn SPA
via Koch 12
I-20152 Milan, Italy
Tel.: [39] 02 48 83 81
Fax: [39] 02 48 38 27 34
(Pharmaceuticals)
The Upjohn Co.

Procter & Gamble Italia SPA
viale Cesare Pavese 385
I-00144 Rome, Italy

Unisys Italia SPA
via B Crespi 57
I-20159 Milan, Italy
Tel.: [39] 02 69 85 1
Fax: [39] 02 69 85 588
(Software and electronic equipment)
Unisys Corp.

Coca Cola Italiana
Galleria Passerella 1
I-20122 Milan, Italy
Tel.:[39] 02 76 09 71
Fax: [39] 02 76 01 44 28
(Soft drinks)
The Coca Cola Co.

Dolma SPA
via Dante 40
I-27011 Belgioioso, Italy
Tel.: [39] 03 82 97 91
Fax: [39] 03 82 97 04 93
(Confectionery)
Mars Inc.

General Motors Italia SPA
piazzace del Industria 40
I-00144 Rome, Italy
Tel.: [39] 06 54 56 1
(Motor vehicles)
General Motors Corp.

Hewlett-Packard Italiana SPA
via G. di Vittorio 9
I-20063 Cernusco S/N (MI), Italy
Tel.: [39] 02 92 121
Fax: [39] 02 92 10 44 73
(Electronic equipment)
Hewlett-Packard Co.

Kodak SPA
viale Mattelotti 62
I-20092 Cinisello Balsamo, Italy
Tel.: [39] 02 66 02 81
Fax: [39] 02 66 02 85 07
(Photographic equipment)
Eastman Kodak Co.

Kraft Jacobs Suclard SPA
via Montecuccoli 21
I-20147 Milan, Italy
Tel.: [39] 09 20 41 351
Fax: [39] 09 20 41 354 500
(Philip Morris Co. Inc.)

Motorola SPA
via Milanofiori
I-20090 Milan, Italy
Tel.: [39] 02 82 201

(Communication equipment)
Motorola Inc.

Pharmacia and Upjohn SPA
via Koch 12
I-20152 Milan, Italy
Tel.: [39] 02 48 83 81
Fax: [39] 02 48 38 27 34
(Pharmaceuticals)
The Upjohn Co.

Polaroid (Italia) SPA
via Piave 11
I-20151 Arcisate, Italy
Tel.: [39] 03 32 47 00 31
Fax: [39] 03 32 47 82 49
(Photographic equipment)
Polaroid Inc.

Texas Instruments Italia SPA
via Pacinotti 5/7
I-67051 Avezzano, Italy
Tel.: [39] 08 63 42 31
Fax: [39] 08 63 41 27 63
(Electronic equipment)
Texas Instruments Inc.

3M Italia SPA
via S. Bovio 1/3
I-20090 Segrate, Italy
Tel.: [39] 02 70 35 1
Fax: [39] 02 70 35 30 93
(Adhesives, copying equipment)
Minnesota Mining and Manufacturing
Co.

Xerox SPA
strada Padana Superiore 28
I-20063 Cernusco Naviglio, Italy
Tel.: [39] 02 92 18 81
(Office machines)
Rank Xerox (Management) Ltd.

SERVICE INDUSTRIES

Arthur Andersen & Co.
via della Moscova 3
I-20121 Milan, Italy
Tel.: [39] 02 29 03 71
Fax: [39] 02 29 03 76 97
(Accountancy, management consulting)
Arthur Andersen & Co.

DHL International SRL
Milanofiori Palazzo u/3
I-20089 Rozzano, Italy

Tel.: [39] 02 57 57 21
Fax: [39] 02 89 20 80 99
(Air cargo services)
DHL International

United Parcel Service Italia SPA
via Fantoli 15/2
I-20138 Milan, Italy
Tel.: [39] 02 50 79 1
Fax: [39] 02 55 40 01 80
(Freight transport)

EUROPEAN COMPANIES IN ITALY

The following are major non-American firms operating in the country. These selected companies can be either Italian or foreign, usually other European. Such companies will generally hire their own nationals first but may employ Americans.

BANKING AND FINANCE

Assicurazioni Generali SPA
via Savona 123
I-20144 Milan, Italy
Tel.: [39] 01 14 35 31 98
(Insurance and reinsurance)

Banca Commerciale Italiana SPA
piazza della Scala 6
I-20121 Milan, Italy
Tel.: [39] 02 88 501
Fax: [39] 02 88 50 30 26
(Commercial bank)

Banca Nazionale del Lavoro SPA
via Venetilo 119
I-00100 Rome, Italy
Tel.: [39] 06 47 02 1
Fax: [39] 06 47 02 84 45
(Bank)

Banca Popolare di Novara SCRL
via Negroni 12
28100 Novara, Italy
Tel.: [39] 03 21 66 21 11
Fax: [39] 03 21 66 20 06
(Bank)

Banca di Roma SPA
via Minghetti 17
I-00187 Rome, Italy
Tel.: [39] 06 67 07 1
Fax: [39] 06 66 44 52 451
(Government bank)

Barclays Bank PLC
via della Moscova 18
I-20121 Milan, Italy
Tel.: [39] 02 63 72 1
Fax: [39] 02 63 72 20 45
(Bank)

Credito Italiano SPA
piazza Cordusio
I-20123 Milan, Italy
Tel.: [39] 02 88 62 1
Fax: [39] 02 88 62 35 24
(Banking and credit services)

ICCRI Instituto Credito Delle Cassedi Risparmio
via di San Basilio 15
I-00187 Rome, Italy
Tel.: [39] 06 47 15 1
Fax: [39] 06 48 24 508
(Credit company)

IRI-Instituto per la Ricostruzione Industriale
via Veneto 89
I-00187 Rome, Italy
Tel.: [39] 06 47 271
Fax: [39] 06 47 27 23 08
(Holding co.)

INDUSTRIAL MANUFACTURING

AGIP Petroli SPA
via Laurentina 449
I-00142 Rome, Italy
Tel.: [39] 06 59 88 1
Fax: [39] 06 59 88 57 00
(Oil and gas exploration and production)

Assicurazioni Gerali SPA
piazza Duca degli Abruzzi 2
I-34100 Trieste, Italy
Tel.: [39] 04 67 11
Fax: [39] 04 67 16 00
(Insurance)

BASF Vernici E Inchiostri
via Margherita de Vizzi 51/A

I-20092 Cinisello Balsamo, Italy
Tel.: [39] 02 61 79 51
Fax: [39] 02 66 01 04 11
(Chemicals)
BASF AG, Germany

Benetton Group SPA
via Villa Minelli 1
I-31050 Ponzano Veneto, Italy
Tel.: [39] 04 22 44 91
Fax: [39] 04 22 96 501
(Clothing)

BP Italia SPA
Str. 6 Pal. E/5 Milanofiori
I-20090 Assago, Italy

Tel.: [39] 02 82 27 41
Fax: [39] 02 57 51 959
(Petroleum products)

Cartiere Burgo SPA
via del Freidano 8
I-10099 San Mauro Torinese, Italy
Tel.: [39] 01 12 23 31 11
Fax: [39] 01 12 23 34 10
(Paper products)

Danieli & C. Officine Meccaniche SPA
via Nazione 41
I-33042 Buttrio, Italy
Tel.: [33] 04 32 59 81
Fax: [33] 04 32 59 82 89
(Industrial machinery)

Enel SpA
via G.B. Martini, 3
I-00198 Rome, Italy
Tel.: [39] 06 850 91
Fax: [39] 06 85 85 70 97
(Electricity)

ERG Petroli SPA
Strada Statale 114 km
I-96010 Priolo Gargallo, Italy
Tel.: [39] 09 31 76 21 11
Fax: [39] 09 31 76 27 14

Falck, Acciaierie Ferriere Lombarde SPA
via Falck 63
I-20099 Sesto San Giovanni, Italy
Tel.: [39] 02 24 901
Fax: [39] 02 24 90 23 38
(Steel)

Fiat Auto SPA
Corso Giovanni Agnelli 200
I-10135 Turin, Italy
Tel.: [39] 01 16 83 11 11
Fax: [39] 01 16 83 75 91
(Automobiles and commercial vehicles)

Glaxo Welcome SPA
via Fleming 2
I-37135 Verona Zai, Italy
Tel.: [39] 04 59 21 81 11
Fax: [39] 04 59 21 83 88
(Pharmaceuticals)

Hoechst Italia SPA
via Traiano 18
I-20149 Milan, Italy
Tel.: [39] 02 31 07 1
(Chemicals and pharmaceuticals)

IBM Italia SPA
Circonvallaziona Idroscalo
I-20090 Segrate, Italy

Tel.: [39] 02 59 62 1
Fax: [39] 02 59 62 47 86
(Computers and software)

I.R.I. Instituto per la Ricostruzione Industriale SPA.
via Veneto 89
I-00187 Rome, Italy
Tel.: [39] 06 47 27 1
Fax: [39] 06 47 27 23 08
(Banks; steel production; high technology)

Italiana Petroli
piazza della Vittorio 1
I-16121 Genoa, Italy
Tel.: [39] 010 57 71
Fax: [39] 010 54 10 04
(Petroleum refining)

Magnetti Marelli SPA
via Timavo 33
I-40131 Bologna, Italy
Tel.: [39] 05 16 16 75 11
Fax: [39] 05 16 15 70 20
(Electrical equipment)

Montedison SPA
Foro Buonaparte 31
I-20121 Milan, Italy
Tel.: [39] 02 63 331
Fax: [39] 02 62 701
(Agro-industrial; chemicals & pharmaceuticals; energy; engineering; real estate)

Olivetti SPA
via Jervis 77
I-10015 Ivrea, Italy
Tel.: [39] 01 25 52 90 89
Fax: [39] 01 25 52 92 78
(Information technology, office products)

Pirelli SPA
viale Sarca
I-20126 Milan, Italy
Tel.: [39] 02 64 421
Fax: [39] 02 64 42 33 00
(Tires and cables)

Rizzoli Periodici SPA
via Rizzoli 2
I-20132 Milan, Italy
Tel.: [39] 02 25 841
Fax: [39] 02 25 84 39 03
(Magazine publishing)

SNIA BPD SPA
via Borgonuovo 14
I-20121 Milan, Italy
Tel.: [39] 02 63 321 11
Fax: [39] 02 63 321
(Textiles)

SERVICE INDUSTRIES

Alitalia SPA
aeroporto Capodichino
I-80100 Naples, Italy
Tel.: [39] 08 17 09 11 11
Fax: [39] 08 17 09 30 50
(Airline)

CIGA Hotels Italia SPA
(Compagnia Italiana Grandi Alberghi)
piazza Della Republica 32
I-20124 Milan, Italy
Tel.: [39] 02 62 661
Fax: [39] 02 67 00 571
(Hotel administration)

Costa Crociere SPA
via G D'Annuzio 2
I-16121 Genoa, Italy
Tel.: [39] 01 05 48 31
Fax: [39] 01 05 48 32 90
(Shipping services)

Italgas Area SUD
Centro Direzionale
I-80100 Naples, Italy

Tel.: [39] 08 12 27 81 11
Fax: [39] 08 17 65 14 21
(Natural gas)

Italtel Tecnoelettronica
via Brocchi
I-20019 Settimo Milan, Italy
Tel.: [39] 02 43 88 1
Fax: [39] 02 43 88 83 50
(Telecommunications)

Societá Finanziaria Telefonica
Corso d'Italia 41
I-00198 Rome, Italy
Tel.: [39] 06 85 89 1
Fax: [39] 06 85 89 434
(Telecommunication; publishing;
marketing; information processing)

Telecom Italia SPA
via San Dalmazzo 15
10122 Turin, Italy
Tel.: [39] 01 15 51 41
Fax: [39] 01 15 32 269
(Telephone service)

INTERNATIONAL NON-PROFIT EMPLOYERS IN ITALY

Food Agriculture Organization of the U.N.
Via delle Terme di Caracalla
I-00100 Rome, Italy
Tel.: [39] 06 57 971

**International Association Against
Torture**
Via Ugo Foscolo 3
Casella Postale 1487

I-20100 Milan, Italy
Tel.: [39] 02 89 01 64 11

Italo-Latin American Institute
Piazza Guglielmo Marconi 26
I-00144 Rome, Italy
Tel.: [39] 06 59 09 1
Fax: [39] 06 59 14 92 3

INTERNATIONAL SCHOOLS IN ITALY

**American International School of
Florence**
via del Carota 23/25
I-50012 Bagno a Ripoli
Florence, Italy
Tel.: [39] 05 56 46 10 07
Fax: [39] 05 56 44 22 6
Email: admin.aisf@interbusiness.it
(U.S./International Baccalaureate
curriculum, pre-K-12)

American International School in Genoa
Via Quarto 13/C
I-16148 Genoa, Italy

Tel.: [39] 01 03 86 52 8
Fax: [39] 01 03 98 70 0
Email: aisgenoa@tin.it
(U.S., pre-K-8)

American Overseas School of Rome
Via Cassia 811
I-00189 Rome, Italy
Tel.: [39] 06 33 26 48 41
Fax: [39] 06 33 26 85 31
Email: aosr.admissions@agora.stm.it
www.nexus.it/aosr
(U.S./I.B., pre-K-13)

American School of Milan
Villagio Mirasole
I-20090 Noverasco di Opera
Milan, Italy
Tel.: [39] 02 53 00 00 1
Fax: [39] 02 57 60 62 74
Email: directorasm@planet.it
(U.S./I.B., pre-K-13)

International School of Milan
Via Caccialepori 22
I-20148 Milan, Italy
Tel.: [39] 02 4091 0067
Fax: [39] 02 4870 3644
Email: ismhigh@telemacus.it
(U.K./I.B., pre-K-13)

International School of Naples
Building A, HQ AFSOUTH
Post Viale della
Liberazione 1
I-80125 Bagnoli, Naples, Italy
Tel.: [39] 08 17 21 20 37
Fax: [39] 08 17 62 84 29
Email: isn@na.cybernet.it
(U.S., pre-K-12)

International School of Trieste
via Conconello 16 (Opicina)
I-34016 Trieste, Italy
Tel.: [39] 04 02 11 452
Fax: [39] 04 02 13 122
Email: istrieste@interbusiness.it
(U.S., pre-K-8)

International School of Turin (ACAT)
Vicolo Tiziano 10,
I-10024 Moncalieri, Turin, Italy
Tel.: [39] 01 16 45 967
Fax: [39] 01 16 43 298
Email: acatist@hotmail.com
www.saa.unito.it/ist/
(U.S./Italian/I.B., pre-K-12)

Marymount International School
Via di Villa Lauchli 180
Via Cassia Antica 7 km
I-00191 Rome, Italy
Tel.: [39] 06 36 30 17 42
Fax: [39] 06 36 30 17 38
Email: Marymount@pronet.it
(U.S./I.B., pre-K-13)

Germany

MAJOR EMPLOYMENT CENTERS: Frankfurt, Munich, Hamburg, Berlin

MAJOR BUSINESS LANGUAGE: German

LANGUAGE SKILL INDEX: English is spoken by younger people, and it is possible to get by in informal situations with English. German proficiency, however, is usually required in business

CURRENCY: Euro; the Deutsch mark will remain the currency in circulation until 2002

TELEPHONE COUNTRY CODE: 49

TIME ZONE: EST+6

PUNCTUALITY INDEX: Germans are very formal and punctuality is absolutely required.

AVERAGE DAILY TEMPERATURE, HIGH/LOW: January, 35/26°F; July, 74/55°F (Munich)

AVERAGE NUMBER OF DAYS WITH PRECIPITATION: January, 11; July, 19

BEST BET FOR EMPLOYMENT:

FOR STUDENTS: CIEE or resort/hotel work

PERMANENT JOBS: High tech/engineering

CHANCE OF FINDING A JOB: Not bad using the above options, but expect stiff competition due to high unemployment

TRIVIA: German workers enjoy the most paid holidays in the world, with 42 per year

Germany, located in north-central Europe, borders Denmark and the Baltic Sea to the north; the Netherlands, Belgium, Luxembourg, and France to the west; Switzerland and Austria to the south; and the former Czechoslovakia and Poland to the east. Germany is larger than New Mexico but smaller than California. Northern and central Germany are generally flat, while the west is hilly and the south is mountainous.

Charlemagne conquered most of the Germanic tribes occupying the territories of present-day Germany, which became the German Empire following his death. Germany eventually dissolved into numerous principalities, with religious conflicts between Catholics and Protestants exacerbating the process during the Reformation. Following the Napoleonic period, Prussia and Hapsburg Austria contended for control of Germany. Under the guidance of the chancellor Otto von Bismarck, the Prussians eventually outmaneuvered the Austrians and the French. The second German Empire was proclaimed in 1871.

Germany was defeated in World War I, losing its overseas colonies and large tracts of its European lands. The Republic of Germany was proclaimed in 1919, embodying the most liberal principles of the time. The republic, known as the Weimar Republic, suffered from economic turmoil, an undemocratic political culture, and onerous sanctions imposed by the Treaty of Versailles. The worldwide depression shattered the republic and led to the appointment of Adolf Hitler as chancellor in 1933. By 1938, Hitler had established a Nazi totalitarian state, violated the Versailles Treaty, and occupied Austria and much of Czechoslovakia. In 1939 Germany invaded Poland, and World War II began.

Following Germany's defeat in 1945, the U.S., the U.S.S.R., Britain, and France divided the country into occupation zones. Berlin, fully within the Soviet sector, was similarly divided. Germany lost large portions of land in the east to Poland and the Soviet Union. The Federal Republic was created in 1949 in the American, British, and French zones. In response, the Soviets imposed a blockade upon West Berlin. West Germany became fully independent in 1955.

The German Democratic Republic was declared in 1949 and proclaimed independent in 1954. West Germany joined the European Community and the North Atlantic Treaty Organization, while East Germany joined the Warsaw Pact Organization and Comecon. Both German states entered the United Nations in 1973. West Germany's major parties included the Christian Democrats, the Social Democrats, the Free Democrats, and the Greens. The communist Socialist Unity party dominated East Germany until the collapse of the East European regimes in late 1989.

Two of the most enduring symbols of the end of the Cold War—the opening of the Berlin Wall on November 9, 1989, and the unification of the two Germanys on October 3, 1990—were sudden and largely unexpected. For forty years, the two German states had existed side by side, looking back on the same historical traditions but taking diametrically opposite paths. The West was democratic, federalist, and oriented to a market economy, and the East was socialist, centralist, and operated a planned economy. Unification, although long desired, was not easy. It has both benefited and strained the German economy, and it has pushed Germany into the forefront as the E.U.'s most powerful nation.

Although now united in name as a country, Germany is not yet united in spirit. Even 10 years after unification, some "Ossis" (East Germans) still view the East German reunification with *der Vaterland* more as a West German occupation than a liberation. East Germany, which once enjoyed the highest standard of living of the East European countries, has faced economic turmoil and mild prejudice from "Wessis" counterparts since "The Change." The unemployment rate in the eastern states is still higher than that in the western. The government decided in June, 1991, to move Germany's capital from Bonn to Berlin, and the Bundestag will resume sitting in Berlin's Reichstag building in September 1999.

Gerhard Schroeder, a Social Democrat, was elected Prime Minister in October, 1998. In a stinging humiliation, Helmut Kohl and his Christian Democrats, who had been in power for 16 years, won only 35% of the national vote. Schroeder's government entered into a coalition with the Greens. Despite the change in leadership, Schroeder has made clear any shift in German policies will be gradual and that maintaining economic stability will be his priority.

Post offices in Germany are usually open from 8:00 a.m. to 6:00 p.m., Monday through Friday, and 8:00 a.m. to noon on Saturday. Banks are open 9:00 a.m. to 4:00 p.m., with a break from noon to 2:00 p.m., Monday through Friday. Normal business hours are from 8:30 a.m. to 6:00 p.m., Monday through Friday. August is the major vacation month in Germany, so you shouldn't expect to conduct much business then.

Current Economic Climate

After unification, Germany became Europe's indisputable leading economic power. Both West and East Germany possessed highly industrialized economies and well-trained work forces, and East Germany, which already conducted business in eastern Europe, stood to gain substantially from economic liberalization. Unification has restored prime food-producing regions to Germany as well as principal industrial areas.

There still exists great discrepancies between former East and West Germanys. The east still has twice as many unemployed people as the west (currently at about 9%). Overall investments in eastern Germany have now declined from peak levels in the early 1990s, and annual growth there is currently 1.6% (as compared to 2.3% in western Germany). With the decline of traditional heavy industries in the region, tourism has developed into an important economic sector. Under the leadership of Prime Minister Schroeder, economists are anticipating growth in the next millennium. The government has closed industries using old and inefficient methods, and economic recovery is expected to require the present level of government funding for at least ten more years.

Approximately 60% of the work force is industrial, 30% services, and 10% agricultural. Major products include machinery, chemicals, shipbuilding, automobiles, and steel. Most German trade is conducted with the E.U. and the U.S. Germany consistently ranks as the world's first or second largest exporter.

GERMANY'S 10 LARGEST COMPANIES

(1997, composite ranking)
1. Siemens
2. Deutsche Post
3. Daimler Benz
4. Volkswagen
5. Deutsche Telekom
6. Deutsche Bundesbahn
7. Tengelmann Group
8. Europa Carton
9. Hoechst
10. Robert Bosch

Using the phone, fax, and Internet

Like most of Europe, pay phones in Germany generally only accept phonecards, available at post offices, news kiosks, tourist offices, and banks. Phonecards offered by private companies are now available since Telekom has lost its monopoly status. To reach a German operator, dial 0010. For information, dial 11834. Most post offices have public fax-phones that operate with a phonecard. Cybercafes are increasingly popular, especially in major cities, making it easy to access your Email. If you will be using your own laptop computer, you will need a special kit in order to use local telephone plugs.

Getting Around in Germany

Eurail and InterRail passes are accepted in Germany. The national railway network, GermanRail, also offers various discounts. The Deutsche Bundesbahn (DB), the railroad system in the west, is one of Europe's fastest networks. Since the reunification of East and West, Germany has experienced some difficulty linking up the former East Germany's rail system, the Reichsbahn, with its Western counterpart. Commuter trains are rather slow. The KD German Rhine steamers provide transportation services along the Rhine, Moselle, and Main rivers. Buses are also available. Lufthansa is one of Europe's busiest airlines and features connections to various parts of eastern Europe.

Riding the rails in Germany

For anyone who may have doubts about train travel in Germany, fear not. I don't speak much German, but managed nevertheless to make my way virtually trouble-free through Germany and part of Austria on a 15-day Eurail Pass. Station announcements are generally given both in English and German, which was a big help.

I traveled first-class—not necessarily by choice, but because non-students aren't eligible for second-class fares with the Eurail Pass. The trains were invariably clean, fast, and on time. ("On time," by the way, has two connotations. First, obviously, that schedules are reliable. And second, that you'd better be organized about getting on and off trains, since conductors keep down-time to a minimum!)

Trains were very comfortable. Seating is divided into compartments, which seat five or six, with some designated for smoking, others for non-smoking. I wasn't aware of any sleeping cars, but seats pull flat to form a sleeping platform that is at least functional, if not exactly cushy. Windows on older trains open, which was pleasant. (Windows on newer trains don't open, but the cars are air-conditioned.) Crowding was only a problem during rush hour, but even then I could always find a seat. During non-peak hours it wasn't uncommon for one or two passengers to have a compartment all to themselves.

Dogs are allowed on the trains, so anyone traveling with a four-footed friend shouldn't have any problems. There are also bicycle cars, where cyclists can stow their bikes. The only complaint I had in over two weeks of travel is that food service on trains seemed inconsistent. Some trains had dining cars, some had vending trolleys that were carted through the aisles, some had no food service at all. If you can plan around this one minor detail, though, you should find traveling by rail to be smooth sailing—so to speak—all the way.—J.P. Buenker

Employment Regulations and Outlook for Americans

Americans do not need a visa for stays of fewer than 90 days in Germany. Work permits, which are required to obtain employment in Germany, may be applied for at the employment office after entering the country. Local embassies and consulates can provide applications for visas and residence permits, which are required for anyone seeking employment. German employers tend to emphasize academic performance and expect detailed academic records from applicants. There are generally more German graduates than jobs in all areas, with the exception of graduates in highly technical fields.

The German Central Placement office, Zentralstelle fur Arbeitsvermittlung (ZAV), can be useful in the job search. For example, they may review a foreign job applicant's chances for employment in Germany. American citizens, as non-E.U. nationals, must demonstrate some special skill to be received favorably and become listed in the ZAV's bulletins to employers. The ZAV also offers a summer jobs program in which Americans can participate, with most positions in the tourist industry.

College students may work for up to five months through the CIEE's Work in Germany program. Foreign students currently enrolled in German schools can also work between school terms without a permit.

Zentralstelle fur Arbeitsvermittlung
Postfach 17 05 45
D-60079 Frankfurt-am-Main, Germany
Tel: [49] (69) 71 11 0

Most unskilled labor in Germany is performed by over 1 million foreign workers, *gastarbeiter*, limiting employment opportunities for Americans seeking temporary work. The Federal Employment Institute, *Bundesanstalt fur Arbeit* (Regenburgerstrasse 104, D-9023 Nurnberg, Germany) operates an extensive chain of employment offices throughout the country. These employment offices, the *Arbeitsamter*, maintain a virtual legal monopoly on job placement, although some private employment agencies have recently begun operating. The Bundesanstadt also sets up temporary employment offices, Service-Vermittlung, when necessary.

Unregulated jobs in the black market, known as *schwarzarbeit*, can be found in bars and hotels. These jobs usually pay in cash without tax withholding but offer no legal protections. The best places to find tourist work are Munich, Berlin, the southern Bavarian Alps, coastal areas, and forest areas in the southwestern part of the country. Jobs may also be found on U.S. military bases, although the U.S. military presence in Germany is diminishing of late.

If you are a student, you can bypass the usual employment restrictions by contacting the Council for International Educational Exchange (CIEE), which provides permits allowing American students to work in Germany for up to five months.

CIEE
205 East 42nd Street
New York, NY 10017
Tel.: (888) COUNCIL
Email:wabrochure@ciee.org
www.ciee.org

Short-term and Temporary Work

There are plenty of opportunities for casual work as an au pair.

Au Pair in Germany
Uberstrasse 94
D-53173 Bonn, Germany
Tel.: [49] (228) 95 7300
Au pair placements for all nationalities.

Au Pair Service International
Nelkenweg 6
D-74391 Erligheim, Germany
Tel: [49] (71) 43 8700 78

Internship Programs

Several professional internship programs offer students opportunities to obtain professional experience. Some programs, such as that run by Boston University, also offer an opportunity to earn academic credit.

Boston University International Programs
232 Bay State Road, 5th Floor
Boston, MA 02215
Tel.: (617) 353-9888
Fax: (617) 353-5402
Email: abroad@bu.edu
www.web.bu.edu/abroad
Offers internships in advertising, marketing, broadcasting, business, journalism, and politics.

Brethren Colleges Abroad
605 College Avenue
North Manchester, IN 46963
Tel.: (219) 982-5244
Fax: (219) 982-7755
Email: bca@manchester.edu
www.studyabroad.com/bac

Business, teaching, political science, and social work internships.

CDS International
330 7th Avenue, 19th Floor
New York, NY 10001
Tel.: (212) 497-3500
Fax: (212) 497-3535
Arranges 6-month internships in business, engineering, and other technical fields.

IASTE-US
10400 Little Patuxent Parkway, Suite 250 L
Columbia, MD 21044-3510
Tel.: (410) 997-3068
Fax: (410) 997-5186
Email: iaeste@aipt.org
www.aipt/iaste.html
Arranges reciprocal internships in 63 different countries. Specifically for students in technical fields.

Volunteer Opportunities

Several organizations maintain workcamps in Germany. The Council on International Educational Exchange coordinates workcamps with local agencies. Service Civil International (SCI) operates over 50 such camps, attracting participants from throughout Europe and beyond. Several of SCI's workcamps revolve around peace, anti-fascist/anti-racist, and "Third World solidarity" themes. Other issues include women's studies and intercultural groups. Over 700 volunteers participate in SCI workcamps annually. IBG organizes voluntary workcamps around Germany. Germany's state-funded youth organization, Internationale Jugendgemein (IJGD), runs over 100 summer workcamps, emphasizing ecological themes and accepting thousands of volunteers per year.

Council on International Educational Exchange
205 East 42nd Street
New York, NY 10017
Tel.: (888) COUNCIL
Email: ivpdirectory@ciee.org
www.ciee.org

IBG
Schlosserstrasse 28
D-70180 Stuttgart, Germany
Tel.: [49] (711) 649 11 28

Internationale Jugendgemein (IJGD)
Berliner Strasse 49
D-11467 Potsdam, Germany
Tel.: [49] (331) 29 35 23

International Workcamps
Nothelfergemeinschaft der Freunde
Postfach 101510
D-52349 Düren, Germany

Tel.: [49] (2421) 76569
Fax: [49] (2421) 76468

Peace Village International
Lanterstrasse 21
D-46539 Dinslaken, Germany
Tel.: [49] (2064) 4974 0
Fax: [49] (2064) 4974 999

Service Civil International—U.S.A.
Route 2, Box 506
Crozet, VA 22932
Tel.: (804) 823-1826

Volunteers for Peace
International Workcamps
43 Tiffany Road
Belmont, VT 05730
Tel.: (802) 259-2759
Fax: (802) 259-2922
Email: VFP@VFP.prg
www.vfp.org

NEWSPAPERS IN GERMANY

Berliner Morgenpost (daily)
Axel Springer Platz1
D-20450 Hamburg, Germany
Tel.: [49] (40) 347 228 84
Fax: [49] (40) 347 255 40
Email: berliner-morgenpost@asv.de

Bild (daily)
Axel Springer Platz 1
D-20350 Hamburg 36, Germany
Tel.: [49] (40) 347 228 84
Fax: [49] (40) 347 255 40
Email: bild@asv.de

Frankfurter Allgemeine (daily, except Sunday)
Hellerhofstrasse 2-4
D-60327 Frankfurt am Main, Germany
Tel.: [49] (69) 75 91 0
Fax: [49] (69) 75 91 17 43

Handelsblatt (business news, daily)
P.O. Box 102663
D-4017 Düsseldorf, Germany
Tel.: [49] (211) 88 70
Fax: [49] (211) 32 67 59
Email: gwp.international@vhb.de
www.händelsblatt.de

Rheinische Post (daily)
Zülpicher Strasse 10
D-40549 Düsseldorf, Germany
Tel.: [49] (211) 50 50 1
Fax: [49] (211) 50 47 562

Sueddeutsche Zeitung (daily)
Sendlingerstrasse 80
D-80331 Munich, Germany
Tel.: [49] (89) 218 30
Fax: [49] (89) 218 37 95
Email: szinfo@sueddeutsche.de

Resources for Further Information

USEFUL WEBSITES FOR JOB SEARCHERS

The Internet is a good place to begin your job search. Many German employers list job vacancies, especially those in technical fields, on the World Wide Web. There are also many websites that provide useful information for job searchers researching the German job market.

Breitbach & Partner
www.breitbach.com
Features jobs in business/legal field; in German.

Channel One (Job World)
www.channel-one.de/html/jobs.html
Lists jobs in technical, business, and liberal arts fields; in German.

ComKarriere
www.commarket.de/JOBS/infos.html
Offers advice on seeking a job; in German.

Danike & Partner-
www.danike.de/index.html-ssi
Advertises jobs to business-oriented seekers; in German.

DV Jobs
www.industrie-job.de/dvjobframes.html
Job-search guides; in German.

German Career Service
www.career-service.de//
Recruitment tools for university graduates and young professionals.

Jobs & Adverts
www.job.de
Job postings in all fields.

Job Info
www.karrierefuehrer.de
A comprehensive site that covers all aspects of obtaining a job in Germany; in German.

Jobs & Karriere
www.wdr.de/tv/jobs/index.html
Information on working in Germany; job postings; in German.

JobNet
www.jobnet.de
Comprehensive job-search page for all types of fields; in German.

JobWare International
www.jobware.net
Online service dedicated to candidates seeking a job and companies seeking an employee.

Oeko
www.oneworldweb.de/oeko-jobs/index.html
Features jobs in business and technology; in German.

EMBASSIES AND CONSULAR OFFICES

American embassies and consulates have commercial and/or economic sections that can provide you with business information and explain aspects of the local economy. Inquiries about business opportunities should be addressed either to "Commercial Officer" or "Commercial Section," followed by the appropriate street address.

Representation of Germany in the United States

Embassy of the Federal Republic of Germany
4645 Reservoir Road NW
Washington, DC 20007
Tel.: (202) 298-4000
Fax: (202) 298-4249
www.germany-info.org

German Consulates General: Chicago, (312) 263-0850; Los Angeles, (213) 930-2703; New York, (212) 610-9700

Representation of the United States in Germany

American Embassy Bonn/Berlin
Deichmanns Ave 29
D-53170 Bonn, Germany
Tel.: [49] (30) 228 3391
Fax: [49] (30) 339 2663
www.usembassy.de/
American Embassy Bonn/Berlin
Clayallee 170
D-14195 Berlin, Germany
Tel: [49] (30) 832 2933
Fax: [49] (30) 8305 1215

American Consulate General—Düsseldorf
Kennedydamm 15-17
D-40476 Düsseldorf, Germany
Tel.: [49] (211) 470 61

American Consulate General—Frankfurt
Siesmayerstrasse 21
D-60323 Frankfurt am Main, Germany
Tel.: [49] (69) 7535 0
Fax: [49] (69) 748 938

American Consulate General—Hamburg
Alsterufer 27/28
D-20354 Hamburg, Germany
Tel.: [49] (40) 411 710
Fax: [49] (40) 417 665

American Consulate General—Leipzig
Vilhelm Seyfferth Strasse 4
D-04107 Leipzig, Germany
Tel.: [49] (341) 213 840
Fax: [49] (341) 213 8417

American Consulate General—Munich
Koeniginstrasse 5
D-80539 Munich, Germany
Tel.: [49] (89) 288 8729
Fax: [49] (89) 280 9998

U.S. Commercial Office
Neustädtische Kirchstrasse 4-5
D-10117 Berlin, Germany
Tel.: [49] (30) 8305 2700
Fax: [49] (30) 238 6296

CHAMBERS OF COMMERCE

Chambers of commerce consist of firms in both countries interested in international trade. These are appropriate companies to initially target in the job search.

American Chamber of Commerce in Germany
12 Rossmarkt, Postfach 100162
D-60311 Frankfurt, Germany
Tel.: [49] (69) 929 1040
Fax: [49] (69) 929 10411
Email: accinfo@germany.cerf.net

American Chamber of Commerce in Germany—Berlin Office
29 Budapersterstrasse
D-10787 Berlin, Germany
Tel.: [49] (30) 261 5586
Fax: [49] (30) 262 2600

Association of German Chambers of Industry and Commerce
1 Farragut Square Street NW, 6th Floor
Washington, DC 20006
Tel.: (202) 347-0247
Fax: (202) 347-3685

German-American Chamber of Commerce
40 West 57th Street
New York, NY 10019
Tel.: (212) 974-8830
Fax: (212) 974-8867
Email: GACCNY@compuserve.com

WORLD TRADE CENTERS IN GERMANY

World Trade Centers usually include many foreign companies operating in the country.

World Trade Center Bremen
Birkenstrasse 15
D-28195 Bremen, Germany
Tel.: [49] (421) 174 660

Fax: [49] (421) 174 6622
Email: Reuter@bremen-business.de
www.bremen-business.de/

World Trade Center Cologne
Bruckenstrasse 17
D-50667 Cologne, Germany
Tel.: [49] (221) 205 9402
Fax: [49] (221) 205 9419

World Trade Center Hamburg
Neuer Wall 50
D-20354 Hamburg, Germany
Tel.: [49] (40) 372630
Fax: [49] (40) 364882
Email: wtc-hamburg@dialup.nacamar.de
www.wtca.org

World Trade Center Hannover
International Suite Am Listholze 78
D-30177 Hannover, Germany
Tel.: [49] (511) 302 9051, [49] 511 302
9050
Fax: [49] (511) 302 9020
Email: ubw.wtc@t-online.de
http://pweb.uunet.de/ubw.h/

World Trade Center Leipzig
Walter-Koehn-Strasse 1c
D-04356 Leipzig, Germany
Tel.: [49] (341) 5250 101
Fax: [49] (341) 5250 110
Email: wtc-leipzig@msn.com
www.wtc-leipzig.de

World Trade Center Rostock
Parkstrasse 53
D-18119 Rostock, Germany
Tel.: [49] (381) 513 95, [49] (381) 519
2845
Fax: [49] (381) 522 55
Email: tprostock@t-online.de
www.wtca.org/wtc/rostock.html

World Trade Center Ruhr Valley
Sparkassenstrasse 1
D-45879 Gelsenkirchen, Germany
Tel.: [49] (209) 17971 0
Fax: [49] (209) 17971 59
Email: wtciv@wtc.gelsen-net.de

OTHER INFORMATIONAL ORGANIZATIONS

Foreign government missions in the U.S. such as National Tourist Offices can furnish visas and information on work permits and other important regulations. They may also offer economic and business information about the country. The German Academic Exchange Service (DAAD) coordinates educational exchanges with Germany.

**German Academic Exchange Service
(DAAD)**
950 Third Avenue
New York, NY 10022
Tel.: (212) 758-3223
Fax: (212) 755-5780
Email: daadny@daad.org
www.daad.org

German National Tourist Office
122 East 42nd Street, 52nd Floor
New York, NY 10168
Tel.: (212) 661-7200
Fax: (212) 661-7174
Email: GNTONY@aol.com

Fair jobs in Germany

You may be able to find work at various trade, wine, and beer fairs held in Germany. These jobs primarily involve manual labor setting up tents and rides. Oktoberfest is a popular annual event in Bavaria—especially around Munich. It usually starts the last Saturday in September and lasts two weeks. Local brewers usually need manual workers as early as three months in advance.

Trade Fairs: Frankfurt (Mar., Aug.), Hannover (April)
Wine Fairs: Mainz (Aug.), Neustadt (Sept., Oct.), Rudesheim
(Aug.), Wiesbaden (Aug., Sept., Oct.)
Beer Fairs: Munich (Sept., Oct.), Stuttgart (Sept., Oct.)

BUSINESS DIRECTORIES

Although not always easy to find, business directories can prove invaluable in the international job search. Most directories list company names, addresses, products, and phone numbers. Some directories include executive names and titles and financial information about the company. These sources provide you with the names of the people to contact for employment information as well as financial data, which can tell you how strong a company's position in a country may be.

American Chamber of Commerce in Germany Membership Directory and Yearbook. Published annually by the American Chamber of Commerce in Germany, Rossmarkt 12, Postfach 100162, D-60311 Frankfurt, Germany. Lists American and German firms engaged in bilateral trade.

American Subsidiaries of German Firms. Available from the German-American Chamber of Commerce in the U.S., 40 West 57th Street, New York, NY 10019-4092; email: gaccny@compuserve.com. Lists 2,300 American businesses and 1,600 subsidiaries in Germany.

Banken-Jahrbuch. Published annually in German. Verlag Hoppenstedt & Co., Hoppenstedt Wirtschaftsverlag, GmbH, 100139, Havelstrasse 9, D-64285 Darmstadt 1, Germany; email: hoppenstedtt@t-online.de; www.hoppenstedt.com. Directory of 1,400 German banks.

BDI: Germany Supplies/German Industry. Published annually by Verlag W. Sachon GmbH, Schloss Mindelburg, D-87714 Mindelheim, Germany; email: info@sachon.de; www.sachon.de. Lists German export manufacturers.

Companies in the New Federal States (east Germany.) Published by Verlag Hoppenstedt & Co., Hoppenstedt Wirtschaftsverlag, GmbH, 100139, Havelstrasse 9, D-64285 Darmstadt 1, Germany; email: hoppenstedt@t-online.de; www.hoppenstedt.com. Lists 23,000 companies in the new eastern states.

Directory of Foreign Firms Operating Abroad: Germany. World Trade Academy Press, 257 Central Park West, Suite 10A, New York, NY 10024-4110; email: uniworldbp@aol.com; www.uniworldbp.com. Lists names and addresses of parent companies in the U.S. and their subsidiaries and affiliates in Germany.

Directory of German Motor Industry Manufacturing. Federation of the German Motor Industry, Westendstrasse 61, Postfach 70563, D-60079 Frankfurt, Germany. Lists major car manufacturers and associated businesses.

Directory of Major German Companies. Published annually in German, English, French, and Spanish by Verlag Hoppenstedt & Co., Hoppenstedt Wirtschaftsverlag, GmbH, 100139, Havelstrasse 9, D-64285 Darmstadt 1, Germany; email: hoppenstedt@t-online.de; www.hoppenstedt.com. Covers 23,500 enterprises with annual revenues in excess of DM 20,000,000, or that have at least 150 employees.

Directory of Medium-Sized German Companies. Published annually by Verlag Hoppenstedt & Co., Hoppenstedt Wirtschaftsverlag, GmbH, 100139, Havelstrasse 9, D-64285 Darmstadt 1, Germany; email: hoppenstedtt@t-online.de; www.hoppenstedt.com. Includes information on over 50,000 firms with annual revenues of between 2 and 20 million German marks, and/or 20-150 employees.

Firmen Information Bank. Published by AZ Direct Marketing Bertelsmann, Carl Bertelsmann Strasse 161, D-33311 Guetersloh, Germany; www.bedirect.de. Lists 110,000 German companies.

German-American Business Contacts. Published annually in English and German by Verlag Hoppenstedt & Co., Hoppenstedt Wirtschaftsverlag, GmbH, 100139, Havelstrasse 9, D-64285 Darmstadt 1, Germany; email: hoppenstedt@t-online.de; www.hoppenstedt.com. Covers 4,000 German businesses and their 7,000 U.S. affiliates.

German-American Chamber of Commerce Membership Directory. Published by the German-American Chamber of Commerce in the U.S., 40 West 57th Street, New York, NY 10019-4092; email: gaccny@compuserve.com. Lists the 2,200 Chamber members in the U.S. and Germany.

Germany's Top 500. Published by Frankfurter Algemeine Zeitung, Information Services, Hellerhofstrasse 9, D-60327 Frankfurt, Germany; email: german.business@faz.de; www.laenderdienste.de/Germany. Top companies in Germany.

Kompass Deutschland. Available annually in German, English, and French. Published by Kompass Deutschland Verlags und Vertriebsgellschaft, GmbH, Jechtinger Strasse 13, D-79111 Freiburg, Germany; email: info@kompass-deutschland.de; www.kompass.com. Covers over 40,000 leading German manufacturers, distributors, and service companies.

Wer Gehort zu Wem (Who Belongs to Whom?). Published triennially in German by Commerzbank, Zentraler Stab Kommunikation, Informations-Zentrum, D-60261 Frankfurt, Germany; www.commerzbank.com. Lists foreign investors in German firms.

Wer Leitet: Das Middlemanagement der Deutschen Wirtschaft. Published annually in German by Verlag Hoppenstedt & Co., Hoppenstedt Wirtschaftsverlag, Gmbh, Postfach 4005, Havelstrasse 9, D-61000 Darmstadt 1, Germany. Lists executives of German firms.

AMERICAN COMPANIES IN GERMANY

The following companies are classified by business area: Banking and Finance; Industrial Manufacturing; Retailing and Wholesaling; and Service Industries. Company information includes firm name, address, telephone and fax numbers, specific business, American parent company. Your chances of achieving employment abroad are substantially better if you contact the subsidiary company in Europe rather than the parent company in the U.S.

BANKING AND FINANCE

Bank of America (NTCSA)
Ulmenstrasse 30
D-60325 Frankfurt, Germany
Tel.: [49] (69) 71 00 10
Fax: [49] (69) 71 00 12 61
(Bank)
Bank of America

Chase Bank AG
Alexanderstrasse 59
D-6000 Frankfurt, Germany
Tel.: [49] (69) 24 78 90
Fax: [49] (69) 254 5285
www.chase.com
(Bank)
Chase Manhattan Bank, New York

Chemical Bank AG
Ulmenstrasse 30
D-60325 Frankfurt, Germany
Tel.: [49] (69) 71 58 1
Fax: [49] (69) 71 58 209
(Bank)
Chemical Bank

CitiBank AG
Neue Mainzer Strasse 75
D-6000 Frankfurt, Germany
Tel.: [49] (69) 13660
Fax: [49] (69) 1366 1113
(Commercial and merchant bank)
Citibank NA

Dow Jones Markets GmbH
Mainzer Land 23a
D-60329 Frankfurt, Germany
Tel.: [49] (69) 256 16
Fax: [49] (69) 256 161 11
(Finance and credit companies)
Dow Jones & Co.

Morgan Stanley Bank
Rahmhofstrasse 2-4
D-60313 Frankfurt, Germany
Tel.: [49] (69) 216 60
Fax: [49] (69) 20 99
(Bank)
Morgan Guaranty International Finance
Corp.

INDUSTRIAL MANUFACTURING

Alcoa Deutschland GmbH
Mainzer Strasse 185
D-67547 Worms, Germany
(Machinery)
Tel.: [49] (6241) 40 010
Fax: [49] (6241) 40 01 87
(Metal products)
Aluminum Co. of America

Amoco Chemical Deutschland GmbH
Heinrichstrasse 85
D-40239 Düsseldorf, Germany
Tel.: [49] (211) 61 20 81
Fax: [49] (211) 62 89 40
(Chemicals)
Amoco Corp.

Armstrong World Industries GmbH
Robert Bosch 10
D-48152 Münster, Germany
Tel.: [49] (251) 760 30
Fax: [49] (251) 760 33 46
(Flooring, ceilings, insulation)
Armstrong World Industries Inc.

Avon Cosmetics GmbH
Postfach 400140
D-80701 Munich, Germany
Tel.: [49] (8165) 720
(Cosmetics and jewelry)
Avon Products, Inc.

Black & Decker GmbH
Black-&-Decker-Strasse 40
D-65510 Idstein, Germany
Tel.: [49] (6126) 21 0
Fax: [49] (6126) 21 24 33
(Power tools)
Black & Decker Germany Holdings, Inc.

Bristol-Myers Squibb GmbH
Volkartstrasse 83
D-80636 Munich, Germany
Tel.: [49] (89) 12 14 20
Fax: [49] (89) 12 13 23 92
(Chemicals and pharmaceuticals)
E.R. Squibb & Sons

Coca-Cola GmbH
Max-Keith-Strasse 66
Postfach 100761
D-4300 Essen 1, Germany
Tel.: [49] (201) 821 510
(Beverages)
Coca-Cola Export Corp.

Compaq Computer GmbH
Arabellastrasse 30
D-81925 Munich, Germany
Tel.: [49] (89) 92 69 70\
(Computers)
Compaq Computer Corp.

Deutsche Goodyear GmbH
Xantnerstrasse 105
D-50732 Cologne, Germany
Tel.: [49] (221) 97 66 61
Fax: [49] (221) 97 66 65 85
(Tires and rubber products)
Goodyear Tire and Rubber Company

Deutsche Shell Tanker AG
Überseering 35
D-22297 Hamburg, Germany
Tel.: [49] (40) 632 40
Fax: [49] (40) 632 10 51
www.deutsche-shell.de
(Chemicals)
Shell Oil

Digital Equipment GmbH
Freischützstrasse 91
D-81927 Munich, Germany
Tel.: [49] (89) 959 10
Fax: [49] (89) 959 110 10
(Office equipment)
Digital Equipment Corp.

Dow Corning GmbH
Rheingaustrasse 53
D-65201 Wiesbaden, Germany
Tel.: [49] (611) 23 71
Fax: [49] (611) 259 54
(Chemicals and plastics)
Dow Chemical Corp.

Du Pont de Nemours (Deutschland) GmbH
Du Pont Strasse 1
D-61352 Bad Homburg, Germany
Tel.: [49] (6172) 870
Fax: [49] (6172) 87 15 00
(Chemicals)
E.I. Du Pont de Nemours & Co.

Esso AG
Kapstadtring 2
D-22297 Hamburg, Germany
Tel.: [49] (40) 639 30
Fax: [49] (40) 63 93 33 68
(Oil refining, marketing)
Exxon Corp.

Ford-Werke AG
Henry Ford Strasse 1
D-50724 Cologne, Germany
Tel.: [49] (221) 90 0
Fax: [49] (221) 901 26 41
(Automobiles and parts)
Ford Motor Co.

Gillette Deutschland GmbH
Oberlandstrasse 75-84
D-12098 Berlin, Germany
Tel.: [49] (30) 756 40
Fax: [49] (30) 751 10 98
(Toiletries)
Gillette Co.

Grace GmbH
Erlengang 31
D-22844 Norderstedt, Germany
Tel.: [49] (40) 52 60 10
Fax: [49] (40) 52 60 15 10
(Plastics)
W.R. Grace and Co.

Hewlett-Packard GmbH
Herrenberger Strasse 110-130
D-71034 Böblingen, Germany
Tel.: [49] (7031) 14 0
Fax: [49] (7031) 14 29 99
www.hp.com
(Computers)
Hewlett-Packard Co.

Johnson & Johnson GmbH
Kaiserswerther Strasse 270
D-40474 Düsseldorf, Germany
Tel.: [49] (211) 430 50
Fax: [49] (211) 430 5352
(Personal care products)
Johnson & Johnson

Kellogg (Deutschland) GmbH
Auf der Muggenberg 30
D-28041 Bremen 1, Germany
Tel.: [49] (421) 39 99 0
Fax: [49] (421) 39 10 67
(Food products)
The Kellogg Company

Kodak AG
Hedelfingerstrasse 54-60
D-70327 Stuttgart, Germany
Tel.: [49] (711) 406 0
Fax: [49] (711) 406 5397
www.kodak.com
(Photographic equipment)
Eastman Kodak Co.

Kraft General Foods GmbH
Unterbibergerstrasse 15
D-81737 Munich, Germany
Tel.: [49] (89) 62 73 80
Fax: [49] (89) 62 73 86 120
www.kraft.com
(Food products)
Kraft General Foods Inc.

Mattel GmbH
An der Trift
D-63303 Dreiech, Germany
Tel.: [49] (6103) 89 10
Fax: [49] (6103) 86 132
www.mattel.com
(Toys)
Mattel Inc.

Mobil Oil AG
Steinstrasse 5
D-20095 Hamburg, Germany
Tel.: [49] (40) 30 02 0
Fax: [49] (40) 30 02 28 30
(Oil and gas exploration and production)
Mobil Oil Corp.

Motorola GmbH
Heinrich-Hertz-Strasse 1
D-65232 Taunusstein, Germany
Tel.: [49] (6128) 700
Fax: [49] (6128) 70 4900
(Telecommunications equipment)
Motorola Inc.

Pepsi-Cola GmbH
Martin Behaim Strasse
D-63263 Neu Isenburg, Germany
Tel.: [49] (6102) 74 90
Fax: [49] (6102) 74 9200
(Beverages)
PepsiCo, Inc.

Procter & Gamble GmbH
Sulzbacherstrasse 50
D-65823 Schwalbach, Germany
Tel.: [49] (6196) 8 90 1
Fax: [49] (6196) 89 49 29
(Household products)
Procter & Gamble Co.

R.J. Reynolds Tobacco GmbH
Maria-Ablass-Platz 15
D-50668 Cologne, Germany
Tel.: [49] (221) 1 64 601
Fax: [49] (221) 1 64 64 31
(Cigarettes)
RJR Nabisco Corp.

RETAILING AND WHOLESALING

Deutsche Wrigley GmbH
Albrecht-Dürer Strasse
D-82008 Unterhaching, Germany
Tel.: [49] (89) 66 51 00
Fax: [49] (89) 66 51 03 09
(Chewing gum)
Wrigley

IBM Deutschland GmbH
Ernst Reuterplatz 2
D-10587 Berlin, Germany
Tel.: [49] (30) 31 150
Fax: [49] (30) 31 15 1447
(Information systems)
IBM

Rank Xerox GmbH
Emanuel-Leutze-Strasse 20
D-40547 Düsseldorf, Germany
Tel.: [49] (211) 990 0
Fax: [49] (211) 990 78 32
(Office communications equipment)
Xerox Corp.

SERVICE INDUSTRIES

Amdahl Deutschland GmbH
Balanstrasse 55
D-81541 Munich, Germany
Tel.: [49] (89) 49 05 80
Fax: [49] (89) 49 05 82 22
(Computer servicing)
Amdahl Corp.

Texas Instruments Deutschland GmbH
Haggertystrasse 1
D-85356 Freising, Germany
Tel.: [49] (8161) 80 0
Fax: [49] (8161) 84 516
www.ti.com
(Electronic equipment)
Texas Instruments Inc.

3M Deutschland GmbH
Carl-Schurz-Strasse 1
D-41453 Neuss, Germany
Tel.: [49] (2131) 14 0
Fax: [49] (2131) 14 26 49
(Adhesives, abrasives, etc.)
3M

Reynolds Aluminium Deutschland International
Finkenwerder Strasse 2
D-21129 Hamburg, Germany
Tel.: [49] (40) 740 11 00
Fax: [49] (40) 74 01 12 05
(Metals)
Reynolds Metals Co.

F.W. Woolworth & Co. GmbH
Lyonerstrasse 52
D-60528 Frankfurt, Germany
Tel.: [49] (69) 660 11
Fax: [49] (69) 660 13 99
(General merchandise)
Woolworth Corp.

Zenith Data Systems GmbH
52 Robert Bosch Strasse
D-63225 Langen, Germany
Tel: [49] (6103) 76 10
Fax: [49] (6103) 761 43 10
(Computer products)
Zenith Electronics Corp.

Arthur Andersen & Co GmbH
Obenmarspforten 21
D-50667 Cologne, Germany
Tel.: [49] (221) 20 64 00
Fax: [49] (221) 258 10 18
www.arthuranderson.com/offices/
germany
(Accounting)
Arthur Andersen

BBDO Düsseldorf GmbH
Königsallee 92
D-40212 Düsseldorf, Germany
Tel.: [49] (211) 137 90
Fax: [49] (211) 137 96 211
(Advertising)
BBDO Worldwide Inc.

Booz Allen & Hamilton International
Koenigsalle 106
D-40125 Düsseldorf, Germany
(Management consulting)
Tel.: [49] (211) 38 900
Fax: [49] (211) 37 10 02
Booz Allen & Hamilton Inc.

Diebold Deutschland GmbH
Frankfurter Strasse 27
D-65760 Escheborn B Frankfurt,
Germany
Tel.: [49] (6196) 90 31 00
Fax: [49] (6196) 90 34 56
(Consulting and public relations)
Diebold Group Inc.

**DMB & B Hamburg D'Arcy Masius
Benton & Bowles GmbH**
Bleichenbrücke 10
D-20354 Hamburg, Germany
Tel.: [49] (359) 130
Fax: [49] (359) 133 00
(Advertising)
D'Arcy Masius Benton & Bowles

Dun & Bradstreet GmbH
Hahnstrasse 31-35
D-60528 Frankfurt, Germany
Tel.: [49] (69) 6609 22 11
Fax: [49] (69) 6609 21 75
(Commercial information services)
Dun & Bradstreet International

Ernst & Young
Eschersheimer Lanstrasse 14
D-60322 Frankfurt, Germany

Tel.: [49] (69) 152 080 1
Fax: [49] (69) 152 083 99
(consulting)
Ernst & Young

Korn/Ferry International GmbH
Lyonerstrasse 15
D-60528 Atricom, Frankfurt, Germany
Tel.: [49] (69) 669 017 0
Fax: [49] (69) 669 017 66
(Consulting)
Korn/Ferry International

McCann-Erickson Service
Grosser Hasenpfad 44
D-60598 Frankfurt, Germany
Tel.: [49] (69) 60 50 70
Fax: [49] (69) 60 50 72 20
(Advertising)
Interpublic Group of Companies

McKinsey & Company, Inc.
Königsallee 60c,
D-40027 Düsseldorf, Germany
Tel.: [49] (0211) 136 40
Fax: [49] (0211) 13 64 700
www.mckinsey.com
(Consulting)
McKinsey & Company

Saatchi & Saatchi Compton GmbH
Wiesenau 38-40
D-60323 Frankfurt, Germany
Tel.: [49] (69) 71 420
Fax: [49] (69) 71 411 84
(Advertising)
Saatchi & Saatchi

Young & Rubicam GmbH
Bleichstrasse 64
D-60313 Frankfurt am Main, Germany
Tel.: [49] (69) 21 920
Fax: [49] (69) 21 924 30
(Advertising)
Young & Rubicam Inc.

EUROPEAN COMPANIES IN GERMANY

The following are major non-American firms operating in the country. These selected companies can be either domestic or foreign, usually other European. Such
companies will generally hire their own nationals first but may employ Americans.

BANKING AND FINANCE

Allianz AG Holding
Königinstrasse 28
D-80802 Munich, Germany
Tel.: [49] (89) 38 000
Fax: [49] (89) 38 00 34 25
(Holding and reinsurance)

Bayerische Landesbank Girozentrale
Brienner Strasse 20
D-80997 Munich, Germany
Tel.: [49] (89) 217 101
Fax: [49] (89) 217 11 66 1
(Financial services)

Bayerische Vereinsbank AG
Kardinal-Faulhaber-Strasse 1–14
D-80333 Munich, Germany
Tel.: [49] (89) 213 21
Fax: [49] (89) 213 26 41
(Bank)

Commerzbank AG
Neue Mainzer Strasse 32
D-60311 Frankfurt, Germany
Tel.: [49] (69) 1 36 20
Fax: [49] (69) 1 36 22 089
(Commercial and investment banking)
www.commerzbank.de

Deutsche Bank AG
Taunusanlage 12
D-60262 Frankfurt, Germany
Tel.: [49] (69) 91 000
Fax: [49] (69) 71 504 225
(Bank)

DG Bank
Am Platz der Republik
D-6000 Frankfurt am Main, Germany

Tel.: [49] (69) 7447 1355
Fax: [49] (69) 7447 1688
(Commercial and investment bank)

Dresdner Bank AG
Jürgen-Ponto-Platz 1
D-60329 Frankfurt, Germany
Tel.: [49] (69) 263 0
Fax: [49] (69) 263 4831
(Bank)

Helaba
Boerenstrasse 7-11
D-60313 Frankfurt, Germany
Tel.: [49] (69) 29 97 01 18
Fax: [49] (69) 22 97 01 94
www.helaba.de
(Financial services)

Norddeutsche Landesbank Girozentrale
Georgsplatz 1
D-30158 Hannover, Germany
Tel.: [49] (511) 361 0
Fax: [49] (511) 361 2502
(Bank)

Roland Berger & Partner GmbH
International Management Consultants
Arabellastrasse 33
D-81925 Munich, Germany
Tel.: [49] (89) 92 230
Fax: [49] (89) 92 23 202
www.rolandberger.com
(Consulting)

Westdeutsche Landesbank Girozentrale
15 Herzogstrasse
D-40217 Düsseldorf, Germany
Tel.: [49] (211) 826 01
Fax: [49] (211) 826 6119
(Bank)

INDUSTRIAL MANUFACTURING

Adidas AG
Adi-Dassler Strasse 1-2
D-91047 Herzogenaurach, Germany
Tel.: [49] (9132) 84 0
Fax: [49] (9132) 84 2241
(Athletic shoes and clothing)

AEG AG
Theodor-Stern-Kai 1
D-60596 Frankfurt am Main, Germany
Tel.: [49] (69) 600 0
Fax: [49] (69) 54 00
(Telecommunications equipment)

AGFA-Gevaert AG
Kaiser Wilhelm Allee
D-51373 Leverkusen, Germany
Tel.: [49] (214) 14 30 1
Fax: [49] (214) 51 368
(Photochemical products and chemicals)

Audi AG
Postfach 1144
D-74148 Neckasulm, Germany
Tel.: [49] (7132) 310
Fax: [49] (7132) 31 22 02
(Automobiles and parts)

BASF AG
Carl-Bosch-Strasse 38
D-67056 Ludwigshafen, Germany
Tel.: [49] (621) 60 0
Fax: [49] (621) 604 25 22
www.basf.com
(Chemicals)

Bayer AG
Bayerwerk
D-51368 Leverkusen, Germany
Tel.: [49] (214) 301
Fax: [49] (214) 306 63 28
www.bayer.de
(Chemicals and plastics)

Bayerische Motoren Werke AG (BMW)
BMW Haus
Postfach 40 2040
D-80788 Munich, Germany
Tel.: [49] (89) 3820
Fax: [49] (89) 38 22 58 58
(Automobiles and parts)

Bertelsmann AG
Carl-Bertelsmann-Strasse 270
D-33311 Guetersloh, Germany
Tel.: [49] (5241) 80 34 25
Fax: [49] (5241) 80 60 95
(Publishing)

Robert Bosch GmbH
Auf der Breit 4
D-76227 Karlsruhe, Germany
Tel.: [49] (721) 94 20
Fax: [49] (721) 94 22 310
(Automotive equipment)

Bosch-Siemens Hausgerate GmbH
Hochstrasse 17
D-81669 Munich, Germany
Tel.: [49] (89) 45 90 00
Fax: [49] (89) 45 90 23 47
(Consumer electronics)

CO OP AG
Hahnstrasse 72
D-60528 Frankfurt, Germany
Tel.: [49] (69) 668 30
Fax: [49] (69) 668 311
(Consumer products)

Daimler Chrysler AG
Epplestrasse 225
D-70546 Stuttgart, Germany
Tel.: [49] (711) 170
Fax: [49] (711) 179 41 16
www.Daimler-Benz.com
(Vehicles)

Dornier GmbH
Immenstaad a.d. Bundestrasse 31
D-88090 Friedrichshafen, Germany
Tel.: [49] (7545) 81
Fax: [49] (7545) 84 411
(Aviation, defense systems, and space technology)

Eschweiler Bergwerks-Verein AG
Roermonder Strasse 63
D-5120 Herzogenrath, Germany
Tel.: [49] (2407) 51 01
Fax: [49] (2407) 84 55
(Mining)

Hoechst AG
Brueningstrasse 50
D-65926 Frankfurt, Germany
Tel.: [49] (69) 30 50
Fax: [49] (69) 30 36 65
www.hoechst.com
(Chemicals, pharmaceuticals, and cosmetics)

Klöckner-Werke AG
Klöcknerhaus
D-47057 Duisburg, Germany
Tel.: [49] (203) 3960
Fax: [49] (203) 396 3535
(Steel products)

MAN AG
Ungererstrasse 69
D-80805 Munich 40, Germany
Tel.: [49] (89) 36 098 0
Fax: [49] (89) 36 098 0
(Machinery and construction)

Mannesmann AG
Mannesmannufer 2
D-40213 Düsseldorf, Germany
Tel.: [49] (211) 820 0
Fax: [49] (211) 8202 163
(Industrial machinery)

Messerschmitt-Bölkow-Systems GmbH
Erlenstegenstrasse 10
D-90491 Nurenburg, Germany
Tel.: [49] (911) 919 99 0
Fax: [49] (911) 919 99 22
(Aircraft, helicopters, and defense systems)

Pfaff AQS
Wittenerstrasse 46
D-42277 Wuppertal, Germany
Tel.: [49] (202) 26 602
Fax: [49] (202) 26 602 12
(Sewing machines)

Porsche AG
Porschestrasse 42
D-70435 Stuttgart, Germany
Tel.: [49] (711) 827 0
Fax: [49] (711) 827 60 25
www.porsche.com
(Automobiles and parts)

Puma AG Rudolf Dassler Sport
Würzburger Strasse 13
D-91073 Herzogenaurach, Germany
Tel.: [49] (9132) 81 0
Fax: [49] (9132) 81 22 46
(Sports shoes and equipment)

Schering AG
Muellerstrasse 170-178
D-13353 Berlin, Germany
Tel.: [49] (30) 468 11 11
Fax: [49] (39) 468 15 305
(Pharmaceuticals)

Siemens AG
Wittelsbacherplatz 2
D-80333 Munich, Germany
Tel.: [49] (89) 636 00
Fax: [49] (89) 636 42 42
(Electrical products)

Thyssen AG
Kaiser-Wilhelmstrasse 100
D-47166 Duisburg, Germany
Tel.: [49] (203) 203 521
Fax: [49] (203) 522 51 02
(Steel products)

Veba AG
Benningsenplatz 1
D-40474 Düsseldorf, Germany
Tel.: [49] (211) 4579 13 67
Fax: [49] (211) 4579 532
(Electricity and chemicals)

Villeroy & Boch AG
Saaruferstrasse
D-6642 Mettlach, Germany
Tel.: [49] (6864) 81 12 44
Fax: [49] (6864) 81 25 24
(Tiles and tableware)

Volkswagen AG
Berliner Ring 2
D-38436 Wolfsburg, Germany
Tel.: [49] (5361) 90
Fax: [49] (5361) 92 82 82
(Automobiles and parts)

RETAILING AND WHOLESALING

Andreae-Noris Zahn AG
Solmsstrasse 25
D-60486 Frankfurt, Germany
Tel.: [49] (69) 79203 0
Fax: [49] (69) 79203 277
(Pharmaceuticals)

Aral AG
Wittener Strasse 45
D-44789 Bochum, Germany
Tel.: [49] (234) 315 0
Fax: [49] (234) 315 24 53
(Chemical products)

ASKO Deutsche Kaufhaus AG
Mainzer Strasse 180-184
D-66121 Saarbrücken, Germany
Tel.: [49] (681) 8104 01
Fax: [49] (681) 8104 261
(Discount retailing)

AVA Allgemeine Handelsgesellschaft Der Verbrauche
Fuggerstrasse 11
D-33689 Bielefeld, Germany
Tel.: [49] (5205) 94 01
Fax: [49] (5205) 94 10 10
(Department stores)

Deutsche BP AG
Überseering 2
D-22297 Hamburg, Germany
Tel.: [49] (40) 6359 50
Fax: [49] (40) 6359 22 24
(Petroleum and mineral products)

Deutsche ICI GmbH
Emil-von-Behring-Strasse 2
D-60439 Frankfurt, Germany
Tel.: [49] (69) 5801 00
Fax: [49] (69) 5801 234
(Chemicals, fibers, paints, and pharmaceuticals)

Deutsche Renault AG
Kölner Weg 6-10
D-50321 Brühl-Vochem, Germany
Tel.: [49] (2232) 73 0
Fax: [49] (2232) 73 552
(Automobiles)

Hertie Waren-Und Kaufhaus GmbH
Ludwig-Erhardstrasse 1
D-61440 Oberursel, Germany
Tel.: [49] (6171) 987 01
Fax: [49] (6171) 987 02
(Department stores)

Melitta Unternehmensgruppe Bentz
Marienstrasse 88
D-3425 Minden, Germany
Tel.: [49] (571) 40 460
Fax: [49] (571) 40 46 499
(Coffee equipment, tobacco products, and porcelain)

Rewe-Zentral AG
Domstrasse 20
D-50558 Cologne, Germany
Tel.: [49] (221) 149 0
Fax: [49] (221) 149 90 00
(Consumer goods)

Bernhard Rothfos AG
Am Sandtorkai 5
D-20457 Hamburg, Germany

Tel.: [49] (40) 37 001 0
Fax: [49] (40) 37 001 338
(Coffee)

Stinnes Markt AG
Teilestrasse 34
D-45472 Mülheim/Ruhr 1, Germany
Tel.: [49] (208) 494 0
(Fuel, ores, and minerals)

Thyssen Handelsunion AG
Bessemerstrasse 80
D-44793 Bochum, Germany
Tel.: [49] (234) 622 1
Fax: [49] (234) 622 34 0
(Building materials)

SERVICE INDUSTRIES

Deutsche Babcock AG
Duisburger Strasse 375
D-46049 Oberhausen, Germany
Tel.: [49] (208) 8330
Fax: [49] (208) 260 91
(Engineering)

Deutsche Lufthansa AG
Von Gablenz Strasse 2-6
D-50679 Cologne, Germany
Tel.: [49] (221) 826
Fax: [49] (221) 826 38 18
(Airline)

Dyckerhoff & Widmann AG
Dornach Erdinger Landstrasse 1
D-8000 Munich, Germany
Tel.: [49] (89) 9255 1
Fax: [49] (89) 9255 2127
(Civil engineering)

Franz Haniel & CIE GmbH
Franz-Haniel-Platz 1
D-47119 Duisburg, Germany
Tel.: [49] (203) 806 0
Fax: [49] (203) 806 22
(Environmental protection services)

Hapag-Lloyd AG
Ballendamm 25
D-20095 Hamburg, Germany
Tel.: [49] (40) 3001 0
Fax: [49] (40) 3266 25
(Air freight)

Phillip Holzmann AG
Taunusanlage 1
D-60329 Frankfurt, Germany
Tel.: [49] (69) 262 1
Fax: [49] (69) 26 24 33
(Construction and civil engineering)

Fried. Krupps AG
Altendorfer Strasse 103
D-45143 Essen, Germany
Tel.: [49] (201) 188 1
Fax: [49] (202) 188 4100
(Mechanical engineering)

Linde AG
Abraham-Lincoln-Strasse 21
D-65189 Wiesbaden, Germany
Tel.: [49] (611) 770 0
Fax: [49] (611) 770 269
(Engineering and construction)

Strabag Bau-AG
Siegburger Strasse 241
D-506769 Cologne, Germany
Tel.: [49] (221) 824 01
Fax: [49] (221) 824 2936
(Construction)

Vereinigte Elektrizitatswerke Westfalen AG
Rheinlanddamm 24
D-44139 Dortmund, Germany
Tel.: [49] (231) 438 1
Fax: [49] (231) 438 2147
(Electricity and gas supply)

INTERNATIONAL NON-PROFIT ORGANIZATIONS IN GERMANY

Goethe Institute
Helen-Weber Allee
D-8000 Munich 40, Germany
Tel.: [49] (89) 159 210
Fax: [49] (89) 159 214 50

Institute for European Environmental Policy
Aloys-Schulte-Strasse 6
D-5300 Bonn 1, Germany
Tel.: [49] (228) 21 38 10

Institute of European Politics
Bachstrasse 32
D-5300 Bonn 1, Germany
Tel.: [49] (228) 729 0050
Fax: [49] (228) 729 0018

International Association for Religious Freedom
Dreieichstrasse 59
D-6000 Frankfurt 70, Germany
Tel.: [49] (69) 62 87 72

INTERNATIONAL SCHOOLS IN GERMANY

Berlin International School
Körnerstrasse 11
D-12169 Berlin, Germany
Tel.: [49] (30) 7900 0370
Fax: [49] (30) 7900 0379
Email: kant-akademie@berlin.snafu.de

Bonn American High School
Martin Luther King Strasse 14
D-53175 Bonn 2, Germany
Tel.: [49] (228) 308 540
Fax: [49] (228) 308 5420
Email: admin@bis.bonn.org
www.bis.bonn.org
(U.S./International Baccalaureate
curriculum, grades 6-12)

The Frankfurt International School
An der Waldlust 15
D-61440 Oberursel 1, Germany
Tel.: [49] (6171) 2020
Fax: [49] (6171) 202384
Email: guenther_brandt@fis.edu
www.fis.edu
(U.S./U.K./I.B., pre-K-12)

International School of Düsseldorf
Niederrheinstraße 338
D-40489 Düsseldorf, Germany
Tel.: [49] (211) 9406-6
Fax: [49] (211) 408 0774

Email: 101762.1041@compuserve.com
www.isdedu.com
(U.S./I.B., pre-K-13)

International School Hamburg
Holmbrook 20
D-22605 Hamburg, Germany
Tel.: [49] (40) 883 0010
Fax: [49] (40) 881 1405
Email: info@ish.intrasat.org
www.ish.intrasat.org
(U.S./U.K./I.B., pre-K-12)

John F. Kennedy School
Teltower Damm 87-93
D-14167 Berlin, Germany
Tel.: [49] (30) 8091 2701
Fax: [49] (30) 8091 3377
Email: hanna/ad@kennedy.beehive.de
www.kennedy.beehive.de/
(U.S./German Arbitur, K-13)

Munich International School
Schloss Buchhof, Percha
D-82319 Starnberg Munich, Germany
Tel.: [49] (8151) 366 0
Fax: [49] (8151) 366 109/119
Email: 106174.203@compuserve.com
www.mis-munich.de
(U.S./U.K./I.B., K-12)

Spain and Portugal

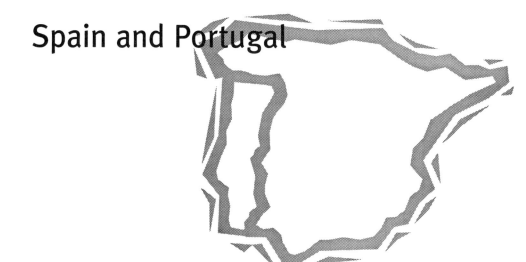

Spain

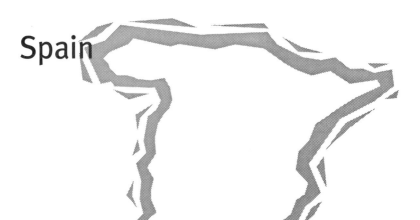

Major employment centers: Madrid, Barcelona, Valencia

Major business language: Spanish

Language skill index: Spanish is it; even poor Spanish is better than none. Beware the variety of Spanish accents, which may be confusing at first

Currency: Euro; the Spanish peseta will remain the currency in circulation until 2002

Telephone country code: 34

Time zone: EST+6

Punctuality index: Spaniards are a bit laid back when it comes to time

Average daily temperature, high/low: January, 47/33°F; July, 87/62°F (Madrid)

Average number of days with rain: January, 8; July, 4

Best bet for employment:

　For students: Resorts on the southern coast

　Permanent jobs: Finance and manufacturing

Chance of finding a job: Unemployment is sufficiently high at present to make finding work difficult. Unofficial jobs are a good option

Trivia: The workday in Spain usually begins at 9:00 a.m., stops from 1:00 to 4:00 p.m. for siesta, and then ends at 8:00 p.m. Consequently, dinner in Spain is relatively late—after 9:00 p.m.

T

he Kingdom of Spain occupies about 85% of the Iberian Peninsula in southwestern Europe. Spain, approximately twice the size of Wyoming, borders Portugal to the west, the Bay of Biscay to the north, France, Andorra, and the Mediterranean to the east, and Africa lies across the Strait of Gibraltar to the south. The Pyrenees Mountains form the border with France in the northeast. Most of the country consists of a high plateau interrupted by mountain ranges. The southern region, however, is a flat plain with a much warmer climate. The Balearic Islands are located off the Mediterranean coast, and the Canary Islands are slightly west of western Africa. Spain also controls two small enclaves on the northern coast of Morocco: Ceuta and Melilla.

Spanish, or Castellano, is the official language, but Catalan, Basque, and Galician are also spoken in the autonomous areas. Approximately 17% of the population is Catalan, 8% Galician, and 2% Basque. The remaining 73% is classified as Spanish. The vast majority of the population is Roman Catholic.

Spain, originally inhabited by Celts, Basques, and Iberians, was conquered by the Romans in 206 B.C. The Visigoths ruled the region from A.D. 412 to 711, when Muslim armies invaded from Africa. The Christian states of Aragon and Castile were united in 1469 and defeated the Muslims in 1492. Roman Catholicism became the official religion, and Muslims and Jews were heavily persecuted.

In the early sixteenth century, Spain conquered Mexico and Peru, establishing an extensive empire in the Americas. The ruling dynasty, the Spanish Hapsburgs, also established control over the Netherlands and parts of Italy and Germany. Although Spain then ranked as the most powerful state in the world, its power began to decline in the late sixteenth century. In 1588 the Invincible Armada was defeated by the English, and Spain never regained its major-power status. By the late nineteenth century, the American empire had been lost through revolutions. Finally, the United States acquired several Spanish possessions in 1898, as a result of the Spanish-American War.

Spain remained neutral in both world wars. In 1931 strong antimonarchial sentiments led to the declaration of a republic under socialist guidance. Elections held in 1936 provided a large majority for the Popular Front, composed of socialists, communists, and anarchists. Army officers, led by Francisco Franco, then revolted against the government, initiating a bloody civil war. By 1939, Franco's forces, aided by Fascist Italy and Nazi Germany, had defeated the government Loyalists, aided by France, the U.S.S.R., and the Abraham Lincoln Brigade from the U.S. Franco became "Caudillo," head of state and government, as well as the right-wing Falange Party. In 1947 Spain again became a monarchy—this time a constitutional monarchy, with Franco continuing as head of government, but not head of state. Prince Juan Carlos was designated to become king of Spain when Franco's government ended.

Franco died in 1975; Juan Carlos became king, and still reigns today. In free elections in 1977, the Democratic Center won power and granted autonomy to the Catalonian and Basque regions. Economic instability and political violence led to the victory of prime minister Felipe Gonzalez Marquez and the Spanish Socialist Workers Party in 1982. Spain entered the European Community in 1986. In 1992, Spain drew world interest by hosting Expo '92 in Seville and the Olympic Games in Barcelona. In 1997, Spain became fully integrated in the North Atlantic Treaty Organization and is a member of the European Monetary Union.

Most businesses are closed on weekends, except for Saturday morning. Banks are open from 9:00 a.m. to 2:00 p.m., Monday through Friday, and 9:00 a.m. to 1:00 p.m. on Saturday. Businesses generally close between 1:00 and 4:00 and reopen from 4:00 to 8:00 p.m. Banks are notoriously slow and usually close on Saturday from June to September. Post offices are open from 9:00 a.m. to 2:00 p.m., and some reopen from 4:00 to 7:00 p.m.

Using the language

A knowledge of Spanish is usually necessary to find employment in Spain. Although some young people are very likely to know English, most Spaniards will not expect to be approached in English. Spanish as spoken in Spain differs in accent from the versions spoken in various parts of Latin America. Even if you know Spanish, it will take you a little time to adapt to the local dialects.

Current Economic Climate

Spain's gross national product has grown at the fastest rate in Europe, nearly 3% annually. Unfortunately, the Spanish economy also suffers from Europe's highest unemployment rate. The Spanish government's official unemployment figure, based on the number of people registered for unemployment benefits, is 12%. The E.U. estimates that the real figure is much higher, closer to 19.8%. Spain's inflation rate, though still high, has lowered along with the national deficit. The underground economy contributes about 15-20% of the economic activity. In recent years, the government has been investing a percentage of its GDP to improve and expand Spain's public transportation and hence create an attractive environment for businesses.

The country's per capita income has also grown steadily in recent years as prices of products are also rising steadily. Spain's major industries include machinery, food processing, textiles, chemicals, automobiles, and shipbuilding. About 50% of the work force is employed in the service industries, 35% in manufacturing, and 15% in agriculture. Spanish trade primarily occurs within the E.U., although the U.S. is an important trade partner. Spain's tourist industry continues to grow at a rapid pace. The over 50 million tourists that visit Spain each year bring work to about 10% of the entire labor force. Southern Spain, primarily the region of Andalusia, has long been compared to Florida because of the large number of European retirees who settle there. Seville, Andalusia's economic center, hosted the 1992 World Exposition with the expectation of attracting foreign investment to the region. Barcelona drew world interest as the site for the 1992 Summer Olympics.

SPAIN'S 10 LARGEST COMPANIES

(1997, composite ranking)

1. Telefónica De España
2. Teneo Group
3. Fomento de Construcciones y Contratas
4. Banco Central Hispanoamericano
5. Banco de Santander
6. Banco Bilbao Vizcaya
7. Ibería, Lineas Aéreas de España
8. Dragados y Construcciones
9. Repasol
10. Banco Español de Crédito

Using the phone, fax, and Internet

Telephone booths are easy to find in the cities but you may have to wait to use one; although most families do have a phone, public phones in the cities are heavily frequented because Spaniards like to go out often. Public pay phones accept coins, phonecards, and credit cards. Information in Spain is "oo3," the operator is "oo8," and the national emergency number is "o91." In 1998, the area codes in Spain became an integral part of the phone number.

Most post offices have a fax service, but you will find cheaper rates at a shop or office with a "Fax Público" sign. Cybercafes are springing up in major Spanish cities, making access to Email convenient.

Getting Around in Spain

Spain's national railway system, RENFE, accepts both Eurail and InterRail passes. Traveling across the French-Spanish border by rail requires switching trains because Spanish railroads use a different track gauge than the rest of Europe. Trains are especially crowded during the summer months when tourists flock to Spain, so advance reservations are recommended. Bus service is extensive and recommended for traveling inter-city or along the northern coast of Spain where trains do not reach. Bus fares are generally comparable to train fares but may run a little higher for long-distance trips.

Passenger boats and ferries are available for traveling from the mainland to nearby islands or across the Strait of Gibraltar and Mediterranean Sea to the African Continent. Flying by Spain's national airline, Iberia, is sometimes a better choice than traveling by boat because it is quicker and in some cases cheaper.

Spain's highway system consists of the national highways, often mere two-lane roads, and the *Autopistas*, multilane expressways. The expressways are found only around major cities and are almost always congested. A twenty-mile commute into Madrid, for instance, can take nearly two hours. Relief is at hand, though; the government is spending lavishly to improve the country's overburdened transportation system.

Employment Regulations and Outlook for Americans

Current employment opportunities in Spain are limited thanks to the country's high unemployment rate. Visas aren't required for U.S. citizens staying fewer than three months. Upon arriving in Spain, U.S. citizens who intend to work must present a work permit, obtained by their employer from the Ministry of Labor, and a residence permit, obtained from the police department. If an American company will pay in American dollars, an employee may apply for a work permit at the Consulate General: in person only, with employment contract in hand. If the employer is Spanish, the company should initiate the process for acquiring proper work papers.

Spanish employers must demonstrate that no Spanish citizen is available for the job before hiring a foreign national. Because Spanish labor authorities are particularly effective, illegal employment in Spain has been highly discouraged, even in the tourist industry. Despite strict regulations and enforcement, some employers in the tourist industry do hire foreign temporary workers. Job security and benefits are nil, and wages are strictly "under the table."

A work permit is generally not required for teaching English, and native speakers are sought for individual tutoring or classes. Knowledge of Spanish is generally not essential since the philosophy is to speak only English during the sessions. However, some facility in Spanish helps with disciplining young students and explaining grammar. Agricultural work in Spain is virtually unavailable.

Trekking through Spain

During the summer between my junior and senior years in college, I decided not to pursue a regular summer job, but see Europe by foot. I recreated a medieval pilgrimage. This "little trek" took me through the beautiful countryside of the French Pyrenees to the Atlantic coast of Spain. I followed the ancient pilgrimage route to Santiago de Compostela in Gallecia. Although my primary goal was to eventually live and work abroad, I never dreamed I'd be trekking from France to Spain. Throughout the 2,000 miles I (mostly) walked, I met people from all over the world, trekking with Brazilians, Netherlanders, French, Italians, and Spaniards.

The Camino de Santiago de Compostela does not fit into the normal range of "work experiences" that people think about when planning to go abroad. However, I found that this unique alternative enhanced my U.S. job search when I *returned* from Spain. Corporate recruiters found my experience interesting and unforgettable. In fact, I chose my current job as a management consultant because my interviewers were very interested in my experiences abroad and wanted to talk about them in depth.

I plan to eventually work abroad. I know that my summer trek to the coast of Spain gave me a unique cultural insight to the country—not to mention a few blisters. I sincerely believe that an "alternative" summer experience can pay off in the long run!
—Sincerely, Betsey Tufano

Short-term and Temporary Work

The best opportunities for temporary work is as an au pair or as an English teacher.

Au-Pair Spain
Serrano Clavero 2
E-46340 Requenqa
Valencia, Spain
Tel.: [34] 96 2300 5082

GIC
Pintor Sorolla, Apt. 1080
E-46901 Monte Vedat
Valencia, Spain

Tel./Fax: [34] 96 156 5837
Au pair placement service.

Intercambio 66/Exprofit club Relaciones Culturales Internacionales
Ferraz 82
E-28008 Madrid, Spain
Tel.: [34] 91 541 7103
Au pair placement service

Internship Programs

Several professional internship programs offer students opportunities to obtain professional experience. Some programs, such as that run by Simmons College, also offer an opportunity to earn academic credit.

IASTE-US
10400 Little Patuxent Parkway, Suite 250 L
Columbia, MD 21044-3510
Tel.: (410) 997-3068
Fax: (410) 997-5186

Email: iaeste@aipt.org
www.aipt/iaste.html
Arranges reciprocal internships in 63 different countries. Specifically for students in technical fields.

Simmons College in Córdoba
Foreign Languages and Literatures
Boston, MA 02115
Fax: (617) 521 3199

Volunteer Opportunities

The Council on International Educational Exchange works with Spanish agencies to coordinate workcamps. The Instituto de Juventud runs over 90 workcamps throughout Spain for 2,000 volunteers annually. Various workcamp themes include forest and environmental work, children's camps, building and historical site restoration, archaeology, and gardening. Service Civil International operates 9 workcamps for volunteers helping with water projects, children's camps, building reconstruction, and forest work.

Council on International Educational Exchange
205 East 42nd Street
New York, NY 10017
Tel.: (888) COUNCIL
Email: ivpdirectory@ciee.org
www.ciee.org

Instituto de Juventud
José Ortega y Gasset 71
E-28006 Madrid, Spain
Tel.: [34] 91 401 6625

Service Civil International—U.S.A.
Route 2, Box 506
Crozet, VA 22932
Tel.: (804) 823-1826

Volunteers for Peace
International Workcamps
43 Tiffany Road
Belmont, VT 05730
Tel.: (802) 259-2759
Fax: (802) 259-2922
Email: VFP@VFP.prg
www.vfp.org

NEWSPAPERS IN SPAIN

ABC
Juan Ignacio Luca de Tena 7
E-28027 Madrid, Spain
Tel.: [34] 91 339 90 00
Fax: [34] 91 329 90 50

Iberian Daily Sun (English)
Zurbano 74
E-28010 Madrid, Spain
Tel.: [34] 91 442 77 00
Fax: [34] 91 442 78 54

Majorca Daily Bulletin (English)
Paseo Majorca 9A
E-07011 Palma de Mallorca, Spain

Tel.: [34] 71 78 84 00
Fax: [34] 71 71 97 06

El Mundo (daily)
Sanchez Pacheco 61
E-28002 Madrid, Spain
Tel.: [34] 91 586 48 00
Fax: [34] 91 586 48 45

El Pais (daily)
Miguel Yuste 40
E-28037 Madrid, Spain
Tel.: [34] 91 337 82 00
Fax: [34] 91 304 87 66

Resources for Further Information

USEFUL WEBSITES FOR JOB SEARCHERS

The Internet is a good place to begin your job search. Many websites provide useful information for job searchers researching the Spanish job market; there are also several that list job vacancies.

Business in Spain
www.business-spain.com
Effective list of job search links; gives advice about the job search.

Iplex Barcelona, Spain
www.iplex.com/barcelonah
Job listings in Barcelona.

El Periodico de Catalunya
www.elperiodico.es
Online magazine from Spain; in Spanish.

Si, Spain
www.civeng.carleton.ca:80/SiSpain
An interactive service that offers information on current affairs, culture, history, etc.

The Spanish Scientific Research Council (CSIC)
www.iiia.csic.es/
Has numerous job postings for the sciences; in Spanish.

Tourist Office of Spain
www.spaintour.com
Gives valuable "before you leave" information.

Web de Spain Telecom
http://stnet.es
Job search and information; in Spanish.

EMBASSIES AND CONSULAR OFFICES

American embassies and consulates have commercial and/or economic sections that can provide you with business information and explain aspects of the local economy. Inquiries about business opportunities should be addressed either to "Commercial Officer" or "Commercial Section," followed by the appropriate street address.

Representation of Spain in the United States

Embassy of Spain
2375 Pennsylvania Avenue NW
Washington, DC 20037
Tel.: (202) 452-0100
Fax: (202) 833-5670

Consulates General of Spain: Chicago, (312) 782-4588; Los Angeles, (323) 938-0158; New York, (212) 355-4080

Representation of the United States in Spain

American Embassy
Serrano 75
E-28006 Madrid, Spain
Tel.: [34] 91 587 2200
Fax: [34] 91 587 2303
www.embusa.es

American Consulate General— Barcelona
Reina Elisenda 23
E-08034 Barcelona, Spain
Tel.: [34] 93 93 28 02 227
Fax: [34] 93 93 20 55 206

American Consulate General—Sevilla
Paseo de las Delicias, 7
E-41012 Sevilla, Spain
Tel.: [34] 95 95 42 31 885
Fax: [34] 95 95 42 32 040

American Consulate General—Valencia
Calle de la Paz, 6–5º, local 5
E-46003 Valencia, Spain
Tel.: [34] 96 96 35 16 973
Fax: [34] 96 96 35 29 565

CHAMBERS OF COMMERCE

Chambers of commerce consist of firms in both countries interested in international trade. These are appropriate companies to initially target in the job search.

American Chamber of Commerce in Spain—Barcelona
General Secretariat
477 Avenue Diagonal, 8th Floor
E-08036 Barcelona, Spain
Tel.: [34] 93 405 1266
Fax: [34] 93 405 3124
Email: 101643.715@compuserve.com

American Chamber of Commerce in Spain—Madrid
Branch Office,
Lexington International Business Center
Paseo de la Castellana
E-28046 Madrid, Spain

Tel.: [34] 91 359 6559
Fax: [34] 91 359 6520

Spain Chamber of Commerce
Avenida Diagonal 452-454
E-08006 Barcelona, Spain
Tel.: [34] 93 416 9300
Fax: [34] 93 416 9301

Spain-U.S. Chamber of Commerce
350 Fifth Avenue, Suite 3514
New York, NY 10118
Tel.: (212) 967-2170

WORLD TRADE CENTERS IN SPAIN

World Trade Centers usually include many foreign companies operating in the country.

World Trade Center Barcelona
c/o Urgell, 240 6 D
E-08036 Barcelona, Spain
Tel.: [34] 93 439 4534
Fax: [34] 93 439 7396
Email: wtc.@mail.cinet.es

World Trade Center Madrid
Paseo de la Habana, 26
3rd Floor, Suite #4
E-28036 Madrid, Spain
Tel.: [34] 91 411 6145
Fax: [34] 91 562 4004
Email: wtcmadrid@mad.servicom.es

World Trade Center Seville
Isla De La Cartuja
E-41092 Seville, Spain
Tel.: [34] 95 448 8222
Fax: [34] 95 446 2173
Email: servicios@wtc.es
www.wtc.es

World Trade Center Valencia
c/o Paseo de la Habana
No. 26, 3rd Floor, Suite 4
E-28036 Madrid, Spain
Tel.: [34] 91 411-6145
Fax: [34] 91 562-4004
Email: WTCVL@wtca.geis.com

OTHER INFORMATIONAL ORGANIZATION

Foreign government missions in the U.S. such as National Tourist Offices can furnish visas and information on work permits and other important regulations. They may also offer economic and business information about the country.

National Tourist Office of Spain
666 Fifth Avenue
New York, NY 10103
Tel.: (212) 759-8822

Fax: (212) 265-8864
Email: oet.ny@here-i.com
www.okspain.org

BUSINESS DIRECTORIES

Although not always easy to find, business directories can prove invaluable in the international job search. Most directories list company names, addresses, products, and phone numbers. Some directories include executive names and titles and financial information about the company. These sources provide you with the names of the people to contact for employment information as well as financial data, which can tell you how strong a company's position in a country may be.

American Chamber of Commerce in Spain—Membership Directory. Published annually by the American Chamber of Commerce in Spain, 477 Avenida Diagonal, 8th Fl., E-08036 Barcelona, Spain. Lists 1,500 American and Spanish firms engaged in bilateral trade.

Anuario Financiero y de Sociedades Anonimas de España. Published annually by Editorial SOPEC, Villanueva 24-30, E-28001 Madrid, Spain. Describes publicly held companies, including financial information.

Anuario de Sociedades, Consejeros y Directivos. Published annually in Spanish by DICODI SA, Calle Doctor Castelo 10, E-28009 Madrid, Spain. Covers over 50,000 of Spain's largest companies, including listings of 16,000 top executives.

Directory of Foreign Firms Operating Abroad: Spain. World Trade Academy Press, 257 Central Park West, Suite 10A, New York, NY 10024-4110; email: uniworldbp@aol.com; www.uniworldbp.com. Lists names and addresses of parent companies in the U.S. and their subsidiaries and affiliates in Spain.

Directory of Spanish Industry, Export & Import. Published annually by Capel Editorial Distribuidora, SA, Almirante 21, Apdo. 562, E-28004 Madrid, Spain. Lists 15,000 Spanish manufacturers and traders.

Dun's 15,000 Largest Companies—Spain. Dun and Bradstreet Information Services, Dun and Bradstreet Corporation, 3 Sylvan Way, Parsippany, New Jersey, 07054; email: dnbmdd@dnb.com. Directory of major Spanish companies.

Guia de Exportadores de la Comunidad de Madrid. Published in Spanish. Madrid Chamber of Commerce, calle el Huertas 13, E-28012 Madrid, Spain. Directory contains information on 3,500 Madrid firms active in exporting.

Kompass España. Published annually by Ibericom SA, Manuel Gonzalez Longoria 6, E-28010 Madrid, Spain. Describes 24,000 manufacturing and service companies.

Spain's 30,000 Top Companies. Published annually by Dun and Bradstreet Information Services, Dun and Bradstreet Corporation, 3 Sylvan Way, Parsippany, New Jersey, 07054. Lists companies with annual sales of at least $500,000.

Spain-United States Chamber of Commerce Membership Directory. Published biennially by the Spain-U.S. Chamber of Commerce, 350 Fifth Avenue, Suite 3514, New York, NY 10118. Contains information on Spanish and American firms engaged in bilateral trade.

The Top 2,000 Spanish Companies. Published by Fomento de la Produccion, Casanova 57, E-08011 Barcelona, Spain. Leading companies in Spain.

Who Sells Foreign Products in Spain. Published biennially in Spanish by Prointer-Ediciones Alfonso Luengo, Puerta del Sol 11, Madrid, Spain. Lists Spanish importers and distributors.

Who's Who in Spain. Updated every 18 months. Who's Who in Italy, SRI, via de Amicis 2, I-20091 Bresso Milan, Italy; email: whoswhogc@ibm.com; www.whoswho-sutter.com. Includes statistical information on about 2,500 companies, institutions, and organizations.

Youth Policy and Youth Work in Spain. International Youth Exchange and Visitors' Service, Hochkreuzalle 20, D-53175 Bonn, Germany. Organizations for children and youth in Spain.

AMERICAN COMPANIES IN SPAIN

The following companies are classified by business area: Banking and Finance; Industrial Manufacturing; Retailing and Wholesaling; and Service Industries. Company information includes firm name, address, phone and fax numbers, specific business, and American parent company. Your chances of achieving employment abroad are substantially better if you contact the subsidiary company in Europe rather than the parent company in the U.S.

BANKING AND FINANCE

Chase Manhattan Bank España, SA
Maria de Molina, 39
E-28006 Madrid, Spain
Tel.: [34] 91 411 62 23
(Bank)
Chase Manhattan Bank, New York

Citibank España SA
Avenida de Europa 19
E-28108 Madrid, Spain
Tel.: [34] 91 663 10 00
Fax: [34] 91 663 1430
(Bank)
Citicorp Overseas Investment Corp.

INDUSTRIAL MANUFACTURING

Armstrong World Industries SA
Paseo Castellana 135-14
E-28046 Madrid, Spain
Tel.: [34] 91 571 29 90
(Wood products)
Armstrong World Industries Inc.

Avon Cosmetics S.A.
París 146148 Bajo
E-08036 Barcelona, Spain
Tel.: [34] 934 19 60 83
Fax: [34] 934 19 70 23
(Cosmetics)
Avon Cosmetics

BMC Software SA
Gobles 25-27 Urb la Florida
E-28023 Madrid, Spain
Tel.: [34] 91 37 29 625
(Software)
BMC Software

Braun Española SA
Enrique Granados 30
Esplugues De Llobregat
E-08950 Barcelona, Spain

Tel.: [34] 93 37 29 105
Fax: [34] 93 401 94 72
(Consumer electronics)
Gillette

Bristol-Myers SA
Almansa 101
Campus Empresarial Jose M Churruca
E-28040 Madrid, Spain
Tel.: [34] 91 45 65 300
(Pharmaceuticals)
Bristol-Myers Co.

Chevron Oil SA
Paseo de Gracia 54
E-08007 Barcelona, Spain
Tel.: [34] 93 48 77 000
(Petroleum import, development)

Colgate-Palmolive SAE
Avenido Bueses Aires 5-6
1° A-despacho 3
E-15004 Coruña, Spain
Tel.: [34] 981 25 04 64
Fax: [34] 981 25 09 89
(Toiletries)
Colgate Palmolive Corp.

John Deere Ibérica SA
Carretera de Toledo Km 12.200
E-28905 Getafe, Spain
Tel.: [34] 91 695 62 00
Fax: [34] 91 695 63 00
(Tractors)
Deere & Co.

Dow Corning Ibérica SA
Avinguda Diagonal 63
E-08028 Barcelona, Spain
Tel.: [34] 93 40 51 215
(Plastics)
Dow Chemical Co.

DuPont Ibérica SA
Avenida Diagonal 561
Edificio L'illa Diagonal
E-08029 Barcelona, Spain
Tel.: [34] 93 22 76 000
(Chemicals)
E.I. DuPont de Nemours & Co. Inc.

Firestone Hispania SA
Urbiren s/n
E-48970 Basauri (Vizcaya), Spain
Tel.: [34] 94 449 2300
(Tires and tubes)
Firestone Tire and Rubber Co.

Ford España SA
Paseo de la Castellana 135
E-28046 Madrid, Spain
Tel.: [34] 91 336 9100
Fax: [34] 91 5791 4233
(Motor vehicles and farm equipment)
Ford Motor Co.

General Motors España
Poligono Industria Entrerios Km 27
E-50639 Figueruelas, Spain
Tel.: [34] 97 665 8111
Fax: [34] 97 661 1194
(Automobiles)
General Motors Co.

Johnson's Wax Española SA
Orense 4, Pisos 5 Y 6
E-28020 Madrid, Spain
Tel.: [34] 91 555 9700
(Personal care and cleaning products)
S.C. Johnson & Son Inc.

Kodak SA
Carretera de la Coruna Km 23
Las Rozas de Madrid
E-28230 Madrid, Spain
Tel.: [34] 91 626 7100
(Photographic equipment)
Eastman Kodak Inc.

Kraft General Foods SA
Condesa de Venadito 5
E-28027 Madrid, Spain
(Food processing)
Kraft General Foods Inc.

Levi Strauss de España SA
Avenida Diagonal 605 3 Planta
E-08028 Barcelona, Spain
Tel.: [34] 93 22 76 900
(Clothing)
Levi Strauss & Co.

Mattel España SA
Aribau 200-210 8-9
E-08036 Barcelona, Spain
Tel.: [34] 93 30 67 900
(Toys)
Mattel Inc.

Merck Sharp & Dohme España
Josefa Valcárcel 38
E-28027 Madrid, Spain
Tel.: [34] 91 321 0600
Fax: [34] 91 321 0612
(Pharmaceuticals)
Merck Sharp & Dohme International Inc.

Nabisco Brands España SA
Montornés Nord s/n
E-08170 Montornés del Valles
(Barcelona), Spain
Tel.: [34] 93 568 1300
(Cereals, cookies, pasta)
Nabisco Brands Inc.

NCR España jSA
Albacete 1
E-28027 Madrid, Spain
Tel.: [34] 91 37 55 000
(Business machines)
NCR Corp.

Pepsi-Cola de España SA
Arequipa 1-4 Edificio Oficinas
Gran Via de Hortalezas
E-28043 Madrid, Spain
Tel.: [34] 91 38 29 300
(Concentrate for bottling plants)
PepsiCo Inc.

Philip Morris España SA
Marqués de la Ensenada 16
E-28004 Madrid, Spain
Tel.: [34] 91 34 90 100
(Cigarettes)
Philip Morris International

Procter & Gamble España SA
Avenido del Parteron 16-18
Campo de las Naciones
E-28042 Madrid, Spain
Tel.: [34] 91 72 22 100
Fax: [34] 91 72 22 380
(Soaps, pharmaceuticals)
Procter & Gamble Co.

Rank Xerox de España SA
Rivera de Sena 5/N
E-28042 Madrid, Spain
Tel.: [34] 91 520 3000
Fax: [34] 91 520 3275
(Office equipment)
Xerox Corp.

R.J. Reynolds Tobacco España SA
Avenida de Venezuela 1
El Paso Santa Cruz de Tenerife
E-38750 Madrid, Spain

Tel.: [34] 91 52 00 300
(Cigarettes)
R.J. Reynolds-Nabisco Corp.

3M España SA
Juan Ignacio de Tena 19-25
E-28027 Madrid, Spain
Tel.: [34] 91 321 6000
Fax: [34] 91 321 6002
(Adhesives, medical products)
Minnesota Mining and Manufacturing
Co.

Unisys España SA
Avenida del Partenon 4
Campo de las Naciones
E-28042 Madrid, Spain
Tel.: [34] 91 72 11 212
(Data processing systems)
Unisys Corp.

RETAILING AND WHOLESALING

Coca Cola de España SA
Josefa Valcarel 36
E-28027 Madrid, Spain
Tel.: [34] 91 34 81 700
(Soft drinks)
Coca Cola

Digital Equipment Corp. España SA
Cerro del Castañar 72
E-28034 Madrid, Spain
Tel.: [34] 91 583 4100
Fax: [34] 91 734 8834
(Data processing equipment)
Digital Equipment Corp.

Esso Española SA
Velazquez 50, Aptd. 493
E-28001 Madrid, Spain
(Petroleum products)
Exxon Company

Gillette Española SA
Agustin de Foxa 27
E-28036 Madrid, Spain
Tel.: [34] 91 59 69 00

(Shaving equipment)
The Gillette Co.

Hewlet-Packard Española SA
Carretera de la Cruña Km 16540
Las Rosas de Madrid
E-28230 Madrid, Spain
Tel.: [34] 91 611 6000
Fax: [34] 91 631 1830
(Electronic equipment)
Hewlett-Packard Corp.

Mattel España SA
Aribau N. 200-210, 8th Floor
E-08036 Barcelona, Spain
Tel.: [34] 93 200 5344
(Toys)
Mattel Inc.

Unisys España SA
Avenida Del Partenón
Campo de las Naciones
E-28042 Madrid, Spain
Tel.: [34] 91 72 12 121
Fax: [34] 91 72 11 288

SERVICE INDUSTRIES

Andersen Consulting SA
Plaza de Pablo Picasso
E-28020 Madrid, Spain
Tel.: [34] 91 59 66000
Fax: [34] 91 59 66695
(Accountancy, management consulting)
Andersen Consulting

Arthur Andersen & Compañia SRC
Raimundo Fernández Villaverde 65 21
E-28003 Madrid Spain
Tel.: [34] 92 59 73 659
(Accounting)
Andersen Consulting

Associated Press
Calle Espronceda 32
E-28003 Madrid, Spain
Tel.: [34] 91 39 92 433
(Newspaper press agent)
Associated Press

Bassat Ogilvy & Mather SA
Josep Tarradellas 123 1
E-08029 Barcelona, Spain
Tel.: [34] 93 95 55 55
Fax: [34] 93 49 55 500
(Advertising)
Ogilvy Group Inc.

Browning-Ferris Industries Iberica SA
Condesa de Venadito 5, Progal A2
E-28027 Madrid, Spain
Tel.: [34] 91 32 62 784
(Trucking)
Browing-Ferris Industries Inc.

Dun & Bradstreet Español SA
Salvador de Madariaga 1-2
E-28027 Madrid, Spain
Tel.: [34] 91 37 79 100
(Information services)
Dun & Bradstreet International

McCann Erickson SA
Paseo de la Castellana 165
E-28046 Madrid, Spain
Tel.: [34] 91 27 09 640
Fax: [34] 91 57 01 116
(Advertising)
Interpublic Inc.

A.C. Nielsen Co.
Avenida Diagonal 514
Modulo 1-2
E-08006 Barcelona, Spain
Tel.: [34] 93 41 50 210
Fax: [34] 93 41 60 070
(Market research)
A.C. Nielsen

J. Walter Thompson, SA
Arapiles 13
E-28015 Madrid, Spain
Tel.: [34] 91 448 7600
(Advertising and public relations)
Juli n Bravo, Director General
J. Walter Thompson Co.

EUROPEAN COMPANIES IN SPAIN

The following are major non-American firms operating in the country. These selected companies can be either Spanish or foreign, usually other European. Such companies will generally hire their own nationals first but may employ Americans.

BANKING AND FINANCE

Banco Bilbao Vizcaya
Gran Via #1
E-48005 Bilbao, Spain
Tel.: [34] 94 48 75 555
Fax: [34] 94 48 76 432
(Bank)

Banco Central Hispanoamericano SA
Calle Alcala 49
E-28014 Madrid, Spain
Tel.: [34] 91 55 84 100
Fax: [34] 91 53 27 659
(Bank)

Banco de Santander SA
Paseo de la Castellana 24
E-28046 Madrid, Spain

Tel.: [34] 91 34 25 887
Fax: [34] 91 34 24 894
(Bank)

Banco Español de Credito SA
Paseo de la Castellana 7
E-28046 Madrid, Spain
Tel.: [34] 91 33 81 000
Fax: [34] 91 33 81 020
(Bank)

Banco Popular Español SA
Velázquez 34
Edificio Goya
E-28001 Madrid, Spain
Tel.: [34] 91 52 07 409
Fax: [34] 91 52 07 408
(Bank)

INDUSTRIAL MANUFACTURING

Compañia Española De Petroleos SA (CEPSA)
Avenida del Partenon 12
E-28042 Madrid, Spain
Tel.: [34] 91 33 76 000
Fax: [34] 91 33 76 819
(Chemicals and petroleum)

Empresa Nacional de Electricidad Sa
Principe de Vergara 187
E-28002 Madrid, Spain
Tel.: [34] 91 56 68 800
Fax: [34] 91 56 38 181
(Electricity distribution)

Empresa Nacional de Ingenieria y Tecnologia SA
Padilla 17 4
E-28006 Madrid, Spain
Tel.: [34] 91 58 71 000
Fax: [34] 91 43 19 962
(Engineering and industrial consultants)

Hoechst Iberica
Via Augusta 252 Bajo
E-80821 Barcelona, Spain
Tel.: [34] 93 30 68 111
Fax: [34] 93 20 11 322
(Chemicals and pharmaceuticals)

Lever España SA
Manuel de Falla 7
E-28036 Madrid, Spain
Tel.: [34] 91 45 77 400
Fax: [34] 91 45 76 832
(Soaps and detergents)
Unilever NV, Netherlands

Renault España SA
Balmes 418-420
E-08022 Barcelona, Spain
Tel.: [34] 93 40 05 700
(Automobiles and parts)

Repsol SA
Paseo de la Castellana 278-280
E-28046 Madrid, Spain
Tel.: [34] 91 34 88 000
Fax: [34] 91 31 42 821
(Petroleum products)

Siemens SA
Orense 2, Aptd. 155
E-28020 Madrid, Spain
Tel.: [34] 91 55 56 500
Fax: [34] 91 55 60 277
(Electronic equipment)
Siemens AG, Germany

RETAILING AND WHOLESALING

BP Oil España SA
María de Molina 6
E-28006 Madrid, Spain
Tel.: [34] 91 36 29 292

Fax: [34] 91 36 29 608
(Petroleum products)

SERVICE INDUSTRIES

Air España SA
Gran Via Asima 23 Bajo
E-07009 Indioteria, Spain
Tel.: [34] 97 11 78 100
Fax: [34] 97 17 18 121
(Passenger airline)

Dragados y Construcciones SA
Paseo de la Alameda de Osuna 50
E-28042 Madrid, Spain
Tel.: [34] 91 58 33 000
Fax: [34] 91 58 32 12
(Construction and engineering)

El Corle Inglés
Hermosilla 112-3 Planta,
E-28009 Madrid, Spain
Tel.: [34] 91 40 28 112
Fax: [34] 91 40 25 821
(Department Store)

Ibéria Líneas Aéreas de España SA
Velazquez 130
E-28006 Madrid, Spain
Tel.: [34] 91 58 74 747
Fax: [34] 91 58 78 182
(National airline)

Telefónica de España SA
Gran Via no 28, 3rd Floor
E-28013 Madrid, Spain
Tel.: [34] 91 58 40 844
Fax: [34] 91 53 27 118
(Telecommunications)

Unión Eléctrica-Fenosa SA
Capitán Haya 53
E-28020 Madrid, Spain
Tel.: [34] 91 56 76 000
Fax: [34] 91 57 04 349
(Electricity supply)

INTERNATIONAL NON-PROFIT EMPLOYER IN SPAIN

World Tourism Organization
Calle Capitan Haya 42
E-28020 Madrid, Spain

Tel.: [34] 91 571 0628
Fax: [34] 91 571 3733

INTERNATIONAL SCHOOLS IN SPAIN

American School of Barcelona
Balmes 7
Esplugas de Llobregat
E-08950 Barcelona, Spain
Tel.: [34] 93 371 4016
Fax: [34] 93 473 4787
Email: info@a-s-b.com
(U.S., Spanish, pre-K-12)

American School of Bilbao
Soparda Bidea 10
E-48640 Berango, Vizcaya
Tel.: [34] 94 668 0860/61
Fax: [34] 94 668 0452
Email: r.junquera@asb.sarenet.es
(U.S., pre-K-10)

American School of Madrid
Apartado 80
E-28080 Madrid, Spain
Tel.: [34] 91 740 1900
Fax: [34] 91 357 2678
Email: asmcc@redestb.es
www.netschool.com/pages/asm
(U.S., Spanish, pre-K-12)

International College Spain
Apartado 271 Alcobendas
E-28100 Madrid, Spain
Tel.: [34] 91 650 2398/99
Fax: [34] 91 650 1035
Email: icsmadrid@mx3.redestb.es
www.icsmadrid.com
(U.S., U.K., International Baccalaureate
curriculum, pre-K-12)

Portugal

MAJOR EMPLOYMENT CENTERS: Lisbon, Porto

MAJOR BUSINESS LANGUAGE: Portuguese

LANGUAGE SKILL INDEX: French and Spanish can help those whose Portuguese is lacking, but your best bet is a solid knowledge of Portuguese

CURRENCY: Euro; the escudo will remain the currency in circulation until 2002

TELEPHONE COUNTRY CODE: 351

TIME ZONE: EST+6 mainland, +5 Madeira

PUNCTUALITY INDEX: Much like Spaniards, the Portuguese are a laid-back folk

AVERAGE DAILY TEMPERATURE: January, 55°F; July, 75°F (Lisbon)

AVERAGE NUMBER OF DAYS WITH RAIN: January, 13; July, 5

BEST BET FOR EMPLOYMENT:

  FOR STUDENTS: Resort jobs in the Algarve

  PERMANENT JOBS: Venture capitalism with your own money

CHANCE OF FINDING A JOB: None too promising without loads of tenacity and pluck

TRIVIA: Prefer a non-smoking work environment? Portugal is not the place for you, as the Portuguese have one of the highest smoking rates in the European Union, second only to Greece

The Portuguese Republic, approximately the size of Indiana, occupies 15% of the Iberian Peninsula and borders Spain to the north and east, the Atlantic Ocean to the west, and Africa to the south across a stretch of ocean. Southern Portugal, the Algarve, attracts tourists to its warm, Mediterranean climate. The northern part of the country is mountainous, while the southern region consists of rolling plains. The Azores Islands are located about 900 miles west of the Portuguese coast; and the Madeira Islands are about 530 miles southwest of Portugal. Macao is an enclave off the southern coast of China.

Portuguese is the national language. Most Portuguese speakers can understand, but probably not speak, Spanish. In the tourist areas of the Algarve, many people speak French or English. The vast majority of people are ethnically homogeneous, but a sizable African minority also exists. About 97% of the population is Roman Catholic.

Until it achieved independence under King John I in the twelfth century, Portugal was one of Spain's linguistically distinct regions. Prince Henry the Navigator coordinated Portugal's extensive voyages of exploration in the late fifteenth century. By the mid-sixteenth century, Portugal had acquired possessions in South America, Africa, east Asia, and India. In 1581 Spain invaded the country and held it until 1640, when Portugal regained its independence. Portugal lost much of its empire during the occupation but retained Brazil until 1822 and its African colonies until 1974. Napoleon invaded in 1807, forcing the king temporarily to move his court to Brazil. A parliamentary republic was proclaimed in 1910.

Portugal fought with the Allies in World War I. A military coup in 1926 initiated the authoritarian reign of Antonio Oliveira Salazar. Portugal remained neutral in World War II but later joined the North Atlantic Treaty Organization. Following Salazar's death in 1970, his successor, Marcello Caetano, continued the policy of opposition to independence movements in the African colonies. A left-wing military coup in 1974 ended the Caetano regime and granted independence to Angola and Mozambique. Communist Party pressure in 1975 lead to extensive nationalizations until a counter-coup in November stopped the trend. The country has experienced nearly twenty governments since then. Portugal's entry into the E.U. in 1986 secured a measure of stability, buttressed by the inclusion of the country as a full member of the European Monetary System in 1992.

Despite E.U. membership, which has given a boost to Portugal's development and modernization, the 1990s have been fraught with recession and high unemployment. In the elections in 1995, the electorate showed its dissatisfaction with the Social Democratic Party by switching back to socialism after 10 years of conservatism.

Business hours are from 9:00 a.m. to 1:00 p.m., followed by a midday break, then from 3:00 to 7:00 p.m. Many businesses are open on Saturday morning but usually not on Sunday. Banking hours are 8:30 to 11:45 a.m. and then again from

1:00 to 2:45 p.m., Monday through Friday. Post offices are open from 8:30 a.m. to 6:30 p.m., Monday through Friday, and from 9:00 a.m. to 12:00 noon on Saturday. In the smaller towns, post offices close for lunch and are never open on Saturdays.

Using the language

Portuguese, French, and Spanish speakers can usually understand each other, although they rarely speak the other language. Knowledge of Spanish or French will certainly help you to communicate in Portugal, but you should understand Portuguese if you hope to gain employment.

Current Economic Climate

Portugal's gross national product and low per capita income rank it as one of Europe's smaller and poorer economies. The country has managed to tame its rampant inflation rate to around 2.5%, and is enjoying a period of economic expansion, due largely to investment in infrastructure and increased privatization. Portugal has benefited considerably from its entry into the E.U. through much needed funding to improve the country's infrastructure. The current unemployment rate is 6.7% and is expected to drop slightly in the future.

Major industries include: textile, wood products, cork, chemicals, canning, and wine. Manufacturing claims 34% of the work force, agriculture 22%, and services 44%. The E.U. and U.S. are Portugal's major trading partners. The country looks set to benefit from low labor costs, a young population, and strong trading links with South America and Africa.

PORTUGAL'S 10 LARGEST COMPANIES

(1997, composite ranking)
1. Transportes Aéros Portugeses
2. Banco Espírito Santo & Comercial de Lisbon
3. Banco Comercial Portages
4. Moat & Compendia
5. Espaliers Navies de Lisbon
6. Est. Jerónimo Martins & Filho
7. Corticeira Amorim Soc. Gestora Parti
8. Salvador Caetano Indústrias Metalúrgicas
9. ENGIL–Sociedade de Construçåo Civil
10. Estoril-Sol.

Using the phone

Local calls from public coin telephones start at 20$00. Since the largest acceptable coin is 50$00, it is impractical to make long-distance and international calls from coin-operated phones. Most newsstands, tobacconists, and telephone offices sell the more practical phonecards that can be used in "Credifones." All domestic and international calls are charged identical rates per time unit, but each destination has a time unit of a different duration. To reach an international operator, dial "098." Portugal's emergency number is "115."

Getting Around in Portugal

Traveling by train in Portugal is slow but express trains are available from Lisbon to Porto and from Lisbon to Algarve. The rail system generally runs until midnight. Buses are faster and more comfortable when traveling inter-city, but fares are more expensive than rail. Eurail and InterRail passes are accepted throughout the country.

Employment Regulations and Outlook for Americans

U.S. citizens do not need a visa for stays in Portugal of fewer than 60 days. In order to work in Portugal, however, a work permit (obtained by one's employer from the Ministry of Labor) and a visa (from the Portuguese Consulate) must be presented upon arrival. Work prospects are generally limited, except as English-language teachers. The Portuguese generally hire their own nationals for most jobs, including tourist work.

Short-term and Temporary Work

The best bet for temporary work in Portugal is teaching English.

Cambridge School Group
avenia da Liberdade 173
P-1200 Lisbon, Portugal
Tel.: [351] (1) 74 74
Operates a chain of English language schools.

Linguacultura
apartado 37/Rua Pedro Santarém 150
1 Dto
P-2001 Santarém Codex, Portugal
Tel.: [351] (1) 43 262 98
English language school.

Internship Program

IASTE offers students an opportunity to obtain professional experience in a technical field.

IASTE-US
10400 Little Patuxent Parkway, Suite 250 L
Columbia, MD 21044-3510
Tel.: (410) 997-3068
Fax: (410) 997-5186

Email: iaste@aipt.org
www.aipt/iaste.html
Arranges reciprocal internships in 63 different countries. Specifically for students in technical fields.

Volunteer Opportunities

Portugal's major youth camp organization, FAOJ, operates camps involving forest work, environmental study, archaeological projects, building restoration, and working with the handicapped. Over 350 students participate in FAOJ workcamps annually. Turicoop organizes camps concentrating on environmental and archaeological work. Companheiros Construtores seeks 200 volunteers annually to work on construction and development projects to benefit mentally or physically handicapped persons and the poor. The Student and Youth Tourism Association (ATEJ) places volunteers in agricultural positions and on archaeological digs.

ATEJ
rua Joaquim Antonio Aguiar No. 255
P-4300 Oporto, Portugal
Tel.: [351] (2) 568 542

Companheiros Construtores
rua Pedro Monteiro No. 3-1
P-3000 Coimbra, Portugal
Tel.: [351] (39) 716 747

FAOJ
c/o Volunteers for Peace
International Workcamps

43 Tiffany Road
Belmont, VT 05730
Tel.: (802) 259-2759
Fax: (802) 259-2922
Email: VFP@VFP.prg
www.vfp.org

Turicoop
rua Pascoal-Melo 15-1ª DTO
P-1100 Lisbon, Portugal
Tel.: [351] (1) 531804

NEWSPAPERS IN PORTUGAL

Anglo-Portuguese News (English)
avenida de Sao Pedro 17
P-2756 Estoril, Portugal
Tel.: [351] (2) 44 31 15
Fax: [351] (2) 44 37 39

Diario de Noticias
266 avenida da Liberdade
P-1200 Lisbon, Portugal

Tel.: [351] (1) 56 11 51
Fax: [351] (1) 53 66 27

Jornal de Noticias
rua Goncalo Cristovao 195/219
P-4052 Oporto, Portugal
Tel.: [351] (2) 38 13 31
Fax: [351] (2) 200 63 30

Organizations for Further Information

USEFUL WEBSITE FOR JOB SEARCHERS

The Internet is a good place to begin your job search. Although Portuguese employers do not regularly use the Internet to list jobs, the following is a general website that provides useful information for job searchers researching the job market.

Portuguese info/jobs
www.portugal-info.net
Gives info on Portugal, and has small jobs list.

EMBASSIES AND CONSULAR OFFICES

American embassies and consulates have commercial and/or economic sections that can provide you with business information and explain aspects of the local economy. Inquiries about business opportunities should be addressed either to "Commercial Officer" or "Commercial Section," followed by the appropriate street address.

Representation of Portugal in the United States

Embassy of Portugal
2125 Kalorama Road NW
Washington, DC 20008
Tel.: (202) 328-8610

Consulates General of Portugal: Boston (617) 536-8740; Los Angeles, (310) 277-1491; New York, (212) 246-4580

Representation of the United States in Portugal

American Embassy
Av. das Forças Armadas
P-1600 Lisbon, Portugal
Tel.: [351] (1) 726 6600
Fax: [351] (1) 726 9109
www.american-embassy.pt/

American Consulate—San Miguel
avenida D. Henrique
Ponta Delgada, San Miguel, Azores
Tel.: [351] (96) 22 216
Fax: [351] (96) 27 216

CHAMBERS OF COMMERCE

Chambers of commerce consist of firms in both countries interested in international trade. These are appropriate companies to initially target in the job search.

American Chamber of Commerce in Portugal
rua D. Estefania 155, esq. 5
P-1000 Lisbon, Portugal
Tel.: [351] (1) 57 82 08

Portugal—U.S. Chamber of Commerce
590 Fifth Avenue, 3rd Floor
New York, NY 10036
Tel.: (212) 354-4610

Portugal Chamber of Commerce and Industry
rua das Postes de Santo Antao 89
P-2080 Lisbon, Portugal

WORLD TRADE CENTERS IN PORTUGAL

World Trade Centers usually include many foreign companies operating in the country.

World Trade Center Lisbon
avenida do Brasil, 1-9
P-1700 Lisbon, Portugal
Tel.: [351] (1) 792 3700
Fax: [351] (1) 792 3701
Email: wtc@telepac.pt

World Trade Center Porto
avenida da Boavista, 1277
P-4100 Porto, Portugal
Tel.: [351] (2) 606 8855
Fax: [351] (2) 600 2135

OTHER INFORMATIONAL ORGANIZATIONS

Foreign government missions in the U.S. such as National Tourist Offices can furnish visas and information on work permits and other important regulations. They may also offer economic and business information about the country.

Portuguese Export Promotion Board
101-A, avenida 5 de Outubro
Lisbon, Portugal

Portuguese National Tourist Office
590 Fifth Avenue, 4th Floor
New York, NY 10036-4704
Tel.: (212) 354-4403

BUSINESS DIRECTORIES

Although not always easy to find, business directories can prove invaluable in the international job search. Most directories list company names, addresses, products, and phone numbers. Some directories include executive names and titles and financial information about the company. These sources provide you with the names of the people to contact for employment information as well as financial data, which can tell you how strong a company's position in a country may be.

American Chamber of Commerce in Portugal—Membership Directory. Published biannually by the American Chamber of Commerce in Portugal, Rua de Estefania 155, P-1000 Lisbon, Portugal. List of members of the chamber.

Directory of Foreign Firms Operating Abroad: Portugal. World Trade Academy Press, 257 Central Park West, Suite 10A, New York, NY 10024-4110; email: uniworldbp@aol.com; www.uniworldbp.com. Lists names and addresses of parent companies in the U.S. and their subsidiaries and affiliates in Portugal.

Dun's 15,000 Largest Companies–Portugal. Published by address; email: dnbmbbc@dnb.com. Directory of industrial, trading, banking, insurance, and service companies in Portugal.

Export Directory of Portugal. Published annually in Portuguese, English, French, and German by Interpropo Lda., Rua Coronal Bento Roma 28, P-1700 Lisbon, Portugal. Includes 4,500 manufacturers engaged in export from continental Portugal, Madeira, the Azores, and Macau.

Kompass Portugal. Published by Interpropo Lda., Rua Coronal Bento Roma 28, P-1700 Lisbon, Portugal. Leading companies and exporters in Portugal.

AMERICAN COMPANIES IN PORTUGAL

The following companies are classified by business area: Banking and Finance; Industrial Manufacturing; Retailing and Wholesaling; and Service Industries. Company information includes firm name, address, phone and fax number, specific business, and American parent company. Your chances of achieving employment abroad are substantially better if you contact the subsidiary company in Europe rather than the parent company in the U.S.

BANKING AND FINANCE

Chase Manhattan Bank, NA
rua Alexandre Herculano 50, 7th Floor
P-1200 Lisbon, Portugal
Tel.: [351] (1) 521 195
Fax: [351] (1) 521 171
(Bank)
Chase Manhattan Bank

Citibank Portugal SA
rua Barata Salgueiro 30
E-1250 Lisbon, Portugal
Tel.: [351] (1) 311 63 00
Fax: [351] (1) 311 63 16

INDUSTRIAL MANUFACTURING

Aeronautical Instrument & Radio Co.
Cinave, rua do Quelhas 27, Rdc.
Lisbon, Portugal
(Flight and navigation equipment)
Aeronautical Instrument & Radio Co.

American Home Products de Portugal
rua Humberto Madeira 2-3
P-2745 Barcarena, Portugal
Tel.: [31] (1) 434 80 90
(Pharmaceuticals)
American Home Products Corp.

Bristol Farmaceutica Portuguesa Lda.
Qunita da Fonte 85, Porto Salvo
Paco de Arcos
P-2780 Oeras, Portugal
Tel.: [351] (1) 44 07 005
(Pharmaceuticals)
Bristol-Myers Co.

Crown Cork & Seal de Portugal SA
avenida Infante Ohenrique Cotes
P-1800 Lisbon, Portugal
Tel.: [351] (1) 18 51 31 41
(Packaging products)
Crown Cork & Seal Co. Inc.

Dow Portugal Produtos Quimicos Lda.
Quinta da Industria Beduido
Estarreja Aveiro
P-3860 Estarreja, Portugal
Tel.: [351] (1) 34 84 01 007
(Chemicals and plastics)
The Dow Chemical Co.

Firestone Portuguesa SA
Estrada Nacional 119, Km 1.5
P-2890 Alcochete, Setubal, Portugal
Tel.: [351] (1) 56 33 48
(Tires and tubes)
Firestone Tire and Rubber Co.

Ford Lusitana SA
rua Rosa Araujo 2-2
P-1250 Lisbon, Portugal
Tel.: [351] (1) 31 22 300

(Automobiles and farm equipment)
Ford Motor Co.

Goodyear Portuguesa Lda.
Tapada Do Marchante Prior Velho
P-2685 Loures, Portugal
Tel.: [351] (1) 94 29 000
(Tires)
Goodyear Tire and Rubber Co.

Grace Portuguesa (Productos Quimicos e Plasticos) Ltd.
rua Dr. Afonso Cordeiro 679-1E
P-4450 Matosinhos, Portugal
Tel.: [351] (1) 525 349
(Sealing compounds and lubricants)
W.R. Grace & Co. Inc.

Hewlett Packard Portugal SA
Quinta da Fonte Edificio
Bartolemeu Dias
P-2780 Oeiras Lisbon, Portugal
Tel.: [351] (1) 48 28 500
(Electronic equipment)
Hewlett-Packard

Johnson & Johnson Lda.
estrada Rivinheria-Queluz de Baixo
P-2745 Queluz, Portugal
Tel.: [351] (1) 43 68 770
(Medical equipment)
Johnson & Johnson

Kodak Portuguesa Ltd.
rua Alexandre Herculano 4
Linda-A-Velha
P-2795 Oeiras, Portugal
Tel.: [351] (1) 41 47 600
(Photographic equipment)
Eastman Kodak Co.

Merck Sharp & Dohme Lda.
Queluz de Baixo
P-2745 Queluz, Portugal
Tel.: [351] (1) 43 47 000
(Pharmaceuticals)
Merck & Co. Inc.

Nabisco Brands, Inc.
rua do Proletariado 14, Portela da Ajuda
Lisbon 3, Portugal
(Food processing)
Nabisco Brands, Inc.

**Texas Instruments Equipamento
Electronico Portugal Lda.**
rua Eng Frederico Uirich 2650
P-4470 Moreira De Maia, Maia, Douro
Lito, Portugal
(Electronic components)
Texas Instruments

3M de Portugal Ltd.
rua Conde de Redondo 98
P-1100 Lisbon Codex, Portugal
Tel.: [351] (1) 561 131
(Office equipment)
Minnesota Mining and Manufacturing Co.

**Warner-Lambert (Portugal) Comercio E
Industria Lda.**
rua Tierno Galvan Torre 3, Fraccao M-12
P-1200 Lisbon, Portugal
Tel.: [351] (1) 691 260
(Chewing gum, pharmaceuticals, and
toiletries)
Warner-Lambert Co.

**Xerox (Portugal) Equipamentos de
Escritorio Ltd.**
rua Pedro Nunes 16
P-1050 Lisbon Codex, Portugal
Tel.: [351] (1) 13 13 10 00
(Electronic equipment)
Xerox Corp.

RETAILING AND WHOLESALING

Abbott Laboratorios Lda.
rua 9 Lote 40
P-2700 Amadora, Lisbon, Portugal
Tel.: [351] (1) 976 904
(Pharmaceuticals)
Abbott Laboratories

Avon-Cosmeticos Lda.
avenida Fontes Pereira De Melo 14-5
P-1000 Lisbon, Portugal
Tel.: [351] (1) 540 701
(Cosmetics)
Avon International Operations

Colgate Palmolive SA
rua Mario Castelhano
Quelez de Baiyo, Portugal
Tel.: [351] (1) 436 3381
(Cleaning products and toiletries)
Colgate-Palmolive Co.

Companhia IBM Portuguesa SA
7PC de Alvalade 7, Bloco C-D
(Antigo Lote 1249)
P-1700 Lisbon, Portugal
Tel.: [351] (1) 894 161
(Data processing equipment)
IBM World Trade Corp.

Digital Equipment Portugal
avenida Engduarte Pacheco Terre 1-9
P-1070 Lisbon, Portugal
Tel.: [351] (1) 381 80 00
(Computer equipment)
Digital Equipment

Esso Portuguesa Sarl
rua Filipe Folque 2-3
P-1050 Lisbon, Portugal
Tel.: [351] (1) 350 07 00
(Petroleum products)
Exxon Corp.

General Electric Portuguesa, SA
avenida Helen Keller 19
P-1400 Lisbon, Portugal
Tel.: [351] (1) 36 31 166
Fax: [351] (1) 36 47 083
(Computers)
General Electric Co.

General Motors De Portugal Lda.
estrada Nacional No. 3
P-2050 Azambuja, Portugal
Tel.: [351] (1) 634 2692
(Automobiles and auto parts)
General Motors Corp.

Mobil Oil Portuguesa LDA
rua Castilho 165-Ed Mobil
P-1070 Lisbon, Portugal
Tel.: [351] (1) 387 55 61
Fax: [351] (1) 387 04 21
(Petroleum products)
Mobil Oil Corp.

**Unisys Portugal-Sistemas de Informacão
SA**
rua Actor Antonio Silva 7
P-1600 Lisbon, Portugal
Tel.: [351] (1) 758 0307
(Data processing equipment)
Unisys Corp.

SERVICE INDUSTRIES

Air Express International
c/o Germano Serrao Arnaud, Ltd.
avenida 24 Julio, 22D
Lisbon 2, Portugal
(Air freight)
Air Express Int'l.

Andersen Consulting
Amoreiras, Torre 1-16
P-10700 Lisbon, Portugal
Tel.: [351] (1) 387 21 34
Fax: [351] (1) 388 51 42
(Management consulting)

Arthur Andersen & Co. (Portugal)
avenida Eng. Duarte Pacheco, Torr E 1-15
P-1070 Lisbon, Portugal
(Accounting)
Arthur Andersen & Co.

**Coopers & Lybrand & Carqueja Periconta—
Peritagens Contabilisticas Ltd.**
P.O. Box 1910
P-1004 Lisbon Codex, Portugal
(Accounting)
Coopers & Lybrand Int'l.

**Deloitte & Touche–Auditores E
Consultores LDA**
avenida Eng. Duarte Pacheco 1-12
P-1070 Lisbon, Portugal
Tel.: [351] (1) 387 56 26
Fax: [351] (1) 65 93 22
(Accounting)
Deloitte & Touche

Dun & Bradstreet Portugal Serviços LDA
rua Barata Salgueiro 28,3°
P-1250 Lisbon, Portugal
Tel.: [351] (1) 314 66 36
Fax: [351] (1) 357 89 39
(Business information services)
Dun & Bradstreet International

Editora McGraw-Hill de Portugal Ltd.
estrada de Alfagide, Lote 107
P-2700 Alfagide, Portugal
Tel.: [351] (1) 472 85 00
Fax: [351] (1) 471 89 81
(Publishing)
McGraw-Hill Int'l. Co.

A.J. Goncalves de Moraes LDA
rua Nova alfandega 18
P-4050 Porto, Portugal
Tel.: [351] (2) 32 37 41

Fax: [351] (2) 32 32 17
(Warehousing and transport)
Sea-Land Service Inc.

**KPMG Peat, Marwick, Auditores &
Consultores**
avenida Praia Da Vitoria 71-a/f-11
P-1050 Lisbon, Portugal
Tel.: [351] (1) 311 04 06
Fax: [351] (1) 315 30 36
(Accounting)
KPMG Peat Marwick

Manpower Portuguesa
Praca Jose Fontana, 9-C
P-1000 Lisbon, Portugal
(Temporary labor)
Manpower Inc.

McCann-Erickson/Hora Publicidada Lda.
avenida Antonio Jose De Almeida 5F
P-1093 Lisbon, Portugal
Tel.: [351] (1) 793 2022
(Advertising)
McCann-Erickson Worldwide

A.C. Nielsen Co. of Portugal
rua Filipa de Vilhema 38
P-1000 Lisbon, Portugal
Tel.: [351] (1) 793 73 36
Fax: [351] (1) 796 64 81
(Market research)
A.C. Nielsen Co.

Ogilvy & Mather Portugal
avenida Marques de Tomar 102-2nd
P-1000 Lisbon, Portugal
(Advertising)
Ogilvy & Mather Worldwide, Inc.

**Price Waterhouse Auditores &
Consultores**
avenida De Liberdade 145-7/8
P-1250 Lisbon, Portugal
Tel.: [351] (1) 311 33 00
Fax: [351] (1) 316 11 12
(Accounting)
Price Waterhouse & Co.

Sheraton Lisboa Hotel
rua latino Coelho 1
P-1069 Lisbon, Portugal
Tel.: [351] (1) 357 57 57
Fax: [351] (1) 354 71 64
(Hotel operations)
Sheraton Hotels

EUROPEAN COMPANIES IN PORTUGAL

The following are major non-American firms operating in Portugal. These selected companies can be either Portuguese or foreign. Such companies will generally hire their own nationals first but may employ Americans.

BANKING AND FINANCE

Banco de Portugal
rua Do Comercia 148
P-1100 Lisbon, Portugal
Tel.: [351] (1) 346 29 31
Fax: [351] (1) 346 48 43
(Central Bank)

Banco Espirito Santo & Commercial de Lisboa, SA
avenida Da Liberdade 195
P-1250 Lisbon, Portugal
Tel.: [351] (1) 315 83 31
Fax: [351] (1) 353 29 31
(Bank)

Banco Nacional Ultramarino
avenida 5 de Outubro 175
P.O. Box 2419
P-1111 Lisbon, Portugal
Tel.: [351] (1) 793 01 12
Fax: [351] (1) 793 89 52
(Bank)

Caixa Geral de Depositos
avenida Joao XXI 63
P-1000 Lisbon, Portugal
Tel.: [351] (1) 790 50 00
Fax [351] (1) 790 50 49
(Bank)

INDUSTRIAL MANUFACTURING

Agros
Lugar Portas Fronhas
P-4480 Vila do Conde, Portugal
Tel.: [351] (52) 640 11 00
Fax: [351] (52) 604 12 90
(Cheese and dairy products)

Central de Cervejas SA
avenida Almirante Reis 115
P-1170 Lisbon, Portugal
Tel.: [351] (1) 355 88 41
Fax: [351] (1) 353 85 29
(Beer)

Corticeira Amorim Industria SA
Meladas Mouquim
P-4535 Lourosa, Portugal
Tel.: [351] (2) 764 75 09
Fax: [351] (2) 764 35 24
(Cork products)

Grundig Electronica Portugal Lda.
Estrada Nacional No. 3
P-2020 Azambuja, Portugal
Tel.: [351] 53 25 081
(Electronic products)
Grundig AG, Germany

Nestlé Portugal SA
rua Alexandre Herculano 8-8/A
P-2795 Linda-A-Velha, Portugal
Tel.: [351] (1) 414 85 00
Fax: [351] (1) 414 37 00
(Food products)
Nestlé, SA, Switzerland

Petroléos de Portugal SA
rua das Flores 7
P.O. Box 2539
P-1113 Lisbon Codex, Portugal
Tel.: [351] (1) 347 3440
(Oil exploration and refining)

RETAILING AND WHOLESALING

BP Portugesa SA
rua de Castiho 69-r/c-Dt.
P-1205 Lisbon, Portugal
Tel.: [351] (1) 311 16 00
Fax: [351] (1) 57 78 06
(Petroleum products)
The British Petroleum Company

Estb. Jerónimo Martins & Filho Adm. E Part.
rua Tierno Galvan, Torre 3, 9 Piso, Letra J
1000 Lisbon, Portugal
Tel.: [351] (1) 388 60 36
(Supermarkets)

Philips Portuguesa SA
rua Dr. Antonio Loureiro Borges 5
P-1495 Lisbon, Portugal
Tel.: [351] (1) 416 33 33
Fax: [351] 416 33 66
(Household appliances)
Philips Gloeilampenfabrieken NV,
Netherlands

Siemens SA
Estrada Nacional 117Km 2.6, Alfragide
P-2700 Amadera, Lisbon, Portugal
Tel.: [351] (1) 417 00 11
(Electrical appliances)
Siemens AG, Germany

SERVICE INDUSTRIES

Air Portugal
Aeroporto Lisboa, rua B-Ed. TAP-9-lo
P-1704 Lisbon, Portugal
Tel.: [351] (1) 841 65 93
Fax: [351] (1) 841 66 01
(National airline)

ENGIL–Sociedade de Construcao Civil SA
rua Mario Dionisio, 2
P-2795 Linda-a-Velha, Portugal
Tel.: [351] 414 26 47
Fax: [351] 414 26 47
(Construction)

Estaleiros Navais de Lisboa, SA
Rocha do Conde de Obidos
P-1300 Lisbon, Portugal
Tel.: [351] (1) 606 171
Fax: [351] (1) 661 179
(Shipbuilding & repair)

Estoril-Sol. S.A.
rua Melo E. Souza, 535
P-2765 Cascais, Portugal

Tel.: [351] (1) 268 4521
(Services and entertainment)

Mota & Companhia, SA
rua do Rego Lameiro, 38
P-4300 Porto, Portugal
Tel.: [351] (2) 510 0303
Fax: [351] (2) 56 0336
(Public work & civil construction)

Salvador Caetano Ind. Metal. Veículos de Transport
avenida Vasco da Gama, Oliveira do
Douro, Aptdo 51
P-4401 Vila Nova de Gaia, Portugal
Tel.: [351] (2) 783 3773
Fax: [351] (2) 782 6318
(Transportation rentals)

Transportes Aéreos Portugueses S.A.
Aeroporto de Lisboa
P-1704 Lisbon, Portugal
Tel.: [351] (1) 847 0304
(International airline)

INTERNATIONAL SCHOOLS IN PORTUGAL

American International School—Lisbon
Apartado 10
P-2795 Carnaxide, Portugal
Tel.: [351] (1) 923 9800
Fax: [351] (1) 923 9899
Email: aisllmc@mail.telepac.pt
www.ecis.org/aislisbon/index.html
(U.S., pre-K-12)

St. Julian's School (English Section)
Quinta Nova
Carcavelos
P-2777 Parede Codex, Portugal
Tel.: [351] (1) 457 0140
Fax: [351] (1) 456 6817
Email: mail@stjulians.com
www.ecis.org/stjulians
(U.K., International Baccalaureate, pre-K-12)

Scandinavia: Denmark, Finland, Norway, and Sweden

Denmark

Major Employment center: Copenhagen

Major business language: Danish

Language skill index: Most Danes speak English, and if you are looking for a job in a tourist spot, it may not be necessary to learn Danish. Many Danes also speak German, so knowledge of German may help in a pinch

Currency: Krone

Telephone country code: 45

Time zone: EST+6

Punctuality index: Danes find punctuality very important

Average daily temperature, high/low: January, 36/29°F; July, 72/55°F (Copenhagen)

Average number of days with precipitation: January, 15; July, 13

Best bet for employment:

For students: Work through the American-Scandinavian Foundation

Permanent jobs: Business services of some sort

Chance of finding a job: Just so-so; you really need a special skill

Trivia: Denmark is the least corrupt country in which to do business, according to the annual "corruption perceptions index" compiled by Transparency International

Denmark is the smallest of the Scandinavian countries and is about half the size of Maine. Made up of the Jutland Peninsula and over 500 islands (of which only 100 are inhabited), Denmark stretches north from Germany, separating the North Sea on the west from the Baltic Sea on the east. Excluding Denmark's territories of the Færœ Islands and Greenland, the country covers over 16,000 square miles. While in Denmark, you are never more than 35 miles from the sea. Denmark is so flat that Danes claim you can see from one end of the country to the other while standing on a carton of beer. Denmark is separated by narrow waters from Norway on the northwest and Sweden on the northeast. Its capital, Copenhagen, is located on the largest Baltic island, Zealand. Nearly 85% of the population is urban, with 38% of the total population concentrated in the four largest cities (Copenhagen, Alborg, Odense, and Arhus).

A large portion of the Viking raids on western Europe and England in the early Middle Ages were carried out by Danes. Until the 17th century, when it lost its land in Sweden, the Kingdom of Denmark was a major power in northern Europe. Denmark lost Norway to Sweden in 1815, after supporting Napoleon. Denmark remained neutral in World War I and was occupied by the Nazis in World War II. Iceland declared its independence in 1944, and in 1945 Denmark was liberated by British troops. Denmark joined the United Nations in 1945 and N.A.T.O. in 1949.

The Kingdom of Denmark is one of the world's oldest monarchies. Since 1849, Denmark has been a constitutional monarchy, with the monarch and parliament jointly sharing power. Queen Margrethe II, who was crowned in 1972 after her nation's constitution was amended to allow female succession, is the world's youngest queen. Legislative powers rest with the *Folketing,* Denmark's parliament which is made up of 179 elected members who serve four-year terms. The prime minister is appointed by the Queen. The nation's major political parties are the Social Democrats, the Conservative People's Party, the Socialist People's Party, and the Liberal Party.

Denmark has been hesitant to support expansion of the E.U. In fact, when the Maastricht Treaty came up for ratification in 1992, Danish voters rejected it by a margin of 51% to 49%. The Danes only voted to accept it in 1993 when they were granted exemptions from Maastricht's common defense and single currency provisions. Danish support for the E.U. remains lukewarm as many people fear the loss of local control to a European bureaucracy dominated by stronger countries.

As in all Scandinavian countries, the cost of living in Denmark is higher than in the U.S. and much higher than in the Mediterranean countries. Scandinavia is well known for its extensive welfare system and good record on civil rights. Denmark, in fact, now grants formal legal status to gay couples.

July and August are bad months for doing business in Denmark. Because of the Danes' love of the summer, it is difficult and considered inconsiderate to try to conduct heavy business in these months. Business hours are generally from 9 a.m. to 4 p.m., Monday-Friday. Most stores are open until 5:30 p.m. on weekdays and until 2 p.m. on Saturdays.

Current Economic Climate

Denmark has one of the highest per capita GNPs in the world and maintains a very high standard of living. The unemployment rate, now at 5.4%, is expected to drop slightly and the inflation rate, now at 2.5%, is one of the lowest of any E.U. country. Economic growth has averaged about 2% or slightly above, keeping pace with the European Union's average. Denmark has extremely high taxes levied by the government that have enabled it to conduct one of the most advanced systems of welfare and social services in the world.

Denmark's labor force is 65% services, 28% industry, and 6% agricultural. Denmark is the world's leading exporter of canned meat. Although the fishing industry employs only about .5% of the workforce, Denmark leads the E.U. in terms of fish catches. Other important exports include butter, cheese, beer, furniture, electronics, silverware, and porcelain. Denmark's major trading partners include Germany, Sweden, the U.K., and the U.S.

DENMARK'S 10 LARGEST COMPANIES
(1997 composite)
1. International Service System
2. Sophus Berendsen
3. Carlsberg
4. TeleDanmark
5. Den Danske Bank
6. J. Lauritzen Holding
7. Aktieselskabet Potagua
8. FLS Industries
9. The East Asiatic Company
10. Novo Nordisk

Using the phone and fax

No matter where you are in Denmark you must use the entire eight-digit phone number to make a call; there are no area codes within Denmark. Toll-free and emergency numbers are preceded by a zero. Public phones in busier areas use *telekort* phonecards which are available at post offices and kiosks. Faxes can be sent from public telephone offices, usually found beside larger post offices.

Getting Around in Denmark

The Danish State Railways (DSB) provide extensive train services in and around Denmark, and the major routes have high-speed IC3 trains. Private and government-owned ferry lines serve passengers traveling in the Great Belt (the channel between the mainland and surrounding islands). Ferries with rails carry trains across the water. Regional buses serve smaller towns not reached by trains. Eurail and InterRail passes are accepted on all DSB trains in Denmark, and holders may ride the state-run ferries for free.

Employment Regulations and Outlook for Americans

U.S. citizens do not need visas for stays in Denmark of fewer than 90 days, but this 90-day period begins as soon as you enter any Scandinavian country. Since work permits are only granted to foreigners who possess "special training or skills not readily available in Denmark," your employer must apply on your behalf. Work permits are available through the Royal Danish Embassy (3200 Whitehaven Street NW, Washington, DC 20008). A special bulletin, *Short Cuts,* contains information on working in Copenhagen. It is available for 40 kroner through the Youth Information Copenhagen (see "Other Informational Organizations" below).

Short-term and Temporary Work

The best bet for a casual job in Denmark, as in all of Scandinavia, is to work as an au pair.

Exis
Rebslagergade 3
Postboks 291
DK-6400 Sonderborg, Denmark
Tel.: [45] 74 42 97 49
Email: exis@po.ia.dk
Au pair placement in Denmark, Norway, and Iceland.

Internship Programs

There are opportunities for students to gain professional experience, usually in technical fields. The American-Scandinavian Foundation and IASTE coordinate placements for technical interns. The World Assembly of Youth coordinates government internships.

The American-Scandinavian Foundation
725 Park Avenue
New York, NY 10021
Tel.: (212) 879-9779
Email: training@amscan.org
Places summer interns in engineering, agriculture, and other technical fields throughout Scandinavia.

IASTE
10400 Little Patuxent Parkway, Suite 250 L
Columbia, MD 21044-3510
Tel.: (410) 997-3068
Fax: (410) 997-5186

Email: iaste@aipt.org
www. aipt.org/iaste.html
Arranges reciprocal internship exchanges
among 63 member countries for students in
engineering, architecture, and the sciences.

World Assembly of Youth
Ved Bellahoj 4
DK-2700 Bronshoj, Copenhagen,

Denmark
Tel.: [45] 31 60 77 70
Fax: [45] 31 60 57 97
Email: way@inform.bbs.dk
International coordinating body of
national youth councils and organizations.

Volunteer Opportunities

Denmark offers voluntary service opportunities in international student workcamps. Through the Council on International Educational Exchange (CIEE), students can do volunteer work protecting the environment or sending supplies to Third World countries. Participants must be 18 or older, and U.S. citizens need to apply to the CIEE address given below.

For year-long volunteer work, the International Christian Youth Exchange offers work opportunities in health care, education, construction, and the environment. Volunteers must be between 18 and 30. For more details, contact their office in New York. Volunteers for Peace, another major international workcamp coordinator based in the U.S., may also provide leads on volunteering in Denmark.

CIEE
Voluntary Service Department
205 East 42nd Street
New York, NY 10017
Tel.: (800) COUNCIL
Email: info@ciee.org
www.ciee.org

International Christian Youth Exchange
134 West 26th Street
New York, NY 10001
Tel.: (212) 206-7307

MS/Mellemfolkeligt Samvirke
Stusgade 20
DK-8000 Aarhus C, Denmark
Summer workcamps in Denmark and
Greenland.

Volunteers for Peace
International Workcamps
43 Tiffany Road
Belmont, VT 05730
Tel.: (802) 259-2759
Email: vfp@vermontel.com
www.vfp.org

VHH (Danish Equivalent of WWOOF)
Asenvej 35
DK-9881 Bindslev, Denmark
Provides lists of organic farmers who offer
room and board in exchange for work.

NEWSPAPERS IN DENMARK

Ekstra Bladet
Politiken Newspapers
Raadhuspladsen 37
DK-1785 Copenhagen V, Denmark
Tel.: [45] 33 11 13 13
Fax: [45] 33 14 10 00

Information
St. Kongensgade 40
Postboks188
DK-1006 Copenhagen K, Denmark
Tel.: [45] 33 69 60
Fax: [45] 33 95 31 19

Morgenavisen Jyllands-Posten
Grondalsvej 3
DK-8260 Viby J, Denmark
Tel.: [45] 87 38 38 38
Fax: [45] 87 38 32 86 89

Politiken
Raadhuspladsen 37
DK-1785 Copenhagen V, Denmark
Tel.: [45] 33 11 85 11
Fax: [45] 33 15 41 17

Resources for Further Information

USEFUL WEBSITES FOR JOB SEARCHERS

The Internet is a good place to begin your job search. Many Scandinavian employers list job vacancies, especially those in technical fields, on the World Wide Web. There are also many websites that provide useful information for job searchers researching the Danish job market.

Denmark Information Servers
http://info.denet.dk.denmark.html
Facts about Denmark.

FAST TRAC
www.fast-trac.ofw.fi
Offers work programs for business
students; offered through Niels Brock
Copenhagen Business College.

Job Match Denmark
www.jobmatch.dk
Matches candidates with jobs in Denmark; in Danish.

Jubii
www.jubii.dk
Very valuable; contains all of the Danish links on the Web; in Danish.

EMBASSIES AND CONSULAR OFFICES

American embassies and consulates have commercial and/or economic sections that can provide you with business information and explain aspects of the local economy. Inquiries about business opportunities should be addressed either to "Commercial Officer" or "Commercial Section," followed by the appropriate street address.

Representation of Denmark in the United States

Embassy of the Kingdom of Denmark
3200 Whitehaven Street NW
Washington, DC 20008
Tel.: (202) 234-4300
Fax: (202) 328-1470
www.denmarkemb.org

Danish Consulates General: Chicago, (312) 787-8780; New York, (212) 223-4545

Representation of the United States in Denmark

American Embassy
Dag Hammarskjolds Alle 24
DK-2100 Copenhagen Ø, Denmark
Tel.: [45] 31 42 31 44
Fax: [45] 35 42 72 73

CHAMBER OF COMMERCE

Chambers of commerce consist of firms in both countries interested in international trade. These are appropriate companies to initially target in the job search.

Danish-American Chamber of Commerce Tel.: (212) 980-6240
885 Second Avenue, 18th Floor Fax: (212) 754-1904
New York, NY 10017

WORLD TRADE CENTER IN DENMARK

World Trade Centers usually include many foreign companies operating in the country.

World Trade Center Copenhagen Tel.: [45] 39 17 98 00
Bygstubben 13-2950 Fax : [45] 31 20 55 21
Vedbaek, Denmark

OTHER INFORMATIONAL ORGANIZATIONS

Foreign government missions in the U.S. such as tourist and trade offices can furnish visas and information on work permits and other important regulations. They may also offer economic and business information about the country.

Danish Foreign Trade Office **Denmark-America Foundation**
78 Hellerupvej Dr. Tvaergade 44
DK-2900 Hellerup, Denmark DK-1302 Copenhagen K, Denmark
 Tel.: [45] 31 12 90 11
Danish Tourist Board
655 Third Avenue, 18th Floor **Youth Information Copenhagen**
New York, NY 10017 Radhusstraede 13
Tel.: (212) 885-9700 D-1466 Copenhagen K, Denmark
Fax: (212) 885-9710 Tel.: [45] 1 33 15 65 18

BUSINESS DIRECTORIES

Although not always easy to find, business directories can prove invaluable in the international job search. Most directories list company names, addresses, products, and phone numbers. Some directories include executive names and titles and financial information about the company. These sources provide you with the names of the people to contact for employment information as well as financial data, which can tell you how strong a company's position in a country may be.

Denmark's 10,000 Largest Companies. Published annually in Danish and English by ELC Publishing, 109 Uxbridge Road, 3rd Floor, Ealing, London W5 5TL, England. Covers 10,000 leading companies in Denmark. Available in the U.S. from Dun & Bradstreet Information Services, 3 Sylvan Way, Parsippany, NJ 07054.

Directory of Foreign Firms Operating Abroad: Denmark. World Trade Academy Press, 257 Central Park West, Suite 10A, New York, NY 10024-4110; email: uniworldbp@aol.com; www.uniworldbp.com. Lists names and addresses of parent companies in the U.S. and their subsidiaries and affiliates in Denmark.

Export Directory of Denmark. Published annually by Kraks Forlag AS, Virumgardsvej 21, DK-2830 Virum, Denmark; email: krak@www.krak.dk; www.krak.dk. Lists 6,000 export producers, plus service, transport, software, research, and other firms.

GreensHandbogen om Dansk Erhvervsliv (Danish Company Yearbook). Published annually in Danish by AS Forlaget Boersen, Montergade 19, DK-1140 Copenhagen, Denmark. Covers 4,800 of Denmark's largest companies, including financial information and names and titles of key personnel.

Kommunal Handbogen (Danish business and government). Published annually in Danish by Mostrups Forlag A/S, 2 Farvergrade, DK-1017 Copenhagen, Denmark. Contains government departments, institutes, universities, associations, and Danish and foreign manufacturers and distributors that sell to the Danish government.

Kompass Scandinavia. Published annually by Bureau van Dijk, Avenue Louise 250, Box 14, B-1050 Brussels. Lists over 65,000 Scandinavian companies and their products and services.

Krak (Danish commercial and industrial directory). Five-volume set published annually in English, French, German, and Spanish by Kraks Forlag, 21 Virumgardsvej, DK-2830 Virum, Denmark; email: krak@www.krak.dk; www.krak.dk. Volumes 1 and 2 are of primary interest to job hunters. Volume 1 lists 60,000 Danish companies by business type, then geography. Volume 2 lists the same firms alphabetically, with addresses and phone numbers.

Major Companies in Scandinavia. Published by Araham & Whiteside Ltd., Tuition House, 5-6 Francis Grove, London SW19 4DT, England; email: sales@major_co_data.com. Lists 1,250 Scandinavian companies.

Trade Directory for Denmark. Published annually in English, German, French, Spanish, and Danish by the Information Office of the Danish Foreign Trade, Hellerupvej 78, DK-2900 Hellerup, Denmark. Businesses operating in Denmark, the Færœ Islands, Iceland, and Greenland.

AMERICAN COMPANIES IN DENMARK

The following companies are classified by business area: Banking and Finance; Industrial Manufacturing; Retailing and Wholesaling; and Service Industries. Company information includes firm name, address, phone and fax number, specific business, and American parent company. Your chances of achieving employment abroad are substantially better if you contact the subsidiary company in Europe rather than the parent company in the U.S.

BANKING AND FINANCE

Citibank, N.A.
Industriens Hus
Vesterbrogade 1B
DK-1620/V Copenhagen, Denmark

Tel.: [45] 33 15 50 30
Fax: [45] 33 32 88 93
(Bank)
Citibank, New York

INDUSTRIAL MANUFACTURING

Analog Devices AS
Marielundvej 46D
DK-2730 Herlev, Copenhagen, Denmark
(Electrical components)
Analog Devices Inc.

Elizabeth Arden AS
Stationsparken 25
Postboks 333
DK-2600 Glostrup, Denmark
Tel.: [45] 43 28 48 00
(Cosmetics)
Elizabeth Arden Cosmetics

Borden Company AS
Limfjordsvej 4
DK-6715 Esbjerg, Denmark
Tel.: [45] 75 14 42 22
(Food processing)
Borden Inc.

Colgate-Palmolive AS
Smedeland 9
DK-2600 Glostrup, Denmark
Tel.: [45] 42 96 12 34
(Soap and cosmetics)
Colgate-Palmolive Co.

Dansk Esso AS
Skt. Annae Plads 13
DK-1298 Copenhagen K, Denmark
(Petroleum)
Exxon

General Dynamics Intl.
Industriparken 39-43
DK-2750 Ballerup, Denmark
(Electronic equipment)
General Dynamics

Goodyear Tire & Rubber Company AS
Fabriksparken 1
DK-2600 Glostrup, Copenhagen,
Denmark
(Rubber products)
Goodyear Tire & Rubber Company

IBM Danmark AS
Nymøllevej 91
DK-2800 Lyngby, Aarhus, Denmark
Tel.: [45] 93 45 45
(Information systems)
IBM Corp.

Jurid Scandinavia APS
Kuldyssen 13
DK-2630 Tastrup, Denmark

(Aircraft and communications systems)
Bendix Aerospace

Kraft General Foods AS
Smedeland 36
DK-2600 Glostrup, Denmark
Tel.: [45] 43 96 96 22
Fax: [45] 43 96 01 02
(Food products)
Kraft General Foods Inc.

Raytheon-Copenhagen
Siljangade 6-8
DK-2300 Copenhagen S, Denmark
(Microwave, X-ray & industrial tubes)
Raytheon Co.

Revlon AS
Toldbodgade 33
DK-1253 Copenhagen, Denmark
(Cosmetics)
MacAndrews & Forbes Holdings

Squibb Pharmaceuticals Ltd.
Hanebred 2
DK-2720 Vanlose, Copenhagen, Denmark
(Pharmaceuticals)
Squibb Corp.

3M AS
Fabriksparken 15
Postboks 1393
DK-2600 Glostrup, Denmark
Tel.: [45] 43 48 01 00
(Adhesive and imaging tapes)
Minnesota Mining & Manufacturing

Unisys AS
Blegdamsuej 56
DK-2100 Copenhagen, Denmark
(Computers)
Unisys Corp.

RETAILING AND WHOLESALING

Digital Equipment Corporation AS
Adalsvej 99
DK-2970 Hørsholm, Denmark
Tel.: [45] 33 76 96 66
(Computers)
Digital Equipment Corp.

Dow Chemical AS
Stavangervej 10
DK-4900 Nakskov, Denmark
Tel.: [45] 53 92 27 99
(Chemicals)
Dow Chemical Company

Ford Motor Company AS
Sluseholmen 1
DK-2450 Copenhagen, Denmark
Tel.: [45] 33 31 05 10
(Motor vehicles and farm machinery)
Ford Motor Company

Hewlett-Packard AS
Birkerd Kongevej 25
DK-3460 Birkerod, Denmark
Tel.: [45] 45 99 10 00
Fax: [45] 45 99 10 01
(Computer equipment)
Hewlett-Packard SA

Kodak AS
Dybendal Alle 10
DK-2630 Tastrop, Denmark
Tel.: [45] 43 71 71 11
(Photographic equipment)
Eastman Kodak Company

Levi Stauss Denmark AS
Frederiksberggade 30
DK-1459 Copenhagen, Denmark
(Clothing)
Levi Strauss Inc.

Mobil Oil Danmark AS
Birkerød Kongevej 64
DK-3460 Birkerud, Denmark

SERVICE INDUSTRIES

American Express
Kobmagergade 60
DK-1150 Copenhagen, Denmark
(Financial and travel services)
American Express

Andersen Consulting
Oslo Plads 2
Postboks 2677
DK-2100 Copenhagen, Danmark
Tel.: [45] 33 42 20 00
Fax: [45] 33 42 71 00

Avia Radio AS
Copenhagen Airport
DK-2791 Dragor, Copenhagen, Denmark
Tel.: [45] 32 45 08 00
(Jet service center)
AAR Corp.

Coopers & Lybrand
Lyngbyvej 16-28
Postboks 2709
DK-2100 Copenhagen, Denmark
Tel.: [45] 39 27 72 20
Fax: [45] 39 27 27 72
(Accounting and auditing)
Coopers & Lybrand

(Petroleum products)
Mobil Oil Corp.

Rank Xerox AS
Borupvang 5
DK-2750 Ballerup, Denmark
(Copier equipment)
Xerox Corp.

Texaco AS
Borgergade 13
DK-1300 Copenhagen, Denmark
(Petroleum)
Texaco Corp.

Ernst & Young
Tagensvej 86
DK-2100 Copenhagen
Tel.: [45] 75 50 68 66
(Consulting)
Ernst & Young

Ogilvy & Mather Reklame Bureau A/S
Martinsvej 9
DK-1926 Copenhagen, Denmark
(Advertising agency)
Ogilvy Group Inc.

Price Waterhouse/IKO
Tuborg Blvd. 1
DK-2900 Hellerup, Denmark
Tel.: [45] 39 47 00 00
Fax: [45] 39 47 00 10
(Accounting)
Price Waterhouse & Co.

Young & Rubicam
Norre Sogade 35
DK-1370 Copenhagen K, Denmark
(Advertising agency)
Young & Rubicam

EUROPEAN COMPANIES IN DENMARK

The following are major non-American firms operating in the country. These selected companies can be either Danish or foreign, usually European companies. Such companies will generally hire their own nationals first but may employ Americans.

BANKING AND FINANCE

Den Danske Bank
Holmens Kanal 2-12
DK-1092/K Copenhagen, Denmark
Tel.: [45] 33 44 00 00
Fax: [45] 31 18 58 73
(Commercial bank)

The East Asiatic Company Ltd. AS
Company House
Midtermolen 7
DK-2100 Copenhagen, Denmark
Tel.: [45] 35 27 27 27
Fax: [45] 31 42 12 34
(Banking)

Sparekassen Bikuben AS
Silkegade 8
DK-1113 Copenhagen, Denmark
Tel.: [45] 33 12 01 33

Fax: [45] 33 12 09 33
(Savings bank)

Unibank AS
Torvegade 2
DK-1786 Copenhagen, Denmark
Tel.: [45] 33 33 33 33
Fax: [45] 33 33 63 63
(Commercial bank)

Unidanmark AS
Torvegade 2
DK-1786 Copenhagen V, Denmark
Tel.: [45] 33 33 33 33
Fax: [45] 33 33 63 63
(Bank)

INDUSTRIAL MANUFACTURING

Aktieselskabet Potagua
Kalvebod Brygge 20
DK-1560 Copenhagen V, Denmark
Tel.: [45] 33 91 58 00
Fax: [45] 33 91 17 50
(Paper & pulp; cement; transport &
forwarding)

Bang & Olufsen AS
Peter Bangsvej 15
DK-7600 Struer, Denmark
Tel.: [45] 97 85 11 22
Fax: [45] 97 85 59 42
(Audio & video home products)

Carlsberg AS
Vesterfaelledvej 100
DK-1750 Copenhagen V, Denmark
Tel.: [45] 33 27 33 27
Fax: [45] 33 27 47 11
(Beverages, glass products)

The Danfoss Group
Nordborgvej 81
DK-6430 Nordborg, Denmark
Tel.: [45] 74 88 22 22
Fax: [45] 74 49 09 49
(Industrial controls)

Danisco Distillers AS
Langebrogade
Postboks 2158
DK-1411 Copenhagen K, Denmark

Tel.: [45] 32 66 24 00
(Beverages)

Dansk Shell AS
Kampmannsgade 2
DK-1604 Copenhagen V, Denmark
Tel.: [45] 33 37 20 00
(Petroleum products)

FLS Industries AS
Vigerslev Alle 77
DK-2500 Valby, Denmark
Tel.: [45] 36 18 36 00
Fax: [45] 36 30 44 41
(Cement)

International Service System AS
Kongevejen 195
DK-2840 Holte, Denmark
Tel.: [45] 45 41 08 11
Fax: [45] 45 41 08 88
(Cleaning service)

J. Lauritzen Holding AS
Sankt Annae Plads 28
DK-1250 Copenhagen K, Denmark
Tel.: [45] 33 11 12 22
Fax: [45] 33 91 12 11
(Ship broker)

Nestlé Danmark AS
Amerikakaj
Dampfærgevej 28
DK-2100 Copenhagen, Denmark

Tel.: [45] 35 46 01 23
Fax: [45] 35 46 02 34
(Food products)

Novo Industri AS
Novo Alle
DK-2880 Bagsvaerd, Copenhagen,
Denmark
Tel.: [45] 44 44 88 88
Fax: [45] 44 49 05 55
(Pharmaceuticals and industrial enzymes)

Phillips Danmark AS
Prags Boulevard 80
DK-2300 Copenhagen S, Denmark
Tel.: [45] 32 88 22 22
(Electronic equipment)

Sophus Berendsen AS
Klausdaisbrovej 1
DK-2860 Søborg, Denmark
Tel.: [45] 39 69 75 00
Fax: [45] 39 69 73 00
(Pest control & tropical plants)

Tele Danmark AS
Kannikegade 16
DK-8000 Aarhus C, Denmark
Tel.: [45] 89 33 77 77
Fax: [45] 89 33 77 19
(Telephone service)

Unilever Danmark AS
Stationsparken 25
DK-2600 Glostrup, Denmark
Tel.: [45] 43 28 41 00
(Tea, snacks)

INTERNATIONAL SCHOOL IN DENMARK

Copenhagen International School
Hellerupvej 22-26
DK-2900 Hellerup, Denmark
Tel.: [45] 39 46 33 00
Fax: [45] 39 61 22 30
Email: cis@cisdk.dk

Finland

MAJOR EMPLOYMENT CENTER: Helsinki

MAJOR BUSINESS LANGUAGES: Finnish, Swedish

LANGUAGE SKILL INDEX: Unlike other Scandinavian languages, Finnish is not an Indo-European language and many people find they can't pick it up easily. Although many Finns understand English, they may be shy about speaking it

CURRENCY: Euro; the markka will remain the currency in circulation until 2002

TELEPHONE COUNTRY CODE: 358, 90

TIME ZONE: EST+7

PUNCTUALITY INDEX: Appointments are necessary, punctuality a must

AVERAGE DAILY TEMPERATURE: January, 30°F; July, 60°F (Helsinki)

AVERAGE NUMBER OF DAYS WITH PRECIPITATION: January, 15; July, 8

BEST BET FOR EMPLOYMENT:

  FOR STUDENTS: American-Scandinavian Foundation

  PERMANENT JOBS: Forestry and paper

CHANCE OF FINDING A JOB: Summer jobs, good. Others, not really

TRIVIA: Be aware of your body language in Finland. A firm handshake is a Finn's traditional greeting, while folded arms are taken as a sign of arrogance and pride

The Republic of Finland extends 700 miles north from the Gulf of Norway and into the Arctic Circle for over 200 miles. Finland's neighbors include the northern tip of Norway to the north, Sweden to the west, and Russia along the entire eastern border. Covering over 130,000 square miles, Finland is three times the size of Ohio or almost the size of Montana. Southern and central Finland have over 200,000 glacially carved lakes and are mostly flat with low hills. Northern Finland is sparsely populated and mountainous. The Finns are racially mixed, most being either of East Baltic stock (living mainly in eastern Finland) or of Nordic stock (in the west and south, especially on the coast and in Ahvenanmaa). A small number of Lapps live in northern Finland. Other ethnic groups include about 2,800 Russian speakers, 2,500 English speakers, 2,200 German speakers, 5,500 Gypsies, and 1,000 Jews.

In the seventh century the Finns came from the Ural area and took the country from the Lapps. After repelling Finnish raiding parties, Sweden conquered the country in 1157. By 1809 the whole of Finland had been overtaken by the Russian Empire. Finland declared its independence in 1917 and became a republic in 1919. In 1939 the Soviet Union attacked, and the Finns ceded 16,000 square miles to them. During World War II, Finland joined Germany against the U.S.S.R. in an effort to reclaim their territory but were defeated and forced to cede even more land to the Soviets. The Finns signed a 20-year treaty of mutual aid and friendship with the Soviets in 1948 and again in 1970. Finland joined the E.U. in 1995.

Finland is a presidential republic, with a president elected by the people for a six-year term. The nation has a multi-party system, and Finns have a multitude of political views. The ruling government is usually composed of a coalition, the most recent including the National Coalition Party, the Social Democratic Party, the Swedish People's Party, and the Finnish Rural Party. Other major political parties are the Center Party, the People's Democratic League (Communist Party), the Finnish Rural Party, and the Christian League.

Finns are noted for their stubborn independence. One reason for this is probably the cultural and language differences between Finland and its neighbors, Sweden and Russia. Although Finns have a unique language, it does not totally isolate them, as most also speak English, Swedish, or German. Finland plays an important part in the group of five Nordic countries. The Finns are much affected through television and consumer goods by American culture.

Stores close early: between 4:00 and 5:00 p.m., Monday through Friday, and around 1:00 p.m. on Saturday. This is especially true in the countryside. Since winters are long and dark, Finns abandon the cities in the summer for the picturesque countryside to bask in the midnight sun. July, August, and early September are, therefore, bad months for business trips or heavy business.

Current Economic Climate

Finland is recovering from its worst post-war recession, triggered by the break-up of the Soviet Union, Finland's largest trading partner. Most businesses in Finland are privately owned, but government spending accounts for over 63% of the GDP. Unemployment, high for a Nordic country, has remained above 16%. Finland also has the dubious distinction of having the highest tax rates in the world. For example, 95% of the price of a bottle of vodka goes to the government. Inflation hovers at about 2%.

Finland's labor force is divided as follows: 9% agriculture and forestry, 21% manufacturing and construction, and 60% service sector (communications, commerce, administration). The wood-processing industry has traditionally played an important part in the Finnish economy. Finland is the world's second largest exporter of paper and cardboard. The metal and engineering industry is the nation's most important employer and also contributes a major part of exports. Over half of the world's ice breakers are built in Finland. Finland is known internationally for its architecture and design.

FINLAND'S 10 LARGEST COMPANIES

(1997, composite ranking)
1. Posts and Telecommunications of Finland
2. Nokia Group
3. Repola
4. Kone Corporation
5. Kymmene Corporation
6. Metra Corporation
7. United Paper Mills
8. Outokumpu
9. Enso-Gutzeit
10. A. Ahlstrom Osakeyhtio

Using the phone, fax, and Internet
Call "118" for domestic information and "000" in emergencies. The post office offers fax service. The Internet is free of charge in most public libraries, allowing you to send Email, although you can't receive it.

Getting Around in Finland

Finair offers economical flights within and across Finland borders. Finnish railways are not only efficient but they are among the cheapest in Europe. Express trains are available but advance reservations may be necessary. Eurail passes are valid throughout the country, although buses serve as a more leisurely means of transportation and cost about the same as trains. Express buses are also available at an extra charge. Ferries and steamers provide transportation along the coastline.

Employment Regulations and Outlook for Americans

Americans need a passport but not a visa to visit Finland for short stays. Visas are required for stays of over three months, and the count begins as soon as you enter any Scandinavian country. Those wanting to stay longer should check with the Finnish embassy. A firm offer of employment is required before applying for a work permit. Contact the Embassy of Finland for more information. Embassy personnel advise that it can be very difficult for Americans to find work in Finland. The Finnish Tourist Board has several publications directed specifically at students and budget travelers.

Short-term and Temporary Work

The best bet for casual jobs in Finland, as in all of Scandinavia, is to work as an au pair.

Au Pair Homestay
World Learning Inc.
1015 15th Street NW, Suite 750
Washington, DC
Tel.: (202) 408-5380
Fax: (202) 408-5397
Sends au pairs to Iceland, Finland, and Norway.

Internship Programs

There are opportunities for students to gain professional experience, usually in technical fields. The American-Scandinavian Foundation and IASTE coordinate placements for technical interns. The Future Farmers of American coordinates an exchange for students interested in agricultural internships.

The American-Scandinavian Foundation
725 Park Avenue
New York, NY 10021
Tel.: (212) 879-9779
Email: training@amscan.org
Places summer interns in engineering, agriculture, and other technical fields throughout Scandinavia.

Future Farmers of America
National FFA Center
P.O. Box 15160
Alexandria, VA 22309
Tel.: (703) 360-3600

Coordinates programs for trainees in agriculture.

IASTE
10400 Little Patuxent Parkway, Suite 250 L
Columbia, MD 21044-3510
Tel.: (410) 997-3068
Fax: (410) 997-5186
Email: iaste@aipt.org
www.aipt.org/iaste.html
Arranges reciprocal internship exchanges among 63 member countries for students in engineering, architecture, and the sciences.

Volunteer Opportunities

The Year Abroad Program sponsored by the International Christian Youth Exchange offers students an opportunity to do volunteer work in construction, health care, education, and conservation in Finland. For more information, contact their office in New York.

CIEE
Voluntary Service Department
205 East 42nd Street
New York, NY 10017
Tel.: (800) COUNCIL
Email: info@ciee.org
www.ciee.org

International Christian Youth Exchange
134 West 26th Street
New York, NY 10001
Tel.: (212) 206-7307

Smaller organizations offering volunteer opportunities include:

KVT (IVS)
Rauhanasama, Veturitori
SF-00520 Helsinki, Finland
Recruits volunteers to work on farms, construction sites, and with the mentally handicapped.

Valamo Monastery
SF-79850 Uusi-Valamo,
Finland
Tel.: [358] 72 57 01 11

Accepts volunteers to help maintain monastery and grounds. Room and board provided.

WOOF Finland
Luomu-Liiton Talkoovalitys
Koiddalamylly
SF-51880 Koikkala, Finland
Tel.: [358] 95 54 50 25
Finnish organic farming organization.

NEWSPAPERS IN FINLAND

Aamulehti
P.O. Box 327
SF-33101 Tampere 10, Finland
Tel.: [358] 3 266 6111
Fax: [358] 31 2666 259

Helsingin Sanomat
Sanoma Corp.
Ludviginkatu 6-9
SF-00130 Helsinki, Finland
Tel.: [358] (9) 1221
Fax: [358] (9) 122 4119

Ilta-Sanomat
Sanoma Corp.
P.O. Box 371
SF-00101 Helsinki, Finland

Tel.: [358] (9) 1221
Fax: [358] (9) 122 4119
www.iltasanomat.fi/

Kauppalehti (The Commercial Daily)
Yrjönakur 13
SF-00120 Helsinki 12, Finland

Turun Sanomat/Turun Sanomat Extra
Kauppiaskatu 5,
SF-20100 Turku, Finland
Tel.: [358] (2) 2693 311
Fax: [358] (2) 2693 274

Uusi Suomi
Mannerheiminitie 6
SF-00100 Helsinki 10, Finland

In addition to the newspapers, you might want to subscribe to T*he Spirit of Finland,* a quarterly newsletter that provides industrial and economic news from Finland. It is available free from the Finland Promotion Board, P.O. Box 324, SF-00131 Helsinki, Finland.

Resources for Further Information

USEFUL WEBSITES FOR JOB SEARCHERS

The Internet is a good place to begin your job search. Many Scandinavian employers list job vacancies, especially those in technical fields, on the World Wide Web. There are also many websites that provide useful information for job searchers researching the Finnish job market.

Finland for Visitors
http://www.mek.fi/mek_promis.htm
Facts about Finland.

Job Board
http://minedu.fi/rekrytointi/jobboard/
index.html
Lists academic vacancies; partly in English.

Job Database
http://www.mol.tietotyo.fi/
Tyovoimapalvelut/Paikat
Huge listing of jobs in Finland; in Finnish.

Nokia
http://www.nokia.com/careers
Features jobs in technology.

EMBASSIES AND CONSULAR OFFICES

American embassies and consulates have commercial and/or economic sections that can provide you with business information and explain aspects of the local economy. Inquiries about business opportunities should be addressed either to "Commercial Officer" or "Commercial Section," followed by the address.

Representation of Finland in the United States

Embassy of Finland
3301 Massachusetts Avenue
Washington, DC 20008
Tel.: (202) 298 5800
Fax: (202) 298 6030

Consulates General of Finland: Chicago, (312) 670-4700; Los Angeles, (310) 203-9903; New York, (212) 750-4400

Representation of the United States in Finland

American Embassy
Itainen Puistotie 14A
SF-00140 Helsinki, Finland
Tel.: [358] (9) 171931
Fax: [358] (9) 174681

CHAMBERS OF COMMERCE

Chambers of commerce consist of firms in both countries interested in international trade. These are appropriate companies to initially target in the job search.

Finnish-American Chamber of Commerce
866 UN Plaza, Suite 249
New York, NY 10017
Tel.: (212) 821-0225
Fax: (212) 750-4417
www.finlandtrade.com

Finnish-American Chamber of Commerce of the Midwest
P.O. Box 11337
Chicago, IL 60611-0337
Tel.: (312) 670-4700

Finnish American Chamber of Commerce—
West Coast
1900 Avenue of the Stars, Suite 1025

Los Angeles, CA 90067
Tel.: (310) 203-9903

WORLD TRADE CENTER IN FINLAND

World Trade Centers usually include many foreign companies operating in the country.

World Trade Center Helsinki
Aleksanterinkatu 17
P.O. Box 800
SF-00100 Helsinki, Finland

Tel.: [358] (9) 6969 2020
Fax: [358] (9) 6969 2027
Email: sirpa.rissa-anttilainen@wtc.fi
www.wtc.fi/

OTHER INFORMATIONAL ORGANIZATIONS

Foreign government missions in the U.S. such as tourist boards can furnish visas and information on work permits and other important regulations. They may also offer economic and business information about the country.

Finnish Tourist Board
655 Third Avenue
New York, NY 10017
Tel.: (212) 370-5540
Fax: (212) 370-5260

Finnish Tourist Board
P.O. Box 625
SF-00101 Helsinki, Finland

Tel.: [358] (9) 4176911
Fax: [358] (9) 41769399
www.mek.fi

Ministry of Labor
International Trainee Exchanges
P.O. Box 30
SF-00101 Helsinki, Finland

BUSINESS DIRECTORIES

Although not always easy to find, business directories can prove invaluable in the international job search. Most directories list company names, addresses, products, and phone numbers. Some directories include executive names and titles and financial information about the company. These sources provide you with the names of the people to contact for employment information as well as financial data, which can tell you how strong a company's position in a country may be.

Directory of Finnish Exporters. Updated every other year by the Finnish Foreign Trade Association, Arkadiankatu 2, P.O. Box 908, SF-00101 Helsinki, Finland; email: info@exports.finland.fi; www.tradefinland.com. Lists approximately 1,500 Finnish exporters. In English.

Directory of Foreign Firms Operating Abroad: Scandinavia. World Trade Academy Press, 257 Central Park West, Suite 10A, New York, NY 10024-4110; email: uniworldbp@aol.com; www.uniworldbp.com. Lists names and addresses of parent companies in the U.S. and their subsidiaries and affiliates in Scandinavia.

Kompass Finland. Published annually Kompass Finland Oy, Kuparitie 2, SF-00400 Helsinki, Finland; email: kompass@kompass.finland.fi; www.kompass.com. Lists over 14,500 Finnish companies and their products and services.

Sininen Kirja: Suomen Talouselaman Hakemisto. Published annually in Finnish by Helsinki Media, Blue Book, Hoyloamotie ID, Postboks 100, SF 00040 Helsinki, Finland; http://bluebook.helsinkimedia.fi. Includes manufacturers, service companies, chambers of commerce, and trade associations.

Taseet ja Taustat (Finnish banks and limited companies). Available annually in Finnish and Swedish from Helsinki Media, Blue Book, Hoyloamotie ID, Postboks 100, SF 00040 Helsinki, Finland; http://bluebook.helsinkimedia.fi. Lists 5,000 banks, insurance companies, and industrial firms.

AMERICAN COMPANIES IN FINLAND

The following companies are classified by business area: Banking and Finance; Industrial Manufacturing; and Retailing and Wholesaling. Company information includes firm name, address, phone and fax number, specific business, and American parent company. Your chances of achieving employment abroad are substantially better if you contact the subsidiary company in Europe rather than the parent company in the U.S.

BANKING AND FINANCE

Citibank OY
Aleksanterinkatu 48 A
SF-00100 Helsinki, Finland

Tel.: [358] (9) 173 381
Fax: [358] (9) 651 194
Citibank, New York

INDUSTRIAL MANUFACTURING

Dow Suomi OY
Simonkatu 8B
P.O. Box 117
SF-00101 Helsinki, Finland
Tel.: [358] (9) 58 45 53 00
Fax: [358] (9) 58 45 53 30
(Chemicals)
Dow Chemical Company

Hewlett Packard OY
Piispankalliontic 17
P.O. Box 68
SF-02201 Espoo, Finland
Tel.: [358] (9) 887 21
Fax: [358] (9) 887 22 7
(Data processing equipment)
Hewlett Packard Corp.

Esso OY AB
Kuunkehrä 6
P.O. Box 37
SF-02211 Espoo, Finland
Tel.: [358] (9) 887 71
Fax: [358] (9) 803 00 04
(Petroleum and petroleum products)
Exxon Corp.

Unisys OY AB
Niittykatu 8
P.O. Box 45
SF-02201 Espoo, Finland
Tel.: [358] (9) 452 81
Fax: [358] (9) 452 84 00
(Measurement equipment)
Unisys Corp.

RETAILING AND WHOLESALING

Digital Equipment Corp. OY
Niitymäentie 7
SF-02200 Espoo, Finland
Tel.: [358] (9) 434 41
Fax: [358] (9) 68 36 81 00
(Data processing equipment)
Digital Equipment Corp.

Ford OY AB
Malminkaari 9 B
P.O. Box 164
SF-00701 Helsinki, Finland
Tel.: [358] (9) 35 17 00
Fax: [358] (9) 374 30 81
(Motor vehicles)
Ford Motor Company

International Business Machines OY
Tietokuja 2
P.O. Box 265
SF-00101 Helsinki, Finland
Tel.: [359] (9) 45 91
Fax: [359] (9) 459 40 14
(Office machines and data processing equipment)
International Business Machines Corp.

Kodak OY
Mäkelänkau 91
P.O. Box 49
SF-00611 Helsinki, Finland
Tel.: [358] (9) 58 40 71
Fax: [358] (9) 58 40 73 52
(Photographic equipment)
Eastman Kodak Co.

Mobil Oil OY
Keskuskatu 7
SF-00100 Helsinki 10, Finland

Tel.: [358] (9) 17 34 51
Fax: [358] (9) 17 34 52 16
(Petroleum products marketing)
Mobil Oil Corp.

Rank Xerox OY
Upseerinkatu 2
P.O. Box 5
SF-02601 Espoo, Finland
Tel.: [358] (204) 685 11
Fax: [358] (204) 685 99
(Copier and information systems products)
Xerox Corp.

Suomen General Motors OY
Kutojantie 8
SF-02630 Espoo, Finland
(Automobiles)
General Motors Corp.

EUROPEAN COMPANIES IN FINLAND

The following are several major non-American firms operating in the country. These selected companies can be either Finnish or foreign, usually European companies. Such companies will generally hire their own nationals first but may employ Americans.

BANKING AND FINANCE

Bank of Finland
Central Bank
SF-00101, Helsinki
Tel.: [358] (9) 18 31
Fax: [358] (9) 17 48 72

Merita Bank Ltd.
Aleksanterinkatu 30
SF-00020 Merita, Finland
Tel.: [358] (9) 16 51
Fax: [358] (9) 61 11 41
(Bank)

OKOBANK (Osuuspankkien Keskuspankki OY)
Arkadiankatu 23 B Pl 308
SF-00101 Helsinki, Finland

Tel.: [358] (9) 4041
Fax: [358] (9) 404 2870
(Commercial bank)

Pohjola-Yhtiöt Pääkonttori
Lapinmäentie 1
SF-00013 Pohjola, Finland
Tel.: [358] (10) 559 11
Fax: [358] (10) 559 30 66
(Insurance)

Union Bank of Finland Ltd.
Aleksanterinkatu 30
P.O. Box 868
SF-00010 Helsinki, Finland
Tel.: [358] (9) 1651
Fax: [358] (9) 1652648
(Commercial bank)

INDUSTRIAL MANUFACTURING

ABB Motors OY
Strömberg Park
Strömbergin Puistotie 5 A
P.O. Box 633
SF-65101 Vaasa, Finland
Tel.: [358] (10) 22 40 00

Fax: [358] (10) 22 47 372
(Electric motors)

Ahlström A Osakeyhtio
PL 329 Eteläesplanadi 14
P.O. Box 329

SF-00101 Helsinki, Finland
Tel.: [358] (9) 50 39 11
Fax: [358] (9) 50 39 709
(Paper manufacturing)

BP Finland OY Chemicals
Laversintie 86
SF-06830 Kulloonkyla, Finland
Tel.: [358] (208) 35 26 68
Fax: [358] (19) 65 21 54
(Petrochemicals)

Enso OYJ
Kanavaranta 1
P.O. Box 309
SF-00101 Helsinki, Finland
Tel.: [358] (204) 61 31
Fax: [358] (204) 62 14 71
(Paper and wood products)

Kemira OY
Porkkalankatu 3
P.O. Box 330
SF-00101 Helsinki, Finland
Tel.: [358] (10) 628 10 00
Fax: [358] (10) 628 10 91
(Chemicals)

Metsä-Serla OYJ Pääkonttori
Revontulentie 6
P.O. Box 10
SF-02101 Espoo, Finland
Tel.: [358] (10) 46 11
Fax: [358] (10) 469 45 05
(Paper and chemicals)

RETAILING AND WHOLESALING

Kesko OY
Satamakatu 3
P.O. Box 135
SF-00016 Helsinki, Finland
Tel.: [358] (10) 53 11
Fax: [358] (10) 65 54 73
(Consumer goods, builder supplies)

SERVICE INDUSTRIES

Finnair OY
P.O. Box P 115
SF-01053 Helsinki, Finland
Tel.: [358] (9) 818 54 50
Fax: [358] (9) 818 54 54
(Airline)

Kone Corporation
P.O. Box 8
SF-00331 Helsinki, Finland

Neste OY
Keilaniemi
P.O. Box 20
SF-02150 Espoo, Finland
Tel.: [358] (20) 45 01
Fax: [358] (20) 450 40 73
(Oil, chemicals, and batteries)

Nokia Telecommunications OY
Upseerinkatu 1
P.O. Box 100
SF-00045 Nokia Group, Finland
Tel.: [358] (9) 511 21
Fax: [358] (9) 511 12 55 69
(Telecommunications equipment)

Orion Corporation Ltd.
Koivu-Mankkaan tie 6
P.O. Box 83
SF-02101 Esbo, Finland
Tel.: [358] (9) 429 95
Fax: [358] (9) 429 27 94
(Pharmaceuticals, confections, and
liquors)

Repola Corp.
Snellmaninkatu 13
SF-00171 Helsinki, Finland
Tel.: [358] (9) 182 8219
(Timber products and machinery)

Valmet OY Päällystyskoneet
Wärtsilänkatu 100
SF-00400 Järvenpää, Finland
Tel.: [358] (9) 271 71
Fax: [358] (9) 27 17 77 41
(Paper and cardboard manufacturing)

Metra Corporation
John Stenbergin ranta 2
P.O. Box 230
SF-00101 Helsinki, Finland
Tel.: [358] (9) 709 51
Fax: [358] (9) 762 278
(Audio-visual production and distribution)

Tel.: [358] (9) 90 475 1
Fax: [358] (9) 90 475 4309

**Posts and Telecommunications of
Finland Ltd.**
Mannerheimintie 11A
SF-00101 Helsinki, Finland
Tel.: [358] (9) 1951
Fax: [358] (9) 195 4040
(Postal and telecommunications service)

Rautaruukki Oy
Kiilakiventie 1
P.O. Box 217
SF-90101 Oulu, Finland
Tel.: [358] (3) 883 60
Fax: [358] (8) 883 64 50
(Steel)

Valtionrautatiet
Finnish State Railways
Vilhonkatu 13

P.O. Box 488
SF-00101 Helsinki, Finland
(Rail transport)

YIT Corporation
Panuntie 11
P.O. Box 36
SF-00621 Helsinki, Finland
Tel.: [358] (9) 159 41
Fax: [358] (9) 94 37 06
(Environmental protection services)

INTERNATIONAL SCHOOL IN FINLAND

International School of Helsinki
Selkämerenkatu 11
SF-00180 Helsinki, Finland
Tel.: [358] (9) 686 61 60
Fax: [358] (9) 685 66 99
Email: mainoffice@ish.edu.hel.fi
www.ish.edu.hel.fi

Norway

MAJOR EMPLOYMENT CENTERS: Oslo, Bergen

MAJOR BUSINESS LANGUAGE: Norwegian

LANGUAGE SKILL INDEX: More important with older people than with younger; more important in long-term and professional positions than for short-term work

CURRENCY: Kroner

TELEPHONE COUNTRY CODE: 47

TIME ZONE: EST+6

PUNCTUALITY INDEX: This is a very punctual place

AVERAGE DAILY TEMPERATURE, HIGH/LOW: January, 30/20°F; July, 73/56°F (Oslo)

AVERAGE NUMBER OF DAYS WITH PRECIPITATION: January, 18; July, 16

BEST BET FOR EMPLOYMENT:

   FOR STUDENTS: American-Scandinavian Foundation

   PERMANENT JOBS: Merchant marine and fishing industries

CHANCE OF FINDING A JOB: Summer jobs, maybe. Others are very hard to get

TRIVIA: Norwegians are more formal than Americans and won't use first names until they get to know you

T he Kingdom of Norway is located on the western part of the Scandinavian peninsula. Geographically, it extends northward from the North Sea over 1,000 miles along the Norwegian Sea into the Arctic Circle, farther north than any other European land. Sweden, Finland, and Russia all share borders with Norway on the east and the northeast. With an area of over 125,000 square miles, Norway is slightly larger than New Mexico.

Over 70% of Norway has very little vegetation, is covered by mountains, glaciers, and rivers, and is uninhabitable. Its numerous and deep fjords give Norway over 12,000 miles of oceanfront. Tens of thousands of islands off the coast form a sheltered coastal shipping channel. Norway also has sovereignty over five islands, the largest being Spitsbergen, in the Arctic Ocean. Norway north of Bodø experiences the midnight sun for a few weeks on either side of the summer solstice (June 21).

The majority of the population live in villages and on small, isolated farmsteads, with about two-thirds of the population concentrated in the valleys of the southeast and close to the coast in southern Norway. Population is extremely sparse in northern Norway and inland. Norway's overall population density is the lowest in Europe, excluding Iceland.

Norse Vikings raided England and the northwestern coast of Europe repeatedly from the 8th to the 11th century. More than just pillagers, the Vikings explored Iceland, Greenland, and North America. This time period and its myths are chronicled in the Icelandic Sagas. In 872 the first ruler of a united Norway, Harold the Fairhaired, came to power.

Norway was part of the Danish kingdom for almost 500 years until Sweden won control in 1814. The country became officially independent in 1905, with a Danish prince on the Norwegian throne. Norway was committed to neutrality in World War I. The country was occupied by the Germans for five years during World War II. Abandoning its neutrality, Norway joined the N.A.T.O. alliance in 1949. However, Norway did have good relations with its neighbor, the Soviet Union. After a referendum in 1972, which divided the country, Norway decided not to join the European Common Market. In 1994, Norway once again rejected closer ties to other European nations when voters turned down a referendum to join the E.U.

Although officially a monarchy, Norway is a constitutional democracy with a parliamentary form of government. The monarch shares executive power with a Cabinet composed of a prime minister and seven other members. Norway's parliament, the *Storting,* has 165 members who are elected by proportional representation. Major political parties in Norway include the Labor Party, the Conservative Party, the Christian Democrats, the Center Party, the Socialist Left Party, and the Party of Progress. Prime Minister Gro Harlem Brundtland has led the Labor Party since 1986 and is the first woman to hold this office.

Norse people speak Norwegian, a language similar to Icelandic and Swedish. Most younger people speak English as well, and if you are looking for a job in a tourist spot, you may have no problems if you only speak English. Although they speak different languages, Scandinavians can often understand each other since the languages (except Finnish) are all descended from the language of the Vikings. The country has two official written languages that are fairly similar: *Bokmål* has evolved from dialects used in urban areas, influenced for centuries by Danish; *Nynorsk*, or New Norwegian, is derived from the dialects of more rural areas of the western part of the country.

Banks are open Monday through Friday from 8:15 a.m. to 3:30 p.m., Thursday until 5:00 p.m.; from mid-May to August all banks close at 3:00 p.m., except Thursdays, when they close at 4:00 p.m. Stores conduct business Monday through Wednesday and Friday from 9:00 a.m. to 4:00 p.m., Thursday until 7:00 p.m., Saturday until 2:00 p.m. Bad times for business trips include Easter and the summer months of July and August.

Current Economic Climate

Norway has one of the highest standards of living in the world, but it is also extremely expensive—even compared to the rest of Scandinavia. The per capita income is one of the highest in the world. With low unemployment (3.8%) and inflation rates, the Norwegian economy experienced in 1998 its fifth consecutive year of steady growth.

The Norwegian labor force is composed of 7% agriculture workers, 47% industrial workers, 18% service workers, and 26% government employees. Only 3-4% of the country's surface area is cultivable and therefore most grain is imported. The majority of the country's forests are owned privately and feed the large timber, furniture, and paper industries. Shipbuilding and shipping are the mainstays of the economy, and the abundant hydroelectric power provides the basis for a number of industries ranging from aluminum to steel to paper production. Norway's chief trading partners are the E.U., the Nordic countries, the U.S., and Japan. Exports account for almost 40% of the G.N.P.

The discovery of petroleum and natural gas in the Norwegian section of the North Sea in the late 1960s played a significant role in the country's prosperity. A 200-nautical-mile zone off Norway's shores gives the government control over the resources in one of the most productive sea areas on earth. Norway has one of the world's largest merchant marines.

After a prolonged period of strong growth, the economy is now approaching full capacity. Norway is experiencing some labor shortages, particularly in building and construction, health care, and in some manufacturing sectors. Price and wage inflation is, however, expected to remain moderate, helped by a tight fiscal policy.

NORWAY'S 10 LARGEST COMPANIES

(1997, composite ranking)
 1. Norsk Hydro
 2. Kvaerner
 3. Norwegian Telecom
 4. Telenor
 5. Aker
 6. Orkla
 7. Den Norske Stats Oljeselskap
 8. Hydro Aluminium
 9. Dyno Industrier
10. Wilh. Wilhelmsen Limited

Using the phone and fax

Norway has no telephone area codes, so you must use all eight digits when dialing. Using the phone in Norway is expensive, whether you're calling within the country or internationally. It is best to use a *telekort,* or phonecard, which is sold in 35, 98, and 210 kr denominations when making calls. You are charged a slightly cheaper rate when using a phonecard than if you use coins. Faxes can be sent from public telephone offices.

Getting Around in Norway

Norway's five railroad lines provide service from the capital city of Oslo to Bergen, Trodheim, and Bodö. Eurail and InterRail passes are valid on all trains in Norway. Buses also provide extensive service, though bus fares are rather expensive. The numerous airlines in Scandinavia also have flights with reasonable fares and discount offers for those traveling extensively within the Scandinavian countries. The major airlines are SAS and Braathens SAFE. Ferries are available everywhere along the coasts. Hydrofoils and car ferries are other options in traveling across the water.

Employment Regulations and Outlook for Americans

A temporary ban is in effect on the issuance of first-time work permits to foreign nationals in Norway. You must file the application for a work permit in your country before you enter Norway. An offer of employment is required to apply for a work permit. Workers on offshore drilling rigs, students studying at Norwegian schools who desire part-time or summer work, and summer job seekers during the period May 15 to September 30 are exempt from this ban and may apply for a work permit after they have arrived in Norway. Special exemptions may be made for people with special skills (musicians, scientists, etc.), trainees, au-pair workers, and youth exchanges.

Summer jobs are gaining in popularity among Norwegian youth, and it is thus becoming increasingly difficult to find summer employment. Your chances of obtaining a job are greater both before and after the period between June 15 and July 15, when the influx of job-seeking Norwegian youths into the labor market is at its peak. Hotels can be a good bet for lucrative work. The Directorate of Labor (see "Other Informational Organizations") distributes a flyer entitled *Summer Employment in Norway*, which also may be of use.

Short-term and Temporary Work

There are opportunities to work in agriculture and as an au pair.

Atlantis
(Norwegian Foundation for Youth
Exchange)
Rolf Hofmosgate 18
N-0655 Oslo, Norway
Tel.: [47] 02 67 00 43
Recruits for summer positions on farms;
also recruits for au pairs.

Au Pair Homestay
World Learning Inc.
1015 15th Street NW, Suite 750
Washington, DC 20005

Tel.: (202) 408-5380
Fax: (202) 408-5397
Sends au pairs to Iceland, Finland, and
Norway.

Exis
Rebslagergade 3
P.O. Box 291
DK-6400 Snderborg, Denmark
Tel.: [45] 74 42 97 49
Au pair placement in Denmark, Norway,
and Iceland.

Internship Programs

There are opportunities for students to gain professional experience, usually in technical fields. The American-Scandinavian Foundation and IASTE coordinate placements for technical interns. The Future Farmers of America coordinates an exchange for students interested in agricultural internships.

The American-Scandinavian Foundation
725 Park Ave.
New York, NY 10021
Tel.: (212) 879-9779
Email: training@amscan.org
Places summer interns in engineering,
agriculture, and other technical fields
throughout Scandinavia.

Future Farmers of America
National FFA Center
P.O. Box 15160
Alexandria, VA 22309

Tel.: (703) 360-3600
Coordinates programs for trainees in
agriculture.

IASTE
10400 Little Patuxent Parkway, Suite 250 L
Columbia, MD 21044-3510
Tel.: (410) 997-3068
Fax: (410) 997-5186
Email: iaste@aipt.org
www.aipt.org/iaste.html
Arranges reciprocal internship exchanges
among 63 member countries for students in
engineering, architecture, and the sciences.

Volunteer Opportunities

The Year Abroad Program sponsored by the International Christian Youth Exchange places students in volunteer work in Norway. Participants work on various projects, including work in health care, construction, education, and conservation.

APØG
Norsk Økologisk Landbrukslag
Langeveien 18
N-5003 Bergen, Norway
Tel.: [47] 55 32 04 80
Service for people who want to work on organic farms.

Internasjonal Dugnad
Nordahl Brunsgate 22
N-0165 Oslo, Norway
Norwegian workcamp organization that

places people into agricultural work.

International Christian Youth Exchange
134 West 26th Street
New York, NY 10001
Tel.: (212) 206-7307

Nansen Internasjonale Center
Barnegarden Breivold, Nesset
N-1400 Ski, Norway
Tel.: [47] 09 94 67 91
Recruits volunteers to help with disturbed teenagers.

NEWSPAPERS IN NORWAY

Adresseavisen
P.O. Box 6070
N-7003 Trondheim, Norway
Tel.: [47] 72 50 00 00
Fax: [47] 72 50 17 54

Aftenposten
Akersgaten 51
N-0107 Oslo 1, Norway
Tel.: [44] 22 33 44 00
Fax: [44] 22 42 63 25
Email: aftenposten@aftenposten.no

Bergens Tidende
P.O. Box 875
N-5015 Bergen, Norway

Tel.: [47] 55 21 46 50
Fax: [47] 55 21 39 80
Email: einar.haalien@bergens-tidende.no
www.bergens-tidende.no

Dagens Naeringsliv
Stenersgaten 1A
Grev Wedele
Plass 9
P.O. Box 1182 Sentrum
N-0107 Oslo, Norway
Tel.: [47] 20 00 10 00
Fax: [47] 20 00 10 70

Resources for Further Information

USEFUL WEBSITES FOR JOB SEARCHERS

The Internet is a good place to begin your job search. Many Scandinavian employers list job vacancies, especially those in technical fields, on the World Wide Web. There are also many websites that provide useful information for job searchers researching the Norwegian job market.

Companies in Norway
www.randburg.com/no/index.html
Links to several Norwegian companies; some facts about Norway.

Jobbguiden
www.jobbguiden.no
A database featuring job listings in all fields; in Norwegian.

Jobshop
www.jobshop.no
Good job listings; in Norwegian.

Norweb bedrifter
www.link.no/norweb/bedrifter.html

Contains many Norwegian links.

Teknisk Ukeblad
www.sol.no/tu/jobbsok.html
Job-search database; in Norwegian.

EMBASSIES AND CONSULAR OFFICES

American embassies and consulates have commercial and/or economic sections that can provide you with business information and explain aspects of the local economy. Inquiries about business opportunities should be addressed either to "Commercial Officer" or "Commercial Section," followed by the appropriate street address.

Representation of Norway in the United States

Embassy of Norway
2720 34th Street NW
Washington, DC 20008
Tel.: (202) 333-6000
Fax: (202) 337-0870

Norwegian Consulates General: Los Angeles, (310) 277-1293; New York, (212) 421-7333

Representation of the United States in Norway

American Embassy
Drammensveien 18
N-0244 Oslo 2, Norway

Tel.: [47] 22 44 85 50
Fax: [47] 22 44 33 63

CHAMBERS OF COMMERCE

Chambers of commerce consist of firms in both countries interested in international trade. These are appropriate companies to initially target in the job search.

American Chamber of Commerce in Norway
P.O. Box 244
N-1322 Hovik, Norway
Tel.: [47] 67 54 68 80
Fax: [47] 67 59 18 27
Email: Amctotal@telepost.no

Norwegian-American Chamber of Commerce
800 Third Avenue

New York, NY 10022
Tel.: (212) 421-9210
Fax: (212) 838-0374
and

821 Marquette Ave.
Minneapolis, MN 55402-2961
Tel.: (612) 332 3338
Fax: (612) 332 1386

WORLD TRADE CENTER IN NORWAY

World Trade Centers usually include many foreign companies operating in the country.

World Trade Center Oslo
Pilestredet 17
N-0164 Oslo, Norway
Tel.: [47] 22 20 98 08
Fax: [47] 22 36 19 20

OTHER INFORMATIONAL ORGANIZATIONS

Foreign government missions in the U.S. such as tourist offices can furnish visas and information on work permits and other important regulations. They may also offer economic and business information about the country.

Directorate of Labor
Postboks 8127
Oslo, Norway
Tel.: [47] 22 11 10 70

Norwegian Information Service in U.S.
825 Third Avenue, 38th Floor
New York, NY 10022
Tel.: (212) 421-7333
Fax: (212) 754-0583

Norwegian Tourist Board
655 Third Avenue, Suite 1810
New York, NY 10017

Tel.: (212) 885-9700
Fax: (212) 885-9710
www.norway.org

Norwegian Trade Council
10 California Street, 6th Floor
San Francisco, CA 94111
Tel.: (415) 986-0770
Fax: (415) 986-6025
Email: ntcsanfran@sf.ntc.telemax.no
www.ntcusa.com

BUSINESS DIRECTORIES

Although not always easy to find, business directories can prove invaluable in the international job search. Most directories list company names, addresses, products, and phone numbers. Some directories include executive names and titles and financial information about the company. These sources provide you with the names of the people to contact for employment information as well as financial data, which can tell you how strong a company's position in a country may be.

Directory of Foreign Firms Operating Abroad: Norway. World Trade Academy Press, 257 Central Park West, Suite 10A, New York, NY 10024-4110; email: uniworldbp@aol.com; www.uniworldbp.com. Lists names and addresses of parent companies in the U.S. and their subsidiaries and affiliates in Norway.

Kompass Norge. Published annually in Norwegian and English by Kompass Norge AS, Hillevagsveien 107, Postboks 1117, N-4004 Stavenger, Norway. Lists 14,800 service, distributing, and manufacturing companies.

Norway's Largest Companies. Published annually by Okonomisk Literatur AS, Lorenveien 129, Postboks 457, Okern, N-0104 Oslo, Norway. Over 10,000 listings.

Norwegian American Chamber of Commerce—Membership Directory. Published in odd years by the Norwegian American Chamber of Commerce, 800 Third Avenue, New York, NY 10022. Contains 1,000 American and Norwegian companies involved in trade and investment in the two countries.

Norwegian Directory of Commerce. Published annually by S.M. Bryde, Lorenveien 38, Postboks 6377, N-0604 Oslo, Norway. Includes information on over 200,000 industrial, trade, and service companies.

AMERICAN COMPANIES IN NORWAY

The following companies are classified by business area: Banking and Finance; Industrial Manufacturing; Retailing and Wholesaling; and Service Industries. Company information includes firm name, address, phone and fax numbers, specific business, and American parent company. Your chances of achieving employment abroad are substantially better if you contact the subsidiary company in Europe rather than the parent company in the U.S.

BANKING AND FINANCE

Chase Manhattan Bank Norway
Fridtjof Nansens P/2, 5th Floor
N-0110 Oslo, Norway
Tel.: [47] 22 94 19 19
Fax: [47] 22 42 58 61
(Bank)
Chase Bank

Citibank AS
Tordenskioldsgaten 8/10
Postboks 1481
N-0116 Oslo, Norway
Tel.: [47] 22 00 96 00
Fax: [47] 22 00 96 22
(Commercial bank)
Citibank, New York

INDUSTRIAL MANUFACTURING

Amerada Hess Norge AS
Langkaia 1
N-0150 Oslo, Norway
Tel.: [47] 22 94 00
Fax: [47] 22 42 63 27
(Oil and natural gas)
Amerada Hess Corp.

Baxter AS
Gjerdrumsvei 10b
N-0406 Oslo 4, Norway
(Pharmaceuticals and surgical supplies)
Baxter International Inc.

Colgate Palmolive Norge AS
Vollsv 13
N-1324 Lysaker, Norway
Tel.: [47] 67 59 00 25
Fax: [47] 67 59 18 64
(Hygiene products)
Colgate-Palmolive

Esso Norge AS
P.O. Box 350, Skøyen
N-0212 Oslo, Norway
Tel.: [47] 22 66 30 30
Fax: [47] 22 66 37 77
(Petroleum refining and marine lubricants)
Exxon Corp.

Hydro Texaco AS
Drammensveien 134
N-0212 Oslo, Norway

Tel.: [47] 22 12 40 00
Fax: [47] 22 12 40 50
(Industrial lubricants)
Texaco Inc.

Mobil Exploration Norway Inc AS
Postboks 510
Nedre Strandgate 41-43
N-4001 Stavanger, Norway
(Petroleum exploration)
Mobil Corp.

Norwegian Oil Consortium AS
Kjorbov 16
N-1300 Sandvika, Norway
Tel.: [47] 22 12 66 00
(Oil drilling and production)
Amoco Corp.

Phillips Petroleum Company Norway
Postboks 1766, Vika
N-0122 Oslo, Norway
Tel.: [47] 22 83 70 00
Fax: [47] 22 83 41 04
(Oil and gas exploration and production)
Phillips Petroleum Co.

3M Norge AS
Hvamveien 6
N-2013 Skjetten, Norway
Tel.: [47] 66 84 75 00
Fax: [47] 63 84 17 88
(Surgical dressings, tapes)
Minnesota Mining and Manufacturing

RETAILING AND WHOLESALING

Digital Equipment Corp. AS
Ammerudveien 22
N-0958 Oslo, Norway
(Computers, data processing equipment)
Digital Equipment Corp.

Ford Motor Norge AS
Trolläsveien 34
N-1411 Kolbotn, Norway
Tel.: [47] 66 99 70 00
Fax: [47] 66 80 74 48
(Automobiles)
Ford Motor Co.

International Business Machines AS
Postboks 500
N-1411 Kolbotn, Norway
Tel.: [47] 66 99 80 00
Fax: [47] 66 99 33

(Office equipment)
IBM World Trade Corp.

Kodak Norge AS
Lienga 7
N-1410 Kilbotn, Norway
Tel.: [47] 66 81 81 81
Fax: [47] 66 80 06 12
(Photographic equipment)
Eastman Kodak Corp.

Rank Xerox AS
Nesoyveien 4
Postboks 905, Slependen
N-1301 Sandvika, Norway
Tel.: [47] 66 98 68 00
(Copier equipment)
Xerox Corp.

SERVICE INDUSTRIES

Arthur Andersen
NO-0212 Oslo, Norway
Tel.: [47] 22 92 80 00
Fax: [47] 22 92 89 00
(Management consulting and accounting)
Arthur Andersen

Coopers & Lybrand Consulting AS
Havnelageret
N-0150 Oslo, Norway
Tel.: [47] 22 40 00 00
Fax: [47] 22 42 50 91
(Consulting)
Coopers & Lybrand

McCann-Erickson AS
Riddervoldsgata 2
N-0256 Oslo, Norway
Tel.: [47] 22 44 84 00

Fax: [47] 22 44 84 60
(Advertising and public relations)
Interpublic Group Companies

Price Waterhouse Management Consulting AS
Holbergs Gate 21
N-0166 Oslo, Norway
Tel.: [47] 22 36 34 40
Fax: [47] 22 36 34 55
(Consulting)
Price Waterhouse Coopers

Unitor Ships Service ASA
Postboks 300 Skøyen
N-0212 Oslo, Norway
Tel.: [47] 22 13 14 15
Fax: [47] 22 13 45 00
(Ship chandlers)

EUROPEAN COMPANIES IN NORWAY

The following are major non-American firms operating in the country. These selected companies can be either Norwegian or foreign, usually European companies. Such companies will generally hire their own nationals first but may employ Americans.

BANKING AND FINANCE

Christiania Bank og Kreditkasse
Middelthunsgaten 17
Postboks 1166
N-0107 Oslo, Norway
Tel.: [47] 22 48 50 00

Fax: [47] 22 48 47 49
(Commercial bank)

Den Norske Bank
Torgalmenning 2
N-5020, Bergen, Norway

Tel.: [47] 55 21 10 00
Fax: [47] 55 21 11 50
(Commercial bank)

Union Bank of Norway Sparebanken Nor
Kirkegaten 18
N-0107 Oslo, Norway

INDUSTRIAL MANUFACTURING

Aker AS
Tjuvholmen 45
N-0250 Oslo, Norway
Tel.: [47] 22 94 50 00
Fax: [47] 67 12 91 00
(Naval construction)

Alcatel Telecom Norway AS
Postboks 310 Økern
N-0511 Oslo, Norway
Tel.: [47] 22 63 85 92
Fax: [47] 22 63 89 50
(Telecommunications equipment)

BP Norge AS
Postbok 2580 Solli
N-0203 Oslo, Norway
Tel.: [47] 22 43 85 80
Fax: [47] 22 11 50 36
(Petroleum products)

Elf Petroleum Norge AS
Postboks 168 Dusavik
N-4001 Stavanger, Norway
Tel.: [47] 51 50 30 00
Fax: [47] 51 50 34 81
(Petroleum products)

Frionor AS
Lysaker Torg 8
Postboks 195
N-1324 Lysaker, Norway
Tel.: [47] 67 52 46 00

SERVICE INDUSTRIES

Norges Statsbaner (Norwegian State Railways)
Storgaten 33
Postboks 9115-Vaterland
N-0134, Oslo 1, Norway
Tel.: [47] 22 36 80 00
(Railway services)

Norsk Data AS
Postboks 25, Bogerud
N-0621 Oslo 6, Norway
Tel.: [47] 22 62 80 00
(Computer systems)

Tel.: [47] 22 31 90 50
Fax: [47] 22 31 85 58
(Savings bank)

Fax: [47] 67 52 46 46
(Packaged seafoods)

Hydro Aluminium Conductors AS
Postboks 80
N-1321 Stabekk, Norway
Tel.: [47] 22 73 81 00
Fax: [47] 22 43 27 25
(Aluminum extraction and products)

Norsk Hydro AS Oil and Gas Group
Drammensv 264
Postboks 200
N-1321 Stabekk, Norway
Tel.: [47] 22 73 81 00
Fax: [47] 22 73 85 53
(Chemicals, plastics, oil and gas exploration, and production)

Orkla AS
Box 308
N-1324, Lysaker, Norway
Tel.: [47] 22 50 10 80
Fax: [47] 22 50 16 91
(Detergents, cosmetics, and frozen foods)

Total Norge AS
Haakon Vll's Gt. 1
Postboks 1361 Vika
N-0113 Oslo 1, Norway
Tel.: [47] 22 83 33 33
Fax: [47] 22 80 40 44
(Oil exploration and production)

Star Shipping AS
Fortunen 1
N-5013, Bergen, Norway
Tel.: [47] 55 23 96 00
Fax: [47] 55 23 25 30
(Shipping company)

Televerket
Postboks 6701
St. Olavs Plass
Universitetsgata 2
N-0130 Oslo 1, Norway
Tel.: [47] 22 48 89 90
(Telecommunications equipment and services)

INTERNATIONAL SCHOOLS IN NORWAY

International School of Bergen
Vilhelm Bjerknesvei 15 Landås
N-5030 Bergen, Norway
Tel.: [47] 55 28 77 16
Fax: [47] 55 27 14 88
Email: murison@isb.gs.hl.no

International School of Stavanger
Treskeveien 3
N-4042 Hafrsfjord Stavanger, Norway
Tel.: [47] 51 55 91 00
Fax: [47] 51 55 29 62
Email: intschol@iss.stavanger.rl.no
www.iss.stavanger.rl.no

Sweden

MAJOR EMPLOYMENT CENTER: Stockholm

MAJOR BUSINESS LANGUAGE: Swedish

LANGUAGE SKILL INDEX: Many businesspeople are fluent in English. You will likely fare much better, though, by speaking Swedish rather than expecting them to accommodate you

CURRENCY: Krona

TELEPHONE COUNTRY CODE: 46

TIME ZONE: EST+6

PUNCTUALITY INDEX: The Swedes are always punctual

AVERAGE DAILY TEMPERATURE, HIGH/LOW: January, 31/23°F; July, 70/55°F (Stockholm)

AVERAGE NUMBER OF DAYS WITH PRECIPITATION: January, 12; July, 12

BEST BET FOR EMPLOYMENT:

   FOR STUDENTS: American-Scandinavian Foundation

   PERMANENT JOBS: Knowledge of Swedish and a special skill

CHANCE OF FINDING A JOB: Summer jobs: possible. Others: very difficult

TRIVIA: If longevity is your goal, Sweden could be the place for you. Life expectancy at birth is 74 for men, 80 for women

T he Kingdom of Sweden is located on the eastern section of the Scandinavian peninsula. The Kjólen Mountains form the Norwegian border on the west. To the east, Finland lies across the Gulf of Bothnia, and Russia is across the Baltic Sea. Denmark is across the Kattegat to the south. Poland and Germany also lie to the south across the Baltic Sea. The north contains numerous lakes, while the rest of the country consists of forest lands and plains.

Sweden, the third-largest nation in western Europe, after France and Spain, is twice the size of Britain but doesn't have many more citizens than London. Sweden is about the size of California. About 95% of the population belongs to the established Lutheran Church. Rural Swedes speak dialects that other Swedes have a hard time understanding. Otherwise, Sweden is extremely homogeneous.

The Swedes have lived in their country for over 5,000 years, longer than any other people in Europe. Gothic tribes from Sweden invaded the Roman Empire, and later Swedes entered Russia. In the 11th century Sweden was converted to Christianity. The Riksdag, Sweden's parliament, was first called in 1435. The Danish kings ruled Sweden from 1397 until a rebellion led by Gustavus I in 1523.

By the 17th century, Sweden had become a major European power, controlling various Baltic provinces and playing an important role in the Thirty Years' War. In 1721 Russia, Poland, and Denmark forced Sweden to relinquish most of its Baltic empire, including Finland. Norway was acquired in the Napoleonic Wars and held until 1905.

Sweden maintained a policy of neutrality in both world wars. Today, Sweden belongs to no military alliance and is a member of the European Free Trade Association. In 1995 Sweden joined the E.U., although this move is highly unpopular with most Swedes. Sweden does participate in the United Nations. Sweden has developed one of the world's most prosperous economies. The country's high standard of living, however, is accompanied by one of the world's highest costs of living.

An extensive social welfare state has been established. Sweden's social programs have largely become the model for other developed countries, although even the Social Democrats, the architects of the system, admit that the cradle-to-grave welfare is about to end.

Sweden continues to have the monarch serve as the head of state under the constitution, but the prime minister is chosen by the speaker of the parliament, the *Riksdag*. The major political parties in Sweden include the Social Democrats, the Conservatives, the Centre Party, Christian Democrats, Liberal Party, and Communists. A right-of-center coalition has been in power since 1991.

Swedes appreciate visitors who have an understanding of the differences between the Scandinavian countries. Although they possess many progressive attitudes, some Swedes are practically puritanical when it comes to alcohol. Liquor is only available from government stores that are open inconvenient hours, and drunk drivers are severely punished.

Most younger Swedes speak English, and if you are looking for a job in a tourist spot, it may not be necessary to learn Swedish. Many businesspeople are fluent in English and one other language. Alphabetics are a little different in Swedish. The vowels å, ä, and ö go at the end of the alphabet. V and W are alphabetized as if they were the same letter. For example, "van" would come after "wait" and before "was." Similarly, the letter C is alphabetized with the Ks. Although Scandinavians speak different languages, they can often understand one another since, with the exception of Finnish, Scandinavian languages are all descended from the language of the Vikings.

Banks, post offices, and most businesses are usually open from 9:00 a.m. to 5:00 or 6:00 p.m., Monday through Friday, and until the afternoon on Saturday.

Current Economic Climate

Sweden's gross national product and per capita income rank it among the wealthiest countries in the world. It is also one of the most socialized countries in the world. The public sector constitutes over 65% of the domestic economy, the highest percentage in the world. Sweden is one of the strongest industrialized nations in Europe. Unemployment is currently at about 9.8% and is continuing to decline. (Until recently, Sweden had almost full employment.) The Swedish tax rates are also among the highest in the world.

Approximately 24% of the work force is involved in manufacturing, 5% in agriculture, and 63% in the service sector, although nearly 35% of service employees work for the government. More than 40% of Sweden's industrial production is exported. Major industries include machinery, automobiles, steel products, wood products, and agriculture. Sweden's primary trading partners are Norway, Germany, Denmark, and Finland.

SWEDEN'S 10 LARGEST COMPANIES

(1997, composite ranking)
1. Electrolux
2. Telefonaktiebolaget LM Ericsson
3. Volvo
4. SKF
5. Kooperative Forbundet Ekonomisk Forening
6. BCP Branded Consumer Products
7. Tetra Laval
8. Telia
9. Statens Jarnvagar
10. Skanska

Using the phone, fax and Internet

Most public phones require that you use a *Telia* phonecard, usually available for 35, 60, or 100 kr. Telia booths also accept most credit cards. Overseas calls will require that you purchase a Telia phonecard with 120 credits. In addition to the typical yellow pages, Swedish phone books include green pages for community services and blue pages for regional services. The emergency number is "112."

The fax rates from Telia booths are the cheapest at just over 30 kr a page. Most public libraries have computers with Internet access that can be used free of charge.

Getting Around in Sweden

Sweden's rail network extends to all the south and most of the north, but train fares are expensive. It is usually better to take the bus when traveling in the north. Eurail and InterRail passes are valid on all trains but not buses. Ferries are also available for traveling in the gulf. The numerous Scandinavian airlines offer discounts for those traveling extensively in the Scandinavian region.

Employment Regulations and Outlook for Americans

Finding employment in Sweden is difficult. Strict labor regulations are compounded by the fact that Sweden is, after all, a small country: there simply aren't that many jobs to go around. The country does enjoy a high standard of living, but employment opportunities for foreigners are especially limited. Swedish workers are well educated and highly skilled, further limiting demand for foreign workers. American citizens intending to work in Sweden must possess a work permit upon arrival.

There are strict limits on the number of foreigners allowed to work in Sweden. Students, however, are allowed to work in the summer, provided they have obtained their work permits before entering the country. Even so, given the difficulty of locating employment, most seasonal work will very likely be arranged on the black market. Tourist work may be found on the western coast, although even hotel work can be difficult to find. Malmö, across from Denmark, has the largest number of restaurants in the country and four youth hostels. Some agricultural work may be found in the southern counties as well. Stockholm and Göteborg both have port facilities that might on occasion require additional manual workers.

Short-term and Temporary Work

The best bet for casual jobs is to work as an au pair.

IRCA International/Sprakcenter
P.O. Box 293
S-29123 Kristianstad, Sweden

Tel.: [46] (44) 12 22 63
Au pair placement agency.

Internship Programs

There are opportunities for students to gain professional experience, usually in technical fields. The American-Scandinavian Foundation and IASTE coordinate placements for technical interns. The Future Farmers of America coordinates an exchange for students interested in agricultural internships.

The American-Scandinavian Foundation
725 Park Avenue
New York, NY 10021
Tel.: (212) 879-9779
Email: training@amscan.org
Places summer interns in engineering, agricultural, and other technical fields throughout Scandinavia.

Future Farmers of America
National FFA Center
P.O. Box 15160
Alexandria, VA 22309

Tel.: (703) 360-3600
Coordinates programs for trainees in agriculture.

IASTE
10400 Little Patuxent Parkway, Suite 250 L
Columbia, MD 21044-3510
Tel.: (410) 997-3068
Fax: (410) 997-5186
Email: iaste@aipt.org
www.aipt.org/iaste.html
Arranges reciprocal internship exchanges among 63 member countries for students in engineering, architecture, and the sciences.

NEWSPAPERS IN SWEDEN

Arbetet
Bergsgatan 20
P.O. Box 125
S-201 21 Malmö, Sweden
Tel.: [46] (40) 20 50 00
Fax: [46] (40) 10 15 81

Dagens Nyheter
Ralambsvagen 17
S-105 15 Stockholm, Sweden
Tel.: [46] (8) 738 10 00
Fax: [46] (8) 719 08 11

Expressen
Gjörwellsgatan 30
S-105 16 Stockholm, Sweden
Tel.: [46] (8) 738 30 00
Fax: [46] (8) 619 04 50

Göteborgs-Posten
Polhemplatsen 5
S-40502 Göteborg, Sweden
Tel.: [46] (31) 62 40 00
Fax: [46] (31) 15 79 18

Resources for Further Information

USEFUL WEBSITES FOR JOB SEARCHERS

The Internet is a good place to begin your job search. Many Scandinavian employers list job vacancies, especially those in technical fields, on the World Wide Web. There are also many websites that provide useful information for job searchers researching the Swedish job market.

interAF
www.af.lu.se/interaf/jobs
Good job-search database; in Swedish.

Job's Place
www.job.bonnier.se
Has listings for business/technical jobs, in Swedish.

Kajetans Jobbsokningssida
www.users.wineasy.se/
Job-search database for most fields, in Swedish.

Online Career Center
http://citygate.se/
Excellent advice on job opportunities, etc., in Swedish.

Swedish Information and Statistics
www.worldtravel-links.com/sweden/
trstat00.htm
Excellent website on Sweden.

EMBASSIES AND CONSULAR OFFICES

American embassies and consulates have commercial and/or economic sections that can provide you with business information and explain aspects of the local economy. Inquiries about business opportunities should be addressed either to "Commercial Officer" or "Commercial Section," followed by the appropriate street address.

Representation of Sweden in the United States

Embassy of Sweden
1501 M Street NW
Washington, DC 20005
Tel.: (202) 467-2600
Fax: (202) 467-2699

Consulates General of Sweden: Chicago, (312) 781-6262; Los Angeles, (213) 470-2555; New York, (212) 751-5900

Representation of the United States in Sweden

American Embassy
Strandvagen 101
S-11589 Stockholm, Sweden

Tel.: [46] (8) 783 5300
Fax: [46] (8) 661 1964

CHAMBERS OF COMMERCE

Chambers of commerce consist of firms in both countries interested in international trade. These are appropriate companies to initially target in the job search.

American Chamber of Commerce in Sweden
P.O. Box 16050
S-103 Stockholm, Sweden
Tel.: [46] (8) 613 1800
Fax: [46] (8) 411 4056
Email: mara@gsh.se

Swedish-American Chamber of Commerce
599 Lexington Avenue, 13th Floor
New York, NY 10022
Tel.: (212) 838-5530
Fax: (212) 755-7953

Swedish American Chamber of Commerce—Colorado
609 W. Littleton Blvd., Suite 309
Englewood, CO 80120
Tel./ Fax: (303) 797-2179
www.saccusa.org/colorado/

Swedish-American Chamber of Commerce of the Western U.S.
564 Market Street
San Francisco, CA 94104
Tel.: (415) 781-4188
Fax: (415) 781-4189

WORLD TRADE CENTER IN SWEDEN

World Trade Centers usually include many foreign companies operating in the country.

Scandinavian World Trade Center AB
Klarabergsviadukten 70
Box 70354
S-107 24 Stockholm, Sweden
Tel.: [46] (8) 700 45 00

Fax: [46] (8) 21 06 81
Email: info@wtc.se
www.sto.wtc.se

OTHER INFORMATIONAL ORGANIZATIONS

Foreign government missions in the U.S. such as National Tourist Offices can furnish visas and information on work permits and other important regulations. They may also offer economic and business information about the country.

Swedish Information Service
P.O. Box 7542
S-10393 Stockholm, Sweden
Tel.: [46] 8 789 2400
Fax: [46] 8 789 2450
www.stoinfo.se

Swedish National Tourist Office
655 Third Avenue
New York, NY 10017
Tel.: (212) 949-2333
Fax: (212) 697-0835

BUSINESS DIRECTORIES

Although not always easy to find, business directories can prove invaluable in the international job search. Most directories list company names, addresses, products, and phone numbers. Some directories include executive names and titles and financial information about the company. These sources provide you with the names of the people to contact for employment information as well as financial data that can tell you how strong a company's position in a country may be.

Commercial Directory of Sweden. Published annually by Bonniers Foretagsinfo AB, Sveavagen 84, Box 3303, S-10366 Stockholm, Sweden. In Swedish, with English headings. Lists 16,500 Swedish firms.

Directory of Foreign Firms Operating Abroad: Sweden. World Trade Academy Press, 257 Central Park West, Suite 10A, New York, NY 10024-4110; email: uniworldbp@aol.com; www.uniworldbp.com. Lists names and addresses of parent companies in the U.S. and their subsidiaries and affiliates in Sweden.

Kompass Sweden. Published annually in Swedish with multilingual product headings by Kompass Sverige, Postboks 3223, Saltmatargat 8, S-10363 Stockholm, Sweden. Over 12,000 service, distributing, and manufacturing companies.

Sweden's Largest Companies. Published annually in English and Swedish by Ekonomisk Litteratur AB, Box 14113, S-16114 Bromma, Sweden; email: info@ekolitt.se;

www.ekolitt.se. Distributed in the U.S. by Negsan Inc., 1200 Westlake Avenue N., Suite 512, Seattle, WA 98109. Includes 10,000 firms in Sweden.

Swedish-American Chamber of Commerce–Membership Directory. Published annually by the Swedish-American Chamber of Commerce, 599 Lexington Avenue, New York, NY 10022; email: info@swedishtrade.de; www.swedishtrade.se/sed. 1,800 U.S. and 200 Swedish companies involved in commercial trade between the two countries.

Swedish Export Directory. Published annually in English by the Swedish Trade Council, Box 5513, S-11485 Stockholm, Sweden. Approximately 1,400 Swedish manufacturers and exporters involved in international trade.

Swedish Related Companies in the USA. Published annually by the Swedish-American Chamber of Commerce, 599 Lexington Avenue, New York, New York, 10022. Lists Swedish subsidiaries in the U.S. and their parent companies in Sweden.

Swedish Technical Directory. Published by Forlags AG Fournier, Tideliusgaten 42-44; S-11669 Stockholm, Sweden. Lists major technical companies and products.

Western Sweden Chamber of Commerce—List of Members. Published biennially in English, French, and Swedish by the Western Sweden Chamber of Commerce, Box 5253, S-402 25 Gothenburg, Sweden. Lists over 2,300 members involved with foreign trade.

AMERICAN COMPANIES IN SWEDEN

The following companies are classified by business area: Industrial Manufacturing; Retailing and Wholesaling; and Service Industries. Company information includes firm name, address, phone and fax number, specific business, contact name, and American parent company. Your chances of achieving employment abroad are substantially better if you contact the subsidiary company in Europe rather than the parent company in the U.S.

INDUSTRIAL MANUFACTURING

Abbott Scandinavia AB
Torshamnsgatan 24
Stockholm, Sweden
Tel.: [46] (8) 752 00 50
(Pharmaceuticals)
Abbott Laboratories

Bell & Howell AB
Wintergarten 1
S-172 30 Sundbyberg, Sweden
Tel.: [46] (8) 898 12 50
(Audio-visual & video production products)
Bell & Howell Co.

Digital Equipment AB
Allén 6
S-172 89 Sundbyberg, Sweden
Tel.: [46] (8) 629 80 00
(Computers and data processing equipment)
Digital Equipment Corp.

Exxon Chemical Norden AB
Box 1035
S-405 22 Göteborg, Sweden
Tel.: [46] (31) 63 82 00
(Specialty polymers)
Exxon Corp.

Johnson & Johnson AB
Staffans Vag 2
S-191 84 Sollentuna, Sweden
Tel.: [46] (8) 754 01 00
(Hospital products)
Johnson & Johnson

Motorola AB
Davaegen 2
S-171 36 Solna, Sweden
Tel.: [46] (8) 734 88 00
(Electronic equipment & parts)
Motorola Inc.

Pfizer AB
Nytropsvagen 2 Nesbypark
S-183 03 Taby, Stockholm, Sweden

Tel.: [46] (8) 758 01 30
(Pharmaceuticals)
Pfizer Inc.

Procter & Gamble AB
Kungsgatan 33
S-103 92 Stockholm, Sweden
Tel.: [46] (8) 824 88 10
(Household products)
Procter & Gamble Co.

Revlon AB
Maria Skolgata 83
S-116 52 Stockholm, Sweden
(Cosmetics)
MacAndrews & Forbes Holding

R.J. Reynolds Tobacco AB
Vatten Tornsvagen 18
S-180 21 Osteruala, Vastimanland, Sweden
(Tobacco products)
RJR Nabisco Inc.

Richardson-Vicks AB
Kungsgatan 33
S-103 92 Stockholm, Sweden

RETAILING AND WHOLESALING

Dow Sverige AB
Ramhällsvägen 2
S-111 35 Stockholm, Sweden
Tel.: [46] (8) 676 57 00
Fax: [46] (8) 676 57 80
(Chemicals, oils & resins, plastics)
Dow Chemicals

Du Pont Scandinavia AB
Torshamnsgatan 35
S-163 86 Stockholm, Sweden
Tel.: [46] (8) 750 37 00
(Textiles, photographic supplies, fuels)
E.I. de Pont de Nemours & Co.

Firestone Scandinavia AB
Box 462
S-501 07 Boras, Alvsborg, Sweden
Tel.: [46] (33) 10 20 50
(Tires & tubes)
Firestone Tire & Rubber Co.

Ford Motor Company AB
Tullvaktsvagen 11
S-102 54 Stockholm, Sweden
Tel.: [46] (8) 782 85 00

Tel.: [46] (8) 823 32 60
(Pharmaceuticals)
Procter & Gamble Co.

3M Svenska AB
Bollstanäsv 3
S-191 89 Sollentuna, Sweden
Tel.: [46] (8) 92 21 00
(Textiles, chemicals, machinery)
Minnesota Mining and Manufacturing

Wabco Westinghouse AB
Hovaverken Industriegatan
S-540 70 Malmö, Sweden
(Automotive products)
Kelso & Company Inc.

Warner-Lambert Scandinavia Aktiebolag
Anderstorpsvagen 16
S-171 04 Solna, Stockholm, Sweden
(Metals, pharmaceuticals, and cosmetics)
Warner-Lambert Co.

(Farm and industrial equipment and
automobiles)
Ford Motor Co.

General Motors Nordiska AB
Armaturvägen 4
S-136 82 Handen, Sweden
Tel.: [46] (750) 715 00
(Automobiles and parts)
General Motors Corp.

Hewlett Packard Sverige AB
Skalholtsgaten 9
S-164 40 Kista, Sweden
Tel.: [46] (8) 444 20 00
Fax: [46] (8) 444 26 66
(Data systems, electronic instruments)
Hewlett-Packard Co.

IBM Svenska AB
Oddegatan 5
S-164 92 Stockholm, Sweden
Tel.: [46] (8) 793 10 00
Fax: [46] (8) 793 49 48
(Office machines)
IBM Corp.

Kodak AB
Nettovägen 2
S-175 41 Järfälla, Sweden
Tel.: [47] (8) 58 02 35 00
Fax: [47] (8) 58 03 36 52
(Photographic equipment)
Eastman Kodak Co.

Kraft Foods AB
Allen 7
S-172 36 Sundbyberg, Sweden
Tel.: [46] (8) 627 10 00
Fax: [46] (8) 98 61 00
(Packaged foods)
Kraft General Foods Corp.

Mobil Oil AB
Skarvikshammen
S-418 34 Göteborg, Sweden
Tel.: [46] (31) 64 67 00

SERVICE INDUSTRIES

McCann-Erickson AB
Torggatan 4
Malmö, Sweden
Tel.: [46] (40) 705 70
(Advertising agency)
Interpublic Group Companies

Nus Scandinavia Incorporated
Box 7500
S-103 92 Stockholm, Sweden
Tel.: [46] (8) 810 48 70
(Energy cost consultants)
National Service Industries

Ogilvy & Mather Group AB
Tegnerlunden 3
S-105 13 Stockholm, Sweden

Fax: [46] (31) 54 57 22
(Petroleum products)
Mobil Holdings

Rank Xerox AB
Domnarvsgatan 11
S-163 87 Stockholm, Sweden
Tel.: [46] (8) 795 10 00
Fax: [46] (8) 795 10 20
(Copier equipment)
Xerox Corp.

Unisys AB
Armégatan 40
S-171 71 Solna, Sweden
Tel.: [46] (8) 470 15 00
Fax: [46] (8) 470 15 35
(Computer data systems)
Unisys Corp.

Tel.: [46] (8) 814 21 00
(Advertising agency)
Ogilvy Group Inc.

Rational Software Scandinavia AB
Skalholtsgatan 10
S-164-40 Kista, Sweden
Tel.: [46] (8) 56 62 82 00
Fax: [46] (8) 751 30 96
(Software consultants)
Rational Software

Warner-Columbia Film AB
Box 1346
S-111 83 Stockholm, Sweden
(Motion picture distribution)
Warner Communications Inc.

EUROPEAN COMPANIES IN SWEDEN

The following are major non-American firms operating in the country. These selected companies can be either Swedish or foreign, usually European companies. Such companies will generally hire their own nationals first but may employ Americans.

BANKING AND FINANCE

Folksamgruppen
Bohusg 14
S-106 60 Stockholm, Sweden
Tel.: [46] (8) 772 6000
Fax: [46] (8) 714 7611
(Insurance)

Gota Bank
Sveavägen 14
S-10350 Stockholm, Sweden
Tel.: [46] (8) 788 10 10
Fax: [46] (8) 10 31 74
(Commercial bank)
Ulf Hedbäck, EVP, International

Skandia Group Insurance Company Ltd.
Sveävagen 44
S-103 50 Stockholm, Sweden
Tel.: [46] (8) 788 11 00
Fax: [46] (8) 10 31 74
(Insurance)

Skandinaviska Enskilda Banken
Kungsträdgårdsgatan 8
S-106 40 Stockholm, Sweden
Tel.: [46] (8) 763 80 00
Fax: [46] (8) 763 83 93
(Joint stock bank)

INDUSTRIAL MANUFACTURING

ABB Asea Skandia AB
Malmvägen 141
S-191 62 Sollentuna, Sweden
Tel.: [46] (8) 92 35 00
Fax: [46] (8) 92 39 80
(Electrical systems)

ABB Motors AB
Saltängsv 22-24
S-721 70 Västeräs, Sweden
Tel.: [46] (21) 32 90 00
Fax: [46] (21) 12 41 03
Email:
christer.holgersson@semot.mail.abb.com
(Electric motors)

AGA AB
S-181 81 Lidingö, Sweden
Tel.: [46] (8) 731 10 00
Fax: [46] (8) 767 63 44
(Industrial gases and measuring instru-
ments)

Astra AB
Kvarnberg 16
S-151 85 Södertälje, Sweden
Tel.: [46] (8) 55 32 60 00
Fax: [46] (8) 55 38 55 51
(Pharmaceuticals)

Atlas Copco Controls AB
Solkraftsvägen 13
S-135 70 Stockholm, Sweden
Tel.: [46] (8) 682 64 00
Fax: [46] (8) 682 65 80
(Electric motors)

Electrolux AB
Luxbacken 1
S-105 45 Stockholm, Sweden
Tel.: [46] (8) 738 60 00

Svenska Handelsbanken
Kungstredgerdsgatan 2
S-106 70 Stockholm, Sweden
Tel.: [46] (8) 701 10 00
Fax: [46] (8) 702 24 37
(Joint stock bank)

SwedBank
Brunkebergstorg 8
S-105 34 Stockholm, Sweden
Tel.: [46] (8) 22 23 20
Fax: [46] (8) 11 90 13
 (Commercial bank)

Fax: [46] (8) 656 44 78
(Laundry and dry-cleaning machinery,
appliances)

Ericsson
Augustendalsv 21-36
S-131 52 Stockholm, Sweden
Tel.: [46] (8) 422 00 00
Fax: [46] (8) 422 10 10
(Business communications)

Esselte AB
Box 1371
S-171 27 Stockholm-Solna, Sweden
Tel.: [46] (8) 734 34 00
Fax: [46] (8) 27 91 35
(Office supplies)

EUROC AB
Box 60066
S-216 60 Malmö, Sweden
Tel.: [46] (40) 16 50 00
Fax: [46] (40) 16 51 65
(Construction equipment, building
materials, and ceramics)

Fermenta AB
Kungsgtan 4A
S-111 43 Stockholm, Sweden
Tel.: [46] (8) 23 83 50
(Pharmaceuticals)

Pharmacia AB
Rapsgatan 7
S-751 82 Uppsala, Sweden
Tel.: [46] (18) 16 30 00
Fax: [46] (18) 12 60 77
(Pharmaceuticals and chemicals)

Saab AB
Broderna Ugglas Gata
S-582 54 Linköping, Sweden
Tel.: [46] (13) 18 00 00
Fax: [46] (13) 18 18 02
(Automobiles and parts)

Sandvik AB
S-811 81 Sandviken, Sweden
Tel.: [46] (26) 26 00 00
Fax: [46] (26) 26 26 13 50
(Steel-based tools)

Stora AB
Äsgatan
S-791 80 Falun, Sweden
Tel.: [46] (23) 78 00 00

Fax: [46] (23) 138 58
(Paper products)

Svenska Cellulosa AB
Box 7827
S-103 97 Stockholm, Sweden
Tel.: [46] (8) 788 51 00
Fax: [46] (8) 678 81 30
(Paper and electrical products)

Volvo AB
S-405 08 Göteborg, Sweden
Tel.: [46] (31) 59 00 00
Fax: [46] (31) 54 49 82
(Automobiles and farm machinery)

RETAILING AND WHOLESALING

Apoteksbolaget AB
Klara Södra Kyrkogata18
S-111 52 Stockholm, Sweden
Tel.: [46] (8) 454 70 00
Fax: [46] (8) 454 75 15
(Pharmaceutical products)

Johnson Axel AB
Jakobsbeigsgaten 7
S-103 75 Stockholm, Sweden
Tel.: [46] (8) 701 61 00
Fax: [46] (8) 611 79 15
(Petroleum, coal, chemicals, and metals)

SERVICE INDUSTRIES

Nobel Industries AB
Gustav Adolgs Torg 18
S-103 27 Stockholm, Sweden
Tel.: [46] (8) 613 25 00
(Construction and chemicals)

Scandic Hotel AB
Gävlegatan 16
P.O. Box 6197
S-102 33 Stockholm, Sweden

Tel.: [46] (8) 610 50 00
Fax: [46] (8) 610 52 65
(Hotels and restaurants)

Scandinavian Airlines System (SAS)
Frösundavik Allé 1
S-161 87 Stockholm, Sweden
Tel.: [46] (8) 797 00 00
Fax: [46] (8) 797 30 47
(Airline for Denmark, Norway, and
Sweden)

INTERNATIONAL SCHOOL IN SWEDEN

International School of Stockholm
Johannesgatan 18
S-111 38 Stockholm, Sweden
Tel.: [46] (8) 412 4000
Fax: [46] (8) 412 4001
Email: admin@intsch.se
www.intsch.se

Benelux Countries:
Belgium, Luxembourg,
and The Netherlands

Belgium

MAJOR EMPLOYMENT CENTERS: Brussels, Antwerp

MAJOR BUSINESS LANGUAGES: Flemish, French

LANGUAGE SKILL INDEX: Expect to speak French for higher-level positions in the E.U. government. For non-governmental jobs: in the north, Flanders, it is better to approach a Flemish speaker with English than French. In the southern part of the country, Wallonia, French is clearly the language of preference. Many young Belgians speak English, and most people speak more than one language

CURRENCY: Euro; Belgian franc will remain the currency in circulation until 2002

TELEPHONE COUNTRY CODE: 32

TIME ZONE: EST+6

PUNCTUALITY INDEX: Very important

AVERAGE DAILY TEMPERATURE: January, 40°F; July, 60°F (Brussels)

AVERAGE NUMBER OF DAYS WITH RAIN: January, 14; July, 14

BEST BET FOR EMPLOYMENT:

FOR STUDENTS: Apply to IASTE

PERMANENT JOBS: International organization and public policy work associated with the European Union in Brussels

CHANCE OF FINDING A JOB: Not too good outside of public policy

TRIVIA: Members of the opposite sex and women kiss each other on alternate cheeks three times as a greeting

The Kingdom of Belgium lies in western Europe just south of the Netherlands, north of France, and west of Germany. The North Sea borders on the west for almost 40 miles. Belgium is about the size of Maryland. The Ardennes region in the southeast consists of forest lands while the rest of the country is mostly flat.

Belgium is linguistically divided between Flanders to the north and Wallonia to the south. Walloons speak French while the people in Flanders speak Flemish, a dialect of Dutch. Brussels, Belgium's capital, is officially bilingual. About 55% of the population is Flemish and almost 33% is Walloon. A small German-speaking population also lives in the far eastern portion of the country. Over 85% of the population belongs to the Roman Catholic Church.

The Belgae, a Celtic people, were the country's first inhabitants. Julius Caesar conquered the region, which was subsequently ruled by the Franks, the Spanish and Austrian Hapsburgs, and the French. After the Napoleonic Wars, Belgium became part of the Netherlands. In 1830 the country became an independent monarchy. Belgium attempted to remain neutral in both world wars but was overrun by the Germans each time. King Leopold III, who surrendered to Germany in 1940, was forced to abdicate in favor of his son, King Baudouin, in 1951. Belgium is a member of the European Union and the North Atlantic Treaty Organization, both of which are headquartered in Brussels.

The federal government is a constitutional and hereditary monarchy. King Albert II succeeded King Baudouin in 1993. Common religious bonds and loyalty to the same king served to unite the Belgians in the past but are failing to achieve the same results today. Politics are dominated by the Christian Democrats, Socialists, and Liberals, although support for the Greens is increasing. In 1993, parliament successfully introduced a series of reforms that effectively created a federal state with power devolved to three increasingly autonomous regions: Flanders, Wallonia, and Brussels. Each region is becoming increasingly self-governing as Parliament transfers more and more power to the three regions.

Business hours are generally between 8:30 a.m.–6 p.m., Monday–Friday. Retail shops are also open on Saturday and on Sunday.

Current Economic Climate

Belgium's economic prosperity has swung between one language community and the other. The Flemish medieval textile wealth was supplanted by Wallonia's mining and steel industry. The decline of mining and steel means that Flanders is again the industrial backbone of Belgium.

Much of the country's economy revolves around international trade. About 50% of the country's industrial production is exported. Numerous multinational corporations base their European operations in Brussels, also the headquarters of N.A.T.O. and the E.U. The city has benefited tremendously from its central role in the E.U. bureaucracy.

Currently, unemployment hovers around 8%. Belgium enjoys a per capita income of nearly $8,000 and one of the lowest inflation rates in the E.U. Major trading partners include the E.U., especially the Netherlands and the U.K., and the U.S. The work force is 60% services, 28% industrial, and 2% agricultural. Major industries include steel, textiles, chemicals, glass, and jewelry. The best prospects for new job growth is in the high-tech industry.

BELGIUM'S LARGEST COMPANIES
(1997, composite rankings)
1. Delhaize "Le Lion"
2. GIB Group
3. Sovay
4. Tractebel
5. Belgacom
6. Cockerill Sambre Group
7. Crédit Générale de Banque
8. Société Générale de Belgique
9. Electrabel
10. Petrofina

Using the phone, fax, and Internet
International calls can be made from any public phone but require a large number of coins. Phonecards, especially Phonepass and The Phonecard, available from newsstands, offer the best rates for international calls. Faxes can be sent from telephone offices. Cybercafes are common only in larger cities.

Getting Around in Belgium

Eurail and InterRail passes are valid on intercity buses, plus trains throughout Belgium. The Belgian railroad network, known for its reliability and extensive service, offers special discounts for exclusive traveling within the Benelux countries or within Belgian borders. Train travel in Belgium is relatively inexpensive.

Employment Regulations and Outlook for Americans

American citizens don't need a visa to visit Belgium for less than 90 days. However, a residence permit is required for longer stays. As in most E.U. countries, a work permit must be presented upon arrival if you intend to work. Your prospective employer must apply for the work permit to the Belgian authorities. Foreigners seeking employment opportunities in Belgium are often disappointed; low-skill employment in the tourist industry is sometimes a good bet. Whatever your job aspirations in Belgium, fluency in French or Flemish is recommended.

Short-term and Temporary Work

Like most of Europe, good bets for casual jobs are with au pair agencies.

Services de la Jeunesse Feminine
rue Faider 29
B-1050 Brussels, Belgium
Tel.: [32] (2) 539 35 14
Au pair placement agency.

Stufam
Vierwindenlaan 7
B-1780 Wemmel, Belgium
Tel.: [32] (2) 460 33 95
Au pair placement agency.

Internship Programs

Students interested in professional work should apply for technical internships through IASTE. The Environmental Information Centre helps students interested in the environment find internships.

Environmental Information Centre
Natuur 2000
Bervoetstraat 33
B-2000 Antwerpen, Belgium
Tel.: [32] (3) 231 2604
Internships in the field of environmental education.

IASTE
10400 Little Patuxent Parkway, Suite 250 L
Columbia, MD 21044-3510

Tel.: (410) 997-3068
Fax: (410) 997-5186
Email: iaste@aipt.org
www.aipt.org/iaste.html
Arranges reciprocal internship exchanges among 63 member countries for students in engineering, architecture, and the sciences.

Volunteer Opportunities

Numerous organizations offer an array of voluntary service opportunities in Belgium. The CIEE places volunteers (18 years and older) in workcamps. Participants work on construction projects. The International Christian Youth Exchange also offers their Year Abroad in Belgium for persons aged 18 to 24. Volunteers work in health care, education, construction, and the environment.

CIEE
Voluntary Service Department
205 East 42nd Street
New York, NY 10017
Tel.: (800) COUNCIL
Email: info@ciee.org
www.ciee.org

International Christian Youth Exchange
134 West 26th Street
New York, NY 10001
Tel.: (212) 206-7307

Other organizations that recruit volunteers to work in Belgium include the International Voluntary Service, and Volunteers for Peace. Contact their offices directly for program details.

Archeolo-j
Avenue Paul Terlinden 23
B-1330 Rixensart, Belgium
Tel.: [32] (2) 653 8268
Fax: [32] (2) 673 40 85
Coordinates residential archaeological digs.

International Voluntary Service—
United States
SCI-USA
Route 2, Box 506

Crozet, VA 22932
Tel.: (804) 823-1826

Volunteers for Peace
International Workcamps
43 Tiffany Road
Belmont, VT 05730
Tel.: (802) 259-2759
Email: vfp@vermontel.com
www.vfp.org

NEWSPAPERS IN BELGIUM

The Bulletin (English)
Ackroyd Publications SA
Ch de Waterloostwg 1038
B-1180 Brussels, Belgium
Tel.: [32] (2) 373 99 09
Fax: [32] (2) 375 98 22

Het Laatste Nieuws (Flemish)
Hoste NV
Brusselsesteenweg 347
B-1730 Kobbegem, Belgium
Tel.: [32] (2) 454 22 11
Fax: [32] (2) 453 05 45

De Nieuwe Gazet (Flemish)
Hoste NV
Brusselsesteenweg 347
B-1730 Kobbegem, Belgium

Tel.: [32] (2) 454 22 11
Fax: [32] (2) 453 05 45

Het Nieuwsblad/De Standaard (Flemish)
Alfons Gossetlaan 30
B-1702 Groot-Bijgaarden, Belgium
Tel.: [32] (2) 467 22 11
Fax: [32] (2) 466 66 30 93

Le Soir (French)
112 rue Royale
B-1000 Brussels, Belgium
Tel.: [32] (2) 225 55 55
Fax: [32] (2) 225 59 04

Resources for Further Information

USEFUL WEBSITES FOR JOB SEARCHERS

The Internet is a good place to begin your job search. Many Belgian employers list job vacancies, especially those in technical fields, on the World Wide Web. There are also many websites that provide useful information for job searchers researching the Belgian job market.

L'emploi en Belgique
www.sd.be/journal/index_f.htm
Offers advice on obtaining a job in Belgium.

FOREM
www.forem.be/forem
Advertises job listings in most fields.

Interlaber Interim
www.interlaber.be/
Temporary employment services.

Plug-in Belgiumx
www.plug-in.be:80/plugin
A contact magazine with classified ads.

Profiles
www.nomad.be/profiles
An impressive Belgian jobs website; in
English.

Search & Selection
www.searchselection.com
Job links for Belgium.

EMBASSIES AND CONSULAR OFFICES

American embassies and consulates have commercial and/or economic sections that
can provide you with business information and explain aspects of the local economy.
Inquiries about business opportunities should be addressed either to "Commercial
Officer" or "Commercial Section," followed by the appropriate street address.

Representation of Belgium in the United States

Embassy of Belgium
3330 Garfield Street NW
Washington, DC 20008
Tel.: (202) 333-6900
Fax: (202) 333-3079
www.belgium-emb.org/usa/

Consulates General of Belgium: Chicago, (312) 263-6624; Los Angeles, (323) 857-1244;
New York, (212) 586-5110

Representation of the United States in Belgium

American Embassy
boulevard de Regent 27
B-1000 Brussels, Belgium
Tel.: [32] (2) 508 2111
Fax: [32] (2) 511 2725

CHAMBERS OF COMMERCE

Chambers of commerce consist of firms in both countries interested in international trade. These are appropriate companies to initially target in the job search.

**American Chamber of Commerce in
Belgium**
50 avenue des Arts, Boite 5
B-1000 Brussels, Belgium
Tel.: [32] (2) 513 6770
Fax: [32] (2) 513 3590

**Belgian-American Chamber of Commerce
in the U.S.**
1330 Ave. of the Americas, 26th Floor
New York, NY 10019
Tel: (212) 969-9940
Fax: (212) 969-9942
Email: bacc@ix.netcom.com
www.belcham.org

WORLD TRADE CENTERS IN BELGIUM

World Trade Centers usually include many foreign companies operating in the country.

**The World Trade Center Association
of Antwerp**
Regus Center, Koningin Astridplein 1
B-2018 Antwerpen, Belgium

Tel: : [32] (3) 206 18 50
Fax : [32] (3) 206 18 80
Email: wtca@glo.be

World Trade Center Association Brussels
boulevard Emile Jacqmain 162, Boite 12
B-1210 Brussels, Belgium
Tel.: [32] (2) 203 04 00

Fax: [32] (2) 203 12 82
Email: wtc.brussels@pophost.eunet.be
http://brussels.wtc.be

OTHER INFORMATIONAL ORGANIZATIONS

Foreign government missions in the U.S. such as tourist and trade offices can furnish visas and information on work permits and other important regulations. They may also offer economic and business information about the country.

Belgian National Tourist Office
780 Third Avenue, Suite 1501
New York, NY 10017
Tel.: (212) 758-8130

Fax: (212) 355-7675
Email: info@visitbelgium.com
www.visitbelgium.com

BUSINESS DIRECTORIES

Although not always easy to find, business directories can prove invaluable in the international job search. Most directories list company names, addresses, products, and phone numbers. Some directories include executive names and titles and financial information about the company. These sources provide you with the names of the people to contact for employment information as well as financial data, which can tell you how strong a company's position in a country may be.

ABC Belge Pour le Commerce et l'Industrie. Published annually in French and Dutch (with some English) by ABC Belge Pour le Commerce et l'Industrie CV, Doornveld 1 B28, B-1731 Asse, Belgium; email: abc-belux@euronet.de; www.abc-d.be. Covers over 20,000 manufacturers, traders, and business-service providers in Belgium.

AMCHAM Membership Directory. Published annually by the American Chamber of Commerce in Belgium, 50 avenue des Arts, Boite 5, B-1000 Brussels, Belgium; email: gch@posti.amcham.be.

Belgian Export Register. Published by the Federation des Chambres de Commerce Belgas a l'Etranger, 8 rue des Sols, B-1000 Brussels, Belgium. Lists leader exporters and organizations aiding exporters.

Dun's 15,000 Largest Companies–Belgium. Dun & Bradstreet Information Services, Dun & Bradstreet Company, 3 Sylvan Way, Parsippany, NJ 07054-3896. Covers 15,000 enterprises in Belgium and Luxembourg, including financial data and key personnel.

Kompass Belgium. Published annually in French and Flemish (with multi-lingual product headings) by Editus Belgium SA, 256 avenue Moliere, B-1000 Brussels, Belgium; email: editus@kompass.de; www.kompass.com. Available in the U.S. from IPC Business Press, 205 East 42nd Street, New York, NY 10017. Lists 30,000 manufacturers, distributors, and service companies.

Quoted Companies on the Brussels & Antwerp Stock Exchange. Published by DAFSA-Belgique SA, rue Ginestell, B-1030 Brussels, Belgium. Lists companies with shares traded on the Antwerp and Brussels stock exchange.

U.S.-Belgium Trade Directory. Published during odd years by the Belgian-American Chamber of Commerce in the U.S., 350 Fifth Avenue, Suite 703, New York, NY 10118. Covers firms in the U.S. and Belgium that are interested in trading and investing in Luxembourg, Belgium, and the U.S.

AMERICAN COMPANIES IN BELGIUM

The following companies are classified by business area: Banking and Finance; Industrial Manufacturing; Retailing and Wholesaling; and Service Industries. Company information includes firm name, address, phone and fax number, specific business, and American parent company. Your chances of achieving employment abroad are substantially better if you contact the subsidiary company in Europe rather than the parent company in the U.S.

BANKING AND FINANCE

Alexander & Alexander Belgium, SA
avenue Louise 225, Boite 1
B-1050 Brussels, Belgium
Tel.: [32] (2) 640 6320
(Insurance)
Alexander & Alexander Services Inc.

Bank of America National Trust & Savings Association
Uitbreidingstraat 180
B-2600 Antwerp, Belgium
Tel.: [32] (3) 280 4211
Fax: [32] (3) 239 6109
(Bank)
Bankamerica Corp., New York

The Chase Manhattan Bank, N.A.
avenue Louise 326, 9th Floor
B-1050 Brussels, Belgium
Tel.: [32] (2) 629 58 11
Fax: [32] (2) 629 58 50
(Bank)
Chase Manhattan Corp., New York

CIGNA Insurance Company of Europe SA NV
rue Belliard 9-11
B-1040 Brussels, Belgium
Tel.: [32] (2) 516 97 11
Fax: [32] (2) 513 08 84
(Insurance)
CIGNA Corp.

Citibank N.A.
boulevard Général Jacques 263
B-1050 Brussels, Belgium
Tel.: [32] (2) 626 51 47
Fax: [32] (2) 626 56 17
(Bank)
Citibank, New York

Diners Club Benelux SA
boulevard Emile Jacqmain 151
B-1210 Brussels, Belgium
Tel.: [32] (2) 206 95 11
Fax: [32] (2) 206 99 99
(Credit card finance)
Diners Club

Morgan JP (Belgium) SA NV
avenue des Arts 36
B-1040 Brussels, Belgium
Tel.: [32] (2) 508 82 11
Fax: [32] (2) 508 84 34
(Financial services)
J.P. Morgan & Company, Inc.

INDUSTRIAL MANUFACTURING

Baxter SA
boulevard René Branquart 80
B-7860 Lessines, Belgium
Tel.: [32] (68) 27 22 11
Fax: [32] (68) 33 53 91
(Pharmaceuticals)
Baxter International Inc.

Bell Telephone Manufacturing Company NV
Francis Wellesplein 1
B-2018 Antwerp, Belgium
Tel.:[32] (3) 240 40 11
Fax: [32] (3) 240 99 99

(Telecommunications equipment and systems)
American Telephone and Telegraph

Caterpillar Belgium SA
avenue des Etats Unis 1
B-6041 Charleroi (Gosselies), Belgium
Tel.: [32] (71) 25 21 11
Fax: [32] (71) 25 29 49
(Earth-moving machinery)
Caterpillar Inc.

Champion Spark Plug Europe SA
Kosterstraat 209
B-1920 Machelen (Diegem), Belgium

Tel.: [32] (2) 723 28 11
Fax: [32] (2) 720 73 25
(Ignition equipment, wipers, filters)
Champion Spark Plug Inc.

Clark Equipment Belgium NV
Ten Briele 3
B-8200 Sint-Michiels, Belgium
Tel.: [32] (50) 40 22 11
Fax: [32] (50) 40 24 00
(Industrial machinery)
Clark Equipment Co.

Coca-Cola Beverages Belgium SA
Chaussée de Mons 1424
B-1070 Brussels, Belgium
Tel.: [32] (2) 529 18 19
Fax: [32] (2) 529 15 45
(Soft drinks)
The Coca-Cola Co.

Crown Cork Company (Belgium) NA
Merkemsesteenweg 148
B-2100 Deurne, Belgium
Tel.: [32] (3) 360 48 11
Fax: [32] (3) 325 82 20
(Packaging and closures)
Crown Cork & Seal Co.

Cyanamic Benelux SA
rue du Bosquet 15
B-1348 Mont-Saint-Guibert, Belgium
Tel.: [32] (10) 47 17 11
Fax: [32] (10) 47 18 70
(Pharmaceuticals and chemicals)
American Cyanamid Co.

Dow Corning Europe
rue Général de Gaulle 62
B-1310 La Hulpe, Belgium
Tel.: [32] (2) 655 21 11
Fax: [32] (2) 655 20 01
(Silicone products)
Dow Corning Corp.

DuPont de Nemours (Belgium)
Antoon Spinoystraat 6, Industriezone
B-2800 Mechelen, Belgium
Tel.: [32] (15) 40 14 11
Fax: [32] (15) 40 14 07
(Chemicals)
E.I. DuPont de Nemours & Co.

Duracell Batteries NV
Nijverheidslaan 7
B-3220 Aarschot, Belgium
Tel.: [32] (16) 55 20 11
Fax: [32] (16) 55 20 10

(Electrical components)
Duracell Inc.

Esso Belgium
Polderdijkweg 3
B-2030 Antwerp, Belgium
Tel.: [32] (3) 543 31 11
Fax: [32] (3) 543 34 95
(Petroleum products)
Exxon Corp.

Ethyl SA
avenue Louise 523, Boite 19
B-1050 Brussels, Belgium
Tel.: [32] (2) 642 44 11
Fax: [32] (2) 648 43 36
(Chemicals and petroleum products)
Ethyl Corp.

European Biscuit Holding BV
Leuvensesteenweg 262
B-1800 Vilvoorde, Belgium
Tel.: [32] (2) 252 04 60
Fax: [32] (2) 252 24 99
(Food products)
Campbell Soup Co.

General Motors Continental
Noorderlaan 75
B-2030 Antwerp, Belgium
Tel.: [32] (3) 543 51 11
(Automobiles)
General Motors Corp.

Hewlett Packard Belgium
boulevard de la Woluwe 100-102
B-1200 Brussels, Belgium
Tel.: [32] (2) 778 31 11
Fax: [32] (2) 763 06 13
(Electronic equipment)
Hewlett-Packard

Janssen Pharmaceutica NV
Turnhoutsebaan 30
B-2340 Beerse, Belgium
Tel.: [32] (14) 60 21 11
Fax: [32] (13) 60 28 41
(Pharmaceuticals)
Johnson & Johnson

Kraft General Foods SA
Riverside Business Park
boulevard International 55
B-1070 Brussels, Belgium
Tel.: [32] (2) 526 98 11
Fax: [32] (2) 526 98 98
Kraft General Foods International

Krafts Jacobs Suchard
Brusselsesteenweg 450
B-1500 Halle, Belgium
Tel.: [32] (2) 362 31 11
Fax: [32] (2) 360 38 01
(Chocolate and coffee products)
General Foods

Lee Europe NV
Industriepark Noord 29
B-9100 Sint-Niklaas, Belgium
Tel.: [32] (3) 780 06 11
Fax: [32] (3) 788 04 34
(Clothing)
VF Corp.

Levi Strauss & Co. Europe SA
avenue Louise 489
B-1050 Brussels, Belgium
Tel.: [32] (2) 641 60 11
Fax: [32] (2) 640 29 97
(Clothing)
Levi Strauss & Co.

Master Foods SA
Vorstlaan 100, Boite 7
B-1170 Brussels, Belgium
Tel.: [32] (2) 712 72 22
Fax: [32] (2) 721 49 32
(Confectionery)
Mars Inc.

Memorex SA
rue Colonel Bourg 105a
B-1140 Brussels, Belgium
Tel.: [32] (2) 73 68 930
Fax: [32] (2) 73 35 825
(Data processing products)
Burroughs Corp.

Monroe Belgium
Industriezone 1
B-3800 Sint-Truiden, Belgium
Tel.: [32] (11) 70 31 11
Fax: [32] (11) 70 33 06
(Auto parts)
Monroe Auto Equipment Co.

Monsanto Europe SA
avenue de Terveuren 270-272
B-1150 Brussels, Belgium
Tel.: [32] (2) 761 41 11
Fax: [32] (2) 761 40 40
(Chemicals)
Monsanto Co.

Owens-Corning Belgium SA
chausée de la Hulpe 178
B-1170 Brussels, Belgium
Tel.: [32] (2) 674 82 11

Fax: [32] (2) 660 85 72
(Fiber products)
Owens-Corning Fiberglass Corp.

Philip Morris Belgium SA
boulevard du Soverain 24
B-1170 Brussels, Belgium
Tel.: [32] (2) 674 18 11
Fax: [32] (2) 673 36 70
(Tobacco products)
Philip Morris Inc.

Procter & Gamble Benelux SA
Temselaan 100
B-1853 Strombeek-Bever, Belgium
Tel.: [32] (2) 456 38 46
Fax: [32] (2) 456 21 44
(Cleaning and personal products)
Procter & Gamble Co.

Raychem NV
Diestsesteenweg 692
B-3010 Kessel-Lo, Belgium
Tel.: [32] (16) 35 10 11
Fax: [32] (16) 35 18 74
(Plastics)
Raychem corp.

Samsonite Europe NV
Westerring 17
Industrieterrein Ring 2
B-9700 Heurne, Belgium
Tel.: [32] (55) 33 32 11
Fax: [32] (55) 31 56 60
(Luggage)
Samsonite Corp.

Scott Continental SA
Stocletlaan 3
B-2570 Duffel, Belgium
Tel.: [32] (15) 30 06 11
Fax: [32] (15) 67 51 534
(Paper products)
Scott Paper Co.

SmithKline Beecham Biologicals SA
rue de Tilleal 13
B-1332 Genval, Belgium
Tel.: [32] (2) 656 21 11
Fax: [32] (2) 656 2099
(Pharmaceuticals)
SmithKline Beecham International Corp.

Upjohn NV
Rijksweg 12
B-2870 Puurs, Belgium
Tel.: [32] (3) 890 92 11
Fax: [32] (3) 889 65 32
(Pharmaceuticals)
Upjohn Co.

RETAILING AND WHOLESALING

Allied Signal Europe
Haasrode Research Park Grauwmeer 1
B-3001 Heverlee, Belgium
Tel.: [32] (16) 21 12 11
Fax: [32] (16) 40 00 33
(Chemicals)
Allied-Signal Inc.

Black & Decker (Belgium) NV
Weihoek 1 Industrieterrein Zaventem Zuid
B-1930 Zaventem, Belgium
Tel.: [32] (2) 719 07 11
Fax: [32] (2) 721 40 45
(Hand held power tools)
Black & Decker Manufacturing Co.

Data General SA
boulevard Souverain 165, Boite 11
B-1160 Brussels, Belgium
Tel.: [32] (2) 674 84 11
(Electronic equipment)
Data General

John Deere Intercontinental Ltd. SA
avenue de Broqueville 270, Boite 10
B-1200 Brussels, Belgium
Tel.: [32] (2) 661 06 11
(Industrial and farm equipment)
Deere & Co.

Digital Equipment SA
rue de L'Aéronef 1
B-1140 Brussels, Belgium
Tel.: [32] (2) 244 71 11
Fax: [32] (2) 242 75 60
(Computers)
Digital Equipment Corp.

Fisher Price NV
Trademart 202
B-1020 Brussels, Belgium
Tel.: [32] (2) 478 59 41
Fax: [32] (2) 478 43 27
(Toys)
Fisher Price Inc.

Ford Werke AG Fabrieken te Genk
Henri Fordlaan 6
Postbus 21
B-3600 Genk, Belgium
Tel.: [32] (11) 61 61 11
Fax: [32] (11) 61 90 90
(Motor vehicles)
Ford Motor Co.

Honeywell Europe SA
avenue du Bourget 1
B-1140 Brussels, Belgium
Tel.: [32] (2) 728 27 11
Fax: [32] (2) 728 24 68
(Office machines & equipment)
Honeywell, Inc.

IBM Belgium SA
Square Victoria Regina 1
B-1210 Brussels, Belgium
Tel.: [32] (2) 214 21 11
Fax: [32] (2) 225 34 78
(Data processing equipment)
IBM World Trade Europe/Middle East/
Africa Corp.

Mobil Plastics Europe Inc
Aone de Parc Industriel Latour
B-6761 Latour, Belgium
Tel.: [32] (63) 21 32 11
Fax: [32] (63) 21 34 24
(Plastics, petrochemicals)
Mobil Plastics Europe Inc.

Motorola SA NV
Excelsiorlaan 89
B-1930 Zavenem, Belgium
Tel.: [32] (2) 718 54 11
Fax: [32] (2) 718 56 33
(Electronic equipment)
Motorola Inc.

Pfizer SA
Rue Leon Theodor 102
B-1090 Brussels, Belgium
Tel.: [32] (2) 421 15 11
Fax: [32] (2) 421 17 98
(Pharmaceuticals and chemicals)
Pfizer International Corp.

Quaker Oats Belgium BV
Assesteenweg 39
B-1730 Mollem, Belgium
Tel.: [32] (2) 452 21 00
Fax: [32] (2) 452 22 22
(Cereals and feedstuffs)
The Quaker Oats Co.

Rank Xerox NV SA
Wezembeekstraat 5
B-1930 Zaventem, Belgium
Tel.: [32] (2) 716 68 00
Fax: [32] (2) 716 65 59
(Copier equipment)
Xerox Corp.

SECA NV (Société Européenne des Carburants)
Mechelsesteenweg 520
B-1800 Vilvoorde, Belgium

Tel.: [32] (2) 254 15 11
Fax: [32] (2) 254 16 71
(Diesel and fuel oils)
Conoco Inc.

Texaco Belgium SA
avenue Arnaud Fraiteur 25
B-1050 Brussels, Belgium
Tel.: [32] (2) 639 91 11
Fax: [32] (2) 639 99 11

SERVICE INDUSTRIES

Air Express Intl.
Belgium NV
Nationale Luchthaven Brucargo Gebouw
720
B-1931 Zaventem, Belgium
Tel.: [32] (2) 752 02 11
Fax: [32] (2) 751 93 83
(Air courier)
Air Express International

Dun & Bradstreet—Eurinform SA
avenue des Pléades 73
B-1200 Brussels, Belgium
Tel.: [32] (2) 778 72 11
Fax: [32] (2) 778 72 72
(Business information services)
Dun & Bradstreet Corp.

A.T. Kearney Inc.
avenue des Arts 46
B-1040 Brussels, Belgium
Tel.: [32] (2) 504 48 11
Fax: [32] (2) 511 01 03
(Executive search)
A.T. Kearny

Korn/Ferry International
avenue Louise 523, Boite 25
B-1050 Brussels, Belgium

(Petroleum products)
Texaco Inc.

Unisys Belgium SA
avenue du Bourget 20
B-1130 Brussels, Belgium
Tel.: [32] (2) 728 07 11
Fax: [32] (2) 726 68 10
(Electronic equipment)
Unisys Corp.

Tel.: [32] (2) 640 32 40
Fax: [32] (2) 640 83 82
(Executive search)
Korn/Ferry International

McKinsey & Co.
avenue Louise 480, Boite 22
B-1050 Brussels, Belgium
Tel.: [32] (2) 645 42 11
Fax: [32] (2) 646 45 48
(Consulting)
McKinsey & Co.

Ogilvy & Mather SA
boulevard l'Impétrice 13
B-1000 Brussels, Belgium
Tel.: [32] (2) 545 6500
Fax: [32] (2) 545 6501
(Advertising)
Ogilvy Group Inc.

Price Waterhouse
boulevard de la Woluwe 62
B-1200 Brussels, Belgium
Tel.: [32] (2) 773 14 11
(Accounting)
Price Waterhouse

EUROPEAN COMPANIES IN BELGIUM

The following are several major non-American firms operating in Belgium. These selected companies can be either domestic or foreign but are usually European companies. Such companies will generally hire their own nationals first but may employ Americans.

BANKING AND FINANCE

ASLK—CG ER Bank
rue du Fossé-aux-loups
48 Wolvengracht
B-1000 Brussels, Belgium

Tel.: [32] (2) 213 61 11
Fax: [32] (2) 213 89 91
(Savings bank)

Agricom SA
rue Royale 53
B-1000 Brussels, Belgium
Tel.: [32] (2) 507 02 11
Fax: [32] (2) 507 04 46
(Financial)

Assurances Groupe Josi Sa
rue Col. Bourg 135
B-1140 Brussels, Belgium
Tel.: [32] (2) 730 12 11
Fax: [32] (2) 730 12 51
(Insurance and banking)

Bacob Savings Bank SC
rue de Treves 25
B-1040 Brussels, Belgium
Tel.: [32] (2) 285 20 20
Fax: [32] (2) 230 71 78
(Bank)

Banque Bruxelles Lambert
avenue Marnix 24
B-1050 Brussels, Belgium

Tel.: [32] (2) 547 21 11
Fax: [32] (2) 517 24 03

Banque Nationale de Belgique SA
boulevard de Berlaimont 14
B-1000 Brussels, Belgium
Tel.: [32] (2) 221 21 11
Fax: [32] (2) 221 31 01
(Central bank)

Generale Bank
Montagne du Parc 3
B-1000 Brussels, Belgium
Tel.: [32] (2) 516 21 11
Fax: [32] (2) 516 42 22
(Commercial bank)

Kredietbank NV
Arenbergstraat 7
B-1000 Brussels, Belgium
Tel.: [32] (2) 546 41 11
Fax: [32] (2) 517 42 09

INDUSTRIAL MANUFACTURING

ACEC-Union Miniere SA
avenue East Rousseau
B-6001 Marcinelle, Belgium
Tel.: [32] (71) 44 63 11
Fax: [32] (71) 43 93 79
(Metals)

AGFA-Gevaert Group
Septestraat 27
B-2640 Mortsel, Belgium
Tel.: [32] (3) 444 21 11
Fax: [32] (3) 444 70 94
(Chemical and electronic imaging systems)
Bayer AG

Bayer Antwerpen NV
Scheldelaan 420
Haven 507
B-2040 Antwerp, Belgium
Tel.: [32] (3) 540 30 11
Fax: [32] (3) 540 39 58
(Chemicals)
Bayer AG

Belgian Shell SA/NV
Cantersteen 47
B-1000 Brussels, Belgium
Tel.: [32] (2) 508 91 11
Fax: [32] (2) 511 05 71

(Petroleum products)
Royal Dutch Petroleum, Netherlands

Bell Telephone Manufacturing Company NV
Francis Wellesplein 1
B-2018 Antwerp, Belgium
Tel.: [32] (3) 240 40 11
Fax: [32] (3) 240 99 99
(Telecommunications equipment)

Cockerill Sambre SA
Chaussee de la Hulpe 187
B-1170 Brussels, Belgium
Tel.: [32] (2) 679 92 11
Fax: [32] (2) 660 36 40
(Iron and steel)

Douwe Egberts NV
Potaarde Z/N
B-1850 Grimbergen, Belgium
Tel.: [32] (2) 260 06 11
Fax: [32] (2) 260 08 08
(Coffee, tea, snack foods)
Sara Lee NV, Netherlands

Electrabel
boulevard du Regent 8
B-1000 Brussels, Belgium
Tel.: [32] (2) 518 63 33
Fax: [32] (2) 511 50 20
(Energy distribution)

Fina Borealis NV
Scheldelaan 10
B-2030 Antwerp, Belgium
Tel.: [32] (3) 545 20 11
Fax: [32] (3) 541 21 13
(Petroleum products)

Gechem SA
avenue de Broqueville 12
B-1150 Brussels, Belgium
Tel.: [32] (2) 762 16 72
Fax: [32] (2) 762 26 90
(Polyurethane and organic products)

Interbrew SA
Vaartstraat 94
B-3000 Leuven, Belgium
Tel.: [32] (16) 24 71 11
Fax: [32] (16) 24 74 07
(Beverages)

L'Oreal Belgilux SA
rue du Peuplier 12
B-1000 Brussels, Belgium
Tel.: [32] (2) 210 05 11
Fax: [32] (2) 210 05 70
(Cosmetics)

New Holland NV
Leon Clauysstraat 3A
B-8210 Zedelgem, Belgium
Tel.: [32] (50) 25 31 11
Fax: [32] (50) 20 18 04
(Agricultural equipment)

Petrofina SA
rue de l'Industrie 52
B-1040 Brussels, Belgium
Tel.: [32] (2) 288 32 35
Fax: [32] (2) 288 33 73
(Petroleum products)

Siemens Nixdorf Informati SA
Chaussée de Charleroi 110-116
B-1060 Brussels, Belgium
Tel.: [32] (2) 536 81 11
Fax: [32] (2) 536 81 12
(Electromechanical equipment)

Solvay SA
rue du Prince Albert 33
B-1150 Brussels, Belgium
Tel.: [32] (2) 509 69 09
Fax: [32] (2) 509 72 40
(Chemicals)

RETAILING AND WHOLESALING

BASF Belgium
venue Hamoir 14
B-1180 Brussels, Belgium
Tel.: [32] (2) 373 23 51
Fax: [32] (2) 375 10 42
(Chemicals and plastics)

BP Belgium, NV/SA
Haven 1053
Nieuwe Weg 1
B-2070 Zwijndrecht, Belgium
Tel.: [32] (3) 250 21 11
Fax: [32] (3) 219 59 09
(Petroleum products)
British Petroleum Company

Delhaize Fréres & Cie "Le Lion" SA
rue Osseghem 53
P.O. Box 60

B-1080 Brussels, Belgium
Tel.: [32] (2) 412 21 11
Fax: [32] (2) 412 21 94
(Retail chain stores)

Fradis SA
chaussée de La Hulpe 150, Boite 11
B-1170 Brussels, Belgium
Tel.: [32] (2) 673 60 61
Fax: [32] (2) 660 85 47
(Department stores)

GIB Group
avenue Des Olympiades 20
B-1140 Brussels, Belgium
Tel.: [32] (2) 729 20 30
Fax: [32] (2) 729 20 96
(Supermarkets, hypermarkets)

SERVICE INDUSTRIES

Belgacom
boulevard Emile Jacqmain 151
B-1030 Brussels, Belgium
Tel.: [32] (2) 202 41 11
Fax: [32] (2) 202 96 32
(Telecommunications)

ITT Promedia NV
De Keyserlei 5, Bus 7
B-2018 Antwerp, Belgium
Tel.: [32] (3) 223 52 11
Fax: [32] (3) 223 53 15
(Advertising, public relations, publishing)

Sabena Belgian World Airlines
rue Cardinal Mercier 35
B-1000 Brussels, Belgium
Tel.: [32] (2) 723 31 11
Fax: [32] (2) 509 23 99
(International air services)

SAS International Hotels
Boulevard du Regent 45
B-1000 Brussels, Belgium
Tel.: [32] (2) 514 50 55
Fax: [32] (2) 514 57 14
(Hotel administration)

INTERNATIONAL NON-PROFIT EMPLOYERS IN BELGIUM

Amnesty International
rue Berckmans 9
B-1060 Brussels, Belgium
Tel.: [32] (2) 537 1302

North Atlantic Treaty Organization
B-1110 Brussels, Belgium
Tel.: [32] (2) 241 0040

Greenpeace
avenue de Tervueren 36
B-1040 Brussels, Belgium
Tel.: [32] (2) 736 9929

INTERNATIONAL SCHOOLS IN BELGIUM

The Antwerp International School
Veltwijcklaan 180
B-2180 Ekeren, Belgium
Tel.: [32] (3) 543 93 00
Fax: [32] (3) 541 82 01
Email: ais@ais-antwerp.be
www.ais-antwerp.be

The International School of Brussels
Kattenberg-Boitsfort 19
B-1170 Brussels, Belgium
Tel.: [32] (2) 661 42 11
Fax: [32] (2) 661 42 00
Email: admissions@isb.be
www.isb.be

British School of Brussels
Leuvensesteenweg 19
B-3080 Tervuren, Belgium
Tel.: [32] (2) 766 04 30
Fax: [32] (2) 767 80 70

St. John's International School
Drève Richelle 146
B-1410 Waterloo, Belgium
Tel.: [32] (2) 352 06 10
Fax: [32] (2) 352 06 20/30
Email: admissions@stjohns.be
www.stjohns.be

Luxembourg

MAJOR EMPLOYMENT CENTER: Luxembourg

MAJOR BUSINESS LANGUAGES: French, German

LANGUAGE SKILL INDEX: Many Luxembourg citizens speak English, but you will please natives by knowing a few words of Letzburgish, which is similar to German. Expect to conduct business in German. Government affairs are conducted in French

CURRENCY: Euro; the Luxembourg franc will remain the currency in circulation until 2002

TELEPHONE COUNTRY CODE: 352

TIME ZONE: EST+6

PUNCTUALITY INDEX: Punctuality is expected

AVERAGE DAILY TEMPERATURE: January, 38°F; July, 62°F

AVERAGE NUMBER OF DAYS WITH RAIN: January, 14; July, 13

BEST BET FOR EMPLOYMENT:

  FOR STUDENTS: Apply to IAESTE

  PERMANENT JOBS: Banking and insurance

CHANCE OF FINDING A JOB: Depends upon your skill and experience in international trade

TRIVIA: Like the Belgians, the people of Luxembourg like to kiss as a greeting; however, they only kiss twice and don't kiss just anyone

The Grand Duchy of Luxembourg is a small country in western Europe bordered by Belgium to the west, Germany to the east, and France to the south. Luxembourg has about 370,000 people living on 1,000 square miles of land. This gives the Grand Duchy a very urban population density of 370 people per square mile. Luxembourg City is the capital and only major city, with a population of only 86,000 people.

Luxembourg was founded circa 963 and ruled by the House of Luxembourg, beginning in 1060. Between the 15th and the 18th centuries the heavily fortified city was ruled by Spain, Burgundy, France, and Austria. In 1815 it was declared a Grand Duchy of the Netherlands. This small country was invaded by Germany in both world wars. The Grand Duchy's neutrality was abandoned in 1948, when custom frontiers between Belgium and the Netherlands were removed, creating Benelux.

The present head of state is Grand Duke Jean D'Aviano, who came to power after his mother's abdication in 1964. The prime minister is head of the government. Luxembourg's legislative body is the Chamber of Deputies, consisting of 60 members elected every 5 years. The major parties in the Chamber of Deputies are the Christian Socialists, the Workers-Socialist Party, and the Democratic Party. Despite a large influx of foreign workers, the social and political systems are quite stable, in part because most of the foreign residents are Roman Catholics and western Europeans.

Normal banking hours are from 9:30 a.m. to 5:00 p.m., Monday through Friday. Shops often stay open until 6:00 p.m. on weekdays and until noon on Saturdays. Most stores close for lunch from noon to 2:00 p.m.

Current Economic Climate

Luxembourg is an affluent nation with a highly developed industrial sector. Luxembourg's labor force is concentrated in industry and commerce (42%) and in service industries such as hotels (45%). Less than 1% of the labor force works in the agriculture sector. Luxembourg's principal industries are steel, chemicals, beer, tires, and tobacco. Livestock, wine, and dairy products are the leading agricultural products. The service sector is dominated by the banking system, which has stringent secrecy laws that make it a significant international banking center. The service sector also includes staff members of the European Union, since many major offices of that organization are located in Luxembourg. Most trade is conducted with the Netherlands and Belgium, as well as the rest of the E.U. and with the U.S.

Using the phone, fax, and Internet
There are no telephone area codes in Luxembourg. Faxes can be sent from post offices. Public Email facilities are scarce, and you are likely to find cybercafes only in Luxembourg City.

Getting Around in Luxembourg

Eurail and InterRail passes are accepted throughout Luxembourg. Trains and buses provide adequate transportation for traveling over Luxembourg's 2,600 square km.

Employment Regulations and Outlook for Americans

The Centre d'Information pour Jeunes (see "Other Informational Organizations," below, for contact information) distributes a free visitor's guide, *Focus on Luxembourg*, that includes a section on working in Luxembourg. Jobs are limited, but the casual job hunter may have luck at hotels. The Luxembourg Embassy will send you a list of hotels upon request. Luxembourg is a good place for a polyglot to work, and fluency in English may work to your advantage. As with other E.U. countries, Luxembourg requires a work permit—presented upon arriving in the country—in order to work legally. Permits can be arranged through the company or organization you plan to work for. Unfortunately for outsiders, citizens of E.U. nations take priority over foreigners in job placement.

Short-term and Temporary Work

In addition to hospitality work, a good bet for casual jobs in Luxembourg is to work as an au pair.

Luxembourg-Accueil Informations
10 Bisserwée
L-1238 Luxembourg City, Luxembourg
Tel.: [352] 24 17 17
Arranges au pair positions in Luxembourg.

Internship Program

For students interested in professional technical internships, IASTE presents the best opportunities.

IASTE
10400 Little Patuxent Parkway, Suite 250 L
Columbia, MD 21044-3510
Tel.: (410) 997-3068
Fax: (410) 997-5186
Email: iaste@aipt.org

www.aipt.org/iaste.html
Arranges reciprocal internship exchanges among 63 member countries for students in engineering, architecture, and the sciences.

NEWSPAPER IN LUXEMBOURG

Luxemburger Wort (German/French)
2 rue Christophe Plantin,
L-2988 Luxembourg-Gasperich, Luxembourg
Tel.: [352] 49 93 1
Fax: [352] 49 93 386

Resources for Further Information

EMBASSIES AND CONSULAR OFFICES

American embassies and consulates have commercial and/or economic sections that can provide you with business information and explain aspects of the local economy. Inquiries about business opportunities should be addressed either to "Commercial Officer" or "Commercial Section," followed by the appropriate street address.

Representation of Luxembourg in the United States

Embassy of Luxembourg
2200 Massachusetts Avenue NW
Washington, DC 20008
Tel.: (202) 265-4171
Fax: (202) 328-8270

Consulate General of Luxembourg
1 Sansome Street, Suite 830
San Francisco, CA 94104-4429
Tel.: (415) 788-0816

Representation of the United States in Luxembourg

American Embassy
22 boulevard Emmanuel-Servais
L-2535 Luxembourg City, Luxembourg
Tel.: [352] 46 0123
Fax: [352] 46 1401

CHAMBER OF COMMERCE

Chambers of commerce consist of firms in both countries interested in international trade. These are appropriate companies to initially target in the job search.

Luxembourg Chamber of Commerce
7, rue Alcide de Gasperi
L-2951 Kirchberg, Luxembourg
Tel./Fax: [352] 43 17 56
www.aalux/amcham.org

WORLD TRADE CENTER IN LUXEMBOURG

World Trade Centers usually include many foreign companies operating in the country.

World Trade Center Luxembourg
6-10 place de la Gare, 4th Floor
L-1616 Luxembourg City, Luxembourg
Tel.: (352) 40 86 54
Fax: (352) 40 86 08
Email: rorelux@pt.lu

OTHER INFORMATIONAL ORGANIZATIONS

Foreign government missions in the U.S. such as tourist and trade offices can furnish visas and information on work permits and other important regulations. They may also offer economic and business information about the country.

Centre Information Jeunes (CIJ)
76 boulevard de la Pétrusse
L-2320 Luxembourg City, Luxembourg
Tel.: [352] 40 55 50
Fax: [352] 40 55 56

**Luxembourg Board of Economic
Development**
17 Beekman Place

New York, NY 10022-8003
Tel.: (212) 888-6664
Fax: (212) 888-6116

Luxembourg National Tourist Office
P.O. Box 1001
L-1010 Luxembourg City, Luxembourg
Tel.: [352] 42 82 82 20
Fax: [352] 42 82 82 30
www.etat.lu/tourism

BUSINESS DIRECTORIES

Although not always easy to find, business directories can prove invaluable in the international job search. Most directories list company names, addresses, products, and phone numbers. Some directories include executive names and titles and financial information about the company. These sources provide you with the names of the people to contact for employment information as well as financial data, which can tell you how strong a company's position in a country may be.

ABC Luxembourgeois pour le Commerce et l'Industrie. Published annually in French by ABC Belge pour le Commerce et l'Industrie BV, Doornveld 1 B28, B-1731 Asse, Belgium; email: abc-belux@euronet.de; www.abc-d.be. Lists 1,400 manufacturers, traders, and service companies in Luxembourg.

Dun's 15,000 Largest Companies–Belgium. Dun & Bradstreet Information Services, Dun & Bradstreet Company, 3 Sylvan Way, Parsippany, NJ 07054-3896. Covers 15,000 enterprises in Belgium and Luxembourg, including financial data and key personnel.

L'Industrie Luxembourgeoise. Available from the Federation des Industries Luxembourgeois, 7 rue Alcide de Gaspari, P.O. Box 1304, L01304, Luxembourg, Luxembourg. Lists approximately 320 leading industrial companies.

Inter Region. Published annually in French and German by Editus SARL, rue Michel Rodange 28, L-2340 Luxembourg, Luxembourg. Covers 15,000 top companies in the Saar-Lor-Lux area (southern Belgium, Saarland, Trier, Luxembourg, and Lorraine).

Kompass Luxembourg. Published annually by Editus SARL, rue Michel Rodange 28, L-2430 Luxembourg, Luxembourg. Contains information on the top 2,100 service companies, distributors, and manufacturers in Luxembourg.

AMERICAN COMPANIES IN LUXEMBOURG

The following companies are classified by business area: Banking and Finance; Manufacturing, Wholesaling, and Retailing; and Service Industries. Company information includes firm name, address, phone and fax number, specific business, and American parent company. Your chances of achieving employment abroad are substantially better if you contact the subsidiary company in Europe rather than the parent company in the U.S.

BANKING AND FINANCE

American Express Bank, SA
34 avenue de la Porte-Neuve
L-2227 Luxembourg, Luxembourg
Tel.: [352] 471 7541
Fax: [352] 472 419
(Joint stock bank)
American Express Holdings, Inc.

Bank of America International SA
35 boulevard Royal
L-2449 Luxembourg, Luxembourg
Tel.: [352] 47 49 20

Fax: [352] 46 03 86
(Bank)
Bank of America

Chase Manhattan Bank Luxembourg, SA
47 boulevard Royale
L-2012 Luxembourg, Luxembourg
Tel.: [352] 213 83
Fax: [352] 245 90
(Commercial bank)
Chase Manhattan Overseas Corp.

MANUFACTURING, WHOLESALING, AND RETAILING

Applied Industrial Materials Luxembourg SA
(AIMCOR)
3-5 Place Winston Churchill 3-5
L-1340 Luxembourg, Luxembourg
Tel.: [352] 45 21 41
Fax: [352] 45 27 76
(Diversified fuels)
Aimcor International Inc.

DuPont de Nemours (Luxembourg) SA
L-2984 Luxembourg, Luxembourg
Tel.: [352] 47901
(Chemical products)
E. I. DuPont de Nemours & Co.

SERVICE COMPANY

Arthur Andersen
6 rue Jean Monnet
L-2180 Luxembourg, Luxembourg
Tel.: [352] 422 23 31

General Motors Luxembourg Operations SA
route de Luxembourg, Boite Postale 29
L-4901 Bascharage, Luxembourg
Tel.: [352] 50181
(Automobile bodies)
General Motors Corp.

Goodyear SA
avenue Gordon Smith
L-7750 Colmar-Berg, Luxembourg
Tel.: [352] 819 91
Fax: [352] 819 92 914
(Tires and inner tubes)
Goodyear Tire & Rubber Co.

Fax: [352] 42 22 32
(Consulting)
Arthur Andersen & Co.

EUROPEAN COMPANIES IN LUXEMBOURG

The following are several major non-American firms operating in the country. These selected companies can be either domestic or foreign, but are usually European companies. Such companies will generally hire their own nationals first but may employ Americans.

BANKING AND FINANCE

Banque & Caisse d'Epargne de l'Etat
1 Place de Metz
L-2954 Luxembourg, Luxembourg
Tel.: [352] 298 51
Fax: [352] 276 87
(Savings bank)

Banque Générale du Luxembourg
27 avenue Monterey
L-2163 Luxembourg, Luxembourg
Tel.: [352] 479 91
Fax: [352] 47 99 25 79
(Commercial bank)

Banque Internationale à Luxembourg SA
69 route d'Esch
1470 Luxembourg, Luxembourg
Tel.: [352] 459 01

Fax: [352] 45 90 20 10
(Commercial bank)

INDUSTRIAL MANUFACTURING

Arbed SA
19 avenue de la Liberte
L-2930 Luxembourg, Luxembourg
Tel.: [352] 479 21
Fax: [352] 47 92 26 58
(Iron and steel)

Metallurgique et Miniere de Rondange-Athus SA
2 rue de l'Industrie, Case Postale 24
L-4801 Rodange, Luxembourg
Tel.: [352] 501 91
Fax: [352] 501 92290
(Iron and steel products)

SERVICE INDUSTRIES

Cargolux Airlines International SA
L-2990 Luxembourg, Luxembourg
Tel.: [352] 421 11

Fax: [352] 43 54 46
(Air cargo transport)

INTERNATIONAL SCHOOL IN LUXEMBOURG

American International School of Luxembourg
188 Avenue de la Faiencerie
L-1511 Luxembourg, Luxembourg
Tel.: [352] 47 00 20

Fax: [352] 46 09 24
Email: admin@aisl.lu
www.restena.lu/aisl

The Netherlands

MAJOR EMPLOYMENT CENTERS: Amsterdam, The Hague, Rotterdam

MAJOR BUSINESS LANGUAGE: Dutch

LANGUAGE SKILL INDEX: English is spoken by most, although Dutch is appreciated

CURRENCY: Euro; the Dutch guilder will remain the currency in circulation until 2002

TELEPHONE COUNTRY CODE: 31

TIME ZONE: EST+6

PUNCTUALITY INDEX: Appointments and punctuality are expected

AVERAGE DAILY TEMPERATURE, HIGH/LOW: January, 40/34°F; July, 69/59°F (The Hague)

AVERAGE NUMBER OF DAYS WITH RAIN: January, 19; July, 13

BEST BET FOR EMPLOYMENT:

  FOR STUDENTS: Apply to IAESTE

  PERMANENT JOBS: International trade and business

CHANCE OF FINDING A JOB: Good, but it takes persistence

TRIVIA: The Dutch are big on formal titles. Use everyone's formal title in greetings and introductions

The Kingdom of the Netherlands lies in northwestern Europe on the North Sea. The country, about half the size of Maine, is one of the smallest and most densely populated in Europe. It is often called Holland after a historic region now a part of the modern nation. Most of the Netherlands consists of flat plains, with an average elevation of just 37 feet above sea level. Much of the country is actually below sea level, protected by an extensive series of dikes.

The Dutch speak their own language and are largely ethnically homogeneous. In terms of religious affiliations, Dutch society is divided between Roman Catholics, over 40% of the population, and Protestants belonging to the Dutch Reformed Church, about 20%. Cleavages in the Netherlands have historically occurred around the religious difference.

Celtic and Germanic tribes inhabited the area when Julius Caesar arrived in 55 B.C. The Netherlands were ruled by the Franks, Burgundy, and the Spanish Hapsburgs. William the Silent, Prince of Orange, led the Union of Utrecht in 1579 and demanded independence from Spain in 1581. In the 17th century, the United Dutch Republic achieved economic, military, and artistic prominence in Europe. Napoleon invaded in 1795, creating the Batavian Republic. Following the Napoleonic Wars, the Netherlands became an independent kingdom, uniting Holland and Belgium. In 1830 Belgium seceded; Luxembourg did the same shortly afterward.

The Netherlands remained neutral in World War I but was invaded by Germany in World War II. The colonial empire faded in 1949, when independence was granted to Indonesia, following a protracted war. Large numbers of people have fled to the Netherlands following the independence of former colonies. The Netherlands is a member of the North Atlantic Treaty Organization and the European Union.

The Netherlands maintains a parliamentary democracy under a constitutional monarchy, headed by Queen Beatrix who assumed the throne in 1980. The country's political scene is characterized by coalition governments pursuing policies of compromise. The main political parties are the socialist PvdA, the Catholic-Protestant CDA, and the conservative Liberal VVD. The current prime minister is Wim Kok.

The Dutch work week starts leisurely at around noon on Monday. For the rest of the week, typical business hours are from 8:30 a.m.–5:30 p.m. On Friday evenings, many retail shops are open until 9:00 p.m.

Current Economic Climate

Despite its size, the Netherlands maintains a strong economy. Per capita income is over $13,000, and inflation remains around 2%. The unemployment rate is under

5%. The country's major industries include machinery, chemicals, petroleum refining, electronics, and metallurgy. The high-tech industry has created most of the new jobs. The Netherlands has a highly developed horticultural industry, and agriculture, especially dairy farming, plays an especially important role in the economy. The Rotterdam harbor, which handles the most shipping tonnage in the world, significantly contributes to the strength of the Dutch economy. Major trading partners are the E.U., especially Germany and Belgium, and the U.S.

THE NETHERLANDS' 10 LARGEST COMPANIES

(1997, composite ranking)
1. Philips Electronics
2. Royal Ahold
3. Royal Dutch Shell
4. Randstad Holding
5. Koninklijke PTT Nederland
6. Akzo Nobel
7. ABN Amro Holding
8. SHV Holdings
9. Vendex International
10. The Rabobank Group

Using the phone, fax, and Internet

In large cities, public phones that accept coins are difficult to find, and it is easier to make phone calls with a purchased phonecard. In local telephone books, similar surnames are listed alphabetically by address, not by initials. Faxes can be sent from public fax machines at post offices. Cybercafes are extremely common in major cities, making it easy to access Email.

Getting Around in the Netherlands

The railway system in Holland is very efficient and covers all parts of the country. With a *strippenkaart*, you can have access to trams, buses, subways, and other public transportation. Eurail and InterRail passes are valid on all trains.

Employment Regulations and Outlook for Americans

As in most E.U. countries, obtaining employment in the Netherlands as a foreigner is very difficult. An application for a residence permit for the purpose of employment should be filed in triplicate with the Consulate-General well in advance. Simultaneously, the employer should apply for an employment permit at the Ministry of Social Affairs and Labour. This should be done at least 30 days before the date of employment. Once the employment permit is issued, the employee will be notified. Applicants should be aware that a working knowledge of Dutch is essential for successfully finding employment in the Netherlands.

Most of the jobs that you would find quickly in Holland are in low-skill, menial positions that the Dutch themselves disdain. The minimum wage is fairly high, but you may forfeit such benefits by working illegally. Temporary work may be found through employment agencies, although their ability to locate work for non-E.U. nationals will be limited. Work is always more difficult to find during August, the student vacation month. Agricultural work, for example, is popular with local youth.

Short-term and Temporary Work

A good bet for temporary jobs in the Netherlands is to work as an au pair.

Au Pair and Activity International
Steentilstraat 25
B-9711 GK Groningen, Netherlands
Tel.: [31] 50 31 30 666
Fax: [31] 31 31 633

Interexchange
161 Sixth Avenue, Suite 902
New York, NY 10013
Email: interex@earthlink.net

Internship Program

Students interested in professional work should apply for technical internships through IASTE.

IASTE
10400 Little Patuxent Parkway, Suite 250 L
Columbia, MD 21044-3510
Tel.: (410) 997-3068
Fax: (410) 997-5186
Email: iaste@aipt.org

www.aipt.org/iaste.html
Arranges reciprocal internship exchanges among 63 member countries for students in engineering, architecture, and the sciences.

Volunteer Opportunities

International Voluntary Service sponsors workcamps for international volunteers during the summer months. Participants might work in construction or forest management, or help with programs for the mentally disabled. Applicants should be between the ages of 18 and 30, and U. S. citizens need to apply through the CIEE in New York.

CIEE
Voluntary Service Department
205 East 42nd Street
New York, NY 10017
Tel.: (800) COUNCIL
Email: info@ciee.org
www.ciee.org

International Voluntary Service—
United States
SCI-USA
Route 2, Box 506
Crozet, VA 22932
Tel.: (804) 823-1826

Arm and leg days in Dutch clinics

Holland's medical system provides sound evidence of an old expat truism: once the novelty of an overseas posting wears off—once you've seen the basic tourist attractions, sampled the local culinary delicacies, and so on—it's the details of everyday living that make a foreign country truly "foreign."

To sign on with a family doctor, you have to be recommended by one of his or her current patients. Once you secure a recommendation, the physician will see you for an interview. It's on the basis of the interview that the doctor decides to accept you as a patient or not.

Hospital outpatient clinics have designated days for dealing with injuries to specific parts of the body. Tuesday, for example, might be arm day. Wednesday might be leg day and Friday, eye day. During my family's year-long assignment in The Hague, my son was receiving physical therapy for a broken arm at the same time that my daughter was recovering from a leg injury. It was quite a drive from our house in a neighboring town to the clinic in the city. But could I take both my son and my daughter on the same day for the sake of convenience? No. Arm day is for arms, leg day is for legs.

There are probably those who would argue that America is, on the whole, an overmedicated society. We found medicine as practiced in the Netherlands to tend toward the opposite approach. Have an infection of some sort? Hold off on taking anything. Let your body's defenses deal with it naturally. Having a cavity filled? Don't expect anesthesia unless you request it.

We always found the medical care we received in Holland to be adequate—even if the system for delivering said care, and the philosophies surrounding its administration, took a little getting used to. And the best thing was the price. As a state-sponsored system, prices were definitely affordable.
—George Hutchinson

NEWSPAPERS IN THE NETHERLANDS

Algemeen Dagblad
Marten Meesweg 35
NL-3009 AT Rotterdam, Netherlands
Tel.: [31] 10 40 67 211
Fax: [31] 10 40 66 958

De Telegraaf
Postbus 376
NL-1000 EB Amsterdam, Netherlands
Tel.: [31] 20 585 24 33
Fax: [31] 20 585 24 35

De Volkskrant
Wibautstraat 131
NL-1091 Amsterdam, Netherlands

Tel.: [31] 20 562 2798
Fax: [31] 20 694 9311

Resources for Further Information

USEFUL WEBSITES FOR JOB SEARCHERS

The Internet is a good place to begin your job search. Many Dutch employers list job vacancies, especially those in technical fields, on the World Wide Web. There are also many websites that provide useful information for job searchers researching the Dutch job market.

The Dutch Yellow Pages
www.markt.nl:80/dyp/index-en.html
Very useful website, with many links.

Job List
www.hufkens.nl
Posts job offers in a range of fields.

Job Listings
www.jobs.nl
Dutch jobs.

Torsa Project Services
www.torsa.nl
Temporary and career opportunities for IT specialists.

Van Zoelen Recruitment
www.vz-recruitment.nl/index.htm
Recruitment agency.

EMBASSIES AND CONSULAR OFFICES

American embassies and consulates have commercial and/or economic sections that can provide you with business information and explain aspects of the local economy. Inquiries about business opportunities should be addressed either to "Commercial Officer" or "Commercial Section," followed by the appropriate street address.

Representation of the Netherlands in the United States

Royal Netherlands Embassy
4200 Linnean Avenue NW
Washington, DC 20008
Tel.: (202) 244-5300
Fax: (202) 362-3430

Netherlands Consulates General: Chicago, (312) 856-0110; Los Angeles, (310) 268-1598; New York, (212) 246-1429

Representation of the United States in the Netherlands

American Embassy
Lange Voorhout 102
NL-2614 EJ The Hague, Netherlands
Tel.: [31] 70 310 9209
Fax: [31] 70 361 4688
www.usemb.nl/

American Consulate General—Amsterdam
Museumplein 19
NL-1071 DJ Amsterdam, Netherlands
Tel.: [31] 20 575 5309
Fax: [31] 20 5755 310 (general)

CHAMBERS OF COMMERCE

Chambers of commerce consist of firms in both countries interested in international trade. These are appropriate companies to initially target in the job search.

American Chamber of Commerce in the Netherlands
Van Karnebeeklaan 14
NL-2585 The Hague, Netherlands
Tel.: [31] 70 365 9808
Fax: [31] 70 364 6992
Email: Amchamnl@wxs.nl
www.unisys.nl/amcham

Netherlands Chamber of Commerce in the U.S.
One Rockefeller Plaza, 14th Floor
New York, NY 10020
Tel.: (212) 265-6460
Fax: (212) 265-6402

WORLD TRADE CENTERS IN THE NETHERLANDS

World Trade Centers usually include many foreign companies operating in the country.

World Trade Center Amsterdam
Strawinskylaan 1
NL-1007 XW Amsterdam, Netherlands
Tel.: [31] 20 575 9111
Fax: [31] 20 662 7255
Email: management@wtc-amsterdam.nl

World Trade Center Eindhoven
Bogert 1
Postbus 2085
NL-5600 CB Eindhoven, Netherlands
Tel : [31] 40 265 36 53

Fax : [31] 40 244 49 041
Email: wtce@iaehv.nl
www.wtce.nl

World Trade Center Rotterdam
Beursplein 37
Postbus 30055
NL-3001 DB Rotterdam, Netherlands
Tel.: [31] (10) 405 4444
Fax: [31] (10) 405 5016
Email: wtcro@euronet.nl

OTHER INFORMATIONAL ORGANIZATIONS

Foreign government missions in the U.S. such as tourist offices can furnish visas and information on work permits and other important regulations. They may also offer economic and business information about the country.

Netherlands Board of Tourism
355 Lexington Avenue, 21st Floor
New York, NY 10017
Tel.: (212) 370-7367

Fax: (212) 370-9507
Email: NBTNY@aol.com
www.NTB.NL/Holland

BUSINESS DIRECTORIES

Although not always easy to find, business directories can prove invaluable in the international job search. Most directories list company names, addresses, products, and phone numbers. Some directories include executive names and titles and financial information about the company. These sources provide you with the names of the people to contact for employment information as well as financial data, which can tell you how strong a company's position in a country may be.

Dun's 20,000 Netherlands. Published annually in Dutch by Dun & Bradstreet Information
   Services, Dun & Bradstreet Company, 3 Sylvan Way, Parsippany, NJ 07054-3896; email:
   dnbmdd@dnb.com. Covers 20,000 industrial, trading, transportation, banking,
   insurance, and service companies in the Netherlands.
Holland Exports. Published annually by ABC voor Handel en Industrie C.V., Koningin
   Wilhelminalaan 16, P.O. Box 190, NL-2000 AD Haarlem, Netherlands; email: info@abc-
   d.nl; www.hollandexports.com. Lists over 8,300 exporters and manufacturers in the
   Netherlands.
Kompass Nederland. Published in Dutch (with multilingual product headings) by
   Kompass Nederland BV, Hogehilweg 15, NL-1101 CB Amsterdam, Netherlands.
   Distributed in the U.S. by Croner Publications, 34 Jericho Turnpike, Jericho, NY 11753.
   Lists 3,000 service companies, distributors, and manufacturers.
Nederlands ABC—Services. Published annually in Dutch by Verlag Hoppenstedt and Co.,
   Havelstrasse 9, Postfach 100139, D-6421 Darmstadt, Germany. Lists 23,000 Dutch
   service companies.
Netherlands-American Trade Directory. Published every other year by the American
   Chamber of Commerce in the Netherlands, Van Karnebeeklaan 14, NL-2585 The Hague,
   Netherlands. Includes data on 5,000 Dutch and American businesses trading and
   investing in the two countries.

AMERICAN COMPANIES IN THE NETHERLANDS

The following companies are classified by business area: Banking and Finance; Industrial Manufacturing; Retailing and Wholesaling; and Service Industries. Company information includes firm name, address, phone and fax number, specific
business, and American parent company. Your chances of achieving employment
abroad are substantially better if you contact the subsidiary company in Europe
rather than the parent company in the U.S.

BANKING AND FINANCE

American Express Bank, Ltd.
Riverstaete Building,
Trompenburgstraat 2
NL-1079 TX Amsterdam, Netherlands
Tel.: [31] (20) 551 0111
Fax: [31] (20) 642 2325
American Express Co., New York

Citibank, NA
Herengracht 545/549
NL-1017 BW Amsterdam, Netherlands
Tel.: [31] (20) 551 5911
Fax: [31] (20) 551 5234
Citibank, New York

Morgan Guaranty Trust Corp
Tesselschadestraat 12
NL-1054 ET Amsterdam, Netherlands
Tel.: [31] (20) 676 7766
Fax: [31] (20) 676 9641
(Bank)
J.P. Morgan and Co., New York

Warner-Lambert Holland BV
Oderweg 1, Abbenes
NL-1005 AD Amsterdam NH
Netherlands
Tel.: [31] (20) 587 3450
(Holding co.)
Warner-Lambert Co.

INDUSTRIAL MANUFACTURING

Air Products Nederland BV
Noordkade 100, Postbus 56
NL-2740 AB Waddinxveen, Netherlands
Tel.: [31] (1828) 2 14 21

Fax: [31] (1828) 1 60 72
(Chemicals and industrial gases)
Air Products & Chemicals Inc.

Alcoa Nederland BV
Postbus 21
NL-5151 RP Drunen, Netherlands
Tel.: [31] (4163) 86100
Fax: [31] (4163) 86210
(Aluminum products)
Aluminum Co. of America

Borg-Warner BV
Postbus 8122
NL-1005 AC Amsterdam, Netherlands
Tel.: [31] (20) 5806 6911
Fax: [31] (20) 135525
(Chemicals and pumps)
Borg-Warner Corp.

Cargill BV
Coenhavenweg 2
NL-1013 BL Amsterdam, Netherlands
Tel.: [31] (20) 580 19 11
Fax: [31] (20) 682 01 93
(Soy products)

Chemco Europe NV
De Beaufortlaan 28
Postbus 2
NL-3760 AA Soest, Netherlands
Tel.: [31] (2155) 91911
Fax: [31] (2155) 26648
(Photographic supplies)
Chemco Inc.

Cincinnati Milacron BV
Schiedamsedijk 20
Postbus 98
NL-3130 AB Vlaardingen, Netherlands
Tel.: [31] (10) 4 34 79 44
Fax: [31] (10) 4 35 97 33
(Machine Tools)
Cincinnati Malacron Corp

Cyanamid BV
Coolsingle 139, Postbus 1523
NL-3000 BM Rotterdam, Netherlands
Tel.: [31] (10) 224 84 00
Fax: [31] (10) 413 67 88
(Chemicals)
American Cyanamid Co.

Dow Benelux BV
Postbus 1310
NL-3000 BH, Netherlands
Tel.: [31] (10) 4 17 48 11
Fax: [31] (10) 4 14 78 74
(Industrial chemicals)
Dow Chemical Co.

DuPont de Nemours (Nederland) BV
Baahoekweg 22, P.O. Box 145
NL-3300 AC Dordrecht, Netherlands

Tel.: [31] (78) 21 89 11
Fax: [31] (78) 16 37 37
(Chemical products)
E.I. DuPont De Nemours & Co.

Exxon Chemical Holland
s' Gravelandseweg 298
NL-3125 BK Schiedam, Netherlands
Tel.: [31] (10) 488 19 11
Fax: [31] (10) 488 13 88
(Chemical products)
Exxon Chemical Co.

Foxboro Nederland NV
Baarnschedijk 10
NL-3741 LS Baarn, Netherlands
Tel.: [31] (2155) 0 09 11
Fax: [31] (2155) 9 03 50
(Electrical components)
The Foxboro Co.

Gerkens Caceo Industrie BV
Veerdijk 82, P.O. Box 82
NL-1530/AB Wormer, Netherlands
Tel.: [31] (75) 29 32 93
Fax: [31] (75) 212 571
(Cocoa products)
Cargill Inc.

Hewlett-Packard Nederland BV
Startbaan 16, Postbus 667
NL-1180/AR Amstelveen, Netherlands
Tel.: [31] (20) 547 69 11
Fax: [31] (20) 647 18 25
(Measurement and computation
products)
Hewlett-Packard Co.

Kimberly-Clark Benelux Operations BV
Groeneveldselaan 41
Postbus 72
NL-3900 AB Veenendaal, Netherlands
Tel.: [31] (8385) 3 41 11
Fax: [31] (8385) 2 74 14
(Paper products)
Kimberly-Clark Corp.

Mars BV
Taylorweg 5
NL-5466 AE Veghel, Netherlands
Tel.: [31] (413) 38 33 33
Fax: [31] (413) 35 16 70
(Confectionery)
Mars Inc.

Medtronic BV
Wenckebachstraat 10
Postbus 1013
NL-6460 BA Kerkrade, Netherlands
Tel.: [31] (45) 43 85 85

Fax: [31] (45) 41 74 66
(Medical equipment)
Medtronic Inc.

Merck Sharp & Dohme BV
Waarderweg 39
NL-2031 BN Haarlem, Netherlands
Tel.: [31] (23) 515 31 53
Fax: [31] (23) 514 80 00
(Pharmaceuticals)
Merck & Co., Inc.

Philip Morris Holland BV
Marconilaan 20
NL-4622 RD Bergen Op Zoom, Netherlands
Tel.: [31] (164) 29 50 00
Fax: [31] (164) 29 44 44
(Cigarettes)
Philip Morris Companies Inc.

Polaroid Nederlands BV
Zonnebaan 45
NL-3606 CH Maarssen, Netherlands
Tel.: [31] (30) 241 04 20
Fax: [31] (30) 241 19 69
(Photographic materials)
Polaroid Corp.

Rank Xerox Holding BV
Maasheseweg 89
NL-5804 AB Venray, Netherlands
Tel.: [31] (478) 52 50 00
Fax: [31] (478) 52 60 00
(Copying equipment)
Xerox Corp.

Richardson-Vicks BV
Watermanweg 100
NL-3067 GG Rotterdam, Netherlands
Tel.: [31] (10) 286 33 20
Fax: [31] (10) 286 31 31
(Pharmaceuticals, perfumes, and

cosmetics)
Procter and Gamble Co.

Sara Lee NV
Postbus 2
NL-3500 CA Utrecht, Netherlands
Tel.: [31] (30) 92 73 11
Fax: [31] (30) 93 76 46
(Food products)
Sara Lee Corp.

Scott Page NV
Brabantweg 25
NL-6591 HV Gennep, Netherlands
Tel.: [31] (485) 49 79 11
Fax: [31] (485) 49 76 05
Scott Paper Co.

Texaco Petroleum Maatschappij (Nederland) BV
Weena-Zuid 166
NL-3012 NC Rotterdam, Netherlands
Tel.: [31] (10) 403 34 00
Fax: [31] (10) 403 35 86
(Petroleum products)
Texaco Inc.

Texas Instruments Holland BV
Kolthofsingel 8, Postbus 43
NL-7602 EM Almelo, Netherlands
Tel.: [31] (5490) 79555
Fax: [31] (5490) 70535
(Electronic equipment)
Texas Instruments Inc.

Time Warner Publishing BV
Ottho Heldringstraat 5
NL-1066 AZ Amsterdam, Netherlands
Tel.: [31] (20) 510 49 11
Fax: [31] (20) 617 50 77
(Periodicals and books)
Time Inc.

RETAILING AND WHOLESALING

Bausch & Lomb BV
Nijverheidsweg 41
NL-2100 AC Bloemendaal, North
Holland, Netherlands
Tel.: [31] (23) 33 91 79
(Medical & hospital equipment)
Bausch & Lomb

Bristol-Myers BV
Vijzelmolenlaan 4
NL-3447 GX Woerden, Netherlands
Tel.: [31] (348) 57 42 22
Fax: [31] (348) 42 30 84
(Pharmaceuticals)
Bristol-Myers Co.

Digital Equipment BV
Europalaan 44
NL-3526 KS Utrecht, Netherlands
Tel.: [31] (30) 83 91 11
Fax: [31] (30) 89 06 23
(Computers)
Digital equipment Corp.

Ford Nederland BV
Amsteldijk 216
NL-1079 LK Amsterdam, Netherlands
Tel.: [31] (20) 504 45 04
Fax: [31] (20) 540 92 01
(Motor vehicles and parts)
Ford Motor Co.

General Motors Nederland BV
Baanhoek 188
NL-3361 GN Sliedrecht, Netherlands
Tel.: [31] (78) 422100
Fax: [31] (78) 154742
(Motor vehicles and parts)
General Motors Corp.

Goodyear Nederland BV
Produktieweg 62
NL-2380 AA Nootdorp ZH, Netherlands
Tel.: [31] (71) 45 52 55
(Tires and tubes)
Goodyear Tire and Rubber Co.

H.J. Heinz BV
Stationsstraat 50
Postbus 6
NL-6662 BC Elst Gld, Netherlands
Tel.: [31] (481) 37 18 57
Fax: [31] (481) 37 51 27
(Soups and sauces)
H.J. Heinz Inc.

IBM Nederland NV
Johan Hulzingalaan 765
NL-1066 VH Amsterdam, Netherlands
Tel.: [31] (20) 615 15 00
Fax: [31] (20) 513 68 07
(Information processing equipment)
International Business Machines Corp.

Kodak Nederland BV
Zeisterweg 1
NL-3984 NH Odijk, Netherlands
Tel.: [31] (30) 659 99 11
Fax: [31] (30) 659 95 99
(Electronic equipment)
Eastman Kodak Co.

Mobil Oil BV
Westblaak 163
NL-3012 KJ Rotterdam, Netherlands
Tel.: [31] (10) 465 18 88
Fax: [31] (10) 417 51 50
(Petroleum products)
Mobil Corp.

NCR Nederland NV
Postbus 22705
NL-1100 DE Amsterdam Zuidoost,
Netherlands
Tel.: [31] (20) 651 23 45
Fax: [31] (20) 691 41 09
(Office equipment)
NCR Corp.

Pennzoil Products Europe
Sluispolderweg 11
NL-1505 HJ Zaandam NH, Netherlands

Tel.: [31] (75) 612 33 82
Fax: [31] (75) 615 66 23
(Petroleum)
Pennzoil Co.

Pfizer BV
Koningslaan 200
NL-3009 AC Maasdam ZH, Netherlands
Tel.: [31] (10) 4215122
(Chemicals)
Pfizer Inc.

Reynolds Aluminum
Industrieweg 15
NL-3846 BB Harderwijk, Netherlands
Tel.: [31] (341) 46 44 11
Fax: [31] (341) 41 83 80
(Aluminum and alloys)
Reynolds

R. J. Reynolds Tobacco BV
Vreelandseweg 46
NL-1216 CH Hilversum, Netherlands
Tel.: [31] (35) 622 28 88
Fax: [31] (35) 622 28 90
(Tobacco products)
RJR-Nabisco, Inc.

SmithKline Beecham Consumer Brands BV
Dr. W. Dreesweg 2
Postbus 394
NL-1180 AJ Amstelveen, Netherlands
Tel.: [31] (20) 547 83 78
Fax: [31] (20) 547 83 73
(Pharmaceuticals)
SmithKline Beecham Co.

Tektronix Holland NV
Maktweg 73A, Postbus 526
NL-8440 AM Heerenveen, Netherlands
Tel.: [31] (5130) 3 55 95
Fax: [31] (5130) 3 34 52
(Data processing equipment)
Tektronix Inc.

Unisys Nederland NV
Hoogoorddreef 11
NL-1101 BA Amsterdam Zuidoost,
Netherlands
Tel.: [31] (20) 565 75 85
Fax: [31] (20) 697 77 55
(Computer hardware and software)
Unisys Corp.

Warner Brothers Holland BV
De Boeleln 16
NL-1083 HJ Abbenes NH, Netherlands
Tel.: [31] (20) 464766
(Records and tapes)
Warner Communications Inc.

SERVICE INDUSTRIES

AT&T Network Systems International BV
Larensweg 50
Postbus 1168
NL-1220 BD EJ Hilversum, Netherlands
Tel.: [31] (35) 87 31 11
Fax: [31] (35) 87 17 48
(Telecommunications)
AT&T Corp.

Data General Nederland BV
Burgemeester Stramanweg 101
NL-1101 AA Amsterdam Zuidoost,
Netherlands
Tel.: [31] (20) 565 97 11
Fax: [31] (20) 565 97 00
(Engineering services)
Data General Corp.

Dow Jones Publishing Company (Europe)
In De Cramer 37
NL-6411 RS Heerlen, Netherlands
Tel.: [31] (45) 576 12 22
Fax : [31] (45) 571 47 22
(Magazine and newspaper publishing)
Dow Jones

Dun & Bradstreet BV
Westblaak 138
NL-3012 KM Rotterdam ZH, Netherlands
Tel.: [31] (10) 400 94 00
Fax: [31] (10) 400 96 19
(Business information services)
The Dun & Bradstreet Corp.

Lintas Nederland BV
Strawinskylaan 1641
NL-1007 TA Abbenes NH, Netherlands

Tel.: [31] (20) 573 11 11
(Advertising)
Interpublic Group Companies

Moret Ernst & Young Management Consultants
Varrolaan 100
NL-3584 BW Utrecht, Netherlands
Tel.: [31] (30) 258 85 88
Fax: [31] (30) 258 81 00
(Management consulting)
Ernst & Young

A.C. Nielsen Nederland BV
Diemerhof 2
NL-1112 XL Diemen, Netherlands
Tel.: [31] (20) 569 25 00
Fax: [31] (20) 690 31 75
(Market research)
Dun & Bradstreet Corp.

Ogilvy & Mather (Nederland) BV
Nieuwezijdse Voorburgwal 35-39
NL-1012 RD Amsterdam, Netherlands
Tel.: [31] (20) 521 64 64
Fax: [31] (20) 521 64 00
Email: omadv@omamstr.ogilvy.nl
(Advertising)
Ogilvy Group Inc.

Young & Rubicam BV
Ottho Heldringstraat 27
Postbus 9220
NL-1066 AE Amsterdam, Netherlands
Tel.: [31] (20) 17 28 51
(Advertising)
Young & Rubicam Inc.

EUROPEAN COMPANIES IN THE NETHERLANDS

The following are several major non-American firms operating in the country. These selected companies can be either domestic or foreign but are usually European companies. Such companies will generally hire their own nationals first but may employ Americans.

BANKING AND FINANCE

ABN-AMRO Bank N.V.
Foppingadreef 22
NL-1102 BS Amsterdam Zuidoost,
Netherlands
Tel.: [31] (20) 629 91 11
Fax: [31] (20) 629 80 62

Aegon Insurance Group
Mariahoeveplein 50
NL-2591 TV 'S-Gravenhage, Netherlands
Tel.: [31] (70) 344 32 10
Fax: [31] (70) 347 52 38
(Insurance)

Fortis AMEV NV
Archimedeslaan 10
NL-3584 BA Utrecht, Netherlands
Tel.: [31] (30) 257 91 11
(Insurance)

Internationale Nederlanden Groep N.V.
Strawinskylaan 2631
NL-1077 ZZ Amsterdam, Netherlands
Tel.: [31] (20) 541 54 16
Fax: [31] (20) 563 69 00
(Insurance & savings bank)

Mees & Pierson NV
Weena 129
NL-3013 CK Rotterdam, Netherlands
Tel.: [31] (10) 403 58 00

INDUSTRIAL MANUFACTURING

Advanced Semiconductor Materials International
Jan Steenlaan 9
NL-3723 BS Bilthoven, Netherlands
Tel.: [31] (30) 281 836
Fax: [31] (30) 287 469
(Semiconductors)

Akzo NV
Velperweg 76
NL-6824 BM Arnhem, Netherlands
Tel.: [31] (26) 366 44 33
Fax: [31] (26) 366 32 50
(Chemical products)

BASF Nederland BV
Kadestraat 1
NL-6811 CA Arnhem, Netherlands
Tel.: [31] (26) 371 71 71
Fax: [31] (26) 371 72 46
(Chemicals)
BASF AG, Germany

BP Nederland BV
Frederiksplein 21
Postbus 1634
NL-1000 BP Amsterdam, Netherlands
Tel.: [31] (20) 5 20 19 11
Fax: [31] (20) 5 20 13 72
(Petroleum products)
The British Petroleum Co.

Ciba Geigy International Nederland BV
Raapopseweg 1
NL-6824 DP Arnhem, Netherlands
Tel.: [31] (26) 365 62 00
Fax: [31] (26) 364 05 67
(Chemicals)

Fax: [31] (10) 401 66 06
(Investment bank)

Nationale-Nederlanden N.V.
James Wattstraat 79
NL-1097 DL Amsterdam, Netherlands
Tel.: [31] (20) 591 12 50
Fax: [31] (20) 591 12 61
(Finance and insurance)

Rabobank Nederland
P.O. Box 17100
NL-3500 HG Utrecht, Netherlands
Tel.: [31] (30) 90 2804
Fax: [31] (30) 90 1976
(Cooperative bank)

DAF N.V. Trucks N.V.
Hugo van der Goeslaan 1
NL-5643 TW Eindhoven, Netherlands
Tel.: [31] (40) 214 91 11
Fax: [31] (40) 214 43 25
(Motor vehicles)

DSM, NV
Het Overloon 1
NL-6411 Heerlen, Netherlands
Tel.: [31] (45) 578 81 11
Fax: [31] (45) 571 97 53
(Plastics, resins, fertilizers)

Fokker Services BV
Aviolandalaan 31
NL-4631 RP Hoogerheide, Netherlands
Tel.: [31] (164) 61 80 00
Fax: [31] (164) 61 40 73
(Aircraft and aerospace equipment)

Heineken N.V.
Tweede Weteringplantsoen 21
NL-1017 ZD Amsterdam, Netherlands
Tel.: [31] (20) 670 91 11
Fax: [31] (20) 626 35 03
(Beverages)

Philips Electronics N.V.
Groenewoudseweg 1
NL-5621 BA Eindhoven, Netherlands
Tel.: [31] (40) 279 11 11
Fax: [31] (40) 278 52 81
(Electrical products and systems)

Polygram NV
Gerrit van der Veenlaan 4
NL-3743 DN Baarn, Netherlands
Tel.: [31] (35) 541 99 11

Fax: [31] (35) 541 64 00
(Records, cassettes, CDs)

**Shell Internationale Petroleum
Maatschappij**
Carel van Bylandtlaan 30
NL-2596 HR The Hague, Netherlands
Tel.: [31] (70) 377 91 11
Fax: [31] (70) 377 31 15
(Petroleum products)

Unilever Nederland BV
Weena 457
NL-3013 AL Rotterdam, Netherlands

RETAILING AND WHOLESALING

Internationale Spar Centrale BV
Rokin 101
NL-1012 KM Amsterdam, Netherlands
Tel.: [31] (20) 626 67 49
Fax: [31] (20) 627 51 96
(Food wholesaling and retailing)

Konninklijke Ahold, NV
Albert Heijnweg 1
NL-1507 EH Zaandam, Netherlands
Tel.: [31] (75) 599111
Fax: [31] (75) 598362
(Food retailing)

Royal Ahold
Albert Heijnweg 1, P.O. Box 33
NL-1507 EH Zaandam, Netherlands

SERVICE INDUSTRIES

Ballast Nedam BV
Laan van Kronenburg 2
NL-1183 AS Amstelveen, Netherlands
Tel.: [31] (20) 545 21 09
Fax: [31] (20) 545 35 77
(Civil, electrical, and mechanical
engineering)
British Aerospace PLC

Elsevier N.V.
Van de Sande Bakhuyzenstraat 4
NL-1061 AG Amsterdam, Netherlands
Tel.: [31] (20) 515 23 68
Fax: [31] (20) 683 26 17
(Publishing)

Hagemeyer NV
Rijksweg 69
NL-1411 GE Naarden, Netherlands

Tel.: [31] (10) 217 40 00
Fax: [31] (10) 217 47 98
(Food processing and consumer products)

Van Leeuwen Buizen Group NV
Lindtsedijk 20, Postbus 1
NL-3300 AA Zwijndrecht, Netherlands
Tel.: [31] (78) 25 25 25
Fax: [31] (78) 19 44 44
(Steel pipes and fittings)

Tel.: [31] (75) 659 91 11
Fax: [31] (75) 631 30 30
(Retail)

SHV Holdings NV
Rijnkade 1
NL-3511 LC Utrecht, Netherlands
Tel.: [31] (30) 233 88 33
Fax: [31] (30) 23 33 04
(Retail)

Tel.: [31] (35) 695 76 11
Fax: [31] (35) 694 78 50
(International marketing)

KLM NV
Postbus 7700
NL-1117 ZL Schiphol, Netherlands
Tel.: [31] (20) 649 91 23
Fax: [31] (20) 648 80 69
(International airline)

Nederlandse Spoorwegen (NV) NS
Moreelsepark 1
NL-3511 EP Utrecht, Netherlands
Tel.: [31] (30) 235 91 11
(Rail transport)

INTERNATIONAL NON-PROFIT EMPLOYER IN THE NETHERLANDS

Greenpeace International
Keizersgracht 176
NL-1016 DW Amsterdam, Netherlands
Tel.: [31] (20) 523 6555

INTERNATIONAL SCHOOLS IN THE NETHERLANDS

Afcent International School
Ferdinand Bolstraat 1
NL-6445 EE Brunssum, Netherlands
Tel.: [31] 45 527 82 20
Fax: [31] 45 527 82 33
Email: AFCE-HS@odedodea.edu

The American School of the Hague
Rijksstraatweg 200
NL-2241 BX Wassenaar, Netherlands
Tel.: [31] 70 514 01 13
Fax: [31] 70 511 24 00
Email: bgerritz@ash.nl
www.ash.nl/

The British School in the Netherlands
Rosenburgherlaan 2 Voorschoten
NL-2252 BA The Hague, Netherlands
Tel.: [31] 70 333 8111
Fax: [31] 70 333 8100
Email: info@britishschool.nl
www.britishschool.nl

International School of Amsterdam
Postbox 920
NL-1180 AX Amstelveen, Netherlands
Tel.: [31] 20 347 11 11
Fax: [31] 20 347 12 22
Email: jrich@isa.nl
www.isa.nl

Switzerland, Austria, and Liechtenstein

Switzerland

MAJOR EMPLOYMENT CENTERS: Zurich, Basel, Geneva, Bern

MAJOR BUSINESS LANGUAGES: German, French, Italian

LANGUAGE SKILL INDEX: Count on knowing German or French to gain employment. Even if you know German, you may find that the Swiss dialect takes some getting used to

CURRENCY: Swiss franc

TELEPHONE COUNTRY CODE: 41

TIME ZONE: EST+6

PUNCTUALITY INDEX: In a country famous for its clocks, you'd better be on time

AVERAGE DAILY TEMPERATURE, HIGH/LOW: January, 39/29°F; July, 77/58°F (Geneva)

AVERAGE NUMBER OF DAYS WITH PRECIPITATION: January, 11; July, 12

BEST BET FOR EMPLOYMENT:

FOR STUDENTS: Apply to IASTE

PERMANENT JOBS: Banking and finance

CHANCE OF FINDING A JOB: With the right skills, good

TRIVIA: In Switzerland, questions about one's occupation are not considered an appropriate topic of conversation among new acquaintances

L arger than Massachusetts but smaller than Maine, Switzerland is a geographically compact country. It's in the center of Europe, bordering France to the west, Germany to the north, Liechtenstein and Austria to the east, and Italy to the south. The Swiss Alps cover about a fourth of the country. Large lakes form parts of the borders with France and Germany.

About 65% of the resident population, which includes a large number of noncitizens, is German in ethnicity. About 18% of the population is French, 10% Italian, and 1% Ramansch. Language use tends to follow ethnicity; German, French, and Italian are all official languages. Many Swiss speak three languages, occasionally including English. The particular German dialect spoken in Switzerland, *Scheizerdeutsch*, is generally incomprehensible to other German speakers unfamiliar with this variation. Depending upon what part of the country you are in, begin your conversations in German, French, or Italian. Some people in western Switzerland speak only French and won't prove very responsive to German.

The former Roman province of Helvetia, now Switzerland, is organized along a federal system, with substantial powers reserved for the 23 regional units, the cantons. In 1291, three cantons formed a defensive union that others later joined to form the present country. The Swiss Confederation (Switzerland's official name) achieved its independence from the Holy Roman Empire in 1648. France occupied the country from 1798 to 1815, renaming it the Helvetic Republic. The Catholic cantons seceded in 1847 but reentered with the establishment of a federal constitution in 1848. (The Swiss population is currently evenly divided between Roman Catholics and Protestants.)

The Swiss policy of strict neutrality and nationalistic independence prevents membership in the European Union, the United Nations or NATO. Switzerland is, though, a member of the European Free Trade Association. The country has experienced extraordinary stability, with most major parties participating in the coalition government that is headed by a sort of collective executive presidency. Despite a policy of neutrality, Switzerland maintains a 400,000 person army and spends approximately 2% of G.N.P. on defense to maintain a relatively high level of preparedness.

Revelations in 1995 that implicated Swiss bankers in hiding Nazi plunder during WWII have challenged Switzerland's official claims of neutrality. After a careful investigation and an audit of Swiss bank accounts conducted by a committee led by former Federal Reserve Board Chairman Paul Volcker, the Swiss published lists of 5,559 dormant accounts, many belonging to Holocaust victims. Swiss bankers and businessmen also announced plans to atone for their country's wartime profiteering from the Nazis by setting up a voluntary $200 million Swiss Fund for Needy Victims of the Holocaust.

Standard business hours in Switzerland are from 8:00 a.m. to 6:30 p.m., with a noon to 2:00 p.m. break, Monday through Friday. Post offices in the larger cities are open from 7:30 a.m. to 6:30 p.m., with some services available until 10:30 or 11:00 p.m. in some locations, Monday through Friday, and Saturday morning. Vacation time is in July and August.

Current Economic Climate

Switzerland has overcome its lack of natural resources by basing its economic development on inventiveness, frugality, and perseverance. More than one-fourth of the country's territory is nonproductive; fully one-half is either forested or non-arable grassland, and, except for potential water power, no energy or mineral resources are available for profitable exploitation. Nevertheless, Switzerland is one of the most highly industrialized countries in the world and is consistently ranked as one of the world's richest countries.

Switzerland's unemployment rate is about 5%, and inflation is less than 1%. The country has a mixed economy with an emphasis on private ownership. Telecommunications were privatized in 1998; the only industries still nationalized outright are the postal service and federal railway.

Economic prosperity largely results from a well-educated work force and highly technical industries. Switzerland garners much of its wealth from its position as an international tax haven, although the government has taken steps to modify its strict banking secrecy laws to discourage the laundering of proceeds from illicit drug trafficking. Major industries include precision instruments, tourism, banking, watches, machinery, chemicals and pharmaceuticals, textiles, and agriculture. The labor force is 50% services, 39% commerce and industrial, and 7% agricultural. Most trade occurs with the E.U. and the U.S.

SWITZERLAND'S 10 LARGEST COMPANIES

(1997, composite ranking)
 1. Adia
 2. Nestlé
 3. ABB Asea Brown Boveri
 4. Ciba Geigy
 5. Federation of Migros Cooperatives
 6. Roche Holding
 7. CS Holding
 8. Sandoz
 9. Hoderbank Financière
10. 10. Zurich Insurance Group

Using the phone, fax, and Internet

International calls can be made from Post Offices or from the offices of PPT, the telephone company, which is open from 7:00 a.m. to 10:30 p.m. daily in Zurich and until 6:00 or 6:30 p.m. in the other large cities. Dial "191" for an English language operator, "117" for the police, and "144" for an ambulance. In 1998 Swisscom faced competition in a deregulated telephone market for the first time, so there may be a shake-up of telephone services in the next few years. Faxes may be sent from Swiscom offices. Cybercafes are common in large cities such as Geneva and Zurich, providing easy public access to the Internet.

Getting Around in Switzerland

The Swiss railway system is an excellent network, which includes both private and government-owned lines. Fares, however, are expensive and Eurail and InterRail passes are accepted only on government rail lines. Though less expensive than trains, buses do not accept Eurail or InterRail passes and tend to be slower. Steamers along the lakes will accept Eurail and InterRail passes.

Pedaling down the Rhone

If you're lucky enough to find employment in Switzerland you'll eventually find yourself with a little vacation time on your hands, trying to think of the best way to spend it. Why not try a bicycle trip?

If you plan ahead for this before going to Switzerland you can take a bike with you—either in your shipment or as excess baggage on the plane. (Ask your airline for a bicycle box.) Taking a bike can be worthwhile if you already have a decent bicycle, and it's probably cheaper than buying one overseas. Also, you won't have to bother with any kind of a breaking-in period, as you would with a rental.

Biking in Switzerland is simply a lovely way to get around. Several friends and I spent two weeks touring in the area along the Rhone River, and the scenery was just stunning: towering mountains, lush green valleys, icy-blue alpine lakes. We averaged about 50 miles a day. This gave us plenty of time for stops along the way for sightseeing; there are plenty of castles in addition to the natural wonders. Also, this allowed ample time to sample some of the country cafes along the way, which are outstanding.

For a short trip—say, a week or two—you probably won't need to take any specialized tools or spare parts with you if your bike is in good condition at the start of your journey. All you'll likely need are some tire tools, a spare tube, a patch kit, and a tire pump. And if you have room in your saddle bag, I would suggest tucking in a small stash of Swiss chocolate. What better time to indulge than when you're pedaling away all those extra calories?—Adrian Pechacek.

Employment Regulations and Outlook for Americans

U.S. citizens don't need a visa for stays in Switzerland of less than 90 days. A work permit, called an Assurance of Residence Permit, is considered both a work and residence permit and must be presented upon arrival. Your Swiss employer must apply for the Assurance of Residence Permit for you. Employment for foreigners in Switzerland is extremely difficult. What with the country's almost non-existent unemployment rate and well-trained work force, few foreigners meet the specialized requirements specified by Swiss employment regulations.

Unskilled work is conducted primarily by temporary workers from Spain and Portugal and other less-developed European countries. Some tourist work in hotels and restaurants may be found but usually requires long hours. Agricultural work in Switzerland is also known to require long hours.

Short-term and Temporary Work

Switzerland has ample opportunities for people interested in working as an au pair.

Vereinder Freundinnen Junger Mädchen
Zähringerstrasse 36
CH-8001 Zurich, Switzerland
Tel.: [41] (1) 252 38 40
Fax: [41] (1) 261 18 07
Au pair placement agency.

Pro Filia
51 rue de Carouge
CH-1205 Geneva
Tel.: [41] (22) 329 8462

Places au pairs in French-speaking Switzerland.

Pro Filia
Beckenhoftsrasse 16
CH-8035 Zurich, Switzerland
Tel.: [41] (1) 363 5501
Places au pairs in German-speaking Switzerland.

Internship Program

The best opportunity for students interested in technical internships is to work with IASTE.

IASTE
10400 Little Patuxent Parkway, Suite 250 L
Columbia, MD 21044-3510
Tel.: (410) 997-3068
Fax: (410) 997-5186

Email: iaste@aipt.org
www.aipt.org/iaste.html
Arranges reciprocal internship exchanges among 63 member countries for students in engineering, architecture, and the sciences.

Volunteer Opportunities

Workcamps in Switzerland are operated by Service Civil International and by Volunteers for Peace of Germany. SCI operates numerous summer workcamps, emphasizing such themes as agriculture, building renovation, gardening, land clearing, path clearing, and working with handicapped children. Volunteers for Peace workers do path clearing and other forest jobs.

For those interested in a longer-term commitment, the International Christian Youth Exchange offers one-year opportunities in health care, education, environmental work, and construction. Participants must be between 18 and 30 years of age.

Gruppo Volontari dalla Svizzera Italiana
CP 12
CH 6517 Arbedo, Switzerland
Tel.: [41] (92) 29 13 17
Organizes workcamps of people who can speak one of Switzerland's official languages.

International Christian Youth Exchange
134 West 26th Street
New York, NY 10001
Tel.: (212) 206-7307

Service Civil International
c/o International Voluntary Service
Route 2, Box 506
Crozet, VA 22932
Tel.: (804) 823-1826

Volunteers for Peace (IBG)
International Workcamps
43 Tiffany Road
Belmont, VT 05730
Tel.: (802) 259-2759
www.vfp.org/

NEWSPAPERS IN SWITZERLAND

Basler Zeitung
Hochbergerstrasse 15
CH-4002 Basel, Switzerland
Tel.: [41] (61) 639 11 11
Fax: [41] (61) 631 15 82

Blick
Dufourstrasse 23
CH-8008 Zurich, Switzerland
Tel.: [41] (1) 259 64 83
Fax: [41] (1) 259 69 96
www.blick.ch

Neue Zürecher Zeitung
Falkenstrasse 11
CH-8021 Zurich, Switzerland

Tel.: [41] (1) 258 11 11
Fax: [41] (1) 252 13 29

Tages Anzeiger Zurich
Werdstrasse 21
CH-8021 Zurich, Switzerland
Tel.: [49] (1) 404 60 96
Fax: [49] (1) 404 60 96

24 Heures
33 avenue de la Gare
CH-1001 Lausanne, Switzerland
Tel.: [41] (21) 349 44 44
Fax: [41] (21) 349 41 10
Email: 24heures@edicom.ch

Resources for Further Information

USEFUL WEBSITES FOR JOB SEARCHERS

The Internet is a good place to begin your job search. Many Swiss employers list job vacancies, especially those in technical fields, on the World Wide Web. There are also many websites that provide useful information for job searchers researching the Swiss job market.

emploi.ch
www.emploi.ch
International employment exchange; couples those offering positions with those seeking positions.

Interskill Services SA
www.interskill.ch
Lists positions available in Information Technology.

Job Surf
www.udena.ch/jobsurf
A search engine that lists jobs in Switzerland.

NEXUS
www.nexus.ch
Swiss job server; in German.

search.ch
www.search.ch
A multi-lingual Swiss search engine.

Swiss Web Jobs
www.swisswebjobs.ch
A multi-faceted site of jobs and more.

Telejob
www.telejob.ethz.ch
Exchange board that features job offers for young academics from the academic or business worlds.

EMBASSIES AND CONSULAR OFFICES

American embassies and consulates have commercial and/or economic sections that can provide you with business information and explain aspects of the local economy. Inquiries about business opportunities should be addressed either to "Commercial Officer" or "Commercial Section," followed by the appropriate street address.

Representation of Switzerland in the United States

Embassy of Switzerland
2900 Cathedral Avenue NW
Washington, DC 20008
Tel.: (202) 745-7900
Fax: (202) 387-2564
www.swissemb.org

Consulates General of Switzerland: Chicago, (312) 915-0061; Los Angeles, (310) 575-1145; New York, (212) 599-5700

Representation of the United States in Switzerland

American Embassy
Jubilaeumstrasse 93
CH-3005 Bern, Switzerland
Tel.: [41] (31) 357 7011
Fax: [41] (31) 357 7344

American Center of Geneva
c/o U.S. Mission
route de Pregny 11
CH-1292 Chambésy, Switzerland
Tel.: [41] (22) 798 16 15
Fax: [41] (22) 798 16 30

CHAMBERS OF COMMERCE

Chambers of Commerce consist of firms in both countries interested in international trade. These are appropriate companies to initially target in the job search.

Swiss-American Chamber of Commerce
Talacker 41
CH-8001 Zurich, Switzerland
Tel.: [41] (1) 211 2454

Swiss American Chamber of Commerce
608 Fifth Avenue, Suite 309
New York, NY 10020
Tel.: (212) 246-7789
Fax: (212) 246-1366

WORLD TRADE CENTERS IN SWITZERLAND

World Trade Centers usually include many foreign companies operating in the country.

World Trade Center Basel
Messeplatz 1
CH-4021 Basel, Switzerland
Tel.: [41] (61) 691 20 29
Fax : [41] (61) 686 21 82
Email: WTCBA@wtca.geis.com

World Trade Center Geneva
Route de Pre-Bois 29
CH-1215 Geneva 15, Switzerland
Tel.: [41] (22) 929 56 56
Fax : [41] (22) 791 08 85
Email: wtcgv@bluewin.ch
www.wtc-geneva.ch

World Trade Center Lugano
One World Trade Center
CH-6982 Lugano-Agno, Switzerland
Tel.: [41] (91) 610 21 11
Fax: [41] (91) 610 21 01
Email: info@wtclugano.ch
www.wtclugano.ch

World Trade Center Zurich
Leutschenbachstrasse 95
CH-8050 Zurich, Switzerland
Tel.: [41] (1) 309 11 11
Fax : [41] (1) 309 11 22
Email: trade@wtc-zu

OTHER INFORMATIONAL ORGANIZATION

Foreign government missions in the U.S. such as tourist offices can furnish visas and information on work permits and other important regulations. They may also offer economic and business information about the country.

Swiss National Tourist Office
608 Fifth Avenue
New York, NY 10020
Tel.: (212) 757-5944
Fax: (212) 262-6116

BUSINESS DIRECTORIES

Although not always easy to find, business directories can prove invaluable in the international job search. Most directories list company names, addresses, products, and phone numbers. Some directories include executive names and titles and financial information about the company. These sources provide you with the names of the people to contact for employment information as well as financial data, which can tell you how strong a company's position in a country may be.

Dun & Bradstreet Swiss Company Information. Published by Dun & Bradstreet AG, Schoenegstrasse 5, CH-8026 Zurich, Switzerland. Lists 180,000 business in Switzerland and Liechtenstein.

Kompass Schweiz/Liechtenstein. Published annually by Kompass Schweiz Verlag AG, 14 ln Grosswiesen, CH-8044 Zurich, Switzerland. Available in the U.S. from Croner Publications, 34 Jericho Turnpike, Jericho, NY 11753. Lists 38,000 manufacturers, distributors, and service companies in Switzerland and Liechtenstein.

List of Professional & Trade Associations in Switzerland. Published by the Office of Federal de l'Industrie, P.O. Box 2170, CH-3001 Bern, Switzerland. Lists 1,120 active professional associations in Switzerland.

Swiss-American Chamber of Commerce Yearbook. Published annually by the Swiss-American Chamber of Commerce, Talacker 41, CH-8001 Zurich, Switzerland; email: info@amcham.che. Lists Swiss and American firms engaged in bilateral trade.

Swiss Export Directory. Published by the Swiss Office for Trade Promotion, Stampfenbachstrasse 85, CH-8035 Zurich, Switzerland; www.osec.ch. Includes Swiss firms engaged in export.

Swiss Watch Directory. Available from Indicateur Suisse, route de la Glane 31, CH-1700, Fribourg, Switzerland. Lists Swiss retailers, associations, and manufacturers' guilds.

Verzeichnis der Verwaltungsrate. (Corporate Directors, Switzerland.) Published annually in German and French by Orell Fussli AG, Dietzingerstrasse 3, CH-8036 Zurich, Switzerland. Lists chairmen and directors of Swiss companies, including the 100 "most influential" people in the Swiss economy.

AMERICAN COMPANIES IN SWITZERLAND

The following companies are classified by business area: Banking and Finance; Industrial Manufacturing; Retailing and Wholesaling; and Service Industries. Company information includes firm name, address, phone and fax number, specific business, and American parent company. Your chances of achieving employment abroad are substantially better if you contact the subsidiary company in Europe rather than the parent company in the U.S.

BANKING AND FINANCE

Bank Morgan Stanley SA
Bahnhofstrasse 92
CH-8001 Zurich, Switzerland
Tel.: [41] (1) 220 91 11
Fax: [41] (1) 220 98 00
(Bank)
Morgan Stanley

Bankers Trust AG
Dreikönigsstrasse 6
CH-8022 Zurich, Switzerland
Tel.: [41] (1) 208 81 11
Fax: [41] (1) 202 99 54
(Commercial bank)
Bankers Trust Co., New York

Chase Manhattan Bank Switzerland
63 rue du Rhône
Case Postale 257
CH-1211 Geneva 3, Switzerland

Tel.: [41] (22) 35 36 40
Fax: [41] (22) 36 24 30
(Bank)
Chase Manhattan Overseas Banking Corp.

Citibank Switzerland
Bahnhofstrasse 63
Postfach 3760
CH-8021 Zurich, Switzerland
Tel.: [41] (1) 205 71 71
Fax: [41] (1) 205 77 80
(Bank)
Citicorp Banking Corp.

J.P. Morgan (Suisse) SA
place des Bergues 3
CH-1201 Geneva, Switzerland
Tel.: [41] (22) 739 11 11
Fax: [41] (22) 732 26 55
(Bank)
J.P. Morgan

INDUSTRIAL MANUFACTURING

Abbott Laboratories SA
Gewerbestrasse 5
CH-6330 Cham, Switzerland
Tel.: [41] (41) 749 43 80
Fax: [41] (41) 741 38 35
(Pharmaceuticals)
Abbott Laboratories

Armstrong World Industries (Schweiz) AG
Juraweg, Rothrist
CH-4852 Aargau, Switzerland
(Adhesives and sealants)
Armstrong World Industries Inc.

Bristol-Myers Squibb AG
Neuhofstrasse 6
CH-6341 Baar 1, Switzerland
Tel.: [41] (41) 767 72 00
Fax: [41] (41) 767 73 05
(Pharmaceuticals)
Linson Investments Ltd.

Dow (Europe) SA
Bachtobelstr 4
Horgen 8810, Switzerland
Tel.: [41] (1) 728 3185
Fax: [41] (1) 728 3060
(Chemicals, plastics, pharmaceuticals)
Dow Chemical

Du Pont De Nemours International SA
Case Postale 50
chemin du Pavillon 2
CH-1218 Le Grand-Saconnex, Switzerland
Tel.: [41] (22) 717 51 11
Fax: [41] (22) 717 51 09
(Chemical products)
E.I. Du Pont de Nemours & Co.

General Electric Information Services AG
Bergstrasse 138

CH-8032 Zurich, Switzerland
Tel.: [41] (1) 386 41 11
Fax: [41] (1) 386 41 41
(Software)
General Electric

Goodyear Suisse SA
Industriestrasse 21
CH-8604 Volketswil, Switzerland
Tel.: [41] (1) 947 85 00
Fax: [41] 947 86 80
(Chemical products)
Goodyear Tire and Rubber Company

Pfizer AG
Militaerstrasse 84
CH-8048 Zurich, Switzerland
Tel.: [41] (1) 495 71 11
(Medical, chemical, and botanical products)
Pfizer Corp.

Ralston Purina AG
Poststrasse 9
CH-6300 Zug, Switzerland
Tel.: [41] (4) 221 70 70
(Pet food)
Ralston Purina Co.

Sunkist (Europe) SA
rue du Valentin 29
CH-1004 Lausanne, Switzerland
Tel.: [41] (2) 122 48 01
(Processed foods)
Sunkist Growers Inc.

TRW International SA
rue de Lyon 75
CH-1203 Geneva, Switzerland
Tel.: [41] (2) 245 95 50
(Electronic components)
TRW Corp.

RETAILING AND WHOLESALING

Apple Computer AG
Birgistrasse 41
CH-8304 Wallisellen, Switzerland
Tel.: [41] (1) 877 91 91
Fax: [41] (1) 925 71 22
(Computers)
Apple Computer

Boise Cascade Specialty Paperboard AG
General Wille Strasse 21
CH-8027 Zurich, Switzerland
(Paperboard)
Boise Cascade Corp.

Bridgestone Firestone Schweiz AG
Pfadackerstrasse 6
CH-8957 Spreitenbach, Switzerland
Tel.: [41] (56) 418 71 11
Fax: [41] (56) 401 34 68
(Tires and tubes)
Firestone Tire & Rubber Co.

Data General AG
Postfach 761
CH-8037 Zurich, Switzerland
(Commerical equipment)
Data General Corp.

Digital Equipment Corp International SA
12 avenue des Morgines
CH-1213 Petit-Lancy, Switzerland
Tel.: [41] (22) 709 41 11
Fax: [41] (22) 709 41 40
(Computer services)
Digital Equipment Corp.

Ford Motor Co Switzerland SA
Kurvenstrasse 35
CH-8006 Zurich, Switzerland
Tel.: [41] (1) 365 71 11
(Automobiles & parts)
Ford Motor Co.

General Motors Suisse SA
Salzhausstrasse 21
CH-2501 Biel-Bienne, Switzerland
Tel.: [41] (32) 21 51 11
(Automobiles)
General Motors Corp.

Hewlett-Packard (Schweiz) AG
In der Luberzen 29
CH-8902 Urdorf, Switzerland
Tel.: [41] (1) 735 71 11
Fax: [41] (1) 735 77 00
(Electronics)
Hewlett-Packard Corp.

Honeywell AG
Heristrasse 2
CH-8304 Wallisellen, Switzerland
Tel.: [41] (1) 839 25 25
Fax: [41] (1) 831 01 10
(Measuring and control technology)
Honeywell, Inc.

IBM (Schweiz)
quai Bändliweg 21
CH-8071 Zurich, Switzerland
Tel.: [41] (1) 643 43 43
Fax: [41] (1) 643 40 10

(Data processing equipment)
International Business Machines Corp.

Kodak SA
avenue de Rhodanie 50
CH-1007 Lausanne, Switzerland
Tel.: [41] (21) 619 74 65
(Photographic equipment)
Eastman Kodak Co.

Mobil Oil (Switzerland)
Picassoplatz 4
CH-4010 Basle, Switzerland
Tel.: [41] (61) 287 77 00
(Petroleum products)
Mobil Petroleum Co.

NCR (Schweiz)
Postfach 579
CH-8304 Glattzentrum/Wallisellen,
Switzerland
Tel.: [41] (1) 832 11 11
Fax: [41] (1) 830 74 95
(Office machinery)
NCR

Rank Xerox AG
Thurgauerstrasse 40
CH-8050 Zurich, Switzerland
Tel.: [41] (1) 305 12 12
Fax: [41] (1) 305 14 72
(Copier equipment)
Rank Xerox (Mgmt) Ltd.

Reynolds Tobacco AG
Baselstrasse 65
CH-6252 Dagmersellen, Switzerland
Tel.: [41] (62) 748 01 11
Fax: [41] (62) 756 13 27
(Tobacco products)
RJR Nabisco Inc.

3M Schweiz AG
Eggstrasse 93
CH-8803 Rüschlikon, Switzerland
Tel.: [41] (1) 724 90 90
Fax: [41] (1) 724 94 50
(Adhesives, tapes, and packaging)
Minnesota Mining and Manufacturing
Co.

Warner-Lambert (Schweiz) AG
Blegistrasse 11a
CH-6340 Baar, Switzerland
Tel.: [41] (41) 760 35 35
Fax: [41] (41) 769 18 19
(Chewing gum)

SERVICE INDUSTRIES

Advco Young & Rubicam
Meisenrain 39
Ch-8044 Zurch Gockhausen, Switzerland
Tel.: [41] (1) 801 91 91
Fax: [41] (1) 801 92 92
(Advertising)
Young & Rubicam

Amdahl Switzerland AG
Baumackerstrasse 46
CH-8050 Zurich, Switzerland
Tel.: [41] (1) 31 14 20
(Computer equipment)
Amdahl Corp.

Arthur Andersen AG
Binzmühlestrasse 14
CH-8050 Zurich, Switzerland
Tel.: [41] (1) 308 18 88
Fax: [41] (1) 308 18 01
(Accounting and business consultants)
Arthur Andersen & Co.

ATAG Ernst & Young AG
Aeschengraben 9
CH-4051 Basel, Switzerland
Tel.: [41] (61) 286 86 86
Fax: [41] (61) 272 40 60
(Business consultants)
Ernst & Young

Brown Brothers Harriman Services AG
Stockerstrasse 38
CH-8002 Zurich, Switzerland
(Management and public relations)
Brown Brothers Harriman & Co.

Cargill Financial Services International
Chemin de-Normandie 14
CH-1211 Geneva 12, Switzerland
Tel.: [41] (22) 703 22 11
Fax: [41] (22) 703 25 55
(Import-export)
Cargill

Coopers & Lybrand AG
St. Jakobs Strasse 25
CH-4052 Basel, Switzerland
Tel.: [41] (61) 277 55 00
Fax: [41] (61) 277 55 88
(Financial advisors and business consultants)
PriceWaterhouseCoopers

Dow Jones Markets Switzerland AG
Hardturnstrasse 181
CH-8005 Zurich, Switzerland
Tel.: [41] (1) 279 17 11
Fax:[41] (1) 271 83 87
(Market research)
Dow Jones

Raytheon Europe Intl. Co
route des Acacias 24
CH-1227 Geneva, Switzerland
(Management services)
Raytheon Co.

Viacom SA
Chamerstrasse 18
CH-6300 Zug, Switzerland
(Video distribution)
Viacom International Inc.

EUROPEAN COMPANIES IN SWITZERLAND

The following are major non-American firms operating in the country. These selected companies can be either domestic or foreign, usually other European. Such companies will generally hire their own nationals first but may employ Americans.

BANKING AND FINANCE

Crédit Suisse Group
Postfach 1
CH-8070 Zurich, Switzerland
Tel.: [41] (1) 212 16 16
Fax: [41] (1) 333 25 87
(Bank)

Deutsche Bank Suisse SA
Place des Bergues 3
CH-1211 Geneva 1, Switzerland
Tel.: [41] (22) 739 91 11
Fax: [41] (1) 214 92 85
(Bank)

Electrowatt Ltd.
Postfach Bellerivestrasse 36
CH-8022 Zurich, Switzerland
Tel.: [41] (1) 385 22 11
Fax: [41] (1) 385 25 55
(Investment offices)

Swiss Bank Corporation
Aeschenplatz 6
CH-4002 Basle, Switzerland
Tel.: [41] (61) 288 20 20
Fax: [41] (61) 288 45 76
(Joint stock bank)

Swiss Reinsurance Company
Mythenquai 2
CH-8021 Zurich, Switzerland

Tel.: [41] (1) 285 21 21
Fax: [41] (1) 285 29 99
(Reinsurance)

Union Bank of Switzerland
Bahnhofstrasse 45
CH-8021 Zurich, Switzerland
Tel.: [41] (1) 234 11 11
Fax: [41] (1) 236 51 11
(Bank)

Winterthur Versicherung
General-Guisan-Strasse 40
CH-8401 Winterthur, Switzerland
Tel.: [49] (52) 261 11 11
Fax: [49] (52) 261 41 71
(Insurance)

INDUSTRIAL MANUFACTURING

ABB Asea Brown Boveri Ltd.
Affolternstrasse 44
CH-8050 Zurich, Switzerland
Tel.: [41] (1) 317 71 11
Fax: [41] (1) 317 73 21
(Electricity production)

Bic Suisse
via Cantonale 69
CH-6916 Grancia, Switzerland
Tel.: [41] (91) 985 11 11
Fax: [41] (91) 985 11 10
(Ballpoint pens)

Ciba-Geigy AG
Lettenweg 118
CH-4123 Allschwil, Switzerland
Tel.: [41] (61) 485 50 50
Fax: [41] (61) 64 52 27
(Pharmaceuticals)

Citroen (Suisse) SA
route Acacias 27
CH-1227 Les Acacias, Switzerland
Tel.: [41] (22) 308 01 11
Fax: [41] (22) 342 60 42
(Automobiles)

Georg Fischer Kunststoffarmaturen AG
Seewis
CH-7302 Landquart, Switzerland
Tel.: [41] (81) 307 55 00
Fax: [41] (81) 307 55 77
(Rubber products)

Kraft Jacobs Suchard AG
Bellerivestrasse 203
CH-8032 Zurich, Switzerland
Tel.: [41] (1) 387 81 82
Fax: [41] (1) 387 81 30
(Chocolate and confections)

Landis & Gyr AG
Gubelstrasse 22
CH-6300 Zug, Switzerland
Tel.: [41] (41) 724 11 24
Fax: [41] (41) 724 35 22
(Measuring and control instruments)

Liebherr-International SA
rue de l'Industrie 19
CH-1630 Fribourg, Switzerland
Tel.: [41] (29) 33111
(Construction machinery)

Lonza AG
Münchensteinerstrasse 38
CH-4052 Basel, Switzerland
Tel.: [41] (61) 316 81 11
Fax: [41] (61) 316 87 33
(Chemicals)

Montres Rolex SA
rue de Francois Dussaud 7
CH-1227 Les Acacias, Switzerland
Tel.: [41] (22) 308 22 00
Fax: [41] (22) 300 22 55
(Watches)

Nestlé SA
avenue Nestle 55
CH-1800 Vevey, Switzerland
Tel.: [41] (21) 924 21 11
Fax: [41] (21) 921 18 85
(Foods and confections)

Plüss-Straufer AG
Baslerstrasse 42
CH-4665 Oftringen, Switzerland
Tel.: [41] (62) 789 29 29
Fax: [41] (62) 789 20 77
(Chemicals)

Roche Holding Ltd.
Hauptsrasse 4
CH-4334 Sisseln AG, Switzerland
Tel.: [41] (62) 866 21 11
Fax: [41] (62) 866 25 10
(Pharmaceuticals and agricultural
chemicals)

Sandoz Ltd.
Lichtstrasse 35
CH-4002 Basle, Switzerland
Tel.: [41] (61) 324 11 11
Fax: [41] (61) 324 80 01
(Paints and chemicals)

Société Internationale Pirelli SA
St. Jakob-Strasse 54
CH-4052 Basle, Switzerland
Tel.: [41] (61) 316 41 11
Fax: [41] (61) 316 43 55
(Tires and inner tubes)

Sulzer AG
Zürcherstrasse 12
CH-8400 Winterthur, Switzerland
Tel.: [41] (52) 262 11 22
Fax: [41] (52) 262 01 01
(Mechanical and process engineering)

RETAILING AND WHOLESALING

COOP Schweiz
Postfach 2550
Thiersteinerallee 12
CH-4002 Basel, Switzerland
(Food and consumer goods)

Federation of Migros Cooperatives
Limmatstrasse 152
CH-8005 Zurich, Switzerland

Phone: [41] (1) 277 2111
Fax: [41] (1) 277 2525
(Foods)

Jelmoli Grands Magasins SA
Seidengasse 1
CH-8021 Zurich 1, Switzerland
(Department store)

SERVICE INDUSTRIES

ABB Kraftwerke AG (NOK)
Haselstrasse
CH-5401 Baden, Switzerland
Tel.: [41] (56) 205 77 33
Fax: [41] (56) 205 35 85
(Electricity generation and distribution)

Danzas Holding AG
Leimenstrasse 1
CH-4051 Basel, Switzerland
Tel.: [41] (61) 268 77 77
Fax: [41] (61) 261 58 47
(Shipping, airfreight, and railway)

Kuoni Reisebüro AG
Neue Hard 7
CH-8005 Zurich, Switzerland
Tel.: [41] (1) 277 44 44
Fax: [41] (1) 271 52 82
(Travel agency)

Panalpina AG
Reinacherstrasse 261
CH-4053 Basel, Switzerland
Tel.: [41] (61) 337 47 47
Fax: [41] (61) 331 39 50
(Shipping)

**PTT Schweizerische Post-Telephon-Und
Telegraphenbetriebe**
Viktoriastrasse 21
CH-3030 Bern, Switzerland
Tel.: [41] (31) 338 11 11
Fax: [41] (31) 338 25 49
(Postal and telecommunication services)

SwissAir Schweiz Luftverkehr AG
Flughafen
CH-8058 Zurich, Switzerland
Tel.: [41] (1) 812 12 12
Fax: [41] (1) 812 90 54
(Airline)

INTERNATIONAL NON-PROFIT EMPLOYERS IN SWITZERLAND

General Agreement on Tariffs and Trade
Centre William Rappard, 154 rue de
Lausanne
CH-1211 Geneva 21, Switzerland
Tel.: [41] (22) 739 5111

International Committee of the Red Cross
19, avenue de la Paix
CH-1202 Geneva, Switzerland
Tel.: [41] (22) 734 6001

**International Federation of Association
Football**
11 Hitzigweg, Postfach 85
CH-8030 Zurich, Switzerland
Tel.: [41] (1) 384 9593

**International Federation of Red Cross
and Red Crescent Societies**
17, chemin des Crets
Case Postale 372
Petit-Saconnex
CH-1211 Geneva 19, Switzerland
Tel.: [41] (22) 730 4222

International Olympic Committee
Chateau de Vidy
CH-1007 Lausanne, Switzerland
Tel.: [41] (21) 253271

World Alliance of YMCAs
37, quai Wilson
CH-1201 Geneva, Switzerland
Tel.: [41] (22) 732 3100

World Council of Churches
Case Postale 2100
CH-1211 Geneva 2, Switzerland
Tel.: [41] (22) 791 6111
Fax: [41] (22) 791 0361

World Health Organization
20 avenue Appia
CH-1211 Geneva 27, Switzerland
Tel.: [41] (22) 791 2111
Fax: [41] (22) 791 0746

World Scout Bureau
Case Postale 241
CH-1211 Geneva 4, Switzerland
Tel.: [41] (22) 320 4233

INTERNATIONAL SCHOOLS IN SWITZERLAND

American International School of Zurich
Nidelbadstrasse 49
CH-8802 Kilchberg, Switzerland
Tel.: [41] (1) 715 27 95
Fax: [41] (1) 715 26 94
Email: aisz@aisz.ch
www.aisz.ch
(U.S. curriculum, grades 7-13)

Collège du Léman International School
route de Sauverny 74
CH-1290 Versoix/Geneva, Switzerland
Tel.: [41] (22) 755 2555

Fax: [41] (22) 755 1993
Email: info@cdl.ch
www.cdl.ch
(U.S., U.K., Swiss, French, K-13)

International School of Basel
Burggartenstr 1
P.O. Box 316
CH-4103 Bottmingen, Switzerland
Tel.: [41] (61) 426 9626
Fax: [41] (61) 426 9625
Email: intsba@dial.eunet.ch
www.intschoolbasel.ch
(U.S., U.K., pre-K-12)

Austria

MAJOR EMPLOYMENT CENTER: Vienna

MAJOR BUSINESS LANGUAGE: German

LANGUAGE SKILL INDEX: Crucial for gaining employment. Local employment offices, for example, will ignore inquiries in any other language

CURRENCY: Euro; the Austrian schilling will remain the currency in circulation until 2002

TELEPHONE COUNTRY CODE: 43

TIME ZONE: EST+6

PUNCTUALITY INDEX: Austrians are very punctual

AVERAGE DAILY TEMPERATURE, HIGH/LOW: January, 34/26°F; July, 75/59°F (Vienna)

AVERAGE NUMBER OF DAYS WITH PRECIPITATION: January, 11; July, 15

BEST BET FOR EMPLOYMENT:

  FOR STUDENTS: Hospitality-type jobs or au pair positions

  PERMANENT JOBS: Finance and banking

CHANCE OF FINDING A JOB: Good

TRIVIA: Austrians are proud of their national heritage and are reputed to be friendlier than their northern neighbors, the Germans. Do not commit the faux pas of referring to an Austrian as a "German"

Abbout the size of Maine, Austria is located in central Europe. It's bordered by Switzerland and Liechtenstein to the west, Germany and the former Czechoslovakia to the north, Hungary to the east, and Italy and Yugoslavia to the south. Almost the entire country is blanketed by the Alps, except for the area around Vienna, which rests in the Danube basin. Ninety-five percent of the population speaks German; a large Slovene minority lives in the eastern portion of the country.

The areas comprising Austria were originally settled by Celtic tribes, who were conquered by the Romans. Eventually, the area formed a part of Charlemagne's empire. In 1271 the House of Hapsburg gained possession of the Austrian territories, founding a state that would encompass much of central and eastern Europe. In the nineteenth century, Vienna became Europe's clear cultural focus, especially in music. A dual Austro-Hungarian monarchy dominated vast areas of Europe until World War I. The empire collapsed in defeat and a republic was declared in 1918. A dictatorship followed and Hitler's Germany easily occupied the country in 1938. Following World War II, the Soviets occupied the eastern portion of the republic until 1955, when Parliament declared Austria to be permanently neutral.

Austria is a federal republic with nine states. The Social Democrats (SPÖ) and the conservative People's Party (ÖVP) have alternated or shared power for over 40 years, providing political consensus and stability. In spite of this stability, however, there was a huge international outcry in 1986 when former U.N. Secretary General Kurt Waldheim was elected president, after it was revealed that he may have collaborated in war crimes during his tenure in the German Army. The controversy resulted in the country's temporary internal isolation. Thomas Klestil, head of the ÖVP, was elected president in 1992 and reelected in 1998. In January, 1995, Austria became a member of the E.U.

Normal banking hours in Austria are from 7:45 a.m. to 4:00 p.m., with a break from 12:30 to 2:15 p.m., Monday through Friday. In Vienna banks are open from 8:00 a.m. to 3:00 p.m., Monday through Friday, except for Thursdays, when they are open until 5:30 p.m. Post offices in the larger cities are usually open 24 hours.

Current Economic Climate

Austria's gross national product and per capita income rank it as one of Europe's wealthiest countries. Unemployment has remained under 7% and inflation under 2%. The economy is bolstered by a large presence of foreign workers, mostly from eastern Europe. Austria's principal products include metallurgy, chemicals, electrical equipment, paper products, and textiles. Most trade occurs with E.U. and EFTA members, although eastern Europe is also important. The labor force is 60% industrial and commercial, 28% services, and 12% agricultural.

Tourism has become a major industry. It is based on ski and winter sports, the popular medicinal spas, and on the scenic, recreational, and cultural amenities available in the Alps. The number of foreigners visiting Austria annually has increased more than eightfold since 1955.

AUSTRIA'S 10 LARGEST EMPLOYERS

(1997, composite ranking)
1. Österreichsche Post
2. VA Technologie
3. EA-Generali
4. ÖMV Aktiengesellschaft
5. Creditanstalt-Bankverein
6. Bank Austria
7. Constantia Industrieholding
8. Bräu Union -Osterrichische
9. Allgemeine Baugesellschaft- A. Porr
10. Steyr- Daimler-Puch Aktiengesellschaft

Using the phone, fax, and Internet

Telephone calls in Austria are very expensive. There are four tariff time-periods for local and national calls. The most expensive period to place a call is from Monday to Friday, 8:00 a.m.—noon, and 1:00 p.m.—4:00 p.m. Calls during these periods are 2 1/2 times more expensive than the cheapest rates available nightly between 8:00 p.m.—6:00 a.m.

Faxes can be sent from the post office. Austrian fax numbers are merely an extension of the main telephone number. They may be listed in official publications with merely a hyphen and the extension number. You would first have to dial the main number to reach the fax.

Cybercafes are common in Vienna, Salzburg, Graz, and Innsbruck, making it easy to access Email.

Getting Around in Austria

The Austrian Federal Railways systems offer a variety of choices in traveling—trains, boats, buses, and cable cars. It also provides rental car services, with 52 locations in various cities. Eurail passes are valid for both trains and steamboats (along the Danube River). The bus, tram, and rail systems are all efficient but tend to be rather expensive.

Employment Regulations and Outlook for Americans

U.S. citizens don't need a visa for stays of fewer than 90 days. Visas, required for a longer visit, are granted only to foreigners with a valid work permit. Work permits are distributed by the State Employment Office, and an employer must declare that the position cannot be filled by an Austrian. Some knowledge of German is necessary for seasonal work, which may be sought in advance by writing to local employment offices, but you must write in German.

Work in the tourist industry, primarily in hotels and restaurants in ski areas, can be found, especially in the Tyrol. You should remember that most such jobs are probably illegal and will pay comparatively low wages. Some employers, such as bars and clubs in tourist areas, actually prefer to hire foreigners—with appropriate language skills.

Short-term and Temporary Work

There are many opportunities for casual work as an au pair. The Austrian-American Educational Commission places Americans into English-teaching jobs.

Austrian-American Educational Commission
Schmidgasse 14
A-1082 Vienna , Austria
Positions are for eight months, from October to May.

English for Kinds
A. Baumgartnerstr. 44 A/7042
A-1230 Vienna, Austria
Tel.: [43] (1) 667 45 79

Recruits TEFL-trained teachers for summer camps.

International School Kaprun
Alpine Sports and Ski Racing Academy
Postfach 47
A-5710 Kaprun, Austria
Tel./Fax: [43] 6547 7106
Recruits people to work for a year as teachers or outdoor work.

Internship Program

The best opportunities for students to obtain practical experience in Austria is to work with IASTE.

IASTE
10400 Little Patuxent Parkway, Suite 250 L
Columbia, MD 21044-3510
Tel.: (410) 997-3068
Fax: (410) 997-5186

Email: iaste@aipt.org
www. aipt.org/iaste.htm
Arranges reciprocal internship exchanges among 63 member countries for students in engineering, architecture, and the sciences.

Volunteer Opportunities

Most Austrian workcamps, located primarily in eastern Austria, are run by Service Civil International (SCI). Camps are organized around such themes as agriculture, gardening, cultural concerns, homosexual issues, and women's issues. Osterreichischer Bauorden (OB) employs volunteers in construction work and children's camps. Familiarity with German is recommended for both programs.

Osterreichischer Bauorden
Postfach 186, Hornesgasse 3
A-1031 Vienna, Austria

Service Civil International—Austria
Schottengasse 3 A1/59
A-1010 Vienna , Austria

NEWSPAPERS IN AUSTRIA

Kleine Zeitung
Schönaugasse 64
A-8011 Graz, Austria
Tel.: [43] (316) 87 50
Fax: [43] (316) 875 4004

Kurier
Lindengasse 48/52
A-1072 Vienna, Austria
Tel.: [43] (1) 52 111 0
Fax: [43] (1) 52 111 22 61

Neue Kronen Zeitung
Muthgasse 2
A-1191 Vienna, Austria
Tel.: [43] (1) 360 11 33 63
Fax: [43] (1) 360 12 05

Die Presse
Parkring 12A
A-1015 Vienna, Austria

Service Civil International—U.S.A.
Route 2, Box 506
Crozet, VA 22932
Tel.: (804) 823-1826

Tel.: [43] (1) 5 14 14 0
Fax: [43] (1) 5 14 14 400

Salzburger Nachrichten
Karolingerstrasse 40
A-5021 Salzburg, Austria
Tel.: [43] (662) 83 730
Fax: [43] (662) 83 73 399

Der Standard
Herrengasse 10-21
A-1014 Vienna, Austria
Tel.: [43] (1) 531 70
Fax: [43] (1) 531 70131

Wiener Zeitung
Rennweg 12A
A-1037 Vienna, Austria
Tel.: [43] (1) 797 890
Fax: [43] (1) 797 89433

Resources for Further Information

USEFUL WEBSITES FOR JOB SEARCHERS

The Internet is a good place to begin your job search. Many Austrian employers list job vacancies, especially those in technical fields, on the World Wide Web. There are also many websites that provide useful information for job searchers researching the Austrian job market.

Avotek Headhunters Site/International Jobs
www.xs4all.nl/~avotek/index.htm
Dutch and Austrian job listings.

The Business Traveler in Austria
www.wk.or.at/wk/aw/aw_intl/business/
travel.htm
Good advice for foreigners in Austria.

GIS Consulting
www.gis.telecom.at:80
Posts job opportunities; in German and English.

Iiasa
www.iiasa.ac.at
Posts employment opportunities for engineers.

Job Direct
www.job-direct.co.at/job-direct
Austrian recruiting firm.

EMBASSIES AND CONSULAR OFFICES

American embassies and consulates have commercial and/or economic sections that can provide you with business information and explain aspects of the local economy. Inquiries about business opportunities should be addressed either to "Commercial Officer" or "Commercial Section," followed by the appropriate street address.

Representation of Austria in the United States

Embassy of Austria
3524 International Court NW
Washington, D.C. 20008
Tel.: (202) 895-6700
Fax: (202) 895-6750

Austrian Consulates General: Chicago, (312) 222-1515; Los Angeles, (310) 229-4800; New York, (212) 737-6400

Representation of the United States in Austria

American Embassy
Boltzmanngasse 16
A-1091 Vienna, Austria
Tel.: [43] (1) 31339
Fax: [43] (1) 310 0628

CHAMBERS OF COMMERCE

Chambers of Commerce consist of firms in both countries interested in international trade. These are appropriate companies to initially target in the job search.

American Chamber of Commerce in Austria
Porzellangasse 35
A-1090 Vienna, Austria
Tel.: [43] (1) 319 57 51
Fax: [43] (1) 319 51 51
Email: office@amcham.or.at
www.amcahm.or.at

U.S.-Austrian Chamber of Commerce
165 West 46th Street
New York, NY 10036
Tel.: (212) 819-0117

WORLD TRADE CENTERS IN AUSTRIA

World Trade Centers usually include many foreign companies operating in the country.

World Trade Center Salzburg
c/o World Trade Center Development GmbH
Novel Salzburg City
Franz Josef Strasse 26
A-5020 Salzburg, Austria
Tel.: [43] (1) 70 07 60 00
Fax: 43] (1) 70 07 60 17

World Trade Center Vienna Airport
Wien Flughafen
A-1300 Vienna, Austria
Tel.: [43] (1) 70 07 60 00
Fax: [43] (1) 70 07 60 27
Email: wtc.vienna.airport@telecom.at

OTHER INFORMATIONAL ORGANIZATIONS

Foreign government missions in the U.S. such as tourist offices can furnish visas and information on work permits and other important regulations. They may also offer economic and business information about the country.

Austrian Institute
11 East 52nd Street
New York, NY 10022
Tel.: (212) 759-5165

Austrian National Tourist Office
Margaretenstrasse 1
A-1040 Vienna , Austria
Tel.: [43] (1) 588660

Austrian National Tourist Office, Chicago
500 North Michigan Avenue, Suite 1950

Chicago, IL 60611
Tel.: (312) 644-8029

Austrian National Tourist Office, New York
500 Fifth Avenue
New York, NY 10110
Tel.: (212) 944-6880

Austrian Press and Information Service
31 East 69th Street
New York, NY 10022
Tel.: (212) 288-1727

BUSINESS DIRECTORIES

Although not always easy to find, business directories can prove invaluable in the international job search. Most directories list company names, addresses, products, and phone numbers. Some directories include executive names and titles and financial information about the company. These sources provide you with the names of the people to contact for employment information as well as financial data, which can tell you how strong a company's position in a country may be.

American Chamber of Commerce in Austria–List of Members. Published every other year by the American Chamber of Commerce in Austria, Porzellangasse 35, A-1090 Vienna, Austria; email: office@amcham.or.at; www.amcham.or.at/amcham/members. Distributed in the U.S. by the United States Chamber of Commerce, International Division Publications, 1615 H Street NW, Washington, DC 20062-2000. Lists Austrian and American firms engaged in bilateral trade.

Austrian Commercial Directory. Published annually in German by Jupiter Verlagsgesellschaft, Robertgasse 2, A-1020 Vienna, Austria. Lists 120,000 manufacturing, trade, industrial, and service firms.

Finanz-Compass Osterreich. Published annually in German by Compass-Verlag, Matznergasse 17 32, A-1141 Vienna, Austria; office@compass.ar; www.compnet.as. Lists banks, insurance companies, and other public companies.

Grosse und Mittelstandische Unternehmen in Osterreich (Companies in Austria). Published by Verlag Hoppenstedt & Co., Havelstrasse 9, Postfach 100139, D-64285 Darmstadt, Germany; email: hoppenstadt@t-online.de. Lists 10,000 leading industrial and service companies.

Made in Austria. Available from Jupiter Verlagsgesellschaft, Robertgasse 2, A-1020 Vienna, Austria. Lists 2,500 major Austrian firms engaged in export and distribution. Available only as a CD-ROM.

Personen-Compass. Published annually in German by Compass-Verlag, Wipplingerstrasse 32, A-1013 Vienna, Austria. Lists 19,000 executives of major Austrian firms.

U.S. List of American Firms, Subsidiaries, Affiliates, and Licencees. Published annually by the American Chamber of Commerce in Austria, Porzellangasse 35, A-1090 Vienna, Austria; email: office@amcham.or.at; www.amcham.or.at/. Covers subsidiaries of American companies in Austria.

Wer Liefert Was? Published annually in German by "Wer Liefert Was?" GmbH Bezugsquellennachweis fur den Einkauf, Normannenweg 18-20, D-20537 Hamburg 26, Germany; email: info@wlwonline.de; www.wlwonline.de. A CD-ROM that lists 100,000 German, 12,000 Austrian, and 13,000 Swiss manufacturers.

AMERICAN COMPANIES IN AUSTRIA

The following companies are classified by business area: Banking and Finance; Industrial Manufacturing; Retailing and Wholesaling; and Service Industries. Company information includes firm name, address, phone and fax number, specific business, and American parent company. Your chances of achieving employment abroad are substantially better if you contact the subsidiary company in Europe rather than the parent company in the U.S.

BANKING AND FINANCE

American Express Bank Ltd.
Kärntnerstrasse 21-23
A-1010 Vienna, Austria
Tel.: [43] (1) 515 67
Fax: [43] (1) 515 673
(Banking and financial services)
American Express, New York

Citibank International PLC
Lothringerstrasse 7
A-1010 Vienna, Austria

Tel.: [43] (1) 717 17
Fax: [43] (1) 717 92 06
(Commercial bank)
Citibank Overseas Investment Corp.

Merrill Lynch Pierce Fenner & Smith GmbH
Passauer Platz 5
A-1010 Vienna, Austria
(Securities)
Merrill Lynch International Bank Inc.

INDUSTRIAL MANUFACTURING

Bristol-Meyers GmbH
Mittersteig 10
A-1050 Vienna, Austria
Tel.: [43] (1) 56 35 51
(Pharmaceuticals)
Bristol-Meyers Co.

Coca-Cola Amatil Österreich GMBH
Hallerstrasse 133
A-6020 Innsbruck, Austria
Tel.: [43] (512) 24 24 14
Fax: [43] (512) 24 14 96
(Beverages)
Coca Cola

Digital Equipment Corp.
Vesendorfer Nordring 2
A-2334 Vosendorf-Sud, Austria
Tel.: [43] (222) 69 01 0
(Data processing equipment)
Digital Equipment Corp.

Esso Austria AG
Argentinierstrasse 23
Postfach 201
A-1040 Vienna, Austria
Tel.: [43] (222) 501 40
(Petroleum products)
Exxon Corporation

Head Sportgeräte GmbH
Wuhrkopfweg 37
A-6921 Kennelbach, Austria
Tel.: [43] (5574) 32 8 81
(Sporting goods)
Minstar Inc.

Honeywell Austria GmbH
Handelskai 388
A-1020 Vienna, Austria
Tel.: [43] (1) 72 780
Fax: [43] (1) 72 78 08
(Building control equipment)
Honeywell, Inc.

IBM Österreich GmbH
Lassallestrasse 1
A-1020 Vienna, Austria
Tel.: [43] (1) 21 14 50
Fax: [43] (1) 216 08 86
(Office machines)
IBM World Trade Corp.

Kodak GmbH
Albert Schweitzer-Gasse 4
A-1148 Vienna, Austria
Tel.: [43] (222) 97 01 0
(Photographic equipment)
Eastman Kodak Co.

Master Foods Austria GmbH
Eisenstädterstrasse 80
A-7091 Breitenbrunn, Austria
Tel.: [43] (2162) 60 10
Fax: [43] (2162) 60 16 11
(Chocolate bars, rice)
Mars, Inc.

Procter & Gamble GmbH
Mariahilferstrasse 77-79
A-1060 Vienna, Austria
Tel.: [43] (1) 58 85 70
Fax: [43] (1) 58 85 72 45
(Consumer products)
Procter & Gamble Co.

Tandem Computer GmbH
Handelskai 388/4/6/2
A-1020 Vienna, Austria
Tel.: [43] (1) 727 05
Fax: [43] (1) 720 50 62
(Computers)
Tandem Computers

Wrigley Austria GmbH
Josef-Waachstrasse 11
A-5023 Salzburg, Austria
Tel.: [43] (662) 640 85 00
Fax: [43] (662) 64 31 88
(Chewing gum)
W.M. Wrigley Jr. Co.

RETAILING AND WHOLESALING

Apple Computer GmbH
Ungargasse 59
A-1030 Vienna, Austria
Tel.: [43] (1) 71 1820
(Computers)
Apple Computers

Colgate-Palmolive GmbH
Argentinierstrasse 22/1
A-1040 Vienna, Austria
Tel.: [43] (1) 505 89 51
Fax: [43] (1) 505 89 51 57
(Household and personal care products)
Colgate-Palmolive

Conoco Austria Mineralöl
Sarnergasse 27
A-5020 Salzburg, Austria
Tel.: [43] (662) 877 88 00
Fax: [43] (662) 87 78 80 18
(Petroleum products)
Conoco Corp.

Ford Motor Co. (Austria) KG
Fürbergstrasse 51
A-5020 Salzburg, Austria
Tel.: [43] (662) 642 75 00
Fax: [43] (662) 642 75 05 55
(Automobiles and parts)
Ford Motor Co.

General Motors Austria GmbH
Gross Enzersdorferstrasse 59
A-1220 Vienna, Austria

Tel.: [43] (1) 22 450
(Automobiles and automobile parts)
General Motors Corp.

Hewlett-Packard GmbH
Lieblgasse 1
A-1222 Vienna, Austria
Tel.: [43] (1) 2500 0
(Electronic equipment)
Hewlett-Packard Corp.

Mobil Oil Austria AG
Schwarzenbergplatz 3
A-1010 Vienna, Austria
Tel.: [43] (1) 711 06 0
(Petroleum products)
Mobil Corp.

NCR Österreich GmbH
Storcheng 1
A-1150 Vienna, Austria
Tel.: [43] (1) 891 11
Fax: [43] (1) 891 11 20 10
(Office equipment and software)
NCR Corp.

Rank Xerox Austria GmbH
Nussdorfer Lände 29-33
A-1191 Vienna, Austria
Tel.: [43] (1) 37 35 11 0
(Copier equipment)
Xerox Corp.

3M Österreich Gesellschaft
Brunnerfeldstrasse 63
A-2380 Perchtoldsdorf, Austria
Tel.: [43] (1) 866 86
Fax: [43] (1) 86 68 62 42
(Office equipment and supplies)
Minnesota Mining and Manufacturing
Corp.

SERVICE INDUSTRIES

Andersen Consulting
Jacquingasse 29
A-1030 Vienna, Austria
Tel.: [43] (1) 799 15 08
Fax: [43] (1) 799 15 09
(Management consulting)
Andersen Consulting

A. C. Nielsen Co., GmbH
Moeringgasse 20
A-1150 Vienna, Austria
Tel.: [43] (1) 98 11 00
Fax: [43] (1) 981 10 77
(Marketing research)
Dun and Bradstreet Corp.

Deloitte & Touche Danubia Treuhand GmbH
Friedrichstrasse 10
A-1010 Vienna, Austria

Unisys Österreich GmbH
Seidengasse 33-35
A-1070 Vienna, Austria
Tel.: [43] (1) 52 12 10
Fax: [43] (1) 52 12 13 53
(Information systems)
Unisys Corp.

Tel.: [43] (1) 588 54
Fax: [43] (1) 588 54 72 99
(Financial services)
Deloitte & Touche

McCann-Erickson GmbH
Gregor Mendel Strasse 50
A-1191 Vienna, Austria
Tel.: [43] (1) 3125250
(Advertising agency)
McCann-Erickson Worldwide

Warner Bros. GmbH
Zieglergasse 10
A-1070 Vienna, Austria
Tel.: [43] (1) 52 38 62 60
Fax: [43] (1) 523 86 26 31
(Motion picture distribution)
Warner Brothers

EUROPEAN COMPANIES IN AUSTRIA:

The following are non-American firms operating in the country. These selected companies can be either domestic or foreign, usually other European. Such companies will generally hire their own nationals first but may employ Americans.

BANKING AND FINANCE

Bank Austria AG
Vordere Zollamtsstrasse 13
A-1030 Vienna, Austria
Tel.: [43] (1) 711 91
Fax: [43] (1) 711 91 61 55
(Bank)

Creditanstalt-AG
Schottengasse 6-8
A-1010 Vienna, Austria
Tel.: [43] (2) 531 31
Fax: [43] (2) 531 31/4699
(Commercial bank)

Die Erste Österreichische Spar-Kasse-Bank AG
Graben 21
A-1010 Vienna, Austria
Tel.: [43] (1) 531 00
Fax: [43] (1) 531 00 411
(Joint stock company)

Salzburger Sparkasse Bank AG
Alter Markt 3
A-5020 Salzburg, Austria
Tel.: [43] (662) 80 400
Fax: [43] (6620 804 081
Federal Reserve Banks

INDUSTRIAL MANUFACTURING

ÖMV Aktiengesellschaft
Lasallestrasse 3
A-2030 Vienna, Austria
Tel.: [43] (1) 40 44 00
Fax: [43] (1) 40 40 96
(Oil and natural gas)

Österreichische Automobilfabrik AG
Brunner Strasse 44-50
A-1230 Vienna, Austria
Tel.: [43] (1) 866 31
Fax: [43] (1) 866 31 179
(Truck & bus manufacturing)

Porsche Austria
Vogelweiderstrasse 75
A-5020 Vienna, Austria
Tel.: [43] (662) 46 81
Fax: [43] (662) 46 81 24 61
(Cars)

Semperit Reifen AG
Wienersdorfer Strase 20-24
A-2514 Traiskirchen, Austria
Tel.: [43] (2252) 50 10
Fax: [43] (2252) 52 268
(Tires)

Siemens AG Österreich
Siemensstrasse 88-92
A-1210 Vienna, Austria

Tel.: [43] (1) 17 07
Fax: [43] (1) 170 75 35 19
(Communication and data systems)

Sony DADC Austria AG
Niederalm 282
A-5081 Anif, Austria
Tel.: [43] (6246) 88 00
Fax: [43] (6246) 72 090
(Computer storage devices)

Steyr-Daimler-Puch AG
Technologiezentrum
Schönauerstrasse 5
A-4400 Steyr, Austria
Tel.: [43] (7252) 58 00
Fax: [43] (7252) 58 0752
(Automobile, engineering and military technology)

Voest-Alpine AG
Schulstrasse 9/2 OG UPktC
A-4040 Linz, Austria
Tel.: [43] (732) 73 03 12
Fax: [43] (732) 73 03 234
(Mining and construction)

RETAILING AND WHOLESALING

Julius Meinl AG
Julius-Meinl-Gasse 3-7
A-1160 Vienna, Austria
Tel.: [43] (1) 488 60
Fax: [43] (1) 488 60 13 06
(Food retailing)

Zumtobel Licht Gesellschaft MBH
Schweizerstrase 30,
A-6850 Dombirn, Austria
Tel.: [43] (5572) 39 0
Fax: [43] (5572) 39 06 01
(Retailing)

SERVICE INDUSTRIES

Allgemeine Baugesellschaft-A. Porr AG
Rennweg 12
A-1031 Vienna, Austria
Tel.: [43] (1) 797 200
Fax: [43] (1) 791 332
(Construction & civil engineering)

Erste Allgemeine-Generali Versicherungs AG
Landskrongasse 1-3
A-1010 Vienna, Austria
Tel.: [43] (1) 534 01
Fax: [43] (1) 534 01 226
(Insurance)

Ward Howell Unternehmensberatungs
Argentinierstrasse 26/3/10
A-1040 Vienna, Austria
Tel.: [43] (1) 50 107 0
Fax: [43] (1) 50 107 10
(Staff recruitment services)

Manpower Unternehmens und Personalberatung GMBH
Kirchberggasse 33/1
A-1020 Vienna, Austria
Tel.: [43] (1) 214 80 05
(Staff recruitment services)

Österreichische Bundesbahn (ÖBB)
Elisabethstrasse 9
A-1010 Vienna, Austria
(National railway company)

Österreichische Luftverkehrs AG
Postfach 50, Fontanastrasse 1
A-1107 Vienna, Austria
Tel.: [43] (1) 17 89
Fax: [43] (1) 688 55 05
(Airline)

Österreichische Post-und Telegraphen-Verwaltung
Postgasse 8-10
A-1011Vienna, Austria

Tel.: [43] (1) 51 55 10
Fax: [43] (1) 512 84 14
(Postal and telecommunication services)

Tasa International
Schwindgasse 20
A-1040 Vienna, Austria
Tel.: [43] (1) 505 62 71
Fax: [43] (1) 505 62 75
(Staff recruitment services)

INTERNATIONAL NON-PROFIT EMPLOYER IN AUSTRIA

N. Industrial Development Organization
Vienna International Center
Postfach 300
A-1400 Vienna, Austria
Tel.: [43] (1) 21131

INTERNATIONAL SCHOOLS IN AUSTRIA

American International School
Salmanndorferstrasse 47
A-1190 Vienna, Austria
Tel.: [43] (1) 401 32 0
Fax: [43] (1) 401 32 5
Email: info@ais.at
www.ais.at
(U.S., International Baccalaureat, Austrian curriculum, grades pre-K-12)

Vienna International School
Strasse der Menschenrechte 1
A-1220 Vienna, Austria
Tel.: [43] (1) 203 55 95
Fax: [43] (1) 203 03 66
Email: info@vis.ac.at
www.vis.ac.at
(I.B., K-13)

Liechtenstein

MAJOR EMPLOYMENT CENTERS: Vaduz, Schaan

MAJOR BUSINESS LANGUAGE: German

LANGUAGE SKILL INDEX: Knowledge of German is important, although there are times when English may suffice. Allemanic is the local German dialect

CURRENCY: Swiss franc

TELEPHONE COUNTRY CODE: 41

TIME ZONE: EST+6

PUNCTUALITY INDEX: As in Switzerland and Austria, be on time

BEST BET FOR EMPLOYMENT:

FOR STUDENTS: Hospitality or work as an au pair

PERMANENT JOBS: Banking and finance

CHANCE OF GETTING A JOB: Not bad for those with high-level business skills. Keep in mind, though: it's a small country. Adjust your expectations accordingly

TRIVIA: Foreign workers comprise over a quarter of Liechtenstein's total population of 28,600

The principality of Liechtenstein covers only 62 square miles, making it less than a twentieth the size of Rhode Island, the United States' smallest member. Liechtenstein is nestled in the Alps, sandwiched between Switzerland to the west, Austria to the east. The Alps actually cover about two-thirds of the country; the remainder is occupied by the Rhine Valley. Relations with Austria and Switzerland are cozy not only in terms of geography but in other ways as well. Although Liechtenstein gained sovereignty in the 19th century, its ports were administered by Austria until 1920. Switzerland continues to administer its postal system, as it has since 1921, and the two countries are joined by monetary and telecommunications unions as well.

Liechtenstein as we know it was established in 1712, when the house of Liechtenstein forged a union between the lordships of Vaduz and Schellenberg, both of which had until that time been fiefdoms of the Holy Roman Empire. The line of succession of Liechtenstein's hereditary constitutional monarchy has remained unbroken since that time. The present head of state is Prince Hans Adam II, who has held his position since November, 1989. The head of government since 1978 has been Hans Brunhart, who presides over a diet of 15 members elected by popular vote.

Liechtenstein joined the U.N. in 1990 and the European Economic Area in 1995. Liechtenstein currently has no plans to seek full E.U. membership.

Liechtensteiners enjoy a literacy rate of 100%. Population growth is fairly steady, at a rate of less than 1% per year. Religious preference in Liechtenstein leans overwhelmingly Roman Catholic, at close to 90% of the population. Liechtenstein has no military—it was disbanded in 1868.

Current Economic Climate

Liechtenstein is a very prosperous country, known for its wines, postage stamps, dentures, and status as a tax haven. Its primary industries include precision instruments, chemicals, and ceramics. In 1998, the country had, by its standards, a high level of unemployment: 1.4% or a mere 311 people.

The country was heavily agrarian well into the 20th century. The 1930s to 1960s witnessed a decline in Liechtenstein's farm population from 60% to only 8% of the population. At present, a mere 4% of the labor force is engaged in agriculture, with the vast majority of workers involved in industry and service occupations.

Employment Regulations and Outlook for Americans

U.S. citizens don't need a visa for tourist visits of less than 90 days, but a combination work and residence permit is required for foreign workers. Arrangements for this permit should be made by your employer. While the paperwork required for working in Liechtenstein is similar to that required by Switzerland, the actual work regulations are not identical. The result of this is that while securing permission for a foreigner to work in Switzerland can be very difficult, fully one-third of Liechtenstein's residents are foreign workers.

Volunteer Opportunities

Several U.S.-based organizations coordinate workcamps throughout Europe. Opportunities for voluntary work in Liechtenstein are probably relatively slim, thanks to the country's small size, but contacting one of the major coordinators below is likely your best hope.

International Voluntary Service
Route 2, Box 506
Crozet, VA 22932
Tel.: (804) 823-1826

Belmont, VT 05730
Tel.: (802) 259-2759
Email: vfp@vermontel.com
www.vermontel.com/~vfp/home.htm

Volunteers for Peace
International Workcamps
43 Tiffany Road

Resources for Further Information

USEFUL WEBSITES FOR JOB SEARCHERS

The Internet is a good place to begin your job search. There are websites that provide useful information for job searchers researching the Liechtenstein job market.

Liechtenstein Online
www.lol.li
Magazine that offers financial/economic information.

Travel Information
www.travel.com.hk/liechten.htm
Features travel information about Liechtenstein.

EMBASSIES AND CONSULAR OFFICES

Liechtenstein's interests in the United States are represented by Switzerland. Likewise, the United States consulate in Zurich represents U.S. interests in Liechtenstein. American embassies and consulates have commercial and/or economic sections that can provide you with business information and explain aspects of the local economy. Inquiries about business opportunities should be addressed either to "Commercial Officer" or "Commercial Section," followed by the appropriate street address.

Embassy of Switzerland
2900 Cathedral Avenue NW
Washington, DC 20008
Tel.: (202) 745-7900
Fax: (202) 387-2564

Representation of the United States in Liechtenstein

American Consulate General—Zurich
Zollikerstrasse 141
CH-8008 Zurich, Switzerland
Tel.: [41] (1) 55 25 66

CHAMBER OF COMMERCE

Chambers of Commerce consist of firms in both countries interested in international trade. These are appropriate companies to initially target in the job search.

Chamber of Commerce and Industry
Postfach 232
FL-9490 Vaduz, Liechtenstein
Tel.: [41] (75) 232 2744
Fax: [41] (75) 238 1503

BUSINESS DIRECTORIES

Although not always easy to find, business directories can prove invaluable in the international job search. Most directories list company names, addresses, products, and phone numbers. Some directories include executive names and titles and financial information about the company. These sources provide you with the names of the people to contact for employment information as well as financial data, which can tell you how strong a company's position in a country may be.

Dun & Bradstreet Swiss Company Information. Published by Dun & Bradstreet AG, Schoenegstrasse 5, CH-8026 Zurich, Switzerland. Lists 180,000 business in Switzerland and Liechtenstein.

Kompass Schweiz/Liechtenstein. Published annually by Kompass Schweiz Verlag AG, 14 in Grosswiesen, CH-8044 Zurich, Switzerland. Available in the U.S. from Croner Publications, 34 Jericho Turnpike, Jericho, NY 11753. Lists 38,000 manufacturers, distributors, and service companies in Switzerland and Liechtenstein.

Who's Who in Switzerland and the Principality of Liechtenstein. Published by Orelli Fussli, Dietzingerstrasse 3, CH-8036 Zurich, Switzerland; email: info@orelli-fuessli-verlag.ch. Lists 2,500 influential business, government, and other leaders in Switzerland and Liechtenstein.

MAJOR COMPANIES IN LIECHTENSTEIN

Small country, few companies; there's not much more to be said. Company information below includes firm name, address, phone and fax number, specific business, and, where appropriate, parent company. In the case of American parent firms, your chances of achieving employment abroad are substantially better if you contact the subsidiary company in Europe rather than the parent company in the U.S.

Bank in Liechtenstein AG
Herrengasse 12, Box 85
Vaduz, Liechtenstein
Tel.: [41] (75) 235 1122
Fax: [41] (75) 235 1522
(Commercial and merchant bank)

Black & Decker (Overseas) AG
Staedtle 36
Postfach 34709
FL-9409 Vaduz, Liechtenstein
(Hand-held power tools)
Black & Decker Co.

Liechtensteinische Landesbank
Stodtle 44
FL-9490 Vaduz, Liechtenstein
Tel.: [41] (75) 236 8811
Fax: [41] (75) 236 8822
(Universal bank)

Riunione Adriatica di Sicurta
Toniaule 10
FL-9490 Vaduz, Liechtenstein
Tel.: [41] (75) 22 446
(Insurance)
Allianz AG

Central Europe:
The Czech Republic, Slovakia, Hungary, Poland, and Romania

The Czech Republic and Slovakia

THE CZECH REPUBLIC

MAJOR EMPLOYMENT CENTER: Prague

MAJOR BUSINESS LANGUAGE: Czech

LANGUAGE SKILL INDEX: French and German can be useful alternatives

CURRENCY: koruna

TELEPHONE COUNTRY CODE: 420

TIME ZONE: EST+6

PUNCTUALITY INDEX: Punctuality is expected. Schedule appointments in advance

AVERAGE DAILY TEMPERATURE, HIGH/LOW: January, 34/25°F; July, 74/58°F (Prague)

AVERAGE NUMBER OF DAYS WITH PRECIPITATION: January, 20; July, 14

BEST BET FOR EMPLOYMENT:

FOR STUDENTS: Teaching English

PERMANENT JOBS: Business and manufacturing

CHANCE OF FINDING A JOB: Continually improving along with liberalization

TRIVIA: In both the Czech Republic and Slovakia, you may find that people allow you less "personal space" than you're accustomed to. You should, however, resist the urge to back away if you feel like someone's standing too close to you in conversation. It might be taken as an insult

SLOVAKIA

MAJOR EMPLOYMENT CENTERS: Bratislava, Kosice

MAJOR BUSINESS LANGUAGES: Slovak, Hungarian

LANGUAGE SKILL INDEX: German is the most useful non-Slavic language to know. Pride in language is an aspect of Slovak nationalism, so it is useful to know some Slovak

CURRENCY: new koruna

TELEPHONE COUNTRY CODE: 421

TIME ZONE: EST+6

PUNCTUALITY INDEX: Punctuality is expected. Schedule appointments in advance

BEST BET FOR EMPLOYMENT:

FOR STUDENTS: Teaching English

PERMANENT JOBS: New business development

CHANCE OF FINDING A JOB: Improving, but options are still limited

TRIVIA: Business cards are de rigeur in both the Czech Republic and Slovakia. You will make a good impression by having yours printed in English on one side, and either Czech or Slovak on the other as appropriate

Slavic tribes settled in the region now known as the Czech Republic and Slovakia during the fifth century. Bohemia and Slovakia were both part of the Great Moravian Empire during the ninth century. Slovakia eventually came under Magyar domination. Bohemia and Moravia were ruled by a Czech dynasty and became units of the Holy Roman Empire. The kings of Bohemia transformed medieval Prague into Europe's cultural center. Bohemia and Moravia became Hapsburg possessions in 1526 and, along with Slovakia, remained part of Austria-Hungary until 1918.

Czech and Slovak nationalists proclaimed the Republic of Czechoslovakia following World War I at the Treaty of Versailles. Under President Masaryk, the country maintained eastern Europe's only functioning democracy until 1938, when Adolf Hitler instigated tensions among the German minority in the Sudetenland in Bohemia. At Munich, Britain and France agreed to Hitler's annexation of the Sudetenland in order to prevent war. In 1939 the Nazis occupied Bohemia and Moravia as protectorates, ousted President Benes, and established a puppet Slovak republic. Soviet troops liberated Prague in 1945, and Benes again became president. The 1946 elections resulted in a Communist Party prime minister. In 1948 the communists seized complete power in a Soviet-supported coup.

Stalin's death led to a liberalization period, culminating in the Prague Spring of 1968, in which conservatives were replaced by reformers led by Alexander Dubcek. The forces of five Warsaw Pact countries invaded Czechoslovakia in August 1968, forcing Dubcek resignation in 1969. A human rights group, Charter '77, signed a petition demanding observance of the Helsinki Accords, instigating another crackdown in 1977. The Communist regime finally collapsed in surprisingly rapid fashion in late 1989 in what is known as the "Velvet Revolution."

Around the time of the Revolution the country's name was changed to the Czech and Slovak Federative Republic. Although the name change represented a symbolic gesture to Slovakia, the country was still referred to as Czechoslovakia. After the fall of communism, nationalist movements emerged, and some Slovaks began a movement to form their own state. Economic reforms were harder on the Slovak region in the east than the Czech region in the west, creating discontent. On August 26, 1992, the central government agreed to split into two independent states, the Czech Republic and Slovakia.

The Czech Republic is a democratic, unitary state that appears to have had little difficulty eradicating the vestiges of the communist Czechoslovak regime. Former dissident playwright Vaclav Havel was elected president by the Czech Parliament in 1993. Milos Zeman is the prime minister. The present government, which was reelected in 1996, is a coalition of the CDP, the Christian Democratic party, the CSSD, and the Social Democrats. The ultra-orthodox Communist Party gained 10% of the total vote.

Vladimír Meciar heads a coalition government in Slovakia with members from extreme left-wing and right-wing parties. Meciar has a reputation for exercising semi-authoritarian rule and has been criticized by human rights organizations and other European leaders for passing anti-democratic laws. The development of the political system has been hampered by the fact that many skilled Slovaks were working in Prague at the time of the split and have not returned home. Slovak is the only official language, exacerbating ethnic tensions with the large Hungarian minority that cannot use their native language in public places.

Business hours in the Czech Republic are generally from 8:30 a.m.—5:00 p.m., and from 8:00 a.m.—5:00 p.m. in Slovakia. Very few retail businesses are open on weekends in Slovakia.

Current Economic Climate

Czechoslovakia had one of the strongest economies in central and eastern Europe during the Communist period, although economic performance was hampered by centralization and political interference. The standard of living stagnated in the 1970s and 1980s. The Communist leadership nationalized industry, collectivized agriculture, and set up a central economic planning system. They emphasized heavy industry, mining, and manufacturing, neglecting agriculture and light industry.

While not endowed with massive natural resources, the Czech Republic is highly industrialized in comparison with other former Eastern bloc countries. Inflation has remained about 9% and the gross domestic product has averaged about 5% growth. Unemployment hovers below 3%. An important reason for the strength of the Czech economy is that the post-Communist government moved quickly to privatize industry and agriculture and to encourage foreign investment in the economy. The Prague stock market began trading in June 1993. Tourism has also helped the economy boom: in 1995, 100 million tourists visited the Czech Republic and spent $9.6 billion. Farming makes a significant contribution to the economy with dairy products, hops, and grapes that make for successful brewing and winemaking industries. The Czech Republic's largest trading partners are Germany, Slovakia, Russia, and Austria. Most trade is in manufactured goods, machinery, and transportation equipment. Trade with Slovakia has dropped by more than 50% since their separation.

Less developed and affluent than the Czech Republic, Slovakia has had more difficulty making the transition to a more liberal market economy, partly because of the reluctance of national leaders and partly because living standards are not high. Privatization has been moving steadily, with between one-quarter and one-third of the nation's enterprises now in private hands. By 1995, the economy was visibly improving, growing by 7.4% , second only to the Czech Republic in terms of its strength among former Eastern bloc countries. However, the economy does still have weak spots. It suffers from limited investment, in part because of criticisms of Meciar's authoritarian government. It is also dependent on government subsidies. Since 1995, 50% of the companies have not made a profit and would have gone bankrupt without such subsidies.

Getting Around in the Czech Republic and Slovakia

The national rail systems are inexpensive and fairly efficient. In the last 5 years, however, 300 train services in the Czech Republic have been canceled due to lack of passengers, making some of the more remote parts of the country harder to reach. In the Czech Republic buses are often easier and faster than the train; in Slovakia, by contrast, buses are more expensive and often serve fewer routes on weekends.

Using the phone, fax, and Internet

Czech Telecom is still replacing the antiquated telephone system with a digital system, so expect that telephone numbers will continue to change for several years to come. Faxes can be sent in the Czech Republic from major post offices. Public access to the Internet is virtually non-existent—there is only one cybercafe in the country.

The telephone system in Slovakia is also antiquated. Calls are often slow to connect, and crossed lines are common. Calls can most easily be placed from main post offices or telephone centers. The phone system is being modernized, and many telephone numbers are being changed. Faxes can be sent from most major post offices.

Employment Regulations and Outlook for Americans

American visitors don't require a visa for stays of less than 30 days, and visitors from the U.K. can stay as long as 180 days without a visa. For other foreigners—Canadians, New Zealanders, and Australians, for example—a visa is still required. Foreigners must go through a complicated process to obtain a work permit. Moreover, finding employment for foreigners is virtually impossible and should not be expected until further liberalization takes place. Some American, German, and Austrian companies already operate in the Czech Republic and Slovakia but will not expand significantly until the governments promote more extensive reforms. Workcamps and internship programs, however, are very active.

Short-term and Temporary Work

The opening of the Czech and Slovak economies to the West has created a huge demand for business people to learn English. The result is a booming industry for job seekers looking for short-term or temporary work.

Caledonian School
Vlatavska 24
CZ-150 00 Prague 5, Czech Republic
Tel.: [420] (2) 57 31 36 50
Hires people with TEFL background to teach English.

Czech Academic Information Agency
Dum Zahranicnich Sluzeb
Senovázné Námesti 26
CZ-111 21 Prague, Czech Republic
Tel.: [420] (2) 24 22 9698

or

Navrsku 8
P.O. Box 108
810 00 Bratislava, Slovakia
Tel: [421] (7) 5333 010
Assists English teachers to find jobs, mostly in state schools.

English for Everybody
655 Powell Street, Suite 505
San Francisco, CA 94108

Tel.: (415) 789 7641
TEFL teacher placement agency with large office in Prague.

Fandango
1613 Escalero Road
Santa Rosa, CA 95409
Tel./Fax: (707) 539-2722
A recruitment agency specializing in Czech Republic, Russia, Poland, the Baltic States, and Hungary.

InterExchange
161 Sixth Avenue
New York, NY 10013
Tel.: (212) 924-0446
Fax: (212) 924-0575
www.interexchange.org
Year-long placements to teach English in the Czech Republic (mostly Prague).

Internship Programs

For students interested in technical jobs, IASTE provides the best opportunities. The University of Pennsylvania also sponsors an internship program through which students can earn college credit.

IASTE
10400 Little Patuxent Parkway, Suite 250 L
Columbia, MD 21044-3510
Tel.: (410) 997-3068
Fax: (410) 997-5186
Email: iaste@aipt.org
www. aipt.org/iaste.htm
Arranges reciprocal internship exchanges among 63 member countries for students in engineering, architecture, and the sciences.

Penn-in-Prague
Penn Summer Abroad
University of Pennsylvania
3440 Market Street, Suite 100
Philadelphia, PA 19104-3335
Tel.: (215) 898-5738
Fax: (215) 573-2053
Arranges internships for students interested in the Jewish Museum in Prague and other organizations.

Volunteer Opportunities

The Brontosaurus Movement places volunteers into environmental summer camps throughout the Czech Republic. CIEE, in conjunction with youth exchange organizations in Prague, places U. S. students in volunteer positions in the summer months. These workcamp positions, which last for two weeks, are open to applicants aged 18 to 35. Other opportunities for volunteer work are available through Volunteers for Peace, a major U.S.-based international workcamp coordinator. Education for Democracy places volunteer English teachers in positions throughout the Czech Republic and Slovakia for a minimum four-month stay.

Brontosaurus Movement
Brontosaurus Council CR
Bubenska 6
CZ-170 00 Prague 7, Czech Republic
Tel.: [42] (2) 667 102 45

CIEE
Voluntary Service Department
205 East 42nd Street
New York, NY 10017
Tel.: (800) COUNCIL
Email: info@ciee.org_
www.ciee.org

Education for Democracy—U.S.A.
P.O. Box 40514
Mobile, AL 36640-0514
Tel.: (205) 434-3889
Fax: (205) 434-3731

Foundation for a Civil Society
Masaryk Fellowship Program
1270 Avenue of the Americas, Suite 609
New York, NY 10020
Tel.: (212) 332-2890
Fax: (212) 332-2898
Email: 73303.3024@compuserve.com
Coordinates 1-month placements in Czech or Slovak Republics during the summer.

Volunteers for Peace
International Workcamps
43 Tiffany Road
Belmont, VT 05730
Tel.: (802) 259-2759
www.vfp.org/

NEWSPAPERS IN THE CZECH REPUBLIC AND SLOVAKIA

Lidové noviny
Zerotinova 38
CZ-130 00 Prague 3, Czech Republic
Tel.: [420] (2) 670 98 111
Fax: [420] (2) 670 98 608

Práca (Work)
Odborarske nam. 3
814 99 Bratislava, Slovakia
Tel.: [421] (7) 650 60
Fax: [421] (7) 212 985

Pravda (Truth)
Central Committee of the Slovak
Communist Party
Pribinova 25
810 11 Bratislava, Slovakia
Tel.: [421] (7) 5367 503
Fax: [421] (7) 2104 759
Email: pravda@savba.sk

www.savba.sk/logos/news/pravda/
pravda.html

Rude Pravo (Red Right)
Na Porici 19
CZ-111 21 Prague 1, Czech Republic
Tel.: [420] (2) 248 116 07
Fax: [420] (2) 242 255 03

Smer Dnes (Course Today)
Cs. armády 10
975 43 Banská Bystrica, Slovakia
Tel.: [421] (88) 254 78
Fax: [421] (88) 255 06

Uj Szó (New World)
Martanovicova 25
819 15 Bratislava, Slovakia
Tel.: [421] (309) 331 2 52

Resources for Further Information

USEFUL WEBSITES FOR JOB SEARCHERS

The Internet is a good place to begin your job search. Although few employers list jobs on the Internet, there are websites that provide useful information about the Czech and Slovak job market.

Czech Business Directory
www.muselik.com:80
An excellent directory.

Czech Republic
http://reenic.utexas.edu/reenic/Countries/
Czech/czech.html
More Resources and links.

Doing Business with Czech Republic
www.czech.cz/homepage/busin.htm
Business tips for foreigners.

Jobs in the Czech Republic
www.jobs.cz/english_welcome.html
The first job server created in the Czech Republic.

A Traveler's Guide to the Czech Republic
www.czweb.com/czguide/index.htm
Useful "before-you-leave" information.

EMBASSIES AND CONSULAR OFFICES

American embassies and consulates have commercial and/or economic sections that can provide you with business information and explain aspects of the local economy. Inquiries about business opportunities should be addressed either to "Commercial Officer" or "Commercial Section," followed by the appropriate street address.

Representation of the Czech Republic in the United States

Embassy of the Czech Republic
3900 Spring of Freedom Street NW
Washington, DC 20008
Tel.: (202) 363-6315
Fax: (202) 966-8540

Representation of the United States in the Czech Republic

American Embassy
Triziste 15
CZ-125 48 Prague 1, Czech Republic
Tel.: [420] (2) 536 641
Fax: [420] (2) 532 457

Representation of Slovakia in the United States

Embassy of the Slovak Republic
2201 Wisconsin Avenue NW, Suite 250
Washington, DC 20007
Tel.: (202) 965 5161
Fax: (202) 965-5166

Representation of the United States in Slovakia

American Embassy
Hviezdoslavovo Namestie 4
811 02 Bratislava, Slovakia
Tel.: [421] (7) 533 3338
Fax: [421] (7) 5333 0096

CHAMBERS OF COMMERCE

Chambers of Commerce consist of firms in both countries interested in international trade. These are appropriate companies to initially target in the job search.

Czechoslovak Chamber of Commerce and Industry
Argentinska 38
CZ-170 05 Prague 7, Czech Republic
Tel.: [420] (2) 66 79 94939
Fax: [420] (2) 87 54 38
www.hospkomora.cz

Slovak Chamber of Commerce and Industry
Gorkcho 9
813 03 Bratislava, Slovakia
Tel.: [421] (7) 533 3272
Fax: [421] (7) 533 0754
www.scci.sk

WORLD TRADE CENTERS IN THE CZECH REPUBLIC AND SLOVAKIA

World Trade Centers usually include many foreign companies operating in the country.

World Trade Center Bratislava
Viedenská cesta 5
852 51 Bratislava, Slovakia
Tel.: [421] (1) 780 2026,
Fax: [421] (1) 758 1166 5
Email: incheba@incheba.sk
www.incheba.sk

World Trade Center Brno
Vystaviste 1
CZ-602 00 Brno, Czech Republic
Tel.: [420] (5) 4115 2670
Fax: [420] (5) 4115 2929
Email: wtc@bvv.cz
www.bvv.cz/wtc

World Trade Center Prague
Economic Chamber of the Czech Republic
Seifertova 22
Prague 3
CZ-130 00 Czech Republic
Tel.: [420] (2) 240 96 460
Fax: [420] (2) 240 96 222
Email: wtcpr@hkcr.cz
www.hosp-komora.cz1

OTHER INFORMATIONAL ORGANIZATIONS

Foreign government missions in the U.S. such as tourist offices can furnish visas and information on work permits and other important regulations. They may also offer economic and business information about the country.

Cedok (Tourist Office)
10 East 40th Street, Suite 1902
New York, NY 10016
Tel.: (212) 689-9720
Fax: (212) 481 0597

Tatra, Travel Bureau Inc.
212 East 51st Street
New York, NY 10022
Tel.: (212) 486 0533

BUSINESS DIRECTORIES

Although not always easy to find, business directories can prove invaluable in the international job search. Most directories list company names, addresses, products, and phone numbers. Some directories include executive names and titles and financial information about the company. These sources provide you with the names of the people to contact for employment information as well as financial data, which can tell you how strong a company's position in a country may be.

Business Guide Central-East Europe. Published by Overseas Post Organization, Dr. Hamische Verlags GmbH, Blumenstrasse 15, D-90402 Nuremburg, Germany; email: uepgus@aol.com. Lists business organizations in the Czech Republic, Poland, Hungary, Romania, Slovakia, Moldova, Bulgaria, Russian and the Ukraine.

Eastern Europe Business Directory. Published by Gale Research, 27500 Drake Road, Farmington Hills, MI 48331-3531; email: galeord@gale.com. Lists 7,000 companies in Bulgaria, Czech Republic, Slovakia, Hungary, Poland, Romany, the former East Germany, and the western parts of Russia.

MZM World Business Directory (Ex-Socialist World Business Directory). Available from MZM Publications Publishing Promotion, P.O. Box 465, PL-81-705 Sopot 5, Poland. Lists companies in 33 post-socialist countries involved in international trade.

AMERICAN COMPANIES IN THE CZECH REPUBLIC

Company information includes firm name, address, phone number, specific business, and American parent company. Your chances of achieving employment abroad are substantially better if you contact the subsidiary company in Europe rather than the parent company in the U.S.

Burson-Marsteller
Olivova 6
CZ-110 00 Prague 1, Czech Republic
Tel.: [420] (2) 221 731
(Public relations and public affairs consulting)
Burson-Marsteller

The Chase Manhattan Bank, NA
Hotel Diplomat, Rms. 332-334
Evropska Street 15
CZ-160 00/6 Prague, Czech Republic
Tel.: [420] (2) 331 4111
Fax: [420] (2) 331 4363
(Bank)
Chase Manhattan Bank, New York

Koospol/DMB&B Prague
Europska 178
CZ-160 67 Prague, Czech Republic
Tel.: [420] (2) 336 3424

(Advertising)
D'Arcy Masuis Benton & Bowles, Inc.

GE Central/Eastern Europe Area Operation
Male Namesti 2
CZ-110 01 Prague 1, Czech Republic
Tel.: [420] (2) 263 718
(Electronic equipment)
General Electric Co.

Pragocar
Legerova 52
CZ-120 00 Prague 2, Czech Republic
Tel.: [420] (2) 298 992
(Automobile rental)
Avis Rent A Car System, Inc.

EUROPEAN COMPANIES IN THE CZECH REPUBLIC AND SLOVAKIA

Balirny Douwe Egberts AS
9 K Zizkovu
CZ-190 00 Prague 9, Czech Republic
Tel.: [420] (2) 66 31 16 83
Fax: [420] (2) 683 72 30
(Coffee and tea)

BASF Obchodni Zastoupeni v CSFR
Ricanska 3
CZ-101 00 Prague, Czech Republic
Tel.: [420] (2) 273 1570
(Plastics & resins)
BASF AG

BASF Obchodni Zastoupeni v CSFR
Pobocka Bratislava
Kosicka ul. c. 44/111
821 08 Bratislava, Slovakia
Tel.: [421] (7) 767 593
(Plastics & resins)
BASF AG

CIBA-GEIGY Services AG
P.O. Box Stavoservis
CZ-460 77 Liberec, Czech Republic
Tel.: [420] (2) 6957
(Dyes and chemicals)
Ciba-Geigy Ltd.

Creditanstalt AS
Sirok 5
CZ-110 01 Prague 1, Czech Republic
Tel.: [420] (2) 232 1251
Fax: [420] (2) 232 5130
(Commercial bank)

Cskoslovensk Obchodna Banka AS
Na prikope 14
CZ-115 20 Prague, Czech Republic
Tel.: [420] (2) 233 1111
Fax: [420] (2) 232 7562
(Commercial bank)

E Z Elektrosystemy Statny Podnik
Ruzova Dolina 10

82 477 Bratislava, Slovakia
Tel.: [421] (7) 201 4111
(Engineering Service)

Hoechst, Obchodni Zastoupeni v CSFR
U. nemoc. pojistovny 4
CZ-110 00 Prague 1, Czech Republic
Tel.: [420] (2) 231 2277
(Pharamaceuticals and chemicals)
Hoechst AG

Investicna A Rozvojova Banka Akciova Spolecnost
Sturova 5
Bratislava, Slovakia
Tel.: [421] (7) 36 1051
(Commercial banks)

Mraziarne Statni Podnik
Trencianska 53
02 513 Bratislava, Slovakia
Tel.: [421] (7) 60 360
(Frozen fruits & vegetables)

Siemens AG
Vertretung in der CSFR
Na Strzi 40
CZ-140 00 Prague 4, Czech Republic
Tel.: [420] (2) 692 6345
(Electronics)
Siemens AG

Slovensk Statna Banka Sporitelna
(Slovak State Savings Bank)
Nemestie SNP 18
816 07 Bratislava, Slovakia
Tel.: [421] (7) 321 161
Fax: [421] (7) 367 087
(State commercial and savings bank)

Volkswagen Bratislava Spolescnost SRO
Jana Jonasa
84 108 Bratislava, Slovakia
Tel.: [421] (7) 775 121
(Motor vehicles & car bodies)

INTERNATIONAL SCHOOLS IN THE CZECH REPUBLIC AND SLOVAKIA

International School of Prague
c/o American Embassy Prague
Triziste 15
CZ-118 01 Prague 1, Czech Republic
Tel.: [420] (2) 203 84111
Fax: [420] (2) 203 84555
Email: ispmail@isp.cz

British International School, Bratislava
J Valastana Dolinskeho 1
84 102 Bratislava, Slovakia
Tel.: [421] (7) 643 66992
Fax: [421] (7) 643 64784
Email: bis@computel.sk

Hungary

MAJOR EMPLOYMENT CENTER: Budapest

MAJOR BUSINESS LANGUAGE: Hungarian

LANGUAGE SKILL INDEX: The national language is Magyar (Hungarian).
Some Hungarians also speak German, but English is very uncommon

CURRENCY: forint

TELEPHONE COUNTRY CODE: 36

TIME ZONE: EST+6

PUNCTUALITY INDEX: Promptness is expected

AVERAGE DAILY TEMPERATURE, HIGH/LOW: January, 35/26°F; July, 82/61°F (Budapest)

AVERAGE NUMBER OF DAYS WITH PRECIPITATION: January, 11; July, 12

BEST BET FOR EMPLOYMENT:

FOR STUDENTS: Teaching English

PERMANENT JOBS: Finance

CHANCE OF FINDING A JOB: Things are looking up

TRIVIA: Hungarians place the surname before the given name. Keep this in mind when
reading business cards, correspondence, and the like

Hungary is in east-central Europe, bordering Austria to the west, the Czech Republic and Slovakia to the north, Ukraine and Romania to the east, and Yugoslavia to the south. About the size of Indiana, Hungary is crossed by the Danube River. The western part of the country consists of a plain, the Alfold, while the north and west are hilly. Hungary's population is 92% Magyar, 3% German, 2% Romanian, and 3% Gypsy. Magyar is the official language. Roman Catholics comprise 67% of the population and Protestants 25%.

The present area of Hungary formed parts of the outer provinces of the Roman Empire. Magyars invaded the region in the ninth century, overwhelming the original Germanic and Slavic inhabitants. By the fourteenth century, Hungarian dominions stretched throughout central Europe. The Ottoman Turks began invading Hungary in 1389. In 1526 western and northern Hungary accepted Hapsburg domination to avoid Turkish rule. Eastern Hungary, including Transylvania, became independent. Louis Kossuth led a nationalist revolt in 1848, eventually contributing to the formation of a joint Austro-Hungarian monarchy in 1867. Austria-Hungary dissolved after defeat in World War I and Hungary lost over 68% of its territory, becoming a republic. Following a chaotic communist uprising and a subsequent Romanian invasion, Nicholas Horthy became Regent in a renewed monarchy in 1920.

Hungary joined the German invasion of the U.S.S.R. in 1941 but was defeated by 1944. In 1945 a republic was again proclaimed. The Communist Party seized control in 1948 and inaugurated a harshly repressive regime. In 1956 a Soviet invasion crushed the liberal movement led by Imre Nagy. Nearly 200,000 Hungarians fled the country. Nagy was executed. Janos Kadar became the premier and attempted a policy of reconciliation.

In 1989 Kadar's successor, Karoly Grosz, allowed free parliamentary elections in which the opposition easily won. In October 1989, radical amendments were made to the constitution, and the Hungarian People's Republic became the democratic Republic of Hungary. The transition to a full market economy has been painful and living standards for most people in Hungary have declined. In 1991, most state subsidies were removed, leading to a severe recession exacerbated by the fiscal austerity measures necessary to reduce inflation and stimulate the economy. In the 1994 elections, the Hungarian Socialist party led by former communists won a majority in parliament. This does not suggest Hungary is returning to its past, and indeed all three major Hungarian political parties advocate economic liberalization. Arpád Gonez of the social-democratic Alliance of Free Democrats was elected president in 1995.

Business hours are from 10:00 a.m. to 6:00 p.m., Monday through Friday, except on Thursday, when most businesses are open until 8:00 p.m. Banking hours are generally the same, except for Friday, when banks close at 2:00 p.m. Most businesses close on Sunday but are open on Saturday morning.

Current Economic Climate

Hungary's painful economic restructuring may finally be paying off. Hungarian living standards plummeted during the first half of the 1990s, particularly painful for a population shielded for more than 40 years by a communist government. Unemployment, officially 0% under communism, rose as high as 14% in 1994. Inflation topped out at 35%, and the forint lost half its value between 1992 and 1996.

Signs are, however, that the Hungarian economy is strengthening and may reach a level comparable to its Western neighbors. Hungary has been the destination for many American companies that are considering starting a base in central Europe. It has received over 40% of all capital by foreign companies investing in former eastern bloc countries. Unemployment has dropped to just over 10%, although most jobs are in more prosperous Budapest and Transdanubia. The Hungarian government hopes to get its economic house in order so that it might join the E.U. within the next few years.

An educated work force and excellent industrial infrastructure should enable the economy to prosper as foreign investment and privatization proceed. Major industries include: steel, chemicals, textiles, pharmaceuticals, machinery, and electronic equipment. Approximately 48% of the work force is engaged in manufacturing, 27% in services, and 20% in agriculture. Hungary has successfully replaced the markets lost from the collapse of Comecon (the former Soviet bloc economic organization) with markets in the West. Its major trade partners now include the E.U. and central Europe. Austria, Italy, and Germany also have extensive economic and trading relationships with Hungarian enterprises. Austria has especially capitalized upon its traditionally close ties to pursue investment opportunities in Hungary.

Using the phone

Public telephones are plentiful and in good working order. It is easier to use a telephone card available from any post office than rely on coins. Telephone boxes with a black and white arrow and a red target on the door and the word "visszahivhato," display a telephone number so you can receive incoming calls. All towns in Hungary have two-digit telephone area codes except Budapest, which simply has a "1." Faxes can be sent from most post offices. Cybercafes are common in Hungary, making it easy to access Email.

Getting Around in Hungary

The rail system is clean and reliable though notoriously slow. Express trains are available, however, in major cities. Eurail and InterRail passes are accepted throughout Hungary. The bus system is also cheap but more crowded than the trains. As with most transportation services in Hungary, buses focus primarily upon Budapest and branch out from there. The national airline, Malev, is rather expensive. Hydrofoil transportation on the Danube is a convenient but very expensive way to travel between Vienna and Budapest.

Employment Regulations and Outlook for Americans

Visas are not required for American citizens with a U.S. passport for stays of 3 months or less. No daily currency exchange is required. IBUSZ, the tourist office, is virtually the only place you will find staffed with English speakers. German is considered the second language. Employment prospects may be more promising with foreign-owned companies. You must obtain a work permit after receiving permission for permanent residence. For information on applying for a work permit, write to the Office of Foreigners' Affairs (KEOH), Andrassy ut 12, H-1061 Budapest, Hungary (Tel.: [36] (1) 118 0800).

Short-term and Temporary Work

The best bet for temporary work in Central Europe is to teach English.

Avalon '92 Agency
Erzsebet Krt. 15, 1st Floor #19
H-1073 Budapest, Hungary
Tel.: [36] (1) 351 3010
Places people into nanny positions.

InterExchange
161 Sixth Avenue
New York, NY 10013
Tel.: (212) 924-0446
Fax: (212) 924-0575

www.interexchange.org
Year-long placements to teach English in Hungary (mostly Budapest).

Teachers for Central and Eastern Europe
21 V 5 Rakovski Blvd.
H-6400 Dimitrovgrad, Bulgaria
Tel.: [35] (9) 391 24 787
Fax: [35] (9) 26 218
Recruits native speakers to teach English in Hungary and Poland.

Internship Program

For students interested in obtaining professional experience, IASTE provides the best opportunities.

IASTE
10400 Little Patuxent Parkway, Suite 250 L
Columbia, MD 21044-3510
Tel.: (410) 997-3068
Fax: (410) 997-5186

Email: iaste@aipt.org
www. aipt.org/iaste.htm
Arranges reciprocal internship exchanges among 63 member countries for students in engineering, architecture, and the sciences.

Volunteer Opportunities

The Central European Teaching Program places English teachers in schools throughout Hungary. CIEE places volunteers in international workcamps in Hungary. Projects include restoration and environmental conservation. For more information, contact CIEE's office in New York.

Central European Teaching Program
Beloit College
700 College Street
Beloit, WI 53511
Tel.: (608) 363-2619

CIEE
Voluntary Service Department
205 East 42nd Street
New York, NY 10017
Tel.: (800) COUNCIL
Email: info@ciee.org_
www.ciee.org

NEWSPAPERS IN HUNGARY

Magyar Hirláp
Kerepesj ut. 29/B
H-1087 Budapest, Hungary
Tel.: [36] (1) 113 0050
Fax: [36] (1) 113 3252/ 134 0712

Népszabadság
Besci ut. 122-124
H-1034 Budapest, Hungary
Tel.: [36] (1) 168 6880
Fax: [36] (1) 168 9098

Magyar Nemzet
Kinizsi u 30-36
H-1092 Budapest, Hungary
Tel.: [36] (1) 216 4251

Resources for Further Information

USEFUL WEBSITES FOR JOB SEARCHERS

The Internet is a good place to begin your job search. Although Hungarian employers are just beginning to use the Internet to list job vacancies, there are websites that provide useful information about the job market.

Central & Eastern European Job Bank
www.scala.hu/job-bank
Helps companies and skilled workers find each other in the region.

Hungary Network
http://hungary.com
A website with information on Hungary.

HuDir: Jobs
http://hudir.hungary.com/Text/Business/Jobs
A Hungary jobs list.

Miklos Csuros's Home Page
www.cs.yale.edu/homes/csuros-miklos
Useful job links.

Mta Sztaki
www.sztaki.hu/sztaki/allas.html
A list of jobs.

Summer Jobs
www.summerjobs.com/do/where/jobtree/Hungary
Postings for summer jobs in Hungary.

EMBASSIES AND CONSULAR OFFICES

American embassies and consulates have commercial and/or economic sections that can provide you with business information and explain aspects of the local economy. Inquiries about business opportunities should be addressed either to "Commercial Officer" or "Commercial Section," followed by the appropriate street address.

Representation of Hungary in the United States

Embassy of the Republic of Hungary
3910 Shoemaker Street NW
Washington, DC 20008-3811
Tel.: (202) 362-6730
Fax: (202) 966-8135

Representation of the United States in Hungary

American Embassy
V. 1054 Szabadsa, Ter 12
H-1054 Budapest, Hungary
Tel.: [36] (1) 112 6450
Fax: [36] (1) 112 6480

CHAMBERS OF COMMERCE

Chambers of Commerce consist of firms in both countries interested in international trade. These are appropriate companies to initially target in the job search.

Budapest Chamber of Commerce
P.O. Box 1016
Budapest, Hungary
Tel.: [36] (1) 202 0889
Fax: [36] (1) 202 0889

Hungarian American Chamber of Commerce
10 Twin Dolphin Drive, #B-500
Redwood City, CA 94065

Tel.: (650) 595-1448
Fax: (650) 591-1448

Hungarian Chamber of Commerce
Kossuth Lajos ter. 6-9
H-1055 Budapest, Hungary
Tel.: [36] (1) 153 3333
Fax: [36] (1) 269 4628

WORLD TRADE CENTER IN HUNGARY

World Trade Centers usually include many foreign companies operating in the country.

World Trade Center Budapest
Kecskemeti utca 14
H-1053-Budapest, Hungary
Tel.: [36] (1) 338 24 16
Fax: [36] (1) 318 37 31
Email: jvasvari@dbassoc.hu
www.dbassoc.hu

OTHER INFORMATIONAL ORGANIZATIONS

Foreign government missions in the U.S. such as tourist offices can furnish visas and information on work permits and other important regulations. They may also offer economic and business information about the country.

Hungarian National Tourist Board
150 East 58th Street, 33rd Floor
New York, NY 10155-2958
Tel.: (212) 355 0240
Fax: (212) 207 4103

Hungarian Tourist Board
P.O. Box 11
H-1387 Budapest, Hungary
Tel.: [36] (1) 118 5241
Fax: [36] (1) 118 5241

BUSINESS DIRECTORIES

Although not always easy to find, business directories can prove invaluable in the international job search. Most directories list company names, addresses, products, and phone numbers. Some directories include executive names and titles and financial information about the company. These sources provide you with the names of the people to contact for employment information as well as financial data, which can tell you how strong a company's position in a country may be.

Business Guide Central-East Europe. Published by Overseas Post Organization, Dr. Hamische Verlags GmbH, Blumenstrasse 15, D-90402 Nuremburg, Germany; email: uepgus@aol.com. Lists business organizations in the Czech Republic, Poland, Hungary, Romania, Slovakia, Moldova, Bulgaria, Russian and the Ukraine.

Eastern Europe Business Directory. Published by Gale Research, 27500 Drake Road, Farmington Hills, MI 48331-3531; email: galeord@gale.com. Lists 7,000 companies in Bulgaria, Czech Republic, Slovakia, Hungary, Poland, Romany, the former East Germany, and the western parts of Russia.

Hungarian Companies (Database). Available from Computing and Management Services, Sauglo u.9-15, M-1145 Budapest, Hungary. Database covers approximately 30,000 copanies in Hungary.

Industry Almanac—Hungary. Published annually in Hungarian and German by CompAlmanach Kft., Benedek U.S., H-1033 Budapest, Hungary. Lists over 14,000 companies in Hungary.

Major and Medium-Sized Companies in Hungary. Published Verland Hoppenstedt GmbH, Havelstrasse 9, Postfach 100139, D-64295 Darmstadt, Germany; email: info@hoppe.de. CD ROM listintg 15,000 companies in Hungary.

MZM World Business Directory (Ex-Socialist World Business Directory. Available from MZM Publications Publishing Promotion, P.O. Box 465, PL-81-705 Sopot 5, Poland. Lists companies in 33 post-socialist countries inovolved in international trade.

AMERICAN COMPANIES IN HUNGARY

Company information includes firm name, address, phone number, specific business, and American parent company. Your chances of achieving employment are substantially better if you contact the subsidiary company in Europe rather than the parent company in the U.S.

Atrium Hyatt Budapest
Roosevelt Ter. 2
Postfach 55
H-1366 Budapest V, Hungary
(Hotel)
Hyatt Intl Corp.

Berlitz Nyelviskola Korlatolt Felelossegu Tarsasag
Sommelweis utca 2
H-1052 Budapest, Hungary
Tel.: [36] (1) 370 014
(Language instruction)
Berlitz International Inc.

Burson-Marsteller/Central Europe
Dozsa Gyorgy utca 84/a.ll.21
H-1068 Budapest, Hungary
Tel.: [36] (1) 122 3818
(Advertising and public relations)
Burson-Marsteller

Citibank Budapest Ltd.
Váci u. 19-21
H-1052 Budapest, Hungary
Tel.: [36] (1) 269 45 11
Fax: [36] (1) 118 96 94
(Bank)
Citicorp

Compack Douwe Egberts
Landler J. utca 23-25
H-1078 Budapest, Hungary
Tel.: [36] (1) 122 3245
(Food products)
Sara Lee Corp.

CPC Hungary
Szabadsag utca 117
H-2040 Budapest, Hungary
Tel.: [36] (1) 166 76 97
(Food products)
CPC International

DDB Needham Worldwide Budapest
Tass Vezer Street 18
H-1113 Budapest, Hungary
Tel.: [36] (1) 1854 73 0
(Advertising and public relations)
Omnicom Group Inc.

DMB&B/Profil M.
Logodi utca 19
H-1012 Budapest, Hungary
Tel.: [36] (1) 201-2601
(Advertising)
D'arcy Masius Benton & Bowles, Inc.

Grey Multireklam
Gogol utca 16, Postfach 431
H-1067 Budapest, Hungary
Tel.: [36] (1) 1402 901
(Advertising)
Grey Advertising Inc.

Hasbro Hungary
Terez Korut 23
H-1067 Budapest, Hungary
Tel.: [36] (1) 1131-8568
(Games and toys)
Hasbro Inc.

Ibusz Rac
Martinelli Ter 8
H-1052 Budapest V, Hungary
Tel.: [36] (1) 1184312
(Automobile rental)
Avis Rent A Car System, Inc.

Reader's Digest Kiado Kft.
Kevekaza utca 1
H-1119 Budapest, Hungary
Tel.: [36] (1) 85 0204
(Publishing)
The Reader's Digest Association, Inc.

Tungstram Co., Ltd.
IV, Vaki utca 77
H-1340 Budapest, Hungary
Tel.: [36] (1) 169-0600
(Electronic products and components)
General Electric Co.

Wrigley Hungaria Ltd.
Arpad Fejedelem utca 42-43
H-1023 Budapest, Hungary
(Confectionery)
Wm. Wrigley Jr. Co.

EUROPEAN COMPANIES IN HUNGARY

The following are major non-American firms operating in the country. These selected companies can be either domestic or foreign, usually other European. Such companies will genrally hire their own nationals but may employ Americans.

BASF Magyarorszage Iroda
Seregely utca 1-5
H-1034 Budapest, Hungary
Tel.: [36] (1) 189 5511
(Plastics materials and resins)
BASF AG

Ciba Geigy Services AG
Belgrad-rakpart 25
H-1056 Budapest, Hungary
Tel.: [36] (1) 118 4433
(Pharmaceuticals and chemicals)
Ciba Geigy Ltd.

Credit Lyonnais Bank Hungary Ltd.
Józef nádor tér 7
H-1051 Budapest, Hungary
Tel.: [36] (1) 266 90 00
Fax: [36] (1) 266 99 50
(Bank)

Ferunion
Merleg utca 4
H-1829 Budapest, Hungary
Tel.: [36] (1) 172-611
Fax: [36] (1) 117 2594
(Building construction material)

Gyori Keksz es Ostyagyar
Koranyi F. ter 1
H-9025 Gyor, Hungary
Tel.: [36] (1) 96 16864
(Baked goods)
United Biscuits (Holdings) PLC

Hoechst AG
Magyarorszagi Kozvetien
Kareskedelmi Kepviselet
H-1051 Budapest, Hungary
Tel.: [36] (1) 117 9011
(Pharmaceuticals and chemicals)
Hoechst AG

ICI Hungaria
Hegyalja utca 7-13
H-1016 Budapest I, Hungary
Tel.: [36] (1) 202 3582
(Pharmaceuticals)
Imperial Chemical Industries PLC

Magyar Befektetési És Fejlesztési Bank
Hungarian Investment and Development Bank
Deák Ferenc u. 5
H-1052 Budapest, Hungary
Tel.: [36] (1) 118 12 00
Fax: [36] (1) 117 14 47
(Investment bank)

Magyar Nemzeti
(National Bank of Hungary)
Szabadsag ter 8-9
H-1054 Budapest, Hungary
Tel.: [36] (1) 532 600
Fax: [36] (1) 132 3913
(Central & commercial bank)

INTERNATIONAL SCHOOL IN HUNGARY

American International School of Budapest
P.O. Box 53
H-1525 Budapest, Hungary
Tel.: [36] (395) 2176
Fax: [36] (395) 2179
Email: tass.b@lower.aisb.hu
www.ecis.org/aisbudapest/homepage.htm

Poland

MAJOR EMPLOYMENT CENTERS: Warsaw, Krakow, Lodz

MAJOR BUSINESS LANGUAGE: Polish

LANGUAGE SKILL INDEX: If you can't manage Polish, German or Russian might help

CURRENCY: zloty

TELEPHONE COUNTRY CODE: 48

TIME ZONE: EST+6

PUNCTUALITY INDEX: Be punctual

AVERAGE DAILY TEMPERATURE, HIGH/LOW: January, 30/21°F; July, 75/56°F (Warsaw)

AVERAGE NUMBER OF DAYS WITH PRECIPITATION: January, 13; July, 10

BEST BET FOR EMPLOYMENT:

  FOR STUDENTS: Teaching English

  PERMANENT JOBS: Business

CHANCE OF FINDING A JOB: Pretty good

TRIVIA: Most Poles have some family in the U.S. This can be a good source for networking

Poland is in the northern part of central Europe, bordering the Baltic Sea to the north, Germany to the west, the former Czechoslovakia to the south, and Belarus and the Ukraine to the east. The country is about the size of New Mexico. Most of Poland consists of lowlands. Following World War II, Poland lost almost 70,000 square miles of its eastern territories to the U.S.S.R. but gained about 40,000 square miles from Germany, thus moving the country westward. Over 98% of the population is Polish, with some German, Ukrainian, and Belarussian minorities. Over 95% of the population is Roman Catholic.

Polish history begins in the eleventh century with a slavic kingdom centered around Bohemia, Moravia, and Saxony. In 1410 the Teutonic Knights became Polish vassals. Poland was a great power in the fifteenth century, when its borders reached deep into Russia and extended from the Baltic to the Black Seas. By 1772, however, the elective monarchy produced weak governments that succumbed to foreign invaders. Austria, Prussia, and Russia had completely partitioned Poland by 1795. Napoleon created a brief Grand Duchy of Warsaw, which was soon reabsorbed by Russia.

Following World War I, Poland again emerged as an independent state under Marshal Josef Pilsudski in 1918. In 1926 Pilsudski began ruling as a dictator. Poland signed a non-aggression pact with Germany in 1934, but the Nazis invaded in 1939, following the German-Soviet Nonaggression Pact. Poland was again partitioned. The legal Polish government in exile was opposed by the Soviets who recognized the communist-dominated Provisional Government, which eventually established itself in Warsaw. Poland's borders shifted in 1945.

Poland established a Stalinist model of government until 1956, when riots forced a liberalization. Wladyslaw Gomulka in 1956 and Edward Gierek in 1970 both attempted reforms but failed to stabilize the economy. The Polish people were the first to challenge the hegemony of communist rule in the Eastern bloc and started the trend toward democratization in the region. In 1981, the first independent trade union in a communist country, Solidarity, led by Lech Walesa, succeeded in exacting concessions from the government. In 1981, however, General Wojciech Jaruzelski imposed martial law and banned Solidarity. The U.S. enacted economic sanctions until 1987, when the Polish government enacted a sweeping amnesty for all political prisoners.

Solidarity was relegalized in 1989. Its sweeping victory in June of that year caused the communist government to fall apart, and Tadeusz Mazowiecki, head of a Solidarity-led coalition, became the first non-communist prime minister in Eastern Europe since WWII. Lech Walesa was elected president in 1990. Political instability, lowered living standards, and soaring unemployment made the successive centrist governments that led post-communist Poland very unpopular among those hit hardest by economic austerity measures, including pensioners, industrial work-ers, and low-ranking civil-servants.

In the 1995 presidential elections, Walesa was defeated by Aleksander Kwasniewski, a former communist who was head of the Democratic Left Alliance. Wlodzimierz Cimoszewicz, another former communist, took the post of prime minister. Although the current government maintains a pro-Western image, many old-time communists have been discreetly returned to key administrative and po-litical posts. The government has slowed down privatization activities, but the so-cial benefits promised in the presidential campaign still have not materialized.

Poland is a strongly religious country—about 90% of the population are prac-ticing Catholics. The line between Church and state has always been a thin one. The Church openly supported Solidarity throughout the years in which it was banned and considered the fall of communism also a victory for Catholics. The Catholic Church has extensive influence over social policy. In 1993, the Catholic Church heavily lobbied parliament, which ultimately passed a law that made abor-tion, legal since 1956, against the law.

Normal business hours are from 6:00 a.m. to 7:00 p.m., Monday through Fri-day. Banking hours are from 8:00 a.m. to 4:00 p.m., Monday through Friday. The postal system is extremely unreliable. Almost all of the population speaks Polish, with German and Russian usually as the second and third languages. Some stu-dents speak English.

Current Economic Climate

Since the end of communism, the old state-owned industries have been replaced with a plethora of new, private enterprises. Trade has shifted toward the West, al-though Poland maintains its ties with former eastern bloc countries to preserve its position as a bridge between west and east. More than half of Poland's GDP is now produced by the private sector which employs about 50% of the work force. The reduction of unemployment, from a high of 17% in mid-1994 to a current rate of 10%, is considered a big success for Poland. It is believed, however, that a third of those receiving government unemployment benefits actually do work, but are paid under the table. Inflation has dropped from a 1993 high of 35% to 20%.

The country's major industries include: chemicals, steel, food processing, min-ing, and textiles. Approximately 25% of the work force is involved in the manufac-turing sector, 11% in services, and 30% in agriculture. Central Europe and the former Soviet Union provide most of Poland's trade, but extensive commerce also takes place with the E.U. and the U.S.

Using the phone

The telephone system in Poland is antiquated and unreliable. Public telephones are scarce by western standards, and frequently out of order. Your best bet for finding a working phone is to go to the post office. Although older phones still accept phone cards, newly installed telephones only use phone cards. City codes often vary depending on the city where the call originates. Fax services are difficult to find, and public access to the Internet is unavailable.

Getting Around in Poland

Traveling by rail is inexpensive, and trains go to almost every town. In general, Polish trains are slow, crowded, and uncomfortable; express trains are sometimes available. Neither Eurail nor InterRail is accepted in Poland. Buses are even slower and more crowed than the trains, although fares are comparable. The national airline, LOT, serves most Polish cities and offers relatively economical flights within the country.

Employment Regulations and Outlook for Americans

Visas are presently required for all visitors, who must also register with the police and get a stamp demonstrating where each night was spent. Paid employment for foreigners is prohibited in Poland. Volunteer workcamps, however, are active and open to those interested.

Short-term and Temporary Work

The best bet or temporary work in Poland is to teach English.

International House
ul Pilsudskiego 6, IP
PL-31-110 Krakow, Poland
Runs several English-language schools in Poland.

Teachers for Central and Eastern Europe
21 V 5 Rakovski Blvd.
B-6400 Dimitrovgrad, Bulgaria
Tel: [35] (9) 391 24 787
Fax: [35] (9) 26 218
Recruits native speakers to teach English in Hungary and Poland.

Internship Programs

For students interested in technical jobs, IASTE provides the best opportunities. The University of Pennsylvania also sponsors an internship program through which students can earn college credit.

IASTE
10400 Little Patuxent Parkway, Suite 250 L
Columbia, MD 21044-3510
Tel.: (410) 997-3068
Fax: (410) 997-5186
Email: iaste@aipt.org
www. aipt.org/iaste.htm
Arranges reciprocal internship exchanges among 63 member countries for students in engineering, architecture, and the sciences.

Penn-in-Warsaw
Penn Summer Abroad
University of Pennsylvania
3440 Market Street, Suite 100
Philadelphia, PA 19104-5335
Tel.: (215) 898-5738
Fax: (215) 573-2053
Places students in internships with American firms operating in Poland.

Volunteer Opportunities

Ochotnicze Hufce Pracy (OHP) operates numerous workcamps in Poland and recruits hundreds of volunteers annually. Work may involve archaeology, peace issues, and forest or other ecological work. Several of OHP's workcamps are in Warsaw. For information on these and other workcamps in Poland, contact:

Volunteers for Peace
International Workcamps
43 Tiffany Road
Belmont, VT 05730
Tel.: (802) 259-2759
www.vfp.org/

WorldTeach
Harvard Institute for International Development
1 Eliot Street
Cambridge, MA 02138-5705
Tel.: (617) 495-5527
Places volunteers in positions in Poland.

The Peace Corps in Central Europe

The U.S. is sending Peace Corps volunteers to various central European countries as English instructors and to aid in development. Peace Corps volunteers in Poland play a prominent role in teaching English at secondary schools and teacher training colleges. They provide English instruction, improve learning resources, develop school-based community outreach projects, and enhance the confidence, skills, and knowledge of Polish teachers. Peace Corps also places volunteers in Romania, Slovakia, and Moldova, as well as 9 other eastern European countries. Although the Peace Corps interviewing and application process is rigorous and competitive, volunteers often find service immensely rewarding. Applications may be obtained from the Peace Corps at:

Peace Corps
Recruitment Office
806 Connecticut Avenue NW
Washington, DC 20526
Tel.: (800) 424-8580, ext. 93
www.peacecorps.gov

NEWSPAPERS IN POLAND

Gazette Wyborcza
ul Czerska 8/10
PL-00-732 Warsaw, Poland
Tel.: [48] (22) 41 29 43
Fax: [48] (22) 699 49 82

Zycie Warszawy
ul Armii Ludowej 3/5
PL-00-915 Warsaw, Poland
Tel.: [48] (22) 625 6990
Fax: [48] (22) 625 2829

Resources for Further Information

USEFUL WEBSITES FOR JOB SEARCHERS

The Internet is a good place to begin your job search. Although Polish employers are just beginning to use the Internet to list job vacancies, there are websites that provide useful information about the job market.

Jobs in Poland
www.gumbeers.elka.pg.gda.pl/WA/WP/
Firmy
Business offers from Polish companies.

Jobs in Poland
www.jobs.pl
Job offers in a variety of fields.

Polish Home Page
http://info.fuw.edu.pl/pl/
PolandHome.html
Comprehensive site about Poland.

Survival information
www.zem.co.uk/polish/index.htm
Offers a melange of useful information for foreigners.

Technical jobs in Poland
www.matrixdd.pl
Job offers in technical fields.

Travel information
www.travel.co.pl
Offers vital travel information; travel links.

EMBASSIES AND CONSULAR OFFICES

American embassies and consulates have commercial and/or economic sections that can provide you with business information and explain aspects of the local economy. Inquiries about business opportunities should be addressed either to "Commercial Officer" or "Commercial Section," followed by the appropriate street address.

Representation of Poland in the United States

Embassy of Poland
2640 16th Street NW
Washington, DC 20009
Tel.: (202) 234-3800
Fax: (202) 328-6271

Polish Consulate General—New York
233 Madison Avenue
New York, NY 10016
Tel.: (212) 889-8360

Representation of the United States in Poland

American Embassy
Aleje Ujazdowskie 29/31
PL-00-540Warsaw, Poland
Tel.: [48] (22) 628 3041
Fax: [48] (22) 625 7298

American Consulate General—Poznan
Ulica Chopina 4
PL-61-708 Poznan, Poland
Tel.: [48] (61) 551088
Fax: [48] (61) 530053

American Consulate General—Krakow
Ulica Stilarska 9
PL-31-043 Krakow, Poland
Tel.: [48] (12) 229764
Fax: [48] (12) 218292

U.S. Trade Center
Aleke Jerozolimskie 56C
IKEA Building, 2nd Floor
PL-00-803 Warsaw, Poland
Tel.: [48] (22) 21 45 15
Fax: [48] (22) 21 63 27

CHAMBERS OF COMMERCE

Chambers of Commerce consist of firms in both countries interested in international trade. These are appropriate companies to initially target in the job search.

American Chamber of Commerce in Poland
ul Swietokrzyska 36/6
PL-00-116 Warsaw, Poland
Tel.: [48] (22) 622 55 25
Email: amcham@it.com.pl
www.polishworld.com

Polish Chamber of Commerce
ulica Trebacka

PL-00-916 Warsaw, Poland
Tel.: [48] (22) 26 02 21
Fax: [48] (22) 27 46 73

Polish-US Economic Council
1615 H Street NW
Washington, DC 20062-2000
Tel.: (202) 463-5482
Fax: (202) 463-3114

WORLD TRADE CENTERS IN POLAND

World Trade Centers usually include many foreign companies operating in the country.

World Trade Center Gdynia
Tadeusza Wendy 7/9
PL-81-341 Gdynia, Poland
Tel.: [48] (58) 620 31 82
Fax: [48] (58) 620 13 02
Email: wtc@wtcgdynia.com.pl
www.wtcgdynia.com.pl

World Trade Center Poznan
ul. Glogowska 26

PL-60-734 Poznan, Poland 60-734
Tel.: [48] (61) 866 17 28
Fax: [48] (61) 866 17 28

World Trade Center Warsaw
The Palace of Culture & Science
1 Plac Defilad (PKiN)
PL-00-901 Warsaw, Poland
Tel.: [48] (22) 656 77 11
Fax: [48] (22) 656 71 33

OTHER INFORMATIONAL ORGANIZATIONS

Foreign government missions in the U.S. such as tourist offices can furnish visas and information on work permits and other important regulations. They may also offer economic and business information about the country.

ORBIS (Tourist Office)
16 Bracka Street
PL-00-028 Warsaw, Poland
Tel.: [48] (22) 27 22 72
Fax: [48] (22) 27 18 18

Polish National Tourist Office
275 Madison Avenue Suite 1711
New York, NY 10018
Tel.: (212) 338-9412
Fax: (212) 338-9283
www.polandtour.org

BUSINESS DIRECTORIES

Although not always easy to find, business directories can prove invaluable in the international job search. Most directories list company names, addresses, products, and phone numbers. Some directories include executive names and titles and financial information about the company. These sources provide you with the names of the people to contact for employment information as well as financial data, which can tell you how strong a company's position in a country may be.

Business Foundation Book: General Trade Index and Business Guide. Published annually by the Business Foundation, Krucza 38/42, PL-00-512, Warsaw, Poland. Includes data on 3,500 Polish businesses and firms interested in trade with the West.

Business Guide Central-East Europe. Published by Overseas Post Organization, Dr. Hamische Verlags GmbH, Blumenstrasse 15, D-90402 Nuremburg, Germany; email: uepgus@aol.com. Lists business organizations in the Czech Republic, Poland, Hungary, Romania, Slovakia, Moldova, Bulgaria, Russia, and the Ukraine.

Eastern Europe Business Directory. Published by Gale Research, 27500 Drake Road, Farmington Hills, MI 48331-3531; email: galeord@gale.com. Lists 7,000 companies in Bulgaria, Czech Republic, Slovakia, Hungary, Poland, Romany, the former East Germany, and the western parts of Russia.

Major Companies in Poland. Available from Verlag Hoppenstedt GmbH, Havelstrasse 9, Postfach 100139, D-64295 Darmstadt, Germany; email: info@hoppe.de. CD ROM includes 30,000 companies in Poland.

MZM World Business Directory (Ex-Socialist World Business Directory). Available from MZM Publications Publishing Promotion, P.O. Box 465, PL-81-705 Sopot 5, Poland. Lists companies in 33 post-socialist countries involved in international trade.

Polish Business Directory. Available from Branzowy Katalog Firm—Ravi Sp., ul Mazowiecka 17, PL-50-412 Wroclaw, Poland. Lists more than 3,000 companies in Poland.

Polist Industry Directory. Available from Branzowy Katalog Firm—Ravi Sp., ul Mazowiecka 17, PL-50-412 Wroclaw, Poland. Lists more than 10,000 companies in Poland including leading importers and exporters.

AMERICAN COMPANIES IN POLAND

Company information includes firm name, address, phone and fax number, specific business, and American parent company. Your chances of achieving employment abroad are substantially better if you contact the subsidiary company in Europe rather than the parent company in the U.S.

Arthur Andersen
ulica Nowy Swiat 6/12, 4th Floor
PL-00-400 Warsaw, Poland
Tel.: [48] (22) 625 1164
Fax: [48] (22) 625 1208
(Management consulting and accounting)
Arthur Andersen & Co.

Burson-Marsteller
ulica Krolewska 27/402
PL-00-060 Warsaw, Poland
Tel./Fax: [48] (22) 277 829
(Advertising)
Burson-Marsteller Inc.

Coopers & Lybrand
ulica Iwonicka 19
PL-02-924 Warsaw, Poland
Tel.: [48] (22) 642 5525, 642 6415
Fax: [48] (22) 42 87 66
(Accounting)
Coopers & Lybrand

DDB Needham Worldwide Warszawa
ulica Brodzinskiego 21
PL-01-557 Warsaw, Poland
Tel./Fax: [48] (22) 39 49 45
(Advertising and public relations)
Omnicom Group Inc.

Deloitte & Touche
ulica Grzybowska 80/82
PL-00-844 Warsaw, Poland
Tel.: [48] (22) 661 5300
Fax: [48] (22) 661 5350
(Accounting)
Deloitte & Touche

DMB&B Warsaw
ulica Jana Styki 4
PL-09-934 Warsaw, Poland
Tel./Fax: [48] (22) 177 153
(Advertising)
D'Arcy Masius Benton & Bowles Inc.

Eastnet Personnel Selection Consultants
ulica Koszykowa 60/62
PL-00-673 Warsaw, Poland

Tel./Fax: [48] (22) 628 4836
(Staff recruitment services)

Ernst & Young
ulica Wspolna 62
PL-00-684 Warsaw, Poland
Tel.: [48] (22) 259 241
Fax: [48] (22) 294 263
(Accounting)
Ernst & Young

Failure Analysis Associates Ltd.
ulica Uphagena 27
PL-80-237 Gdansk, Poland
Tel.: [48] (22) 414 470 or 414 011, ext. 60
Fax: [48] (22) 418 946
(Engineering consultants)
Failure Analysis

Heidrick & Struggles Ltd.
Aleje Jerozolimskie 65/79, LIM Center
PL-00-697 Warsaw, Poland
Tel.: [48] (22) 630 6632
Fax: [48] (22) 630 6620
(Staff recruitment services)
Heidrick & Struggles Inc.

Macro/PJG Market Research
Aleje Jerozolomskie 56c
PL-00-803 Warsaw, Poland
Tel.: [48] (22) 630 2244
Fax: [48] (22) 630 2234
(Market research services)

NAJ International
ulica Odolanska 22/7
PL-02-562 Warsaw, Poland
Tel.: [48] (22) 455 857
Fax: [48] (22) 455 988
(Staff recruitment services)

Price Waterhouse
ulica Emilii Plater 28
Warsaw Corporate Center
PL-00-688 Warsaw, Poland
Tel.: [48] (22) 320 281
Fax: [48] (22) 327 559
(Accounting)
Price Waterhouse

SMG/KRC Search & Selection
ulica Foksal 21/2
PL-00-372 Warsaw, Poland
Tel./Fax: [48] (22) 263 437
(Staff recruitment services)

EUROPEAN COMPANIES IN POLAND

ABB Dolmel Ltd.
ulica Pstrowskiego 10
Wroclaw, Poland
Tel.: [48] (71) 55 4511
Fax: [48] (71) 55 1742
(Engineering and construction)
ABB Asea Brown Bovrei (Holding) Ltd.

Bank Gospodarstwa Krajowego (BGK)
National Economy Bank (NEB)
Grzybowska 80/82
PL-00-958/66 Warsaw, Poland
Tel.: [48] (22) 661 5106
Fax: [48] (22) 661 5108
(Government bank)

Bank Inicjatyw Spoleczno-
Ekonomicznych SA
6 Nowy Swiat
PL-00-497 Warsaw, Poland
Tel.: [48] (22) 21 83 86
Fax: [48] (22) 21 76 08
(Bank for socio-economic initiatives)

Bank Rozowoju Eksportu SA
Al Jerozolimskie 65/79
P.O. Box 728
PL-00-950 Warsaw, Poland
Tel.: [48] (22) 63 05 919
Fax: [48] (22) 39 120 160
(Commercial bank)

Unitronex Corp.
ulica Grqybowska 87
PL-00-844 Warsaw, Poland
Tel.: [48] (22) 320 281
Fax: [48] (22) 327 559
(Computers, peripherals, and software)
Tektronix Inc.

BASF Poland
Aleje Jerozlimskie 65/79
PL-00-697 Warsaw, Poland
Tel.: [48] (22) 2230 0291
Fax: [48] (22) 2230 0296
(Plastics and resins)

Ciba-Geigy AG
Oddzial w Warzawie ulica
Lektykarska 29 m 16
Warsaw, Poland
Tel.: [48] (22) 3912 1120
Fax: [48] (22) 3912 0635
(Pharmaceuticals and chemicals)
Ciba-Geigy Ltd.

Det Norske Veritas
c/o Stocznia Gdanska SA
ulica Doki 1
PL-80-863 Gdansk, Poland
Tel.: [48] (58) 39 1232
(Shipping and offshore platform services)

ICI Poland
Oddzial w Warzawie ulica
Nieklanska 23
PL-03-924 Warsaw, Poland
Tel.: [48] (22) 17 0658
Fax: [48] (22) 17 2205
(Pharmaceuticals)
Imperial Chemical Industries PLC

INTERNATIONAL SCHOOLS IN POLAND

The American School of Warsaw
ulica Konstancinska 13
PL-02-942 Warsaw, Poland
Tel.: [48] (22) 42 39 52
Fax: [48] (22) 642 7542
Email: Thorton@asw.waw.pl
www.asw.waw.pl
(U.S. curriculum, pre-K-12)

The British School, Warsaw
ul Orkana 14
PL-02-656 Warsaw, Poland

Tel.: [48] (22) 843 4453
Fax: [48] (22) 843 7365
Email: britscholar@wonet.com.pl

St. Paul's British International School
Zielona 14 Piaseczno
PL-05-500 Warsaw, Poland
Tel.: [48] (22) 756 7797
Fax: [48] (22) 756 2609
Email: stpbis@stpbis.com.pl
www.stpbis.com.pl

Romania

MAJOR EMPLOYMENT CENTER: Bucharest

MAJOR BUSINESS LANGUAGES: Romanian, English, French, German

LANGUAGE SKILL INDEX: You pretty much need to use one of the business languages. English and French are the first foreign languages taught in schools. Romanian is closer to classical Latin than it is to other Romance languages, and speakers of Italian, Spanish, and French should be able to understand written Romanian

CURRENCY: lei

TELEPHONE COUNTRY CODE: 40

TIME ZONE: EST+7

PUNCTUALITY INDEX: Very punctual

AVERAGE DAILY TEMPERATURE, HIGH/LOW: January, 33/20°F; July, 86/61°F (Bucharest)

AVERAGE NUMBER OF DAYS WITH PRECIPITATION: January, 12; July, 12

BEST BET FOR EMPLOYMENT:

  FOR STUDENTS: Technical work through IASTE

  PERMANENT JOBS: Teaching English

CHANCE OF FINDING A JOB: Not very good

TRIVIA: You will find that many Romanians have a fascination with the French and French culture. Most locals use the French merci to say "thank you"

R omania, located in southeastern Europe in the northern section of the Balkan Peninsula, is bordered by the Black Sea on the east, Ukraine and Moldova to the north, Hungary to the west, Yugoslavia to the southwest, and Bulgaria to the south. The Carpathian mountain range runs across the northern part of the country, and the Transylvanian Alps run through the central regions. Previously part of the Ottoman Empire, Romania became an independent kingdom in 1881.

Romania was an ally of Nazi Germany in World War II, and in 1945 succumbed to pressure by the Soviet Union to allow a communist-led coalition form of government. The Communist Party led the government until December of 1989, when demonstrations against President Nikolai Ceausescu's plan of forced urbanization led to violence and the overthrow of the government. The coup lasted 8 days and resulted in 1033 deaths. (Original estimates immediately after the coup were as listed as many as 64,000 people dead.) Ceausescu and his wife Elena were tried by an anonymous court and executed by a firing squad.

The National Salvation Front replaced Ceausescu's regime in 1990 with 85% of the popular vote. In 1992, a new constitution was ratified, and the Democratic National Salvation Front won elections in September of that year. Iliescu was re-elected president in October 1992. Iliescu's quasi-communist policies, however, were the source of widespread discontent, and he was unable to secure a third term as president. In November 1996, Emil Constantinescu, head of the Democratic Convention in Romania, was elected president.

The political scene has begun to stabilize, although some political infighting continues. Constantinescu has been able to implement some economic and democratic reforms. Progress continues to be slow, however. Constantinescu gives high priority to qualifying Romania for membership in the E.U. and NATO. Currently Romania has associate-member agreements with both the E.U. and the World Trade Organization.

Romania has a population of 23.2 million, a tenth of whom live in the capital city of Bucharest. The population is 89% Romanian. There are small minority communities of Germans and Hungarians in Romania, as well as roughly 1.5 million Gypsies, the largest Gypsy community in the world. Romania is the only country with a Romance language that does not have a Roman Catholic background—70% of the people belong to the Romanian Orthodox Church.

Banking hours are weekdays from 9 a.m. to 1 p.m. All retail shops and markets are closed on Sundays. Main post offices are open from Monday to Saturday until 8 p.m., and Sunday until noon.

Current Economic Climate

The government has begun to introduce free-market reforms, which are gradually bringing about economic growth and boosting employment levels. The inflation rate was reduced from 50% in 1994 to less than 25% by 1997. Living standards remain very low, however, and political infighting threatens to stall economic reforms. Half of the nation's GDP comes from the industrial sector, including chemical production, metallurgy, machinery, and petroleum refinement. The agricultural sector is an important contributor to economic growth. Romania is a major producer of wheat, corn, sunflower seeds, potatoes, and sugar beets. Romania's principal trade partners include the E.U. and Russia.

Foreign investment has been slow to take off. However, there are still several large companies operating in Romania, including Shell, Coca Cola, and Colgate-Palmolive. McDonald's already has five restaurants in Bucharest, the first of which broke all eastern European sales records.

Using the phone and fax

The telephone service in Romania is by far the worst in eastern Europe. If you cannot use a private phone or one of the new bright orange public phones, don't count on making an international call. An international call requires that you put up an initial deposit equal to the cost of your call. If no connection is made for any reason, such as nobody is home or the line is busy, a service charge equal to about $1 is deducted from your refund. Since it can take up to two hours to make a connection, this can be very costly and very frustrating. Faxes can be easily sent from main post offices.

Getting Around in Romania

Train travel in Romania requires hours of waiting in line for tickets. Express trains charge a little more but are worth the extra expense. InterRail passes are accepted but Eurail is not valid. Buses offer extensive service and are recommended where trains are not available. Fares are cheap, but buses are often uncomfortable, overcrowded, and unreliable.

Employment Regulations for Americans

U. S. citizens are required to carry a visa when traveling in Romania but there is no longer a required currency exchange. According to the Romanian embassy, there are currently no employment regulations for Americans.

Short-term and Temporary Work

The best bet for temporary work in Romania is to teach English.

Travel Teach USA
P.O. Box 357
Rigby, ID 83442
Tel./Fax: (208) 745-7222
Working holidays teaching English in Romania.

Volunteer Opportunities

The Central European Teaching Program places English teachers in schools throughout Romania.

Central European Teaching Program
Beloit College
700 College Street
Beloit, WI 53511
Tel.: (608) 363-2619
Fax: (608) 363-2449

NEWSPAPERS IN ROMANIA

Adevarul
Plata Presei Libere nr1, sector 1
Bucharest, Romania
Tel.: [40] (1) 618 06 08
Fax: [40] (1) 617 55 40

Curierul National
Str. Ministerului 2-4, sector 1
Bucharest, Hungary
Tel.: [40] (1) 615 9512
Fax: [40] (1) 312 1300

Libertatea
Str. Brezojanu 23-25, sector 1

Bucharest, Hungary
Tel.: [40] (1) 13 22 77
Fax: [40] (1) 13 03 93

Romania Libera
Piata Presei Libere nr. 1
Bucharest, Romania
Tel.: [40] (1) 312 8670
Fax: [40] (1) 312 8271

Timeretul Liber
Piata Presei Libere nr. 1
Bucharest, Romania
Tel.: [40] (1) 617 6737
Fax: [40] (1) 312 8269

Resources for Further Information

USEFUL WEBSITES FOR JOB SEARCHERS

The Internet is a good place to begin your job search. Although few Romanian employers list jobs on the Internet, there are websites that provide useful information about the job market.

Internet Service Romania
www.isr.co.ro
Advertises employment opportunities.

Job offers
www.byte.ro

Posts job offers; facts about Romania; in Romanian.

Travel information
http://city.net/countries/romania
Good, useful source for travel information on Romania.

EMBASSIES AND CONSULAR OFFICES

American embassies and consulates have commercial and/or economic sections that can provide you with business information and explain aspects of the local economy. Inquiries about business opportunities should be addressed either to "Commercial Officer" or "Commercial Section," followed by the appropriate street address.

Representation of Romania in the United States

Embassy of Romania
1607 23rd Street NW
Washington, DC 20008-2809
Tel.: (202) 332-4846
Fax: (202) 232-4748

Representation of the United States in Romania

American Embassy
Strada Tudor Arghezi 7-9
Bucharest, Romania
Tel.: [40] (1) 214 042
Fax: [40] (1) 210 395

CHAMBERS OF COMMERCE

Chambers of Commerce consist of firms in both countries interested in international trade. These are appropriate companies to initially target in the job search.

American Chamber of Commerce in Romania
Eminescu nr 105-107, Ap. 1
Bucharest, Romania
Tel.: [40] (1) 2109399

Romanian Chamber of Commerce and Industry
22 Boulevard Nicolae Balcescu
R-79302 Bucharest, Romania
Tel.: [40] (1) 312 1312
Fax: [40] (1) 312 3830

WORLD TRADE CENTERS IN ROMANIA

World Trade Centers usually include many foreign companies operating in the country.

World Trade Center Bucharest
2 Expozitiei Blvd., Sector 1
Bucharest, 78 334 Romania
Tel: [40] (1) 224 4362,
Fax: [40] (1) 224 2770
Email: wtcb@wtcb.ro

World Trade Center Bucharest
1-3 Nicolae Lorga Street
Bucharest 1, Romania
Tel.: [40] (1) 311-0045
Fax: [40] (1) 311-0781

OTHER INFORMATIONAL ORGANIZATIONS

Foreign government missions in the U.S. such as economic councils can offer business information about the country.

Romanian-U.S. Economic Council
1615 H Street NW, 6th Floor
Washington, DC 20062-0001
Tel.: (202) 463-5482
Fax: (202) 463-3114

BUSINESS DIRECTORIES

Although not always easy to find, business directories can prove invaluable in the international job search. Most directories list company names, addresses, products, and phone numbers. Some directories include executive names and titles and financial information about the company. These sources provide you with the names of the people to contact for employment information as well as financial data, which can tell you how strong a company's position in a country may be.

Business Guide Central-East Europe. Published by Overseas Post Organization, Dr. Hamische Verlags GmbH, Blumenstrasse 15, D-90402 Nuremburg, Germany; email: uepgus@aol.com. Lists business organizations in the Czech Republic, Poland, Hungary, Romania, Slovakia, Moldova, Bulgaria, Russia, and the Ukraine.

Chamber of Commerce and Industry of Romania—Members Directory. Published irregularly in English by the Chamber of Commerce and Industry of Romania, 22 Boulevard Nicolae Balcescu, R-70122 Bucharest, Romania. Lists foreign trade companies and agencies.

Eastern Europe Business Directory. Published by Gale Research, 27500 Drake Road, Farmington Hills, MI 48331-3531; email: galeord@gale.com. Lists 7,000 companies in Bulgaria, Czech Republic, Slovakia, Hungary, Poland, Romany, the former East Germany, and the western parts of Russia.

MZM World Business Directory (Ex-Socialist World Business Directory). Available from MZM Publications Publishing Promotion, P.O. Box 465, PL-81-705 Sopot 5, Poland. Lists companies in 33 post-socialist countries inovolved in international trade.

AMERICAN COMPANIES IN ROMANIA

There are many more companies operating in Romania than are listed here, but business information about these operations can be difficult to find. Company information in this section includes firm name, address, phone and fax number, specific business, and American parent company. Your chances of achieving employment abroad are substantially better if you contact the subsidiary company in Europe rather than the parent company in the U.S.

Chemical Bank
16 Bulevardu Republicii
P.O. Box 1-750
Bucharest, Romania
Tel.: [40] (1) 615 8412
Fax: [40] (1) 312 1076
(Bank)
Chemical Bank, New York

Ont Carpati
7 Blvd. Magheru
Bucharest 1, Romania
Tel.: [40] (0) 136 684
(Passenger car rental)
Avis Rent A Car System, Inc.

ROM Control Data
Fabrica de Glucoza Street
15, Sector 2
Bucharest, Romania
Tel.: [40] (0) 884 095
Fax: [40] (0) 883 175
Control Data Corp.

Unitronex
Street Banitel, Nr. 1 ScA at S Ap 21
Bucharest, Romania
Tel.: [40] (0) 350 465
(Computers and software)
Tektronix Inc.

EUROPEAN COMPANIES IN ROMANIA

The following are major non-American firms operating in the country. These selected companies can be either domestic or foreign, usually other European. Such companies will generally hire their own nationals first but may employ Americans.

Banca Commerciala Romana SA
(The Romanian Commercial Bank SA)
14 Republicii Blvd., Sector 3
70348 Bucharest, Romania
Tel.: [40] (1) 614 2116
Fax: [40] (1) 614 3213

Banca Romana de Comert Exterior SA
22-24 Calea Victoriei
70012 Bucharest, Romania
Tel.: [40] (1) 614 9190
Fax: [40] (1) 614 1598
(Commercial bank)

BASF AG/RFG Representative
Street Dr. Grigore Mora 39
R-71278 Bucharest 1, Romania
Tel.: [40] (0) 79 6210
(Plastics and resins)
BASF AG

Chimimportexport
P.O. Box 525
Bucharest, Romania
Tel.: [40] (0) 160 636
(Rubber products)

Ciba-Geigy Services SA
Strada Ltd Lemnea #4
Bucharest, Romania
Tel./Fax: [40] (0) 50 2644
(Pharmaceuticals and chemicals)
Ciba-Geigy Ltd.

Electronum
P.O. Box 105
Bucharest, Romania
Tel.: [40] (0) 142 126
(Electronic equipment)

Ewir Est West Informatique Roumanie Srl
27 Eroilor Sanitari Blvd.
Bucharest, Romania
Tel.: [40] (1) 210 31 25
Fax: [40] (1) 210 31 22
Email: info@ewir.ro
(Software)

ICI Romania, ICI Liaison Office
1 Edgar Quinet Street, Sector 1
Bucharest, Romania
Tel.: [40] (0) 13 1250
Fax: [40] (0) 13 3178
(Pharmaceuticals)
Imperial Chemical Industries PLC

Impexmin
P.O. Box 710
Bucharest, Romania
Tel.: [40] (0) 128 126
(Mining equipment)

Petrolexportimport
1-3, BD. Magheru
R-70161 Bucharest, Romania
Tel.: [40] (0) 131 249
(Petroleum products)

Shell Romania SRL
Diplomal Hotel, Apt. 110B
Sevastopol Street 13-17
R-78118 Bucharest 1, Romania
Tel.: [40] (5) 05 046
Fax: [40] (5) 94 242
(Petroleum products)

Siemens Birou de Consultantii Tehnice
Street Edgar Quinet 1, #5
R-70106 Bucharest, Romania
Tel.: [40] (0) 15 1825
(Electronics)
Siemens AG

Tehnoforestexport
4, Piata Rosetti
R-79536 Bucharest, Romania
Tel.: [40] (0) 136 717
(Paper products)

Universal Tractor
P.O. Box 454
Bucharest, Romania
Tel.: [40] (0) 158 620
(Agricultural machines)

INTERNATIONAL SCHOOLS IN ROMANIA

American School of Bucharest
Calea Dorobantilor #39
Bucharest, Romania
Tel.: [40] (1) 211 0102/ 03
Fax: [40] (1) 211 0104
Email: director@asb.kappa.ro
http://asb.kappa.ro

International School of Bucharest
428 Mihai Bravu Street
Dristar
Bucharest, Romania
Tel.: [40] (1) 324 54 3233
Fax: [40] (1) 324 5443
Email: intsbuc@rolink.iiruc.ro

twenty-one

Greece, Turkey, Cyprus, and Malta

Greece

MAJOR EMPLOYMENT CENTERS: Athens, Thessaloniki

MAJOR BUSINESS LANGUAGE: Greek

LANGUAGE SKILL INDEX: English is spoken by most business people. As in most countries, though, not knowing the host language will limit your advancement potential

CURRENCY: drachma

TELEPHONE COUNTRY CODE: 30

TIME ZONE: EST+7

PUNCTUALITY INDEX: Punctuality in Greece is fairly flexible, but don't push your luck

AVERAGE DAILY TEMPERATURE, HIGH/LOW: January, 54/42°F; July, 90/72°F (Athens)

AVERAGE NUMBER OF DAYS WITH RAIN: January, 12; July, 2

BEST BET FOR EMPLOYMENT:

FOR STUDENTS: Working at resorts

PERMANENT JOBS: Tourism

CHANCE OF FINDING A JOB: Not too good, thanks to a soft economy

TRIVIA: Be aware of nonverbal communications in Greece. A nod of the head means "no," and a slight tilt to the side means "yes"

The Hellenic Republic, about the size of New York State, is located on the southern end of the Balkan Peninsula in southeastern Europe, bordering Yugoslavia, Albania, and Bulgaria to the north, Turkey and the Aegean Sea to the east, the Ionian Sea to the west, and the Mediterranean to the south. Most of the country is mountainous, with the highest point, Mt. Olympus, rising to 9,570 feet. Fewer than 170 of Greece's over 2,000 islands are inhabited. The larger islands include Crete and the Ionian, Cyclades, and Sporades groups. About 97% of the population states a religious affiliation with the Greek Orthodox Church.

Greece, especially the area around Athens, reached its apex in the fourth century B.C. but eventually became a Roman province. The country formed a part of the Byzantine Empire and later the Ottoman Empire. Turkish rule lasted until 1827, ending after a bloody war of independence. Greece maintained a monarchy until 1923, when a republic was declared under military rule. The monarchy was restored in 1941 but collapsed during the Axis invasion. Italians, Germans, and Bulgarians occupied the country in World War II until liberation in 1944. Communist guerrillas conducted a civil war against the government from 1947-49 but were defeated with extensive U.S. assistance. A military regime seized power in 1967 and declared a republic in 1973. The next year, the military regime resigned, following a failed attempt to capture Cyprus.

The Panhellenic Socialist Movement (PASOK) won the 1981 election, and Andreou Papandreou became Greece's first socialist prime minister. In 1988, Papandreou had a widely publicized affair with an airline attendant (whom he later married), and the government collapsed after PASOK became embroiled in a serious financial scandal. In 1989, a conservative and communist government took over and implemented a katharsis, a campaign of purification, to investigate Papandreou and his ministers. The government ruled that they should stand trial for embezzlement, telephone tapping, and illegal grain sales. Constantine Mitsotakis of the New Democracy Party (NDP) took over as premier in 1990. The NDP lost its parliamentary majority in 1993, and in general elections held in October Papandreou, now cleared of all the charges leveled against him, and PASOK captured a majority of seats. Papandreou's government was marked by cronyism — his wife served as his chief of staff, his son was deputy foreign minister, and his personal physician was appointed minister of health. Papandreou was replaced in 1996 by Costas Simitis, an experienced economist and lawyer, who has implemented economic reforms including an overhaul of the country's taxation system.

Greece's foreign policy is dominated by its extremely sensitive relationship with Turkey, its Muslim neighbor. The two NATO allies have repeatedly come close to war. The break-up of the former Yugolsavia raises the possibility that the former Yugoslav Republic of Macedonia has territorial designs on the Greek province of the same name.

Business in Greece features extensive moonlighting at second jobs, especially on Tuesday, Thursday, and Friday nights, from which many Greeks derive a significant portion of their incomes. An afternoon break from 2:00 to 5:00 p.m. is also normal. Banks are open from 8:00 a.m. to 2:00 p.m., Monday to Thursday, but close at 1:30 p.m. on Fridays. Post Offices are open from 7:30 a.m. to 2:30 p.m., Monday to Friday.

Current Economic Climate

Greece has the second-lowest income per capita in the E.U. Its annual growth rate hovers at around 2%. The underground economy—not included in official economic statistics—is estimated to contribute an additional 30% to the official G.N.P. The labor force is officially 43% service, 29% industrial, and 28% agricultural. Major industrial products include textiles, chemicals, and processed foods. The economy is sustained by a massive tourism sector, although the country is also known for its extensive ownership of ships. The E.U. and the U.S. are Greece's predominant trading partners. Greece also trades significantly with the Middle East. Greece has been criticized by the Organization for Economic Cooperation and Development for failing to develop its export sector. Much of the Greek economy has been sheltered by government subsidies and remains internationally uncompetitive.

The 1990s have been characterized by tough austerity measures that have tended to make the government highly unpopular. The reforms, however, seem to be successful in bringing the Greek economy in-line to join the E.M.U. by mid-1999. Since the mid-1990s, the budget deficit has been reduced by more than 10 percentage points, inflation has fallen to around 5%, and the unemployment rate is around 9%.

Using the phone, fax, and Internet

The phone system in Greece is modern and efficient. To call long distance, visit one of the offices of Greece's telephone company, OTE. Offices in major cities are generally open twenty-four hours a day, while offices in smaller towns may close at 10:00 p.m.—sometimes as early as mid-afternoon, depending on the size of the town. The "i" at the top left of the dialing panel on public phones brings up the operating instructions in English. Most city post offices have fax facilities. Although Greece has been slow in embracing the Internet, cybercafes are becoming increasingly popular making Email easier to access.

Getting Around in Greece

The bus service, KTEK, is generally fast and extensive, whereas the train system, OSE, is considered slower and less convenient than other European networks. Ferry and train services offer reasonable rates. Eurail and InterRail are accepted on the national railways. The national airline, Olympic Airways, connects many of the Greek islands at fairly reasonable prices and is often heavily booked.

Employment on the Greek Islands and Tourism

Over eight million tourists visit Greece annually, providing jobs in the tourist industry centered around the Greek Aegean Sea islands. Pubs and hotels often seek individuals with language skills to serve tourists. Ferries, which provide much of the transportation between islands, also offer job opportunities. The best islands for tourist work include Rhodes, Corfu, Ios, Augina, Mykonos, and Paros. Women have an easy time finding work in restaurants, bars, and cafes while men are regularly employed in construction work. Boating and yacht companies generally like to hire English speakers to accommodate tourists. Americans may also find work in Glyfada, south of Athens, which plays host to a U.S. military base. Many bars around the base, as well as in Athens, have English names and cater to the American crowd.

Using the language

Most employment in the tourist industry doesn't necessarily require a knowledge of Greek. Employment in other sectors of the economy, however, necessitates Greek language skills. Foreign subsidiaries usually only hire Greek speakers. Some young people speak English, but you should generally initiate conversations in Greek.

Employment Regulations and Outlook for Americans

Greece has an oversupply of university graduates in most fields, making it difficult for foreigners to find jobs. U.S. citizens do not require visas to travel to Greece but must present a passport, letter of intent of employment, and medical papers to the local Aliens Bureau if they intend to work. A work permit must be presented upon entering the country. The Ministry of Labor provides work permits but only for specialized work. Since foreign firms are allowed to hire their nationals for most jobs, applying to an American firm in Greece would be the best approach. Keep in mind, however, that most foreign subsidiaries in Greece are fairly small and have comparatively minor personnel needs.

The vast majority of employment recruiting takes place through advertisements or personal contacts. Writing a letter to a potential employer in Greece may prove beneficial. Greek employers tend to hire people with relevant degrees, even for general management positions. Few candidates with only bachelor's degrees will be hired without extensive work experience. Since very little training is available from most firms, employers expect job candidates to arrive with the necessary skills.

Americans may be able to find jobs teaching English, especially at private schools and service organizations. The fishing industry in Greece is large and constantly needs additional laborers. Various types of agricultural work, such as grape or olive picking, can also be found throughout Greece. Such agricultural employment should be sought in the *Athens News* and is usually advertised in local hostels and cafes.

Short-term and Temporary Work

The best bets for casual jobs are to work as an au pair or in a tourist resort. There are some opportunities for teaching English.

Au Pair Activities
P.O. Box 76080
GR-17110 Nea Smyrni, Athens, Greece
Tel./Fax: [30] (1) 932 6016

Consolas Travel
100 Eolou St.
GR-10559 Athens, Greece
Tel.: [30] (1) 325 4931
Hires people as hostel staff for pensions in Athens and the islands.

English Studies Advisory Centre
22 Belestinou Street
GR-11523 Athens, Greece
Tel.: [30] (1) 649 7017
Fax: [30] (1) 649 4618
Hires English teachers for schools around Greece.

The Galentina European Childcare Consultancy
P.O. Box 51181
Kifissia
GR-14510 Athens, Greece
Tel./Fax: [30] (1) 808 1005
Au pair placement agency.

Internship Program

IASTE provides the best opportunity for students to obtain professional work in Greece.

IASTE
10400 Little Patuxent Parkway, Suite 250 L
Columbia, MD 21044-3510
Tel.: (410) 997-3068
Fax: (410) 997-5186
Email: iaste@aipt.org
www. aipt.org/iaste.htm
Arranges reciprocal internship exchanges among 63 member countries for students in engineering, architecture, and the sciences.

Volunteer Opportunities

Service Civil International (SCI) operates workcamps for volunteers interested in environmental projects, building renovation, and working with handicapped children. The American Farm School (AFS) employs several Americans every summer on a farm in Thessaloniki. Club Paradisus recruits conservation volunteers for one-month projects between June and September to help clean up beaches on the Peloponnese. Skyros recruits "work scholars" to help with cleaning, bar work, and domestic duties in exchange for room, board, and the chance to participate in courses such as windsurfing.

American Farm School
Summer Work Activities Program
1133 Broadway
New York, NY 10010
Tel.: (212) 463-8433

CIEE
Voluntary Service Department
205 East 42nd Street
New York, NY 10017
Tel.: (800) COUNCIL
Email: info@ciee.org
www.ciee.org

Club Paradisus
8/9 Paradise

Coalbrookcale
Telford
Shropshire TF8 7NR, United Kingdom
Tel.: [44] (1952) 432 337

Service Civil International
c/o International Voluntary Services
Route 2, Box 506
Crozet, VA 22932
Tel.: (804) 823-1826

Skyros
92 Prince of Wales Road
London NW5 3NE, England
Tel.: [44] (171) 267 4424

Archaeology Today magazine's annual March/April issue includes listings of opportunities to go on digs in the Eastern Mediterranean. They also publish an annual *Fieldwork Opportunities Bulletin*. For more information, contact the publisher directly at:

Archaeology Today
675 Commonwealth Avenue
Boston, MA 02215
Tel.: (617) 353-9361

NEWSPAPERS IN GREECE

Apogevmatini (daily)
1-2 Fridiou Street
GR-106 78 Athens, Greece
Tel.: [30] (1) 361 88 11
Fax: [30] (1) 360 9876

Athens News (English)
3 Christou Lada
GR-10237 Athens, Greece

Tel.: [30] (1) 333 3165
Fax: [30] (1) 323 1698
www.dolnet.gv

Eleftherotypia (daily)
Tegopoulos Editions
Minoos 10.16
GR-11743 Athens, Greece
Tel.: [30] (1) 92 96 600
Fax: [30] (1) 90 28 023

Ethnos (daily)
Odos Benaki, Metamorfosi
GR-152 35 Halandriou, Greece
Tel.: [30] 1 63 80 640
Fax: [30] 1 639 65 15

Kathiemerini (daily)
Socratous 57
GR-10431 Athens, Greece
Tel.: [30] (1) 523 1001 9
Fax: [30] (1) 522 8894

Ta Nea (daily)
Odos Christou Lada 3
GR-102 37 Athens, Greece
Tel.: [30] (1) 333 3555
Fax: [30] (1) 322 87 97

To Vima (Sunday)
Odos Christou Lada 3
GR-102 37 Athens, Greece
Tel.: [30] (1) 333 3555
Fax: [30] (1) 322 87 97

Resources for Further Information

USEFUL WEBSITES FOR JOB SEARCHERS

The Internet is a good place to begin your job search. Although Greek employers are just beginning to use the Internet to list job vacancies, there are websites that provide general information about the job market.

Employment in Greece
www.efginc.com/greece.html
Lists job opportunities in a variety of fields.

Hellas Online
www.hol.gr:80

Internet service provider in Greece; offers some employment opportunities.

Information on Greece
www.softlab.ntua.gr/local/greece.html
Offers cultural information on Greece.

EMBASSIES AND CONSULAR OFFICES

American embassies and consulates have commercial and/or economic sections that can provide you with business information and explain aspects of the local economy. Inquiries about business opportunities should be addressed either to "Commercial Officer" or "Commercial Section," followed by the appropriate street address.

Representation of Greece in the United States

Embassy of Greece
2221 Massachusetts Avenue NW
Washington, DC 20008
Tel.: (202) 939-5800
Fax: (202) 939-5824

Consulates General of Greece: Chicago, (312) 750-1014; New York, (212) 988-5500; San Francisco, (415) 775-2102

Representation of the Unted States in Greece

American Embassy
91 Vasilissis Sophias Boulevard
GR-10160 Athens, Greece
Tel.: [30] (1) 721 2951
Fax: [30] (1) 645 6282 (general)

**American Consulate General—
Thessaloniki**
59 Leoforos Nikis
GR-54622 Thessaloniki, Greece
Tel.: [30] (31) 242 905
Fax: [30] (31) 242 927

CHAMBERS OF COMMERCE

Chambers of Commerce consist of firms in both countries interested in international trade. These are appropriate companies to initially target in the job search.

**American Hellenic Chamber of
Commerce**
16 Kanari Street, Third Floor
GR-106 74 Athens, Greece
Tel.: [30] 1 362 3231
Fax: [30] 1 361 0170

**Hellenic-American Chamber of
Commerce**
Atlantic Bank Building, Suite 1204
960 Avenue of the Americas
New York, NY 10001
Tel.: (212) 629-6380

WORLD TRADE CENTER IN GREECE

World Trade Centers usually include many foreign companies operating in the country.

Athens World Trade Center
Akademias 7
Athens, Greece
Tel.: [30] (1) 3602411
Fax: [30] (1) 3607849

OTHER INFORMATIONAL ORGANIZATION

Foreign government missions in the U.S. such as tourist offices can furnish visas and information on work permits and other important regulations. They may also offer economic and business information about the country.

Greek National Tourist Organization
Olympic Tower
645 Fifth Avenue
New York, NY 10022
Tel.: (212) 421-5777
Fax: (212) 826-6940

BUSINESS DIRECTORIES

Although not always easy to find, business directories can prove invaluable in the international job search. Most directories list company names, addresses, products, and phone numbers. Some directories include executive names and titles and financial information about the company. These sources provide you with the names of the people to contact for employment information as well as financial data, which can tell you how strong a company's position in a country may be.

American-Hellenic Chamber of Commerce- Business Directory of Members. Published
annually by the American Hellenic Chamber of Commerce, 16 Kanari St., 3rd Floor, GR-
106 74 Athens, Greece. Includes American subsidiaries in Greece and major Greek firms.

Greek Export Directory. Published by the Athens Chamber of Commerce and Industry, 7
Akadimias, GR-106 71 Athens, Greece. Lists Greek firms engaged in export.

Greek Shipowners Register. Available from Greek Shipping Publications Co. Ltd., 14 Skouse &
Kolokotroni Street, GR-185 36 Piraeus, Greece. Listing of Greek shipowning companies.

ICAP Financial Directory of Greek Companies. Published annually by ICAP Hellas S.A., 54a
Queen Sophias Ave., GR-115 28 Athens, Greece. Distributed in the U.S. by EBSCO
Subscription Services, Box 1943, Birmingham, AL 35201. Lists financial data on over
20,000 Greek companies.

Yearbook of the Athens Stock Exchange. Published annually by the Athens Stock Exchange,
10 Sophocleus Odos, 105 59 Athens, Greece. Lists 196 companies quoted on the
exchange and stockbrokers.

AMERICAN COMPANIES IN GREECE

The following companies are classified by business area: Banking and Finance; Industrial Manufacturing; Retailing and Wholesaling; and Service Industries. Company information includes firm name, address, phone and fax number, specific
business, and American parent company. Your chances of achieving employment
abroad are substantially better if you contact the subsidiary company in Europe
rather than the parent company in the U.S.

BANKING AND FINANCE

American Express Bank, Ltd.
31 Panepistimiou Street
P.O. Box 671
GR-102 26 Athens, Greece
Tel.: [30] (1) 323 4781
Fax: [30] (1) 322 4919
(Financial and travel services)
American Express, New York

**Bank of America National Trust and
Savings Association**
39 Panepistimiou Street
P.O. Box 630
GR-102 27 Athens, Greece
Tel.: [30] (1) 325 1901
Fax: [30] (1) 323 1376
Bank of America, San Francisco

The Chase Manhattan Bank, NA
3 Koraï Street
GR-102 10 Athens, Greece

Tel.: [30] (1) 324 2511
Fax: [30] (1) 324 2511, x162
Chase Manhattan Bank, New York

Citibank, NA
8 Othonos Street
GR-105 57, Athens, Greece
Tel.: [30] (1) 322 7471
Fax: [30] (1) 324 0829
Citibank, New York

**Merrill Lynch Pierce Fenner & Smith
(Hellas) LLC**
17 Valaoritou Street
GR-475 53 Athens, Greece
Tel.: [30] (1) 361 89 16
Fax: [30] (1) 364 80 40
(Securities)
Merrill Lynch International Bank Inc.

INDUSTRIAL MANUFACTURING

Abbot Laboratories (Hellas) SA
194 Syngrou Ave.
GR-176 71 Kallithea, Greece
Tel.: [30] (1) 9505 911
(Pharmaceuticals)
Abbot Laboratories

Bristol-Meyers Squibb SA
Athinon-Lamais National Road (11th Km)
GR-144 52 Athens, Greece
Tel.: [30] (1) 281 33 90
Fax: [30] (1) 281 24 70
(Pharmaceuticals)
Bristol-Meyers Co.

Colgate-Palmolive (Hellas) SAIC
89 Athinon Avenue
GR-185 41 Piraeus, Greece
Tel.: [30] (1) 483 19 00
Fax: [30] (1) 48 31 09 24
(Soaps and toiletries)
Colgate-Palmolive Co.

Dow (Hellas) AE
32 Kifissias Avenue
GR-151 25 Maroussi, Greece
Tel.: [30] (1) 680 06 40
Fax: [30] (1) 680 06 46
(Plastics and resins)
Dow Chemical Co.

Goodyear Hellas SAIC
94 Kifissou Avenue
P.O. Box 41092
GR-122 10 Algaleo, Greece

Tel.: [30] (1)562 56 10
(Tires)
Goodyear Tire & Rubber Co.

IBM Hellas SA
284 Kifissias Avenue
GR-152 33 Halandri, Greece
Tel.: [30] (1) 688 11 11
Fax: [30] (1) 680 13 01
(Electronic data processing equipment)
IBM

Johnson & Johnson Hellas SA
4 Epidavroustroet
GR-151 25 Maroussi, Greece
Tel.: [30] (1) 685 08 91
Fax: [30] (1) 685 03 09
(Healthcare products)
Johnson & Johnson

Pepsico-IVI SA
22nd km Athinon-Lavriou Avenue Karela
GR-194 00 Athens, Greece
Tel.: [30] (1) 602 85 41
Fax: [30] (1) 664 63 45
(Soft drinks)
PepsiCo Inc.

Procter & Gamble Hellas AE
165 Syngrou Ave.
GR-171 21 Nea Smyrni, Greece
Tel.: [30] (1) 939 40 00
Fax: [30] (1) 939 48 00
(Soaps and detergents)
Procter & Gamble Co.

RETAILING AND WHOLESALING

Allied Signal Aerospace Service Corp.
15410 Psychico
P.O. Box 65039
Athens, Greece
(Aerospace electrical products)
Allied-Signal Inc.

Mobil Oil Hellas
194 Syngrou Avenue
GR-176 71 Athens, Greece
Tel.: [30] (1) 950 10 00
Fax: [30] (1) 950 12 38
(Petroleum products)
Mobil Petroleum Co. Inc.

Rohm & Haas Greece LTD
9 Leontariou Street
Alsoupolis
GR-142 35 Nea Ionia, Athens, Greece
(Electronic equipment)
Rohm & Haas Co.

Texaco Greek Petroleum Co. SA
75 Catechaki & Kifissias Ave.
P.O. Box 65 030
GR-154 10 Psychiko, Greece
Tel.: [30] (1) 6925401
(Petroleum products)
Texaco Inc.

SERVICE INDUSTRIES

Andersen Consulting SA
246 Avenue Kifissias
GR-152 31 Halandri, Greece
Tel.: [30] (1) 677 64 00
Fax: [30] (1) 677 64 05
(Management consulting)
Andersen Consulting

Coopers & Lybrand
24 Xenias Street
GR-115 28 Athens, Greece
Tel.: [30] (1) 771 01 12
Fax: [30] (1) 777 73 90
(Management consulting)
Coopers & Lybrand

Deloitte & Touche SA
250-254 Avenue Kifissias
GR-152 31 Halandri, Greece
Tel.: [30] (1) 677 62 30
Fax: [30] (1) 677 62 21
(Management consulting)
Deloitte & Touche

Price Waterhouse Company
P.O. Box 14018
GR-115 15 Athens, Greece
(Accounting and financial services)
Price Waterhouse Co.

EUROPEAN COMPANIES IN GREECE

The following are major non-American firms operating in the country. These selected companies can be either domestic or foreign, usually other European. Such companies will generally hire their own nationals first but may employ Americans.

BANKING AND FINANCE

Barclays Bank PLC
1 Kolokotroni Street
GR-105 62 Athens, Greece
Tel.: [30] (1) 331 12 00
(Bank)

Commercial Bank of Greece S A
11 Sofokleous
GR-10235 Athens, Greece

Tel.: [30] (1) 320 11 11
Fax: [30] (1) 320 20 84
(Bank)

Credit Bank AE
40 Stadiou Street
GR-102 52 Athens, Greece
Tel.: [30] (1) 326 0000
Fax: [30] (1) 322 4522
(Commercial bank)

MANUFACTURING, SALES, AND SERVICES

Aluminium de Grèce S A
1 Sekeri
GR-10 671 Athens, Greece
Tel.: [30] (1) 369 30 00
Fax: [30] (1) 369 31 15
(Aluminum)

Astir Hotels Co.
Kamenavourla
GR-350 08 Athens, Greece
Tel.: [30] (1) 324 3961
Fax: [30] (1) 323 3911
(Hotel operation)

Athenian Brewery SA
102 Kiffissou Avenue
GR-122 41 Athens, Greece

Tel.: [30] (1) 538 4911
Fax: [30] (1) 545 0848
(Alcoholic beverages)

Ciba-Geigy Hellas AG
Anthoussis Avenue
GR-153 44 Anthoussa, Greece
Tel.: [30] (1) 666 6612
Fax: [30] (1) 666 72 46
Ciba-Geigy Ltd., Switzerland

Hellenic Steel Co. SA
5 Erythrou Stravrou & Ymittou Street
GR-151 23 Maroussi, Greece
Tel.: [30] (1) 685 8000
Fax: [30] (1) 685 8010
(Steel products)

Hoechst Hellas AG
Rd. Tatoiou
GR-146 10 Nearythrea, Greece
Tel.: [30] (1) 800 91 11
Fax: [30] (1) 807 15 73
(Chemical products)
Hoechst AG, Germany

Jacobs Suchard-Pavlides SA
274 Kifissias Avenue
GR-152 32 Halandri, Greece
Tel.: [30] (1) 680 10 80
Fax: [30] (1) 680 10 90
(Confectionery)

Lever Hellas S A
25 Alexandroupoleos Street,
GR-11527 Athens, Greece
Tel.: [30] (1) 770 48 11

Fax: [30] (1) 771 07 46
(Soaps, detergents, cosmetics)
Unilever NV, Netherlands

Shell Company (Hellas) Ltd.
2 El Venizelou Avenue
P.O. Box 3499
GR-176 76 Kallithea, Greece
Tel.: [30] (1) 929 5911
Fax: [30] (1) 922 28 04
(Petroleum products)

Siemens SA
Artemidos et Paradiss
P.O. Box 61011
GR-151 10 Maroussi, Greece
Tel.: [30] (1) 686 41 11
Fax: [30] (1) 686 42 99
(Information systems)

INTERNATIONAL NON-PROFIT EMPLOYER IN GREECE

International Olympic Academy
4 Kapsali Street
GR-106 74 Athens, Greece
Tel.: [30] (1) 724 9235

INTERNATIONAL SCHOOLS IN GREECE

American Community Schools of Athens
129 Aghias Paraskevis Street
GR-152 34 Athens, Greece
Tel.: [30] (1) 639 32 00
Fax: [30] (1) 639 00 51
Email: acs@acs.gr
www.acs.gr
(U.S. Internaitional Baccalaureate
curriculum, pre-K-12)

TASIS Hellenic International School
P.O. Box 51025
145 10 Kifissia, Greece
Tel.: [30] (1) 808 1426
Fax: [30] (1) 801 8421
Email: bhani@hol.gr
www.tasis.com
(U.S., U.K., pre-K-12)

Turkey

MAJOR EMPLOYMENT CENTERS: Ankara, Istanbul, Izmir

MAJOR BUSINESS LANGUAGES: Turkish, English, French

LANGUAGE SKILL INDEX: You can certainly get by in English, but a little Turkish will help

CURRENCY: Turkish lira

TELEPHONE COUNTRY CODE: 90

TIME ZONE: EST+7

PUNCTUALITY INDEX: Punctuality is important

AVERAGE DAILY TEMPERATURE, HIGH/LOW: January, 45/36°F; July, 81/65°F (Istanbul)

AVERAGE NUMBER OF DAYS WITH PRECIPITATION: January, 12; July, 3

BEST BET FOR EMPLOYMENT:

  FOR STUDENTS: Technical jobs through the IASTE

  PERMANENT JOBS: New businesses and trade

CHANCE OF GETTING A JOB: Unless you are creating your own, slight chance

TRIVIA: Nodding off during that morning meeting? Try a little Turkish coffee, considered by many to be the strongest in the world

Turkey lies at the crossroads of Europe and Asia. The major part of its geographic area—known as Anatolia—lies in far western Asia and consists of some 290,000 square miles. Separated from this by the Bosporus, the Sea of Marmara, and the Dardanelles (collectively known as the Straits) is the other 3% of Turkey's land area: the roughly 30,000-square-mile area of Eastern Thrace in far southeastern Europe. Taken as a whole, Turkey is bordered to the north by Bulgaria, the Black Sea, and Georgia; to the East by Armenia and Iran; to the south by Iraq, Syria, and the Mediterranean Sea, which along with Greece and the Aegean Sea defines Turkey's western limit. Turkey's total land area of just over 300,000 square miles makes it not quite the size of Oklahoma and Texas combined.

Much of Turkey's terrain is mountainous. At the center is a wide plateau that rises to meet an interior ring of peaks, which in the east, south, and much of the north continue on to Turkey's borders. In the west, the mountains give way first to rolling plains then to coastal plains as the land bows to meet the sea.

Turkey's capital of Ankara, located in the central plateau, is home to over 2.5 million inhabitants. Istanbul is far larger, with a population nearing 7 million, which perches just on the easternmost tip of Turkey's geographically European portion. The population of Turkey as a whole is just under 60 million, 60% of whom live in cities and towns. Turkey's population consists largely of ethnic Turks (80%). There is also a substantial Kurdish minority (18%)—a fraction of which has been a source of tension since the mid-1980s as Kurdish separatists in the southeast have fought to create a Kurdish state.

The organization and outlook of modern Turkey is largely the product of Mustafa Kemal, or Atatürk, who led a war of independence against occupying British, French, Greek, and Russian armies after the Ottoman Empire's defeat in World War I. Atatürk forged the Republic of Turkey from the remnants of the Ottoman Empire and strongly embraced for his foundling nation a policy of modernization—which he equated with Westernization. Atatürk imposed strict curbs on the civil power of Islam, Romanized the alphabet, and guaranteed civil rights for women.

Turkey is a parliamentary democracy and a secular Muslim state. The military acts as a unofficial, although effective, guarantor of democracy and secularism. In 1960, 1970, and 1980 the army stepped in to correct what it saw as a drift away from the principles set forth by Atatürk. In 1997, the military expressed its distrust of the government headed by Refah, the Islamic Welfare Party, and charges were brought that the party had engaged in unconstitutional, antisecularist activities. The party was disbanded.

Turkey has experienced rapid economic growth during the 1980s and the 1990s and was considered a likely candidate for membership in the E.U. In 1995 Turkey signed a customs-union agreement with the E.U., yet in 1998 was still left off the "short-list" of next-generation E.U. candidates. The E.U. said it was officially because of economic and human rights problems, but Muslim Turks suspect that that it was because they are not a Christian nation.

Regular business hours are from 8:30 a.m.—5:00 p.m., Monday—Friday. Lunch breaks are frequently from 1:00—2:00 p.m. Food shops generally open early (6:00 a.m.) and close late (7:00 p.m.).

Current Economic Climate

Despite a slight decline over the past 20 years, Turkey remains a largely agrarian society, with 56% of its population engaged in agricultural work. Primary crops include tobacco, cereals, and cotton. Turkey's Black Sea region produces 70% of the world's hazelnuts. Industrial products emphasize metals and metal products, including iron, steel, machinery, and automobiles. The tourism boom in the 1980s has made this an important industry.

Although Turkey's per-capita GDP of less than $3,500 is low by western European standards, Turkey has enjoyed the highest economic growth rate of any European nation since the late '80s. The inflation rate has fluctuated during the early 1990s, but remains high. Unemployment has largely remained in check, helped by the large number of Turks who work in Europe, especially Germany. Turkey's primary trading partners include E.U. nations and the United States.

Using the phone, fax and Internet

Phone cards and tokens are available at post offices and newsstands and sometimes from enterprising children near banks of phones. International calls can be made from newer yellow phones or post offices (this will take several hours to get through). Türk Telekom telephone centers have fax services, but require a lot of paperwork. Cybercafes are appearing in the major cities and tourist areas. CompuServe has nodes in Ankara (modem 312-234 5268). America Online has a node in Istanbul (modem 212-234 5158).

Getting Around in Turkey

For local transportation, trains, buses, and dolmus (shared taxis) are likely your best options. Trains are the most economical but are a bit slow. Buses are efficient, comfortable, and reasonably priced, although more expensive than trains. Dolmus follow set routes within and between cities, and users can get on or off as they please. For longer trips within Turkey, consider Turkish Airlines. Fares are reasonable and, depending on how much time you have in-country, you may find a two-or three-hour flight preferable to hours on end stuck in a bus.

Employment Regulations and Outlook for Americans

U.S. citizens traveling to Turkey for stays of up to 90 days require a passport and a visa, available from Turkish authorities for $20. Those intending to work will need to present a work visa upon arrival. For work stays of less than six months, your visa application should include a copy of your employment contract plus a letter from your employer describing your position and its duration. Stays of more than six months require written approval from the State Planning Organization, which is submitted along with the aforementioned materials when applying for a visa.

Short-term and Temporary Work

Best bets for casual jobs are teaching English and working at resorts along the coast. There are some opportunities for au pair work in Istanbul and Ankara.

Dogan International Organization
Sehitmuhtar Caddesi 37/7
Taksim
TR-80090 Istanbul, Turkey
Tel.: [90] (212) 235 1599
Fax: [90] (212) 253 5706
Au pair and employment placement agency.

English Fast
Burhaniye Mah
Resmi Efendi Sok. No 4
Beylerbeyi
Istanbul, Turkey
Tel.: [90] (216) 318 7018
Fax: [90] (216) 318 7021
Employs English teachers in Istanbul, Ankara, and Izmir.

Sunworld Sailing Ltd.
120 St. Georges Road
Brighton, East Sussex BN2 1EA, England
Employees instructors, crew, and staff for sailing and windsurfing excursions.

Internship Program

IASTE provides the best opportunity for students to obtain professional work in Turkey.

IASTE
10400 Little Patuxent Parkway, Suite 250 L
Columbia, MD 21044-3510
Tel.: (410) 997-3068
Fax: (410) 997-5186
Email: iaste@aipt.org
www. aipt.org/iaste.htm
Arranges reciprocal internship exchanges among 63 member countries for students in engineering, architecture, and the sciences.

Volunteer Opportunities

There are a number of workcamp opportunities in Turkey. Arrangements to participate can be made through several of the large workcamp coordinating organizations based in the United States. The CIEE, in cooperation with Gençtur, Turkey's youth travel bureau, arranges workcamps involving archaeology, construction, and gardening. Camps generally last two or three weeks and participants must be at least 18 years old. GSM organizes 17 workcamps throughout Turkey in cooperation with local communities and universities. Other opportunities are available through Volunteers for Peace and Service Civil International; contact these organizations directly for details.

CIEE
Voluntary Service Department
205 East 42nd Street
New York, NY 10017
Tel.: (800) COUNCIL
Email: info@ciee.org_
www.ciee.org

Gençtur
Istiklal Caddesi Zambak Sok. 15/5
TR-80080 Istanbul, Turkey
Tel.: [90] 1 212 249 25 15
Fax: [90] 1 212 249 25 54
Email: workcamps@genctur.com.tr

GSM Youth Services Centre
Bayindir Sokak, No 45/9
Kizilay

TR-06450 Kizilay-Ankara, Turkey
Tel.: [90] 1 312 417 11 24
Fax: [90] 1 312 425 81 92

Service Civil International
c/o International Voluntary Service
Route 2, Box 506
Crozet, VA 22932
Tel.: (804) 823-1826

Volunteers for Peace
International Workcamps
43 Tiffany Road
Belmont, VT 05730
Tel.: (802) 259-2759
Email: vfp@vermontel.com_
www.vermontel.com/~vfp/home.htm

Archaeology Today magazine's annual March/April issue includes listings of opportunities to go on digs in the Eastern Mediterranean. They also publish an annual *Fieldwork Opportunities Bulletin*. For more information, contact the publisher directly at:

Archaeology Today
675 Commonwealth Avenue
Boston, MA 02215
Tel.: (617) 353-9361

NEWSPAPERS IN TURKEY

Cumhuriyet
Turkucagu Caddesi 39/41
Cagaloglu
TR-34334 Istanbul, Turkey
Tel.: [90] 512 05 05
Fax: [90] 526 60 72

Milliyet
Dogan Medya Center
Bagcilar
TR- 34554 Istanbul, Turkey
Tel.: [90] 212 506 61 11
Fax: [90] 212 505 62 33

Resources for Further Information

USEFUL WEBSITES FOR JOB SEARCHERS

The Internet is a good place to begin your job search. Although Turkish employers are just beginning to use the Internet to list job vacancies, there are websites that provide useful information about the job market.

Information on Turkey
www.turkey.com
Offers cultural information about Turkey.

Jobs in Turkey
www.metu.edu.tr/Turkey/inet-turkey.html
Internet services; lists job opportunities in Turkey.

EMBASSIES AND CONSULAR OFFICES

American embassies and consulates have commercial and/or economic sections that can provide you with business information and explain aspects of the local economy. Inquiries about business opportunities should be addressed either to "Commercial Officer" or "Commercial Section," followed by the appropriate street address.

Representation of Turkey in the United States

Embassy of the Republic of Turkey
1714 Massachusetts Avenue NW
Washington, DC 20036-1903
Tel.: (202) 659-8200
Fax: (202) 862-1858
www.turkey.org

Representation of the United States in Turkey

American Embassy
110 Ataturk Bulvari
Ankara, Turkey
Tel.: [90] 312 468 6110
Fax: [90] 312 467 0019

U.S. Consulate General—Istanbul
104-108 Mesrutiyet Caddesi

Tepebasi, Istanbul, Turkey
Tel.: [90] (212) 251 3602
Fax: [90] (212) 252 2417

U.S. Consulate—Adana
Ataturk Caddesi
Adana, Turkey
Tel.: [90] (322) 453 9106
Fax: [90] (322) 457 6591

CHAMBERS OF COMMERCE

Chambers of Commerce consist of firms in both countries interested in international trade. These are appropriate companies to initially target in the job search.

Turkish-American Businessmen's Association
Barbaros Boulevard Eser Apt #48
TR-80700 Istanbul, Turkey

Tel.: [90] (212) 274 2824
Fax: [90] (212) 275 9316
www.taba.org.tr

Turkish-American Businessmen's
Association
Sair Esref Bul. No. 18/601
Gankaya

TR-35250 Izmir, Turkey
Tel.: [90] (212) 441 4068
Fax: [90] (212) 275 9316

WORLD TRADE CENTERS IN TURKEY

World Trade Centers usually include many foreign companies operating in the country.

World Trade Center Ankara
Tahran Caddesi No. 30
Kavaklidere
TR-06700 Ankara, Turkey
Tel.: [90] (312) 468-8750
Fax: [90] (312) 468-8100
Email: adtm-f@tr-net.net.tr

World Trade Center Istanbul
Atatürk Hava Limani Yani
Cobancesme Kavsagi
P.O. Box 40
TR-34830 Havalimani, Istanbul, Turkey
Tel.: [90] (212) 663-0881
Fax: [90] (212) 663-0973

OTHER INFORMATIONAL ORGANIZATION

Foreign government missions in the U.S. such as tourist offices can furnish visas and information on work permits and other important regulations. They may also offer economic and business information about the country.

Turkish Tourism Office
1717 Massachusetts Avenue NW, Suite 306
Washington, DC 20036
Tel.: (202) 429 9844
Fax: (202) 429 5649

BUSINESS DIRECTORIES

Although not always easy to find, business directories can prove invaluable in the international job search. Most directories list company names, addresses, products, and phone numbers. Some directories include executive names and titles and financial information about the company. These sources provide you with the names of the people to contact for employment information as well as financial data, which can tell you how strong a company's position in a country may be.

Directory of Exporting Industrialists. Available from the Istanbul Chamber of Industry, Mesrutiyet ca. 118 Tepebasi, TR-80050 Istanbul, Turkey. Lists approximately 700 exporting companies in Turkey.
Turkey's 500 Major Industrial Establishments. Available from the Istanbul Chamber of Industry, Mesrutiyet ca. 118 Tepebasi, TR-80050 Istanbul, Turkey. Lists the leading Turkish industrial companies.

AMERICAN COMPANIES IN TURKEY

The following companies are classified by business area: Banking and Finance; Industrial Manufacturing; Retailing and Wholesaling; and Service Industries. Company information includes firm name, address, phone and fax number, specific business, and American parent company. In the case of American parent firms, your chances of achieving employment abroad are substantially better if you contact the subsidiary company in Europe rather than the parent company in the U.S.

BANKING AND FINANCE

Cigna-Sabanci Sigorta AS
Barbaros Bulvari 19, Besiktas
TR-80690 Istanbul, Turkey
Tel.: [90] (1) 159 11 89
(Insurance services)
Cigna Worldwide, Inc.

INDUSTRIAL MANUFACTURING

ARCO Turkey
Kader Sokak 43/1
TR-06700 Ankara, Turkey
Tel.: [90] (41) 366 030
(Petroleum products)
Atlantic Richfield Co.

Bendix Otomotiv Sanayi je Ticaret
Buyukdere Caddesi no. 30
TR-80290 Mecidiye Koy, Turkey
Tel.: [90] (1) 173 2653
Fax: [90] (1) 172 3925
(Automotive brake components)
Allied Signal Inc.

Dow Turkiye AS
Dedeman Ticaret Merkozi
Kat 9, Esentepe
Istanbul, Turkey
(Chemicals)
Dow Chemical Co.

General Dynamics International Corp.
P.K. 18, Kavakildere, Murted
TR-06690 Ankara, Turkey
Tel.: [90] (4) 427 1290
(Aircraft, data systems, military equipment)
General Dynamics Corp.

Goodyear Lastikleri TAS
Buyukdere Caddesi 41
Maslak Meydomi, Levant
TR-80670 Istanbul, Turkey
(Tires and tubes)
The Goodyear Tire & Rubber Co.

Ipek Kagit Sanaylve Ticaret AS
Buyukdere Caddesi 193
Levent
TR-80240 Istanbul, Turkey

Tel.: [90] (1) 179 2500
(Paper products)
James River Corp.

Johnson Wax AS
Degirmen Sok Sasmaz Plaza kat 10/11
Kozyata
TR-81090 Istanbul, Turkey
Tel.: [90] (212) 275 23 65
Fax: [90] (216) 445 58 22
(Cleaning products)
Johnson & Johnson

Packard Elektrik Sistemleri Ltd.
Omrani
TR-81260 Istanbul, Turkey
Tel.: [90] (1) 364 1118
(Automobiles and components)
General Motors Corp.

Texaco Petrol AS
Tunus Caddesi 50112
Ankara, Turkey
Tel.: [90] (41) 12829
(Petroleum products)
Texaco, Inc.

3M Ticaret
44a Yildizposta Caddesi
Sisik Apt. A, Block N, 44
Daire 5, P.O. Box 2
Gayrettepe-Istanbul, Turkey
Tel.: [90] (1) 661 977
(Adhesives, abrasives, imaging products)
Minnesota Mining and Manufacturing Co.

Wyeth Laboratuvarlari AS
P.K. 67, Aksaray
TR-34472 Istanbul, Turkey
Tel.: [90] (1) 567 4725
(Pharmaceuticals, household products)
American Home Products Corp.

RETAILING AND WHOLESALING

Best Inc.
Esentepe, Gazeteciler Sitesi
Keskin Kalem, Sokak 6/3 Gayret
Istanbul, Turkey
Tel.: [90] (1) 172 1328
(Computers and calculators)
Hewlett-Packard Co.

**Bilkon Vural Yilmaz & Olcay
Musaogullari**
Abdi Ipecki Caddesi
Altin Sokak Ahmat Kara Is Ilani, #2
Nisantasi
TR-80200 Istanbul, Turkey
Tel.: [90] (1) 132 1506
Fax: [90] (1) 140 4064
Apple Computer Co.

SERVICE INDUSTRIES

Coopers & Lybrand
Büyukdere Cad, Nol 111
Kat 2-3 Gayrettepe
TR-80300 Istanbul, Turkey
Tel.: [90] (212) 275 28 40
Fax: [90] (212) 273 04 93
(Financial consultants)
Coopers & Lybrand

Korn/Ferry
Cumhuriyet Cad 30/19
Kervansaray Apt. B,
Blok, Elmadag
TR-80200 Istanbul, Turkey
Tel.: [90] (212) 231 39 49
Fax: [90] (212) 231 22 50
(Personnel recruitment)
Korn/Ferry International

Penajanx Advertising & Public Relations
Tesvikiye Caddesi No. 105/3-4
TR-80200 Tesvikiye, Turkey
Tel.: [90] (1) 136 1622

Kodak (Near East) Inc.
Buyukdere Caddesi 80
Akabe Ticaret Merkezi
Kat: 6, Gayrettepe
TR-80290 Istanbul, Turkey
Tel.: [90] (1) 172 0039
(Photographic and optical equipment)
Eastman Kodak Co.

Raychem
Buyukdere Caddesi Arzu 99/3
Gayrettepe
TR-80300 Istanbul, Turkey
Tel.: [90] (1) 272 4027
Fax: [90] (1) 272 4028
(Wires, cables, & fibre optics)
Raychem Corp.

Fax: [90] (1) 135 1630
(Advertising & public relations)
D'Arcy Masuis Benton & Bowles, Inc.

Price Waterhouse
Bjk Plaza
Spor Caddesi 92
B Blok, Kat 9
Arkaretier, Besiktas
TR-80680 Istanbul, Turkey
Tel.: [90] (212) 259 49 80
Fax: [90] (212) 259 49 02
(Audit services)
Price Waterhouse

**Tur-Yat AS Kurucesme Oto Kiralama
Subesi**
Tramway Caddesi 74
Kurucesme
TR-80820 Istanbul, Turkey
Tel.: [90] (1) 577 670
(Passenger car rental)
Avis Rent A Car System

EUROPEAN COMPANIES IN TURKEY

The following are major non-American firms operating in the country. These selected companies can be either domestic or foreign, but are usually the latter. Such companies will generally hire their own nationals first but may employ Americans.

BANKING AND FINANCE

Türkiye Halk Bankasi AS
(People's Bank of Turkey)
Ilkiz Sok No.1, Sihhiye
TR-06430 Ankara, Turkey
Tel.: [90] (4) 231 75 00 (general)
Tel.: [90] (4) 433 57 29 (international)
Fax: [90] (4) 427 4716
(Government bank)

Türkiye Is Bankasi AS
Atatürk Bulvan 191, Kavaklidere
TR-06684 Ankara, Turkey
Tel.: [90] (4) 428 11 40
Fax: [90] (4) 425 07 50-53
(Private & commercial bank)

INDUSTRIAL MANUFACTURING

BASF AG
Fabrika Gebze, Dilovaki
Mevkii P.K. 29
Gebze-Kocaali, Turkey
Tel.: [90] 199 111 57
(Plastics and resins)

Bayer Truk Kimya Sanayi Ltd.
Golden Plaza
19 Mayis Cad. No. 1
TR-80220 Sisli-Istanbul, Turkey
Tel.: [90] (1) 224 0301
Fax: [90] (1) 224 0303
(Pharmaceuticals)
Bayer AG

Ciba-Sabanci Sigorta AS
Barbaros Bulvari 19, Besiktas
TR-80690 Istanbul, Turkey
Tel.: [90] (1) 159 1189
(Pharmaceuticals)
Ciba-Geigy Worldwide Inc.

Imperial Chemical Industries (Turkey) Ltd.
P.O. Box 957, Karakoy
TR-80006 Istanbul, Turkey

Tel.: [90] (1) 151 4060
(Chemicals)
Inperial Chemical Industries PLC

The Shell Company of Turkey
Buyukdere Caddesi no. 32
Mecidiyekoy
TR-80290 Istanbul, Turkey
Tel.: [90] (1) 175 3410
(Petroleum products)
Royal Dutch/Shell Group of Companies

Turk Hoechst Sanayi ve Ticaret AS
Davutpasa Caddesi no. 145
TR-34020 Topkapi/Istanbul, Turkey
Tel.: [90] (1) 567 9500
(Pharmaceuticals)
Hoechst AG

Turk Pirelli Lastikleri AS
Buyukdere Caddesi no. 117, Gayrettepe
P.K. 5
Istanbul, Turkey
Tel.: [90] (1) 175 2280
(Tires and tubes)
Pirelli SpA

RETAILING AND WHOLESALING

Mercedes-Benz Turk AS
Burmali Cesme Sokak Asker
Firin Yolu No. 2
Davutpasa
Istanbul, Turkey
(Automotive parts and accessories)
Daimler-Benz AG

Siemens AG
Barbaros Bulvari
Iba Loklari no. 10
Daire: 5 Besiktas
TR-80700 Istanbul, Turkey
Tel.: [90] (1) 167 0708
(Electrical equipment and supplies)

SERVICE INDUSTRIES

ABB Esas Trafo Sanayi AS
Ankara Asfalti
Soganikoyu Mevkil, P.O. Box 20
Kartal, Istanbul, Turkey
Tel.: [90] (1) 389 5890
(Engineering and construction)
ABB Asea Brown Boveri (Holding) Ltd.

Det Norske Veritas
Bogazkesen Caddesi no. 73, K2
TR-80040 Istanbul, Turkey
Tel.: [90] (1) 151 7859
(Shipping and offshore platform services)
Det Norske Veritas

INTERNATIONAL NON-PROFIT EMPLOYER IN TURKEY

International Committee for the Preservation of Islamic Cultural Heritage
Barbaros Bulvari
Vidiz Sarayi
Seyir Kosku, Besiktas
TR-80700 Istanbul, Turkey
Tel.: [90] (1) 260 5989

INTERNATIONAL SCHOOLS IN TURKEY

Istanbul International Community School
Meydan Mahallesi
P.K. 29 Bebek
TR-80810 Istanbul, Turkey
Tel.: [90] (212) 287 2770
Fax: [90] (212) 265 0580
Email: headmast@iics.k12.tr
www.iics.k12.tr
(U.S. curriculum, K-10)

The Koç School
P.O. Box 38
Pendik-Istanbul, Turkey

Tel.: [90] (216) 304 1003
Fax: [90] (216) 304 1048
Email: jrckoc@ibm.net
(U.S., Turkish curriculum, 6-12)

Robert College of Istanbul
P.K. 1
TR-80820 Istanbul, Turkey
Tel.: [90] (1) 265 3430
Fax: [90] (1) 257 5443
Email: robcol@superonline.com
www.robcol.k12.tr
(U.S., Turkish curriculum, 7-12)

Cyprus

MAJOR EMPLOYMENT CENTER: Nicosia

MAJOR BUSINESS LANGUAGES: Greek, Turkish, English

LANGUAGE SKILL INDEX: English is understood by many, but you'll get further knowing Greek

CURRENCY: Cypriot pound

TELEPHONE COUNTRY CODE: 357

TIME ZONE: EST+7

PUNCTUALITY INDEX: Much as in Greece, punctuality is quite lax

AVERAGE DAILY TEMPERATURE: January, 51°F; July, 83°F (Nicosia)

AVERAGE NUMBER OF DAYS WITH RAIN: January, 10; July, 0

BEST BET FOR EMPLOYMENT:

  FOR STUDENTS: Technical work through the IASTE

  PERMANENT JOBS: Not much here

CHANCE OF GETTING A JOB: Frankly, not good

TRIVIA: Despite the ongoing political unrest, many tourists still visit Cyprus because of the great ruins and beaches

Threstice **T**he Republic of Cyprus occupies the largest island in the eastern Mediterranean Sea and is located about 40 miles south of Turkey and 60 miles west of Syria. The island of Cyprus covers just under 3,600 square miles, making it roughly two-thirds the size of Hawaii. Two mountain ranges span Cyprus from east to west and are separated by a broad, fertile plain. The capital city of Nicosia rests in the eastern central part of the plain and is home to almost 170,000 of Cyprus' over 700,000 inhabitants. The population of Cyprus consists largely of ethnic Greeks (almost 80%), with a substantial Turkish minority (18%).

Ethnic rivalries and questions of national sovereignty have, over recent decades, become a constant source of contention on the island. Violence broke out in the mid-1950s when the Greek majority urged union with Greece, and the Turkish minority dissented. In 1959 Greek and Turkish interests agreed to disagree, in effect, and forged a republic with a permanent division of government offices upon ethnic lines, with constitutional guarantees for the Turkish minority. Not surprisingly, tensions continued over the years, resulting in violence both in the '60s and in the '70s. In 1975, Turkish Cypriots voted to form a separate Turkish Cypriot state. The government was officially installed in 1976, and 200,000 Greek Cypriots were expelled from the Turkish-controlled area. (Turkey is the only nation that recognizes the Turkish Republic of Northern Cyprus.)

Cyprus remains a divided island, and violence between the two sides erupts from time-to-time. The U.N. has overseen sporadic and largely unsuccessful peace talks. There is some hope for reunification because both sides want to join the E.U. The island's split has interestingly resulted in the Greek Cypriots becoming more culturally defined. For example, the Republic decided to change some of its place names, making them more Cypriot than English. In the North, the Turks have created a sense of pervasive "Turkishness," and have changed several Greek place names to Turkish.

Opening business hours vary according to whether it is winter, spring, or summer. Shops are open from 8:00 a.m.—1:00 p.m. and from 4:00 p.m.—7:30 p.m., Monday—Saturday.

Current Economic Climate

Cyprus has a diverse and prosperous economy that prompted the country's deletion from the World Bank's list of less-developed nations in 1991. The service sector is the heart of the economy, with more than half the population working in service industries. Tourism is also a major industry. Primary agricultural products include grains, grapes, citrus fruits, and olives. Light manufacturing also plays an important role in the Cypriot economy. Cyprus' major trading partners include the U.S., the U.K., Russia, and Bulgaria.

Using the phone, fax, and Internet

You can make international calls from all telephone boxes using phone cards available from newsstands. Faxes can be sent from the post office. Cybercafes are common in major towns, although few Cypriot businesses maintain websites.

Getting Around in Cyprus

One attractive short-trip option in Cyprus is touring on rented mopeds and bicycles. Rates are reasonable, plus there is the advantage of flexibility: you can go where you like, when you like. Buses and shared taxis serve routes between major cities and towns, although tourists are prohibited from crossing between the Greek and Turkish sides of the island. Ferries and planes provide service between Cyprus and mainland European and Middle Eastern ports.

Employment Regulations and Outlook for Americans

For tourist stays in Cyprus of 90 days or less, U.S. citizens don't need a visa. As with most of the rest of Europe, Cyprus requires that persons intending to work in the country present a work permit upon arrival. Since preference in hiring is given to Cypriot nationals, legal employment can be difficult to find. Informal arrangements serving some aspect of Cyprus' booming tourist industry—hotel or restaurant work, for example—may be the only option available to most.

Internship Program

IASTE provides the best opportunity for students to obtain professional work in Cyprus.

IASTE
10400 Little Patuxent Parkway, Suite 250 L
Columbia, MD 21044-3510
Tel.: (410) 997-3068
Fax: (410) 997-5186

Email: iaste@aipt.org
www. aipt.org/iaste.htm
Arranges reciprocal internship exchanges among 63 member countries for students in engineering, architecture, and the sciences.

Volunteer Opportunities

Archaeology Today magazine's annual March/April issue includes listings of opportunities to go on digs in the Eastern Mediterranean. They also publish an annual *Fieldwork Opportunities Bulletin*. For more information, contact the publisher directly at:

Archaeology Today
675 Commonwealth Avenue
Boston, MA 02215
Tel.: (617) 353-9361

NEWSPAPERS IN CYPRUS

Apogevmatini (Greek)
P.O. Box 5603
5 Aegaleo Street, Stravolos
Nicosia, Cyprus
Tel.: [357] (2) 35 36 03
Fax: [357] (2) 35 32 23

The Cyprus Weekly (English)
P.O. Box 4977

Nicosia, Cyprus
Tel.: [357] (2) 45 60 47
Fax: [357] (2) 45 86 65

I Simerini
P.O. Box 1836
31 Archangelos Avenue
Stravolos, Nicosia, Cyprus
Tel.: [357] (2) 35 3532
Fax: [357] (2) 35 2298

Resources for Further Information

USEFUL WEBSITES FOR JOB SEARCHERS

The Internet is a good place to begin your job search. Although Cypriot employers are just beginning to use the Internet to list job vacancies, there are websites that provide useful information about the job market.

Cyprus Government Page
www.pio.gov.cy
Offers some job listings; work information; advice for tourists.

Cyprus News
www.cynews.com
Gives current news on Cyprus; some
employment opportunities.

EMBASSIES AND CONSULAR OFFICES

American embassies and consulates have commercial and/or economic sections that can provide you with business information and explain aspects of the local economy. Inquiries about business opportunities should be addressed either to "Commercial Officer" or "Commercial Section," followed by the appropriate street address.

Representation of Cyprus in the United States

Embassy of the Republic of Cyprus
2211 R Street NW
Washington, DC 20008-4017
Tel.: (202) 462-5722
Fax: (202) 483-6710

Representation of the United States in Cyprus

American Embassy
Metochiou and Ploutarchou Streets
Engomi, Nicosia, Cyprus
Tel.: [357] (2) 47 6100
Fax: [357] (2) 46 5944

CHAMBERS OF COMMERCE

Chambers of Commerce consist of firms in both countries interested in international trade. These are appropriate companies to initially target in the job search.

Cyprus Chamber of Commerce and Industry
P.O. Box 1455
1509 Nicosia, Cyprus
Tel.: [357] (2) 44 95 00
Fax: [357] (2) 44 90 48
Email: chamber@ccci.org.cy
www.ccci.org.cy

Famagusta Chamber of Commerce
339 Ayiou Andreou Street

P.O. Box 3124
Limassol, Cyprus
Tel.: [357] (5) 37 01 65
Fax: [357] (5) 37 02 91

Larnaca Chamber of Commerce and Industry
P.O. Box 287
Larnaca, Cyprus
Tel.: [357] (4) 62 48 51
Fax: [357] (4) 62 82 81

WORLD TRADE CENTER IN CYPRUS

World Trade Centers usually include many foreign companies operating in the country.

Cyprus World Trade Center
Chamber Building
38 Grivas Dhigenis Avenue
P.O. Box 1455
Nicosia, Cyprus
Tel.: (357) (2) 44 9500
Fax: (357) (2) 44 9048

OTHER INFORMATIONAL ORGANIZATIONS

Foreign government missions in the U.S. such as tourist offices can furnish visas and information on work permits and other important regulations. They may also offer economic and business information about the country.

Cyprus Tourist Organization
P.O. Box 4535
Nicosia, Cyprus
Tel.: [357] (2) 31 57 15
Fax: [357] (2) 31 30 22

Cyprus Trade Centre
13 East 40th Street
New York, NY 10016
Tel.: (212) 213-9100
Fax: (212) 213-2918

BUSINESS DIRECTORY

Although not always easy to find, business directories can prove invaluable in the international job search. Most directories list company names, addresses, products, and phone numbers. Some directories include executive names and titles and financial information about the company. These sources provide you with the names of the people to contact for employment information as well as financial data, which can tell you how strong a company's position in a country may be.

Cyprus Chamber of Commerce and Industry Directory. Published irregularly in English by the Cyprus Chamber of Commerce and Industry, 38 Grivas Dhigenis Ave., P.O. Box 1455, Nicosia, Cyprus. Lists over 5,000 financial, commercial, and service companies in Cyprus, plus government offices.

MAJOR COMPANIES IN CYPRUS

Company information includes firm name, address, phone and fax number, specific business, and, where appropriate, parent company. In the case of American parent firms, your chances of achieving employment abroad are substantially better if you contact the subsidiary company in Europe rather than the parent company in the U.S.

Amathus Navigation Co. Ltd.
1 Suntagmatos Street
Limassol, Cyprus
Tel.: [357] (53) 73 303
Fax: [357] (53) 69 656
(Transportation services)

Bank of Cyprus Ltd.
51 Stasinou Street
1398 Nicosia, Cyprus
Tel.: [357] (2) 378000
Fax: [357] (2) 378327
(Commercial Banks)

BASF AG
P.O. Box 1261
Nicosia, Cyprus
Tel.: [357] (2) 42 31218
(Plastics & resins)
BASF AG

Christofides & Son Ltd.
P.O. Box 1512
Nicosia, Cyprus
Tel.: [357] (2) 46 4239
(Pharmaceuticals)
Hoechst AG

Cyprus Airways Ltd.
21 Alkeou Street
Nicosia, Cyprus

Tel.: [357] (244) 3054
Fax: [357] (244) 3167
(Transportation, air)

Cyprus Building & Road Construction Co. Ltd.
Dhali Industrial Area
Nicosia, Cyprus
Tel.: [357] (248) 7744
Fax: [357] (248) 7666
(Construction)

Cyprus Telecommunications Authority
Telecommunications Street
Nicosia, Cyprus
Tel.: [357] (231) 0202
Fax: [357] (249) 4940
(Telephone communications)

Cyprus Transport (Taxi) Ltd.
2 Byron Avenue, P.O. Box 2276
Nicosia, Cyprus
Tel.: [357] (2) 47 2062
(Passenger car rental)
Avis Rent A Car

Cyprus Turkish Cooperative Central Bank
Mahmut Pasha Street
Nicosia, Cyprus
Tel.: [90] (520) 73398
Fax: [90] (520) 76787

Det Norske Veritas
231D, 28th October Street
Limassol, Cyprus
Tel.: [357] (5) 34 4081
(Shipping and offshore platform services)
Det Norske Veritas

Electricity Authority of Cyprus
15 Foti Pitta
Nicosia, Cyprus
Tel.: [357] (246) 2001
Fax: [357] (245) 7658
(Electric services)

Gevo Ltd.
9 Meletiou Metaxaki
P.O. Box 1307
Nicosia, Cyprus
Tel.: [357] (2) 47 7045
(Electronics)
Siemens AG

Hellenic Bank Ltd.
92 Comer Dhigenis Akritas Avenue and
Crete Street
1394 Nicosia, Cyprus
Tel.: [357] (236) 0000
Fax: [357] (245) 4074
(Commercial banks)

L M CH Schima Furniture Ltd.
178 Athalassas Avenue
Nicosia Cyprus
Tel.: [357] (231) 2648
Fax: [357] (249) 7441
(Furniture)

Ministry of Health
Byron Avenue
Nicosia, Cyprus
Tel.: [357] (230) 2075
Fax: [357] (230) 3498
(Hospitals)

Raychem Technologies Ltd.
Memrb House 21
Akademias Ave., P.O. Box 562
Aglanjia, Nicosia, Cyprus
Tel.: [357](2) 33 5940
(Wires, cables, fibre optics)
Raychem Corp.

Shell Cyprus Ltd.
35 Academy Avenue
Strovolos
143 Nicosia, Cyprus
Tel.: [357] (2) 31 6222
(Petroleum products)
Royal Dutch/Shell Group of Companies

T C S Plastic Ltd.
32 Delos Street
Limassol, Cyprus
Tel.: [357] (539) 3488
Fax: [357] (539) 2746
(Plastic products)

Telerexa Ltd.
P.O. Box 1152, Valentine House
8 Stassandrou Street
Nicosia, Cyprus
Tel.: [357] (2) 45 628
(Computers and software)
Hewlett-Packard Co.

INTERNATIONAL NON-PROFIT EMPLOYER IN CYPRUS

Broadcasting Organizations of Non-Aligned Countries
Broadcasting House
P.O. Box 4824
Nicosia, Cyprus
Tel.: [357] (2) 42 2231

INTERNATIONAL SCHOOL IN CYPRUS

American International School In Cyprus
P.O. Box 3847
1086 Nicosia, Cyprus
Tel.: [357] (2) 316 345
Fax: [357] (2) 316 549
Email: aisc@aisc.ac.cy
www.aisc.ac.cy

Malta

MAJOR EMPLOYMENT CENTERS: Birkirkara, Valletta

MAJOR BUSINESS LANGUAGES: Maltese, English

LANGUAGE SKILL INDEX: Knowing English should be just fine

CURRENCY: Maltese lera

TELEPHONE COUNTRY CODE: 356

TIME ZONE: EST+6

PUNCTUALITY INDEX: Punctuality is not the greatest of concerns on Malta

AVERAGE DAILY TEMPERATURE: January, 55°F; July, 77°F

AVERAGE NUMBER OF DAYS WITH RAIN: January, 13; July, 1

BEST BET FOR EMPLOYMENT:

FOR STUDENTS: Technical work with IAESTE, resort work

PERMANENT JOBS: Business, trade

TRIVIA: As the ancient home of the Knights of St. John, Malta has a history of internationalism and international diversity

T he Republic of Malta consists of three islands—Malta, Gozo, and Comino—due south of Sicily in the Mediterranean Sea. The total area of the islands is only 122 square miles: a scant 11 square miles larger than Denver, Colorado. Malta's terrain is uniformly hilly, making for a corrugated coastline where the hills meet the sea. Malta's capital city is Valletta, although Birkirkara is the nation's largest city with over 20,000 inhabitants. Malta has a total population of over 350,000.

Malta has a colorful political history, having been governed at various times by Phoenicians, Romans, Arabs, Normans, the Knights of Malta, France, and Britain. The islands became independent in 1964, and declared a republic ten years later. Malta is currently governed by a parliamentary democracy, with 13 electoral districts. Malta follows a policy of international nonalignment and is one of the few countries to have good relations with the regime of Libyan dictator Col. Muammar Quadhafi, although this has hampered the nation's efforts to become a member of the E.U.

Current Economic Climate

The nation has a relatively strong economy, despite a shortage of fresh water and domestic energy supplies. Malta's natural resources are limited and its agricultural sector is small. The island's principal source of income is the highly successful tourist sector and the state-owned dockyards. Service industries play an important role in Malta's economy, providing work for over 40% of the labor force. Malta's per-capita GDP is about $6,500 per year—similar to that of Cyprus. Major trading partners include Germany, France, the United Kingdom, and Italy.

Getting Around in Malta

Buses, reasonably priced and comfortable, service the entire island of Malta. For the do-it-yourself type, rented mopeds provide a more flexible option. Ferries provide transport among the islands of Malta, Gozo, and Comino and among Malta and several cities of southern Italy.

Employment Regulations and Outlook for Americans

For tourist stays of up to 90 days, U.S. citizens don't need a visa. Those planning to work in Malta must have received an offer of employment prior to arrival. Once this is achieved, a work permit is issued. As in much of Europe, though, official employment can be difficult to come by in Malta. One organization that might be able to help is the Malta Youth Hostels Association, which takes on part-time workers (20 hours a week) in exchange for lodging and breakfast. For details, contact the MYHA at least three months in advance of your planned arrival date.

Short-term and Temporary Work

Malta Youth Hostels Association
17 Triq Tal-Borg
PLA 06 Pawla, Malta
Tel./Fax: [356] 69 39 57
Email: myha@keyworld.net
Volunteers work in youth hostels for 2 weeks to 3 months in exchange for room and board.

Internship Program

IASTE provides the best opportunity for students to get more professional work in Malta.

IASTE
10400 Little Patuxent Parkway, Suite 250 L
Columbia, MD 21044-3510
Tel.: (410) 997-3068
Fax: (410) 997-5186

Email: iaste@aipt.org
www. aipt.org/iaste.htm
Arranges reciprocal internship exchanges among 63 member countries for students in engineering, architecture, and the sciences.

NEWSPAPERS IN MALTA

L'Orizzont
Union Press Publications
Workers Memorial Building
Soutn Street
Valletta, Malta
Tel.: [356] 24 4451
Fax: [356] 24 3454

The Times
Allied Newspapers Ltd.
341 St. Paul's Street
Valletta, VL T07 Malta
Tel.: [356] 24 14 64/9
Fax: [356] 24 79 01

Resources for Further Information

USEFUL WEBSITES FOR JOB SEARCHERS

The Internet is a good place to begin your job search. Although Maltese employers are just beginning to use the Internet to list job vacancies, there are websites that provide useful information about the job market.

Travel and Business Information
www.malta.co.uk
Gives advice on these topics in Malta.

University of Malta
www.cis.um.edu.mt

Lists educational and occupational opportunities.

Web Design
http://cwebdesign.com/mnr
Features jobs in the IT field.

EMBASSIES AND CONSULAR OFFICES

American embassies and consulates have commercial and/or economic sections that can provide you with business information and explain aspects of the local economy.

Inquiries about business opportunities should be addressed either to "Commercial Officer" or "Commercial Section," followed by the appropriate street address.

Representation of Malta in the United States

Embassy of Malta
2017 Connecticut Avenue NW
Washington, DC 20008-6132
Tel.: (202) 462-3611
Fax: (202) 387-5470
www.magnet.mt

Representation of the United States in Malta

American Embassy
P.O. Box 535
Valletta, Malta
Tel.: [356] 23 59 60
Fax: [356] 22 33 22

CHAMBER OF COMMERCE

Chambers of Commerce consist of firms in both countries interested in international trade. These are appropriate companies to initially target in the job search.

Maltese Chamber of Commerce
Exchange Buildings
Republic Street
Valletta, VLT05 Malta
Tel.: [356] 24 72 33
Fax: [356] 24 52 23
Email: chamber@kemmunet.net.mt
www.chamber-commerce.org.mt

OTHER INFORMATIONAL ORGANIZATIONS

Foreign government missions in the U.S. such as tourist offices can furnish visas and information on work permits and other important regulations. They may also offer economic and business information about the country.

National Tourist Organization of Malta
280 Republic Street
Valletta, Malta
Tel.: [356] 23 8282

National Tourism Organization
Harper Lane
Floriana, Malta

BUSINESS DIRECTORIES

Although not always easy to find, business directories can prove invaluable in the international job search. Most directories list company names, addresses, products, and phone numbers. Some directories include executive names and titles and financial information about the company. These sources provide you with the names of the people to contact for employment information as well as financial data, which can tell you how strong a company's position in a country may be.

Made in Malta. Published by the Malta External Trade Corp., P.O. Box 8, San Gwann SG
   No.1, Malta; http://metco.com.mt. Lists 850 manufacturing firms located in Malta.
Malta Trade Directory. Published annually in English by the Maltese Chamber of Commerce,
   Exchange Buildings, Republic Street, Valletta, Malta; email: chamber@kemmundt.nt.mt.
   Includes company information, plus businesses, professional associations, and government
   offices.
The Malta Year Book. Published annually in English by De la Salle Brothers Publications,
   St. Benild School, Church Street, Sliema SLM 02, Malta. Distributed in the U.S. by Paul
   E. Mifsud, Maltese-American Foundation, 2074 Ridgewood Road, Medina, OH 44256.
   Lists schools, banks, libraries, and trade unions in the Maltese Islands.

MAJOR COMPANIES IN MALTA

Malta's economy depends heavily on tourism. The most effective way to secure employment in this field, which includes hotel and resort work, sports and other entertainment, and the like, is to approach employers directly in the hope of striking some sort of informal arrangement. Information on a few other companies operating in Malta is given below. In the case of companies with American parent firms, your chances of achieving employment abroad are substantially better if you contact the subsidiary company in Europe rather than the parent company in the U.S.

Addax Trading Co. Ltd.
11 Piazetta Tower Road, Flat 22
Sliema, Malta
Tel.: [356] 34 2274
(Pharmaceuticals)
Hoechst AG

Air Malta Company Ltd.
Air Malta
LQA 01 Luqa, Malta
Tel.: [356] 690 890
Fax: [356] 673241
(Air transportation)

Bank of Valletta Ltd.
58 Zachary Street
VLT04 Valletta, Malta
Tel.: [356] 24 3261
Fax: [356] 23 0894
(Commercial bank)

BDS Ltd.
Casa Leone, Granaries Square
Floriana, Malta
Tel.: [396] 222 9200
(Computers and peripherals)
Apple Computer, Inc.

Brand International LTD
B36 Bulebel Industrial Estate,
ZNT 08 Zejtun, Malta
Tel.: [356] 69 3760
Fax: [356] 69 3761
(Toys)

Det Norske Veritas
Europa Centre
Office No. 8, First Floor
Floriana, Malta
Tel.: [356] 23 6104
(Shipping and offshore platform services)

Dowty (Malta) Ltd.
Mriehel Industrial Estate
QRM 09 Qormi, Malta
Tel.: [356] 44 1371
Fax: [356] 44 7831
(Packing devices)

Eagle Star (Malta) Ltd.
4th Floor, Kingsway Palace
Republic Street
Valletta, Malta
Tel.: [356] 24 5335
(Insurance)
Eagle Star Insurance Co. Ltd.

Enemalta Corporation
Church Wharf,
HMR 01 Marsa, Malta
Tel.: [356] 220 462
Fax: [356] 243 055
(Electric)

London Services Ltd.
50 Msida Seafront
Msida, Malta
Tel.: [356] 24 6640
(Passenger car rental)
Avis Rent A Car System, Inc.

Malta Shipbuilding Co Limited
Marsa Shipyard, Marsa, Malta
Tel.: [356] 231 3335
Fax: [356] 240 930
(Shipbuilding & repairing)

Mid-Med Bank Ltd.
233 Republic Street
P.O. Box 428
Valletta, Malta
Tel.: [356] 24 5281
Fax: [356] 23 0406
(Commercial bank)

**S G S Thomson Microelectronics
(MALTA) Ltd.**
Ramlija Road
ZRQ 10 Kirkop, Malta
Tel.: [356] 682 307
Fax: [356] 689 978
(Printed circuit boards)

INTERNATIONAL SCHOOL IN MALTA

Verdala International School
Fort Pembroke
STJ 14 St. Andrews, Malta
Tel.: [356] 332 361
Fax: [356] 372 387
Email: VIS@maltanet.net
www.digigate.net/vis
(U.S., U.K. curriculum, grades pre-K-12)

Index